Learning Web Design

Third Edition

A Beginner's Guide to (X)HTML, Style Sheets, and Web Graphics

Jennifer Niederst Robbins

O'REILLY®

Beijing · Cambridge · Farnham · Köln · Sebastopol · Tokyo

Learning Web Design, Third Edition
A Beginner's Guide to (X)HTML, Style Sheets, and Web Graphics

by Jennifer Niederst Robbins

Copyright © 2007 O'Reilly Media, Inc. All rights reserved.
Printed in Canada.

Published by O'Reilly Media, Inc., 1005 Gravenstein Highway North, Sebastopol, CA 95472.

O'Reilly Media books may be purchased for educational, business, or sales promotional use. Online editions are also available for most titles (*safari.oreilly.com*). For more information, contact our corporate/institutional sales department: 800-998-9938 or *corporate@oreilly.com*.

Editor: Linda Laflamme

Production Editor: Philip Dangler

Cover Designer: Mark Paglietti

Interior Designer: Ron Bilodeau

Print History:

March 2001:	First edition.
June 2003:	Second edition.
June 2007:	Third edition.

This book uses RepKover™, a durable and flexible lay-flat binding.

ISBN: 978-0-596-52752-5
[TI]

[2012-02-24]

CONTENTS

PREFACE

Hello and welcome to the third edition of *Learning Web Design*! When I first started writing it, I figured, "It's just an update... I'll just make a few tweaks and it will be done in a jiffy." I couldn't have been more wrong. As it turns out, pretty much everything about web design changed since I wrote the second edition four years ago. Most significantly, web designers as well as browser developers are finally abiding by the standards for writing and styling web pages set forth by the World Wide Web Consortium (W3C). You'll learn a lot more about these standards throughout the book.

What it means is that using HTML markup for visual effects is out—HTML for describing the meaning and structure of content is in. Table-based layouts are out—style sheet-driven layouts are in. And the font element, spacer GIFs, and other clever hacks of the past... forget about it! They're all history.

This edition has been completely rewritten to be in compliance with the standards and modern web design practices. The markup chapters emphasize using HTML to describe your content accurately, not as a tool for formatting the appearance of text. And now you will find seven chapters on Cascading Style Sheets (CSS), where the second edition had just one.

But like the first two editions, this book addresses the specific needs and concerns of beginners of all backgrounds, including seasoned graphic designers, programmers looking for a more creative outlet, office assistants, recent college graduates, work-at-home moms, and anyone else wanting to learn how to design web sites. I've done my best to put the experience of sitting in my beginner web design class into a book, with exercises and tests along the way, so you get hands-on experience and can check your progress.

I start at square one, with answers to common beginner questions and an explanation of how the Web works. By the end of the book, you'll have the skills necessary to create multicolumn CSS layouts with optimized graphic files, and you'll know how to get them on the Web. You can start at the very beginning, or feel free to jump in at any point.

The Companion Web Site

Be sure to visit the companion web site for this book at *learningwebdesign.com*. It features materials for the exercises, downloadable articles, lists of links from the book, updates, and other good stuff.

Whether you are reading this book on your own or using it as a companion to a web design course, I hope it gives you a good head start and that you have fun in the process.

Acknowledgments

I want to thank my editors, Brian Sawyer, Chuck Toporek, Linda Laflamme, and Steve Weiss, for their valuable input to this new edition. A special thank you goes to my technical reviewer, Aaron Gustafson, for his expert guidance, generosity, and for keeping on the straight and narrow when it comes to standards compliance.

Thanks also to the others who contributed hands-on time to the creation of this book: Ron Bilodeau for the updated interior design, Rob Romano for the figure production, Chris Reilley for helping me envision some of the more complex figures, Sohaila Abdulali for copyediting, Reg Aubry for writing the index, and everyone else who helped with the project.

Finally, I want to thank my Mom, Dad, brother Liam, and the whole Robbins clan for their inspiration and continued support while I labored to crank out this edition. And it pleases me greatly, Jeff and Arlo, to tell you that I am finally done writing. Thanks for putting up with me being half there.

O'Reilly Would Like to Hear From You

Please address comments and questions concerning this book to the publisher:

O'Reilly Media, Inc.
1005 Gravenstein Highway North
Sebastopol, CA 95472
800-998-9938 (in the United States or Canada)
707-829-0515 (international/local)
707-829-0104 (fax)

There is a web page for this book, which lists errata and additional information. You can access this page at:

http://www.oreilly.com/catalog/9780596527525

To comment or ask technical questions about this book, send email to:

bookquestions@oreilly.com

For more information about books, conferences, software, Resource Centers, and the O'Reilly Network, see the O'Reilly web site at:

http://www.oreilly.com

Conventions Used in This Book

The following typographic conventions are used in this book:

Italic

Used to indicate URLs, email addresses, filenames, and directory names, as well as for emphasis

Colored roman text

Used for special terms that are being defined and for crossreference.

`Constant width`

Used to indicate code examples and keyboard commands

`Colored constant width`

Used to indicate (X)HTML tags and attributes, and used for emphasis in code examples.

`Constant width italic`

Used to indicate placeholders for attribute and style sheet property values.

GETTING STARTED

PART I

CHAPTER 1

WHERE DO I START?

The Web has been around for well over a decade now, experiencing euphoric early expansion, an economic-driven bust, an innovation-driven rebirth, and constant evolution along the way. One thing is certain: the Web as a communication and commercial medium is here to stay.

For many people, it's a call to action—a new career opportunity, an incentive to keep up with competitors, or just a chance to get stuff out there for the world to see. But the world of web design can also seem overwhelming.

Through my experience teaching web design courses and workshops, I've had the opportunity to meet people of all backgrounds who are interested in learning how to build web pages. Allow me to introduce you to just a few:

"I've been a print designer for 17 years, and now all my clients want web sites."

"I work as a secretary in a small office. My boss has asked me to put together a small internal web site to share company information among employees."

"I've been a programmer for years, but I want to try my hand at more visual design. I feel like the Web is a good opportunity to explore new skills."

"I am an artist and I want to know how to get samples of my paintings and sculpture online."

"I'm a designer who has watched all my colleagues switch to web design in the last few years. I'm curious about it, but I feel like I may be too late."

Whatever the motivation, the first question is always the same: "Where do I start?" It may seem like there is an overwhelming amount of stuff to learn and it's not easy to know where to jump in. But you have to start somewhere.

This chapter attempts to put the learning curve in perspective by answering the most common questions I get asked by people ready to make the leap. It provides an introduction to the disciplines, technologies, and tools associated with web design.

IN THIS CHAPTER

Am I too late?

Where do I start?

What do I need to learn?

Do I need to learn Java?
What other languages do
I need to know?

What software
and equipment do I
need to buy?

Am I Too Late?

The first step is understanding the fundamentals of how the Web works.

That's an easy one—absolutely not! Although it may seem that everyone in the whole world has a personal web page, or that your colleagues are all light-years ahead of you in web experience, I can assure you that you're not late.

The Web has become an essential part of standard business practice. We're at the point where we just assume that a business, regardless of its size, will have a useful web site. It also remains a uniquely powerful tool for self-publishing, whether to a small circle of friends or to a worldwide audience. We can be certain that there will be a steady need for web designers and developers.

Where Do I Start?

Your particular starting point will no doubt depend on your background and goals. However, a good first step for everyone is to get a basic understanding of how the Web and web pages work. That you are reading this book now shows that you are already on the right track. Once you learn the fundamentals, there are plenty of resources on the Web and in bookstores for you to further your learning in specific areas. One way to get up to speed quickly is to take an introductory web design class. If you don't have the luxury of a full-semester course, even a weekend or one-day seminar can be extremely useful in getting over that first hump.

You'll learn that the term "web design" has come to encompass many skills, and you don't necessarily need to learn all of them (most people don't). This chapter introduces the various disciplines and paths you may take.

I Just Want a Blog!

You don't necessarily need to become a web designer to start publishing your words and pictures on the Web. You can start your own "blog" or personal journal site using one of the free or inexpensive blog hosting services. These services provide templates that spare you the need to learn HTML (although it still doesn't hurt). These are three of the most popular as of this writing:

- Blogger (*www.blogger.com*)
- TypePad (*www.typepad.com*)
- LiveJournal (*www.livejournal.com*)

If you use a Mac, Apple's iWeb software makes it simple to publish blogs (including video) using one of several stylish templates.

Similarly, there are many levels of involvement in web design, from just building a site for yourself to making it a full-blown career. You may enjoy being a full-service web site developer or just specializing in one skill, like Flash development. There are a lot of ways you can go.

If your involvement in web design is purely at the hobbyist level, or if you have just one or two web projects you'd like to publish, you may find that a combination of personal research (like reading this book), taking advantage of available templates, and perhaps even investing in solid web design tools (such as Dreamweaver from Adobe) may be all you need to accomplish the task at hand.

If you are interested in pursuing web design as a career, you'll need to bring your skills up to a professional level. Employers may not require a web design degree, but they will expect to see sample web sites that demonstrate your skills and experience. These sites can be the result of class assignments, personal projects, or a simple site for a small business. What's important is that they look professional and have clean, working HTML and style sheets behind the scenes. Getting an entry-level job and working as part of a team is a great way to learn how larger sites are constructed and can help you decide which aspects of web design you would like to pursue.

What Do I Need to Learn?

This one's a big question. The short answer is "not everything." A more accurate answer depends on where you are starting and what you want to do.

As mentioned earlier, the term "web design" has become a catch-all for a process that actually encompasses a number of different disciplines, from graphic design to serious programming. We'll take a look at each of them.

If you are designing a small web site on your own, you will need to wear many hats. The good news is that you probably won't notice. Consider that the day-to-day upkeep of your household requires you to be part-time chef, housecleaner, accountant, diplomat, gardener, and construction worker—but to you it's just the stuff you do around the house. In the same way, as a solo web designer, you'll be part-time graphic designer, writer, producer, and information architect, but to you, it'll just feel like "making web pages." Nothing to worry about.

There are also specialists out there whom you can hire to fill in the skills you don't have. For example, I have been creating web sites for more than a decade and I still hire programmers and multimedia developers when my clients require those features. That allows me to focus on the parts I do well.

Large-scale web sites are almost always created by a team of people, numbering from a handful to hundreds. In this scenario, each member of the team focuses on just one facet of the site building process. If that is the case, you may be able to simply adapt your current set of skills and interests to the new medium.

The following are some of the core disciplines involved in the web design process, along with brief descriptions of the skills required in each area.

Graphic design

Because the Web is a visual medium, web pages require attention to presentation and design. The graphic designer makes decisions regarding everything you see on a web page: graphics, type, colors, layout, etc. As in the print world, graphic designers play an important role in the success of the final product. If you work as a graphic designer in the web design process, you may never need to learn any backend programming languages. (I didn't.)

If you are interested in doing the visual design of commercial sites professionally, I strongly recommend graphic design training as well as a strong proficiency in Adobe Photoshop (the industry standard). If you are already a graphic designer, you will be able to adapt your skills to the Web easily.

AT A GLANCE

"Web design" actually combines a number of disciplines, including:

- Graphic design
- Information design
- Interface design
- HTML, style sheet, and graphic production
- Scripting and programming
- Multimedia

If you are not interested in becoming a jack-of-all-trades solo web designer, you may choose to specialize and work as part of a team or as a freelance contractor.

Frontend Versus Backend

You may hear web designers and developers say that they specialize in either the **frontend** or **backend** of web site creation.

Frontend design

"Frontend" refers to any aspect of the design process that appears in or relates directly to the browser. This book focuses primarily on frontend web design.

The following tasks are commonly considered to be frontend disciplines:

- Graphic design
- Interface design
- Information design as it pertains to the user's experience of the site
- Site production, including HTML documents, style sheets and JavaScript

Backend development

"Backend" refers to the programs and scripts that work on the server behind the scenes to make web pages dynamic and interactive. In general, backend web development falls in the hands of experienced programmers, but it is good for all web designers to be familiar with backend functionality.

The following tasks take place on the backend:

- Information design as it pertains to how the information is organized on the server
- Forms processing
- Database programming
- Content management systems
- Other server-side web applications using Perl/CGI, PHP, ASP, JSP, Ruby on Rails, Java and other programming languages.

Because graphics are a big part of web design, even hobbyist web designers will need to know how to use some image-editing software, at minimum.

If you don't have visual design experience, you may want to do some personal research on the fundamentals of graphic design. The following books will give you a good start on rounding out your design skills.

The Non-Designer's Design Book, Second Edition by Robin Williams (Peachpit Press, 2003)

The Non-Designer's Web Book, Third Edition by Robin Williams and John Tollett (Peachpit Press, 2005)

Design Basics, Sixth Edition by David Lauer and Stephen Pentak (Harcourt College Publishers, 2004)

Graphic Design Solutions, Third Edition by Robin Landa (Thomson Delmar Learning, 2005).

Information design

One easily overlooked aspect of web design is information design, the organization of content and how you get to it. Information designers (also called "information architects") deal with flow charts and diagrams and may never touch a graphic or text file; however, they are a crucial part of the creation of the site.

It is possible to find courses specifically about information design, although they are likely to be at the graduate level. Again, some personal research and experience working on a team will go a long way toward rounding out this skill. If you think you may be interested in this aspect of web development, check out these books:

Information Architecture for the World Wide Web: Designing Large-Scale Web Sites, Third Edition by Lou Rosenfeld and Peter Morville (O'Reilly, 2006) for a good overview.

Information Architecture: Blueprints for the Web, by Christina Wodtke (New Riders, 2002)

Interface design

If graphic design is concerned with how the page looks, interface design focuses on how the page works. The concept of usability, how easily visitors can accomplish their goals on the site, as well as the general experience of using the site, is a function of the interface design. The interface of a web site includes the methods for doing things on a site: buttons, links, navigation devices, etc., as well as the functional organization of the page. In most cases, the interface, information archictecture, and visual design of a site are tightly entwined.

Often, the interface design falls into the hands of a graphic designer by default; in other cases, it is handled by an interface design specialist or the information designer. Some interface designers have backgrounds in software design. It is possible to find courses on interface design; however, this is an area that you can build expertise in by a combination of personal research, experience in the field, and common sense. You may also find these popular books on web usability helpful:

Don't Make Me Think, A Common Sense Approach to Web Usability, Second Edition, by Steve Krug (New Riders, 2005)

The Elements of User Experience: User-Centered Design for the Web, by Jesse James Garrett (New Riders, 2002)

Document production

A fair amount of the web design process involves the creation and troubleshooting of the documents, style sheets, scripting, and images that make up a site. The process of writing HTML and style sheet documents is commonly referred to as authoring.

The people who handle production need to have an intricate knowledge of HTML (the markup language used to make web documents) and style sheets, and often additional scripting or programming skills. At large web design firms, the team that handles the creation of the files that make up the web site may be called the "development" or "production" department. In some cases, the tasks may be separated out into specialized positions for CSS designer, HTML author/coder, and client-side programmer.

This book will teach you the basics of web authoring, including how to write HTML documents, create style sheets, and produce web graphics. Fortunately, it's not difficult to learn. Once you've gotten the fundamentals under your belt, the trick is to practice by creating pages and learning from your mistakes. There are also authoring tools that speed up the production process, as we'll discuss later in this chapter.

In addition to the HTML document and style sheets, each of the images that appear on the page need to be produced in a way that is appropriate and optimized for web delivery. Graphics production techniques are covered in Part IV.

A Little More About Flash

Adobe Flash (previously Macromedia Flash, previously FutureSplash) is a multimedia format created especially for the Web. Flash gives you the ability to create full-screen animation, interactive graphics, integrated audio clips, even scriptable games and applications, all at remarkably small file sizes. Some sites use Flash instead of (X)HTML for their entire interface, content, and functionality.

Flash has a number of advantages:

- Because it uses vector graphics, files are small and the movie can be resized without loss of detail. Real-time anti-aliasing keeps the edges smooth.

- It is a streaming format, so movies start playing quickly and continue to play as they download.

- You can use ActionScript to add behaviors and advanced interactivity, allowing Flash to be used as the frontend for dynamically generated content or e-commerce functions.

- The Flash plug-in is well-distributed, so support is reliable.

On the downside:

- The fact that a plugin is required to play Flash media makes some developers squeamish.

- Content may be lost for nongraphical browsers. However, Flash has many features to improve accessibility.

- The software required to create Flash content is often expensive, and the learning curve is steep.

Flash is not appropriate for all sites and it is not poised to replace (X)HTML. However, when used well, it can create a big impact and a memorable user experience.

For more information, look for "Adobe Flash" at *Wikipedia.org*.

Scripting and programming

Advanced web functionality (such as forms, dynamic content, and interactivity) requires web scripts and sometimes special programs and applications running behind the scenes. Scripting and programming is handled by web programmers (also called developers). Developers who specialize in the programming end of things may never touch a graphic file or have input on how the pages look, although they need to communicate well with the information and interface designers to make sure their scripts meet intended goals and user expectations.

Web scripting and programming definitely requires some traditional computer programming prowess. While many web programmers have degrees in computer science, it is also common for developers to be self-taught. Developers I know usually start by copying and adapting existing scripts, then gradually add to their programming skills on the job. If you have no experience with programming languages, the initial learning curve may be a bit steep.

Teaching web programming is beyond the scope of this book. It is possible to turn out competent, content-rich, well-designed sites without the need for programming, so hobbyist web designers should not be discouraged. However, once you get into collecting information via forms or serving information on demand, it is usually necessary to have a programmer on the team.

Multimedia

One of the cool things about the Web is that you can add multimedia elements to a site, including sound, video, animation, and Flash movies for interactivity (see sidebar). You may decide to add multimedia skills to your web design toolbelt, or you may decide to become a specialist. If you are not interested in becoming a multimedia developer, you can always hire one.

There is a constant call for professional Flash developers and people who know how to produce audio and video files that are appropriate for the Web. Web development companies usually look for people who have mastered the standard multimedia tools, and have a good visual sensibility and an instinct for intuitive and creative multimedia design. Professional Flash developers are also expected to know ActionScript for adding advanced behaviors to Flash movies and interfaces.

Do I Need to Learn Java?

You'd be surprised at the number of times I've heard the following: "I want to get into web design so I went out and bought a book on Java." I usually respond, "Well, go return it!" Before you spend money on a big Java book,

The World Wide Web Consortium

The World Wide Web Consortium (called the W3C for short) is the organization that oversees the development of web technologies. The group was founded in 1994 by Tim Berners-Lee, the inventor of the Web, at the Massachusetts Institute of Technology (MIT).

In the beginning, the W3C concerned itself mainly with the HTTP protocol and the development of the HTML. Now, the W3C is laying a foundation for the future of the Web by developing dozens of technologies and protocols that must work together in a solid infrastructure.

For the definitive answer on any web technology question, the W3C site is the place to go:

www.w3.org

For more information on the W3C and what they do, see this useful page:

www.w3.org/Consortium/

I'm here to tell you that you don't need to know Java programming (or any programming, for that matter) to make web sites.

The following is a list of technologies associated with web development. They are listed in general order of complexity and in the order that you might want to learn them. Bear in mind, the only *requirements* are HTML and Cascading Style Sheets. Where you draw the line after that is up to you.

HTML/XHTML

HTML (HyperText Markup Langage) is the language used to create web page documents. The updated version, XHTML (eXtensible HTML) is essentially the same language with stricter syntax rules. We'll get to the particulars of what makes them different in Chapter 10, Understanding the Standards. It is common to see HTML and XHTML referred to collectively as (X)HTML, as I will do throughout this book when both apply.

(X)HTML is not a programming language; it is a markup language, which means it is a system for identifying and describing the various components of a document such as headings, paragraphs, and lists. You don't need programming skills—only patience and common sense—to write (X)HTML.

Everyone involved with the Web needs a basic understanding of how HTML works. The best way to learn is to write out some pages by hand, as we will be doing in the exercises in this book.

If you end up working in web production, you'll live and breathe (X)HTML. Even hobbyists will benefit from knowing what is going on under the hood. The good news is that it's simple to learn the basics.

AT A GLANCE

Web-related programming "languages" in order of increasing complexity:

- HTML/XHTML
- Style sheets
- JavaScript/DOM scripting
- Server-side scripting
- XML
- Java

It is common to see HTML and XHTML referred to collectively as (X)HTML.

NOTE

When this book says "style sheets" it is always referring to Cascading Style Sheets, the standard style sheet language for the World Wide Web.

The Web Design Layer Cake

Contemporary web design is commonly visualized as being made up of three separate "layers."

The content of the document with its (X)HTML markup makes up the **Structure Layer**. It forms the foundation upon which the other layers may be applied.

Once the structure of the document is in place, you can add style sheet information to control how the content should appear. This is called the **Presentation Layer**.

Finally, the **Behavior Layer** includes the scripts that make the page an interactive experience.

CSS (Cascading Style Sheets)

While (X)HTML is used to describe the content in a web page, it is Cascading Style Sheets (CSS) that describe how you want that content to *look*. In the web design biz, the way the page looks is known as its presentation. CSS is now the official and standard mechanism for formatting text and page layouts.

CSS also provides methods for controlling how documents will be presented in media other than the traditional browser on a screen, such as in print and on handheld devices. It also has rules for specifying the non-visual presentation of documents, such as how they will sound when read by a screen reader.

Style sheets are also a great tool for automating production, because you can make changes to all the pages in your site by editing a single style sheet document. Style sheets are supported to some degree by all modern browsers.

Although it is possible to publish web pages using (X)HTML alone, you'll probably want to take on style sheets so you're not stuck with the browser's default styles. If you're looking into designing web sites professionally, proficiency at style sheets is mandatory.

Style sheets are discussed further in Part III.

JavaScript/DOM scripting

Despite its name, JavaScript is not at all related to Java. JavaScript is a scripting language that is used to add interactivity and behaviors to web pages, including these (just to name a few):

- Checking form entries for valid entries

- Swapping out styles for an element or an entire site

- Making the browser remember information about the user for the next time they visit

JavaScript is a language that is commonly used to manipulate the elements on the web page or certain browser window functions. There are other web scripting languages, but JavaScript (also called ECMAScript) is the standard and most ubiquitous.

You may also hear the term DOM scripting used in relation to JavaScript. DOM stands for Document Object Model, and it refers to the standardized list of web page elements that can be accessed and manipulated using JavaScript (or another scripting language). DOM scripting is an updated term for what used to be referred to as DHTML (Dynamic HTML), now considered an obsolete approach.

Writing JavaScript is programming, so it may be time-consuming to learn if you have no prior programming experience. Many people teach themselves

JavaScript by reading books and following and modifying existing examples. Most web-authoring tools come with standard scripts that you can use right out of the box for common functions.

If you want to be a professional web developer, JavaScript is the first scripting language you should learn. However, plenty of designers rely on developers to add JavaScript behaviors to their designs. So while JavaScript is useful, learning to write it is not mandatory for all web designers. Teaching JavaScript is outside the scope of this book; however, *Learning JavaScript* by Shelley Powers (O'Reilly, 2006) is certainly a good place to start if you want to learn more.

Server-side programming

Some web sites are collections of static (X)HTML documents and image files, but most commercial sites have more advanced functionality such as forms handling, dynamically generated pages, shopping carts, content management systems, databases, and so on. These functions are handled by special web applications running on the server. There are a number of scripting and programming languages that are used to create web applications, including:

- CGI Scripts (written in C++, Perl, Python, or others)
- Java Server Pages (JSPs)
- PHP
- VB.NET
- ASP.NET
- Ruby on Rails

Developing web applications is programmer territory and is not expected of all web designers. However, that doesn't mean you can't offer such functionality to your clients. It is possible to get shopping carts, content management systems, mailing lists, and guestbooks as prepackaged solutions, without the need to program them from scratch.

XML

If you hang around the web design world at all, you're sure to hear the acronym XML (which stands for eXtensible Markup Language). XML is not a specific language in itself, but rather a robust set of rules for creating other markup languages.

To use a simplified example, if you were publishing recipes, you might use XML to create a custom markup language that includes the elements `<ingredient>`, `<instructions>`, and `<servings>` that accurately describe the types of information in your recipe documents. Once labeled correctly, that information can be treated as data. In fact, XML has proven to be a powerful tool for

Ajax for Applications

The latest web technique to create a big stir is **Ajax**, which stands for **Asynchronous JavaScript and XML**.

Ajax is a technique for creating interactive web applications. The significant advantage to using Ajax for web applications is that it allows the content on the screen to change instantly, without refreshing the whole page. This makes using the application more like a desktop program than a web page because controls react instantly, without all that pesky waiting for server calls and page redraws.

As a beginner, you aren't likely to be writing Ajax-based applications right off the bat, but it is useful to be familiar with what it is and what it can do.

To learn more, I recommend searching for "Ajax" at *Wikipedia. org*. The Ajax listing provides a solid explanation as well as a list of links to Ajax resources.

sharing data between applications. Despite the fact that XML was developed with the Web in mind, it has actually had a larger impact outside the web environment because of its data-handling capabilities. There are XML files working behind the scenes in an increasing number of software applications, such as Microsoft Office, Adobe Flash, and Apple iTunes.

Still, there are a number of XML languages that are used on the Web. The most prevalent is XHTML, which is HTML rewritten according the the stricter rules of XML. There is also RSS (Really Simple Syndication or RDF Site Summary) that allows your content to be shared as data and read with RSS feed readers, SVG (Scalable Vector Graphics) that uses tags to describe geometric shapes, and MathML that is used to describe mathematical notation.

As a web designer, your direct experience with XML is likely to be limited to authoring documents in XHTML or perhaps adding an RSS feed to a web site. Developing new XML languages would be the responsibility of programmers or XML specialists.

Java

Although Java can be used for creating small applications for the Web (known as "applets"), it is a complete and complex programming language that is typically used for developing large, enterprise-scale applications. Java is considered one of the "big guns" and is overkill for most web site needs. Learn Java only if you want to become a Java programmer. You can live your life as a web designer without knowing a lick of Java (most web designers and developers do).

What Do I Need to Buy?

It should come as no surprise that professional web designers require a fair amount of gear, both hardware and software. One of the most common questions I'm asked by my students is, "What should I get?" I can't tell you specifically what to buy, but I will provide an overview of the typical tools of the trade.

Bear in mind that while I've listed the most popular commercial software tools available, many of them have freeware or shareware equivalents which you can download if you're on a budget (try CNET's *Download.com*). With a little extra effort, you can get a full web site up and running without big cash.

Equipment

For a comfortable web site creation environment, I recommend the following equipment:

A solid, up-to-date computer. Windows, Linux, or Macintosh is fine. Creative departments in professional web development companies tend to be Mac-based. Although it is nice to have a super-fast machine, the files that make up web pages are very small and tend not to be too taxing on computers. Unless you're getting into sound and video editing, don't worry if your current setup is not the latest and greatest.

Extra memory. Because you'll tend to bounce between a number of applications, it's a good idea to have enough RAM installed on your computer that allows you to leave several memory-intensive programs running at the same time.

A large monitor. While not a requirement, a large or high-resolution monitor makes life easier. The more monitor real estate you have, the more windows and control panels you can have open at the same time. You can also see more of your page to make design decisions.

Just make sure if you're using a high-resolution monitor (1280×1024 or 1600×1200), that you design for users with smaller monitors in mind. Most professional web sites these days are designed to fit in an 800×600 monitor as the lowest common denominator. Also keep in mind that when working in high resolution, the text and graphics may look smaller to you than to users with lower resolutions or larger pixel size. Be sure to take a look at your pages under a variety of viewing conditions.

A second computer. Many web designers find it useful to have a test computer running a different platform than the computer they use for development (i.e., if you design on a Mac, test on a PC). Because browsers work differently on Macs than on Windows machines, it's critical to test your pages in as many environments as possible, and particularly on the current Windows operating system. If you are a hobbyist web designer working at home, check your pages on a friend's machine.

A scanner and/or digital camera. If you anticipate making your own graphics, you'll need some tools for creating images or textures. I know a designer who has two scanners: one is the "good" scanner, and the other he uses to scan things like dead fish and rusty pans. Because web graphics are low resolution, you don't need a state-of-the-art, mega-pixel digital camera to get decent results.

Run Windows on Your Mac

If you have a Macintosh computer with an Intel chip, you don't need a separate computer to test in a Windows environment. It is now possible to run Windows right on your Mac.

Apple offers the free Boot Camp, as part of the Leopard OS X release, that allows you to switch to Windows on reboot.

There is also Parallels Desktop for Mac, a commercial program that allows you to toggle between operating systems easily. For more information see *www.parallels.com*.

Both options require that you purchase a copy of Microsoft Windows, but it sure beats buying a whole machine.

Software

There's no shortage of software available for creating web pages. In the early days, we just made do with tools originally designed for print. Today, there are wonderful tools created specifically with web design in mind that make the process more efficient. Although I can't list every available software release (you can find other offerings as well as the current versions of the following programs in software catalogs), I'd like to introduce you to the most common and proven tools for web design. Note that you can download trial versions of many of these programs from the company web sites, as listed in the At a Glance: Popular Web Design Software sidebar later in this chapter.

Web page authoring

Web-authoring tools are similar to desktop publishing tools, but the end product is a web page (an (X)HTML file and its related style sheet and image files). These tools provide a visual "WYSIWYG" (What You See Is What You Get; pronounced "whizzy-wig") interface and shortcuts that save you from typing repetitive (X)HTML and CSS. The following are some popular web-authoring programs:

Adobe (previously Macromedia) Dreamweaver. This is the industry standard due to its clean code and advanced features.

NOTE

Since acquiring Dreamweaver, Adobe has discontinued GoLive, its own advanced WYSIWYG editor. As of this writing, the last version, CS2, is still available for purchase.

Microsoft Expression Web (Windows only). Part of Microsoft's suite of professional design tools, MS Expression Web boasts standards-compliant code and CSS-based layouts. Microsoft no longer offers its previous web editor, FrontPage, which was notorious for proprietary and sloppy code.

Nvu (Linux, Windows, and Mac OS X). Don't want to pay for a WYSIWYG editor? Nvu (pronounced N-view, for "new view") is an open source tool that matches many of the features in Dreamweaver, yet is downloadable for free at *nvu.com*.

HTML editors

HTML editors (as opposed to authoring tools) are designed to speed up the process of writing HTML by hand. They do not allow you edit the page visually as WYSIWYG authoring tools (listed previously) do. Many professional web designers actually prefer to author HTML documents by hand, and they overwhelmingly recommend the following four tools:

TextPad (Windows only). TextPad is a simple and inexpensive plain-text code editor for Windows.

Adobe (Macromedia) HomeSite (Windows only). This tool includes shortcuts, templates, and even wizards for more complex web page authoring.

BBEdit by Bare Bones Software (Macintosh only). Lots of great shortcut features have made this the leading editor for Mac-based web developers.

TextMate by MacroMates (Macintosh only). This advanced text editor features project management tools and an interface that is integrated with the Mac operating system. It is growing in popularity because it is easy to use, feature-rich, and inexpensive.

Graphics software

You'll probably want to add pictures to your pages, so you will need an image-editing program. We'll look at some of the more popular programs in greater detail in Part IV. In the meantime, you may want to look into the following popular web graphics–creation tools:

Adobe Photoshop. Photoshop is undeniably the industry standard for image creation in both the print and web worlds. If you want to be a professional designer, you'll need to know Photoshop thoroughly.

Adobe (Macromedia) Fireworks. This web graphics program combines a drawing program with an image editor and vector tools for creating illustrations. It also features advanced tools for outputting web graphics.

Adobe Photoshop Elements. This lighter version of Photoshop is designed for photo editing and management, but some hobbyists may find that it has all the tools necessary for putting images on web pages.

Adobe Illustrator. This vector drawing program is often used to create illustrations. You can output web graphics directly from Illustrator, or bring them into Photoshop for additional fine-tuning.

Corel Paint Shop Pro Photo (Windows only). This full-featured image editor is popular with the Windows crowd, primarily due to its low price (only $99 at the time of this printing).

Multimedia tools

Because this is a book for beginners, I won't focus on advanced multimedia elements; however, it is still useful to be aware of the software that is available to you should you choose to follow that specialty:

Adobe (Macromedia) Flash. This is the hands-down favorite for adding animation, sound, and interactive effects to web pages due to the small file size of Flash movies.

exercise 1-1 |
Taking stock

Now that you're taking that first step in learning web design, it might be a good time to take stock of your assets and goals. Using the lists in this chapter as a general guide, try jotting down answers to the following questions:

- What are your web design goals? To become a professional web designer? To make personal web sites only?
- Which aspects of web design interest you the most?
- What current skills do you have that will be useful in creating web pages?
- Which skills will you need to brush up on?
- Which hardware and software tools do you already have for web design?
- Which tools do you need to buy? Which tools would you like to buy eventually?

Apple QuickTime and iMovie. You can use the QuickTime Player Pro to do basic audio and video editing and exports. iMovie is another good and affordable tool for exporting video for the Web.

Apple Final Cut Pro. For more advanced video editing, Final Cut Pro is an industry favorite.

Microsoft Windows Movie Maker. Windows Media is growing in popularity on the Web. This simple movie editor for Windows lets you easily create movies in Windows Media format. Microsoft also offers Windows Media Encoder to convert existing movies to Windows Media format.

Adobe After Effects. This is the industry standard for creating motion graphics and visual effects.

Sony Sound Forge. Sound Forge is a full-featured professional audio editing program. Sony also offers Sound Forge Audio Studio for entry-level users.

Audacity. For the budget-conscious, Audacity is a powerful, cross-platform, open source audio editing program, and you can't beat the price...it's free!

Internet tools

Because you will be dealing with the Internet, you need to have some tools specifically for viewing and moving files over the network:

A variety of browsers. Because browsers render pages differently, you'll want to test your pages on as many browsers as possible. There are hundreds of browsers on the market, but these are best supported on Windows and Macintosh:

Windows:	**Macintosh OS X:**
Internet Explorer (the current version and at least two prior versions)	Safari
	Firefox
	Macintosh OS 9:
Firefox	Internet Explorer 5 (Note that most developers do not test on this browser because it accounts for a miniscule fraction of web traffic.)
Netscape	
Opera	
Safari 3	

A file-transfer program (FTP). An FTP program enables you to upload and download files between your computer and the computer that will serve your pages to the Web. The web authoring tools listed earlier all have FTP programs built right in. There are also dedicated FTP programs as listed below. See Chapter 21, Getting Your Pages on the Web, for more information on file uploading.

Windows:

WS_FTP

CuteFTP

AceFTP

Filezilla

Macintosh OS X:

Transmit

Fetch

Interarchy

Terminal application. If you know your way around the Unix operating system, you may find it useful to have a terminal (command line) application that allows you to type Unix commands on the server. This may be useful for setting file permissions, moving or copying files and directories, or managing the server software.

Windows users can install a Linux emulater called Cygwin for command line access. There is also PuTTY, a free Telnet/SSH client. Mac OS X includes an application called Terminal that is a full-fledged terminal application giving you access to the underlying Unix system and the ability to use SSH to access other command line systems over the Internet.

AT A GLANCE

Popular Web Design Software

Web Page Authoring

Adobe (Macromedia) Dreamweaver
www.adobe.com

Microsoft Expression Web
www.microsoft.com/products/expression

Nvu (open source web page editor)
www.nvu.com

Apple iWeb
apple.com/ilife/iweb

HTML Editing

Adobe (Macromedia) HomeSite
www.adobe.com

BBEdit by Bare Bones Software
www.barebones.com

TextMate by MacroMates
www.macromates.com

TextPad for Windows
www.textpad.com

Graphics

Adobe Photoshop

Adobe Photoshop Elements

Adobe Illustrator

Adobe (Macromedia) Fireworks
www.adobe.com

Corel Paint Shop Pro Photo
www.corel.com

Multimedia

Adobe (Macromedia) Flash (Windows, Mac OS), Adobe After Effects (Windows, Mac OS)
www.adobe.com

Apple iMovie (Mac OS only)
www.apple.com/ilife/imovie

Apple QuickTime (Mac OS, Windows)
www.apple.com/quicktime

Apple Final Cut Studio (includes Final Cut Pro, Soundtrack Pro, Motion, Color, Compressor, and DVD Studio) (Mac OS X only)
www.apple.com/finalcutstudio/

Audacity (all platforms)
audacity.sourceforge.net

Sony Sound Forge (Windows only)
www.sonycreativesoftware.com/products/soundforgefamily.asp

Windows Media Encoder, Windows Movie Maker (Windows only)
www.microsoft.com/windows/windowsmedia/

Browsers

Microsoft Internet Explorer
www.microsoft.com/windows/ie

Firefox
www.firefox.com

Netscape Navigator
browser.netscape.com

Opera
www.opera.com

Safari
www.apple.com/safari

Networking

WS_FTP, CuteFTP, AceFTP and others for WIndows available at:
www.download.com

Transmit (for Macintosh OSX)
www.panic.com

Interarchy (for Macintosh OSX)
www.interarchy.com

Cygwin (Linux emulator for Windows)
www.cygwin.com

PuTTY (telnet/SSH terminal emulator)
www.chiark.greenend.org.uk/~sgtatham/putty/

What You've Learned

The lesson to take away from this chapter is: "you don't have to learn everything." And even if you want to learn everything eventually, you don't need to learn it all at once. So relax, don't worry. The other good news is that, while many professional tools exist, it is possible to create a basic web site and get it up and running without spending much money by using freely available or inexpensive tools and your existing computer setup.

As you'll soon see, it's easy to get started making web pages—you will be able to create simple pages by the time you're done reading this book. From there, you can continue adding to your bag of tricks and find your particular niche in web design.

Test Yourself

Each chapter in this book ends with a few questions that you can answer to see if you picked up the important bits of information. Answers appear in Appendix A.

1. Match these web professionals with the final product they might be responsible for producing.

   A. Graphic designer   _____ (X)HTML and CSS documents

   B. Production department   _____ PHP scripts

   C. Information designer   _____ Photoshop page sketch

   D. Web programmer   _____ Site diagram

2. What does the W3C do?

3. Match the web technology with its appropriate task:

   A. HTML and XHTML   _____ Checks a form field for a valid entry

   B. CSS   _____ Creates a custom server-side web application

   C. JavaScript   _____ Identifies text as a second-level heading

   D. Ruby on Rails   _____ Defines a new markup language for sharing financial information

   E. XML   _____ Makes all second-level headings blue

4. What is the difference between frontend and backend web development?

5. What is the difference between a web-authoring program and an HTML-editing tool?

CHAPTER 2

HOW THE WEB WORKS

I got started in web design in early 1993—pretty close to the start of the Web itself. In web time, that makes me an old-timer, but it's not so long ago that I can't remember the first time I looked at a web page. It was difficult to tell where the information was coming from and how it all worked.

This chapter sorts out the pieces and introduces some basic terminology you'll encounter. If you've already spent time perusing the Web, some of this information will be a review. If you're starting from scratch, it is important to have all the parts in perspective. We'll start with the big picture and work down to specifics.

IN THIS CHAPTER

An explanation of the Web, as it relates to the Internet

The role of the server

The role of the browser

Introduction to URLs and their components

The anatomy of a web page

The Internet Versus the Web

No, it's not a battle to the death, just an opportunity to point out the distinction between these two words that are increasingly being used interchangeably.

The Internet is a network of connected computers. No company owns the Internet (i.e., it is not equivalent to a service like America Online); it is a cooperative effort governed by a system of standards and rules. The purpose of connecting computers together, of course, is to share information. There are many ways information can be passed between computers, including email, file transfer (FTP), and many more specialized modes upon which the Internet is built. These standardized methods for transferring data or documents over a network are known as protocols.

The World Wide Web (known affectionately as "the Web") is just one of the ways information can be shared over the Internet. It is unique in that it allows documents to be linked to one another using hypertext links—thus forming a huge "web" of connected information. The Web uses a protocol called HTTP (HyperText Transfer Protocol). If you've spent any time using the Web, that acronym should look familiar because it is the first four letters of nearly all web site addresses, as we'll discuss in an upcoming section.

A Brief History of the Web

The Web was born in a particle physics laboratory (CERN) in Geneva, Switzerland in 1989. There, a computer specialist named Tim Berners-Lee first proposed a system of information management that used a "hypertext" process to link related documents over a network. He and his partner, Robert Cailliau, created a prototype and released it for review. For the first several years, web pages were text-only. It's difficult to believe that in 1992 (not that long ago), the world had only 50 web servers, total.

The real boost to the Web's popularity came in 1992 when the first graphical browser (NCSA Mosaic) was introduced. This allowed the Web to break out of the realm of scientific research into mass media. The ongoing development of the Web is overseen by the World Wide Web Consortium (W3C).

If you want to dig deeper into the Web's history, check out these sites:

Web Developers' Virtual Library

WDVL.com/Internet/History

W3C's History Archives

www.w3.org/History.html

TERMINOLOGY

Open source

Open source software is developed as a collaborative effort with the intent to make its source code available to other programmers for use and modification. Open source programs are usually available for free.

Serving Up Your Information

Let's talk more about the computers that make up the Internet. Because they "serve up" documents upon request, these computers are known as servers. More accurately, the server is the software (not the computer itself) that allows the computer to communicate with other computers; however, it is common to use the word "server" to refer to the computer, as well. The role of server software is to wait for a request for information, then retrieve and send that information back as quickly as possible.

There's nothing special about the computers themselves...picture anything from a high-powered Unix machine to a humble personal computer. It's the server software that makes it all happen. In order for a computer to be part of the Web, it must be running special web server software that allows it to handle Hypertext Transfer Protocol transactions. Web servers are also called "HTTP servers."

There are many server software options out there, but the two most popular are Apache (open source software, see sidebar) and Microsoft Internet Information Services (IIS). Apache is freely available for Unix-based computers and comes installed on Macs running Mac OS X. There is a Windows version as well. Microsoft IIS is part of Microsoft's family of server solutions.

Each computer on the Internet is assigned a unique numeric IP address (IP stands for Internet Protocol). For example, the computer that hosts oreilly.com has the IP address 208.201.239.37. All those numbers can be dizzying, so fortunately, the Domain Name System (DNS) was developed that allows us to refer to that server by its domain name, oreilly.com, as well. The numeric IP address is useful for computers, while the domain name is more accessible to humans. Matching the text domain names to their respective numeric IP addresses is the job of a separate DNS server.

It is possible to configure your web server so that more than one domain name is mapped to a single IP address, allowing several sites to share a single server.

A Word About Browsers

We now know that the server does the servin', but what about the other half of the equation? The software that does the requesting is called the client. On the Web, the browser is the client software that makes requests for documents. The server returns the documents for the browser to display.

The requests and responses are handled via the HTTP protocol, mentioned earlier. Although we've been talking about "documents," HTTP can be used to transfer images, movies, audio files, and all the other web resources that commonly make up web sites or are shared over the Web.

When we think of a browser, we usually think of a window on a computer monitor with a web page displayed in it. These are known as graphical browsers or desktop browsers. The most popular graphical browser is Internet Explorer for Windows, with over 80% of web traffic as of this writing. However, there are many other popular browsers, including Firefox, Safari, Opera, and Netscape.

Although it's true that the Web is most often viewed on traditional graphical browsers, it is important to keep in mind that there are all sorts of browsing experiences. Users with sight disabilities may be listening to a web page read by a screen reader. Some browsers are small enough to fit into cell phones or PDAs. The sites we build must be readable in all of these environments.

Bear in mind also that your web pages may look and work differently even on up-to-date graphical browsers. This is due to varying support for web technologies and users' ability to set their own browsing preferences. Dealing with the ways browsers and users affect your pages is discussed in Chapter 3, The Nature of Web Design.

TERMINOLOGY

Server-side and Client-side

Often in web design, you'll hear reference to "client-side" or "server-side" applications. These terms are used to indicate which machine is doing the processing. Client-side applications run on the user's machine, while server-side applications and functions use the processing power of the server computer.

Web Page Addresses (URLs)

With all those web pages on all those servers, how would you ever find the one you're looking for? Fortunately, each document has its own special address called a URL (Uniform Resource Locator). It's nearly impossible to get through a day without seeing a URL (pronounced "U-R-L," not "erl") plastered on the side of a bus, printed on a business card, or broadcast on a television commercial.

NOTE

Among developers, there is a movement to use the more technically accurate term URI (Uniform Resource Identifier) for identifying the name of a resource. On the street and even on the job, however, you're still likely to hear URL.

Some URLs are short and sweet. Others may look like crazy strings of characters separated by dots (periods) and slashes, but each part has a specific purpose. Let's pick one apart.

Intranets and Extranets

When you think of a web site, you generally assume that it is accessible to anyone surfing the Web. However, many companies take advantage of the awesome information sharing and gathering power of web sites to exchange information just within their own business. These special web-based networks are called intranets. They are created and function like ordinary web sites, only they are on computers with special security devices (called firewalls) that prevent the outside world from seeing them. Intranets have lots of uses, such as sharing human resource information or providing access to inventory databases.

An extranet is like an intranet, only it allows access to select users outside of the company. For instance, a manufacturing company may provide its customers with passwords that allow them to check the status of their orders in the company's orders database. Of course, the passwords determine which slice of the company's information is accessible. Sharing information over a network is changing the way many companies do business.

The parts of a URL

A complete URL is generally made up of three components: the protocol, the site name, and the absolute path to the document or resource, as shown in Figure 2-1.

Hey, There's No http:// on That URL!

Because all web pages use the Hypertext Transfer Protocol, the `http://` part is often just implied. This is the case when site names are advertised in print or on TV, as a way to keep the URL short and sweet.

Additionally, browsers are programmed to add `http://` automatically as a convenience to save you some keystrokes. It may seem like you're leaving it out, but it is being sent to the server behind the scenes.

When we begin using URLs to create hyperlinks in (X)HTML documents in Chapter 6, Adding Links, you'll learn that it is necessary to include the protocol when making a link to a web page on another server.

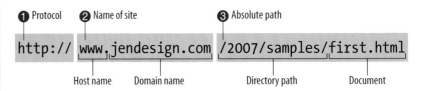

Figure 2-1. The parts of a URL.

❶ `http://`

The first thing the URL does is define the protocol that will be used for that particular transaction. The letters HTTP let the server know to use Hypertext Transfer Protocol, or get into "web-mode."

NOTE

Sometimes you'll see a URL that begins with `https://`. *This is an indication that it is a secure server transaction. Secure servers have special encryption devices that hide delicate content, such as credit card numbers, while they are transferred to and from the browser.*

❷ `www.jendesign.com`

The next portion of the URL identifies the web site by its domain name. In this example, the domain name is jendesign.com. The "www." part at the beginning is the particular host name at that domain. The host name "www" has become a convention, but is not a rule. In fact, sometimes the host name may be omitted. There can be more than one web site at a domain (sometimes called subdomains). For example, there might also be *development.jendesign.com*, *clients.jendesign.com*, and so on.

NOTE

A group of folks are working to abolish the "www" subdomain. Read more at no-www.org.

❸ `/2007/samples/first.html`

This is the absolute path to the requested HTML document, *first.html*. The words separated by slashes indicate the pathway through directory levels, starting with the root directory of the host, to get to *first.html*. Because the Internet originally comprised computers running the Unix operating system, our current way of doing things still follows many Unix rules and conventions (hence the /).

To sum it up, the example URL says it would like to use the HTTP protocol to connect to a web server on the Internet called *www.jendesign.com* and request the document *first.html* (located in the *samples* directory, which is in the *2007* directory).

Default files

Obviously, not every URL you see is so lengthy. Many addresses do not include a file name, but simply point to a directory, like these:

```
http://www.oreilly.com
http://www.jendesign.com/resume/
```

When a server receives a request for a directory name rather than a specific file, it looks in that directory for a default document, typically named *index. html*, and sends it back for display. So when someone types in the above URLs into their browser, what they'll actually see is this:

```
http://www.oreilly.com/index.html
http://www.jendesign.com/resume/index.html
```

The name of the default file (also referred to as the index file) may vary, and depends on how the server is configured. In these examples, it is named *index. html*, but some servers use the file name *default.htm*. If your site uses server-side programming to generate pages, the index file might be named *index.php* or *index.asp*. Just check with your server administrator to make sure you give your default file the proper name.

Another thing to notice is that in the first example, the original URL did not have a trailing slash to indicate it was a directory. When the slash is omitted, the server simply adds one if it finds a directory with that name.

The index file is also useful for security. Some servers (depending on their configuration) return the contents of the directory for display in the browser if the default file is not found. Figure 2-2 shows how the documents of the *housepics* directory are exposed as the result of a missing default file. One way to prevent people snooping around in your files is to be sure there is an index file in every directory. Your system administrator may also add other protections to prevent your directories from displaying in the browser.

Providing the URL for a directory (rather than a specific filename) prompts the server to look for a default file, typically called index.html.

Some servers are configured to return a listing of the contents of that directory if the default file is not found.

The Anatomy of a Web Page

We're all familiar with what web pages look in the browser window, but what's happening "under the hood?"

At the top of Figure 2-3, you see a basic web page as it appears in a browser. Although you can view it as one coherent page, it is actually made up of three separate files: an HTML document (*index.html*) and two graphics (*kitchen.gif* and *spoon.gif*). The HTML document is running the show.

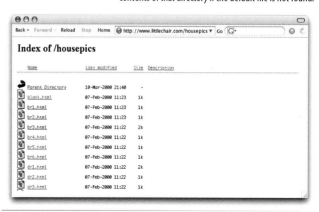

Figure 2-2. Some servers display the contents of the directory if an index file is not found.

exercise 2-1 |
View source

You can see the (X)HTML file for any web page by choosing View → Page Source or (View → Source) in your browser's menu. Your browser will open the source document in a separate window. Let's take a look under the hood of a web page.

1. Enter this URL into your browser:

   www.learningwebdesign.com/ materials/chapter02/ kitchen.html

   You should see the Jen's Kitchen Web page from Figure 2-3.

2. Select View → Page Source (or View → Source) from the browser menu. A window opens showing the source document shown in the figure.

3. The source for most sites is considerably more complicated. View the source of oreilly.com or the site of your choice. Don't worry if you don't understand what's going on. Much of it will look more familiar by the time you are done with this book.

Keep in mind that while learning from others' work is fine, the all-out stealing of other people's code is poor form (or even illegal). If you want to use code as you see it, ask for permission and always give credit to those who did the work.

HTML documents

You may be as surprised as I was to learn that the graphically rich and interactive pages we see on the Web are generated by simple, text-only documents. That's right: plain old ASCII text (meaning it has just letters, numbers, and a few symbol characters). This text file is referred to as the source document.

Take a look at *index.html*, the source document for the Jen's Kitchen web page. You can see it contains the text content of the page plus special tags (indicated with angle brackets, < and >) that describe each text element on the page.

Adding descriptive tags to a text document is known as "marking up" the document. Web pages use a markup language called the HyperText Markup Language, or HTML for short, that was created especially for documents with hypertext links. HTML defines dozens of text elements that make up documents such as headings, paragraphs, emphasized text, and of course, links. There are also HTML elements that add information about the document (such as its title) and that add media such as images, videos, Flash movies, or applets to the page.

NOTE

The discussion of HTML in this section also applies to its updated version, XHTML (eXtensible Hypertext Markup Language). The document in Figure 2-3 is actually authored in XHTML.

A quick introduction to HTML

You'll be learning about HTML in detail in Part II, so I don't want to bog you down with too much detail right now, but there are a few things I'd like to point out about how HTML works and how browsers handle it.

Read through the HTML document in Figure 2-3 and compare it to the browser results. It's easy to see how the elements marked up with HTML tags in the source document correspond to what displays in the browser window.

First, you'll notice that the text within brackets (for example, `<body>`) does not display in the final page. The browser only displays the content of the element; the markup is hidden. The tags provide the name of the HTML element—usually an abbreviation such as "h1" for "heading level 1," or "em" for "emphasized text."

Second, you'll see that most of the HTML tags appear in pairs surrounding the content of the element. In our HTML document, `<h1>` indicates that the following text should be a level-1 heading; `</h1>` indicates the end of the heading. Some elements, called empty elements, do not have content. In our sample, the `<hr />` tag indicates an empty element that tells the browser to "draw a horizontal rule (line) here."

The web page shown in this browser window actually consists of three separate files: an HTML text document and two graphics. Tags in the HTML document gives the browser instructions for how the text is to be handled and where the images should be placed.

index.html

```
<!DOCTYPE html PUBLIC "-//W3C//DTD XHTML 1.0 Transitional//EN"
    "http://www.w3.org/TR/xhtml1/DTD/xhtml1-transitional.dtd">

<html>
<head>
<title>Jen's Kitchen</title>
</head>
<body>
<img src="kitchen.gif" alt="Jen's Kitchen banner" />

<h1>Welcome to the future home of Jen's Kitchen</h1>

<p>If you love to read about <strong>cooking and eating</strong>, would like to learn of some
of the best restaurants in the world, or just want a few choice recipes to add to your
collection, <em>this is the site for you!</em></p>

<p><img src="spoon.gif" alt="spoon illustration" />We're busy putting the site together.
Please check back soon.</p>

<hr />

<p>Copyright 2006, Jennifer Robbins</p>
</body>
</html>
```

kitchen.gif

spoon.gif

Figure 2-3. *The source file and images that make up a simple web page.*

When I first began writing HTML, it helped me to think of the tags and text as "beads on a string" that the browser deals with one by one, in sequence. For example, when the browser encounters an open bracket (<) it assumes all of the following characters are part of the markup until it finds the closing bracket (>). Similarly, it assumes all of the content following an opening `<h1>` tag is a heading until it encounters the closing `</h1>` tag. This is the manner in which the browser parses the HTML document. Understanding the browser's method can be helpful when troubleshooting a misbehaving HTML document.

But where are the pictures?

Obviously, there are no pictures in the HTML file itself, so how do they get there when you view the final page?

You can see in Figure 2-3 that each image is a separate graphic file. The graphics are placed in the flow of the text with the HTML image element (`img`) that tells the browser where to find the graphic (its URL). When the browser sees the `img` element, it makes another request to the server for the image file, and then places it in the content flow. The browser software brings the separate pieces together into the final page.

The assembly of the page generally happens in an instant, so it appears as though the whole page loads all at once. Over slow connections or on slower computers, or if the page includes huge graphics, the assembly process may be more apparent as images lag behind the text. The page may even need to be redrawn as new images arrive (although you can construct your pages in a way to prevent that from happening).

Putting It All Together

To wrap up our introduction to how the Web works, let's trace the stream of events that occur with every web page that appears on your screen (Figure 2-4).

❶ You request a web page by either typing its URL (for example, *http://jenskitchensite.com*) directly in the browser, or by clicking on a link on the page. The URL contains all the information needed to target a specific document on a specific web server on the Internet.

❷ Your browser sends an HTTP Request to the server named in the URL and asks for the specific file. If the URL specifies a directory (not a file), it is the same as requesting the default file in that directory.

❸ The server looks for the requested file and issues an HTTP response.

    a. If the page cannot be found, the server returns an error message. The message typically says "404 Not Found," although more hospitable error messages may be provided.

b. If the document *is* found, the server retrieves the requested file and returns it to the browser.

❹ The browser parses the HTML document. If the page contains images, (indicated by the HTML img element), the browser contacts the server again to request each image file specified in the markup.

❺ The browser inserts each image in the document flow where indicated by the img element. And *voila*! The assembled web page is displayed for your viewing pleasure.

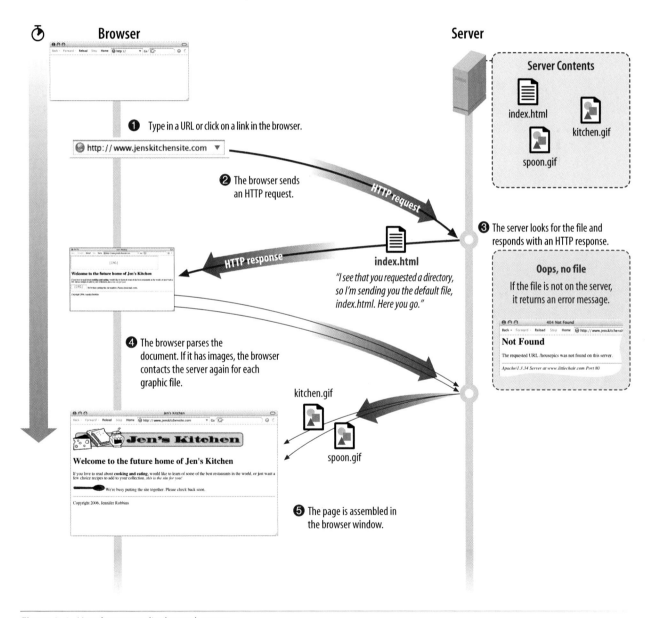

Figure 2-4. How browsers display web pages.

Test Yourself

Let's play a round of "Identify that Acronym!" The following are a few basic web terms mentioned in this chapter. Answers are in Appendix A.

1. HTML   a) Home of Mosaic, the first graphical browser
2. W3C   b) The location of a web document or resource
3. CERN   c) The markup language used for all web documents
4. HTTP   d) Matches domain names with numeric IP addresses
5. IP   e) A limited set of letters, numbers and symbols
6. URL   f) Internet Protocol
7. NCSA   g) Particle physics lab where the Web was born
8. DNS   h) Protocol for transferring web documents on the Internet
9. ASCII   i) The organization that monitors web technologies

Answers: _____

CHAPTER 3

THE NATURE OF WEB DESIGN

As a web designer, you spend a lot of time creating pages and tweaking them until they look good in your browser. Before you grow too attached to the way your page looks on your screen, you should know that it is likely to look different to other people. That's just the nature of web design—you can't guarantee that everyone will see your page the way you do. The way your site looks and performs is at the mercy of a number of variables such as browser version, platform, monitor size, and the preferences or special needs of each individual user. Your page may also be viewed on a mobile device like a cell phone, or using an assistive device like a screen magnifier or a screen reader.

This unpredictable nature of the Web is particularly challenging if you have experience designing for print, where what you design stays put. As a print designer who made the transition to web design, I found I needed to let go of controlling things such as page size, typography, and precise color. Having a solid understanding of the web environment allows you to anticipate and plan for these shifting variables. Eventually, you'll develop a feel for it.

This chapter looks at the ways in which browsers, user configurations, platform, connection speed, computer monitors, and alternative browsing environments affect the design and functionality of web pages. It suggests some tips for coping along the way.

Browser Versions

One of the biggest challenges in designing for the Web is dealing with the multitude of browsers in current use. Although the current version of Microsoft Internet Explorer running on Windows makes up the lion's share (60 to 80% as of this writing), there are at least a dozen browser versions that web developers pay attention to, and hundreds more obscure or antiquated browsers still in use. See the sidebar, Browser Roll Call, for more information on relevant browsers.

In the no-so-distant past, browsers were so incompatible that web authors were forced to create two separate sites, one for Internet Explorer and one for Netscape (the only two players at the time). Fortunately, things have

IN THIS CHAPTER

How variables on the user's end affect the way your page looks and performs, including:

Browser version

Alternative browsing devices

User preferences

Platform

Connection speed

Browser window size and monitor resolution

Monitor color

The nature of web design is that there is no guarantee that everyone will see your page the way you do.

Browser Roll Call

It is important that web developers be familiar with the browsers in current use. Although there are hundreds of browsers out there, only about a dozen make up 99% of browser usage. The A-list browsers in Table 3-1 offer solid standards support and represent the vast majority of web traffic.

Older and niche browsers listed in Table 3-2 may be tested to be sure that the content is available and accessible, but there is no effort made to reproduce the A-list browsing experience on these browsers.

It should be noted that the browsers listed here, and the Usage Statistics in particular, reflect the browser landscape as of the writing of this book. Things are sure to be different by the time you are reading this. For updated browser statistics, go to *www.thecounter. com* or *www.w3schools.com/browsers*. Of course, the most meaningful statistics are those taken from your own site. 3% of visitors to your blog and 3% on a site like Yahoo! are different sized crowds indeed, and may warrant different support decisions.

NOTE

For a complete list of all browers, old and new, see browsers.evolt.org.

For Further Reading

The article "Graded Browser Support" by Nate Koechley at Yahoo!'s Developer Network aptly sums up the contemporary approach to browser support. Read it at *developer.yahoo. com/yui/.articles/gbs/gbs.html*

Table 3-1. A-list browsers (generally tested for a consistent presentation and scripting experience)

Browser version	Platforms	Released	Stats*	Notes
Internet Explorer 7	Windows XP and Vista	2006	14%	IE7 improves support for CSS2 and fixes many of the bugs in IE6. Its share will eventually surpass IE6
Internet Explorer 6	Windows	2001	58%	IE6 usage will decrease as IE7 is distributed.
Internet Explorer 5.5 and 5	Windows, Unix & Mac (IE 5.0 only)	2000 (5.5) 1999 (5)	1%	There are significant differences in the way IE5 and 5.5 supports CSS, requiring workarounds until these versions finally go away. Some developers have already stopped supporting IE5 with the release of IE7.
Mozilla Firefox 1.x & 2.x	Windows, Linux, Unix, Macintosh	2002 (1.0) 2006 (2.0)	12%	Fast and standards-compliant, this is the recommended browser of the development community.
Netscape 7 & 8	Windows, Linux, Unix, Macintosh	2002 (7) 2005 (8)	1%	Netscape once dominated; now it is barely a blip on the radar.
Opera 8 & 9	Windows, Linux, Unix, Macintosh	2005 (8) 2006 (9)	1%	Opera is popular in the development community for its small size and standards compliance.
Safari 1.0 and 2.0	Macintosh OS X	2002 (1.0) 2005 (2.0)	3%	Safari comes with OS X. Safari 2.0 offers the most advanced CSS support of any current browser.
Safari 3.0	Macintosh OS X, Windows XP and Vista	2007	n/a	In public beta as of this writing.

Table 3-2. Older browser versions (tested only to make sure content is available and accessible)

Netscape 4	Windows, Linux, Unix, Macintosh	1999	< .5%	Netscape 4 has only partial support for CSS and other standards. It is representative of legacy browsers.
IE 5 (Mac)	Macintosh	2000	< 1%	The best standards-compliant browser option for users who must still use Mac OS 9
Lynx (or other text only browser)	old versions for Windows, Mac, Unix	1992	n/a	A text only browser is useful for testing the accessibility of content on less-than-optimal browsers.

* Usage statistics taken from *TheCounter.com* in April 2007.

improved dramatically now that browsers have better support for web standards established by the World Wide Web Consortium (W3C for short). The situation will continue to improve as older, problematic browser versions such as Internet Explorer 5 and Netscape 4 fade out of existence.

Fortunately, nearly all browsers in use today support HTML 4.01 and XHTML standards, with only a few exceptions. That doesn't mean that an (X)HTML document will look identical on all browsers—there may still be slight differences in the default rendering of text and form elements. That's because browsers have their own internal style sheets that determine how each element looks by default.

Instead, the new challenge for cross-browser consistency comes in the varying support of certain aspects of Cascading Style Sheets (CSS). Although most of the basic style sheet properties can be used reliably, there are still some bugs and inconsistencies that may cause unexpected results. Figure 3-1 shows how the same web page may be rendered differently based on the browser's support of CSS.

Figure 3-1. The same web page may look different on different browsers. In this case, the problem is in inconsistent implementation of certain style properties by IE5 (Win). Fortunately, the percentage of web traffic using IE5 (Win) is down around 2% and shrinking with the release of IE7 in 2006.

Firefox 1.5
This page appears as the author intended.

Internet Explorer 5 (Windows 2000)
Because of IE5Win's implementation of CSS, centering is broken, columns overlap, and the tabs run together.

Coping with various browser versions

How do professional web designers and developers cope with the multitude of browsers and their varying capabilities? Here are a few guidelines.

Don't sweat the small stuff. As a web designer, you must allow a certain amount of variation. It's the nature of the medium. What is important isn't that form input boxes are all precisely 15 pixels tall, but that they work. The first lesson you'll learn is that you have to let go.

Stick with the standards. Following web standards—(X)HTML for document structure and CSS for presentation—as documented by the W3C is your primary tool for ensuring your site is as consistent as possible on all standards-compliant browsers (that's approximately 99% of browsers in current use).

DEVELOPMENT TIP

Browsercam

A good shortcut for checking how your page looks in a variety of browsers (without installing them all yourself) is to use a subscription service like Browsercam.com. For a monthly fee, just enter the URL of your page, and Browsercam captures the screen image in every browser configuration you can imagine. Check it out at *www.browsercam. com*. It is not a substitute for testing performance (you can't tell if the scripts are working), but it can catch style sheet and even markup issues.

FOR FURTHER READING

Accessibility vs. Availability

Web accessibility guru, Derek Featherstone, draws an interesting and useful distinction between "accessibility" for users with disabilities and "availability" for users with alternative devices such as mobile phones. Read his blog entry at *www.boxofchocolates. ca/archives/2005/08/25/accessibility-and-availability*

Start with good markup. When an (X)HTML document is written in logical order and its elements are marked up in a meaningful way, it will be usable on the widest range of browsing environments, including the oldest browsers, future browsers, and mobile and assistive devices. It may not look exactly the same, but the important thing is that your content is available.

Don't use browser-specific (X)HTML elements. There are markup elements and attributes out there that work only with one browser or another, a remnant from the browser wars of old. Don't use them! (You won't learn them here.)

Become familiar with the aspects of CSS that are likely to cause problems. Using style sheets effectively takes some practice, but experienced developers know which properties are "safe," and which require some extra tweaks to get consistent results on all current browsers.

Alternative Browsing Environments

The previous section focused on issues relevant to graphical browsers used on desktop or laptop computers. It is critical to keep in mind, however, that people access content on the Web in many different ways. Web designers must build pages in a manner that creates as few barriers as possible to getting to information, regardless of the user's ability and the device used to access the Web. In other words, you must design for accessibility.

Accessibility is a major topic of discussion in the web design world, and a priority for all web designers. While intended for users with disabilities such as poor vision or limited mobility, the techniques and strategies developed for accessibility also benefit other users with less-than-optimum browsing experiences, such as handheld devices, or traditional browsers over slow modem connections or with the images and JavaScript turned off. Accessible sites are also more effectively indexed by search engines such as Google. The extra effort in making your site accessible is well worth the effort.

Users with disabilities

There are four broad categories of disabilities that affect how people interact with their computers and the information on them:

- **Vision impairment.** People with low or no vision may use an assistive device such as a screen reader, Braille display, or a screen magnifier to get content from the screen. They may also simply use the browser's text zoom function to make the text large enough to read.

- **Mobility impairment.** Users with limited or no use of their hands may use special devices such as modified mice and keyboards, foot pedals, or joysticks to navigate the Web and enter information.

- **Auditory impairment.** Users with limited or no hearing will miss out on audio aspects of multimedia, so it is necessary to provide alternatives, such as transcripts for audio tracks or captions for video.

- **Cognitive impairment.** Users with memory, reading comprehension, problem solving, and attention limitations benefit when sites are designed simply and clearly. These qualities are helpful to anyone using your site.

The lesson here is that you shouldn't make assumptions about how your users are accessing your information. They may be hearing it read aloud. They may be pushing a button to jump from link to link on the page. The goal is to make sure your content is accessible, and the site is as easy to use as possible.

The mobile Web

The increased popularity of the Web, combined with the growing reliance on handheld devices such as cell phones, PDAs, and palm-top computers, has resulted in web browsers squeezing into the coziest of spaces.

Although most content accessible on mobile devices has been developed specifically for that type of browser, an increasing number of devices now include microbrowsers capable of displaying the same web content that you'd see on your PC. Microbrowsers are designed to accommodate limited display area, lower memory capacity, and low bandwidth abilities. Some have only basic HTML support and others support the current web standards.

One limitation of handheld devices is screen size. Mobile displays are roughly only 240 pixels square, although some have dimensions as small as 128 pixels or as large as 320. That's not much room to look at a typical web site. Mobile browsers deal with the limited screen size the best they can. Some shrink the page to fit by displaying the text content as it appears in the HTML source document, and resizing the images to fit the screen. Others simply allow horizontal scrolling. Figure 3-2 shows the Jen's Kitchen page as it might appear in a microbrowser on a cell phone.

Dealing with diversity

The best way to accommodate the needs of all your visitors is to design with accessibility in mind. Accessible design not only helps your disabled visitors, but also those using the Web on the go or under any less-than-ideal conditions. You'll also improve the quality of your content as perceived by search engine indexing programs.

The W3C started the Web Accessibility Initiative to address the need to make the Web usable for everyone. They developed the Web Content Accessibility Guidelines (WCAG) to help developers create accessible sites. You can read

NOTE

Adobe Creative Suite 3 features many tools for designing and optimizing applications for mobile devices. Learn more at adobe.com.

Figure 3-2. This is the Jen's Kitchen web page from Chapter 2 as it might appear on a mobile device. (The image was taken using the Openwave Mobile Browser Simulator available at developer. openwave.com.)

them all at *http://www.w3.org/TR/WAI-WEBCONTENT/*. The United States government used the Priority 1 points of the WCAG as the basis for its Section 508 accessibility guidelines (see the sidebar, Government Accessibility Guidelines: Section 508).

While accessibility and the techniques for achieving it are vast topics, I've summarized some of the guiding principles and provided pointers to useful resources here.

Start with clean HTML. When your source document has been marked up with appropriate, meaningful HTML elements and the content appears in a logical order, your content will make sense in the widest variety of circumstances, whether it is read aloud or displayed on a tiny handheld screen.

Provide alternatives. Always provide alternatives to non-text content such as alternative text or long descriptions for images, transcripts for audio, and captions for video content, to better serve users with various disabilities.

Allow text to resize. If you use style sheets to specify font size, do so in relative measurements such as percentages or ems (a unit of measurement for text equal to a capital "M") so that users can resize it with the browser's "text zoom" feature (when available).

Don't put text in graphics. Although it may be tempting to control the typography of a headline by putting it in a graphic, doing so makes it less accessible by removing that content from the document. It also prevents users from resizing the text.

Use accessibility features when creating HTML tables and forms. There are a number of attributes in HTML 4.01 and XHTML that improve accessibility by explicitly labeling columns or form fields. They're only useful if you take the time to use them correctly. We'll address these features in the tables and forms chapters, respectively.

Be careful with colors and backgrounds. Be sure that there is plenty of contrast between the foreground and background colors you specify. When using background images, be sure to also specify a similarly colored background color so text is legible, should the image not load properly.

For further reading

The following resources are good starting points for further exploration on web accessibility.

- The Web Accessibility Initiative (WAI), *www.w3.org/WAI*

- WebAIM: Web Accessibility in Mind, *www.webaim.org*

- Dive Into Accessibility: 30 days to a more accessible web site, *diveintoaccessibility.org*

Government Accessibility Requirements: Section 508

If you create a site for a Federal agency, you are required by law to comply with the Section 508 Guidelines that ensure that electronic information and technology is available to people with disabilities. State and other publicly funded sites may also be required to comply.

The following guidelines, excerpted from the Section 508 Standards at *www.section508.gov*, provide a good checklist for basic accessibility for all web sites.

1. A text equivalent for every non-text element shall be provided (e.g., via "alt", "longdesc", or in element content).

2. Equivalent alternatives for any multimedia presentation shall be synchronized with the presentation.

3. Web pages shall be designed so that all information conveyed with color is also available without color, for example from context or markup.

4. Documents shall be organized so they are readable without requiring an associated style sheet.

5. Redundant text links shall be provided for each active region of a server-side image map.

6. Client-side image maps shall be provided instead of server-side image maps except where the regions cannot be defined with an available geometric shape.

7. Row and column headers shall be identified for data tables.

8. Markup shall be used to associate data cells and header cells for data tables that have two or more logical levels of row or column headers.

9. Frames shall be titled with text that facilitates frame identification and navigation.

10. Pages shall be designed to avoid causing the screen to flicker with a frequency greater than 2 Hz and lower than 55 Hz.

11. A text-only page, with equivalent information or functionality, shall be provided to make a web site comply with the provisions of this part, when compliance cannot be accomplished in any other way. The content of the text-only page shall be updated whenever the primary page changes.

12. When pages utilize scripting languages to display content, or to create interface elements, the information provided by the script shall be identified with functional text that can be read by assistive technology.

13. When a web page requires that an applet, plug-in or other application be present on the client system to interpret page content, the page must provide a link to a plug-in or applet that complies with §1194.21(a) through (l).

14. When electronic forms are designed to be completed online, the form shall allow people using assistive technology to access the information, field elements, and functionality required for completion and submission of the form, including all directions and cues.

15. A method shall be provided that permits users to skip repetitive navigation links.

16. When a timed response is required, the user shall be alerted and given sufficient time to indicate more time is required.

- *Building Accessible Websites*, by Joe Clark (New Riders) provides a comprehensive overview. Joe Clark's web site (*joeclark.org/access*) features Joe's latest thinking and discussions on accessibility issues.

User Preferences

At the heart of the original web concept lies the belief that the end user should have ultimate control over the presentation of information. For that reason, browsers are built with features that enable users to set the default appearance of the pages they view. Users' settings will override yours, and there's not much you can do about it. This ensures that users who need to alter the presentation to meet special needs, such as enlarging type to compensate for imparied vision (or even just to read while leaning back in their chairs), are able to do so.

Simply by changing preference settings in the browser, anyone can affect the appearance and functionality of web pages (including yours) in the following ways.

- **Change the font face and size.** The text zoom feature in modern browsers makes it easy to make text larger or smaller on the fly. Users might also change the font face in addition to the size using font settings in the browser Preferences. I've seen CAD designers with super-high monitor resolution set their default type at 24 points to make text easily readable from a comfortable distance. I've looked over the shoulder of a kid who set his browser to render all text in a graffiti font, just because he could. You simply don't know how your text will look on the other end. Figure 3-3 shows how the Jen's Kitchen page might look with different user preferences.

- **Change the background and text colors.** These days, users are less likely to alter the color settings in their browsers just for fun as they did when all web pages were comprised of black text on gray backgrounds. However, some users with impaired vision may use the browser preferences to ensure that all text is dark on a light background with plenty of contrast.

- **Ignore style sheets or apply their own.** Savvy users with specific needs may create their own style sheets that apply to all the sites they view. Others may choose to simply turn style sheets off, for whatever reason.

- **Turn images off.** Users can opt to turn off the graphics completely. You'd be surprised at how many people do this to alleviate the wait for bandwidth-hogging graphics over slow modem connections. Make sure your pages are at least functional with the graphics turned off. Although adding alternative text for each image helps (and it's required in HTML 4.01 and XHTML), it is not visible to 100% of your users. Figure 3-4 shows how a missing image with alternative text looks on several browsers with the images turned off. As you can see, if there is text in the graphic, it will be lost to Safari users because of Safari's poor support for alternative text.

- **Turn off Java and JavaScript.** Your visitors can turn off technologies such as Java or JavaScript with the push of a button. With Java turned off, Java applets will not function. It is actually fairly common for users to turn off JavaScript due to security issues (real or perceived). Figure 3-5 shows a page that uses a Java applet for its main navigation. With Java turned off, the page is a dead end. Similarly, all of the main content on the web page at the bottom of Figure 3-5 disappears if JavaScript is not enabled. The lesson is to avoid relying on technology that can be turned on and off for critical content.

- **Turn off pop-up windows.** Because pop-up ads have become such a nuisance, some browsers make it easy to prevent pop-up windows from opening.

Figure 3-3. A document can look very different as a result of the user's browser settings.

Images on

Firefox (same for Win and Mac)

IE6-Win (alt text on)

IE6-Win (alt text off)

Safari (Mac OS X)

Netscape 7 (Win)

Figure 3-4. It is possible for users to turn image loading off in their browsers. Although providing alternative text helps, it is not 100% foolproof. Notice that the link labels are lost in IE 6 for Windows (when the Alt text option is turned off) and Safari on the Mac. This is another reason to be careful with the way you use images on your pages.

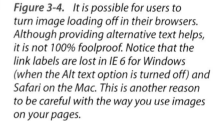

Java ON

Java OFF

Navigation disappears

Figure 3-5. The site on the top loses all of its navigation when Java is turned off. In the site at the bottom of the figure, the main content disappears when JavaScript is not on. Both sites serve as a lesson not to require special functionality for essential content.

JavaScript ON

JavaScript OFF

Content disappears

exercise 3-1 | Playing with preferences

See how bad you can get your favorite web pages to look. Keep in mind that some users may be doing this to you.

- Launch your browser and open the Preferences dialog box.
- In Internet Explorer, select General and Colors/Fonts. In Firefox, select Content then Fonts & Colors.
- Have fun setting new text and background colors. Change the size and fonts of the text. Be sure to check or uncheck boxes so that your preferences will override the document's settings. Try turning off image display.

Now have a look at some web pages. How do you like their makeover?

Users also have a say about which fonts and plug-ins are installed on their computers, which can affect their experience of your site as well. Even if you specify a particular font in a style sheet, that font won't be used if it isn't found on the user's hard drive (we'll talk more about fonts in Chapter 12, Formatting Text). And as mentioned earlier, some media formats are dependent on plug-ins that must be downloaded and installed.

Coping with user preferences

How do you deal with user preferences? It basically comes down to "if you can't beat 'em, join 'em."

Design for flexibility. Whether for good reason or on a whim, the user has the final say on how pages look in the browser. The trend in contemporary web design is to build flexibility into the page. Techniques include using CSS layout techniques that specifically allow text size to change or providing multiple style sheets. We'll look at some of those techniques in Part III.

Make sure your content is accessible without images, scripts, applets, and plug-ins. Be prepared for the fact that some users opt to turn these features off in their browsers. It is a good idea to test your site under minimal conditions to make sure content is not lost and that there are no dead ends. Always provide alterative text for images and alternative means of accessing your important information or media.

Different Platforms

Another variable that affects how users see your pages is the platform, or operating system, of their computers. Although most web users have personal computers running some version of the Windows operating system, a significant portion view the Web from Macintosh computers and Unix/Linux systems. The user's platform affects:

- **Font availability and display.** Operating systems come with different fonts installed, so you can't assume that a font that comes installed on Windows will be available for everyone else. In addition, text tends to have a different look from platform to platform due to the methods used for sizing and rendering. Typography on the Web is discussed in more detail in Chapter 12.

- **The rendering of form elements.** Form elements such as scrolling lists and pull-down menus tend to take on the general appearance of the operating system, and therefore appear quite differently from one platform to another. They may also be sized differently, which comes into play if you are attempting to fit form elements into a space of a specific size.

- **Availability of plug-in media players.** Browsers use plug-ins (or ActiveX controls on Windows) to play media such as streaming video, audio, or

Flash movies that have been embedded on a web page. Fortunately, very popular players like the Flash Player are available for all platforms. Be aware, however, that some plug-in releases for Macintosh and Unix lag behind the Windows versions (the Windows Media Player, for example) or are not supported at all.

Coping with different platforms

These are a few strategies for dealing with the fact that your page will be viewed on different platforms.

Allow some variation. You've heard this tip before in the previous section. As long as your content is available and functional, the small details don't matter. You'll get the hang of designing for flexibility to allow for changing font and form control sizes.

Specify common fonts and provide alternatives. There are a handful of fonts that are available cross-platform, and you should always provide a list back-up fonts should your specified font not be found. Specifying fonts is discussed in Chapter 12.

Be sure media players are available for all platforms. Before you commit to a particular media format, make sure that it will be accessible for all platforms. If the necessary plug-in isn't available for everyone, provide an alternative format, if possible. It has become common for media sites to offer a choice between QuickTime, Windows Media, and RealMedia and let the user pick the format they prefer.

Don't mimic a particular operating system in your interface design. OK, this might just be a personal peeve of mine, but web sites (and pop-up ads) that use Windows-style menu bars and buttons just look silly on my Mac.

Connection Speed

Remember that a web page is published over a network, and it needs to go zipping through the lines as little bundles of data before it reaches the end user. In most cases, the speed of that connection is a mystery.

On the high end, folks with T1 connections, cable modems, ISDN, and other high-speed Internet access may be viewing your pages at a rate of up to 500 KB per second. The percentage of people accessing the Web with broadband connections is steadily increasing. As of this writing, roughly 70% of Internet users in the United States access the Internet via broadband*, and it is steadily climbing. That percentage rises to 90% in the U.S. workplace.

---

* According to Nielsen/Net Ratings (*www.netratings.com*) as published by WebSiteOptimization. com in August, 2006 (*www.websiteoptimization.com/bw0604/*).

ONLINE RESOURCE

For global broadband statistics, see the statistics published by the Organisation for Economic Co-operation and Development at *www.oecd.org*.

The remaining 30% are dialing in with modems whose speed can range from 56 Kbps to as slow as 14.4 Kbps. For these users, data transfer rates of 1 KB per second are common.

NOTE

There are other factors that affect download times, including the speed of the server, the amount of traffic it is receiving when the web page is requested, and the general congestion of the lines.

Coping with unknown connection speed

When you're counting on maintaining the interest of your readers, every millisecond counts. For this reason, it's wise to follow the golden rules of web design:

Keep your files as small as possible. It should be fairly intuitive that larger amounts of data will require more time to arrive. One of the worst culprits for hogging bandwidth is graphics files, so it is especially important that you spend time optimizing them for the Web. (I discuss some strategies for doing this in Chapter 19, Creating Lean and Mean Web Graphics.) (X)HTML files, although generally just a few kilobytes (KB) in size, can be optimized as well by removing redundant markup and extra spaces. Audio, video, and multimedia content also consume lots of bandwidth and should be compressed appropriately. Because you know a web page is designed to travel, do your best to see that it travels light.

Know your audience. In some cases, you can make assumptions as to the connection speeds of your typical users. For example, if you are creating a video sharing site, you can optimize the site for performance over high-bandwidth connections. Because most people have access to high-bandwidth Internet in the workplace, you may be a bit more lenient on file sizes for sites with a professional audience. However, if your site is aimed at consumers or the classroom, be especially frugal with your byte count.

Browser Window Size and Monitor Resolution

Although you may prefer the way your page looks when the window is just larger than the masthead you designed, the fact is users can set the window as wide or narrow as they please. You really have no idea how big your page will be: as large as the user's monitor will allow, or smaller according to personal preference or to accommodate several open windows at once.

But don't worry. Not only will you become familiar with how your content behaves at different window sizes, there are also design techniques that can make the page layout more predictable. I'll talk about them a bit in this section and then in detail in Chapter 16, Page Layout with CSS.

Go with the flow

Let's take a look at what happens to text content on web pages when the window is resized. Unlike print pages, web pages are fluid. Take a look at the web page in Figure 3-6. By default, elements like headings, paragraphs, and lists stack up (sort of like blocks), and the text within them flows in to fill the available width of the window or other container space. This is what is called the normal flow of the document.

Figure 3-6. In the normal text flow, headings and paragraphs stack up, but the text within them flows to fill the available width. If the width changes, the text reflows.

Now look at what happens when the page is resized, as shown in the figure on the right. The block elements stay stacked up in order, but the lines of text in them rebreak and reflow to fill the new, narrower space, resulting in more text lines and a longer page overall.

That means you can't be sure that your intro paragraph will be exactly a certain number of lines as you can in print. In addition, if the browser window is very wide, the lines of text will be very long, perhaps even too wide to be read comfortably. We'll address some of these issues in a moment, but first, let's look at what we *do* know about typical browser window dimensions.

Web page dimensions

Because browser windows can only be opened as large as the monitors displaying them, standard monitor resolution (the total number of pixels available on the screen) is useful in anticipating the likely dimensions of your page. This is particularly true on Windows machines, because the browser window is typically maximized to fill the monitor. The sidebar, Common Monitor Resolutions, lists the most popular resolutions as well as how much space that leaves for your content.

As of this writing, most commercial web sites are designed to fit in an 800 × 600 monitor, the smallest monitor that is still in significant use. Allowing

---

exercise 3-2 |
Get a feel for the normal flow

If you have a browser and access to the Web, you can play along with Figure 3-6. Make sure your browser window is not optimized to fill the screen.

Enter the following URL into your browser:

www.w3.org/MarkUp

Make the browser as wide as your monitor will allow. Now make it extremely narrow. How many lines of text are at the top? What happens to the headline? What happens to the pink box?

for the browser chrome and operating system menus, that leaves a canvas area of approximately 775×425 pixels for your web content. See the sidebar, Designing "Above the Fold," that describes some of the important content

TERMINOLOGY

What Is a Pixel?

If you look closely at an image on a computer monitor, you can see that it looks like a mosaic made up of tiny, single-colored squares. Each square is called a pixel.

Common Monitor Resolutions

Table 3-3 lists the most common monitor resolutions from smallest to largest. It does not include the dimensions of widescreen laptop monitors, as there are currently no usage statistics for those resolutions.

The canvas dimensions refer to the amount of space left in the browser window after all of the controls for the operating system and the buttons and scrollbars for the browser (known as chrome) are accounted for. The canvas measurements reflect the available space in Internet Explorer 6 on Windows (the most popular browser/platform configuration). On browsers on Macintosh OS X, the canvas space is approximately five pixels wider and 40 pixels taller than IE6(Win).

Finally, the usage statistics reflect those gathered by TheCounter.com for the month of October, 2006. The percentage of 800×600 monitors is declining steadily, so it is worth taking a look at the Global Stats on TheCounter.com for updated statistics. Of course, the most meaningful resolution stats will come from your own site.

Table 3-3. Common monitor resolutions

Resolution	Canvas Size (IE6/Win)	% of Users (Oct '06)
640×480	620×309	< 1 %
800×600	780×429	22 %
1024×768	1004×597	56 %
1152×864	1132×793	3 %
1280×1024	1260×853	13 %
1600×1200	1580×1129	< 1%

elements you may want to fit in that modest space.

There is an emerging trend toward wider web pages that fill 1024 and even 1280 pixel monitor widths. This is particularly true for sites aimed at a technical and creative audience where it may be assumed that the audience is viewing from an up-to-date computer with a high-resolution monitor.

Coping with browser window size

How do you cope with the unknown-window-size dilemma? Two page layout approaches have developed in reaction to the need to accommodate changing browser window dimensions:

Designing "Above the Fold"

Newspaper editors know the importance of putting the most important information "above the fold," that is, visible when the paper is folded and on the rack. This principle applies to web design as well.

Web designers have adopted the term "above the fold" to refer to the first screenful of a web page. It's what users will see without scrolling, and it bears the burden of holding their attention and enticing them to click in or scroll down further. Some elements you should consider placing above the fold include:

- The name of the site and your logo (if you have one)
- Your primary message
- Some indication of what your site is about (e.g., shopping, directory, magazine, etc.)
- Navigation to key parts of the site

- Crucial calls to action, such as "Register Now"
- Any other important information, such as a toll-free number
- An advertising banner (your advertisers may require it)

But how much is a "screenful?" Unfortunately, this varies by browser window size. Your available space could be as small as 760 × 400 pixels in a browser on an 800 × 600 monitor.

In general, the level of confidence in what will be seen on the first "page" is highest in the top-left corner of the browser window and then diminishes as the pages moves down and to the right. When the browser window is made very small, the bottom and the right edge are the most likely to be cut off. One strategy for page layout is to put your most important elements and messages in that top-left corner and work out from there through hierarchies of importance.

Liquid layouts

Liquid layouts resize and adapt to the changing window size (Figure 3-7). When the window gets narrower, so do the columns, and the text is allowed to re-wrap as necessary. Liquid layouts are in keeping with the behavior of the normal flow and the spirit of the medium. They also don't require choosing a target resolution for development; however, on very large monitors, the line lengths may get too long to read comfortably.

Figure 3-7. An example of a liquid layout (screenshots taken from clagnut.com/blog/269).

Fixed layouts

Fixed (or fixed-width) layouts keep the content at a particular width, measured in pixels, regardless of window size (Figure 3-8). While fixed layouts promise more predictable pages and line lengths, they may result in awkward empty space on large monitors. There is also a risk of users missing out on content on the right edge if their browsers are not as wide as the layout.

Figure 3-8. *The design on the left (Faded Flowers by Mani Sheriar at csszengarden. com) uses a fixed-width page positioned on the left. When the browser window is resized larger, the extra space is added to the right of the page. The page on the right (Dragen by Matthew Buchanan , also at CSS Zen Garden) has the fixed-width page centered in the browser window. Extra space is split on the left and right margins.*

Liquid and fixed layout techniques are discussed in greater detail in Chapter 16.

NOTE

There are other layout techniques, namely Elastic and Zoom layouts, that respond to font size rather than browser dimensions. They are also introduced in Chapter 16.

Monitor Color

As long as we're talking about monitors, let's look at another impact they have on your design: the display of color. I'll never forget my first lesson in web color. I had designed a headline graphic that used a rich forest green as a background. I proudly put the page up on the server, and when I went into my boss's office to show him my work, the graphic came up on his screen with a background of *pitch black*. It was then that I learned that not everyone (including my boss) was seeing my colors the way I intended them.

When you're publishing materials that will be viewed on computer monitors, you need to deal with the varying ways computers handle color. The differences fall under two main categories: the brightness of the monitor and the number of colors.

Brightness

That rich forest green I described earlier was a victim of varying gamma settings. Gamma refers to the overall brightness of a computer monitor's display, and its default setting varies from platform to platform.

Macintoshes are generally calibrated to a lighter gamma setting than Windows machines. That means that Mac-based designers may be surprised to find their graphics look much darker to users on Windows or Unix (which is what happened to me). Images created under Windows will look washed out on a Mac. Figure 3-9 shows the same page viewed at different gamma settings. Note how detail is lost in the photos at the darker gamma setting.

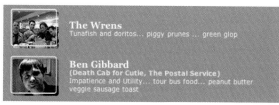

Macintosh gamma

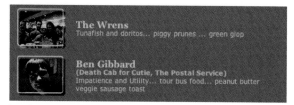

Windows gamma

Figure 3-9. Gamma refers to the overall brightness of monitors. Windows and Unix machines tend to be darker (the result of higher gamma settings) than Macs.

Number of colors

Monitors also differ in the number of colors they are able to display. As of this writing, over 80% of users have 24-bit monitors, capable of displaying nearly 17 million colors. The remainder have 16-bit monitors that display approximately 65,000 colors. With that color-displaying potential, any color you choose should display smoothly.

In the early '90s when the Web was young, most users used 8-bit monitors capable of displaying only 256 colors. Web designers were forced to choose colors from a restrictive web palette of 216 cross-platform colors (Figure 3-10) if they wanted them to display smoothly (that is, without a speckled pattern called dithering). Now that 8-bit monitors account for fewer than 1% of web traffic, it is no longer necessary to jump through those hoops. So while you may hear about the web palette and come across it in web authoring or graphics programs, know that you're no longer restricted to it.

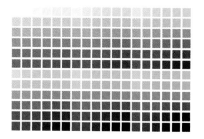

Figure 3-10. The obsolete web palette. Now that nearly all web users have monitors with thousands or millions of colors, you no longer need to restrict yourself to web-safe colors.

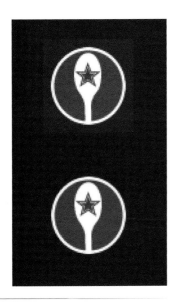

Figure 3-11. On 16-bit monitors, RGB colors get shifted around. In this figure, although the graphic in the foreground uses the identical RGB values as the color in the background, you can still see the outline of the image on the page (top). The only way to fix this is to make the image transparent and allow the background to show through (bottom).

What *is* worth noting, however, is that 16-bit monitors use a completely different color spectrum than 24-bit monitors; i.e., it is not a subset of the 24-bit color space. For that reason, when you specify a color numerically in a style sheet or use it in an image, the 16-bit monitor always needs to shift it slightly to a color in its spectrum. Whether it gets shifted lighter or darker depends on whether the color is in an image or specified in a style sheet, whether it is in the foreground or the background, which browser and platform is used. In other words, it's completely unpredictable. The same color may shift different directions in the foreground and background of the same document.

What this means is that it is difficult to match a foreground color and background color seamlessly for users with 16-bit monitors (Figure 3-11). This may be problematic if you want an image to blend seamlessly with a background image or color, even if they have identical RGB values. While it will be seamless for the majority of users with 24-bit color monitors, 16-bit users will see the rectangular edges of the image in front of the background and the seamless effect will be ruined. This issue is easily remedied by using a transparent graphic format that permits the background color to show through. Transparency is discussed in Chapter 18, Web Graphics Basics.

Coping with monitor color variation

Here are some tips and tricks for dealing with color variations from monitor to monitor.

Let go of precise color control. Yes, once again, the best practice is to acknowledge that the colors you pick won't look the same to everyone, and live with it. Precise color is not a priority in this medium where the colors you see can change based on the plaform, monitor bit-depth, or even the angle of the laptop screen.

Simulate alternative Gamma settings while you design. Since the majority of the web audience today uses Windows machines, designers using Macintosh computers need to be more diligent in testing designs for clarity on Windows. You can simulate what your graphics will look like on Windows using Adobe Photoshop by selecting View→ Proof Setup → Windows RGB (or Macintosh RGB if you are designing on Windows). If it is too light or too dark, make manual adjustments as necessary to the image itself to fix it. To see how the entire page will look with Windows gamma, you can set the brightness of your monitor darker using the Display settings in the System Preferences, or try the inexpensive GammaToggle software that lets you switch back and forth between gamma settings (GammaToggle is available for US$15 from ThankYouWare, *www.thankyouware.com*).

Use transparent images for smooth transitions to the background. There is no way to prevent a noticeable mismatch of foreground and background colors on 16-bit monitors. If you want to be absolutely sure that there is no rectangle around your image for over 99% of users, use a transparent GIF or PNG instead (Figure 3-11).

Know Your Audience

We've established that there are many unknown factors to consider when designing a web page. But there's one thing that you hopefully do know something about when you begin the design process: your target audience. In professional web development companies, researching the characteristics and needs of the target audience is one of the most important parts of the design process.

A good understanding of your audience can help you make better design decisions. Let's take a look at a few examples:

Scenario 1: A site that sells educational toys. If your site is aimed at a consumer audience, you should assume that a significant portion of your audience will be using your site from home computers. They may not keep up with the very latest browser versions, or they may be using an AOL browser, or even surfing the Web with their TVs, so don't rely too heavily on cutting-edge web technologies. They may also be connecting to the Internet through modem connections, so keep your files extra small to prevent long download times. When your bread and butter depends on sales from ordinary consumers, it's best to play it safe with your page design. You can't afford to alienate anyone.

Scenario 2: A site with resources for professional graphic designers. Because graphic designers tend to have larger computer monitors, this is a case for which you may safely design for an 1024×768 pixel screen size. In addition, if they are accessing your pages from work, they are likely to have a connection to the Internet that is faster than the standard modem connection, so you can be a little more lax with the number of size of graphics you put on the page (plus, a good-looking site will be part of the draw for your audience).

Scenario 3: A site used to share company information for in-house use only (also known as an intranet). This is the ideal situation for a web designer because many of the "unknowns" become easily known. Often, a company's system administrator will install the same browser on all machines and keep them up-to-date. Or you might know that everyone will be working on Windows machines with standard 1024×768 monitors. Bandwidth becomes less of an issue when documents are served internally. You should be able to take advantage of some features that would be risky in the standard web environment.

Keeping the Big Picture in Mind

This chapter should help you to set expectations when starting to design your first web pages. It's not as precise a medium as print, and you shouldn't try to force it to be so. Let go of the details and go with the flow. Focus your time and attention on making sure that your content is available for all users, regardless of their browsing devices.

As we dive into the details of (X)HTML and CSS in the following chapters, it will be useful to keep the nature of the Web in mind.

Test Yourself

This chapter covers a number of the quirks of the Web that every new web designer will need to become accustomed to. Describe how each of these factors affect your role as a web designer. Be specific. Answers appear in Appendix A.

1. The variety of browsers in use

2. Macs, Windows, and Unix/Linux systems

3. Each user's browser preferences

4. Resizable browser windows

5. Modem connections

6. Users with assistive devices

HTML MARKUP FOR STRUCTURE

PART **II**

CHAPTER 4

CREATING A SIMPLE PAGE
(HTML Overview)

Part I provided a general overview of the web design environment. Now that we've covered the big concepts, it's time to roll up our sleeves and start creating a real web page. It will be a simple page, but even the most complicated pages are based on the principles described here.

In this chapter, we'll create a simple web page step by step so you can get a feel for what it's like to mark up a document with (X)HTML tags. The exercises allow you to work along.

This is what I want you to get out of this chapter:

- Get a feel for how (X)HTML markup works, including an understanding of elements and attributes.
- See how browsers interpret (X)HTML documents.
- Learn the basic structure of an (X)HTML document.
- Get a first glimpse of a style sheet in action.

Don't worry about learning the specific text elements or style sheet rules at this point; we'll get to those in the following chapters. For now, just pay attention to the process, the overall structure of the document, and the new terminology.

A Web Page, Step by Step

You got a look at an (X)HTML document in Chapter 2, How the Web Works, but now you'll get to create one yourself and play around with it in the browser. The demonstration in this chapter has five steps that cover the basics of page production.

Step 1: Start with content. As a starting point, we'll add raw text content and see what browsers do with it.

Step 2: Give the document structure. You'll learn about (X)HTML elements and the elements that give a document its structure.

IN THIS CHAPTER

An introduction to (X)HTML elements and attributes

A step-by-step demonstration of marking up a simple web page

The elements that provide document structure

Basic text and image elements

A simple style sheet

Troubleshooting broken web pages

(X)HTML

(X)HTML is a shorthand way to refer to both HTML and its latest version, XHTML. Authors may write documents in either version. For a detailed explanation of the differences, see Chapter 10, Understanding the Standards.

HTML the Hard Way

With all the wonderful web-authoring tools out there today, chances are you will be using one to create your pages.

You may be asking, "If the tools are so great, do I need to learn HTML at all?" The answer is yes, you do. You may not need to have every element memorized, but some familiarity is essential for everyone who wants to make web pages. If you apply for a "web designer" position, employers will expect that you know your way around an (X)HTML document.

I stand by my method of teaching (X)HTML the old-fashioned way—*by hand*. There's no better way to truly understand how markup works than typing it out, one tag at a time, then opening your page in a browser. It doesn't take long to develop a feel for marking up documents properly.

Understanding (X)HTML will make using your authoring tools easier and more efficient. In addition, you will be glad that you can look at a source file and understand what you're seeing. It is also crucial for troubleshooting broken pages or fine-tuning the default formatting that web tools produce.

Step 3: Identify text elements. You'll describe the content using the appropriate text elements and learn about the proper way to use (X)HTML.

Step 4: Add an image. By adding an image to the page, you'll learn about attributes and empty elements.

Step 5: Change the look with a style sheet. This exercise gives you a taste of formatting content with Cascading Style Sheets.

By the time we're finished, you will have written the source document for the page shown in Figure 4-1. It's not very fancy, but you have to start somewhere.

We'll be checking our work in a browser frequently throughout this demonstration—probably more than you would in real life—but because this is an introduction to (X)HTML, it is helpful to see the cause and effect of each small change to the source file along the way.

Figure 4-1. In this chapter, we'll write the source document for this web page step by step.

Before We Begin, Launch a Text Editor

In this chapter and throughout the book, we'll be writing out (X)HTML documents by hand, so the first thing we need to do is launch a text editor. The text editor that is provided with your operating system, such as Notepad (Windows) or TextEdit (Macintosh), will do for these purposes. Other text editors are fine as long as you can save plain text (ASCII) files with the *.html* extension. If you have a WYSIWYG web authoring tool such as Dreamweaver or FrontPage, set it aside for now. I want you to get a feel for marking up a document manually (see the sidebar, (X)HTML the Hard Way).

This section shows how to open new documents in Notepad and TextEdit. Even if you've used these programs before, skim through for some special settings that will make the exercises go more smoothly. We'll start with Notepad; Mac users can jump ahead.

Creating a new document in Notepad (Windows users)

These are the steps to creating a new document in Notepad on Windows XP (Figure 4-2).

1. Open the Start menu and navigate to Notepad (in Accessories). ❶

2. Clicking on Notepad will open a new document window, and you're ready to start typing. ❷

3. Next, we'll make the extensions visible. This step is not required to make (X)HTML documents, but it will help make the file types more clear at a glance. In any Explorer window, select "Folder Options..." from the Tools menu ❸ and select the "View" tab. ❹ Find "Hide extensions for known file types" and uncheck that option. ❺ Click OK to save the preference and the file extensions will now be visible.

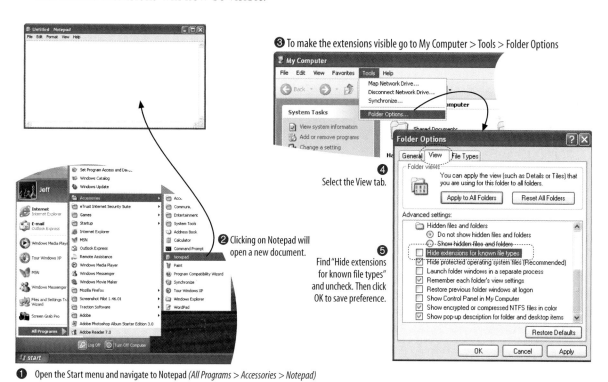

Figure 4-2. Creating a new document in Notepad.

TIP

To make it easy to get to TextEdit later, follow these instructions to save it in the Dock. With TextEdit running, click and hold on its icon in the Dock, then select "Keep in Dock" from the pop-up menu. The next time you need it, you can double-click its icon in the Dock, launch the program, and alleviate to the need to navigate to the Applications folder.

Creating a new document in TextEdit (Macintosh users)

By default, TextEdit creates "rich text" documents, that is, documents that have hidden style formatting instructions for making text bold, setting font size, and so on. (X)HTML documents need to be plain text documents, so we'll need to change the Format, as shown in this example (Figure 4-3).

1. Use the Finder to look in the Applications folder for TextEdit. When you've found it, double-click the name or icon to launch the application.

2. TextEdit opens a new document. You can tell from the text formatting menu at the top that you are in Rich Text mode ❶. Here's how you change it.

3. Open the Preferences dialog box from the TextEdit menu.

4. There are three settings you need to adjust:

   Select "Plain text". ❷

   Select "Ignore rich text commands in HTML files". ❸

   Turn off "Append '.txt' extensions to plain text files". ❹

5. When you are done, click the red button in the top-left corner. ❺

6. Quit TextEdit and restart it to open a new document with the new Plain Text settings. The formatting menu will no longer be on the new document.❻

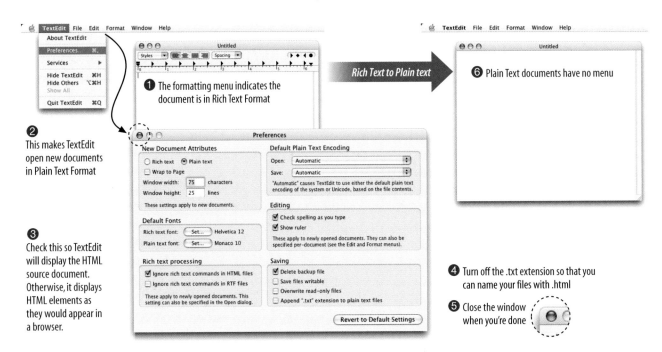

Figure 4-3. Launching TextEdit and choosing Plain Text settings in the Preferences.

Step 1: Start with Content

Now that we've got our new document, it's time to get typing. A web page always starts with content, so that's where we begin our demonstration. Exercise 4-1 walks you through entering the raw text content and saving the document in a new folder.

exercise 4-1 | **Entering content**

1. Type the content for the home page into the new document in your text editor. Just copy it as you see it here. Keep the line breaks the same for the sake of playing along.

```
Black Goose Bistro

The Restaurant
The Black Goose Bistro offers casual lunch and dinner fare in
a hip atmosphere. The menu changes regularly to highlight the
freshest ingredients.

Catering
You have fun... we'll handle the cooking. Black Goose Catering
can handle events from snacks for bridge club to elegant corporate
fundraisers.

Location and Hours
Seekonk, Massachusetts;
Monday through Thursday 11am to 9pm, Friday and Saturday, 11am to
midnight
```

2. Select "Save" or "Save as" from the File menu to get the Save As dialog box (Figure 4-4). The first thing you need to do is create a new folder that will contain all of the files for the site (in other words, it's the local root folder).

   Windows: Click the folder icon at the top to create the new folder. ❶

   Mac: Click the "New Folder" button. ❷

Windows XP

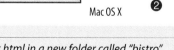
Mac OS X

Figure 4-4. Saving index.html in a new folder called "bistro".

Naming Conventions

It is important that you follow these rules and conventions when naming your files:

Use proper suffixes for your files. (X)HTML files must end with *.html* (some servers allow *.htm*). Web graphics must be labeled according to their file format: *.gif* , *.png* , or *.jpg* (*.jpeg* is also acceptable).

Never use character spaces within filenames. It is common to use an underline character or dash to visually separate words within filenames, such as *robbins_bio.html* or *robbins-bio.html*.

Avoid special characters such as ?, %, #, /, :, ;, •, etc. Limit filenames to letters, numbers, underscores, hyphens, and periods.

Filenames may be case-sensitive, depending on your server configuration. Consistently using all lowercase letters in filenames, while not necessary, makes your filenames easier to manage.

Keep filenames short. Short names keep the character count and file size of your (X)HTML file in check. If you really must give the file a long, multiword name, you can separate words with capital letters, such as *ALongDocumentTitle.html*, or with underscores, such as *a_long_document_title.html*, to improve readability.

Self-imposed conventions. It is helpful to develop a consistent naming scheme for huge sites. For instance, always using lowercase with underscores between words. This takes some of the guesswork out of remembering what you named a file when you go to link to it later.

What Browsers Ignore

Some information in the source document will be ignored when it is viewed in a browser, including:

Line breaks (carriage returns). Line breaks are ignored. Text and elements will wrap continuously until a new block element, such as a heading ($h1$) or paragraph (p), or the line break (br) element is encountered in the flow of the document text.

Tabs and multiple spaces. When a browser encounters a tab or more than one consecutive blank character space, it displays a single space. So if the document contains:

        long,   long   ago

the browser displays:

    long, long ago

Unrecognized markup. A browser simply ignores any tag it doesn't understand or that was incorrectly specified. Depending on the element and the browser, this can have varied results. The browser may display nothing at all, or it may display the contents of the tag as though it were normal text.

Text in comments. Browsers will not display text between the special <!-- and --> tags used to denote a comment. See the (X)HTML Comments sidebar later in this chapter.

Name the new folder **bistro**, and save the text file as **index.html** in it. Windows users, you will also need to choose "All Files" after "Save as type" to prevent Notepad from adding a ".txt" extension to your filename. The filename needs to end in **.html** to be recognized by the browser as a web document. See the sidebar, Naming Conventions, for more tips on naming files.

3. Just for kicks, let's take a look at **index.html** in a browser. Launch your favorite browser (I'm using Firefox) and choose "Open" or "Open File" from the File menu. Navigate to **index.html** and select the document to open it in the browser. You should see something like the page shown in Figure 4-5. We'll talk about the results in the following section.

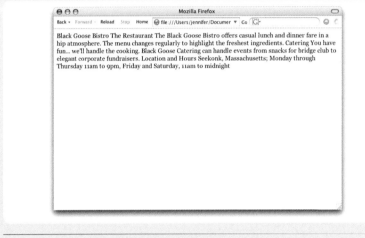

Figure 4-5. *The home page content in a browser.*

NOTE

The raw text file for this exercise is available online at www.learningwebdesign.com/materials/.

Learning from step 1

Our content isn't looking so good (Figure 4-5). The text is all run together—that's not how it looked in the original document. There are a couple of things to be learned here. The first thing that is apparent is that the browser ignores line breaks in the source document. (The sidebar, What Browsers Ignore, lists other information in the source that are not displayed in the browser window.)

Second, we see that simply typing in some content and naming the document *.html* is not enough. While the browser can display the text from the file, we haven't indicated the *structure* of the content. That's where (X)HTML comes in. We'll use markup to add structure: first to the (X)HTML document itself (coming up in Step 2), then to the page's content (Step 3). Once the browser knows the structure of the content, it can display the page in a more meaningful way.

Step 2: Give the Document Structure

We've got our content saved in an *.html* document—now we're ready to start marking it up.

Introducing... the HTML element

Back in Chapter 2, How the Web Works, you saw examples of (X)HTML elements with an opening tag (`<p>` for a paragraph, for example) and closing tag (`</p>`). Before we start adding tags to our document, let's look at the structure of an HTML element and firm up some important terminology. A generic (X) HTML element is labeled in Figure 4-6.

An element consists of both the content and its markup.

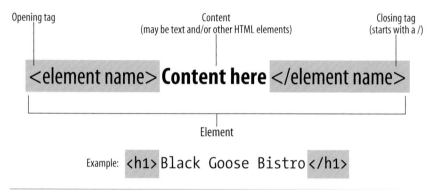

Figure 4-6. *The parts of an (X)HTML element.*

Elements are identified by tags in the text source. A tag consists of the element name (usually an abbreviation of a longer descriptive name) within angle brackets (< >). The browser knows that any text within brackets is hidden and not displayed in the browser window.

The element name appears in the opening tag (also called a start tag) and again in the closing (or end) tag preceded by a slash (/). The closing tag works something like an "off" switch for the element. Be careful not to use the similar backslash character in end tags (see the tip, Slash vs. Backslash).

The tags added around content are referred to as the markup. It is important to note that an element consists of both the content *and* its markup (the start and end tags). Not all elements have content, however. Some are empty by definition, such as the `img` element used to add an image to the page. We'll talk about empty elements a little later in this chapter.

One last thing...capitalization. In this book, all elements are lowercase, and I recommend that you follow the same convention. Even though it isn't strictly required for HTML documents, it *is* required for XHTML documents, so keeping all your markup lowercase brings you one step closer to being compatible with future web standards. See the sidebar, Do As I Say, Not As They Do, for details.

TIP

Slash vs. Backslash

(X)HTML tags and URLs use the slash character (/). The slash character is found under the question mark (?) on the standard QWERTY keyboard.

It is easy to confuse the slash with the backslash character (\), which is found under the bar character (|). The backslash key will not work in tags or URLs, so be careful not to use it.

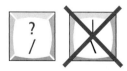

Do As I Say, Not As They Do

If you view the source of a few web pages, you are likely to see markup that looks different from the examples in this book. That's because this book teaches contemporary authoring methods that are in keeping with the stricter requirements of XHTML. If you're learning markup for the first time, you might as well learn to do it like the pros do it.

Lax markup practices are partly due to the fact that the rules of HTML are less stringent than XHTML. In addition, browsers have been forgiving of incorrect markup, so designers have gotten away with bad habits for years.

I recommend following these guidelines even for documents written with HTML.

Capitalization. In HTML, element names are not case sensitive, so you could write <IMG>, <Img>, or <img>. Most professionals, however, keep all elements and attributes in lowercase for consistency and to be in line with future (X)HTML standards.

Quotation marks. *All* attribute values should be in quotation marks, even though in HTML, certain values were okay without them.

Closing elements. In HTML, it is okay to omit the closing tag for certain block elements (such as a paragraph or list item), however, it is safer to close every element in the document.

Complex tables for layout. Old-school web design is well-known for its use of complex nested tables for page layout. Now that style sheets can handle the same thing, the table-based approach is obsolete.

Basic document structure

Much like you and me, (X)HTML documents have a head and a body. The head of the document (also sometimes called the header) contains descriptive information about the document itself, such as its title, the style sheet it uses, scripts, and other types of "meta" information. The body contains the actual content that displays in the browser window.

Figure 4-7 shows the minimal skeleton of an (X)HTML document[*]. First, the entire document is contained within an `html` element. The `html` element is called the root element because it contains all the elements in the document, and it may not be contained within any other element. It is used for both HTML and XHTML documents.

The `head` comes next and contains the `title` element. According to the (X)HTML specifications, every document must contain a descriptive title. The `body` element comes after the `head` and contains everything that we want to show up in the browser window. The document structure elements do not affect how the content looks in the browser (as you'll see in a moment), but they are required to make the document valid (that is, to properly abide by the (X)HTML standards).

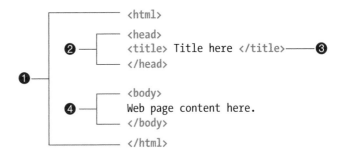

The minimal structure of an (X)HTML document:

❶ Identifies the document as written in HTML or XHTML
❷ The head provides information about the document
❸ A descriptive title is required
❹ The body contains the content that displays in the browser

Figure 4-7. The minimal structure of an (X)HTML document.

Are you ready to add some structure to the Black Goose Bistro home page? Open the *index.html* document and move on to Exercise 4-2.

---

[*] Technically, there are other bits of information that are required for HTML and XHTML documents to validate, such as a document type definition and an indication of the character set used in the document. We'll discuss those in Chapter 10, but for the current introductory discussion these are the only elements you need to worry about.

exercise 4-2 | Adding basic structure

1. Open the newly created document, *index.html*, if it isn't open already.

2. Put the entire document in an HTML root element by adding an **<html>** start tag at the very beginning and an end **</html>** tag at the end of the text. This identifies the document as marked up in HTML (although XHTML uses **html** as well in order to be backwards compatible). Throughout the exercises in this chapter, we'll be writing markup according to the rules of XHTML.

3. Next, create the document head that contains the title for the page. Insert **<head>** and **</head>** tags before the content. Within the **head** element, add the title, "Black Goose Bistro", surrounded by opening and closing **<title>** tags.

4. Finally, define the body of the document by wrapping the content in **<body>** and **</body>** tags. When you are done, the source document should look like this (the markup is shown in color to make it stand out):

```
<html>

<head>
    <title>Black Goose Bistro</title>
</head>

<body>
Black Goose Bistro

The Restaurant
The Black Goose Bistro offers casual lunch and dinner fare in a hip
atmosphere. The menu changes regularly to highlight the freshest
ingredients.

Catering Services
You have fun... we'll do the cooking. Black Goose Catering can handle
events from snacks for bridge club to elegant corporate fundraisers.

Location and Hours
Bakers Corner in Seekonk, Massachusetts;
Monday through Thursday 11am to 9pm, Friday and Saturday, 11am to
midnight
</body>

</html>
```

5. Save the document in the *bistro* directory, so that it overwrites the old version. Open the file in the browser or hit "refresh" or "reload" if it is open already. Figure 4-8 shows how it should look now.

Figure 4-8. The home page in a browser after the document structure elements have been defined.

NOTE

The correct terminology is to say that the title *element is nested within the* head *element. We'll talk about nesting more in later chapters.*

Don't Forget a Good Title

Not only is a title element required for every document, it is quite useful as well. The title is what is displayed in a user's Bookmarks or Favorites list. Descriptive titles are also a key tool for improving accessibility, as they are the first thing a person hears when using a screen reader. Search engines rely heavily on document titles as well. For these reasons, it's important to provide thoughtful and descriptive titles for all your documents and avoid vague titles, such as "Welcome" or "My Page." You may also want to keep the length of your titles in check so they are able to display in the browser's title area.

Not much has changed after structuring the document, except that the browser now displays the title of the document in the top bar. If someone were to bookmark this page, that title would be added to their Bookmarks or Favorites list as well (see the sidebar, Don't Forget a Good Title). But the content still runs together because we haven't given the browser any indication of how it is broken up. We'll take care of that next.

Step 3: Identify Text Elements

With a little markup experience under your belt, it should be a no-brainer to add the markup that identifies headings and subheads (h1 and h2), paragraphs (p), and emphasized text (em) to our content, as we'll do in Exercise 4-3. However, before we begin, I want to take a moment to talk about what we're doing and *not* doing when marking up content with (X)HTML.

Introducing...semantic markup

The purpose of (X)HTML is to provide meaning and structure to the content. It is *not* intended to provide instructions for how the content should look (its presentation).

Your job when marking up content is to choose the (X)HTML element that provides the most meaningful description of the content at hand. In the biz, we call this semantic markup. For example, the first heading level on the page should be marked up as an h1 because it is the most important heading on the page. Don't worry about what that looks like in the browser...you can easily change that with a style sheet. The important thing is that you choose elements based on what makes the most sense for the content.

In addition to adding meaning to content, the markup gives the document structure. The way elements follow each other or nest within one another creates relationships between the elements. This document structure is the foundation upon which we can add presentation instructions with style sheets, and behaviors with JavaScript. We'll talk about document structure more in Part III, when we discuss Cascading Style Sheets.

Although HTML was intended to be used strictly for meaning and structure since its creation, that mission was somewhat thwarted in the early years of the Web. With no style sheet system in place, HTML was extended to give authors ways to change the appearance of fonts, colors, and alignment. Those presentational extras are still out there, so you may run across them when you "view source." In this book, however, we'll focus on using HTML and XHTML the right way, in keeping with the new standards-based approach of contemporary web design.

Okay, enough lecturing. It's time to get to work on that content in Exercise 4-3.

(X)HTML Comments

You can leave notes in the source document for yourself and others by marking them up as comments. Anything you put between comment tags (`<!-- -->`) will not display in the browser and will not have any effect on the rest of the source.

```
<!-- This is a comment -->
<!-- This is a
  multiple-line comment
  that ends here. -->
```

Comments are useful for labeling and organizing long (X)HTML documents, particularly when they are shared by a team of developers. In this example, comments are used to point out the section of the source that contains the navigation.

```
<!-- start global nav -->
<ul>
  ...
</ul>
<!-- end global nav -->
```

Bear in mind that although the browser will not display comments in the web page, readers can see them if they "view source," so be sure that the comments you leave are appropriate for everyone.

exercise 4-3 | **Defining text elements**

1. Open the document *index.html* in your text editor, if it isn't open already.

2. The first line of text, "Black Goose Bistro," is the main heading for the page, so we'll mark it up as a Heading Level 1 (**h1**) element. Put the opening tag, **<h1>**, at the beginning of the line and the closing tag, **</h1>**, after it, like this.

   `<h1>Black Goose Bistro</h1>`

3. Our page also has three subheads. Mark them up as Heading Level 2 (**h2**) elements in a similar manner. I'll do the first one here; you do the same for "Catering" and "Location and Hours".

   `<h2>The Restaurant</h2>`

4. Each **h2** element is followed by a brief paragraph of text, so let's mark those up as paragraph (**p**) elements in a similar manner. Here's the first one; you do the rest.

   `<p>The Black Goose Bistro offers casual lunch and dinner fare in a hip atmosphere. The menu changes regularly to highlight the freshest ingredients. </p>`

5. Finally, in the Catering section, I want to emphasize that visitors should just leave the cooking to us. To make text emphasized, mark it up in an emphasis element (**em**) element, as shown here.

   `<p>You have fun... <em>we'll handle the cooking. </em> Black Goose Catering can handle events from snacks for bridge club to elegant corporate`

   `fundraisers.</p>`

6. Now that we've marked up the document, let's save it as we did before, and open (or refresh) the page in the browser. You should see a page that looks much like the one in Figure 4-9. If it doesn't, check your markup to be sure that you aren't missing any angle brackets or a slash in a closing tag.

Figure 4-9. *The home page after the content has been marked up in (X)HTML elements.*

Now we're getting somewhere. With the elements properly identified, the browser can now display the text in a more meaningful manner. There are a few significant things to note about what's happening in Figure 4-9.

Block and inline elements

While it may seem like stating the obvious, it is worth pointing out that the heading and paragraph elements start on new lines and do not run together as they did before. That is because they are examples of block-level elements. Browsers treat block-level elements as though they are in little rectangular boxes, stacked up in the page. Each block-level element begins on a new line, and some space is also usually added above and below the entire element by default. In Figure 4-10, the edges of the block elements are outlined in red.

By contrast, look at the text we marked up as emphasized (em). It does not start a new line, but rather stays in the flow of the paragraph. That is because the em element is an inline element. Inline elements do not start new lines;

they just go with the flow. In Figure 4-10, the inline em element is outlined in light blue.

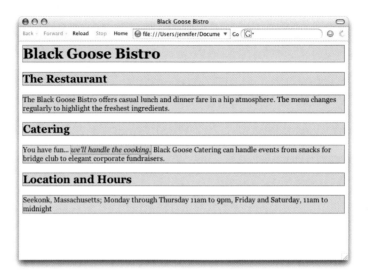

Figure 4-10. The outlines show the structure of the elements in the home page.

The distinction between block-level and inline elements is important. In (X)HTML markup, whether an element is block-level or inline restricts what other elements it may contain. For example, you can't put a block-level element within an inline element (such as a paragraph within a link). Block-level and inline elements also behave differently when it comes to applying Cascading Style Sheets.

Default styles

Browsers have built-in style sheets that describe the default rendering of (X)HTML elements.

The other thing that you will notice about the marked-up page in Figures 4-9 and 4-10 is that the browser makes an attempt to give the page some visual hierarchy by making the first-level heading the biggest and boldest thing on the page, with the second-level headings slightly smaller, and so on.

How does the browser determine what an h1 should look like? It uses a style sheet! All browsers have their own built-in style sheets that describe the default rendering of (X)HTML elements. The default rendering is similar from browser to browser (for example, h1s are always big and bold), but there are some variations (block quotes may or may not be indented). The appearance is also affected by the user's preferences, discussed in Chapter 3, The Nature of Web Design.

If you think the h1 is too big and clunky as the browser renders it, just change it with a style sheet rule. Resist the urge to mark up the heading with another element just to get it to look better (for example, using an h3 instead of an h1 so it isn't as large). In the days before ubiquitous style sheet support, elements were abused in just that way. Now that there are style sheets for controlling the design, you should always choose elements based on how accurately they describe the content, and don't worry about the browser's default rendering.

We'll fix the presentation of the page with style sheets in a moment, but first, let's add an image to the page.

Step 4: Add an Image

What fun is a web page with no image? In Exercise 4-4, we'll add an image to the page using the img element. Images will be discussed in more detail in Chapter 7, Adding Images, but for now, it gives us an opportunity to introduce two more basic markup concepts: empty elements and attributes.

Empty elements

So far, all of the elements we've used in the Black Goose Bistro home page have followed the syntax shown in Figure 4-1: a bit of text content surrounded by start and end tags.

A handful of elements, however, do not have text content because they are used to provide a simple directive. These elements are said to be empty. The image element (img) is an example of such an element; it tells the browser to get an graphic file from the server and insert it into the flow of the text at that spot in the document. Other empty elements include the line break (br), horizontal rule (hr), and elements that provide information about a document but don't affect its displayed content, such as the meta element.

The syntax for empty elements is slightly different for HTML and XHTML. In HTML, empty elements don't use closing tags—they are indicated by a single tag (<img>, <br>, or <hr>, for example) inserted into the text, as shown in this example that uses the br element to insert a line break.

```
<p>1005 Gravenstein Highway North <br>Sebastopol, CA 95472</p>
```

In XHTML, all elements, including empty elements, must be closed (or terminated, to use the proper term). Empty elements are terminated by adding a trailing slash preceded by a space before the closing bracket, like so: <img />, <br />, and <hr />. Here is that example again, this time using XHTML syntax.

```
<p>1005 Gravenstein Highway North <br />Sebastopol, CA 95472</p>
```

Attributes

Obviously, an `<img />` tag is not very useful by itself... there's no way to know which image to use. That's where attributes come in. Attributes are instructions that clarify or modify an element. For the `img` element, the `src` (short for "source") attribute is required, and provides the location of the image file via its URL.

The syntax for attributes is as follows:

```
<element attribute-name="value">Content</element>
```

or for empty elements:

```
<element attribute-name="value" />
```

For another way to look at it, the attribute structure of an `img` element is labeled in Figure 4-11.

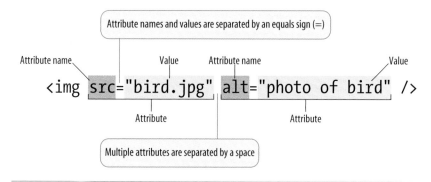

Figure 4-11. An element with attributes.

Here's what you need to know about attributes:

- Attributes go after the element name in the opening tag only, never in the end tag.

- There may be several attributes applied to an element, separated by spaces in the opening tag. Their order is not important.

- Attributes take values, which follow an equals sign (=).

- A value might be a number, a word, a string of text, a URL, or a measurement depending on the purpose of the attribute.

- Always put values within quotation marks. Although quotation marks aren't required around all values in HTML, they *are* required in XHTML. You might as well do it the more future-compatible way from the start. Either single or double quotation marks are acceptable as long as they are used consistently, however, double quotation marks are the convention.

- Some attributes are required, such as the `src` and `alt` attributes in the `img` element.

- The attribute names available for each element are defined in the (X)HTML specifications; in other words, you can't make up an attribute for an element.

Now you should be more than ready to try your hand at adding the `img` element with its attributes to the Black Goose Bistro page in the next exercise.

exercise 4-4 | **Adding an image**

1. If you're working along, the first thing you'll need to do is get a copy of the image file on your hard drive so you can see it in place when you open the file locally. The image file is provided in the materials for this chapter. You can also get the image file by saving it right from the sample web page online at *www.learningwebdesign.com/chapter4/bistro*. Right-click (or Ctrl-click on a Mac) on the goose image and select "Save to disk" (or similar) from the pop-up menu as shown in Figure 4-12. Be sure to save it in the bistro folder with *index.html*.

2. Once you've got the image, insert it at the beginning of the first-level heading by typing in the `img` element and its attributes as shown here:

   ```
   <h1><img src="blackgoose.gif" alt="Black Goose
   logo" />Black Goose Bistro</h1>
   ```

   The `src` attribute provides the name of the image file that should be inserted, and the `alt` attribute provides text that should be displayed if the image is not available. Both of these attributes are required in every `img` element.

3. Now save *index.html* and open or refresh it in the browser window. The page should look like the one shown in Figure 4-13. If it doesn't, check to make sure that the image file, *blackgoose.gif*, is in the same directory as *index.html*. If it is, then check to make sure that you aren't missing any characters, such as a closing quote or bracket, in the `img` element markup.

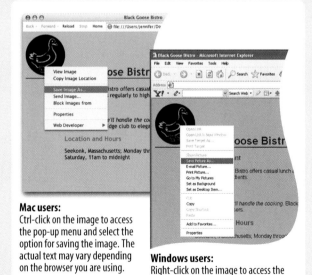

Mac users:
Ctrl-click on the image to access the pop-up menu and select the option for saving the image. The actual text may vary depending on the browser you are using.

Windows users:
Right-click on the image to access the pop-up menu and select the option for saving the picture.

Figure 4-12. Saving an image file from a page on the Web.

Figure 4-13. The Black Goose Bistro home page with the Black Goose logo inline image.

Step 5: Change the Look with a Style Sheet

Depending on the content and purpose of your web site, you may decide that the browser's default rendering of your document is perfectly adequate. However, I think I'd like to pretty up the Black Goose Bistro home page a bit to make a good first impression on potential patrons. "Prettying up" is just my way of saying that I'd like to change its presentation, which is the job of Cascading Style Sheets (CSS).

In Exercise 4-5, we'll change the appearance of the text elements and the page background using some simple style sheet rules. Don't worry about understanding them all right now—we'll get into CSS in more detail in Part III. But I want to at least give you a taste of what it means to add a "layer" of presentation onto the structure we've created with our XHTML markup.

exercise 4-5 | Adding a style sheet

1. Open *index.html* if it isn't open already.

2. We're going to use the **style** element to apply an embedded style sheet to the page. (This is just one of the ways to add a style sheet; the others are covered in Chapter 11, Style Sheet Orientation.)

   The **style** element is placed inside the **head** of the document. It uses the required **type** attribute to tell the browser the type of information in the element (**text/css** is currently the only option). Start by adding the **style** element to the document as shown here:

```
<head>
    <title>Black Goose Bistro</title>
    <style type="text/css">

    </style>
</head>
```

3. Now, type the following style rules within the **style** element just as you see them here. Don't worry if you don't know exactly what is going on... you'll learn all about style rules in Part III.

```
<style type="text/css">
body {
    background-color: #C2A7F2;
    font-family: sans-serif;
    }
h1 {
    color: #2A1959;
    border-bottom: 2px solid #2A1959;
    }
h2 {
    color: #474B94;
    font-size: 1.2em;
    }
h2, p {
    margin-left: 120px;
    }
</style>
```

4. Now it's time to save the file and take a look at it in the browser. It should look like the page in Figure 4-14. If it doesn't, go over the style sheet code to make sure you didn't miss a semi-colon or a curly bracket.

Figure 4-14. The Black Goose Bistro page after CSS style rules have been applied.

We're finished with the Black Goose Bistro page. Not only have you written your first XHTML document, complete with a style sheet, but you've learned about elements, attributes, empty elements, block-level and inline elements, the basic structure of an (X)HTML document, and the correct use of markup along the way.

When Good Pages Go Bad

The previous demonstration went very smoothly, but it's easy for small things to go wrong when typing out (X)HTML markup by hand. Unfortunately, one missed character can break a whole page. I'm going to break my page on purpose so we can see what happens.

What if I had forgotten to type the slash (/) in the closing emphasis tag (</em>)? With just one character out of place (Figure 4-15), the remainder of the document displays in emphasized (italic) text. That's because without that slash, there's nothing telling the browser to turn "off" the emphasized formatting, so it just keeps going.

```
<h2>Catering</h2>
<p>You have fun... <em>we'll handle the cooking.<em> Black Goose
Catering can handle events from snacks for bridge club to elegant
corporate fundraisers.</p>
```

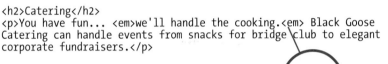

NOTE

Omitting the slash in the closing tag (in effect, omitting the closing tag itself) for certain block elements, such as headings or paragraphs, may not be so dramatic. Browsers interpret the start of a new block element to mean that the previous block element is finished.

Without the slash, the browser does not know to turn the emphasized text "off," and the remainder of the page is rendered as emphasized text (italics).

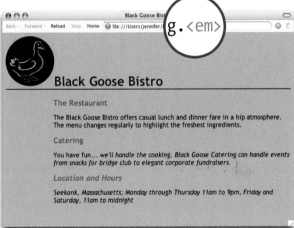

Figure 4-15. When a slash is omitted, the browser doesn't know when the element ends, as is the case in this example.

I've fixed the slash, but this time, let's see what would have happened if I had accidentally omitted a bracket from the end of the first `<h2>` tag (Figure 4-16).

Having Problems?

The following are some typical problems that crop up when creating web pages and viewing them in a browser:

I've changed my document, but when I reload the page in my browser, it looks exactly the same.

It could be you didn't save your document before reloading, or you may have saved it in a different directory.

Half my page disappeared.

This could happen if you are missing a closing bracket (>) or a quotation mark within a tag. This is a common error when writing (X)HTML by hand.

I put in a graphic using the `img` element, but all that shows up is a broken graphic icon.

The broken graphic could mean a couple of things. First, it might mean that the browser is not finding the graphic. Make sure that the URL to the image file is correct. (We'll discuss URLs further in Chapter 6, Adding Links.) Make sure that the image file is actually in the directory you've specified. If the file is there, make sure it is in one of the formats that web browsers can display (GIF, JPEG, or PNG) and that it is named with the proper suffix (*.gif*, *.jpeg* or *.jpg*, or *.png*, respectively).

```
<h2The Restaurant</h2>
<p>The Black Goose Bistro offers casual lunch and dinner fare
in a hip atmosphere. The menu changes regularly to highlight
the freshest ingredients.</p>
```

Without the bracket, all the following characters are interpreted as part of a long, unrecognizable element name, and "The Restaurant" disappears from the page.

Figure 4-16. A missing end bracket makes all the following content part of the tag, and therefore it doesn't display.

See how the headline is missing? That's because without the closing tag bracket, the browser assumes that all the following text—all the way up to the next closing bracket (>) it finds—is part of that `<h2>` tag. Browsers don't display any text within a tag, so my heading disappeared. The browser just ignored the foreign-looking element name and moved on to the next element.

Making mistakes in your first (X)HTML documents and fixing them is a great way to learn. If you write your first pages perfectly, I'd recommend fiddling with the code as I have here to see how the browser reacts to various changes. This can be extremely useful in troubleshooting pages later. I've listed some common problems in the sidebar, Having Problems? Note that these problems are not specific to beginners. Little stuff like this goes wrong all the time, even for the pros.

Test Yourself

Now is a good time to make sure you're understanding the basics of markup. Use what you've learned in this chapter to answer the following questions. Answers are in Appendix A.

1. What is the difference between a tag and an element?

2. Write out the minimal structure of an (X)HTML document.

3. Mark whether each of these file names is an acceptable name for a web document by circling "Yes" or "No." If it is not acceptable, provide the reason why.

   a. *Sunflower.html*   Yes   No _____

   b. *index.doc*   Yes   No _____

   c. *cooking home page.html*   Yes   No _____

   d. *Song_Lyrics.html*   Yes   No _____

   e. *games/rubix.html*   Yes   No _____

   f. *%whatever.html*   Yes   No _____

4. All of the following markup examples are incorrect. Describe what is wrong with each one, then write it correctly.

   a. `<img "birthday.jpg">`

   b. `<i>Congratulations!<i>`

   c. `<a href="file.html">linked text</a href="file.html">`

   d. `<p>This is a new paragraph<\p>`

5. How would you mark up this comment in an (X)HTML document so that it doesn't display in the browser window?

    product list begins here

(X)HTML Review: Document Structure Elements

This chapter introduced the elements that establish the structure of the document. The remaining elements introduced in the exercises will be treated in more depth in the following chapters.

Element	Description
html	The root element that identifies the document as (X)HTML
head	Identifies the head of the document
title	Gives the page a title
body	Identifies the body of the document that holds the content

CHAPTER 5

MARKING UP TEXT

In the previous chapter, you learned the hows and whys of (X)HTML markup. This chapter introduces the elements you have to choose from for marking up text content. There probably aren't as many of them as you might think, and really just a handful that you'll use with regularity.

Before we get to the element roll-call, this is a good opportunity for a reminder about the importance of meaningful (semantic) and well-structured markup.

In the early years of web design, it was common to choose elements based on how they looked in the browser. Don't like the size of the `h1`? Hey, use an `h4` instead. Don't like bullets on your list? Make something list-like using line break elements. But no more! Those days are over thanks to reliable browser support for style sheets that do a much better job at handling visual presentation than (X)HTML ever could.

You should always choose elements that describe your content as accurately as possible. If you don't like how it looks, change it with a style sheet. A semantically marked up document ensures your content is available and accessible in the widest range of browsing environments, from desktop computers to cell phones to screen readers. It also allows non-human readers, such as search engine indexing programs, to correctly parse your content and make decisions about the relative importance of elements on the page.

Your content should also read in a logical order in the source. Doing so improves its readability in all browsing environments. Information that should be read first should be at the beginning of the (X)HTML source document. You can always use style sheets to position elements where you want them on the final web page.

With these guidelines in mind, it is time to meet the (X)HTML text elements, starting with the block-level elements.

IN THIS CHAPTER

Choosing the best element for your content

Using block elements to identify the major components of the document.

Adding line breaks

Comparing inline elements

Creating custom elements with the versatile generic elements, `div` and `span`

Adding special characters to your document

Choose elements that describe your content as accurately as possible.

Building Blocks

When creating a web page, I always start with my raw content in a text file and make sure that it has been proofread and is ready to go. I put in the document structure elements (html, head, title, and body). I also identify which version of (X)HTML I'm using in a DOCTYPE declaration, but we'll get to that in Chapter 10, Understanding the Standards. Then I am ready to divide the content into its major block-level elements.

Block-level elements make up the main components of content structure. As mentioned in Chapter 4, Creating a Simple Page, block-level elements always start on a new line and usually have some space added above and below, stacking up like blocks in the normal flow of the document.

NOTE

Tables and forms are also block-level elements, but they are treated in their own respective chapters. The generic div block-level element is introduced later in this chapter.

There are surprisingly few text block-level elements. Table 5-1 lists (nearly) all of them (see note).

Table 5-1. Block-level elements for text content

Type	Element(s)
Headings	h1, h2, h3, h4, h5, h6
Paragraphs	p
Block (long) quotes	blockquote
Preformatted text	pre
Various list elements	ol, ul, li, dl, dt, dd
Author contact address	address
Horizontal rules (lines)	hr

We've already used some of these in the exercises in the previous chapter. In this section we'll take a closer look at block-level elements and the rules for how they are used.

Paragraphs

`<p>...</p>`

A paragraph element

Paragraphs are the most rudimentary elements of a text document. You indicate a paragraph with the p element. Simply insert an opening `<p>` tag at the beginning of the paragraph and a closing `</p>` tag after it, as shown in this example.

```
<p>Serif typefaces have small slabs at the ends of letter strokes. In
general, serif fonts can make large amounts of text easier to read.</p>
```

```
<p>Sans-serif fonts do not have serif slabs; their strokes are square
on the end. Helvetica and Arial are examples of sans-serif fonts. In
general, sans-serif fonts appear sleeker and more modern.</p>
```

NOTE

You must assign an element to all the text in a document. In other words, all text must be enclosed in some sort of block element. Text that is not contained within tags is called "naked" or "anonymous" text, and it will cause a document to be invalid. For more information about checking documents for validity, see Chapter 10.

Paragraphs may contain text, images and other inline elements, but they may *not* contain other block elements, including other p elements, so be sure never to put the elements listed in Table 5-1 between paragraph tags.

In HTML, it is acceptable to omit the closing `</p>` tag, but in XHTML, the closing tag must be there. For reasons of forward-compatibility, it is recommended that you always close paragraph (and all) elements.

Headings

In the last chapter, we used the `h1` and `h2` elements to indicate headings for our Black Goose Bistro page. There are actually six levels of headings in (X) HTML, from `h1` to `h6`. Because headings are used to provide logical hierarchy or outline to a document, it is proper to start with the Level 1 heading (`h1`) and work down in numerical order. Doing so not only improves accessibility, but helps search engines (information in higher heading levels is given more weight). Using heading levels consistently throughout a site—using `h1` for all article titles, for example—is also recommended.

```
<h1>...</h1>
<h2>...</h2>
<h3>...</h3>
<h4>...</h4>
<h5>...</h5>
<h6>...</h6>
```
Heading elements

This example shows the markup for four heading levels. Additional heading levels would be marked up in a similar manner.

```
<h1>Type Design</h1>

<h2>Serif Typefaces</h2>

<p>Serif typefaces have small slabs at the ends of letter strokes. In
general, serif fonts can make large amounts of text easier to read.</p>

<h3>Baskerville</h3>

<h4>Description</h4>
<p>Description of the Baskerville typeface.</p>

<h4>History</h4>
<p>The history of the Baskerville typeface.</p>

<h3>Georgia</h3>
<p>Description and history of the Georgia typeface.</p>
```

You can use a style sheet to specify the appearance of the heading levels. By default, they will be displayed in bold text, starting in very large type for `h1`s with each consecutive level in smaller text, as shown in Figure 5-1.

Figure 5-1. The default rendering of four heading levels. Their appearance can be changed easily with a style sheet.

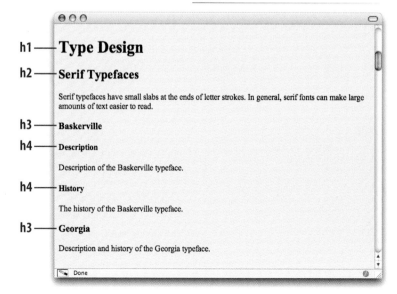

Long quotations

`<blockquote>...</blockquote>`

A lengthy, block-level quotation

If you have a long quotation, a testimonial, or a section of copy from another source, particularly one that spans four lines or more, you should mark it up as a `blockquote` element. It is recommended that content within blockquotes be contained in other elements, such as paragraphs, headings, or lists, as shown in this example.

```
<p>Renowned type designer, Matthew Carter, has this to say about his
profession:</p>

<blockquote>
  <p>Our alphabet hasn't changed in eons; there isn't much latitude in
what a designer can do with the individual letters.</p>

  <p>Much like a piece of classical music, the score is written
down - it's not something that is tampered with - and yet, each
conductor interprets that score differently. There is tension in the
interpretation.</p>
</blockquote>
```

NOTE

There is also the inline element, q, for short quotations in the flow of text. We'll talk about it later in this chapter.

Figure 5-2 shows the default rendering of the blockquote example. This can be altered with CSS.

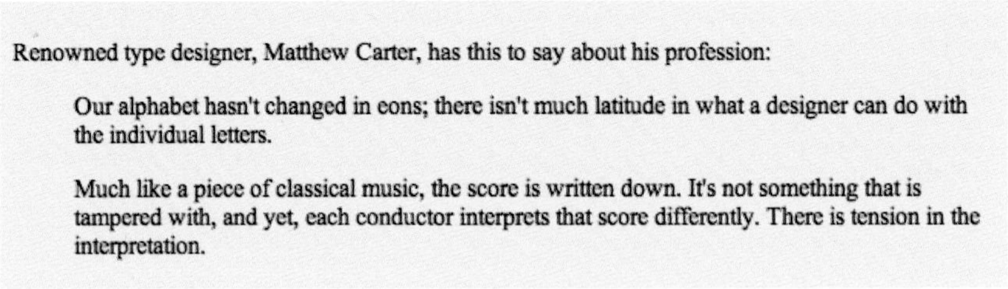

Renowned type designer, Matthew Carter, has this to say about his profession:

> Our alphabet hasn't changed in eons; there isn't much latitude in what a designer can do with the individual letters.
>
> Much like a piece of classical music, the score is written down. It's not something that is tampered with, and yet, each conductor interprets that score differently. There is tension in the interpretation.

Figure 5-2. The default rendering of a `blockquote` element.

Preformatted text

`<pre>...</pre>`

Preformatted text

Early on, you learned that browsers ignore white space such as line returns and character spaces in the source document. But in some types of information, such as code examples or poetry, the white space is important for conveying meaning. For these purposes, there is the preformatted text (`pre`) element. It is a unique element in that it is displayed exactly as it is typed—including all the carriage returns and multiple character spaces. By default, preformatted text is also displayed in a constant-width font (one in which all the characters are the same width, also called monospace), such as Courier.

NOTE

The `white-space:pre` CSS property can also be used to preserve spaces and returns in the source. Unlike the `pre` element, text formatted with the `white-space` property is not displayed in a constant-width font.

The `pre` element in this example displays as shown in Figure 5-3. The second part of the figure shows the same content marked up as a paragraph (`p`) element for comparison.

```
<pre>
This is               an             example of
     text with a            lot of
                            curious
                            white space.
</pre>

<p>
This is               an             example of
     text with a            lot of
                            curious
                            white space.
</p>
```

```
This is                an              example of
     text with a            lot of
                            curious
                            white space.

This is an example of text with a lot of curious white space.
```

Figure 5-3. *Preformatted text is unique in that the browser displays the white space exactly as it is typed into the source document. Compare it to the paragraph element in which line returns and character spaces are ignored.*

Horizontal Rules

If you want to add a divider between sections, you can insert a horizontal rule (`hr`) element between blocks of text. When browsers see an `hr` element, they insert a shaded horizontal line in its place by default. Because horizontal rules are block-level elements, they always start on a new line and have some space above and below. The `hr` element is an empty element—you just drop it into place where you want the rule to occur, as shown in this XHTML example and Figure 5-4. Note that in HTML, the `hr` element is written simply as `<hr>`.

```
<hr /> (XHTML)
<hr>   (HTML)
```
A horizontal rule

```
<h3>Times</h3>
<p>Description and history of the Times typeface.</p>
<hr />
<h3>Georgia</h3>
<p>Description and history of the Georgia typeface.</p>
```

Times

Description and history of the Times typeface.

_____

Georgia

Description and history of the Georgia typeface.

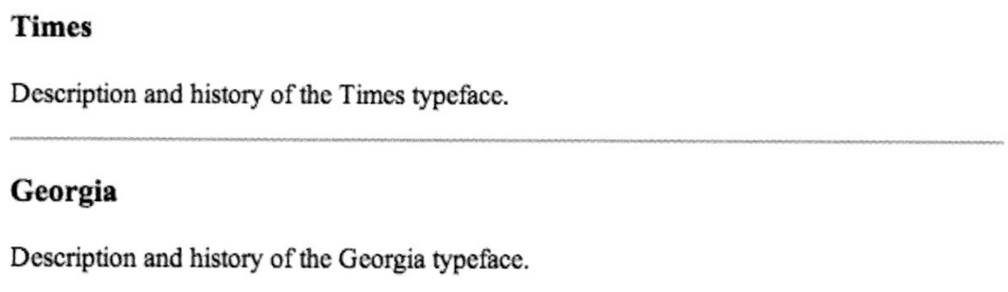

Figure 5-4. *The default rendering of a horizontal rule.*

Some authors use the `hr` element as a logical divider between sections, but hide it in the layout with a style rule. For visual layouts, it is common to create a rule by specifying a colored border before or after an element with CSS.

Addresses

`<address>...</address>`
Contact information

Last, and well, least, is the `address` element that is used to provide contact information for the author or maintainer of the document. It is generally placed at the beginning or end of a document or a large section of a document. You shouldn't use the `address` element for all types of addresses, such as mailing addresses, so its use is fairly limited. Here's an example of its intended use (the "a href" parts are the markup for links... we'll get to those in Chapter 6, Adding Links).

```
<address>
Contributed by <a href="../authors/robbins/">Jennifer Robbins</a>,
<a href="http://www.oreilly.com/">O'Reilly Media</a>
</address>
```

Lists

Sometimes it is necessary to itemize information instead of breaking it into paragraphs. There are three main types of lists in (X)HTML:

- **Unordered lists.** Collections of items that appear in no particular order.

- **Ordered lists.** Lists in which the sequence of the items is important.

- **Definition lists.** Lists that consist of terms and definitions.

All list elements—the lists themselves and the items that go in them—are block-level elements, which means that they always start on a new line by default. In this section, we'll look at each list type in detail.

Unordered lists

`<ul>...</ul>`
Unordered list

`<li>...</li>`
List item within an unordered list

Just about any list of examples, names, components, thoughts, or options qualify as unordered lists. In fact, most lists fall into this category. By default, unordered lists display with a bullet before each list item, but you can change that with a style sheet, as you'll see in a moment.

To identify an unordered list, mark it up as a `ul` element. The opening `<ul>` tag goes before the first list item and the closing tag `</ul>` goes after the last item. Then, each item in the list gets marked up as a list item (`li`) by enclosing it in opening and closing `li` tags as shown in this example. Notice that there are no bullets in the source document. They are added automatically by the browser (Figure 5-5).

```
<ul>
   <li>Serif</li>
   <li>Sans-serif</li>
   <li>Script</li>
   <li>Display</li>
   <li>Dingbats</li>
</ul>
```

NOTE

The only thing that is permitted within an unordered list (that is, between the start and end `ul` tags) is one or more list items. You can't put other elements in there, and there may not be any untagged text. However, you can put any element, even other block elements, within a list item (`li`).

- Serif
- Sans-serif
- Script
- Display
- Dingbats

Figure 5-5. The default rendering of the sample unordered list. The bullets are added automatically by the browser.

But here's the cool part. We can take that same unordered list markup, and radically change its appearance by applying different style sheets, as shown in Figure 5-6. In the figure, I've turned off the bullets, added bullets of my own, made the items line up horizontally, even made them look like graphical buttons. The markup stays exactly the same.

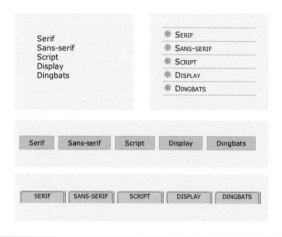

Figure 5-6. With style sheets, you can give the same unordered list many different looks.

Ordered lists

Ordered lists are for items that occur in a particular order, such as step-by-step instructions or driving directions. They work just like unordered lists described earlier, except they are defined with the `ol` element (for ordered list, naturally). Instead of bullets, the browser automatically inserts numbers before ordered list items, so you don't need to number them in the source document. This makes it easy to rearrange list items without renumbering them.

Ordered list elements must contain one or more list item elements, as shown in this example and in Figure 5-7:

```
<ol>
    <li>Gutenburg develops moveable type (1450s)</li>
    <li>Linotype is introduced (1890s)</li>
    <li>Photocomposition catches on (1950s)</li>
    <li>Type goes digital (1980s)</li>
</ol>
```

Nesting Lists

Any list can be nested within another list; it just has to be placed within a list item. This example shows the structure of an unordered list nested in the second ordered list item.

```
<ol>
  <li></li>
  <li>
    <ul>
      <li></li>
      <li></li>
      <li></li>
    </ul>
  </li>
</ol>
```

When you nest an unordered list within another unordered list, the browser automatically changes the bullet style for the second-level list. Unfortunately, the numbering style is not changed by default when you nest ordered lists. You need to set the numbering styles yourself using style sheets.

`<ol>...</ol>`
Ordered list

`<li>...</li>`
List item within an ordered list

Changing Bullets and Numbering

You can use the `list-style-type` style sheet property to change the bullets and numbers for lists. For example, for unordered lists, you can change the shape from the default dot to a square or an open circle, substitute your own image, or remove the bullet altogether. For ordered lists, you can change the numbers to roman numerals (I., II., III. or i., ii., iii.), letters (A., B., C., or a., b., c.), and several other numbering schemes. Changing the style of lists with CSS is covered in Chapter 17.

1. Gutenburg develops moveable type (1450s)
2. Linotype is introduced (1890s)
3. Photocomposition catches on (1950s)
4. Type goes digital (1980s)

Figure 5-7. The default rendering of an ordered list. The numbers are added automatically by the browser.

If you want a numbered list to start at a number other than "1," you can use the `start` attribute in the `ol` element to specify another starting number, as shown here:

```
<ol start="17">
  <li>Highlight the text with the text tool.</li>
  <li>Select the Character tab.</li>
  <li>Choose a typeface from the pop-up menu.</li>
</ol>
```

The resulting list items would be numbered 17, 18, and 19, consecutively.

NOTE

The `start` attribute is not supported in the "Strict" versions of HTML and XHTML, so you have to use CSS generated text (beyond the scope of this book) instead. Unfortunately, generated text is not supported by IE6(Win) and earlier. If you need to alter numbering in a way that is supported by all browsers, stick with the "Transitional" version of (X)HTML and use the `start` attribute. The difference between Strict and Transitional is explained in Chapter 10.

Definition lists

`<dl>...</dl>`
A definition list

`<dt>...</dt>`
A term

`<dd>...</dd>`
A definition

Definition (or dictionary) lists are used for lists of terms with their respective definitions. They are a bit different from the other two list types in format. The whole list is marked up as a definition list (`dl`) element. The content of a `dl` is some number of terms (indicated by the `dt` element) and definitions (indicated by the `dd` element). Here is an example of a brief definition list (Figure 5-8).

```
<dl>
  <dt>Linotype</dt>
  <dd>Line-casting allowed type to be selected, used, then recirculated
into the machine automatically. This advance increased the speed of
typesetting and printing dramatically.</dd>

  <dt>Photocomposition</dt>
  <dd>Typefaces are stored on film then projected onto photo-sensitive
paper. Lenses adjust the size of the type.</dd>

  <dt>Digital type</dt>
  <dd><p>Digital typefaces store the outline of the font shape in a
format such as Postscript. The outline may be scaled to any size for
output.</p>
    <p>Postscript emerged as a standard due to its support of
graphics and its early support on the Macintosh computer and Apple
laser printer.</p>
  </dd>

</dl>
```

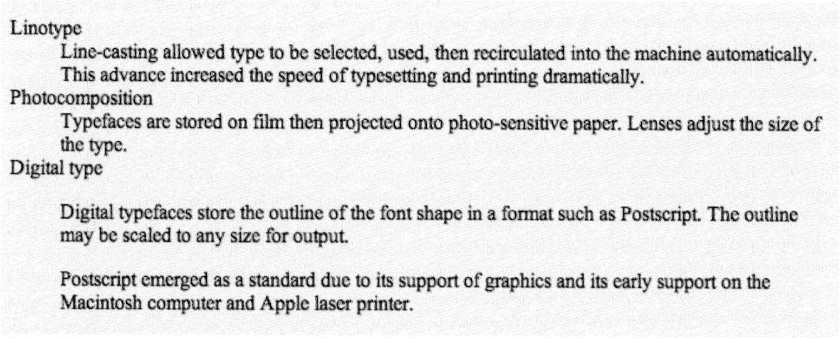

Linotype
Line-casting allowed type to be selected, used, then recirculated into the machine automatically. This advance increased the speed of typesetting and printing dramatically.
Photocomposition
Typefaces are stored on film then projected onto photo-sensitive paper. Lenses adjust the size of the type.
Digital type

Digital typefaces store the outline of the font shape in a format such as Postscript. The outline may be scaled to any size for output.

Postscript emerged as a standard due to its support of graphics and its early support on the Macintosh computer and Apple laser printer.

Figure 5-8. The default rendering of a definition list. Definitions are set off from the terms by an indent.

The `dl` element is only allowed to contain `dt` and `dd` elements. It is okay to have multiple definitions with one term and vice versa. You can not put block-level elements (like headings or paragraphs) in terms (`dt`), but the definition (`dd`) can contain any type of content (inline or block-level elements).

At this point, you've been introduced to *all* of the elements for defining different blocks of text. In Exercise 5-1 (following page), you'll get a chance to mark up a document yourself and try them out.

Adding Line Breaks

All of the elements we've seen so far start automatically on new lines. But sometimes it is desirable to add a line break within the flow of text. Because we know that the browser ignores line breaks in the source document, we need a specific directive to tell the browser to "add a line break here."

`<br />` *(XHTML)*
`<br>` *(HTML)*
A line break

The inline line break element (`br`) does exactly that. The classic use of the `br` element is to break up lines of addresses or poetry. It is an empty element, which means it does not have content. Just add the `br` element (`<br>` in HTML, `<br />` in XHTML) in the flow of text where you want a break to occur, as shown in here and in Figure 5-9.

```
<p>
So much depends <br />upon <br /><br />a red wheel <br />barrow
</p>
```

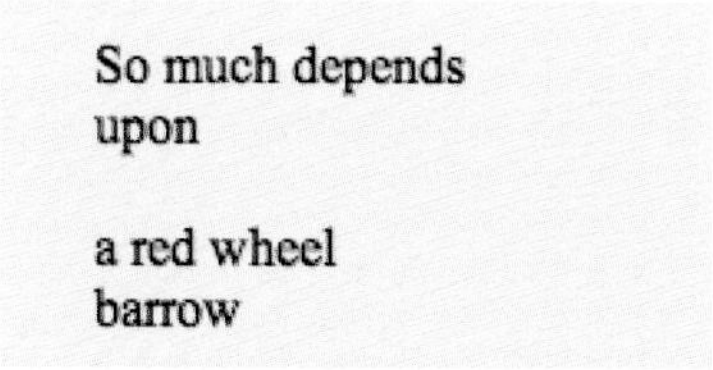

So much depends
upon

a red wheel
barrow

Figure 5-9. Line breaks are inserted at each br *element.*

WARNING

Be careful that you aren't using br *elements to force breaks into text that really ought to be a list. For instance, don't do this:*

```
<p>milk<br />
bread<br />
orange juice<br />
</p>
```

If it's a list, use the semantically correct unordered list element instead, and turn off the bullets with style sheets.

```
<ul>
  <li>milk</li>
  <li>bread</li>
  <li>orange juice</li>
</ul>
```

AT A GLANCE

Text Block Elements

headings	h1, h2, h3, h4, h5, h6
paragraph	p
long quotes	blockquote
preformatted	pre
author contact	address
unordered list	ul
ordered list	ol
list item	li
definition list	dl
term	dt
definition	dd

Unfortunately, the br element is easily abused (see Warning). Consider whether using the CSS white-space property (introduced in Chapter 12, Formatting Text) might be a better alternative for maintaining line breaks from your source without extra markup.

exercise 5-1 | **Fun with block elements**

Below you will find the raw text of a recipe web page. The document structure elements have been added, but it's up to you to decide which element is the best match for each block of content. The complete list of block elements is provided on this page as a reminder of what you have to choose from, but you won't necessarily use all of them in this example.

You can write the tags right on this page. Or, if you want to use a text editor and see the results in a browser, this text file is available online at *www.learningwebdesign. com/materials*. The resulting code appears in Appendix A.

```
<html>
<head><title>Tapenade Recipe</title></head>
<body>

Tapenade (Olive Spread)

This is a really simple dish to prepare and it's always a big hit at
parties. My father recommends:

"Make this the night before so that the flavors have time to blend.
Just bring it up to room temperature before you serve it. In the
winter, try serving it warm."

Ingredients

1 8oz. jar sundried tomatoes
2 large garlic cloves
2/3 c. kalamata olives
1 t. capers

Instructions

Combine tomatoes and garlic in a food processor. Blend until as smooth
as possible.

Add capers and olives. Pulse the motor a few times until they are
incorporated, but still retain some texture.

Serve on thin toast rounds with goat cheese and fresh basil garnish
(optional).

</body>

</html>
```

The Inline Text Element Round-up

Most (X)HTML text elements are inline elements, which means they just stay in the flow of text and do not cause line breaks. Inline text elements fall into two general categories: semantic elements and presentational elements. Those terms should be familiar by now.

The semantic elements describe the meaning of the text; for example, an acronym or emphasized text. The presentational elements provide descriptions of the element's typesetting or style, such as bold, italic, or underlined. It should come as no surprise that the presentational inline elements are discouraged from use in contemporary web design where style information should be kept separate from the markup. For that reason, we'll pay more attention to the preferred semantic elements in this section.

Semantic inline elements

The semantic text elements describe the enclosed text's meaning, context or usage. The way they look when they appear in the browser window depends on a style sheet, either one you provide or the browser's built-in default rendering.

Despite all the types of information you could add to a document, there are only a dozen of these elements in (X)HTML. Table 5-2 lists all of them. We'll discuss each in more detail in this section.

Table 5-2. Semantic inline text elements

Element	Description
abbr	abbreviation
acronym	acronym
cite	citation; a reference to another document, such as a book title
code	program code sample
del	deleted text; indicates an edit made to a document
dfn	the defining instance or first occurrence of a term
em	emphasized text
ins	inserted text; indicates an insertion in a document
kbd	keyboard; text entered by a user (for technical documents)
q	short, inline quotation
samp	sample output from programs
strong	strongly emphasized text
var	a variable or program argument (for technical documents)

Deprecated Elements

A number of elements and attributes in (X)HTML have been deprecated, which means they are being phased out and are discouraged from use. You may run across them in existing markup, so it is worthwhile knowing what they are, but there is no reason to use them in your documents.

Most of the deprecated elements and attributes are presentational and have analogous style sheet properties that should be used instead. Others are simply obsolete or poorly supported.

The following is a complete list of deprecated elements.

applet	inserts a Java applet
basefont	establishes default font settings for a document
center	centers its content
dir	directory list (replaced by unordered lists)
font	font face, color, and size
isindex	inserts a search box
menu	menu list (replaced by unordered lists)
s	strike-through text
strike	strike-through text
u	underlined text

Adding emphasis to text

`<em>...</em>`
Emphasized inline text

`<strong>...</strong>`
Strongly emphasized inline text

There are two elements that indicate that text should be emphasized: em for emphasized text and strong for strongly emphasized text. Emphasized text elements almost always display in italics by default, but of course you can make them display any way you like with a style sheet. Strong text typically displays in bold text. Screen readers may use a different tone of voice to convey emphasized text, which is why you should use an em or strong element only when it makes sense semantically, not just to achieve italic or bold text.

The following is a brief example of emphasized and strong text elements in the flow of a paragraph element. Figure 5-10 should hold no surprises.

```
<p>Garamond is a <em>really</em> popular typeface, but Times is a
<strong>really really</strong> popular typeface.</p>
```

Garamond is a *really* popular typeface, but Times is a **really really** popular typeface.

Figure 5-10. The default rendering of emphasized and strong text.

Short quotations

`<q>...</q>`
Short inline quotation

Use the quotation (q) element to mark up short quotations, such as "To be or not to be" in the flow of text, as shown in this example.

```
Matthew Carter says, <q>Our alphabet hasn't changed in eons.</q>
```

According to the HTML 4.01 Recommendation, browsers should automatically add quotation marks around q elements, so you don't need to include them in the source document. Many standards-compliant browsers (Firefox, Netscape, Opera, Safari, and IE on the Mac) do just that. Unfortunately, Internet Explorer 5, 5.5, 6, and 7 on Windows, which account for as much as 70% of web traffic as of this writing, do *not* (Figure 5-11). That makes using the q element kind of tricky: if you leave the quotation marks out, IE5 and 6 users won't see them, but if you include them, everyone else will see them twice. As old versions vanish, the q element will become more useful.

Figure 5-11. Standards-compliant browsers, such as Mozilla Firefox (top) automatically add quotation marks around q elements; Internet Explorer 6 for Windows (bottom) does not. Support is fixed in IE7.

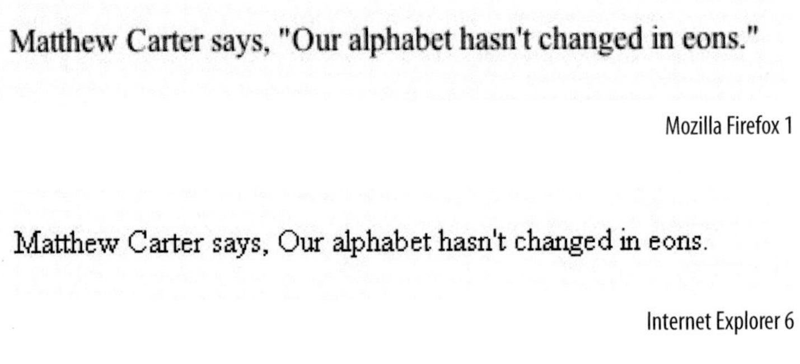

Matthew Carter says, "Our alphabet hasn't changed in eons."

Mozilla Firefox 1

Matthew Carter says, Our alphabet hasn't changed in eons.

Internet Explorer 6

Abbreviations and acronyms

Marking up shorthand terms as acronyms and abbreviations provides useful information for search engines, screen readers, and other devices. Abbreviations, indicated by the `abbr` element, are shortened versions of a word ending in a period (Conn. for Connecticut, for example). Acronyms, indicated by the `acronym` element, are abbreviations formed by the first letters of the words in a phrase (such as WWW or USA). Both elements use the `title` attribute to provide the long version of the shortened term, as shown in this example.

```
<acronym title="American Type Founders">ATF</acronym>

<abbr title="Points">pts.</abbr>
```

`<abbr>...</abbr>`
Abbreviation

`<acronym>...</acronym>`
Acronym

NOTE

The `acronym` element is likely to go away in future versions of (X)HTML in favor of using the `abbr` element for all acronyms and abbreviations.

Citations

The `cite` element is used to identify a reference to another document, such as a book, magazine, article title, and so on. Citations are typically rendered in italic text by default. Here's an example:

```
<p>Passages of this article were inspired by <cite>The Complete Manual
of Typography</cite> by James Felici.</p>
```

`<cite>...</cite>`
Citation

Defining terms

In publishing, the first and defining instance of a word or term is often called out in some fashion. In this book, defining terms are set in blue text. In (X) HTML, you can identify them with the `dfn` element and format them visually using style sheets. They are also useful for foreign phrases where a translation can be provided by a `title` attribute.

```
<p><dfn>Script typefaces</dfn> are based on handwriting.</p>
```

`<dfn>...</dfn>`
Defining term

Program code elements

A number of inline elements are used for describing the parts of technical documents, such as code (`code`), variables (`var`), program samples (`samp`), and user-entered keyboard strokes (`kbd`). For me, it's a quaint reminder of HTML's origins in the scientific world (Tim Berners-Lee developed HTML to share documents at the CERN particle physics lab in 1989).

Code, sample, and keyboard elements typically render in a constant-width (also called monospace) font such as Courier by default. Variables usually render in italics.

`<code>...</code>`
Code

`<var>...</var>`
Variable

`<samp>...</samp>`
Program sample

`<kbd>...</kbd>`
User-entered keyboard strokes

Inserted and deleted text

The `ins` and `del` elements are used to mark up changes to the text and indicate parts of a document that have been inserted or deleted (respectively).

```
Chief Executive Officer: <del title="retired">Peter Pan</del><ins>Pippi
Longstockings</ins>
```

`<ins>...</ins>`
Inserted text

`<del>...</del>`
Deleted text

Adios, <font>!

The font element—an inline element used to specify the size, color, and font face for text—is the poster child for what went wrong with HTML. It was first introduced by Netscape Navigator as a means to give authors control over font formatting not available at the time. Netscape was rewarded with a temporary slew of loyal users, but the HTML standard and web development community paid a steep price in the long run. The font element is emphatically deprecated, and you shouldn't use it... ever.

Not only does font add no semantic value, it also makes site updates more laborious because every **font** element needs to be hunted down and changed. Compare this to style sheets that let you reformat elements throughout a site with a single rule edit.

The font element has three attributes, all of which have been deprecated as well:

- color specifies the color of the text
- face specifies a font or list of fonts (separated by commas).
- size specifies the size for the font on a scale of 1 to 7, with 3 as the default.

Be aware that some WYSIWYG web authoring tools still make heavy use of the font element unless you specify that you want all styles to be handled with CSS.

Presentational inline elements

The remaining inline text elements in the (X)HTML specification provide typesetting instructions for the enclosed text. Like all inline text elements, these elements have an opening tag and a closing tag, so you should already be familiar with how they work.

As I mentioned earlier, professional web authors are careful to keep style information like this out of the (X)HTML document. I'm not saying that you should never use these elements; they are perfectly valid elements and many of them (such as bold and italic) are included in future versions of XHTML currently in development.

I am encouraging you, however, to consider whether there might be another way to mark up the content that provides meaning and not just style instructions. There's an alternative—whether it's a semantic element or a style sheet property—for just about every element in this category.

All of the presentational inline text elements along with the recommended alternatives are listed in Table 5-3.

exercise 5-2 | **Fix it**

This document was written by someone who doesn't know as much about modern markup practices as you do. It needs some work.

Some markup is incorrect and needs to be fixed, some elements could be marked up more accurately, and there is one element that was overlooked but should be marked up for better accessibility. In all, there will be seven changes. Some of them are obvious, and some of them are subtle.

You can make your changes right on this page, or download the source from *www.learningwebdesign.com/materials/* and edit the file in a text editor. The improved markup is provided in Appendix A.

```
<h1>You've Won!

<p><b>Congratulations!</b> You have just won dinner for two at the

highly acclaimed Blue Ginger restaurant in Wellesley, Mass. In

addition to dinner, you will receive an autographed copy of Ming

Tsai's book, <i>Blue Ginger</i>. To redeem your prize, go to our site

and enter your prize code (Example: <tt>RPZ108-BG</tt>). We're sure

you're going to <i>love</i> it!<p>
```

Table 5-3. Presentational inline text elements

Element	Description	Alternative
b	bold text	Use the **strong** element instead if appropriate, or use the `font-weight` CSS property: `font-weight: bold`
big	makes text slightly larger than the default text size	In CSS, use a relative `font-size` keyword to make text display slightly larger than the surrounding text: `font-size: bigger`
center*	centers the enclosed text	Use the CSS `text-align` property to center the text in an element: `text-align: center`
font*	specifies the size, color, and typeface (see the Adios, <font>! sidebar)	All of the functionality of the font element has been replaced by the `font-family`, `font-size`, and `color` CSS properties: Example: `font-family: sans-serif;  font-size: 120%;  color: white;`
i	italic text	Use the **em** element instead if appropriate, or use the CSS `font-style` property: `font-style: italic`
s*	strike-through text	Use the CSS `text-decoration` property to make text display with a line through it: `text-decoration: line-through`
small	makes text slightly smaller than the default text size	Use a CSS relative `font-size` keyword to make text display slightly smaller than the surrounding text: `font-size: smaller`
strike*	strike-through text	Use the CSS `text-decoration` property to make text display with a line through it: `text-decoration: line-through`
sub	subscript (smaller font positioned below the text baseline)	Use a combination of the `font-size` and `vertical-align` CSS properties to resize and position subscript text: `font-size: smaller; vertical-align: sub;`
sup	superscript (smaller font positioned slightly above the text baseline)	Use a combination of the `font-size` and `vertical-align` CSS properties to resize and position subscript text: `font-size: smaller; vertical-align: sup;`
tt	teletype; displays in constant-width (monospace) font, such as Courier	Use a **code**, **samp**, or **kbd** element, if appropriate. Otherwise use the `font-family` property to select a specific or generic fixed-width font: `font-family: "Andale Mono", monospace;`
u*	underlined text	Use the CSS `text-decoration` property to make text display with a line under it: `text-decoration: underline`

* These elements have been "deprecated" in HTML 4.01, which means they will be phased out of future versions of XHTML.

Generic Elements (div and span)

`<div>...</div>`
Generic block-level element

`<span>...</span>`
Generic inline element

There are endless types of information in the world, but as you've seen, not all that many semantic elements. Fortunately, (X)HTML provides two generic elements that can be customized to describe your content perfectly. The `div` (short for "division") element is used to indicate a generic block-level element, while the `span` element is used to indicate a generic inline element. You give a generic element a name using either an `id` or `class` attribute (we'll talk about those more in just a moment).

The `div` and `span` elements have no inherent presentation qualities of their own, but you can use style sheets to format the content however you like. In fact, generic elements are a primary tool in standards-based web design because they enable authors to accurately describe content and offer plenty of "hooks" for adding style rules.

We're going to spend a little time on `div` and `span` (as well as the `id` and `class` attributes, also called element identifiers) because they will be powerful tools once we start working with Cascading Style Sheets. Let's take a look at how authors use these elements to structure content.

Divide it up with a div

MARKUP TIP

It is possible to nest `div` elements within other `div` elements, but don't go overboard. You should always strive to keep your markup as simple as possible, so only add a `div` element if it is necessary for logical structure or styling.

The `div` element is used to identify a block-level division of text. You can use a `div` like a container around a logical grouping of elements on the page. By marking related elements as a `div` and giving it a descriptive name, you give context to the elements in the grouping. That comes in handy for making the structure of your document clear but also for adding style properties. Let's look at a few examples of `div` elements.

In this example, a `div` element is used as a container to group an image and two paragraphs into a "listing".

```
<div class="listing">
  <img src="felici.gif" alt="" />
  <p><cite>The Complete Manual of Typography</cite>, James Felici</p>
  <p>A combination of type history and examples of good and bad type.
  </p>
</div>
```

By putting those elements in a `div`, I've made it clear that they are conceptually related. It also allows me to style two `p` elements within listings differently than other paragraphs on the page.

Here is another common use of a `div` used to break a page into sections for context, structure, and layout purposes. In this example, a heading and several paragraphs are enclosed in a `div` and identified as the "news" section.

```
<div id="news">
  <h1>New This Week</h1>
  <p>We've been working on...</p>
  <p>And last but not least,... </p>
</div>
```

Now that I have an element known as "news," I could use a style sheet to position it as a column to the right or left of the page.

Get inline with span

A `span` offers all the same benefits as the `div` element, except it is used for inline elements that do not introduce line breaks. Because spans are inline elements, they can only contain text and other inline elements (in other words, you cannot put block-level elements in a `span`). Let's get right to some examples.

In this example, each telephone number is marked up as a `span` and classified as "phone."

```
<ul>
  <li>Joan: <span class="phone">999.8282</span></li>
  <li>Lisa: <span class="phone">888.4889</span></li>
  <li>Steve: <span class="phone">888.1628</span></li>
  <li>Morris: <span class="phone">999.3220</span></li>
</ul>
```

You can see how the labeled spans add meaning to what otherwise might be a random string of digits. It makes the information recognizable not only to humans but to (theoretical) computer programs that know what to do with "phone" information. It also enables us to apply the same style to phone numbers throughout the site.

Element identifiers

In the previous examples, we saw the element identifiers, `id` and `class`, used to give names to the generic `div` and `span` elements. Each identifier has a specific purpose, however, and it's important to know the difference.

The id identifier

The `id` identifier is used to identify a unique element in the document. In other words, the value of `id` must be used only once in the document. This makes it useful for assigning a name to a particular element, as though it were a piece of data. See the sidebar, id and class Values, for information on providing names for the `id` attribute.

This example uses the book's ISBN number to uniquely identify each listing. No two book listings may share the same `id`.

```
<div id="ISBN0321127307">
  <img src="felici.gif" alt="" />
  <p><cite>The Complete Manual of Typography</cite>, James Felici</p>
  <p>A combination of type history and examples of good and bad type.</p>
</div>
```

Not Just for divs

The `id` and `class` attributes may be used with nearly all (X)HTML elements, not just `div` and `span`. For example, you could identify an unordered list as "navigation" instead of wrapping it in a `div`.

```
<ul id="navigation">
  <li>...</li>
  <li>...</li>
  <li>...</li>
</ul>
```

In HTML 4.01, `id` and `class` attributes may be used with all elements except `base`, `basefont`, `head`, `html`, `meta`, `param`, `script`, `style`, and `title`. In XHTML, `id` support has been added to those elements.

id and class Values

The values for `id` and `class` attributes should start with a letter (A-Z or a-z) or underscore (although Internet Explorer 6 and earlier have trouble with underscores, so they are generally avoided). They should not contain any character spaces or special characters. Letters, numbers, hyphens, underscores, colons, and periods are okay. Also, the values are case-sensitive, so "sectionB" is not interchangeable with "Sectionb."

```
<div id="ISBN0881792063">
    <img src="bringhurst.gif" alt="" />
    <p><cite>The Elements of Typographic Style</cite>, Robert
    Bringhurst</p>
    <p>This lovely, well-written book is concerned foremost with
creating beautiful typography.</p>
</div>
```

Web authors also use `id` when identifying the various sections of a page. With this method, there may not be more than one "header," "main," or other named `div` in the document.

```
<div id="header">
(masthead and navigation here)
</div>

<div id="main">
(main content elements here)
</div>

<div id="links">
(list of links here)
</div>

<div id="news">
(news sidebar item here)
</div>

<div id="footer">
(copyright information here)
</div>
```

The class identifier

TIP

The `id` attribute is used to *identify*.
The `class` attribute is used to *classify*.

The `class` attribute is used for grouping similar elements; therefore, unlike the `id` attribute, multiple elements may share a class name. By making elements part of the same class, you can apply styles to all of the labeled elements at once with a single style rule. Let's start by classifying some elements in the earlier book example. In this first example, I've added `class` attributes to certain paragraphs to classify them as "descriptions."

```
<div id="ISBN0321127307" class="listing">
  <img src="felici.gif" alt="" />
  <p><cite>The Complete Manual of Typography</cite>, James Felici</p>
  <p class="description">A combination of type history and examples of
good and bad type.</p>
</div>

<div id="ISBN0881792063" class="listing">
  <img src="bringhurst.gif" alt="" />
  <p><cite>The Elements of Typographic Style</cite>, Robert
Bringhurst</p>
  <p class="description">This lovely, well-written book is concerned
foremost with creating beautiful typography.</p>
</div>
```

I've also classified each `div` as a "listing." Notice how the same element may have both a `class` and an `id` identifier. It is also possible for elements to belong to multiple classes. In this example, I've classified each div as a "book" to set them apart from "cd" or "dvd" listings elsewhere in the document.

```
<div id="ISBN0321127307" class="listing book">
  <img src="felici.gif" alt="CMT cover">
  <p><cite>The Complete Manual of Typography</cite>, James Felici</p>
  <p class="description">A combination of type history and examples of
good and bad type.</p>
</div>

<div id="ISBN0881792063" class="listing book">
  <img src="bringhurst.gif" alt="ETS cover">
  <p><cite>The Elements of Typographic Style</cite>, Robert
    Bringhurst</p>
  <p class="description">This lovely, well-written book is concerned
foremost with creating beautiful typography.</p>
</div>
```

This should have given you a good introduction to how div and span are used to provide meaning and organization to documents. We'll work with them even more in the style sheet chapters in Part III.

Some Special Characters

There's just one more text-related topic before we move on.

Some common characters, such as the copyright symbol ©, are not part of the standard set of ASCII characters, which contains only letters, numbers, and a few basic symbols. Other characters, such as the less-than symbol (<), are available, but if you put one in an (X)HTML document, the browser will interpret it as the beginning of a tag.

Characters such as these must be escaped in the source document. Escaping means that instead of typing in the character itself, you represent it by its numeric or named character reference. When the browser sees the character reference, it substitutes the proper character in that spot when the page is displayed.

There are two ways of referring to a specific character: by an assigned numeric value (numeric entity) or using a predefined abbreviated name for the character (called a named entity). All character references begin with an "&" and end with a ";".

Some examples will make this clear. I'd like to add a copyright symbol to my page. The typical Mac keyboard command, *Option-G*, which works in my word processing program, won't work in XHTML. Instead, I must use the named entity © (or its numeric equivalent ©) where I want the symbol to appear (Figure 5-12).

```
<p>All content copyright &copy; 2007, Jennifer Robbins</p>
```

or:

```
<p>All content copyright &#169; 2007, Jennifer Robbins</p>
```

Character References in XHTML

There are a few ways in which XHTML is different than HTML when it comes to character references.

- First, XHTML defines a character entity for apostrophe ('), that was curiously omitted from the HTML spec.

- In XHTML, every instance of an ampersand *must* be escaped so that it is not interpreted as the beginning of a character entity, even when it appears in the value of an attribute. For example,

```
<img src="sno.jpg"
alt="Sifl &amp; Olly Show" />
```

Non-breaking Spaces

One interesting character to know about is the non-breaking space ( ). Its purpose is to ensure that a line doesn't break between two words. So, for instance, if I mark up my name like this:

```
Jennifer Robbins
```

I can be sure that they will always stay together on a line.

Non-breaking spaces are also commonly used to add a string of character spaces to text (remember that browsers ignore consecutive character spaces in the source document). But if it's space you're after, first consider whether a style sheet margin, padding, or white-space property might be a better option than a string of space characters.

All content copyright © 2007, Jennifer Robbins

Figure 5-12. The special character is substituted for the character reference when the document is displayed in the browser.

(X)HTML defines hundreds of named entities as part of the markup language, which is to say you can't make up your own entity. Table 5-4 lists some commonly used character references. If you'd like to see them all, the complete list of character references has been nicely assembled online by the folks at the Web Standards Project at *www.webstandards.org/learn/reference/charts/entities/*.

Table 5-4. Common special characters and their character references

Character	Description	Name	Number
	Character space (nonbreaking space)		
&	Ampersand	&amp;	&#038;
'	Apostrophe	' (XHTML only)	&#039;
<	Less-than symbol (useful for displaying markup on a web page)	&lt;	&#060;
>	Greater-than symbol (useful for displaying markup on a web page)	&gt;	&$062;
©	Copyright	&copy;	&#169;
®	Registered trademark	&reg;	&#174;
™	Trademark	&trade;	&#8482;
£	Pound	&pound;	&#163;
¥	Yen	&yen;	&#165;
€	Euro	&euro;	&#8364;
–	En-dash	&ndash;	&#8211;
—	Em-dash	&mdash;	&#8212;
'	Left curly single quote	&lsquo;	&#8216;
'	Right curly single quote	&rsquo;	&#8217;
"	Left curly double quote	&ldquo;	&#8220;
"	Right curly double quote	&rdquo;	&#8221;
•	Bullet	&bull;	&#8226;
...	Horizontal ellipsis	&hellip;	&#8230;

Putting It All Together

So far, you've learned how to mark up elements and you've met all of the (X)HTML elements for adding structure and meaning to text content. Now it's just a matter of practice. Exercise 5-3 gives you an opportunity to try out everything we've covered so far: document structure elements, block elements, inline elements and character entities. Have fun!

exercise 5-3 | Text markup practice

Now that you've been introduced to all of the text elements, you can put them to work by marking up a menu for the Black Goose Bistro. The raw text is shown below. You can type it in or get the raw text file online (see note). Once you have the raw content, follow the instructions following the copy. The resulting page is shown in Figure 5-13.

```
Black Goose Bistro | Summer Menu

Baker's Corner Seekonk, Massachusetts, Hours: M-T: 11 to 9, F-S; 11 to
midnight

Appetizers

Black bean purses
Spicy black bean and a blend of mexican cheeses wrapped in sheets of
phyllo and baked until golden. $3.95

Southwestern napoleons with lump crab -- new item!
Layers of light lump crab meat, bean and corn salsa, and our handmade
flour tortillas. $7.95

Main courses

Shrimp sate kebabs with peanut sauce
Skewers of shrimp marinated in lemongrass, garlic, and fish sauce then
grilled to perfection. Served with spicy peanut sauce and jasmine
rice. $12.95

Grilled skirt steak with mushroom fricasee
Flavorful skirt steak marinated in asian flavors grilled as you like
it*. Served over a blend of sauteed wild mushrooms with a side of blue
cheese mashed potatoes. $16.95

Jerk rotisserie chicken with fried plantains -- new item!
Tender chicken slow-roasted on the rotisserie, flavored with spicy and
fragrant jerk sauce and served with fried plantains and fresh mango.
$12.95

* We are required to warn you that undercooked food is a health risk.
```

NOTE

This text file is available online at www. learningwebdesign.com/materials. The resulting markup is in Appendix A.

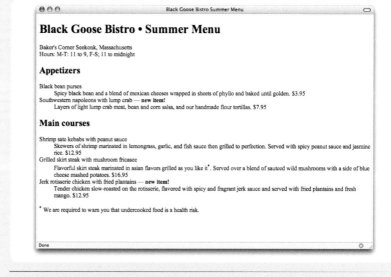

Figure 5-13. The finished menu page.

1. Enter the document structure elements first. Give the document the title "Black Goose Bistro Summer Menu."

2. Use **div** elements to divide the page into four unique sections named "header," "appetizers," "main," and "warnings," in that order as appropriate.

3. Identify the first- and second-level headings (**h1** and **h2**). In the first-level heading, change the vertical bar character to a bullet character.

4. Make the restaurant information a paragraph. Delete the comma after "Massachusetts" and start "hours" on a new line with a **br** element.

5. Choose the best list elements for the menu item listings (Appetizers and Main Courses). Mark up the lists and each item in them.

6. Make the footnote at the bottom of the menu a paragraph.

7. Make the asterisk for the footnote superscript. Make the asterisk in the menu description superscript as well.

8. Two of the dishes are new items. Change the double hyphens to an em-dash character and strongly emphasize "new items!" Classify the title of each new dish as "newitem".

9. Classify each price as "price" using **span** elements.

10. Label the paragraph in the "warnings" **div** as a "footnote" using a **class** identifier.

Save the file and name it *menu_summer. html* (you can save it in the *bistro* directory you created in Chapter 4). Check your page in a browser.

Markup tips:

- Choose the element that best fits the meaning of the selected text.
- Don't forget to close elements with closing tags.
- Put all attribute values in quotation marks
- "Copy and paste" is your friend when adding the same markup to multiple elements. Just be sure what you copied is correct before you paste it throughout the document.

Want More Practice?

Try marking up your own résumé. Start with the raw text, then add document structure elements, block elements, then inline elements as we've done in Exercise 5-3. If you don't see an element that matches your information just right, try creating one using a div or a span.

Test Yourself

Were you paying attention? Here is a rapid-fire set of questions to find out.

1. Add the markup to add a quick horizontal rule between these paragraphs.

   ```
   <p>People who know me know that I love to cook.</p>

   <p>I've created this site to share some of my favorite
   recipes.</p>
   ```

2. What does "deprecated" mean?

3. What's the difference between a `blockquote` and a `q` element?

4. What element displays white space exactly as it is typed into the source document?

5. What is the difference between a `ul` and an `ol`?

6. How do you remove the bullets from an unordered list? (Be general, not specific.)

7. What element would you use to provide the full name of the W3C in the document? Can you write out the complete markup?

8. What is the difference between a `dl` and a `dt`?

9. What is the difference between `id` and `class`?

10. Name the characters generated by these character entities:

    — _____   & _____

      _____   © _____

    • _____   ™ _____

(X)HTML Review: Text Elements

The following is a summary of the elements we covered in this chapter.

Block-level elements

address	author contact address
blockquote	blockquote
h1...h6	headings
p	paragraph
pre	preformatted text
hr	horizontal rule

List elements (block-level)

dd	definition
dl	definition list
dt	term
li	list item (for ul and ol)
ol	ordered list
ul	unordered list

Semantic inline elements

abbr	abbreviation
acronym	acronym
cite	citation
code	code sample
del	deleted text
dfn	defining term
em	emphasized text
ins	inserted text
kbd	keyboard text
q	short quotation
samp	sample output
strong	strongly emphasized
var	variable

Presentational inline elements

b	bold
big	big
br	line break
center	centered text
font	size, color, face
i	italic
s	strike-through
small	small text
strike	strike-through
sub	subscript
sup	superscript
tt	teletype
u	underlined

Generic elements

div	block-level division
span	inline span of text

CHAPTER 6

ADDING LINKS

If you're creating a page for the Web, chances are you'll want it to point to other web pages, whether to another section of your own site or to someone else's. You can even link to another spot on the same page. Linking, after all, is what the Web is all about. In this chapter, we'll look at the markup that makes links work: to other sites, to your own site, and within a page.

If you've used the Web at all, you should be familiar with the highlighted text and graphics that indicate "click here." There is one element that makes linking possible: the anchor (a).

`<a>...</a>`

Anchor element (hypertext link)

The content of the anchor element becomes the hypertext link. Simply wrap a selection of text in opening and closing `<a>...</a>` tags and use the `href` attribute to provide the URL of the linked page. Here is an example that creates a link to the O'Reilly Media web site:

```
<a href="http://www.oreilly.com">Go to O'Reilly.com</a>
```

To make an image a link, simply put the `img` element in the anchor element:

```
<a href="http://www.oreilly.com"><img src="ora.gif" /></a>
```

The only restriction is that because anchors are inline elements, they may only contain text and other inline elements. You may not put a paragraph, heading, or other block element between anchor tags.

Most browsers display linked text as blue and underlined, and linked images with a blue border. Visited links generally display in purple. Users can change these colors in their browser preferences, and, of course, you can change the appearance of links for your sites using style sheets. I'll show you how in Chapter 13, Colors and Backgrounds.

When a user clicks on the linked text or image, the page you specify in the anchor element loads in the browser window. The linked image markup sample shown previously might look like Figure 6-1.

IN THIS CHAPTER

Making links to external pages

Making relative links to documents on your own server

Linking to a specific point in a page

Adding "mailto" links

Targeting new windows

AT A GLANCE

Anchor Syntax

The simplified structure of the anchor element is:

```
<a href="url">linked text or image</a>
```

WARNING

One word of caution: if you choose to change your link colors, it is recommended that you keep them consistent throughout your site so as not to confuse your users.

Figure 6-1. When a user clicks on the linked text or image, the page you specify in the anchor element loads in the browser window.

The href Attribute

You'll need to tell the browser which document to link to, right? The `href` (hypertext reference) attribute provides the address of the page (its URL) to the browser. The URL must always appear in quotation marks. Most of the time you'll point to other (X)HTML documents; however, you can also point to other web resources, such as images, audio, and video files.

Because there's not much to slapping anchor tags around some content, the real trick to linking comes in getting the URL correct.

There are two ways to specify the URL:

- **Absolute URLs** provide the full URL for the document, including the protocol (*http://*), the domain name, and the pathname as necessary. You need to use an absolute URL when pointing to a document out on the Web.

  Example: `href="http://www.oreilly.com/"`

  Sometimes, when the page you're linking to has a long URL pathname, the link can end up looking pretty confusing (Figure 6-2). Just keep in mind that the structure is still a simple container element with one attribute. Don't let the pathname intimidate you.

- **Relative URLs** describe the pathname to the linked file *relative* to the current document. It doesn't require the protocol or domain name—just the pathname. Relative URLs can be used when you are linking to another document on your own site (i.e., on the same server).

  Example: `href="recipes/index.html"`

In this chapter, we'll add links using absolute and relative URLs to my cooking web site, Jen's Kitchen (see sidebar). Absolute URLs are easy, so let's get them out of the way first.

TERMINOLOGY

URL vs. URI

The W3C and the development community are moving away from the term URL (Uniform Resource Locator) toward the more generic and technically accurate URI (Uniform Resource Identifier).

At this point, "URL" has crossed over into the mainstream vocabulary. Because it is more familiar, I will be sticking with it throughout the discussions in this chapter.

If you like to geek out on this kind of thing, I refer you to the documentation that defines URIs and their subset, URLs: *www.gbiv.com/protocols/uri/rfc/rfc3986.html*.

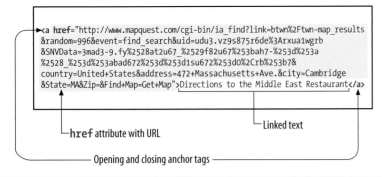

Figure 6-2. *An example of a long URL. Although it may make the anchor tag look confusing, the structure is the same.*

Linking to Pages on the Web

Many times, you'll want to create a link to a page that you've found on the Web. This is known as an "external" link because it is going to a page outside of your own server or site. To make an external link, you need to provide the absolute URL, beginning with `http://` (the protocol). This tells the browser, "Go out on the Web and get the following document."

I want to add some external links to the Jen's Kitchen home page (Figure 6-3). First, I'll link the list item "The Food Network" to the site *www.foodtv.com*. I marked up the link text in an anchor element by adding opening and closing anchor tags. Notice that I've added the anchor tags *inside* the list item (`li`) element. That's because block-level elements, such as `li`, may not go inside the inline anchor element.

    <li><a>The Food Network</a></li>

Next, I add the `href` attribute with the complete URL for the site.

    <li><a href="http://www.foodtv.com">The Food Network</a></li>

And *voila*! That's all there is to it. Now "The Food Network" will appear as a link, and will take my visitors to that site when they click it.

---

exercise 6-1 | **Make an external link**

Open the file *index.html* from the *jenskitchen* folder. Make the list item, "Epicurious," link to its web page at *www.epicurious.com*, following my example.

    <ul>
        <li><a href="http://www.foodtv.com/">The Food Network</a></li>
        <li>Epicurious</li>
    </ul>

When you are done, you can save *index.html* and open it in a browser. If you have an Internet connection, you can click on your new link and go to the Epicurious site. If the link doesn't take you there, go back and make sure that you didn't miss anything in the markup.

MARKUP TIP

URL Wrangling

If you are linking to a page with a long URL, it is helpful to copy the URL from the location toolbar in your browser and paste it into your (X)HTML document. That way, you avoid mistyping a single character and breaking the whole link.

TRY IT

Work Along with Jen's Kitchen

Figure 6-3. *Finished Jen's Kitchen page*

All the files for the Jen's Kitchen web site are available online at *www.learningwebdesign.com/materials*. Download the entire directory, making sure not to change the way its contents are organized.

The resulting markup for all of the exercises is provided in Appendix A.

The pages aren't much to look at, but they will give you a chance to develop your linking skills.

Linking Within Your Own Site

A large portion of the linking you'll do will be between pages of your own site: from the home page to section pages, from section pages to content pages, and so on. In these cases, you can use a relative URL—one that calls for a page on your own server.

Without "http://", the browser looks on the current server for the linked document. A pathname, the notation used to point to a particular file or directory, tells the browser where to find the file. Web pathnames follow the Unix convention of separating directory and filenames with forward slashes (/). A relative pathname describes how to get to the linked document starting from the location of the current document.

Relative pathnames can get a bit tricky. In my teaching experience, nothing stumps beginners like writing relative pathnames, so we'll take it one step at a time. There are exercises along the way that I recommend you do as we go along.

All of the pathname examples in this section are based on the structure of the Jen's Kitchen site shown in Figure 6-4. When you diagram the structure of the directories for a site, it generally ends up looking like an inverted tree with the root directory at the top of the hierarchy. For the Jen's Kitchen site, the root directory is named *jenskitchen*. For another way to look at it, there is also a view of the directory and subdirectories as they appear in the Finder on my Mac (Windows users see one directory at a time).

NOTE

On PCs and Macs, files are organized into "folders," but in the web development world, it is more common to refer to the equivalent and more technical term, "directory." A folder is just a directory with a cute icon.

Important Pathname Don'ts

When you are writing relative pathnames, it is critical that you follow these rules to avoid common errors:

Don't use backslashes (\). Web URL pathnames use forward slashes (/) only.

Don't start with the drive name (D:, C:, etc.). Although your pages will link to each other successfully while they are on your own computer, once they are uploaded to the web server, the drive name is irrelevant and will break your links.

Don't start with file://. This also indicates that the file is local and causes the link to break when it is on the server.

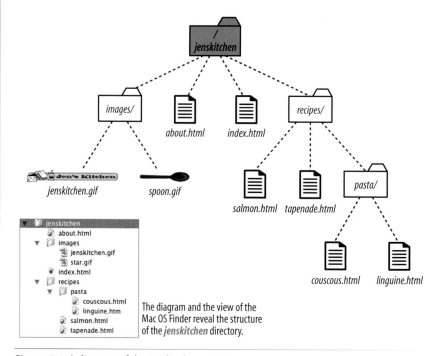

The diagram and the view of the Mac OS Finder reveal the structure of the *jenskitchen* directory.

Figure 6-4. A diagram of the jenskitchen site structure

Linking within a directory

The most straightforward relative URL to write is to another file within the same directory. When you are linking to a file in the same directory, you only need to provide the name of the file (its filename). When the URL is a single file name, the server looks in the current directory (that is, the directory that contains the (X)HTML document with the link) for the file.

In this example, I want to make a link from my home page (*index.html*) to a general information page (*about.html*). Both files are in the same directory (*jenskitchen*). So from my home page, I can make a link to the information page by simply providing its filename in the URL (Figure 6-5):

A link to just the filename indicates the linked file is in the same directory as the current document.

```
<a href="about.html">About the site...</a>
```

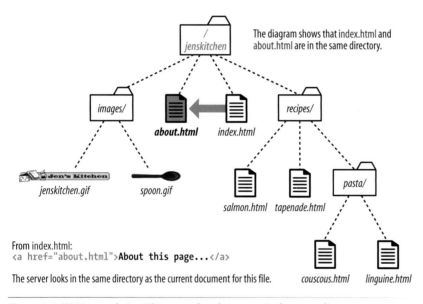

Figure 6-5. *Writing a relative URL to another document in the same directory.*

exercise 6-2 | **Link in the same directory**

Open the file *about.html* from the *jenskitchen* folder. Make the paragraph, "Back to the home page" at the bottom of the page link back to *index.html*. Remember that the anchor element must be contained in the **p** element, not the other way around.

```
<p>Back to the home page</p>
```

When you are done, you can save *about.html* and open it in a browser. You don't need an Internet connection to test links locally (that is, on your own computer). Clicking on the link should take you back to the home page.

Linking to a lower directory

But what if the files aren't in the same directory? You have to give the browser directions by including the pathname in the URL. Let's see how this works.

Getting back to our example, my recipe files are stored in a subdirectory called *recipes*. I want to make a link from *index.html* to a file in the *recipes* directory called *salmon.html*. The pathname in the URL tells the browser to look in the current directory for a directory called *recipes*, and then look for the file *salmon.html* (Figure 6-6):

```
<li><a href="recipes/salmon.html">Garlic Salmon</a></li>
```

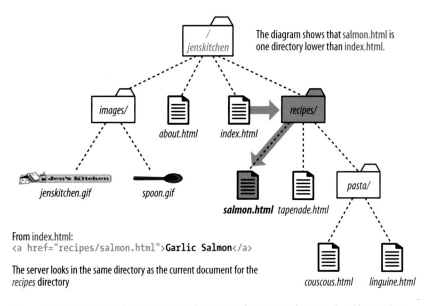

Figure 6-6. *Writing a relative URL to a document that is one directory level lower than the current document*

exercise 6-3 | Link one directory down

Open the file *index.html* from the *jenskitchen* folder. Make the list item, "Tapenade (Olive Spread)" link to the file *tapenade.html* in the *recipes* directory. Remember to nest the elements correctly.

```
<li>Tapenade (Olive Spread)</li>
```

When you are done, you can save *index.html* and open it in a browser. You should be able to click your new link and see the recipe page for tapenade. If not, make sure that your markup is correct and that the directory structure for *jenskitchen* matches the examples.

Now let's link down to the file called *couscous.html*, which is located in the *pasta* subdirectory. All we need to do is provide the directions through two subdirectories (*recipes*, then *pasta*) to *couscous.html* (Figure 6-7):

```
<li><a href="recipes/pasta/couscous.html">Couscous with Peas and Mint
</a></li>
```

Directories are separated by forward slashes. The resulting anchor tag tells the browser, "Look in the current directory for a directory called *recipes*. There you'll find another directory called *pasta*, and in there is the file I'd like to link to, *couscous.html*."

Now that we've done two directory levels, you should get the idea of how pathnames are assembled. This same method applies for relative pathnames that drill down through any number of directories. Just start with the name of the directory that is in same location as the current file, and follow each directory name with a slash until you get to the linked file name.

When linking to a file in a lower directory, the pathname must contain the names of the subdirectories you go through to get to the file.

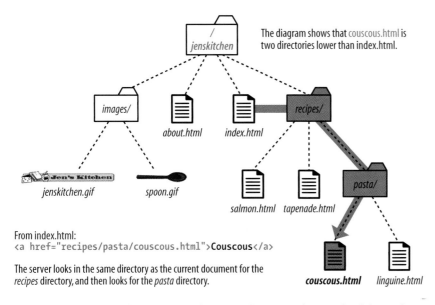

Figure 6-7. Writing a relative URL to a document that is two directory levels lower than the current document.

exercise 6-4 | **Link two directories down**

Open the file *index.html* from the *jenskitchen* folder. Make the list item, "Linguine with Clam Sauce" link to the file *linguine.html* in the *pasta* directory.

```
<li>Linguine with Clam Sauce</li>
```

When you are done, you can save *index.html* and open it in a browser. Click on the new link to get the delicious recipe.

Linking to a higher directory

So far, so good, right? Here comes the tricky part. This time we're going to go in the other direction and make a link from the salmon recipe page back to the home page, which is one directory level up.

In Unix, there is a pathname convention just for this purpose, the "dot-dot-slash" (`../`). When you begin a pathname with a `../`, it's the same as telling the browser "back up one directory level" and then follow the path to the specified file. If you are familiar with browsing files on your desktop, it is helpful to know that a "../" has the same effect as clicking the "Up" button in Windows Explorer or the left-arrow button in the Finder on Mac OS X.

Each ../ at the beginning of the pathname tells the browser to go up one directory level to look for the file.

Let's start by making a link back to the home page (*index.html*) from *salmon.html*. Because *salmon.html* is in the *recipes* subdirectory, we need to back up a level to *jenskitchen* to find *index.html*. This pathname tells the browser to "go up one level," then look in that directory for *index.html* (Figure 6-8):

```
<p><a href="../index.html">[Back to home page]</a></p>
```

Note that we don't need to write out the name of the higher directory (*jenskitchen*) in the pathname. The `../` stands in for it.

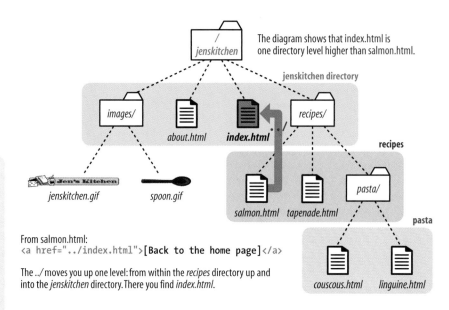

From salmon.html:
```
<a href="../index.html">[Back to the home page]</a>
```

The ../ moves you up one level: from within the *recipes* directory up and into the *jenskitchen* directory. There you find *index.html*.

Figure 6-8. *Writing a relative URL to a document that is one directory level higher than the current document.*

exercise 6-5 | **Link to a higher directory**

Open the file *tapenade.html* from the *recipes* directory. At the bottom of the page, you'll find this paragraph.

```
<p>[Back to the home page]</p>
```

Using the notation described in this section, make this text link back to the home page (*index.html*) located one directory level up.

But how about linking back to the home page from *couscous.html*? Can you guess how you'd back your way out of two directory levels? Simple, just use the dot-dot-slash twice (Figure 6-9).

A link on the *couscous.html* page back to the home page (*index.html*) would look like this:

```
<p><a href="../../index.html">[Back to home page]</a></p>
```

The first `../` backs up to the *recipes* directory; the second `../` backs up to the top-level directory where *index.html* can be found. Again, there is no need to write out the directory names; the `../` does it all.

NOTE

I confess to still sometimes silently chanting "go-up-a-level, go-up-a-level" for each ../ when trying to decipher a complicated relative URL. It helps me sort things out.

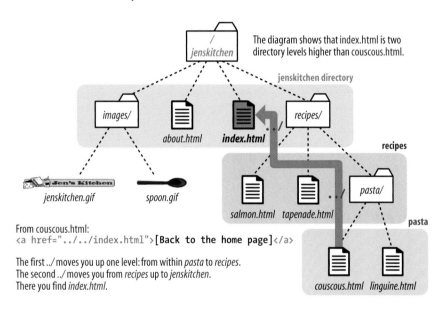

Figure 6-9. *Writing a relative URL to a document that is two directory levels higher than the current document.*

exercise 6-6 | **Link up two directory levels**

OK, now it's your turn to give it a try. Open the file *linguine.html* and make the last paragraph link to back to the home page using `../../` as I have done.

```
<p>[Back to the home page]</p>
```

When you are done, save the file and open it in a browser. You should be able to link to the home page.

Site root relative pathnames

All web sites have a root directory, which is the directory that contains all the directories and files for the site. So far, all of the pathnames we've looked at are relative to the document with the link. Another way to write a pathname is to start at the root directory and list the sub-directory names until you get to the file you want to link to. This kind of pathname is known as site root relative.

Site root relative links are generally preferred due to their flexibility.

In the Unix pathname convention, the root directory is referred to with a forward slash (/) at the start of the pathname. The site root relative pathname in the following link reads, "Go to the very top-level directory for this site, open the *recipes* directory, then find the *salmon.html* file" (Figure 6-10):

```
<a href="/recipes/salmon.html">Garlic Salmon</a>
```

Note that you don't need to write the name of the root directory (*jenskitchen*) in the URL—the forward slash (/) stands in for it and takes the browser to the top level. From there, it's a matter of specifying the directories the browser should look in.

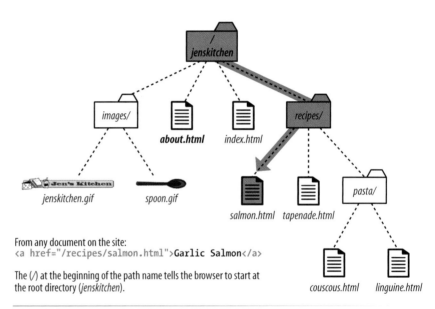

From any document on the site:
`<a href="/recipes/salmon.html">`**`Garlic Salmon`**`</a>`

The (/) at the beginning of the path name tells the browser to start at the root directory (*jenskitchen*).

Figure 6-10. Writing a relative URL starting at the root directory.

Because this link starts at the root to describe the pathname, it will work from any document on the server, regardless of which sub-directory it may be located in. Site root relative links are useful for content that might not always be in the same directory, or for dynamically generated material. They also make it easy to copy and paste links between documents. On the downside, however, the links won't work on your local machine because they will be relative to your hard drive. You'll have to wait until the site is on the final server to check that links are working.

It's the same for images

The `src` attribute in the `img` element works the same as the `href` attribute in anchors when it comes to specifying URLs. Since you'll most likely be using images from your own server, the `src` attributes within your image elements will be set to relative URLs.

Let's look at a few examples from the Jen's Kitchen site. First, to add an image to the *index.html* page, the markup would be:

```
<img src="images/jenskitchen.gif" alt="" />
```

The URL says, "Look in the current directory (*jenskitchen*) for the *images* directory; in there you will find *jenskitchen.gif*."

Now for the *piece de résistance*. Let's add an image to the file *couscous.html*:

```
<img src="../../images/spoon.gif" alt="" />
```

This is a little more complicated than what we've seen so far. This pathname tells the browser to go up two directory levels to the top-level directory and, once there, look in the *images* directory for a image called *spoon.gif*. Whew!

Of course, you could simplify that path by going the site root relative route, in which case, the pathname to *spoon.gif* (and any other file in the *images* directory) could be accessed like this:

```
<img src="/images/spoon.gif" alt="" />
```

The trade-off is that you won't see the image in place until the site is uploaded to the server, but it does make maintenance easier once it's there.

A Little Help from Your Tools

If you use a WYSIWYG authoring tool to create your site, the tool generates relative URLs for you. Be sure to use one of the automated link tools (such as the Browse button or GoLive's "Point and Shoot" function) for links and graphics. Some programs, such as Adobe Dreamweaver and Microsoft Expression Web, have built-in site management functions that adjust your relative URLs even if you reorganize the directory structure.

exercise 6-7 | **Try a few more**

Before we move on, you may want to try your hand at writing a few more relative URLs to make sure you've really gotten it. You can just write your answers below, or if you want to test your markup to see if it works, make changes in the actual files. You'll need to add the text to the files to use as the link (for example, "Go to the Tapenade recipe" for the first question). Answers are in Appendix A.

1. Create a link on *salmon.html* to *tapenade.html*.

2. Create a link on *couscous.html* to *salmon.html*.

3. Create a link on *tapenade.html* to *linguine.html*.

4. Create a link on *linguine.html* to *about.html*.

5. Create a link on *tapenade.html* to *www.allrecipes.com*.

NOTE

Any of these pathnames could be site root relative, but write them relative to the listed document for the practice.

Linking to a specific point in a page

Did you know you can link to a specific point in a web page? This is useful for providing shortcuts to information at the bottom of a long scrolling page or for getting back to the top of a page with just one click. You will sometimes hear linking to a specific point in the page referred to as linking to a document fragment.

Linking to a particular spot within a page is a two-part process. First, you identify the destination, and then you make a link to it. In the following example, I create an alphabetical index at the top of the page that links down to each alphabetical section of a glossary page (Figure 6-11). When users click on the letter "H," they'll jump down on the page to the "H" heading lower on the page.

Step 1: Naming the destination

I like to think of this step as planting a flag in the document so I can get back to it easily. To create a destination, use the `id` attribute to give the target element in the document a unique name (that's "unique" as in the name may only appear once in the document, not "unique" as in funky and interesting). In web lingo, this is the fragment identifier.

You may remember the `id` attribute from Chapter 5, Marking Up Text where we used it to name generic `div` and `span` elements. Here, we're going to use it to name an element so that it can serve as a fragment identifier, that is, the destination of a link.

Here is a sample of the source for the glossary page. Because I want users to be able to link directly to the "H" heading, I'll add the `id` attribute to it and give it the value "startH" (Figure 6-11 ❶).

```
<h1 id="startH">H</h1>
```

Step 2: Linking to the destination

With the identifier in place, now I can make a link to it.

At the top of the page, I'll create a link down to the "startH" fragment ❷. As for any link, I use the `a` element with the `href` attribute to provide the location of the link. To indicate that I'm linking to a fragment, I use the octothorpe symbol (#), also called a hash or number symbol, before the fragment name.

```
<p>... F | G | <a href="#startH">H</a> | I | J ...</p>
```

And that's it. Now when someone clicks on the "H" from the listing at the top of the page, the browser will jump down and display the section starting with the "H" heading ❸.

NOTE

Linking to another spot on the same page works well for long, scrolling pages, but the effect may be lost on a short web page.

AUTHORING TIP

To the Top!

It is common practice to add a link back up to the top of the page when linking into a long page of text. This alleviates the need to scroll back after every link.

NOTE

Remember that `id` values must start with a letter or an underscore (although underscores may be problematic in some versions of IE).

---

1 Identify the destination using the `id` attribute.

```
<h2 id="startH">H</h2>
<dl>
<dt>hexadecimal</dt>
<dd>A base-16 numbering system that uses the characters 0-9 and
A-F. It is used in CSS and HTML for specifying color values</dd>
```

2 Create a link to the destination. The # before the name is necessary to identify this as a fragment and not a filename.

```
<p>... | F | G | <a href="#startH">H</a> | I | J ...</p>
```

3

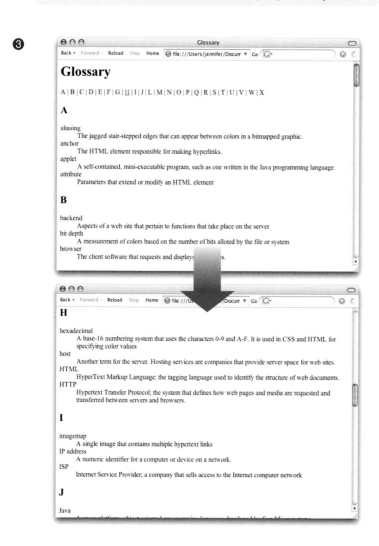

Figure 6-11. Linking to a specific destination within a single web page.

Named Anchors

The old way of identifying a destination in a document was to place a named anchor element. A named anchor is an `a` element that uses the `name` attribute (for providing the unique fragment identifier) instead of `href`, for example:

```
<h2><a name="startH">H</a></h2>
```

Named anchors are not underlined when the page displays in the browser.

The `name` attribute is no longer used with the `a` element in XHTML, so the recommended practice is to simply identify the element itself with the `id` attribute (as we've done in this chapter). It also keeps the markup simple and semantically sound. (Note that `name` is still used for certain form input elements.)

If, for some reason, you must support Netscape 4 or other out-of-date browsers for the .1% of people still using them, you will need to include a named anchor because old browsers do not support the `id` attribute for naming fragments.

Linking to a fragment in another document

You can link to a fragment in another document by adding the fragment name to the end of the URL (absolute or relative). For example, to make a link to the "H" heading of the glossary page from another document in that directory, the URL would look like this:

```
<a href="glossary.html#startH">See the Glossary, letter H</a>
```

You can even link to specific destinations in pages on other sites by putting the fragment identifier at the end of an absolute URL, like so:

```
<a href="http://www.example.com/glossary.html#startH">See the Glossary,
letter H</a>
```

Of course, you don't have any control over the named fragments in other people's web pages. The destination points must be inserted by the author of those documents in order to be available to you. The only way to know whether they are there and where they are is to "View Source" for the page and look for them in the markup. If the fragments in external documents move or go away, the page will still load; the browser will just go to the top of the page as it does for regular links.

Targeting a New Browser Window

One problem with putting links on your page is that when people click on them, they may never come back. One solution to this dilemma is to have the linked page open in a new browser window. That way, your visitors can check out the link and still have your content available where they left it.

The downside is that opening new windows is problematic for accessibility. New windows may be confusing to some users, particularly those who are accessing your site via a screen reader or other assistive device. At the very least they may be perceived as an annoyance rather than a convenience, particularly now that we are regularly bombarded with pop-up advertising. Finally, because it is common to configure your browser to block pop-up windows, you risk having the users miss out on the content in the new window altogether.

The method you use to open a link in a new browser window depends on whether you want to control its size. If the size of the window doesn't matter, you can use (X)HTML alone. However, if you want to open the new window with particular pixel dimensions, then you need to use JavaScript. Let's look at both of these techniques.

---

exercise 6-8 | Linking to a fragment

Want some practice linking to specific destinations? Open the file *glossary.html* in the *materials* folder for this chapter. It looks just like the document in Figure 6-11.

1. Identify the **h2** "A" as a destination for a link by naming it "startA" with an **id** attribute.

   ```
   <h2 id="startA">A</h2>
   ```

2. Make the letter "A" at the top of the page a link to the identified fragment. Don't forget the #.

   ```
   <a href="#startA">A</a>
   ```

Repeat steps 1 and 2 for every letter across the top of the page until you really know what you are doing (or until you can't stand it anymore). You can help users get back to the top of the page, too.

3. Make the heading "Glossary" a destination named "top."

   ```
   <h1 id="top">Glossary</h1>
   ```

4. Add a paragraph element containing "TOP" at the end of each lettered section. Make "TOP" a link to the identifier that you just made at the top of the page.

   ```
   <p><a href="#top">TOP</a></p>
   ```

Copy and paste this code to the end of every letter section. Now your readers can get back to the top of the page easily throughout the document.

A new window with markup

To open a new window using (X)HTML markup, use the `target` attribute in the anchor (a) element to tell the browser the name of the window in which you want the linked document to open. Set the value of target to `_blank` or to any name of your choosing. Remember with this method, you have no control over the size of the window, but it will generally open at the same size as the most recently opened window in the user's browser.

Setting `target="_blank"` always causes the browser to open a fresh window. For example:

```
<a href="http://www.oreilly.com" target="_blank">O'Reilly</a>
```

If you target "_blank" for every link, every link will launch a new window, potentially leaving your user with a mess of open windows.

A better method is to give the target window a specific name, which can then be used by subsequent links. You can give the window any name you like ("new," "sample," whatever), as long as it doesn't start with an underscore. The following link will open a new window called "display."

```
<a href="http://www.oreilly.com" target="display">O'Reilly</a>
```

If you target the "display" window from every link on the page, each linked document will open in the same second window. Unfortunately, if that second window stays hidden behind the user's current window, it may look as though the link simply didn't work.

Opening a window with JavaScript

If you want to control the dimensions of your new window, you'll need to use JavaScript, a scripting language that adds interactivity and conditional behaviors to web pages. Teaching JavaScript is beyond the scope of this book, but you can use this simple window-opening script. Copy it exactly as it appears here, or (thank goodness) copy and paste it from the document *windowscript.html* provided in the materials for this chapter (at *www.learningwebdesign.com/materials*).

Targeting Frames

The `target` attribute is also useful with framed documents. A framed document is one in which the browser is divided into multiple windows, or frames, each displaying a separate (X)HTML document. If you give each frame a name, you can use the **target** attribute in links to make a linked document open in a specific frame. Frames, while once popular, have largely gone out of style due to usability and accessibility problems.

Figure 6-12. JavaScript allows you to open a window at a specific pixel size.

The script in the following example opens a new window that is 300 pixels wide by 400 pixels high (Figure 6-12).

There are two parts to the JavaScript. The first is the script itself ❶; the second is a reference to the script within the link ❷.

```html
<html>
<head>
  <title>Artists</title>
❶ <script type="text/javascript">
   // <![CDATA[
   var properties = { width: 300,
                      height: 400,
                      scrollbars: 'yes',
                      resizable: 'yes' };
   function popup(){
     var link = this.getAttribute( 'href' );
     var prop_str = '';
     for( prop in properties ){
       prop_str = prop_str + prop + '=' + properties[prop] + ',';
     }
     prop_str = prop_str.substr( 0, prop_str.length - 1 );
     var newWindow = window.open( link, '_blank', prop_str );
     if( newWindow ){
       if( newWindow.focus ) newWindow.focus();
       return false;
     }
     return true;
   }
   function setupPopups(){
     var links = document.getElementsByTagName( 'a' );
     for( var i=0; i<links.length; i++ ){
       if( links[i].getAttribute( 'rel' ) &&
           links[i].getAttribute( 'rel' ) == 'popup' ) links[i].
onclick = popup;
     }
   }
   window.onload = function(){
     setupPopups();
   }
   // ]]>
  </script>
</head>

<body>
<h1>Artists</h1>
<ul>
❷ <li><a href="waits.html" rel="popup">Tom Waits</a></li>
   <li><a href="eno.html" rel="popup">Brian Eno</a></li>
</ul>
</body>
</html>
```

When a user clicks on a link with a `rel` attribute set to "popup," this script kicks into action and opens the linked document in a new window that is sized according to the width and height property settings (300 × 400 pixels in this example).

This script opens any link with a `rel` attribute set to "popup" in a new window set to a specific size. You can set the width and height of the window to any pixel dimensions in the properties list at the beginning of the script (in bold). You can also decide whether the window has scrollbars and whether the user can resize the window by setting the "scrollbars" and "resizable" variables to "yes" or "no." The property values are the only portion of the script that should be customized. The rest should be used as-is.

In the body of the document, you'll see that each link includes the `rel` attribute set to "popup" ❷. Links without this `rel` value will not trigger the script.

Mail Links

Here's a nifty little linking trick: the `mailto` link. By using the `mailto` protocol in a link, you can link to an email address. When the user clicks on a `mailto` link, the browser opens a new mail message preaddressed to that address in a designated mail program.

A sample `mailto` link is shown here:

```
<a href="mailto:alklecker@hotmail.com">Contact Al Klecker</a>
```

As you can see, it's a standard anchor element with the `href` attribute. But the value is set to `mailto:name@address.com`.

The browser has to be configured to launch a mail program, so the effect won't work for 100% of your audience. If you use the email itself as the linked text, nobody will be left out if the `mailto` function does not work.

Test Yourself

The most important lesson in this chapter is how to write URLs for links and images. Here's another chance to brush up on your pathname skills.

Using the directory hierarchy shown in Figure 6-13, write out the markup for the following links and graphics. I filled in the first one for you as an example. The answers are located in Appendix A.

This diagram should provide you with enough information to answer the questions. If you need hands-on work to figure them out, the directory structure is available in the *test* directory in the materials for this chapter. The documents are just dummy files and contain no content.

1. In *index.html* (the site's home page), write the markup for a link to *tutorial.html*.

   <a href="tutorial.html">...</a>

TIP

The ../ (or multiples of them) always appears at the beginning of the pathname and never in the middle. If the pathnames you write have ../ in the middle, you've done something wrong.

2. In *index.html*, write the anchor element for a link to *instructions.html*.

3. Create a link to *family.html* from the page *tutorial.html*.

4. Create a link to *numbers.html* from the *family.html* page, but this time, start with the root directory.

5. Create a link back to the home page (*index.html*) from the page *instructions.html*.

6. In the file *intro.html*, create a link to the web site for this book (*www. learningwebdesign.com*).

7. Create a link to *instructions.html* from the page *greetings.html*.

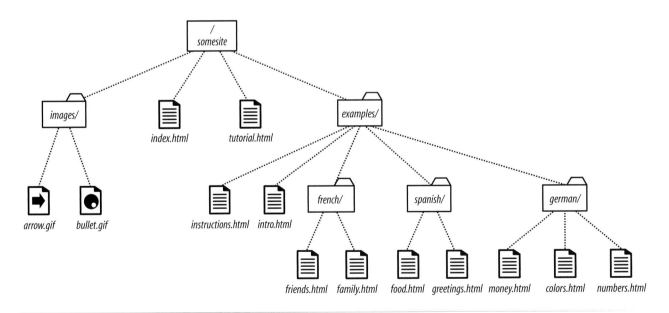

Figure 6-13. *The directory structure for the Test Yourself questions.*

8. Create a link back to the home page (*index.html*) from *money.html*.

We haven't covered the image (`img`) element in detail yet, but you should be able to fill the relative URLs after the `src` attribute to specify the location of the image files for these examples.

9. To place the graphic *arrow.gif* on the page *index.html*, the URL is:

`<img src="` `" alt="" />`

10. To place the graphic *arrow.gif* on the page *intro.html*, the tag is:

`<img src="` `" alt="" />`

11. To place the graphic *bullet.gif* on the *friends.html* page, the tag is:

`<img src="` `" alt="" />`

(X)HTML Review: The Anchor Element

There's really only one element relevant to linking:

Element and attributes	Description
`a`	Anchor (hypertext link) element
`href="url"`	Location of the target file
`name="text"`	Obsolete method for naming an anchor to create a fragment

CHAPTER 7

ADDING IMAGES

IN THIS CHAPTER

Adding images
to a web page

Using the src, alt, width,
and height attributes

Creating an imagemap

A web page with all text and no pictures isn't much fun. The Web's explosion into mass popularity is due in part to the fact that there are images on the page. Before the Web, the Internet was a text-only tundra.

Images appear on web pages in two ways: as part of the inline content or as tiling background images. Background images are added using Cascading Style Sheets and are talked about at length in Chapter 13, Colors and Backgrounds. In this chapter, we'll focus on adding image content to the document using the inline img element.

Inline images may be used on web pages in several ways:

As a simple image. An image can be used on a web page much as it is used in print, as a static image that adds information, such as a company logo or an illustration.

As a link. As we saw in the previous chapter, an image can be used as a link to another document by placing it in the anchor element.

As an imagemap. An imagemap is a single image that contains multiple links ("hotspots") that link to other documents. We'll look at the markup used to add clickable areas to images in this chapter as well.

With the emergence of standards-driven design and its mission to keep all matters of presentation out of the document structure, there has been a shift away from using inline images for purely decorative purposes. See the sidebar, Decorative Images Move on Back, on the following page for more information on this trend.

First, a Word on Image Formats

We'll get to the img element and markup examples in a moment, but first it's important to know that you can't put just any image on a web page. In order to be displayed inline, images must be in the GIF, JPEG, or PNG file format. Chapter 18, Web Graphics Basics explains these formats and the image types they handle best. In addition to being in an appropriate format, image files need to be named with the proper suffixes—.*gif*, .*jpg* (or .*jpeg*), and .*png*, respectively—in order to be recognized by the browser. Browsers use the suffix to determine how to display the image.

If you have a source image that is in another popular format such as TIFF, BMP, or EPS, you'll need to convert it to a web format before you can add it to the page. If, for some reason, you must keep your graphic file in its original format, you can make it available as an external image, by making a link directly to the image file, like this:

```
<a href="architecture.eps">Get the drawing</a>
```

Browsers use helper applications to display media they can't handle alone. The browser matches the suffix of the file in the link to the appropriate helper application. The external image may open in a separate application window or within the browser window if the helper application is a plug-in, such as the QuickTime plug-in. The browser may also ask the user to save the file or open an application manually.

Without further ado, let's take a look at the img element and its required and recommended attributes.

The img Element

`<img />` *(XHTML)*
`<img>` *(HTML)*
Adds an inline image

The img element tells the browser, "Place an image here." You add it in the flow of text at the point where you want the image to appear, as in this example. Because it is an inline element, it does not cause any line breaks, as shown in Figure 7-1.

```
<p>I had been wanting to go to Tuscany <img src="tuscany.jpg" alt="" />
for a long time, and I was not disappointed.</p>
```

I had been wanting to go to Tuscany for a long time, and I was not disappointed.

Figure 7-1. By default, inline images are aligned with the baseline of the surrounding text, and they do not cause a line break.

When the browser sees the img element, it makes a request to the server and retrieves the image file before displaying it on the page. Even though it makes a separate request for each image file, the speed of networks and computers

---

Decorative Images Move on Back

Images that are used purely for decoration have more to do with presentation than document structure and content. For that reason, they should be controlled with a style sheet rather than the (X)HTML markup.

Using CSS, it is possible to place an image in the background of the page or in any text element (a div, h1, li, you name it). These techniques are introduced in Chapters 13 and 19 of this book.

There are several benefits to specifying decorative images only in an external style sheet and keeping them out of the document structure. Not only does it make the document cleaner and more accessible, it also makes it easier to make changes to the look and feel of a site than when presentational elements are interspersed in the content.

For inspiration on how visually rich a web page can be with no img elements at all, see the CSS Zen Garden site at *www.csszengarden.com*.

usually makes it appear to happen instantaneously (unless you are dialing in on a slow modem connection).

The `src` and `alt` attributes shown in the sample are required. The `src` attribute tells the browser the location of the image file. The `alt` attribute provides alternative text that displays if the image is not available. We'll talk about `src` and `alt` a little more in upcoming sections.

There are a few other things of note about the `img` element:

- It is an empty element, which means it doesn't have any content. You just place it in the flow of text where the image should go.

- In XHTML, empty elements need to be terminated, so the `img` element is written `<img />`. In HTML, it's simply `<img>`.

- It is an inline element, so it behaves like any other inline element in the text flow. Figure 7-2 demonstrates the inline nature of image elements. When the browser window is resized, the line of images reflows to fill the new width.

- The `img` element is what's known as a replaced element because it is replaced by an external file when the page is displayed. This makes it different from text elements that have their content right there in the (X) HTML source (and thus are non-replaced).

- By default, the bottom edge of an image aligns with the baseline of text, as shown in Figures 7-1 and 7-2. Using Cascading Style Sheets, you can float the image to the right or left margin and allow text to flow around it, control the space and borders around the image, and change its vertical alignment. There are deprecated (X)HTML attributes for handling image alignment (see the sidebar, Deprecated img Attributes, next page), but they are discouraged from use and don't offer such fine-tuned control anyway.

The `src` and `alt` attributes are required in the `img` element.

Figure 7-2.   Inline images are part of the normal document flow. They reflow when the browser window is resized.

Providing the location with src

`src="URL"`
Source (location) of the image

The value of the `src` attribute is the URL of the image file. In most cases, the images you use on your pages will reside on your server, so you will use relative URLs to point to them. If you just read Chapter 6, Adding Links, you should be pretty handy with writing relative URLs by now. In short, if the image is in the same directory as the (X)HTML document, you can just refer to the image by name in the `src` attribute:

```
<img src="icon.gif" alt="" />
```

Developers usually organize the images for a site into a directory called *images* or *graphics*. There may even be separate image directories for each section of the site. If an image is not in the same directory as the document, you need to provide the relative pathname to the image file.

```
<img src="/images/arrow.gif" alt="" />
```

Of course, you can place images from other web sites as well (just be sure that you have permission to do so). Just use an absolute URL, like this:

```
<img src="http://www.example.com/images/smile.gif" alt="" />
```

DEVELOPMENT TIP
Organize Your Images

It is common to store all the graphics in their own directory (usually called *images* or *graphics*). You can make one images directory to store all the graphics for the whole site or create an images directory in each subdirectory (subsection) of the site.

Once you have your directory structure in place, be careful to save your graphics in the proper directory every time. Also be sure that the graphics are in the proper format and named with the *.gif*, *.jpg*, or *.png* suffix.

Providing alternate text with alt

`alt="text"`
Alternative text

Every `img` element must also contain an `alt` attribute that is used to provide a brief description of the image for those who are not able to see it, such as users with screen readers, Braille, or even small mobile devices. Alternate text (also referred to as alt text) should serve as a substitute for the image content—serving the same purpose and presenting the same information.

```
<p>If you're <img src="happyface.gif" alt="happy" /> and you know it
clap your hands.</p>
```

Deprecated img Attributes

In the past, image placement was handled with presentational attributes that have since been deprecated. For the sake of thoroughness, I'm listing them here with the recommendation that you not use them.

`border`

Specifies the width of a border around an image. Use one of the CSS `border` properties instead.

`align`

Changes the vertical and horizontal alignment of the image. It is also used to float the image to the left or right margin and allow text to wrap around it. This is now handled with the CSS `float` property.

`hspace`

Holds space to the left and right of an image floated with the `align` attribute. Space around images should be handled with the CSS `margin` property.

`vspace`

Holds space above and below an image floated with the `align` attribute. Again, the `margin` property is now the way to add space on any side of an image.

A screen reader might indicate the image and its `alt` value this way:

"If you're image happy and you know it clap your hands."

If an image is purely decorative, or does not add anything meaningful to the text content of the page, it is recommended that you leave the value of the `alt` attribute empty, as shown in this example and other examples in this chapter. Note that there is no character space between the quotation marks.

```
<img src="bullet.gif" alt="" />
```

Do not omit the `alt` attribute altogether, however, because it will cause the document to be invalid (validating documents is covered in Chapter 10, Understanding the Standards). For each inline image on your page, consider what the alternative text would sound like when read aloud and whether that enhances or is just obtrusive to a screen-reader user's experience.

Alternative text may benefit users with graphical browsers as well. If a user has opted to turn images off in the browser preferences or if the image simply fails to load, the browser may display the alternative text to give the user an idea of what is missing. The handling of alternative text is inconsistent among modern browsers, however, as shown in Figure 7-3.

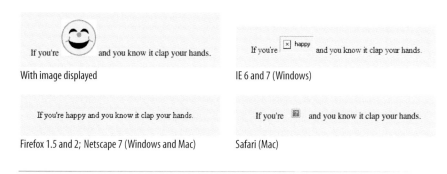

Figure 7-3. Most browsers display alternative text in place of the image (either with an icon or as inline text) if the image is not available. Safari for Macintosh OS X is a notable exception.

Long descriptions

Alternative text is a good start toward improving the accessibility of non-text content, but it is intended to be brief and succinct. For complex images, such as floor-plans, charts, graphs, and informational photographs, alternative text is not enough to fully convey the content. For those images, you may provide a longer description of the image using the `longdesc` attribute.

The value of the `longdesc` attribute is the URL of an external (X)HTML document containing the long description, as shown here:

```
<img src="executiveking.jpg" alt="photo of executive king room"
longdesc="executiveking-ld.html" />
```

<div class="sidebar">

TIP

Take Advantage of Caching

Here's a tip for making images display more quickly and reducing the traffic to your server. If you use the same image in multiple places on your site, be sure each `img` element is pointing to the same image file on the server.

When a browser downloads an image file, it stores it in the disk cache (a space for temporarily storing files on the hard disk). That way, if it needs to redisplay the page, it can just pull up a local copy of the source document and image files without making a new trip out to the remote server.

When you use the same image repetitively in a page or a site, the browser only needs to download the image once. Every subsequent instance of the image is grabbed from the local cache, which means less traffic for the server and faster display for the end user.

The browser recognizes an image by its entire pathname, not just the filename, so if you want to take advantage of file caching, be sure that each instance of your image is pointing to the same image file on the server (not multiple copies of the same image file in different directories).

</div>

`longdesc="`**`text`**`"`

Longer image description

ONLINE RESOURCES

Image Accessibility

There is more to say about image accessibility than I can fit in this chapter. I encourage you to start your research with these resources.

- "Chapter 6, The Image Problem" from the book *Building Accessible Websites* by Joe Clark (*joeclark.org/book/sashay/serialization/Chapter06.html*)
- Techniques for WCAG 2.0; Working Draft of Web Content Accessibility Guidelines (*http://www.w3.org/TR/WCAG20-TECHS*). Look under General and HTML techniques for information on images and longdesc.
- "The alt and title attributes" by Roger Johansson (*www.456bereastreet.com/archive/200412/the_alt_and_title_attributes*)

Using a Browser to Find Pixel Dimensions

You can find the pixel dimensions of an image by opening it in an image editing program, of course, but did you know you can also use a web browser?

Using Firefox, Netscape, or Safari (but not Internet Explorer for Windows), simply open the image file, and its pixel dimensions display in the browser's title bar along with the filename. It's a handy shortcut I use all the time because I always seem to have a browser running.

The content of the *executiveking-ld.html* document reads:

```
<p>The photo shows a room with a sliding-glass door looking out onto
a green courtyard. On the right side of the room, starting in the far
corner, is a small desk with a light and a telephone, then a king-sized
bed with 3 layers of pillows and a floral bed-spread, then a small
night stand with a lamp. Opposite the bed is an armoire with the doors
open revealing a flat-screen television and a small refrigerator.</p>

<a href="rooms.html#execking">Back to rooms page</a>
```

Unfortunately, many browsers and assistive devices do not support the longdesc attribute. As a backup, some developers provide a D-link (a capital letter "D" linked to the long description document) before or after the image. Others use a descriptive caption as the link.

Making image content accessible with alt and longdesc attributes is a rich topic. I've provided a sidebar with pointers to online resources that discuss the various strategies and give tips on writing descriptive and alternate text.

Providing width and height dimensions

width="*number*"
Image width in pixels

height="*number*"
Image height in pixels

The width and height attributes indicate the dimensions of the image in number of pixels. Sounds mundane, but these attributes can speed up the time it takes to display the final page.

When the browser knows the dimensions of the images on the page, it can busy itself laying out the page while the image files themselves are downloading. Without width and height values, the page is laid out immediately, and then reassembled each time an image file arrives from the server. Telling the browser how much space to hold for each image can speed up the final page display by seconds for some users.

NOTE

You can specify the width and height of an image element using style sheets as well, and it could be said that pixel dimensions are a matter of presentation, therefore the job of style sheets exclusively. On the other hand, these attributes provide basic and useful information about the image, and seeing as the W3C has not deprecated them for the img element, it is still recommended that you provide width and height attributes for every image.

Match values with actual pixel size

Be sure that the pixel dimensions you provide are the actual dimensions of the image. If the pixel values differ from the actual dimensions of your image, the browser resizes the image to match the specified values (Figure 7-4).

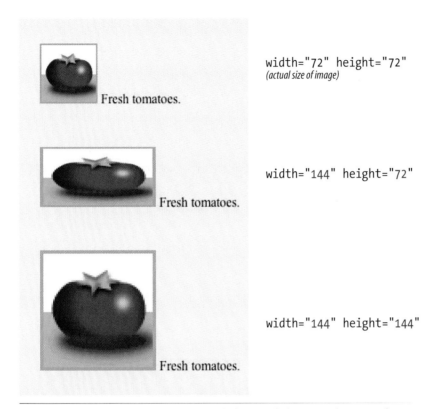

width="72" height="72"
(actual size of image)

width="144" height="72"

width="144" height="144"

Avoid resizing images with HTML. It forces an unnecessarily large file to download and results in a poor-quality image.

Figure 7-4. Browsers resize images to match the provided width *and* height *values. It is strongly recommended not to resize images in this way.*

Although it may be tempting to resize images in this manner, you should avoid doing so. Even though the image may appear small on the page, the large image with its corresponding large file size still needs to download. You shouldn't force a big download on a user when all you want is a small image on your page. It is much better to take the time to resize the image itself in an image editing program, then place it as actual size on the page.

Not only that, resizing with attributes usually results in a blurry and deformed image. In fact, if your images ever look fuzzy when viewed in a browser, the first thing to check is that the width and height values match the dimensions of the image exactly.

exercise 7-1 | **Adding and linking images**

You're back from Italy and it's time to post some of your travel photos to share them with your friends and family. In this exercise, you'll add thumbnail images to a travelog and make them link to larger versions of the photos.

All the thumbnails and photos you need have been created for you. I've given you a head-start on the XHTML files as well. Everything is available at *www.learningwebdesign.com/materials*. Put a copy of the *tuscany* folder on your hard drive, making sure to keep it organized as you find it. As always, the resulting markup is listed in Appendix A.

This little site is made up of a main page (*index.html*) and separate XHTML documents containing each of the larger image views (Figure 7-5). Although it is possible to link directly to the image file, it is better form to place the image on a page.

First, we'll add the thumbnails, then we'll add the full-size versions to their respective pages. Finally, we'll make the thumbnails link to those pages. Let's get started.

Figure 7-5. Travelog photo site

1. Open the file *index.html*, and add the small thumbnail images to this page to accompany the text. I've done the first one for you:

   ```
   <h2>Pozzarello</h2>
   <p><img src="thumbnails/window_100.jpg" alt="view
   from the bedroom window" width="75" height="100"
   /></p>
   ```

   I've put the image in its own **p** element so that it stays on its own line with the following paragraph starting below it. Because all of the thumbnail images are located in the *thumbnails* directory, I provided the pathname in the URL. I also added a description of the image and the width and height dimensions.

   Now it's your turn. Add the image *countryside_100.jpg* to the empty **p** element under the **h2**, "On the Road." Be sure to include the pathname, an alternative text description, and pixel dimensions (100 wide by 75 high).

   In addition, add both *alley_100.jpg* and *cathedral_100.jpg* to the empty **p** element under the subhead, "Sienna." Again, add **alt** text and pixel dimensions (these are 75 wide by 100 high).

   When you are done, save the file and open it in the browser to be sure that the images are visible and appear at the right size.

2. Next, add the images to the individual XHTML documents. I've done *window.html* for you:

   ```
   <h1>The View Through My Window</h1>
   <p><img src="photos/window.jpg" alt="view out the
   window of the rolling Tuscan hills" width="375"
   height="500" /></p>
   ```

   Notice that the full-size images are in a directory called *photos*, so that needs to be reflected in the pathnames.

   Add images to *countryside.html*, *alley.html*, and *cathedral.html*, following my example. Hint: all of the images are 500 pixels on their widest side and 375 pixels on their shortest side, although the orientation varies.

   Save each file and check your work by opening them in the browser window.

3. Back in *index.html*, link the thumbnails to their respective files. I've done the first one here.

```
<h2>Pozzarello</h2>
<p><a href="window.html"><img src="thumbnails/
window_100.jpg" alt="view from the bedroom
window" width="75" height="100" /></a></p>
```

Notice that the URL is relative to the current document (*index.html*), not to the location of the image (the *thumbnails* directory).

Make the remaining thumbnail images links to each of the documents.

When you are done, save *index.html* and open it in a browser. You'll see that linked images display with a blue outline (until you click them, then it should be purple indicating you've visited that link). We'll learn how to turn that border off in Chapter 14, Thinking Inside the Box.

If all the images are visible and you are able to link to each page and back to the home page again, then congratulations, you're done!

Like a little more practice?

If you'd like more practice, you'll find two additional images (*sweets.jpg* and *lavender.jpg*) with their thumbnail versions (*sweets_100.jpg* and *lavender_100.jpg*) in their appropriate directories. This time, you'll need to add your own descriptions to the home page and create the XHTML documents for the full-size images from scratch.

For an added challenge, create a new directory called *photopages* in the *tuscany* directory. Move all of the *.html* documents except *index.html* into that directory then update the URLs on those pages so that the images are visible again.

Imagemaps

In your web travels, I'm sure you've run across a single image that has multiple "hotspots," or links, within it (Figure 7-6). These images are called imagemaps.

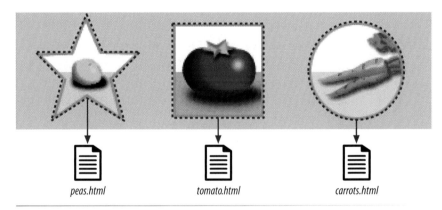

peas.html *tomato.html* *carrots.html*

Figure 7-6. An imagemap has multiple links within one image.

Putting several links in one image has nothing to do with the image itself; it's just an ordinary image file placed with an img element. Rather, the image merely serves as the frontend to the mechanisms that match particular mouse-click coordinates to a URL.

The real work is done by a map in the source document that matches sets of pixel coordinates to their respective link information. When the user clicks somewhere within the image, the browser passes the pixel coordinates of the pointer to the map, which in turn generates the appropriate link. When the

CSS Imagemaps

Imagemaps don't work well with text-only browsers, and thus are considered a hindrance to accessibility. As an alternative to a traditional imagemap, you can also use CSS to create links over an image in a way that is semantically sound and accessible to everyone. The technique is based on putting the large image in the background of an image and positioning invisible links at particular locations over the image.

For a complete tutorial, see the article "Night of the Image Map" by Stuart Robinson at A List Apart (*alistapart.com/articles/imagemap*). A web search for "CSS Imagemaps" will turn up additional demonstrations.

`<map>...</map>`
Client-side imagemap

`<area />` *XHTML*
`<area>` *HTML*
Defines a clickable area in an image map

cursor passes over a hotspot, the cursor changes to let the user know that the area is a link. The URL may also appear in the browser's status bar. Because the browser does the matching of mouse coordinates to URLs, this type of imagemap is called a client-side imagemap (see Note).

NOTE

In the early days of the Web, all imagemaps were processed on the server. Server-side imagemaps (indicated by the `ismap` *attribute in the* `img` *element) are now completely obsolete due to accessibility issues and the fact that they are less portable than the client-side variety.*

Due to new techniques and philosophies in web design, imagemaps are waning in popularity (see the sidebar, CSS Imagemaps). Imagemaps generally require text to be sunk into an image, which is sternly frowned upon. In terms of site optimization, they force all regions of the image to be saved in the same file format, which may lead to unnecessarily large file sizes. That said, take a look at what it takes to make a client-side imagemap.

The parts of an imagemap

Client-side imagemaps have three components:

An ordinary image file (*.gif, .jpg/.jpeg,* or *.png*) placed with the `img` element.

The `usemap` **attribute within that** `img` **element that identifies which map to use (each map is given a name)**

A `map` **element that is a container for some number of** `area` **elements.** Each `area` element corresponds to a clickable area in the imagemap and contains the pixel coordinate and URL information for that area. We'll look at a map in detail in a moment.

Creating the map

Fortunately, there are tools that generate maps so you don't have to write out the map by hand. Nearly all web-authoring and web graphics tools currently on the market (Adobe's Dreamweaver, Fireworks, and Photoshop/ImageReady being the most popular) have built-in imagemap generators. You could also download shareware imagemap programs (see the sidebar Imagemap Tools).

Figure 7-7 shows the imagemap interface in Dreamweaver, but the process for creating the map is essentially the same for all imagemap tools:

1. Open the image in the imagemap program (or place it on the page in a web-authoring tool).

2. Define an area that will be "clickable" by using the appropriate shape tools: rectangle, circle, or polygon (for tracing irregular shapes) ❹.

3. While the shape is still highlighted, enter a URL for that area in the text entry field provided ❶. Enter alternative text for the area as well ❷.

Place the imagemap image where you want it in the document.

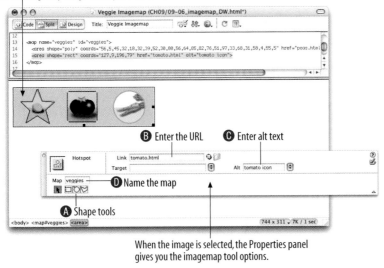

ⓑ Enter the URL   **ⓒ** Enter alt text

ⓓ Name the map

ⓐ Shape tools

When the image is selected, the Properties panel gives you the imagemap tool options.

Figure 7-7. Adding a "hotspot" to an imagemap using Dreamweaver.

4. Continue adding shapes and their respective URLs for each clickable area in the image.

5. Select the type of imagemap you want to create—client-side is the only practical option.

6. Give the map a name in the provided map name field ❶.

7. Add the map to the (X)HTML document. Web-authoring tools, such as Dreamweaver, insert the map automatically. If you are using ImageReady or another tool, you need to export or save the map code, then copy and paste it into the (X)HTML file. The map can go at the top or the bottom of the document; just make sure to keep it together. Then make sure that the `img` element points to the correct map name.

8. Save the (X)HTML document and open it in your browser.

Interpreting a map

Even if you use a tool to generate a map for you (and I recommend that you do), it is good to be familiar with the parts of the map. The following markup example shows the map for the imagemap shown in Figure 7-6. This particular map was generated by Dreamweaver, but it would be pretty much the same regardless of the tool that wrote it.

Imagemap Tools

There are a few imagemap tools available as shareware and freeware for both Windows systems and Mac. Try MapEdit by Tom Boutell, available at *www.boutell.com/mapedit/*. There is a recommended $10 shareware fee. You can also do a search for "imagemap" at CNET's *Download. com* for additional options.

❶ `<map name="veggies" id="veggies">`
❷
Ⓐ `<area shape="poly" coords="56,5,45,32,18,32,39,52,30,80,56,64,85,82,76,51,97,33,68,31,58,4,55,5" href="peas.html" alt="pea icon" />`

Ⓑ `<area shape="rect" coords="127,9,196,79" href="tomato.html" alt="tomato icon" />`

Ⓒ `<area shape="circle" coords="270,46,37" href="carrots.html" alt="carrot icon" />`

`</map>`

❸ `<p><img src="veggies.gif" width="330" height="90" usemap="#veggies"></p>`

❶ This marks the beginning of the map. I gave the map the name `veggies`. Dreamweaver has used both the `name` and `id` attributes to identify the map element. Both attributes have been included in order to be both backward (`name`) and forward (`id`) compatible. Within the `map` element there are `area` elements representing each hot spot in the image.

❷ Each `area` element has several attributes: the shape identifier (`shape`), pixel coordinates (`coords`), the URL for the link (`href`), and alternative text (`alt`). In this map there are three areas corresponding to the rectangle, circle, and polygon that I drew over my image:

Ⓐ The list of x,y coordinates for the polygon (`poly`) identifies each of the points along the path of the star shape containing a pea.

Ⓑ The x,y pixel coordinates for the rectangle (`rect`) identify the top-left, and bottom-right corners of the area over the tomato.

Ⓒ The pixel coordinates for the circle (`circle`) identify the center point and the length of the radius for the area with the carrots.

❸ The `img` element now sports the `usemap` attribute that tells the browser which map to use (`veggies`). You can include several imagemapped images and their respective maps in a single (X)HTML document.

exercise 7-2 | **Making an imagemap**

The image (*veggies.gif*) shown in this section and Figure 7-8 is available in the materials directory for this chapter.

If you have Dreamweaver, you can use Figure 7-7 to help make your own imagemap. The general steps for making an imagemap are outlined above, but you'll need to consult the documentation for a detailed explanation of how to use your program.

Your resulting pixel coordinates are not likely to be identical to the ones shown in this chapter because dragging hotspot areas is not an exact science. What matters is that the area is covered well enough that the user will go to the page as expected.

veggies.gif

Figure 7-8. *Try your hand at making an imagemap.*

Test Yourself

Images are a big part of the web experience. Answer these questions to see how well you've absorbed the key concepts of this chapter. The correct answers can be found in Appendix A.

1. Which two attributes must be included in every `img` element?

2. Write the markup for adding an image called *furry.jpg* that is in the same directory as the current document.

3. Why is it necessary to include alternative text? There are two main reasons.

4. What is the advantage of including `width` and `height` attributes for every graphic on the page?

5. What might be going wrong if your images don't appear when you view the page in a browser? There are three key explanations.

6. What does the `usemap` attribute do?

(X)HTML Review: Image and Imagemap Elements

The following is a summary of the elements we covered in this chapter:

Element and attributes	Description
`img`	Inserts an inline image
`src="url"`	The location of the image file
`alt="text"`	Alternative text
`width="number"`	Width of the graphic
`height="number"`	Height of the graphic
`usemap="usemap"`	Indicates a client-side imagemap (preferred)
`ismap="ismap"`	Indicates a server-side imagemap
`longdesc="url"`	Points to a document with a long description of the image
`title="text"`	Provides a "tool tip" when the user mouses over the image. Can be used for supplemental information about the image.
`map`	Map information for an imagemap
`name="text"`	The legacy method for giving the map a name
`id="text"`	The current method for giving the map a name
`area`	Contains information for a clickable area in an imagemap
`shape="rect|circle|poly"`	Shape of the linked area
`coords="numbers"`	Pixel coordinates for the linked area
`href="url"`	Target file for the link

CHAPTER 8

BASIC TABLE MARKUP

Before we launch into the markup for tables, let's check in with our progress so far. We've covered a lot of territory: how to establish the basic structure of an (X)HTML document, how to mark up text to give it meaning and structure, how to make links, and how to add image content to the page. That's really the majority of what you need to do for most straightforward web content.

This chapter and Chapter 9, Forms describe the markup for specialized content that you might not have a need for right away. Feel free to skip these chapters and go directly to Chapter 10, Understanding the Standards to learn more about XHTML, standards compliance, and validation. Or, if you're getting really antsy to make your pages look good, skip right to Part III and start playing with Cascading Style Sheets. The tables and forms chapters will be here when you're ready for them.

Are you still with me? Great. Let's talk tables. We'll start out by reviewing how tables should be used, then learn the elements used to create (X)HTML tables. Remember, this is an (X)HTML chapter, so we're going to focus on the markup that structures the content into tables, and we won't be concerned with how the tables look. Like any web content, the appearance (or presentation, as we say in the web development world) of tables should be handled with style sheets.

How Tables Are Used

HTML tables were created for instances when you need to add tabular material (data arranged into rows and columns) to a web page. Tables may be used to organize calendars, schedules, statistics, or other types of information as shown in Figure 8-1. Note that "data" doesn't necessarily mean numbers. A table cell may contain any sort of information, including numbers, text elements, even images and multimedia objects.

IN THIS CHAPTER

How tables are used

Basic table structure

The importance of headers

Spanning rows and columns

Cell padding and spacing

Captions and Summaries

Making tables accessible

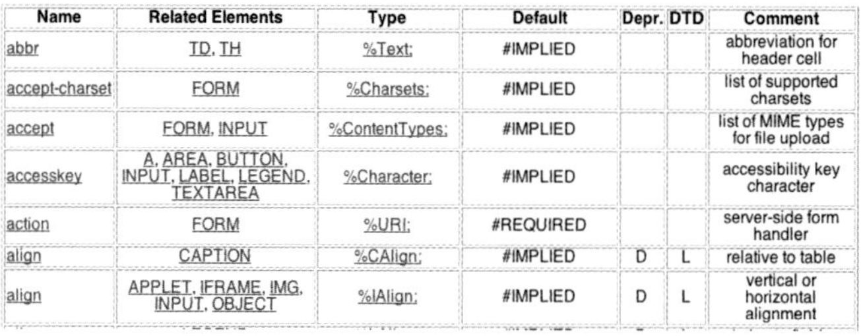

Name	Related Elements	Type	Default	Depr.	DTD	Comment
abbr	TD, TH	%Text;	#IMPLIED			abbreviation for header cell
accept-charset	FORM	%Charsets;	#IMPLIED			list of supported charsets
accept	FORM, INPUT	%ContentTypes;	#IMPLIED			list of MIME types for file upload
accesskey	A, AREA, BUTTON, INPUT, LABEL, LEGEND, TEXTAREA	%Character;	#IMPLIED			accessibility key character
action	FORM	%URI;	#REQUIRED			server-side form handler
align	CAPTION	%CAlign;	#IMPLIED	D	L	relative to table
align	APPLET, IFRAME, IMG, INPUT, OBJECT	%IAlign;	#IMPLIED	D	L	vertical or horizontal alignment

w3.org

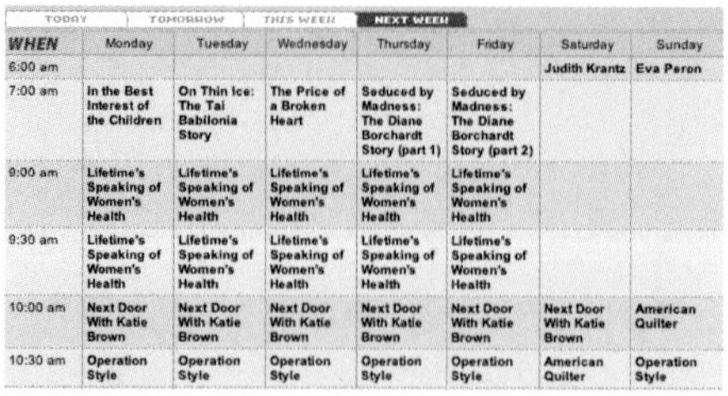

TODAY | TOMORROW | THIS WEEK | NEXT WEEK

WHEN	Monday	Tuesday	Wednesday	Thursday	Friday	Saturday	Sunday
6:00 am						Judith Krantz	Eva Peron
7:00 am	In the Best Interest of the Children	On Thin Ice: The Tai Babilonia Story	The Price of a Broken Heart	Seduced by Madness: The Diane Borchardt Story (part 1)	Seduced by Madness: The Diane Borchardt Story (part 2)		
9:00 am	Lifetime's Speaking of Women's Health	Lifetime's Speaking of Women's Health	Lifetime's Speaking of Women's Health	Lifetime's Speaking of Women's Health	Lifetime's Speaking of Women's Health		
9:30 am	Lifetime's Speaking of Women's Health	Lifetime's Speaking of Women's Health	Lifetime's Speaking of Women's Health	Lifetime's Speaking of Women's Health	Lifetime's Speaking of Women's Health		
10:00 am	Next Door With Katie Brown	Next Door With Katie Brown	Next Door With Katie Brown	Next Door With Katie Brown	Next Door With Katie Brown	Next Door With Katie Brown	American Quilter
10:30 am	Operation Style	Operation Style	Operation Style	Operation Style	Operation Style	American Quilter	Operation Style

lifetimetv.com

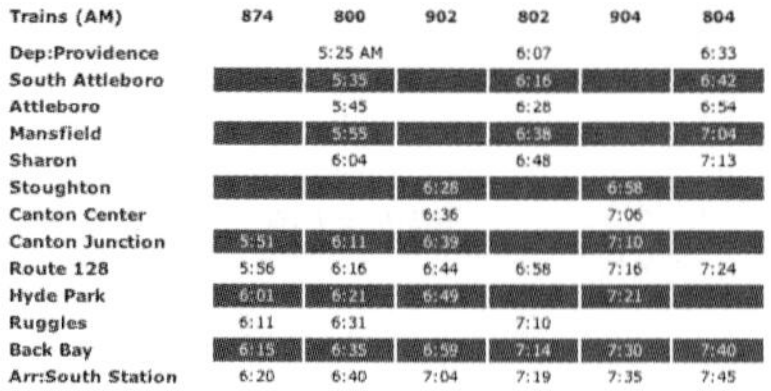

Trains (AM)	874	800	902	802	904	804
Dep:Providence		5:25 AM		6:07		6:33
South Attleboro		5:35		6:16		6:42
Attleboro		5:45		6:28		6:54
Mansfield		5:55		6:38		7:04
Sharon		6:04		6:48		7:13
Stoughton			6:28		6:58	
Canton Center			6:36		7:06	
Canton Junction	5:51	6:11	6:39		7:10	
Route 128	5:56	6:16	6:44	6:58	7:16	7:24
Hyde Park	6:01	6:21	6:49		7:21	
Ruggles	6:11	6:31		7:10		
Back Bay	6:15	6:35	6:59	7:14	7:30	7:40
Arr:South Station	6:20	6:40	7:04	7:19	7:35	7:45

mbta.com

***Figure 8-1.** Examples of tables used for tabular information, such as charts, calendars, and schedules.*

In visual browsers, the arrangement of data in rows and columns gives readers an instant understanding of the relationships between data cells and their respective header labels. Bear in mind when you are creating tables, however, that some readers will be hearing your data read aloud with a screen reader or reading Braille output. Later in this chapter, we'll discuss measures you can take to make table content accessible to users who don't have the benefit of visual presentation.

In the days before style sheets, tables were the only option for creating multi-column layouts or controlling alignment and white space. Layout tables, particularly the complex nested table arrangements that were once standard web design fare, are no longer necessary and are strongly discouraged. See the sidebar, Using Layout Tables, for more information. This chapter focuses on (X)HTML tables as they are intended to be used.

All of the table's content goes into cells that are arranged into rows.

Minimal Table Structure

Let's take a look at a simple table to see what it's made of. Here is a small table with three rows and three columns that lists nutritional information.

Menu item	Calories	Fat (g)
Chicken noodle soup	120	2
Caesar salad	400	26

Figure 8-2 reveals the structure of this table according to the (X)HTML table model. All of the table's content goes into cells that are arranged into rows. Cells contain either header information (titles for the columns, such as "Calories") or data, which may be any sort of content.

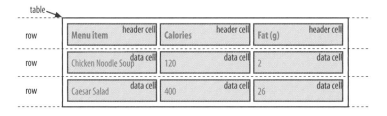

Figure 8-2. Tables are made up of rows that contain cells. Cells are the containers for content.

Simple enough, right? Now let's look at how those parts translate into (X)HTML elements (Figure 8-3).

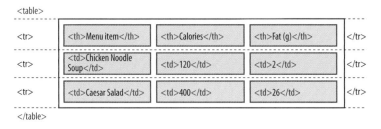

Figure 8-3. The elements that make up the basic structure of a table.

Figure 8-3 shows the elements that identify the table (`table`), rows (`tr`, for "table row"), and cells (`th`, for "table headers," and `td`, for "table data"). Cells are the heart of the table, because that's where the actual content goes. The other elements just hold things together.

What we don't see are column elements (see note). The number of columns in a table is determined by the number of cells in each row. This is one of the things that make (X)HTML tables potentially tricky. Rows are easy—if you want the table to have three rows, just use three `tr` elements. Columns are different. For a table with four columns, you need to make sure that every row has four `td` or `th` elements; the columns are implied.

NOTE

There are two column-related elements in HTML 4.01 and XHTML: `col` for identifying a column and `colgroup` for establishing related groups of columns. They were created to add a layer of information about the table that can potentially speed up its display, but they are not part of HTML's row-centric table model. See the sidebar, Advanced Table Elements, for more information.

Written out in a source document, the markup for the table in Figure 8-3 would look more like the sample below. It is common to stack the `th` and `td` elements in order to make them easier to find in the source. This does not affect how they are rendered by the browser.

Using Layout Tables

Complex tables were once the norm for creating interesting web page layouts, but now that style sheets offer an alternative, this use of (X)HTML tables is discouraged. Not only are they not semantically sound, but they can be a real hindrance to accessibility. The professional web design community is leaving layout tables in the dust.

If you still choose use table elements to create the grid of the page, follow these guidelines:

- Use only the minimal table elements (`table`, `tr`, and `td`).
- Avoid nesting tables within tables.
- Avoid tricks like empty rows and transparent GIF images used solely for adjusting the spacing.
- Use style sheets to control all presentational aspects of the table and its contents, such as colors, alignment, spacing, and column width.
- Make sure that your content still reads in a logical order in the source document when all of the table markup is removed. Tables that read in a logical order are said to linearize well. This is the way visitors with screen readers will encounter the page.

Layout tables are not necessarily evil or even inaccessible if handled responsibly. While we are still in a period of transition with varying browser support for CSS layout features, they are still the choice of some designers.

Stylin' Tables

Once you build the structure of the table in the markup, it's no problem adding a layer of style to customize its appearance.

Style sheets can and should be used to control these aspects of a table's visual presentation. We'll get to all the formatting tools you'll need in the following chapters:

In Chapter 12, Formatting Text:

- Font settings for cell contents
- Text color in cells

In Chapter 14, Thinking Inside the Box:

- Table dimensions (width and height)
- Borders
- Cell padding (space around cell contents)
- Margins around the table

In Chapter 13, Colors and Backgrounds:

- Background colors
- Tiling background images

In Chapter 17, CSS Techniques:

- Special properties for controlling borders and spacing between cells

```
<table>
    <tr>
        <th>Menu item</th>
        <th>Calories</th>
        <th>Fat (g)</th>
    </tr>
    <tr>
        <td>Chicken noodle soup</td>
        <td>120</td>
        <td>2</td>
    </tr>
    <tr>
        <td>Caesar salad</td>
        <td>400</td>
        <td>26</td>
    </tr>
</table>
```

Remember, all the content for a table must go in cells; that is, within `td` or `th` elements. You can put any content in a cell: text, a graphic, even another table.

Start and end `table` tags are used to identify the beginning and end of the table. The `table` element may only directly contain some number of `tr` (row) elements. The only thing that can go in the `tr` element is some number of `td` or `th` elements. In other words, there may be no text content within the `table` and `tr` elements that isn't contained within a `td` or `th`.

Finally, Figure 8-4 shows how the table would look in a simple web page, as displayed by default in a browser. I know it's not exciting. Excitement happens in the CSS chapters. What is worth noting is that tables are block-level elements, so they always start on new lines.

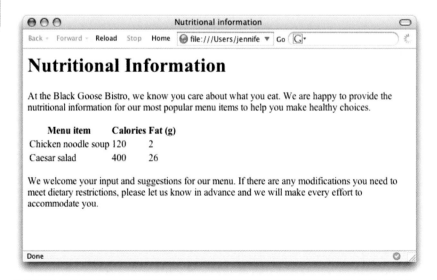

Figure 8-4.   The default rendering of our sample table in a browser (Firefox).

Advanced Table Elements

The sample table in this section has been stripped down to its bare essentials to make its structure clear while you learn how tables work. It is worth noting, however, that there are other table elements and attributes that offer more complex semantic descriptions and improve the accessibility of tabular content. A thoroughly marked-up version of the sample table might look like this:

```
<table summary="A listing of calorie and fat
content for each of the most popular menu items">

<caption>Nutritional Information</caption>

<thead>
    <tr>
        <th scope="col">Menu item</th>
        <th scope="col">Calories</th>
        <th abbr="fat" scope="col">Fat (g)</th>
    </tr>
</thead>

<tbody>
    <tr>
        <td>Chicken noodle soup</td>
        <td>120</td>
        <td>2</td>
    </tr>
    <tr>
        <td>Caesar salad</td>
        <td>400</td>
        <td>26</td>
    </tr>
</tbody>
</table>
```

Row group elements

You can describe rows or groups of rows as belonging to a header, footer, or the body of a table using the `thead`, `tfoot`, and `tbody` elements respectively. Some user agents (another word for a browsing device) may repeat the header and footer rows on tables that span multiple pages. Authors may also use these elements to apply styles to various regions of a table.

Column group elements

Columns may be identified with the `col` element or put into groups using the `colgroup` element. This is useful for adding semantic context to information in columns and may be used to calculate the width of tables more quickly.

Accessibility features

Accessibility features such as captions and summaries for providing descriptions of table content, and the `scope` and `headers` attributes for explicitly connecting headers with their respective content are discussed later in this chapter.

An in-depth exploration of the advanced table elements are beyond the scope of this book, but you may want to do more research if you anticipate working with data-heavy tables. For a detailed explanation, see the HTML 4.01 Recommendation at *www.w3.org/TR/REC-html40/struct/tables.html*.

The following is the source for another table. Can you tell how many rows and columns it will have when it is displayed in a browser?

```
<table>
    <tr>
        <td>Sufjan Stevens</td>
        <td>Illinoise</td>
        <td>Asthmatic Kitty Records</td>
    </tr>
    <tr>
        <td>The Shins</td>
        <td>Oh Inverted World</td>
        <td>Sub-pop Records</td>
    </tr>
</table>
```

If you guessed that it's a table with two rows and three columns, you're correct. Two `tr` elements create two rows; three `td` elements in each row create three columns.

Table Headers

As you can see in Figure 8-4, the text marked up as headers (th elements) are displayed differently from the other cells in the table (td elements). The difference, however, is not purely cosmetic. Table headers are important because they provide information or context about the cells in the row or column they precede. The th element may be handled differently than tds by alternative browsing devices. For example, screen readers may read the header aloud before each data cell ("Menu item, Caesar salad, Calories, 400, Fat-g, 26").

In this way, they are a key tool for making table content accessible. Don't try to fake headers by formatting a row of td elements differently than the rest of the table. Conversely, don't avoid using th elements because of their default rendering (bold and centered). Mark up the headers semantically and change the presentation later with a style rule.

That covers the basics. Before we get more fancy, try your hand at Exercise 8-1.

exercise 8-1 | Making a simple table

Try writing the markup for the table shown in Figure 8-5. You can open an HTML editor or just write it down on paper. The finished markup is provided in Appendix A.

(Note, I've added a 1-pixel border around cells with a style rule just to make the structure clear. You won't include this in your version.)

Be sure to close all table elements. Not only is it required in XHTML and recommended practice in all HTML documents, some browsers will not display the table at all if the end table tag (</table>) is missing.

Album	Year
Rubber Soul	1965
Revolver	1966
Sgt. Pepper's	1967
The White Album	1968
Abbey Road	1969

Figure 8-5. Write the markup for this table.

Spanning Cells

One fundamental feature of table structure is cell spanning, which is the stretching of a cell to cover several rows or columns. Spanning cells allows you to create complex table structures, but it has the side effect of making the markup a little more difficult to keep track of. You make a header or data cell span by adding the colspan or rowspan attributes, as we'll discuss next.

Column spans

Column spans, created with the colspan attribute in the td or th element, stretch a cell to the right to span over the subsequent columns (Figure 8-6). Here a column span is used to make a header apply to two columns. (I've added a border around cells to reveal the table structure in the screenshot.)

```
<table>
    <tr>
        <th colspan="2">Fat</th>
    </tr>
    <tr>
```

```
        <td>Saturated Fat (g)</td>
        <td>Unsaturated Fat (g)</td>
    </tr>
</table>
```

Fat	
Saturated Fat (g)	Unsaturated Fat (g)

Figure 8-6. The colspan attribute stretches a cell to the right to span the specified number of columns.

Notice in the first row (tr) that there is only one th element, while the second row has two td elements. The th for the column that was spanned over is no longer in the source; the cell with the $colspan$ stands in for it. Every row should have the same number of cells or equivalent $colspan$ values. For example, there are two td elements and the $colspan$ value is 2, so the implied number of columns in each row is equal.

WARNING

Be careful with colspan *values; if you specify a number that exceeds the number of columns in the table, most browsers will add columns to the existing table, which typically screws things up.*

exercise 8-2 | **Column spans**

Try writing the markup for the table shown in Figure 8-7. You can open an HTML editor or just write it down on paper. Don't worry if your table doesn't look exactly like the one shown here. The rules have been added to reveal the cell structure. Check Appendix A for the final markup.

The Sunday Night Movie		
Perry Mason	Candid Camera	What's My Line?
Bonanza	The Wackiest Ship in the Army	

Figure 8-7. Practice column spans by writing the markup for this table.

Some hints:

- For simplicity's sake, this table uses all td elements.
- The second row shows you that the table has a total of three columns.
- When a cell is spanned over, its td element does not appear in the table.

Row spans

Row spans, created with the $rowspan$ attribute, work just like column spans, except they cause the cell to span downward over several rows. In this example, the first cell in the table spans down three rows (Figure 8-8).

```
<table>
    <tr>
        <th rowspan="3">Serving Size</th>
        <td>Small (8oz.)</td>
    </tr>
    <tr>
        <td>Medium (16oz.)</td>
    </tr>
    <tr>
        <td>Large (24oz.)</td>
    </tr>
</table>
```

	Small (8oz.)	
Serving Size	Medium (16oz.)	
	Large (24oz.)	

Figure 8-8. The rowspan attribute stretches a cell downward to span the specified number of rows.

Again, notice that the `td` elements for the cells that were spanned over (the first cells in the remaining rows) do not appear in the source.

exercise 8-3 | **Row spans**

Some hints:

- Rows always span downward, so the "oranges" cell is part of the first row.
- Cells that are spanned over do not appear in the table code.

Try writing the markup for the table shown in Figure 8-9. If you're working in an HTML editor, don't worry if your table doesn't look exactly like the one shown here. The resulting markup is provided in Appendix A.

apples		pears
bananas	oranges	pineapple
lychees		

Figure 8-9. Practice row spans by writing the markup for this table.

Cell Padding and Spacing

By default, cells are sized just large enough to fit their contents (see the left example in Figure 8-10), but often, you'll want to add a little breathing room around tabular content. There are two kinds of space that can be added in and around table cells: cell padding and cell spacing, using the `cellpadding` and `cellspacing` attributes, respectively. These attributes may be used with the `table` element only. In other words, you can't apply them to `tr`, `td`, or `th` elements.

Because matters of spacing are presentational, we'll talk about CSS alternatives to these attributes as part of the discussion.

Cell padding

Cell padding is the amount of space held between the contents of the cell and the cell border. If you don't specify any cell padding, the cells will have the default value of one pixel of padding. Figure 8-10 shows the result of the following markup compared to a sample in which no padding or spacing is specified.

```
<table cellpadding="15">
  <tr>
    <td>CELL 1</td>
    <td>CELL 2</td>
  </tr>
```

```
   <tr>
      <td>CELL 3</td>
      <td>CELL 4</td>
   </tr>
</table>
```

By default, table cells
expand just enough to fit

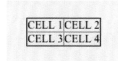

Cell padding adds space between the edge of
the cell and its contents.

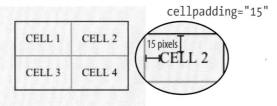

NOTE: I have used style sheets to add a gray rule around cells and a black rule around the table for
demonstration purposes.

Figure 8-10.   The `cellpadding` *attribute adds space between the cell contents and the
cell border.*

Because the `cellpadding` attribute may be used with the `table` element only,
the `cellpadding` value applies to all the cells in the table. In other words,
you can't specify different amounts of padding for individual cells with this
attribute.

However, you *can* apply padding amounts on a cell-by-cell basis using the
`padding` property in CSS. In fact, you can add padding to any (X)HTML
element, as we'll discuss in Chapter 14. Because CSS offers much more fine-
tuned control over spacing within the cell, the clunky and presentational
`cellpadding` attribute is going by the wayside. See the sidebar, Presentational
Table Attributes, for other table-related attributes that are being phased out
in favor of style sheet controls.

Cell spacing

Cell spacing is the amount of space held between cells, specified in number
of pixels (Figure 8-11). If you don't specify anything, the browser will use the
default value of two pixels of space between cells.

```
<table cellpadding="15" cellspacing="15">
   <tr>
      <td>CELL 1</td>
      <td>CELL 2</td>
   </tr>
   <tr>
      <td>CELL 3</td>
      <td>CELL 4</td>
   </tr>
</table>
```

> **TIP**
>
> Many authors explicitly set both
> the `cellpadding` and `cellspacing`
> attributes to 0 (zero) to override
> browser settings and clear the way
> for style sheet properties.

Presentational Table Attributes

These table attributes are no longer necessary now that there are well-supported CSS properties that offer even better control of the details.

width

Specifies the width of the table in pixels or percentage. Use the CSS width property instead.

border

Adds a "3-D" shaded border around cells and the table. The CSS border property offers more flexibility for setting border styles and colors.

align

Sets the horizontal alignment of cell contents to left, right, or center. This attribute is deprecated in favor of the text-align CSS property.

valign

Sets the vertical alignment of cell contents to top, bottom, or middle. The vertical-align style property is a better choice.

bgcolor

Applies a solid background color to a cell, row, or whole table. This attribute is deprecated in favor of the background-color property.

rules

Adds rules between rows, columns, or groups. Use the CSS border property instead.

Cell spacing adds space between cells

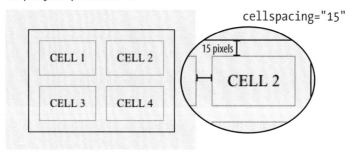

NOTE: I have used style sheets to add a gray rule around cells and a black rule around the table for demonstration purposes.

Figure 8-11. *The cellspacing attribute adds space between cells.*

There is no CSS property that *exactly* replicates the cellspacing attribute, although you can adjust the amount of space between cells by setting the border-collapse property for the table to separate, then use the border-spacing property to specify the amount of space between borders. The problem with this technique is that it is not supported by Internet Explorer 6 and earlier, which accounts for a large percentage of web traffic as of this writing. For the time being, if you absolutely need cell spacing for *all* your visitors, the cellspacing attribute is the only option. This will change eventually as versions 6 and earlier go away.

Captions and Summaries

There are two methods for providing additional information about a table: captions and summaries. The difference is that the caption is displayed with the table in visual browsers, while the summary is not displayed but may be used by assistive devices. Both captions and summaries are useful tools in improving table accessibility.

The caption element

The caption element is used to give a table a title or brief description. The caption element must be the first thing within the table element, as shown in this example that adds a caption to the nutritional chart from earlier in the chapter.

```
<table>
    <caption>Nutritional Information</caption>
    <tr>
        <th>Menu item</th>
        <th>Calories</th>
        <th>Fat (g)</th>
    </tr>
    <tr>
        <td>Chicken noodle soup</td>
```

```
        <td>120</td>
        <td>2</td>
    </tr>
    <tr>
        <td>Caesar salad</td>
        <td>400</td>
        <td>26</td>
    </tr>
</table>
```

The caption is displayed above the table by default as shown in Figure 8-12, although you can use a style sheet property (caption-side) to move it below the table.

Nutritional Information

Menu item	Calories	Fat (g)
Chicken noodle soup	120	2
Caesar salad	400	26

Figure 8-12. The table caption is displayed above the table by default.

The summary attribute

Summaries are used to provide a more lengthy description of the table and its contents. They are added using the summary attribute in the table element, as shown here.

```
<table summary="A listing of the calorie and fat content for each of
the most popular menu items">
    <caption>Nutritional Information</caption>

 ...table continues...

</table>
```

The summary is not rendered in visual browsers, but may be used by screen readers or other assistive devices to give visually impaired users a better understanding of the table's content, which sighted users could understand at a glance. This alleviates the need to listen to several rows of data before deciding whether to continue with the table data or skip it.

Be careful not to get carried away with table descriptions. They should be clear and succinct and used only when the caption isn't sufficient.

Table Accessibility

We've looked at headers, captions, and summaries as methods for improving the accessibility of table content. The HTML 4.01 Recommendation also provides a few additional attributes related to accessibility.

abbr

The abbr attribute is used in a table header (th) element to provide an abbreviated version of the header to be read aloud by a screen reader in place of a longer, more cumbersome version.

```
<th abbr="diameter">Diameter measured in earths</th>
```

scope

The scope attribute explicitly associates a table header with the row, column, rowgroup, or colgroup in which it appears. This example uses the scope attribute to declare that a header cell applies to the current row.

```
<tr>
    <th scope="row">Mars</th>
    <td>.95</td>
    <td>.62</td>
    <td>0</td>
</tr>
```

headers

For really complicated tables in which scope is not sufficient to associate a table data cell with its respective header (such as when the table contains multiple spanned cells), the headers attribute is used in the td element to explicitly tie it to a header. The header (th) element is named using the id attribute, as shown in this example.

```
<th id="diameter">Diameter measured in earths</th>
...many other cells...
<td headers="diameter">.38</td>
...many other cells...
```

This section obviously only scratches the surface. In-depth instruction on authoring accessible tables is beyond the scope of this beginner book, but I enthusiastically refer you to these useful articles:

- "Techniques for Accessible HTML Tables" by Steve Ferg (*www.ferg.org/section508/accessible_tables.html*)

- "Creating Accessible Tables," at WebAIM (*www.webaim.org/techniques/tables*)

Wrapping Up Tables

This chapter gave you a good overview of the components of (X)HTML tables. Exercise 8-4 puts most of what we covered together to give you a little more practice at authoring tables.

After just a few exercises, you're probably getting the sense that writing table markup manually, while not impossible, gets tedious and complicated quickly. Fortunately, web authoring tools such as Dreamweaver provide an interface that make the process much easier and time-efficient. Still, you'll be glad that you have a solid understanding of table structure and terminology, as well as the preferred methods for changing their appearance.

exercise 8-4 | **The table challenge**

Now it's time to put together the table writing skills you've acquired in this chapter. Your challenge is to write out the source document for the table shown in Figure 8-13.

	A common header for two subheads		Header 3
	Header 1	Header 2	
Thing A	data A1	data A2	data A3
Thing B	data B1	data B2	data B3
Thing C	data C1	data C2	data C3

Your Content Here

Figure 8-13. The table challenge.

I'll walk you through it a step at a time.

1. The first thing to do is open a new document in your text editor and set up its overall structure (**html**, **head**, **title**, and **body** elements). Save the document as *table.html* in the directory of your choice.

2. Next, in order to make the boundaries of the cells and table more clear when you check your work, I'm going to have you add some simple style sheet rules to the document. Don't worry about understanding exactly what's happening here (although it's fairly intuitive); just insert this **style** element in the **head** of the document exactly as you see it here.

    ```
    <head>
        <title>Table Challenge</title>
        <style type="text/css">
            td, th { border: 1px solid #CCC }
            table {border: 1px solid black }
        </style>
    </head>
    ```

3. Now it's time to start building the table. I usually start by setting up the table and adding as many empty row elements as I'll need for the final table as placeholders, as shown here (it should be clear that there are five rows in this table).

    ```
    <body>

    <table>
        <tr></tr>
        <tr></tr>
        <tr></tr>
        <tr></tr>
        <tr></tr>
    </table>

    </body>
    ```

4. Start with the top row and fill in the **th** and **td** elements from left to right, including any row or column spans as necessary. I'll help with the first row.

    The first cell (the one in the top left corner) spans down the height of two rows, so it gets a **rowspan** attribute. I'll use a **th** here to keep it consistent with the rest of the row. This cell has no content.

    ```
    <table>
        <tr>
            <th rowspan="2"></th>
        </tr>
    ```

    The cell in the second column of the first row spans over the width of two columns, so it gets a **colspan** attribute:
    ```
    <table>
        <tr>
            <th rowspan="2"></th>
            <th colspan="2">A common header for two subheads</th>
        </tr>
    ```

    The cell in the third column has been spanned over, so we don't need to include it in the markup. The cell in the fourth column also spans down two rows.

    ```
    <table>
        <tr>
            <th rowspan="2"></th>
            <th colspan="2">A common header for two
                subheads</th>
            <th rowspan="2">Header 3</th>
        </tr>
    ```

5. Now it's your turn. Continue filling in the **th** and **td** elements for the remaining four rows of the table. Here's a hint: the first and last cells in the second row have been spanned over. Also, if it's bold in the example, make it a header.

6. To complete the content, add the title over the table using the **caption** element.

7. Next, add 4 pixels of space between the cells using the **cellspacing** attribute.

8. Finally, improve the accessibility of the site by providing a **summary** of your choice. Also, use the **scope** attribute to make sure that the Thing A, Thing B, and Thing C headers are associated with their respective rows.

9. Save your work and open the file in a browser. The table should look just like the one on this page. If not, go back and adjust your markup. If you're stumped, the final markup for this exercise is listed in Appendix A.

Test Yourself

The answers to these questions are in Appendix A.

1. What are the parts/elements of a basic (X)HTML table?

2. Why don't professional web designers use tables for layout anymore?

3. What is the difference between a caption and a summary?

4. When would you use the `col` (column) element?

5. Find five errors in this table markup.

```
<caption>Primetime Television 1965</caption>
<table>
    Thursday Night
    <tr></tr>
        <th>7:30</th>
        <th>8:00</th>
        <th>8:30</th>
    <tr>
        <td>Shindig</td>
        <td>Donna Reed Show</td>
        <td>Bewitched</td>
    <tr>
        <colspan>Daniel Boone</colspan>
        <td>Laredo</td>
    </tr>
</table>
```

(X)HTML Review: Table Elements

The following is a summary of the elements we covered in this chapter:

Element and attributes	Description
table	Establishes a table element
cellpadding="*number*"	Space within cells
cellspacing="*number*"	Space between cells
summary="*text*"	A description of the table for nonvisual browsers
td	Establishes a cell within a table row
colspan="*number*"	Number of columns the cell should span
rowspan="*number*"	Number of rows the cell should span
headers="*header name*"	Associates a data cell with a header
th	Table header associated with a row or column
colspan="*number*"	Number of columns the cell should span
rowspan="*number*"	Number of rows the cell should span
scope="row|col|rowgroup|colgroup"	Associates the header with a row, row group, column, or column group.
tr	Establishes a row within a table
caption	Gives the table a title that displays in the browser.

CHAPTER 9

FORMS

It's hard to go on the Web without encountering some sort of form, whether you're making a purchase, signing up for a mailing list, or requesting product information. Although forms have a wide range of uses, from simple search boxes to complex online shopping interfaces, they are all built out of the same components.

This chapter introduces web forms, how they work, and the markup used to create them.

How Forms Work

There are two parts to a working form. The first part is the form that you see on the page itself. Forms are made up of buttons, text fields, and pull-down menus (collectively known as form controls) used to collect information from the user. Forms may also contain text and other elements.

The other component of a web form is an application or script on the server that processes the information collected by the form and returns an appropriate response. It's what makes the form *work*. In other words, putting up an (X)HTML page with form elements isn't enough. Web applications and scripts require progamming know-how that is beyond the scope of this book, however, the Getting Your Forms to Work sidebar later in this chapter provides some options for getting the scripts you need.

From data entry to response

If you are going to be creating web forms, it is beneficial to understand what is happening behind the scenes. This example traces the steps of a transaction using a simple form that gathers names and email addresses for a mailing list; however, it is typical of the process for most forms.

1. Your visitor, let's call her Sally, opens the page with a web form in the browser window. The browser sees the form control elements in the markup and replaces them with the appropriate form controls, including two text entry fields and a submit button (shown in Figure 9-1).

IN THIS CHAPTER

How forms work

The form element

POST versus GET

Variables and values

Form controls, including text entry fields, buttons, menus, and hidden data

Form accessibility features

A word about form layout

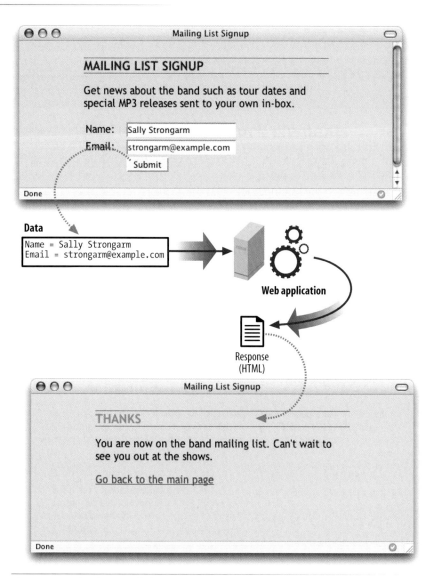

A Word about Encoding

Form data is encoded using the same method used for URLs in which spaces and other characters that are not permitted are translated into their hexadecimal equivalents. For example, each space character in the collected form data is represented by the character string **%20** and a slash (/) character is replaced with **%2F**. You don't need to worry about this; the browser handles it automatically.

Figure 9-1. What happens behind the scenes when a web form is submitted.

2. Sally would like to sign up for this mailing list, so she enters her name and email address into the fields and submits the form by clicking the "Submit" button.

3. The browser collects the information she entered, encodes it (see sidebar), and sends it to the web application on the server.

4. The web application accepts the information and processes it (that is, does whatever it is programmed to do with it). In this example, the name and email address are added to a database.

5. The web application also returns a response. The kind of response sent back depends on the content and purpose of the form. Here, the response is a simple web page that contains a thank you for signing up for the mailing list. Other applications might respond by reloading the (X)HTML form page with updated information, by moving the user on to another related form page, or by issuing an error message if the form is not filled out correctly, to name only a few examples.

6. The server sends the web application's response back to the browser where it is displayed. Sally can see that the form worked and that she has been added to the mailing list.

The form Element

Forms are added to web pages using (no surprise here) the `form` element. The `form` element is a container for all the content of the form, including some number of form controls, such as text entry fields and buttons. It may also contain block elements, (`h1`, `p`, and lists, for example), however, it may *not* contain another `form` element.

This sample source document contains a form similar to the one shown in Figure 9-1.

```
<html>
<head>
  <title>Mailing List Signup</title>
</head>
<body>
  <h1>Mailing List Signup</h1>

  <form action="/cgi-bin/mailinglist.pl" method="post">
    <fieldset>
    <legend>Join our email list</legend>
    <p>Get news about the band such as tour dates and special MP3
releases sent to your own in-box.</p>
    <ol>
    <li><label for="name">Name:</label>
        <input type="text" name="name" id="name" /></li>
    <li><label for="email">Email:</label>
        <input type="text" name="email" id="email" /></li>
    </ol>
    <input type="submit" value="Submit" />
    </fieldset>
  </form>

</body>
</html>
```

In addition to being a container for form control elements, the `form` element has some attributes that are necessary for interacting with the form-processing program on the server. Let's take a look at each.

NOTE

It is current best practice to wrap form controls in lists, most commonly ordered lists as shown in this example. Not only is it semantically correct, it also makes it easier to format the form with style sheets later.

CGI (Common Gateway Interface)

The Common Gateway Interface (CGI) is what allows the server to communicate with other programs. These are usually scripts (called CGI scripts) written in the Perl, C, or C++ programming languages. The most common use of CGI scripts is forms processing. Most servers follow the convention of keeping CGI scripts in a special directory named *cgi-bin* (short for CGI-binaries), as shown in our example. As other more web-focused options for interfacing with databases become available, such as ASP and PHP, traditional CGI programming is getting less attention.

Getting Your Forms to Work

You don't need to learn to be a programmer to make working web forms for your site. There are a number of options for adding interactivity to a form.

Use Hosting Plan Goodies

Many site hosting plans include access to scripts for simple functions such as guestbooks, mailing lists, and so on. More advanced plans may even provide everything you need to add a full shopping cart system to your site as part of your monthly hosting fee. Documentation or a technical support person should be available to help you use them.

Download and Install

There are many free or inexpensive scripts available that you can download and run on your site. Just be sure that your hosting plan permits you to install scripts before you get started. Some script sources include:

Matt's Script Archive (*www.scriptarchive.com*)

The PHP Resource Index (*php.resourceindex.com*)

PHP Builder (*phpbuilder.com*)

PHP Classes (*phpclasses.com*)

Hire a Programmer

If you need a custom solution, you may need to hire a programmer who has Perl, PHP, ASP or other web-related programming skills. Tell your programmer what you are looking to accomplish with your form and he or she will suggest a solution. Again, you need to make sure you have permission to install scripts on your server under your current hosting plan, and that the server supports the language you choose.

The action attribute

The `action` attribute provides the location (URL) of the application or script (sometimes called the action page) that will be used to process the form. The `action` attribute in this example sends the data to a script called *mailinglist.pl*. The script is the *cgi-bin* directory on the same server as the HTML document (you can tell because the URL is site root relative).

```
<form action="/cgi-bin/mailinglist.pl" method="post">...</form>
```

The *.pl* suffix indicates that this form is processed by a Perl script (Perl is a scripting language). It is also common to see web applications that end with the following:

- *.php*, indicating that a PHP program is doing the work. PHP is an open source scripting language most commonly used with the Apache web server.

- *.asp*, for Microsoft's ASP (Active Server Pages) programming environment for the Microsoft Internet Information Server (IIS).

- *.jsp*, for JavaServer Pages, a Java-based technology similar to ASP.

When you create a web form, you most likely will be working with a developer or server administrator who will provide the name and location of the program to be provided by the `action` attribute.

The method attribute

The `method` attribute specifies how the information should be sent to the server. Let's use this data gathered from the sample form in Figure 9-1 as an example.

```
name = Sally Strongarm
email = strongarm@example.com
```

When the browser encodes that information for its trip to the server, it looks like this (see the earlier sidebar if you need a refresher on encoding):

```
name=Sally%20Strongarm&email=strongarm%40example.com
```

There are only two methods for sending this encoded data to the server: POST or GET indicated using the `method` attribute in the `form` element. We'll look at the difference between the two methods in the following sections. Our example uses the POST method, as shown here:

```
<form action="/cgi-bin/mailinglist.pl" method="post">...</form>
```

The POST method

When the form's method is set to POST, the browser sends a separate server request containing some special headers followed by the data. Only the server sees the content of this request, thus it is the best method for sending secure information such as credit card or other personal information.

The POST method is also preferable for sending a lot of data, such as a lengthy text entry, because there is no character limit as there is for GET.

The GET method

With the GET method, the encoded form data gets tacked right onto the URL sent to the server. A question mark character separates the URL from the following data, as shown here:

```
get http://www.bandname.com/cgi-bin/mailinglist.pl?name=Sally%20Strongar
m&email=strongarm%40example.com
```

The GET method is appropriate if you want users to be able to bookmark the results of a form submission (such as a list of search results). Because the content of the form is in plain sight, GET is not appropriate for forms with private personal or financial information. In addition, because there is a 256 character limit on what can be appended to a URL, GET may not be used for sending a lot of data or when the form is used to upload a file.

In this chapter, we'll stick with the more popular POST method. Now that we've gotten through the technical aspects of the form element, we can take on the real meat of forms—form controls.

Variables and Content

Web forms use a variety of controls (also sometimes called widgets) that allow users to enter information or choose options. Control types include various text entry fields, buttons, menus, and a few controls with special functions. They are added to the document using a collection of form control elements that we'll be examining one by one in the upcoming Great Form Control Round-up section.

As a web designer, it is important to be familiar with control options to make your forms easy and intuitive to use. It is also useful to have an idea of what form controls are doing behind the scenes.

The name attribute

The job of a form control is to collect one bit of information from a user. In the form example a few pages back, the text entry fields are used to collect the visitor's name and email address. To use the technical term, "name" and "email" are two variables collected by the form. The data entered by the user ("Sally Strongarm" and "strongarm@example.com") is the value or content of the variable.

The name attribute identifies the variable name for the control. In this example, the text gathered by a textarea element is identified as the "comment" variable:

```
<textarea name="comment" rows="4" cols="45">Would you like to add a
comment?</textarea>
```

NOTE

In XHTML documents, the value of the method *attribute (post or get) must be provided in all lowercase letters. In HTML, however, POST and GET are not case-sensitive and are commonly listed in all uppercase by convention.*

When a user enters a comment in the field ("This is the best band ever!"), it would be passed to the server as a name/value (variable/content) pair like this:

```
comment=This%20is%20the%20best%20band%20ever%21
```

All form control elements must include a name attribute so the form-processing application can sort the information. The only exceptions are the submit and reset button elements because they have special functions (submitting or resetting the form) not related to data collection.

Naming your variables

You can't just name controls willy-nilly. The web application that processes the data is programmed to look for specific variable names. If you are designing a form to work with a preexisting application or script, you need to find out the specific variable names to use in the form so they are speaking the same language. You can get the variable names from the developer you are working with, your system administrator, or from the instructions provided with a ready-to-use script on your server.

If the script or application will be created later, be sure to name your variables simply and descriptively. In addition, each variable must be named uniquely, that is, the same name may not be used for two variables. You should also avoid putting character spaces in variable names; use an underscore or period instead.

We've covered the basics of the form element and how variables are named. Another fundamental part of marking up forms like the professionals do is including elements and attributes that make the form accessible.

Form Accessibility Features

It is essential to consider how users without the benefit of visual browsers will be able to understand and navigate through your web forms. Fortunately, HTML 4.01 introduced a number of elements that improve form accessibility by enabling authors to label the heck out of them. As for many accessibility features, the new form elements provide ways to make semantic connections between the components of a form clear. The resulting markup is not only more semantically rich, but there are also more elements available to act as "hooks" for style sheet rules. Everybody wins!

Labels

Although we may see the label "Address" right next to a text field for entering an address in a visual browser, in the source, the label and field may be separated, such as when they appear in separate table cells. The label element is used to associate descriptive text with its respective form field. This provides important context for users with speech-based browsers.

Each label element is associated with exactly one form control. There are two ways to use it. One method, called implicit association, nests the control and its description within a label element, like this:

```
<label>Male: <input type="radio" name="gender" value="M" /></label>
<label>Female: <input type="radio" name="gender" value="F" /></label>
```

The other method, called explicit association, matches the label with the control's id reference. The for attribute says which control the label is for. This approach is useful when the control is not directly next to its descriptive text in the source. It also offers the potential advantage of keeping the label and the control as two distinct elements, which may come in handy when aligning them with style sheets.

```
<label for="form-login-username">Login account:</label>
<input type="text" name="login" id="form-login-username" />

<label for="form-login-password">Password:</label>
<input type="password" name="password" id="form-login-password" />
```

fieldset and legend

The fieldset element is used to indicate a logical group of form controls. A fieldset may also include a legend element that provides a caption for the enclosed fields.

Figure 9-2 shows the default rendering of the following example in Firefox 1.0, but you could also use style sheets to change the way the fieldset and legend appear.

```
<fieldset>
<legend>Customer Information</legend>
 <ol>
   <li><label>Full name: <input type="text" name="name" /></label></li>
   <li><label>Email: <input type="text" name="email" /></label></li>
   <li><label>State: <input type="text" name="state" /></label></li>
 </ol>
</fieldset>

<fieldset>
<legend>Mailing List Sign-up</legend>
<ul>
  <li><label>Add me to your mailing list <input type="radio"
name="list" value="yes" checked="checked" /></label></li>
  <li><label>No thanks <input type="radio" name="list" value="no" />
</label></li>
</ul>
</fieldset>
```

> **TIP**
>
> To keep your form-related IDs separate from other IDs on the page, consider prefacing them with "form-" as shown in the examples.
>
> Another technique for keeping forms organized is to give the form element an ID, and include it in the IDs for the the controls it contains, as follows:
>
> `<form id="form-login">`
>
> `<input id="form-login-username" />`
>
> `<input id="form-login-password" />`

Figure 9-2. The default rendering of fieldsets and legends (shown in Firefox 1.0 on Mac OS X).

The Great Form Control Round-up

This is the fun part—playing with the markup that adds form controls to the page. Armed with your basic knowledge of how forms and form controls function as well as the markup used for accessibility, this markup should make sense. This section introduces the elements used to create:

- Text entry controls
- Submit and reset buttons
- Radio and checkbox buttons
- Pull-down and scrolling menus
- File selection and upload control
- Hidden controls

We'll pause along the way to allow you to try them out by constructing the questionnaire form shown in Figure 9-3.

As you'll see, the majority of controls are added to a form using the `input` element. The functionality and appearance of the `input` element changes based on the `type` attribute.

Figure 9-3. The contest entry form we'll be building in the exercises in this chapter.

Text entry controls

There are three basic types of text entry fields in web forms: single-line text fields, password entry fields, and multiline text entry fields.

Single-line text field

```
<input type="text" />
```
Single-line text entry control

One of the most simple types of form control is the text entry field used for entering a single word or line of text. It is added to the form using the input element with its type attribute set to text, as shown here and Figure 9-4 **Ⓐ**.

```
<li><label for="form-city">City:</label> <input type="text" name="city"
value="Your Hometown" size="25" maxlength="50" id="form-city" /></li>
```

The name attribute is required for identifying the variable name. The id attribute binds this control to its associated label (although it could also be referenced by style sheets and scripts). This example also includes a number of additional attributes:

value

> The value attribute specifies default text that appears in the field when the form is loaded. When you reset a form, it returns to this value.

size

> By default, browsers display a text-entry box that is 20 characters wide, but you can change the number of characters using the size attribute.

maxlength

> By default, users can type an unlimited number of characters in a text field regardless of its size (the display scrolls to the right if the text exceeds the character width of the box). You can set a maximum character limit using the maxlength attribute if the forms processing program you are using requires it.

NOTE

The input *element is an empty element, so in XHTML documents, it must include a trailing slash as shown in these examples. In HTML documents, the final slash should be omitted.*

NOTE

The specific rendering style of form controls varies by operating system and browser version.

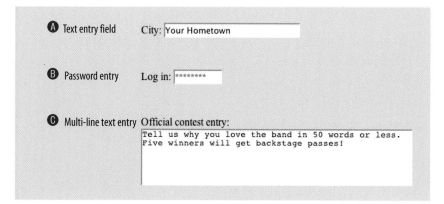

Figure 9-4. Examples of the text-entry control options for web forms.

Password text entry field

`<input type="password" />`

Password text control

A password field works just like a text entry field, except the characters are obscured from view using asterisk (*) or bullet (•) characters, or another character determined by the browser.

It's important to note that although the characters entered in the password field are not visible to casual onlookers, the form does not encrpyt the information, so it should not be considered a real security measure.

Here is an example of the markup for a password field. Figure 9-4 **Ⓑ** shows how it might look after the user enters a password in the field.

```
<li><label for="form-pswd">Log in:</label> <input type="password"
name="pswd" size="8" maxlength="8" id="form-pswd" /></li>
```

Multiline text entry field

`<textarea>...</textarea>`

Multiline text entry control

At times, you'll want your users to be able enter more than just one line of text. For these instances, use the `textarea` element that is replaced by a multi-line, scrollable text entry box when displayed by the browser (Figure 9-4 **Ⓒ**).

```
<li><label for="form-entry">Official contest entry:</label><br />
<textarea name="contest_entry" rows="5" cols="100" id="form-entry">Tell
us why you love the band in 50 words or less. Five winners will get
backstage passes!</textarea></li>
```

Unlike the empty `input` element, the `textarea` element has content between its opening and closing tags. The content of the `textarea` element is the intial content of the text box when the form is displayed in the browser.

In addition to the required `name` attribute, the `textarea` element uses the following attributes:

`rows`

Specifies the number of lines of text the area should display. Scrollbars will be provided if the user types more text than fits in the allotted space.

`cols`

Specifies the width of the text area measured in number of characters.

disabled and readonly

The `disabled` and `readonly` attributes can be added to any form control element to prevent users from selecting them. When a form element is disabled, it cannot be selected. Visual browsers may render the control as grayed-out. The disabled state can only be changed with a script. This is a useful attribute for restricting access to some form fields based on data entered earlier in the form.

The `readonly` attribute prevents the user from changing the value of the form control (although it can be selected). This enables developers to use scripts to set values for controls contingent on other data entered earlier in the form.

Submit and reset buttons

There are a number of different kinds of buttons that can be added to web forms. The most fundamental is the submit button. When clicked, the submit button immediately sends the collected form data to the server for processing. The reset button returns the form controls to the state they were in when the form loaded.

NOTE

Forms that contain only one form field do not require a submit button; the data will be submitted when the user hits the Enter or Return key. A submit button must be included for all other forms.

Both submit and reset buttons are added using the `input` element. As mentioned earlier, because these buttons have specific functions that do not include the entry of data, they are the only form control elements that do not require the `name` attribute.

```
<input type="submit" />
```
Submits the form data to the server

```
<input type="reset" />
```
Resets the form controls to their default settings

Submit and reset buttons are straightforward to use. Just place them in the appropriate place in the form, in most cases, at the very end. By default, the submit button displays with the label "Submit" or "Submit Query" and the reset button is labeled "Reset." Change the text on the button using the `value` attribute as shown in the reset button in this example (Figure 9-5).

```
<p><input type="submit" /> <input type="reset" value="Start over" /></p>
```

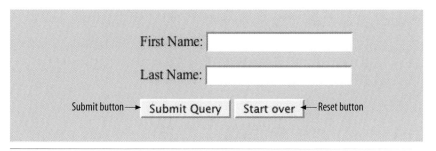

Figure 9-5. Submit and reset buttons.

At this point, you know enough about form markup to start building the questionnaire shown in Figure 9-3. Exercise 9-1 walks you through the first steps.

A Few More Buttons

There are a handful of custom button elements that are a little off the beaten path for beginners, but in the interest of thoroughness, here they are tucked off in a sidebar.

Image buttons

```
<input type="image" />
```

This type of `input` control allows you to replace the submit button with an image of your choice. The image will appear flat, not like a 3-D button.

Custom input button

```
<input type="button" />
```

Setting the type of the `input` element to "button" creates a button that can be customized with a scripting language such as JavaScript. It has no predefined function on its own, as submit and reset buttons do.

The button element

```
<button>...</button>
```

The `button` element is a flexible element for creating custom buttons similar to those created with the `input` element. The content of the button element (text and/or images) is what gets displayed on the button. In this example, a button element is used as a submit button. The button includes a label and a small image.

```
<button type="submit"
name="submit"><img
src="thumbs-up.gif" alt="" />
Ready to go.
</button>
```

For more information on what you can do with the `button` element, read "Push My Button" by Aaron Gustafson at *digital-web.com/ articles/push_my_button*.

exercise 9-1 | Starting the contest form

Here's the scenario. You are the web designer in charge of creating the entry form for the Forcefield Sneakers "Pimp your shoes" Contest. The copy editor has handed you a sketch (Figure 9-6) of the form's content, complete with notes of how some controls should work. There are sticky notes from the programmer with information about the script and variable names you need to use.

Your challenge is to turn the sketch into a functional online form. I've given you a head start by creating a bare-bones document containing the text content and some minimal markup and styles. This document, *contest_entry.html*, is available online at *www.learningwebdesign.com/materials*. The source for the entire finished form is provided in Appendix A if you want to check your work.

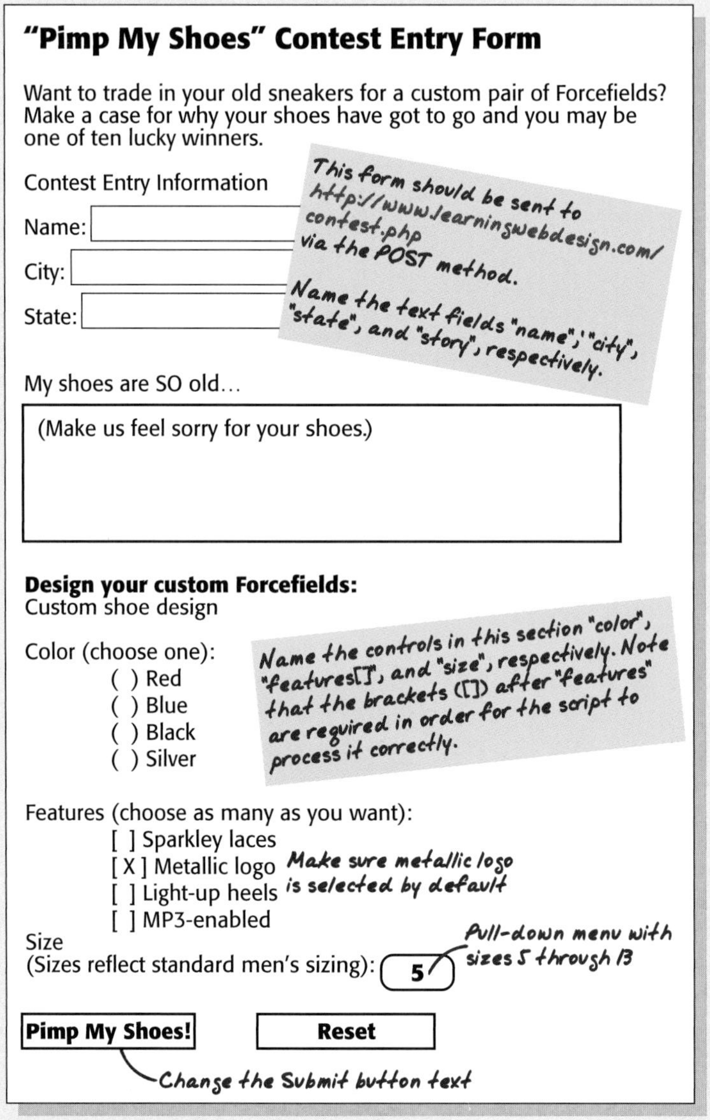

"Pimp My Shoes" Contest Entry Form

Want to trade in your old sneakers for a custom pair of Forcefields? Make a case for why your shoes have got to go and you may be one of ten lucky winners.

Contest Entry Information

This form should be sent to http://www.learningwebdesign.com/ contest.php via the POST method.

Name:

City:

State:

Name the text fields "name", "city", "state", and "story", respectively.

My shoes are SO old…

(Make us feel sorry for your shoes.)

Design your custom Forcefields:
Custom shoe design

Color (choose one):
( ) Red
( ) Blue
( ) Black
( ) Silver

Name the controls in this section "color", "features[]", and "size", respectively. Note that the brackets ([]) after "features" are required in order for the script to process it correctly.

Features (choose as many as you want):
[ ] Sparkley laces
[X] Metallic logo   *Make sure metallic logo is selected by default*
[ ] Light-up heels
[ ] MP3-enabled

Size
(Sizes reflect standard men's sizing): 5   *Pull-down menu with sizes 5 through 13*

Pimp My Shoes!   **Reset**

Change the Submit button text

Figure 9-6. A sketch of the contest entry form.

1. Open *contest_entry.html* in a text editor.

2. The first thing we'll do is put everything after the intro paragraph into a `form` element. The programmer has left a note specifying the `action` and the `method` to use for this form. The resulting `form` element should look like this:

   ```
   <form action="http://www.learningwebdesign.com/contest.php"
   method="post">

   ...

   </form>
   ```

3. In this exercise, we'll work on the "Contest Entry Information" section of the form. Start by creating a `fieldset` that contains the Name, City, State, and "My Shoes" labels. Use the title "Contest Entry Information" as the `legend` for that `fieldset`. In addition, mark up the form fields as an ordered list. The resulting markup is shown here.

   ```
   <fieldset>
   <legend>Contest Entry Information</legend>
     <ol>
         <li>Name:</li>
         <li>City:</li>
         <li>State:</li>
         <li>My shoes are SO old...</li>
     </ol>
   </fieldset>
   ```

4. Now we're ready to add the first three short text entry form controls. Here's the first one; you insert the other two.

   ```
   <li>Name: <input type="text" name="name" /></li>
   ```

   Hint: Be sure to name the `input` elements as specified in the programmer's note.

5. Now add a multiline text area for the shoe description on a new line.

   ```
   <li>My shoes are SO old...<br />
   <textarea name="story" rows="5" cols="60">(Make us feel sorry for
   your shoes.)</textarea></li>
   ```

6. Finally, let's make sure each form control is explicitly tied to its label using the "for/id" label method. I've done the first one; you do the other three.

   ```
   <li><label for="form-name">Name:</label> <input type="text"
   name="name" id="form-name" /></li>
   ```

7. We'll skip the rest of the form for now until we get a few more controls under our belt, but we can add the submit and reset buttons at the end, just before the `</form>` tag. Note that we need to change the text on the submit button.

   ```
   <p><input type="submit" value="Pimp my shoes!" />
   <input type="reset" /></p>
   </form>
   ```

8. Now, save the document and open it in a browser. The parts that are finished should generally match Figure 9-3. If it doesn't, then you have some more work to do.

Once it looks right, take it for a spin by entering some information and submitting the form. You should get a response like the one shown in Figure 9-7 (yes, *contact.php* actually works, but sorry, the contest is make-believe.)

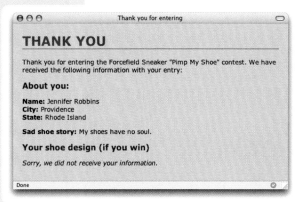

Figure 9-7. You should see a response page like this if your form is working.

Radio and checkbox buttons

Both checkbox and radio buttons make it simple for your visitors to choose from a number of provided options. They are similar in that they function like little on/off switches that can be toggled by the user and are added using the `input` element. They serve distinct functions, however.

A form control made up of a collection of radio buttons is appropriate when only one option from the group is permitted, or, in other words, when the selections are mutually exclusive (such as Yes or No, or Male or Female). When one radio button is "on," all of the others must be "off," sort of the way buttons used to work on old radios—press one button in and the rest pop out.

When checkboxes are grouped together, however, it is possible to select as many or as few from the group as desired. This makes them the right choice for lists in which more than one selection is okay.

Radio buttons

```
<input type="radio" />
```
Radio button

Radio buttons are added to a form with the `input` element with the `type` attribute set to `radio`. The `name` attribute is required. Here is the syntax for a minimal radio button:

```
<input type="radio" name="variable" />
```

In this example, radio buttons are used as an interface for users to enter their age group (a person can't belong to more than one age group, so radio buttons are the right choice). Figure 9-8 shows how radio buttons are rendered in the browser.

```
<fieldset>
<legend>How old are you?</legend>
<ol>
  <li><label><input type="radio" name="age" value="under24"
    checked="checked" /> under 24</label></li>
  <li><label><input type="radio" name="age" value="25-34" /> 25 to 34
    </label></li>
  <li><label><input type="radio" name="age" value="35-44" /> 35 to 44
    </label></li>
  <li><label><input type="radio" name="age" value="over45" /> 45+
    </label></li>
</ol>
</fieldset>
```

Notice that all of the `input` elements have the same variable name ("age"), but their values are different. Because these are radio buttons, only one button can be checked at a time, and therefore, only one value will be sent to the server for processing when the form is submitted.

NOTE

In XHTML documents, the value of the checked *attribute must be explicitly set to* checked, *as shown in the example.*

In HTML documents, you don't need to write out the value for the checked attribute. It can be minimized, as shown here:

```
<input type="radio" name="foo"
checked />
```

The examples in this chapter follow XHTML syntax in which all attributes have explicit values.

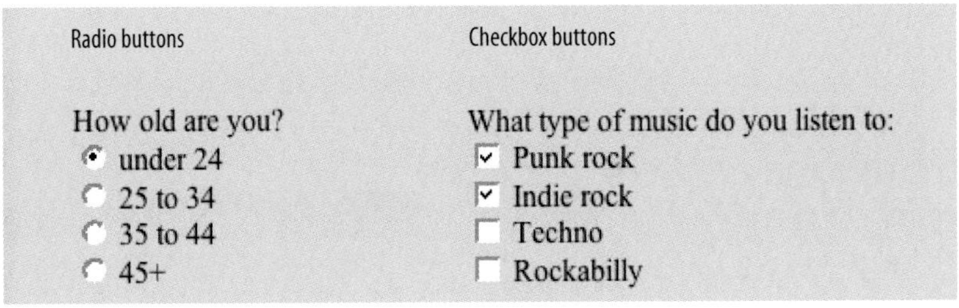

Radio buttons

How old are you?
- under 24
- 25 to 34
- 35 to 44
- 45+

Checkbox buttons

What type of music do you listen to:
- ☑ Punk rock
- ☑ Indie rock
- ☐ Techno
- ☐ Rockabilly

Figure 9-8. Radio buttons (left) are appropriate when only one selection is permitted. Checkboxes (right) are best when users may choose any number of choices, from none to all of them.

You can decide which button is checked when the form loads by adding the `checked` attribute to the `input` element. In this example, the button next to "under 24" will be checked by default.

Also notice in this example that both the button `input` and its text label are contained in a single `label` element. The advantage to this method is that users may click anywhere on the whole label to select the button.

Checkbox buttons

`<input type="checkbox" />`

Checkbox button

Checkboxes are added using the `input` element with its `type` set to `checkbox`. As with radio buttons, you create groups of checkboxes by assigning them the same `name` value. The difference, as we've already noted, is that more than one checkbox may be checked at a time. The value of every checked button will be sent to the server when the form is submitted. Here is an example of a group of checkbox buttons used to indicate musical interests. Figure 9-8 shows how they look in the browser:

```
<fieldset>
<legend>What type of music do you listen to?</legend>
<ul>
  <li><label><input type="checkbox" name="genre" value="punk"
checked="checked" /> Punk rock</label></li>
  <li><label><input type="checkbox" name="genre" value="indie"
checked="checked" /> Indie rock</label></li>
  <li><label><input type="checkbox" name="genre" value="techno" />
Techno </label></li>
  <li><label><input type="checkbox" name="genre" value="rockabilly" />
Rockabilly</label></li>
</ul>
</fieldset>
```

NOTE

This list of options has been marked up semantically as an unordered list because the order of the options is not significant.

Checkboxes don't necessarily need to be used in groups, of course. In this example, a single checkbox is used to allow visitors to opt in for special promotions. The value of the control will only be passed along to the server if the user checks the box.

```
<p><input type="checkbox" name="optin" value="yes" /> Yes, send me news
and special promotions by email.</p>
```

In Exercise 9-2, you'll get a chance to add both radio and checkbox buttons to the contest entry form.

exercise 9-2 | **Adding radio buttons and checkboxes**

The next two questions in the sneaker contest entry form use radio buttons and checkboxes for selecting options. Open the *contest_entry.html* document and follow these steps.

1. Before we start working on the buttons, group the Color, Features, and Size questions in a **fieldset** with the **legend** "Custom Shoe Design."

```
<h2>Design your custom Forcefields:</h2>
<fieldset>
<legend>Custom Shoe Design</legend>
    Color...
    Features...
    Size...
</fieldset>
```

2. Create another fieldset just for the Color options, using the description as the legend as shown here. Also mark up the options as an unordered list.

```
<fieldset>
<legend>Color <em>(choose one)</em>:</legend>
<ul>
   <li>Red</li>
   <li>Blue</li>
   <li>Black</li>
   <li>Silver</li>
</ul>
</fieldset>
```

3. With the structure in place, now we can add the form controls. The Color options should be radio buttons because shoes can be only one color. Insert a radio button before each option, and while you're at it, associate each with its respective label by putting both in a single label element. Follow this example for the remaining color options (use the color names, all lowercase, as the values for each input).

```
<li><label><input type="radio" name="color"
value="red" /> Red</label></li>
```

4. Mark up the Features options as you did the Color options, creating a fieldset, legend, and unordered list. This time, however, the **type** will be **checkbox**. Be sure the variable name for each is "features," and that the metallic logo option is preselected as noted on the sketch. The values for the checkboxes should be identified as "laces," "logo," "heels," and "mp3," in that order.

5. Save the document and check your work by opening it in a browser to make sure it looks right, then submit the form to make sure it's functioning properly.

Menus

Another option for providing a list of choices is to put them in a pull-down or scrolling menu. Menus tend to be more compact than groups of buttons and checkboxes.

`<select>...</select>`
Menu control

`<option>...</option>`
An option within a menu

`<optgroup>...</optgroup>`
A logical grouping of options within a menu

You add both pull-down and scrolling menus to a form with the `select` element. Whether the menu pulls down or scrolls is the result of how you specify its size and whether you allow more than one option to be selected. Let's take a look at both menu types.

Pull-down menus

The select element displays as a pull-down menu by default when no size is specified or if the size attribute is set to 1. In pull-down menus, only one item may be selected. Here's an example (shown in Figure 9-9):

```
<label for="form-fave">What is your favorite 80s band?<label><br />
<select name="EightiesFave" id="form-fave">
    <option>The Cure</option>
    <option>Cocteau Twins</option>
    <option>Tears for Fears</option>
    <option>Thompson Twins</option>
    <option value="EBTG">Everything But the Girl</option>
    <option>Depeche Mode</option>
    <option>The Smiths</option>
    <option>New Order</option>
</select>
```

You can see that the select element is just a container for a number of option elements. The content of the chosen option element is what gets passed to the web application when the form is submitted. If for some reason you want to send a different value than what appears in the menu, use the value attribute to provide an overriding value. For example, if someone selects "Everything But the Girl" from the sample menu, the form submits the value "EBTG" for the "EightiesFave" variable.

You will make a menu like this one for selecting a shoe size in Exercise 9-3.

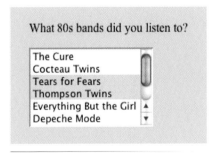

Figure 9-9. Pull-down menus pop open when the user clicks on the arrow or bar.

Scrolling menus

To make the menu display as a scrolling list, simply specify the number of lines you'd like to be visible using the size attribute. This example menu has the same options as the previous one, except it has been set to display as a scrolling list that is six lines tall (Figure 9-10).

```
<label for="EightiesBands">What 80s bands did you listen to?</label>
<select id="EightiesBands" size="6" multiple="multiple"
for="EightiesBands">
    <option>The Cure</option>
    <option>Cocteau Twins</option>
    <option selected="selected">Tears for Fears</option>
    <option selected="selected">Thompson Twins</option>
    <option value="EBTG">Everything But the Girl</option>
    <option>Depeche Mode</option>
    <option>The Smiths</option>
    <option>New Order</option>
</select>
```

You may notice a few new attributes tucked in there. The multiple attribute allows users to make more than one selection from the scrolling list. Note that pull-down menus do not allow multiple selections; when the browser detects the multiple attribute, it displays a small scrolling menu automatically by default.

Figure 9-10. A scrolling menu with multiple options selected.

NOTE

The multiple *and* selected *attributes can be minimized in HTML, as we saw for the* checked *attribute earlier in this chapter.*

Use the `selected` attribute in an `option` element to make it the default value for the menu control. Selected options are highlighted when the form loads. The `selected` attribute can be used with pull-down menus as well.

Grouping menu options

You can use the `optgroup` element to create conceptual groups of options. The required `label` attribute in the `optgroup` element provides the heading for the group. Figure 9-11 shows how option groups are rendered in modern browsers.

```
<select name="icecream" multiple="multiple">
<optgroup label="traditional">
     <option>vanilla</option>
     <option>chocolate</option>
</optgroup>
<optgroup label="fancy">
  <option>Super praline</option>
  <option>Nut surprise</option>
  <option>Candy corn</option>
</optgroup>
</select>
```

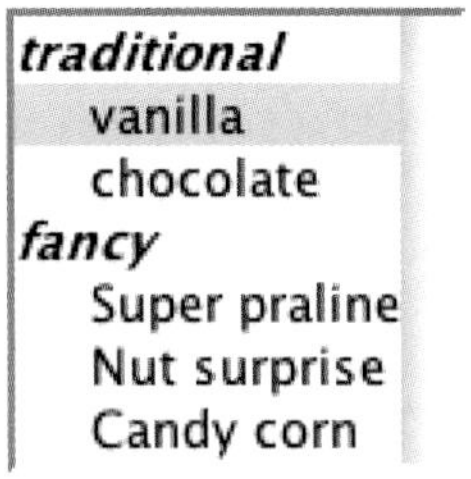

Figure 9-11. Option groups as rendered in a modern browser.

NOTE

The `label` attribute in the `option` element is not the same as the `label` element used to improve accessibility.

---

exercise 9-3 | **Adding a menu**

The only other control that needs to be added to the contest entry is a pull-down menu for selecting a shoe size.

1. First, delimit the Size question in a fieldset with "Size" as the legend. This time, a list doesn't make sense, so mark the line up as a paragraph.

    ```
    <fieldset>
    <legend>Size</legend>
      <p>Sizes reflect standard men's sizes:</p>
    </fieldset>
    ```

2. Insert a **select** menu element with the shoe sizes (5 to 13), and explicitly associate it with its label (using "for/id").

    ```
    <p><label for="size">Size (sizes reflect men's sizing):</label>
    <select name="size" id="size">
    <option>5</option>
    ...insert more options here...
    </select>
    </p>
    ```

3. Save the document and check it in a browser. You can submit the form, too, to be sure that it's working. You should get the Thank You response page listing all of the information you entered in the form.

Congratulations! You've built your first working web form.

File selection control

Web forms can collect more than just data. They can also be used to transmit external documents from a user's hard drive. For example, a printing company could use a web form to receive artwork for a business card order. A magazine could use a form on their site to collect digital photos for a photo contest.

The file selection control makes it possible for users to select a document from the hard drive to be submitted with the form data. It is added to the form using our old friend the `input` element with its `type` set to `file`.

```
<input type="file" />
```
File selection field

The browser displays a "file" input as a text field with a button that allows the user to navigate the hard drive and select the file for upload. The markup sample below and Figure 9-12 shows a file selection control used for photo submissions.

```
<form action="/client.php" method="post" enctype="multipart/form-data">

  <p><label for="form-photo">Send a photo to be used as your online
icon (optional):</label><br />
  <input type="file" name="photo" size="28" id="form-photo" /></p>

</form>
```

It is important to note that when a form contains a file selection input element, you must specify the encoding type (`enctype`) of the form as `multipart/form-data` and use the POST method. The `size` attribute in this example sets the character width of the text field.

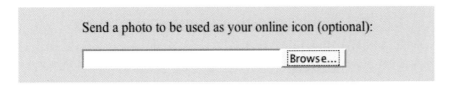

Figure 9-12. A file selection form field.

Hidden controls

There may be times when you need to send information to the form processing application that does not come from the user. In these instances, you can use a hidden form control that sends data when the form is submitted, but is not visible when the form is displayed in a browser.

```
<input type="hidden" />
```
Hidden control field

Hidden controls are added using the `input` element with the `type` set to `hidden`. Its sole purpose is to pass a name/value pair to the server when the form is submitted. In this example, a hidden form element is used to provide the location of the appropriate thank you document to display when the transaction is complete.

```
<input type="hidden" name="success-link" value="http://www.example.com/
littlechair_thankyou.html" />
```

I've worked with forms that have had dozens of hidden controls in the form element before getting to the parts that the user actually fills out. This is the kind of information you get from the application programmer, system administrator, or whoever is helping you get your forms processed. If you are using a canned script, be sure to check the accompanying instructions to see if any hidden form variables are required.

That rounds out the form control round-up. Learning how to insert form controls is one part of the forms production process, but you have to consider the design, layout, and appearance of the form as well.

Form Layout and Design

I can't close this chapter without saying a few words about form design, even though the chapters in this (X)HTML section are not concerned with presentation.

You can use Cascading Style Sheets to alter the font, size, and color of form labels and controls as you would any other element. Just refining the look of controls will go a long way toward giving your forms a look that is consistent with the rest of your site.

The real challenge to formatting forms is alignment. In the past, tables were used to bring alignment and balance to form components. However, using data table elements for page layout is considered a no-no in this age of semantic markup. You can certainly achieve the same alignment effects using Cascading Style Sheets alone. The strategy is to float labels and input elements so they appear next to one another on a given indent. Unfortunately, it requires some CSS moves that are beyond the scope of this book, although you will learn the fundamental concepts in Chapter 15, Floating and Positioning. A web search for "form alignment with CSS" will turn up plenty of online tutorials.

Test Yourself

Ready to put your web form know-how to the test? Here are a few questions to make sure you got the basics.

1. Decide whether each of these forms should be sent via the GET or POST method:

   A form for accessing your bank account online _____

WARNING

Fieldsets and legends tend to throw some curve-balls when it comes to styling. For example, background colors in fieldsets are handled differently from browser to browser. Legends are unique in that their text doesn't wrap. Be sure to do lots of testing if you style these form elements.

FOR FURTHER READING

Designing Forms

You may want to check out these articles at *A List Apart* that address form usability and styling.

- "Sensible Forms: A Form Usability Checklist," by Brian Crescimanno (*www.alistapart.com/articles/sensibleforms*)
- "Prettier Accessible Forms," by Nick Rigby (*www.alistapart.com/articles/prettyaccessibleforms*)

A form for sending t-shirt artwork to the printer   _____

A form for searching archived articles   _____

A form for collecting long essay entries   _____

2. Which form control element is best suited for the following tasks? When the answer is "input," be sure to also include the type. Some tasks may have more than one correct answer.

   Choose your astrological sign from 12 signs.

   Indicate whether you have a history of heart disease (yes or no).

   Write up a book review.

   Select your favorite ice cream flavors from a list of eight flavors.

   Select your favorite ice cream flavors from a list of 25 flavors.

3. Each of these markup examples contains an error. Can you spot what it is?

```
<input name="country" value="Your country here." />
```

```
<checkbox name="color" value="teal" />
```

```
<select name="popsicle">
     <option value="orange" />
     <option value="grape" />
     <option value="cherry" />
</select>
```

```
<input type="password" />
```

```
<textarea name="essay" height="6" width="100">Your story.</textarea>
```

(X)HTML Review: Forms

We covered this impressive list of elements and attributes related to forms in this chapter:

NOTE

The `id` attribute can be used with any of these elements to give a unique name (also called an id reference).

Element and attributes	Description
button	Generic input button
name="*text*"	Supplies a unique variable name for the control
value="*text*"	Specifies the value to be sent to the server
type="submit|reset|button"	The type of custom button
fieldset	Groups related controls and labels

Element and attributes	Description
form	Form element
action="url"	Location of forms processing program (required)
id="text"	Gives the form a unique name ("id reference")
method="get|post"	The method used to submit the form data
enctype="content type"	The encoding method, generally either application/x-www-form-urlen-coded (default) or multipart/form-data
input	Creates a variety of controls, based on the type value
type="text|password|checkbox|radio|submit|reset|file|hidden|image button"	The type of input
checked="checked"	Preselects a checkbox or radio button
disabled="disabled"	Disables the control so it cannot be selected
maxlength="number"	The maximum number of characters that can be entered into a text, password, or file text field
name="text"	Supplies a unique variable name for the control
readonly="readonly"	Makes the control unalterable by the user
size="number"	The character width of a text, password, or file field
value="text"	Specifies the value to be sent to the server
label	Attaches information to controls
for="text"	Identifies the associated control by its id reference
legend	Assigns a caption to a fieldset
optgroup	Defines a group of options
label="text"	Supplies label for a group of options
disabled="disabled"	Disables the optgroup so it cannot be selected
option	An option within a select menu control
disabled="disabled"	Disables the optgroup so it cannot be selected
label="text"	Supplies an alternate label for the option
selected="selected"	Preselects the option
value="text"	Supplies an alternate value for the option
select	Pull-down menu or scrolling list
disabled="disabled"	Disables the control so it cannot be selected
multiple="multiple"	Allows multiple selctions in a scrolling list
name="text"	Supplies a unique variable name for the control
readonly="readonly"	Makes the control unalterable by the user
size="number"	The height of the scrolling list in text lines
textarea	Multi-line text entry field
cols="number"	The width of the text area in characters
disabled="disabled"	Disables the control so it cannot be selected
name="text"	Supplies a unique variable name for the control
readonly="readonly"	Makes the control unalterable by the user
rows="number"	The height of the text area in text lines

CHAPTER 10

UNDERSTANDING THE STANDARDS

I'm going to warn you right now... this is a big, geeky chapter full of some pretty dry material. But I know you can handle it. If you have any notion of doing web development professionally, you'll be required to know it. Even if you don't, it's important stuff.

Professional web designers know that the best way to ensure consistency and accessibility across multiple browsers and devices is to write standards compliant web documents. Standards compliance simply means that your documents abide by all of the rules in the latest Recommendations published by the World Wide Web Consortium (the W3C). That includes HTML and XHTML for markup, but also other standards for style sheets (CSS) and accessibility.

This chapter covers what it takes to get compliant. It gets into the nitty-gritty on HTML and XHTML and their various versions. It begins with a fair amount of story-telling, painting the picture of (X)HTML's past, present, and future. Once you have a feel for the big picture, the markup requirements that follow will make a lot more sense. So sit back and enjoy the tale of HTML and XHTML. (If you're thinking, "C'mon! I don't have time for this... just tell me what I need to put in my document!" then you can skip to the last section in this chapter, Putting It All Together, for the bottom line.)

Everything You've Wanted to Know About HTML But Were Afraid to Ask

By now you're familiar with (X)HTML—you've even gotten handy with it. But did you know that there have been many versions of HTML since its creation by Tim Berners-Lee in 1991? The quick rundown that follows sums up HTML's journey and should provide some useful context for where we are today. Read the sidebar, HTML Version History, for more details.

HTML and what we know as the Web got their start at a particle physics lab (CERN) in Switzerland where Tim Berners-Lee had an idea for sharing research documents via a hypertext system. Instead of inventing a method

The history of HTML

The three versions of HTML: Strict, Transitional, and Frameset

Introduction to XHTML and its stricter syntax requirements

Using Document Type (DOCTYPE) Declarations

Standards vs. Quirks mode in browsers

Validating your markup

Indicating a document's character encoding

for marking up shared documents from scratch, he used SGML (Standard Generalized Markup Language) as the basis for what he coined the Hypertext Markup Language (HTML for short). He took many elements such as p and h1 through h6 right from SGML, then invented the anchor (a) element for adding hypertext links.

Early versions of HTML (HTML + and HTML 2.0) built on Tim's early work with the intent of making it a viable publishing option for a greater world-wide audience.

HTML gets muddied...

In 1994, Mosaic Communication Corporation introduced the Netscape Navigator browser and took the Web by storm. Their most notable "contribution" to web technology was the introduction of many proprietary extensions to HTML that improved the presentation of web documents (in Netscape Navigator only, naturally). When Microsoft finally entered the browser scene in 1996 with Internet Explorer 3.0, they countered with their own proprietary HTML extensions and web technologies. This divisive one-upping is generally referred to as the Browser Wars, and we are still living with the fallout.

HTML Version History

Here is a quick look at HTML's bumpy history.

The original HTML draft. Tim Berners-Lee based his original markup language for hypertext documents on the syntax and elements in SGML, but added the anchor (a) element for adding hypertext links. To see a very early version of HTML, see this document dated 1992: *www.w3.org/History/19921103-hypertext/hypertext/WWW/MarkUp/MarkUp.html*.

HTML +. This version of HTML, written by Dave Raggett in 1993 and 1994, builds upon Berners-Lee's original version, adding elements such as figures, tables, and forms. Many of the ideas developed here made it into later versions, but the specific elements (such as fig for figures) were left behind. You can see it at *www.w3.org/MarkUp/HTMLPlus/htmlplus_1.html*.

HTML 2.0. This was a proposed standard developed by Tim Berners-Lee and the HTML Working Group at IETF (Internet Engineering Task Force) in 1995. It is available online at *www.w3.org/MarkUp/1995-archive/html-spec.html*. At this point, the Web was still in its infancy. In fact, Microsoft had not yet released its Internet Explorer browser. Netscape, however, had emerged on the scene and was busy adding elements to HTML that worked only on its browser.

HTML 3.2. This is the first Recommendation released by the newly-formed W3C in 1996 (*www.w3.org/TR/REC-html32*). It is a snapshot of all the HTML elements in common use at the time and includes many extensions to HTML that were the result of the notorious Browser War between Netscape and Microsoft. Many of these extensions are presentational, and in hindsight, most would say they should have never been incorporated in the standard.

HTML 4.0 and 4.01. HTML 4.0, released as a Recommendation in 1998, got HTML back on track by acknowledging that all matters of presentation should be handled with CSS and remain separate from document markup. Many of the presentational elements and attributes introduced in HTML 3.2 were kept because they were in widespread use, however, they were labeled as deprecated. HTML 4.0 also introduced a number of accessibility and internationalization features. The updated HTML 4.01 Recommendation fixed some small issues and was released in 1999. You can see it online at *www.w3.org/TR/html401*. HTML 4.01 is the current version of HTML. It also served as the basis for the XHTML 1.0 Recommendation.

Meanwhile, a formal HTML standard was being discussed by the international academic community, but it lagged behind commercial development, and Netscape and Microsoft weren't waiting for it. Finally, the newly-formed W3C put a stake in the ground and released its first Recommendation, HTML 3.2, in 1996. HTML 3.2 documented the current state of HTML markup, including many of the popular presentational elements and attributes introduced by the browser developers and gobbled up by site designers. The integrity of HTML had been compromised, and we're still cleaning up the mess.

...and back on track

HTML 4.0 and 4.01 (the slight revision that superseded it in 1999) set out to rectify the situation by emphasizing the separation of presentation from content. All matters of presentation were handed off to the newly developed Cascading Style Sheets (CSS) standard. The other major advances in HTML 4.0 and 4.01 were a number of accessibility and internationalization features that aimed to make the Web available to everyone. HTML 4.01 is the most current version of HTML. (We'll get to its prim and proper identical cousin, XHTML, in a moment.)

It would be nice if we could just end there and say, "so use HTML 4.01," but it's not so simple. There are actually three versions of HTML 4.01 to be aware of: Transitional, Strict, and Frameset. Let's look at what they are and how they differ.

NOTE

To see an itemized list of the changes made between the HTML 3.2 and HTML 4.0, as well as between HTML 4.0 and 4.01, see this page on the W3C site: www.w3.org/TR/REC-html40/appendix/changes.html.

HTML in three flavors

The authors of the HTML 4.01 Recommendation had a dilemma on their hands. They had a vision of how HTML *should* work, given the standardization of style sheets and scripting languages. Unfortunately, the practical fact was, by that time, millions of web pages had been written in legacy HTML. They could not enforce a radical change to the standard overnight. To address this problem, they created several versions of HTML.

Transitional

The "Transitional" version includes most of the presentational extensions to HTML that were in common use. This option was made available to ease web authors as well as browser and tools developers out of their old habits. The presentational elements (like `center`) and attributes (like `bgcolor` and `align`) were marked as deprecated, indicating that they would be removed from future versions of HTML. The HTML 4.01 Recommendation urges the web community to avoid using deprecated elements and attributes. Now that CSS is well supported by virtually all browsers, that is finally easy to do.

Strict

At the same time, the W3C created a "Strict" version of HTML 4.01 that omits all of the deprecated elements and gets HTML into the state they ultimately wanted it to be in.

Frameset

The third version of HTML is the "Frameset" version, which describes the content of framed documents. Frames make it possible to divide the browser into multiple windows, each displaying a different HTML document. Frames are constructed with a frameset document that defines the frame structure and the content of each frame. Frameset documents are fundamentally different from other HTML documents because they use the frameset element instead of body. This technicality earned them their own HTML specification.

NOTE

Due to serious usability and accessibility issues, frames are rarely used in contemporary web design, and therefore are not included in this beginners book. You can find them documented in my other book, Web Design in a Nutshell *(O'Reilly Media), and other comprehensive web design how-to books. A PDF copy of the Frames chapter from the second edition of this book is available at learningwebdesign.com.*

Meet the DTDs

Now you know that HTML has three versions, but let's talk about it in a slightly more technical way, using some terminology that will come in handy later.

When you create a markup language such as HTML, it is useful to document it in a Document Type Definition, or simply DTD, particularly if large groups of people will be using that language. A DTD defines all of the elements and attributes in the language, as well as the rules for using them.

What the W3C actually did was write three slightly different DTDs for HTML 4.01: the Transitional DTD, Strict DTD, and Frameset DTD.

DTDs are dense documents with a syntax that takes a while to learn to read. Luckily, you probably will never need to. But just to give you an idea, Figure 10-1 shows a small snippet of the HTML 4.01 DTD that defines the p and h1–h6 elements and their available attributes. If you are the curious type, you can take a peek at the full Strict DTD here: *www.w3.org/TR/html4/strict.dtd*. Don't worry about understanding exactly what everything means; it is sufficient to know that there are three HTML 4.01 DTDs.

That's where the development of HTML stopped, but the story doesn't end there....

HTML 5

A group of developers are working on a new version of HTML that would be better suited for the computer-program-like applications that are changing the way we use the Web. The Web Applications 1.0 specification (also dubbed "HTML 5") is still in early development as of this writing. To track its progress, check the Web Hypertext Application Technology Working Group's site (*www.whatwg.org*) or the W3C's HTML5 page (*www.w3.org/html*, click "HTML5").

```
<!--==================== Paragraphs ============================-->

<!ELEMENT P - O (%inline;)*     -- paragraph -->
<!ATTLIST P
  %attrs;                       -- %coreattrs, %i18n, %events --
  >

<!--==================== Headings ============================-->

<!--
  There are six levels of headings from H1 (the most important)
  to H6 (the least important).
-->

<!ELEMENT (%heading;)  - - (%inline;)* -- heading -->
<!ATTLIST (%heading;)
  %attrs;              -- %coreattrs, %i18n, %events --
  >
```

Figure 10-1. An excerpt from the HTML 4.01 Strict DTD that defines paragraph and heading elements.

Enter XHTML

Meanwhile... at the XML ranch...

As the Web grew in popularity, it was clear that there was a need and desire to share all sorts of information: chemical notation, mathematical equations, multimedia presentations, financial information, and so on *ad infinitum*. As we've seen, HTML is fairly limited in the types of content it can describe, so it wasn't going to cut it alone. There needed to be a way to create more specialized markup languages.

The W3C took another look at SGML but ultimately decided it was too vast and powerful for the job. Instead, they took a subset of its rules and created XML (eXtensible Markup Language), a metalanguage for creating markup languages for information and data shared over the Web or other networks.

With XML, authors can create custom markup languages that suit any sort of information (see the XML on the Web sidebar for some examples). It is even possible for a single document to use several XML-based markup languages. It should be evident that with all those custom element and attribute names, the markup must be authored very carefully to rule out potential confusion. Browsers may know what to do if a `p` element is missing its closing tag, but what should it do with that unclosed `recipe` element? Thus, the rules for marking up XML documents are much more strict than those for HTML.

Rewriting HTML

W3C had a vision of an XML-based Web with many specialized markup languages working together. The first thing they needed to do was rewrite HTML, the cornerstone of the Web, according to the stricter rules of XML so that it could play well with others. And that's exactly what they did.

XML on the Web

XML has proven itself to be such a powerful language for handling information and data that there is more XML used outside the Web than on it. However, there are several XML languages for the Web that are well-established (although not necessarily in widespread use).

RSS (Really Simple Syndication or RDF Site Summary)

RSS is used for syndicating web content so that it can be shared and read as a data feed by RSS feed readers. The language provides metadata about the content (such as its headline, author, description, an originating site). RSS has become extremely popular because it is built into the functionality of many blog publishing systems.

SVG (Scalable Vector Graphics)

This is a markup language for describing two-dimensional graphics, including vector paths, images, and text. Currently, you must install an SVG Viewer to view SVG graphics.

SMIL (Synchronized Multimedia Integration Language)

This XML language is used to describe the content and timing of multimedia presentations that can combine video, audio, images, and text.

MathML (Mathematical Markup Language)

MathML is used to describe mathematical notation capturing both its structure and content so it can be served and processed on the Web.

The result is XHTML. The "X" stands for "eXtensible" and it indicates its connection to XML. The first version, XHTML 1.0, is nearly identical to HTML 4.01. It shares the same elements and attributes; there are even three DTDs (Transitional, Strict, and Frameset). It was also written with features that make it backward compatible with HTML and HTML browsers.

XHTML Syntax

What makes XHTML documents different is that because XHTML is an XML language, correct syntax is critical. Elements must be closed and properly nested... attributes must be in quotation marks... all in the interest of eliminating confusion. Documents with correct XML syntax are said to be well-formed.

NOTE

In addition to stricter syntax rules, XHTML adds other XML-specific features and rules that weren't necessary in HTML 4.01.

The following is a checklist of the requirements of XHTML documents. If none of these seem particularly shocking, it's because the examples in this book have been following XHTML syntax all along. However, if you have prior experience with HTML or view the source of web pages written in lax HTML, there are some significant differences.

Beyond XHTML 1.0

XHTML 1.0 is the first in a growing family of XHTML document types that have been released or are being developed by the W3C. A brief introduction to each follows. For up-to-date information, visit *www.w3.org/MarkUp*.

XHTML 1.1

You can think of this as a stricter version of XHTML 1.0 Strict. It is the first version of XHTML to be liberated from legacy HTML by eliminating all elements and attributes that control presentation. XHTML 1.1 documents also must identify themselves as XML applications, not as HTML (as XHTML 1.0 documents may do). Unfortunately, not all browsers support XHTML 1.1 documents, which is why developers opt for XHTML 1.0 as of this writing.

Modularization of XHTML

This Recommendation breaks the XHTML language into task-specific modules (sets of elements that handle one aspect or type of object in a document).

XHTML Basic

This is a stripped down version of XHTML that includes just the elements that are appropriate to microbrowsers used in handheld devices.

XHTML 2.0

XHTML 2.0 is a rethinking of HTML that includes new elements and new ways of doing things in order to be purely semantic and highly accessible. It is being developed and is a Working Draft as of this writing, and therefore is not in common use. However, because it is an XML language, it is supported by browsers that support XML. To learn more about it, see *www.w3.org/TR/xhtml2* (the Introduction section is particularly helpful).

Element and attribute names must be lowercase.

In HTML, element and attribute names are not case-sensitive, which means that you could write `<img>`, `<Img>`, or `<IMG>` and it's all the same. Not so in XML. When XHTML was written, all element and attribute names were defined as lowercase. Attribute values do not need to be lowercase, except in cases where a predefined list of values is provided for the attribute.

All elements must be closed (terminated).

Although it is okay to omit the closing tag of certain HTML elements (`p` and `li`, for example), in XHTML, every element must be closed (or *terminated*, to use the proper term).

Empty elements must be terminated too.

This termination rule extends to empty elements as well. To do this, simply add a slash before the closing bracket, indicating the element's ending. In XHTML, a line break is entered as `<br/>`. Some browsers have a problem with this syntax, so to keep your XHTML digestible to all browsers, add a space before the slash (`<br />`) and the terminated empty element will slide right through.

Attribute values must be in quotation marks.

In XHTML, all attribute values must be contained in quotation marks (in HTML, certain attribute values could get away without them). Single or double quotation marks are acceptable as long as they are used consistently. Furthermore, there should be no extra white space (character spaces or line returns) before or after the attribute value inside the quotation marks.

All attributes must have explicit attribute values.

XML (and therefore XHTML) does not support attribute minimization, the SGML practice in which certain attributes can be reduced to just the attribute value. So, while in HTML you can write `checked` to indicate that a form button be checked when the form loads, in XHTML you need to explicitly write out `checked="checked"`.

Elements must be nested properly.

Although it has always been a rule in HTML that elements should be properly nested, in XHTML the rule is strictly enforced. Be sure that the closing tag of a contained element appears before the closing tag of the element that contains it. This will be more clear with an example. Be sure to do this:

```
<p>I can <em>fly</em></p>
```

and not this:

```
<p>I can <em>fly</p></em>.
```

Always use character entities for special characters.

All special characters (<, >, and & for example) must be represented in XHTML documents by their character entities (see Chapter 5, Marking Up Text for an explanation of entities). Character entities are required in attribute values and document titles as well. For example, in the attribute value "Crocco & Lynch" must be written this way in XHTML:

```
<img src="puppets.jpg" alt="Crocco &amp; Lynch" />
```

Use `id` instead of `name` as an identifier.

In XHTML, the `id` attribute replaces the `name` attribute when used as an identifier (such as when creating a document fragment). In fact, the `name` attribute has been deprecated on all elements except form controls, in which case it has a special and distinct function of naming data variables. Unfortunately, older browsers such as Netscape 4 do not support this use of `id`. If your pages absolutely must work for Netscape 4, you'll need to use both `name` and `id`, and live with the XHTML error. This should become a non-issue as older browsers finally fade away entirely.

Scripts must be contained in a CDATA section.

We won't talk much about scripting in this book, but I'll include this XHTML syntax rule here for the sake of being thorough. In XHTML, you need to put scripts in a CDATA section so they will be treated as simple text characters and not parsed as XML markup. Here is an example of the syntax:

```
<script type="type/javascript">
    // <![CDATA[
    ... JavaScript goes here...
    // ]]>
</script>
```

Follow additional nesting restrictions.

In HTML, there are some basic nesting restrictions (for example, don't put a `p` inside another `p` or put a block-level element in an inline element). XHTML adds a few more nesting restrictions:

- `a` must not contain other `a` elements.

- `pre` must not contain the `img`, `object`, `big`, `small`, `sub`, or `sup` elements.

- `button` must not contain the `input`, `select`, `textarea`, `label`, `button`, `form`, `fieldset`, `iframe` or `isindex` elements.

- `label` must not contain other `label` elements..

- `form` must not contain other `form` elements

CDATA

CDATA, short for "character data," is one of the basic data types you can provide in an XML document. Most elements and many attributes in (X)HTML are defined in the DTDs as containing CDATA. Browsers interpret the sequence of characters in CDATA in a manner that should be familiar:

- Character entities are replaced with characters

- Line wraps are ignored

- Carriage returns, tabs, and multiple consecutive character spaces are reduced to a single character space

When CDATA is identified in the `style` and `script` elements, however, it is treated a little differently. Instead of being parsed, it is passed along to the application as is.

Data types, also called `tokens`, have their origin in SGML. Other data types include PCDATA (parsed character data), ID and NAME tokens (restricted to beginning with a letter), and NUMBER (must contain one digit 0–9).

Namespace and language requirements

In addition to the rules listed above, because XHTML is an XML language, there are a few required attributes for the `html` root element that are not used in HTML. The `html` element for XHTML documents must be written like this:

```
<html xmlns="http://www.w3.org/1999/xhtml" lang="en" xml:lang="en">
```

The `xmlns` attribute stands for XML namespace. A namespace is a convention established in XML to identify the language (also called a vocabulary) used by a document or element. Because XML allows several languages to be used in a document, there is the potential for overlap in element names. For example, how is an XML parser to know whether the `a` element is an XHTML anchor or an "answer" from some hypothetical XML language used for testing? With XML namespaces, you can make your intention clear. In XHTML documents, you must identify the `xmlns` as XHTML using the unique identifier for XHTML, as shown.

The `lang` and `xml:lang` attributes are two ways of specifying the language of the document. The value is a standardized two- or three-letter language code. Chances are if you are reading this book, you will be authoring documents in English (`en`). For a complete list of language codes, see *www.loc.gov/standards/iso639-2/langcodes.html*.

This is a good time to put some of this book-learning to use. Exercise 10-1 gives you a chance to convert an HTML document to XHTML.

---

exercise 10-1 | **Defining text elements**

Using the guidelines in the previous section, convert this perfectly correct HTML markup to XHTML 1.0. In the end, you will need to make six syntax changes to make the conversion complete. The changes and resulting markup are provided in Appendix A.

```
<HTML>

<HEAD>
<TITLE>Popcorn & Butter</TITLE>
</HEAD>

<BODY>
<H1>Hot Buttered Popcorn</H1>

<P><IMG SRC="popcorn.jpg" ALT="bowl of
popcorn" WIDTH=250 HEIGHT=125></P>

<H2>Ingredients</H2>
```

```
<UL>
  <LI>popcorn
  <LI>butter
  <LI>salt
</UL>

<H2>Instructions</H2>

<P>Pop the popcorn. Meanwhile, melt the
butter. Transfer the popped popcorn into
a bowl, drizzle with melted butter, and
sprinkle salt to taste.

</BODY>
</HTML>
```

From the Browser's Point of View

NOTE

By non-standard markup, I am referring to the elements and attributes that were introduced by browser developers and are still in common use, but that did not make it into the official HTML or XHTML Recommendation. Many non-standard elements and attributes are still supported by current browser versions in Quirks mode (however, they may still be browser-specific).

The W3C was not the only one dealing with the logistics of moving to a proper (X)HTML standard. The browser developers also had a difficult choice at hand: get rigorous about standards conformance and break millions of existing web pages or maintain the status quo.

The solution was to do both. Standards compliant browsers now operate in two modes. "Standards" mode follows the rules as written in the HTML 4.01 and XHTML DTDs. The other mode, known as "Quirks" mode, is more like the way browsers have always behaved, forgiving legacy and even sloppy markup.

The problem with Quirks mode is that it is unpredictable. Browsers have different ways of handling non-standard (see note) and incorrect markup, which may be okay for a personal site but is certainly unacceptable for professional web sites. By contrast, when you write standards-compliant documents and tell the browser to display it in Standards mode, you have a much better idea of what your users will be getting.

So how do you tell the browser to use Standards mode? I'm glad you asked.

DOCTYPE Switching

When building Internet Explorer 5 for the Macintosh, lead engineer Tantek Çelik invented and coded a stop-gap solution that served two communities of authors: those writing standards-compliant documents and those who were authoring based on familiar browser behaviors.

The method now known as DOCTYPE switching uses the inclusion and content of a valid DOCTYPE declaration to toggle the rendering mode of certain browsers. If the browser detects a correct declaration, it figures the author must know what they're doing and expect their page to be rendered according to the rules of the standards.

If no declaration or an invalid declaration is found, the browser reverts back to Quirks mode, allowing nonstandard markup, hacks, minor errors, and workarounds that were common in legacy authoring practices.

Declaring the Document Type

If you've made the effort to write a standards compliant document, it makes sense that you'd want it displayed in the browser's Standards mode. To do this, simply tell the browser what type of (X)HTML document it is by identifying the (X)HTML version (that is, the DTD) that you followed in a document type (DOCTYPE) declaration at the beginning of the document.

The fact is that (X)HTML documents were *always* required to start with a DOCTYPE declaration in order to be valid (we'll talk more about validation in a moment). It's really only incidental that the presence of a valid DOCTYPE declaration is now being used to trigger Standards mode in browsers (see the sidebar, DOCTYPE Switching). In the years of fast and loose HTML authoring, the declaration was commonly omitted. Now, however, professional developers include a valid DOCTYPE declaration in every document.

This is an example of a DOCTYPE declaration that indicates the document has been written according to the rules of the HTML 4.01 Strict DTD. DOCTYPE declarations must appear before the opening `<html>` tag.

```
<!DOCTYPE HTML PUBLIC "-//W3C//DTD HTML 4.01//EN"
  "http://www.w3.org/TR/HTML4.01/strict.dtd">
<html>
...document continues...
```

Let's pick it apart and see what it's made of. The `<!` at the beginning tells the browser that what follows is a declaration, not an HTML element, and that what is being declared is the document type (DOCTYPE) for a document with

`HTML` as its root element. The next string of characters, `PUBLIC "-//W3C//DTD HTML 4.01//EN"` is what's called a public identifier, which is basically a unique way of identifying a particular DTD. Finally, there is a URL for the Strict DTD that serves as an alternate unique identifier for browsers that don't understand the other method.

Available DOCTYPE declarations

The good news is that you don't really need to remember how to write that all out. "Copy-and-paste" is the way to go when it comes to adding DOCTYPE declarations to your documents, or, if you are using an up-to-date web authoring program, one will be inserted for you automatically. You can find the whole list at the W3C site at *www.w3.org/QA/2002/04/valid-dtd-list.html*. I've also included a text document containing these declarations in the materials for this chapter at *www.learningwebdesign.com/materials*.

The most commonly used DTDs are also presented here as a reference.

HTML 4.01 DTDs

Strict

```
<!DOCTYPE html PUBLIC "-//W3C//DTD HTML 4.01//EN"
    "http://www.w3.org/TR/html4/strict.dtd">
```

Transitional

```
<!DOCTYPE html PUBLIC "-//W3C//DTD HTML 4.01 Transitional//EN"
    "http://www.w3.org/TR/html4/loose.dtd">
```

Frameset

```
<!DOCTYPE html PUBLIC "-//W3C//DTD HTML 4.01 Frameset//EN"
    "http://www.w3.org/TR/html4/frameset.dtd">
```

XHTML 1.0 DTDs

Strict

```
<!DOCTYPE html PUBLIC "-//W3C//DTD XHTML 1.0 Strict//EN"
    "http://www.w3.org/TR/xhtml1/DTD/xhtml1-strict.dtd">
```

Transitional

```
<!DOCTYPE html PUBLIC "-//W3C//DTD XHTML 1.0 Transitional//EN"
    "http://www.w3.org/TR/xhtml1/DTD/xhtml1-transitional.dtd">
```

Frameset

```
<!DOCTYPE html PUBLIC "-//W3C//DTD XHTML 1.0 Frameset//EN"
    "http://www.w3.org/TR/xhtml1/DTD/xhtml1-frameset.dtd">
```

Which One Should You Use?

With so many DTDs to choose from, it may seem daunting to choose the best one. Here are some guidelines to help you.

Transitional or strict

If you are learning markup for the first time, there is no reason to learn legacy HTML practices or use deprecated attributes, so you're well on the way to compliance with one of the Strict DTD versions.

However, if you inherit a site that has already been heavily marked up using deprecated elements and attributes, and you don't have time or resources to rewrite the source, then a Transitional DTD may be the appropriate choice.

HTML or XHTML

Whether to use HTML or XHTML is a more subtle issue. XHTML offers a number of benefits, some of which leverage the power of XML:

- It is future-proof, which means that it will be compatible with the web technologies and browsers that are on the horizon. XHTML is the way of the future, but because it is backward compatible, you can start using it right away.

- Its stricter syntax requirements make it easier for screen readers and other assistive devices to handle.

- Stricter markup rules such as closing all elements makes style sheet application cleaner and more predictable.

- Many mobile devices such as cell phones and PDAs are adopting XHTML as the authoring standard, so your pages will work better on those devices.

- It can be combined with other XML languages in a single document.

- As an XML language, it can be parsed and used by any XML software.

- You can take information and data from XML applications and port it into XHTML more easily. To use the proper term, XML data can be easily transformed into XHTML.

While it is true that the future of web markup will be based on XHTML, HTML is certainly not dead. It remains a viable option, and is universally supported by current browsers. If none of the benefits listed above sound like a compelling reason to take on XHTML, HTML is still okay.

However, because you are learning this stuff for the first time, and because the differences between XHTML and HTML are really quite minor, you might as well learn to write in the stricter XHTML syntax right off the bat, then you'll be one step ahead of the game. Writing well-formed XHTML is even easier if you are using a web authoring tool such as Adobe (Macromedia) Dreamweaver or Microsoft Expression Web because you can configure it to write code in XHTML automatically—just be sure you have the latest version of the software so it is up to speed with the latest requirements.

What the pros do

For professional-caliber web site production, most web developers follow the XHTML 1.0 Strict DTD. Doing so makes sure that the markup is semantic and does not use any of the deprecated and presentational elements and attributes (style sheets are used instead, as is the proper practice). It also has all of the benefits of XHTML that were just listed. This isn't to say that you have to make all of your web sites XHTML Strict too, but I thought you might like to know.

Validating Your Documents

The other thing that professional web developers do is validate their markup. What does that mean? To validate a document is to check your markup to make sure that you have abided by all the rules of whatever DTD you are using. Documents that are error-free are said to be valid. It is strongly recommended that you validate your documents, especially for professional sites. Valid documents are more consistent on a variety of browsers, they display more quickly, and are more accessible.

Right now, browsers don't require documents to be valid (in other words, they'll do their best to display them, errors and all), but any time you stray from the standard you introduce unpredictability in the way the page is displayed or handled by alternative devices. Furthermore, one day there will be strict XHTML browsers that will require valid and well-formed documents.

So how do you make sure your document is valid? You could check it yourself or ask a friend, but humans make mistakes, and you aren't really expected to memorize every minute rule in the specifications. Instead, you use a validator, software that checks your source against the DTD you specify. These are some of the things validators check for:

- The inclusion of a DOCTYPE declaration. Without it the validator doesn't know which version of HTML or XHTML to validate against.

- An indication of the character encoding for the document (character encoding is covered in the next section).

- The inclusion of required rules and attributes.

- Non-standard elements.

- Mismatched tags.

Validation Tools

Developers use a number of helpful tools for checking and correcting errors in (X)HTML documents. These are a few of the most popular.

HTML Tidy

HTML Tidy, by Dave Raggett, checks (X)HTML documents for errors and corrects them. There is an online version available at *infohound.net/tidy*. Find out about downloadable versions of HTML Tidy at *www.w3.org/ People/Raggett/tidy* and *tidy. sourceforge.net*.

Firebug

Firebug is a popular plug-in to the Firefox browser that debugs (X)HTML, CSS, and JavaScript, among many other features. It is available as a free download at *addons.mozilla.org/firefox/1843*.

- Nesting errors.

- DTD rule violations.

- Typos, and other minor errors.

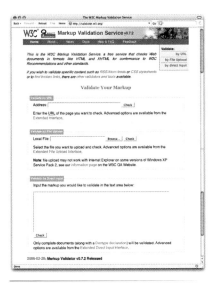

Figure 10-2. The W3C's Markup Validation Service.

The W3C offers a free online validator at *validator.w3.org*. Figure 10-2 shows the W3C Markup Validation Service as it appeared as of this writing (they are known to make tweaks and improvements). There are three options for checking a page: enter the URL of a page on the Web, upload a file from your computer, or just paste the source into a text area on the page. The best way to get a feel for how the validation process works is to try it yourself. Give it a go in Exercise 10-2.

exercise 10-2 | **Validating a document**

In this exercise, you'll validate some documents using the W3C validation service. The documents in this exercise are provided for you online at *www.learningwebdesign. com/materials*.

Start by validating the document ***blackgoose.html*** (it should look familiar because it was the basis of the examples in Chapter 4, Creating a Simple Page). I've included a DOCTYPE declaration that instructs the validator to validate the document against the HTML 4.01 Strict DTD. I've also purposefully introduced a few errors to the document. Knowing what the errors are in advance will give you a better feel for how the validator finds and reports errors.

- The required `title` element is missing in the `head` element.

- The `img` element is missing the required `alt` attribute. Note also that the `img` element uses HTML syntax, that is, it does not have a trailing slash.

- The `p` elements are not closed.

OK, let's get validating!

1. Make sure you have a copy of ***blackgoose.html*** on your hard drive. Open a browser and go to *validator.w3.org*. We'll use the "Validate by File Upload" option. Select "Browse" and navigate to ***blackgoose.html***. Once you've selected it, click the "Check" button on the validator page.

2. The validator immediately hands back the results (Figure 10-3). It should come as no surprise that "this page is not Valid HTML 4.01 Strict." There are apparently three things that prevent it from being so.

   First, although it is not listed as an error, it complains that it could not find the Character Encoding. We'll talk about character encodings in the next section, so let's not worry about that one for now.

   The first real error listed is that the `head` element is "not finished." If you look at the source, you can see that there is indeed a closing `</head>` tag there, so that isn't the issue. The problem here (as hinted in the second paragraph under the error listing) is that the element is missing required content. In this case, it's the missing `title` element that is generating the error. This is a good example of the fact that validation error messages can be a bit cryptic, but at least it points you to the line of code that is amiss so you can start troubleshooting.

   The second error, as expected, is the missing `alt` attribute in the `img` element.

3. Try adding a **title** element and **alt** attribute, save the file, and validate it again. This time it should "tentatively" pass. It still doesn't like that missing character encoding, but we know we can take care of that later.

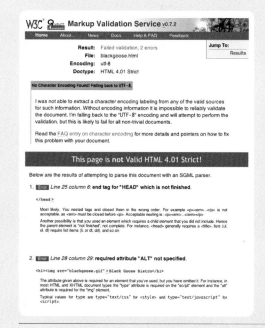

Figure 10-3. The error report generated by the W3C validator.

4. Now let's validate another document, *x-blackgoose.html*. It is identical to the *blackgoose.html* that we just validated, except it specifies the XHTML 1.0 Strict DTD in its DOCTYPE declaration. This will give us a chance to see how the rules for XHTML differ from HTML.

Go to *validator.w3.org* and upload *x-blackgoose.html*. It is not valid, of course, and there is still that character encoding problem. But look at the new list of errors—there are 18 compared to only two when we validated it as HTML. I'm not going to show them all in a figure, but I will call your attention to a few key issues.

First, look at Error 4, "Line 27 column 30: end tag for "img" omitted." The problem here is that although **img** is an empty element, it must be terminated with a closing slash in XHTML (**<img />**).

Now look at Error 6 that states something to the effect that you aren't allowed to use an **h2** in this context. It's saying that because it thinks you are trying to put an **h2** inside an unclosed **img** element, which doesn't make any sense.

The lesson here is that one error early in the document can generate a whole list of errors down the line. It is a good idea to make obvious changes, and then revalidate to see the impact of the correction.

5. Try fixing the **img** element by adding the **alt** attribute and the trailing slash, then reupload the document and check it. There will still be a long list of errors, but now they are related to the **p** elements not being closed. Continue fixing errors until you get the document to be "tentatively" validated.

Now it's time to take care of the character encoding so we can get a true sense of accomplishment by having our documents validate completely.

Character Encoding

Before I show you how to specify the character encoding for your documents, I think it is useful to know what a character encoding *is*.

Because the Web is worldwide, there are hundreds of written languages with a staggering number of unique character shapes that may need to be displayed on a web page. These include not only the various alphabets (Western, Hebrew, Arabic, and so on), but also ideographs (characters that indicate a whole word or concept) for languages such as Chinese, Japanese, and Korean.

Various sets of characters have been standardized for use on computers and over networks. For example, the set of 256 characters most commonly used in Western languages has been standardized and named Latin-1 (or ISO 8859-1, to use its formal identifier). Latin-1 was the character encoding used for HTML 2.0 and 3.0, and you can still use it for documents today.

XML Declarations

The character encoding for XML documents should be provided in an XML declaration. XML declarations indicate the version of XML used in the document and may also include the character encoding.

The following is an example of the XML declaration that the W3C recommends for XHTML documents. It must appear before the DOCTYPE declaration.

```
<?xml version="1.0"
encoding="utf-8"?>
```

XML declarations are not required for all XML documents, but the W3C encourages authors to include them in XHTML documents. They *are* required when the character encoding is something other than the defaults UTF-8 or UTF-16.

Unfortunately, despite the W3C's encouragement, XML declarations are usually omitted because they are problematic for current HTML browsers.

Unicode

The big kahuna of character sets, however, is Unicode (ISO/IEC 10646), which includes the characters for most known languages of the world. There are tens of thousands of characters in Unicode, and room in the specification for roughly a million. The Unicode character set may be encoded (converted to ones and zeros) several ways, the most popular being the UTF-8 encoding. You may also see UTF-16 or UTF-32, which use different numbers of bytes to describe characters.

UTF-8 is the recommended encoding for all HTML 4.01, XHTML, and XML documents. You may remember seeing "Falling back to UTF-8" in the error message in the validator results. Now you know that it was just assuming you wanted to use the default character encoding of Unicode for your document type.

Specifying the character encoding

There are several ways to associate a character encoding with a document. One way is to ask your server administrator to configure the server to include the character encoding in the HTTP header, a chunk of information that a server attaches to every web document before returning it to the browser. However, because this information can be separated from the document content, the W3C also recommends that you include the character encoding in the document itself.

In HTML 4.01 and XHTML 1.0 documents, character encoding is indicated using a `meta` element (see the sidebar, XML Declarations for the method for XML documents). The `meta` element is an empty element that provides information about the document, such as its creation date, author, copyright information, and, as we'll focus on in this section, the character encoding and the type of file.

The meta element goes in the head of the document, as shown in this XHTML example (note the trailing slash in the empty meta element):

```
<head>
    <meta http-equiv="content-type" content="text/html;charset=utf-8" />
    <title>Sample document</title>
</head>
```

The http-equiv attribute identifies that this meta element is providing information about the content type of the document.

The content attribute provides the details of the content type in a two-part value. The first part says that this is an HTML text file (in technical terms, it identifies its media type as text/html). But wait, didn't we just say that this is in an XHTML document? That's fine. XHTML 1.0 documents can masquerade as HTML text documents for reasons of backward compatibility (XHTML 1.1 documents, however, must be identified as application/xml, and unfortunately, browsers don't support that well quite yet).

Finally, we get to the second part that specifies the character encoding for this document as utf-8.

For another look, here is a meta element for an (X)HTML document that uses the Latin-1 character encoding. Try it out yourself in Exercise 10-3.

```
<meta http-equiv="content-type" content="text/html;charset=ISO-8859-1">
```

exercise 10-3 | **Adding the character encoding**

In the earlier exercise, you should have fixed all of the errors in *blackgoose.html* (the HTML document) and *x-blackgoose.html* (the XHTML version of the same content). The **meta** element with the character encoding should be all that stands between you and the thrill of validating against the Strict DTDs.

Try adding the **meta** element as shown in the previous section to both documents, and reupload them in the validator.

HINT: Be sure that the **meta** element has a trailing slash in the XHTML document, and be sure to omit the space and slash in the HTML version.

Putting It All Together

Okay! We've covered a lot of ground in this chapter in the effort to kick your documents up a notch into true standards compliance. We looked at the various versions of HTML and XHTML and what makes them different, how to specify which version (DTD) you used to write your document and how browsers use that information, how to validate your document, and how to specify its character encoding and media type.

What it boils down to is that the minimal document structure for standards compliant documents have a few extra elements than the basic skeleton we created back in Chapter 4. The following examples show the minimal markup for HTML 4.01 Strict and XHTML 1.0 Strict documents (you can adapt these by changing the DTD in the DOCTYPE declaration and the character encoding). The good news is that, if you've read the chapter, now you understand exactly what the extra markup means.

HTML 4.01 strict

This is the minimal document structure for HTML 4.01 Strict documents as recommended by the W3C.

```
<!DOCTYPE html PUBLIC "-//W3C//DTD HTML 4.01//EN"
   "http://www.w3.org/TR/html4/strict.dtd">

<html>

<head>
  <title>An HTML 4.01 Strict document</title>
  <meta http-equiv="content-type" content="text/html;charset=utf-8">
</head>

<body>
  <p>... The document content goes here ...</p>
</body>

</html>
```

NOTE

These document templates are also available for download at www.learningwebdesign.com/materials/.

XHTML 1.0 strict

This is the minimal document structure for XHTML 1.0 Strict documents as recommended by the W3C.

```
<!DOCTYPE html PUBLIC "-//W3C//DTD XHTML 1.0 Strict//EN"
        "http://www.w3.org/TR/xhtml1/DTD/xhtml1-strict.dtd">

<html xmlns="http://www.w3.org/1999/xhtml" xml:lang="en" lang="en">

<head>
  <title>An XHTML 1.0 Strict document</title>
  <meta http-equiv="content-type" content="text/html;charset=utf-8" />
</head>

<body>
  <p>... The document content goes here ...</p>
</body>

</html>
```

Note that this example omits the XML declaration (see the XML Declarations sidebar earlier in this chapter), because it is problematic for current browsers as of this writing.

Test Yourself

This chapter was information-packed. Are you ready to see how much you absorbed?

1. Who fought in the infamous Browser Wars of the 1990s?

2. What is the difference between Transitional and Strict HTML 4.01?

3. How are HTML 4.01 Strict and XHTML 1.0 Strict the same? How are they different?

4. Name four significant syntax requirements in XHTML.

5. Look at these valid markup examples and determine whether each is HTML or XHTML:

   ```
   <IMG SRC="panda.jpg" ALT="panda eating leaves">      _____

   <img src="orchid.jpg" alt="orchid" width=100 height=150 >   _____

   <img src="flipflop.gif" alt="closeup of foot in sandal" />   _____
   ```

6. What extra attributes must be applied to the `html` element in XHTML documents?

7. How do you get a standards compliant browser to display your page in Standards Mode?

8. Name two advantages that XHTML offers over HTML.

9. What is ISO 8859-1?

CSS FOR PRESENTATION

PART III

CHAPTER 11

CASCADING STYLE SHEETS ORIENTATION

You've seen style sheets mentioned quite a bit already, and now we'll finally put them to work and start giving our pages some much needed style. Cascading Style Sheets (CSS) is the W3C standard for defining the presentation of documents written in HTML, XHTML, and, in fact, any XML language. Presentation, again, refers to the way the document is displayed or delivered to the user, whether on a computer screen, a cell phone display, or read aloud by a screen reader. With style sheets handling the presentation, (X)HTML can get back to the business of defining document structure and meaning, as intended.

CSS is a separate language with its own syntax. This chapter covers CSS terminology and fundamental concepts that will help you get your bearings for the upcoming chapters, where you'll learn how to change text and font styles, add colors and backgrounds, and even do basic page layout using CSS. Will you be a style sheet expert by the end of Part III? Probably not. But you will have a solid foundation for further reading, and lots of practice.

NOTE

See the section, Moving Forward with CSS, at the end of this chapter for books and sites that will help you continue your education.

The Benefits of CSS

Not that you need further convincing that style sheets are the way to go, but here is a quick run-down of the benefits of using style sheets.

- **Better type and layout controls.** Presentational (X)HTML never gets close to offering the kind of control over type, backgrounds, and layout that is possible with CSS.

- **Less work.** You can change the appearance of an entire site by editing one style sheet. Making small tweaks and even entire site redesigns with style sheets is much easier than when presentation instructions are mixed in with the markup.

IN THIS CHAPTER

The benefits and power of Cascading Style Sheets (CSS)

How (X)HTML markup creates a document structure

Writing CSS style rules

Attaching styles to the (X) HTML document

The big CSS concepts of inheritance, the cascade, specificity, rule order, and the box model

- **Potentially smaller documents and faster downloads.** Old school practices of using redundant font elements and nested tables make for bloated documents. Not only that, you can apply a single style sheet document to all the pages in a site for further byte savings.

- **More accessible sites.** When all matters of presentation are handled by CSS, you can mark up your content meaningfully, making it more accessible for nonvisual or mobile devices.

- **Reliable browser support.** Nearly every browser in current use supports all of CSS Level 1 and the majority of CSS Level 2. (See the sidebar, Meet the Standards, for what is meant by CSS "levels.")

Come to think of it, there really aren't any disadvantages to using style sheets. There are some lingering hassles from browser inconsistencies, but they can either be avoided or worked around if you know where to look for them. It's by no means a reason to put off using CSS right away.

The power of CSS

We're not talking about minor visual tweaks here, like changing the color of headlines or adding text indents. When used to its full potential, CSS is a robust and powerful design tool. My eyes were opened by the variety and richness of the designs at CSS Zen Garden (*www.csszengarden.com*). Figure 11-1 shows just a few of my favorites. All of these designs use the *exact same* XHTML source document. Not only that, it doesn't include a single img element (all of the images are used as backgrounds). But look how different each page looks—and how sophisticated—that's all done with style sheets.

Granted, it takes a lot of practice to be able to create CSS layouts like those shown in Figure 11-1. Killer graphic design skills help too (unfortunately, you won't get those in this book). I'm showing this to you up front because I want you to be aware of the potential of CSS-based design, particularly because the examples in this beginners' book tend to be simple and straightforward. Take your time learning, but keep your eye on the prize.

How Style Sheets Work

It's as easy as 1-2-3!

1. Start with a document that has been marked up in HTML or XHTML.

2. Write style rules for how you'd like certain elements to look.

3. Attach the style rules to the document. When the browser displays the document, it follows your rules for rendering elements (unless the user has applied some mandatory styles, but we'll get to that later).

OK, so there's a bit more to it than that, of course. Let's give each of these steps a little more consideration.

Meet the Standards

The first official version of CSS (the CSS Level 1 Recommendation, a.k.a CSS1) was officially released in 1996, and included properties for adding font, color, and spacing instructions to page elements. Unfortunately, lack of dependable browser support prevented the widespread adoption of CSS for several years.

CSS Level 2 (CSS2) was released in 1998. It most notably added properties for positioning that allowed CSS to be used for page layout. It also introduced styles for other media types (such as print, handheld, and aural) and more sophisticated methods for selecting elements for styling. CSS Level 2, Revision 1 (CSS2.1) makes some minor adjustments to CSS2 and is a working draft as of this writing. Fortunately, most current browsers support the majority of the CSS1, CSS2, and CSS2.1 specifications.

In fact, some browsers are already supporting features from CSS Level 3 (CSS3) that is still in development. It adds support for vertical text, improved handling of tables and international languages, better integration with other XML technologies, and other little perks like multiple background images in a single element and a larger list of color names.

Keep up to date with the W3C's development of CSS at *www.w3.org/Style/CSS*.

CSS Zen Dragen
by Matthew Buchanan

Faded Flowers
by Mani Sheriar

By the Pier
by Peter OngKelmscott

Shaolin Yokobue
by Javier Cabrera

Organica Creativa
by Eduardo Cesario

Kelmscott
by Bronwen Hodgkinson

Contemporary Nouveau
by David Hellsing

*Figure 11-1. These pages from the CSS Zen Garden use the same XHTML source
document, but the design is changed using exclusively CSS (used with permission of CSS
Zen Garden and the individual designers).*

exercise 11-1 |
Your first style sheet

In this exercise, we'll add a few simple styles to a short article. The XHTML document, *twenties.html* and its associated image, *twenty_20s.jpg*, are available at *www. learningwebdesign.com/materials/*. First, open the document in a browser to see how it looks by default (it should look something like Figure 11-2). You can also open the document in a text editor and get ready to follow along when this exercise continues in the next section.

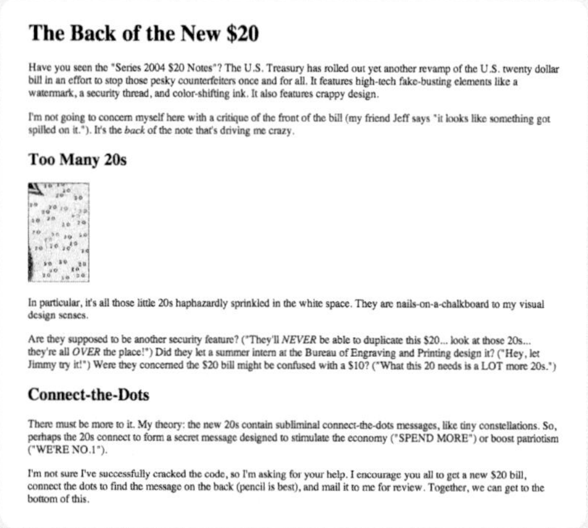

The Back of the New $20

Have you seen the "Series 2004 $20 Notes"? The U.S. Treasury has rolled out yet another revamp of the U.S. twenty dollar bill in an effort to stop those pesky counterfeiters once and for all. It features high-tech fake-busting elements like a watermark, a security thread, and color-shifting ink. It also features crappy design.

I'm not going to concern myself here with a critique of the front of the bill (my friend Jeff says "it looks like something got spilled on it."). It's the *back* of the note that's driving me crazy.

Too Many 20s

In particular, it's all those little 20s haphazardly sprinkled in the white space. They are nails-on-a-chalkboard to my visual design senses.

Are they supposed to be another security feature? ("They'll *NEVER* be able to duplicate this $20... look at those 20s... they're all *OVER* the place!") Did they let a summer intern at the Bureau of Engraving and Printing design it? ("Hey, let Jimmy try it!") Were they concerned the $20 bill might be confused with a $10? ("What this 20 needs is a LOT more 20s.")

Connect-the-Dots

There must be more to it. My theory: the new 20s contain subliminal connect-the-dots messages, like tiny constellations. So, perhaps the 20s connect to form a secret message designed to stimulate the economy ("SPEND MORE") or boost patriotism ("WE'RE NO.1").

I'm not sure I've successfully cracked the code, so I'm asking for your help. I encourage you all to get a new $20 bill, connect the dots to find the message on the back (pencil is best), and mail it to me for review. Together, we can get to the bottom of this.

Figure 11-2. This what the article looks like without any style sheet instructions. Although we won't be making it beautiful, you will get a feel for how styles work.

1. Marking up the document

You know a lot about marking up content from the previous chapters. For example, you know that it is important to choose (X)HTML elements that accurately describe the meaning of the content. You've also heard me say that the markup creates the structure of the document, sometimes called the structural layer, upon which the presentation layer can be applied.

In this and the upcoming chapters, you'll see that having an understanding of your document's structure and the relationships between elements is central to your work as a style sheet author.

To get a feel for how simple it is to change the look of a document with style sheets, try your hand at Exercise 11-1. The good news is that I've whipped up a little XHTML document for you to play with.

2. Writing the rules

A style sheet is made up of one or more style instructions (called rules) that describe how an element or group of elements should be displayed. The first step in learning CSS is to get familiar with the parts of a rule. As you'll see, they're fairly intuitive to follow. Each rule *selects* an element and *declares* how it should look.

The following example contains two rules. The first makes all the h1 elements in the document green; the second specifies that the paragraphs should be in a small, sans-serif font.

```
h1 { color: green; }
p  { font-size: small; font-family: sans-serif; }
```

NOTE

Sans-serif fonts do not have a little slab (a serif) at the ends of strokes and tend to look more sleek and modern. We'll talk a lot more about fonts in Chapter 12, Formatting Text.

In CSS terminology, the two main sections of a rule are the selector that identifies the element or elements to be affected, and the declaration that provides the rendering instructions. The declaration, in turn, is made up of a property (such as color) and its value (green), separated by a colon and a space. One or more declarations are placed inside curly brackets, as shown in Figure 11-3.

```
                    declaration                      declaration block
                        |                                  |
    selector { property: value; }        selector {
                                            property1: value1;
                                            property2: value2;
                                            property3: value3;
                                            }
```

Figure 11-3. The parts of a style sheet rule.

Selectors

In the previous small style sheet example, the `h1` and `p` elements are used as selectors. This most basic type of selector is called an element type selector. The properties defined for each will apply to every `h1` and `p` element in the document, respectively. In upcoming chapters, I'll introduce you to more sophisticated selectors that you can use to target elements, including ways to select groups of elements and elements that appear in a particular context.

Mastering selectors—that is, choosing the best type of selector and using it strategically—is an important step in becoming a CSS Jedi Master.

Declarations

The declaration is made up of a property/value pair. There can be more than one declaration in a single rule; for example, the rule for `p` element above has both the `font-size` and `font-family` properties. Each declaration must end with a semicolon to keep it separate from the following declaration (see note). If you omit the semicolon, the declaration and the one following it will be ignored. The curly brackets and the declarations they contain are often referred to as the declaration block (Figure 11-3).

Because CSS ignores whitespace and line returns within the declaration block, authors typically write each declaration in the block on its own line, as shown in the following example. This makes it easier to find the properties applied to the selector and to tell when the style rule ends.

```
p  {
   font-size: small;
   font-family: sans-serif;
}
```

Note that nothing has really changed here—there is still one set of curly brackets, semicolons after each declaration, etc.. The only difference is the insertion of line returns and some character spaces for alignment.

The heart of style sheets lies in the collection of standard properties that can be applied to selected elements. The complete CSS specification defines dozens of properties for everything from text indent to how table headers should be read aloud. This book covers the most common and best supported properties (see note).

NOTE

Technically, the semicolon is not required after the last declaration in the block, but it is recommended that you get into the habit of always ending declarations with a semicolon. It will make adding declarations to the rule later that much easier.

NOTE

For a complete list of properties in the current CSS2.1 standards, go straight to the W3C Recommendation at www.w3.org/TR/CSS21/propidx.html, or consult a comprehensive CSS reference book such as CSS: The Definitive Guide by Eric Meyer or Web Design in a Nutshell by Jennifer Robbins (that's me), both published by O'Reilly Media.

Providing Measurement Values

When providing measurement values, the unit must immediately follow the number , like this:

```
{ margin: 2em; }
```

Adding a space before the unit will cause the property not to work.

INCORRECT: `{ margin: 2 em; }`

It is acceptable to omit the unit of measurement for zero values:

```
{ margin: 0; }
```

Values are dependent on the property. Some properties take length measurements, some take color values, others have a predefined list of keywords. When using a property, it is important to know which values it accepts; however, in many cases, simple common sense will serve you well.

Before we move on, why not get a little practice writing style rules yourself in the continuation of Exercise 11-1.

exercise 11-1 | **Your first style sheet (continued)**

Open *twenties.html* in a text editor. In the **head** of the document you will find that I have set up a **style** element for you to type the rules into. The **style** element is used to embed a style sheet in the **head** of an (X)HTML document.

To begin, we'll just add the small style sheet that we just looked at in this section. Type the following rules into the document, just as you see them here.

```
<style type="text/css">
h1 {
  color: green;
}
p {
  font-size: small;
  font-family: sans-serif;
}
</style>
```

Save the file and take a look at it in the browser. You should notice some changes (if your browser already uses a sans-serif font, you may only see size change). If not, go back and check that you included both the opening and closing curly bracket and semicolons. It's easy to accidentally omit these characters, causing the style sheet not to work.

Now we'll change and add to the style sheet to see how easy it is to write rules and see the effects of the changes. Here are a few things to try (remember that you need to save the document after each change in order for the changes to be visible when you reload it in the browser).

- Make the **h1** element "gray" and take a look at it in the browser. Then make it "blue". Finally, make it "red". (We'll run through the complete list of available color names in Chapter 13, Colors and Backgrounds.)
- Add a new rule that makes the **h2** elements red as well.
- Add a 100 pixel left margin to paragraph (**p**) elements using this declaration:
  ```
  margin-left: 100px;
  ```
- Remember that you can add this new declaration to the existing rule for **p** elements.

- Add a 100 pixel left margin to the **h2** headings as well.
- Add a red, 1-pixel border to the bottom of the **h1** element using this declaration:
  ```
  border-bottom: 1px solid red;
  ```
- Move the image to the right margin and allow text to flow around it with the **float** property. The shorthand **margin** property shown in this rule adds zero pixels space on the top and bottom of the image and 12 pixels space on the left and right of the image (the values are mirrored in a manner explained in Chapter 14, Thinking Inside the Box).
  ```
  img {
    float: right;
    margin: 0 12px;
  }
  ```

When you are done, the document should look something like the one shown in Figure 11-4.

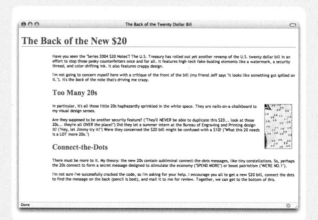

Figure 11-4. The article after adding the small style sheet from the example. As I said, not beautiful, just different.

3. Attaching the styles to the document

In the previous exercise, we embedded the style sheet right in the XHTML document using the `style` element. That is just one of three ways that style information can be applied to an (X)HTML document. You'll get to try each of these out soon, but it is helpful to have an overview of the methods and terminology up front.

External style sheets. An external style sheet is a separate, text-only document that contains a number of style rules. It must be named with the *.css* suffix. The *.css* document is then linked to or imported into one or more (X)HTML documents (we'll discuss how in Chapter 13). In this way, all the files in a web site may share the same style sheet. This is the most powerful and preferred method for attaching style sheets to content.

Embedded style sheets. This is the type of style sheet we worked with in the exercise. It is placed in a document using the `style` element and its rules apply only to that document. The `style` element *must* be placed in the `head` of the document and it must contain a `type` attribute that identifies the content of the `style` element as "text/css" (currently the only available value). This example also includes a comment (see Comments in Style Sheets sidebar).

```
<head>
    <title>Required document title here</title>
    <style type="text/css">
    /* style rules go here */
    </style>
</head>
```

The `style` element may also include the `media` attribute used to target specific media such as screen, print, or handheld devices. These are discussed in Chapter 13 as well.

Inline styles. You can apply properties and values to a single element using the `style` attribute in the element itself, as shown here:

```
<h1 style="color: red">Introduction</h1>
```

To add multiple properties, just separate them with semicolons, like this:

```
<h1 style="color: red; margin-top: 2em">Introduction</h1>
```

Inline styles apply only to the particular element in which they appear. Inline styles should be avoided, unless it is absolutely necessary to override styles from an embedded or external style sheet. Inline styles are problematic in that they intersperse presentation information into the structural markup. They also make it more difficult to make changes because every `style` attribute must be hunted down in the source. These disadvantages sound a lot like those for the obsolete `font` element, don't they?

Comments in Style Sheets

Sometimes, it is helpful to leave yourself or your collaborators comments in a style sheet. CSS has its own comment syntax, shown here:

```
/* comment goes here */
```

Content between the /* and */ will be ignored when the style sheet is parsed, which means you can leave comments anywhere in a style sheet, even within a rule.

```
body { font-size: small;
/* temporary */ }
```

exercise 11-2 |
Applying an inline style

Open the article, *twenties.html*, in whatever state you last left it in Exercise 11-1. If you worked to the end of the exercise, you will have a rule that applies a color to the **h2** elements.

Now, write an inline style that makes the second **h2** purple. We'll do that right in the opening **h2** tag using the **style** attribute as shown here:

```
<h2 style="color: purple">
Connect-the-Dots</h2>
```

Now that heading is purple, overriding whatever color it had been set before. The other **h2** heading is unaffected.

Exercise 11-2 gives you an opportunity to write an inline style and see how it works. We won't be working with inline styles after this point for the reasons listed earlier, so here's your chance.

The Big Concepts

There are a few big ideas that you need to get your head around to be comfortable with how Cascading Style Sheets behave. I'm going to introduce you to these concepts now so we don't have to slow down for a lecture once we're rolling through the style properties. Each of these ideas will certainly be revisited and illustrated in more detail in the upcoming chapters.

Inheritance

Are your eyes the same color as your parents'? Did you inherit their hair color? Your unique smile? Well, just as parents pass down traits to their children, (X)HTML elements pass down certain style properties to the elements they contain. Notice in Exercise 11-1, when we styled the p elements in a small, sans-serif font, the em element in the second paragraph became small and sans-serif as well, even though we didn't write a rule for it specifically (Figure 11-5). That is because it inherited the styles from the paragraph it is in.

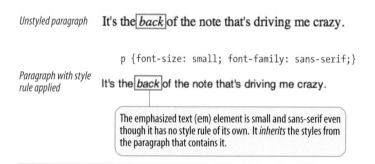

Figure 11-5. The em *element inherits styles that were applied to the paragraph.*

Document structure

This is where an understanding of your document's structure comes in. As I've noted before, (X)HTML documents have an implicit structure or hierarchy. For example, the sample article we've been playing with has an html root element that contains a head and a body, and the body contains heading and paragraph elements. A few of the paragraphs, in turn, contain inline elements like images (img) and emphasized text (em). You can visualize the structure as an upside-down tree, branching out from the root, as shown in Figure 11-6.

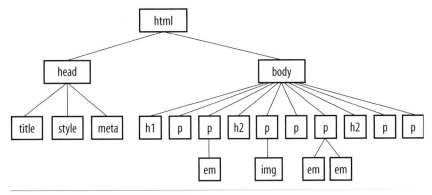

Figure 11-6. The document tree structure of the sample document, twenties.html.

Parents and children

The document tree becomes a family tree when it comes to referring to the relationship between elements. All the elements contained within a given element are said to be its descendants. For example, all of the h1, h2, p, em, and img elements in the document in Figure 11-6 are descendants of the body element.

An element that is directly contained within another element (with no intervening hierarchical levels), is said to be the child of that element. Conversely, the containing element is the parent. For example, the em element is the child of the p element, and the p element is its parent.

All of the elements higher than a particular element in the hierarchy are its ancestors. Two elements with the same parent are siblings. We don't refer to "aunts" or "cousins," so the analogy stops there. This may all seem academic, but it will come in handy when writing CSS selectors.

Pass it on

When you write a font-related style rule using the p element as a selector, the rule applies to all of the paragraphs in the document as well as the inline text elements they contain. We've seen the evidence of the em element inheriting the style properties applied to its parent (p) back in Figure 11-5. Figure 11-7 demonstrates what's happening in terms of the document structure diagram. Note that the img element is excluded because font-related properties do not apply to images.

> **CSS TIP**
>
> When you learn a new property, it is a good idea to note whether it inherits. Inheritance is noted for every property listing in this book. For the most part, inheritance follows your expectations.

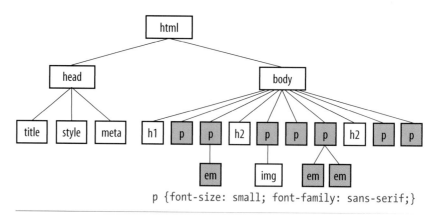

p {font-size: small; font-family: sans-serif;}

Figure 11-7. Certain properties applied to the p *element are inherited by their children.*

Notice that I've been saying "certain" properties are inherited. It's important to note that some style sheet properties inherit and others do not. In general, properties related to the styling of text—font size, color, style, etc.—are passed down. Properties such as borders, margins, backgrounds, and so on that affect the boxed area around the element tend not to be passed down. This makes sense when you think about it. For example, if you put a border around a paragraph, you wouldn't want a border around every inline element (such as em, strong, or a) it contains as well.

You can use inheritance to your advantage when writing style sheets. For example, if you want all text elements to be rendered in the Verdana font face, you could write separate style rules for every element in the document and set the font-family to Verdana. A *better* way would be to write a single style rule that applies the font-family property to the body element, and let all the text elements contained in the body inherit that style (Figure 11-8).

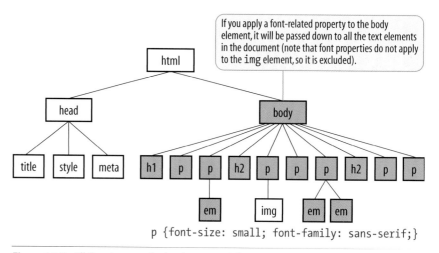

p {font-size: small; font-family: sans-serif;}

Figure 11-8. All the elements in the document inherit certain properties applied to the body *element.*

Any property applied to a specific element will override the inherited values for that property. Going back to the article example, we could specify that the `em` element should appear in a serif font, and that would override the inherited sans-serif setting.

Conflicting styles: the cascade

Ever wonder why they are called "cascading" style sheets? CSS allows you to apply several style sheets to the same document, which means there are bound to be conflicts. For example, what should the browser do if a document's imported style sheet says that `h1` elements should be red, but its embedded style sheet has a rule that makes `h1`s purple?

The folks who wrote the style sheet specification anticipated this problem and devised a hierarchical system that assigns different weights to the various sources of style information. The cascade refers to what happens when several sources of style information vie for control of the elements on a page: style information is passed down until it is overridden by a style command with more weight.

For example, if you don't apply any style information to a web page, it will be rendered according to the browser's internal style sheet (we've been calling this the default rendering). However, if the web page's author provides a style sheet for the document, that has more weight and overrides the browser's styles. Individual users can apply their own styles to documents as well, as discussed in the Reader Style Sheets sidebar.

As we've learned, there are three ways to attach style information to the source document, and they have a cascading order as well. Generally speaking, the closer the style sheet is to the content, the more weight it is given. Embedded style sheets that appear right in the document in the `style` element have more weight than external style sheets. In the example that started this section, the `h1` elements would end up purple as specified in the embedded style sheet, not red as specified in the external *.css* file that has less weight. Inline styles have more weight than embedded style sheets because you can't get any closer to the content than a style right in the element's opening tag.

To prevent a specific rule from being overridden, you can assign it "importance" with the `!important` indicator, as explained in the Assigning Importance sidebar.

The sidebar, Style Sheet Hierarchy, provides an overview of the cascading order from general to specific.

Specificity

Once the applicable style sheet has been chosen, there may still be conflicts; therefore, the cascade continues at the rule level. When two rules in a single style sheet conflict, the type of selector is used to determine the winner. The

Reader Style Sheets

It is possible for users to write their own style sheets and apply them to the pages they see with their browser. The CSS Recommendation refers to these as reader style sheets (in practice, it is more common to use the term user style sheets).

Normally, style rules provided by an author style sheet (external, embedded, or inline) override the reader's style sheet. However, if the user marks a style as "important," it will trump all other styles provided by the author and the browser (see the Assigning Importance sidebar).

So, for example, a user with impaired vision could write a style rule that makes all web text appear in extra large black text on a white background and be guaranteed to see it that way. That's precisely the W3C's intent in allowing reader style sheets and giving them the power to override all other styles.

Assigning Importance

If you want a rule not to be overridden by a subsequent conflicting rule, include the `!important` indicator just after the property value and before the semicolon for that rule. For example, to make paragraph text blue always, use the following rule:

```
p {color: blue !important;}
```

Even if the browser encounters an inline style later in the document (which should override a document-wide style sheet), like this one:

```
<p style="color: red">
```

that paragraph will still be blue, because the rule with the `!important` indicator cannot be overridden by other styles in the author's style sheet.

The only way an `!important` rule may be overridden is by a conflicting rule in a reader (user) style sheet that has also been marked `!important`. This is to ensure that special reader requirements, such as large type for the visually impaired, are never overridden.

Based on the previous examples, if the reader's style sheet includes this rule:

```
p {color: black;}
```

the text would still be blue, because all author styles (even those not marked `!important`) take precedence over the reader's styles. However, if the conflicting reader's style is marked `!important`, like this:

```
p {color: black !important;}
```

the paragraphs will be black and cannot be overridden by any author-provided style.

Style Sheet Hierarchy

Style information can come from various sources, listed here from general to specific. Items lower in the list will override items above them:

- Browser default settings
- User style settings (set in a browser as a "reader style sheet")
- Linked external style sheet (added with the `link` element)
- Imported style sheets (added with the `@import` function)
- Embedded style sheets (added with the `style` element)
- Inline style information (added with the `style` attribute in an opening tag)
- Any style rule marked `!important` by the author
- Any style rule marked `!important` by the reader (user)

more specific the selector, the more weight it is given to override conflicting declarations.

It's a little soon to be discussing specificity because we've only looked at one type of selector (and the least specific type, at that). For now, put the term specificity and the concept of some selectors overriding others on your radar. We will revisit it in Chapter 12 when you have more selector types under your belt.

Rule order

Finally, if there are conflicts within style rules of identical weight, whichever one comes last in the list "wins." Take these three rules, for example:

```
<style type="text/css">
  p { color: red; }
  p { color: blue; }
  p { color: green; }
</style>
```

In this scenario, paragraph text will be green because the last rule in the style sheet, that is, the one closest to the content in the document, overrides the earlier ones.

NOTE

This "last-one-listed wins" rule applies in other contexts in CSS as well. For example, later declarations in a declaration block can override earlier declarations. In addition, external style sheets listed later in the source will be given precedence over those listed above them (even style sheets embedded with the `style` *element).*

The box model

As long as we're talking about "big CSS concepts," it is only appropriate to introduce the cornerstone of the CSS visual formatting system: the box model. The easiest way to think of the box model is that browsers see every element on the page (both block and inline) as being contained in a little rectangular box. You can apply properties such as borders, margins, padding, and backgrounds to these boxes, and even reposition them on the page.

We're going to go into a lot more detail about the box model in Chapter 14, but having a general feel for the box model will benefit you even as we discuss text and backgrounds in the following two chapters.

To see the elements roughly the way the browser sees them, I've written style rules that add borders around every content element in our sample article.

```
h1 { border: 1px solid blue; }
h2 { border: 1px solid blue; }
p { border: 1px solid blue; }
em { border: 1px solid blue; }
img { border: 1px solid blue; }
```

Figure 11-9 shows the results. The borders reveal the shape of each block element box. There are boxes around the inline elements (`em` and `img`), as well. Notice that the block element boxes expand to fill the available width of the browser window, which is the nature of block elements in the normal document flow. Inline boxes encompass just the characters or image they contain.

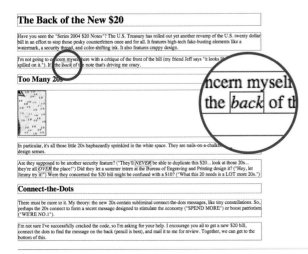

Figure 11-9. Rules around all the elements reveal their element boxes.

Pop Quiz

Can you guess why I didn't just add the `border` property to the `body` element and let it inherit to all the elements in the grouped selector?

Answer:

Because `border` is one of those properties that is not inherited, as noted earlier.

Grouped Selectors

Hey! This is a good opportunity to show you a handy style rule shortcut. If you ever need to apply the same style property to a number of elements, you can group the selectors into one rule by separating them with commas. This one rule has the same effect as the five rules listed previously. Grouping them makes future edits more efficient and results in a smaller file size.

```
h1, h2, p, em, img { border: 1px solid blue; }
```

Now you've got two selector types in your toolbox: a simple element selector, and grouped selectors.

Moving Forward with CSS

This chapter covered all the fundamentals of Cascading Style Sheets, including rule syntax, ways to apply styles to a document, and the central concepts of inheritance, the cascade, and the box model. Style sheets should no longer be a mystery, and from this point on, we'll merely be building on this foundation by adding properties and selectors to your arsenal as well as expanding on the concepts introduced here.

CSS is a vast topic, well beyond the scope of this book. The bookstores and Web are loaded with information about style sheets for all skill levels. I've compiled a list of the resources I've found the most useful during my learning process. I've also provided a list of popular tools that assist in writing style sheets in the CSS Tools sidebar.

Books

There is no shortage of good books on CSS out there, but these are the ones that taught me, and I feel good recommending them.

Cascading Style Sheets: The Definitive Guide, Second Edition, by Eric Meyer (O'Reilly)

Web Standards Solutions: The Markup and Style Handbook, by Dan Cederholm (Friends of Ed)

The Zen of CSS Design: Visual Enlightenment for the Web, by Dave Shea and Molly E. Holzschlag (New Riders)

Eric Meyer on CSS: Mastering the Language of Web Design, by Eric Meyer (New Riders)

Online Resources

The sites on the following page are good starting points for online exploration of style sheets.

World Wide Web Consortium (*www.w3.org/Style/CSS*)

> The World Wide Web Consortium oversees the development of web technologies, including CSS.

A List Apart (*www.alistapart.com*)

> This online magazine features some of the best thinking and writing on cutting-edge, standards-based web design. It was founded in 1998 by Jeffrey Zeldman and Brian Platz.

css-discuss (*www.css-discuss.org*)

> This is a mailing list and related site devoted to talking about CSS and how to use it.

Inspirational CSS showcase sites

If you are looking for excellent examples of what can be done with CSS, check out these sites.

CSS Zen Garden (*www.csszengarden.com*)

> This is a showcase site for what can be done with CSS, a single XHTML file, and the creative ideas of hundreds of designers. Its creator and keeper is standards expert Dave Shea. See the companion book listed above.

CSS Beauty (*www.cssbeauty.com*)

> A showcase of excellent sites designed in CSS.

Informative personal sites

Some of the best CSS resources are the blogs and personal sites of individuals with a passion for CSS-based design. These are only a few, but they provide a good entry point into the online standards community.

Stopdesign (*www.stopdesign.com*)

> Douglas Bowman, CSS and graphic design guru, publishes articles and trend-setting tutorials.

Mezzoblue (*www.mezzoblue.com*)

> This is the personal site of Dave Shea, creator of the CSS Zen Garden.

Meyerweb (*www.meyerweb.com*)

> This is the personal site of the king of CSS, Eric Meyer.

Molly.com (*www.molly.com*)

> This is the blog of prolific author and web-standards activist Molly E. Holzschlag.

Simplebits (*www.simplebits.com*)

> This is the personal site of standards guru and author Dan Cederholm.

CSS Tools

The W3C maintains a list of current CSS authoring tools on the CSS home page at *www.w3.org/Style/CSS/#editors*. Here are a couple that I can personally recommend.

Web Developer Extension

Web developers are raving about the Web Developer extension for Firefox and Mozilla browsers, written by Chris Pederick. The extension adds a toolbar to the browser with tools that enable you to analyze and manipulate any page in the window. You can edit the style sheet for the page you are viewing as well as get information about the (X)HTML and graphics. It also validates the CSS, (X)HTML, and accessibility of the page. Get it at *chrispederick.com/work/firefox/webdeveloper* or from the Addons page at *addons.mozilla.org*.

Web Authoring Programs

Current WYSIWYG authoring programs such as Adobe Dreamweaver and Microsoft Expression Web can be configured to write a style sheet for you automatically as you design the page. The downside is that they are not always written in the most efficient manner (for example, they tend to overuse the `class` attribute to create style rules). Still, they may give you a good head start on the style sheet that you can then edit manually.

Test Yourself

Here are a few questions to test your knowledge of the CSS basics. Answers are provided in Appendix A.

1. Identify the various parts of this style rule:

   ```
   blockquote { line-height: 1.5; }
   ```

   selector: _____   value: _____

   property: _____   declaration: _____

2. What color will paragraphs be when this embedded style sheet is applied to a document? Why?

   ```
   <style type="text/css">
       p { color: purple; }
       p { color: green; }
       p { color: gray; }
   </style>
   ```

3. Rewrite each of these CSS examples. Some of them are completely incorrect and some could just be written more efficiently.

   a. ```
      p {font-face: sans-serif;}
      p {font-size: 1em;}
      p {line-height: 1.2em;}
      ```

   b. ```
      blockquote {
          font-size: 1em
          line-height: 150%
          color: gray }
      ```

   c. ```
      body
          {background-color: black;}
          {color: #666;}
          {margin-left: 12em;}
          {margin-right: 12em;}
      ```

   d. ```
      p {color: white;}
      blockquote {color: white;}
      li {color: white;}
      ```

   e. ```
      Act now!
      ```

4. Circle all the elements in the diagram that you would expect to appear in red when the following style rule is applied to an XHTML document with the structure diagrammed in Figure 11-10. This rule uses a type of selector you haven't seen yet, but common sense should serve you well.

   ```
   div#intro { color: red; }
   ```

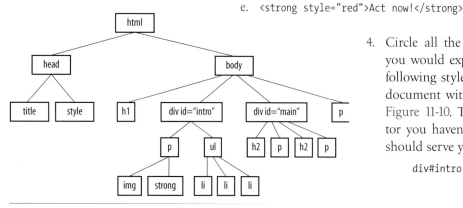

Figure 11-10. The document structure of a sample document.
   ```

FORMATTING TEXT

(Plus More Selectors)

Now that you've gotten your feet wet formatting text, are you ready to jump into the deep end? By the end of this chapter, you'll pick up *fourteen* new CSS properties used to manipulate the appearance of text. Along the way, you'll also learn how to use more powerful selectors for targeting elements in a particular context, and with a specific `id` or `class` name.

Throughout this chapter, we'll be sprucing up the Black Goose Bistro online menu similar to the one we marked up back in Chapter 5, Marking Up Text. I encourage you to work along with the exercises to get a feel for how the properties work. Figure 12-1 shows how the menu looked the last time we saw it and how it will look when we're done. It's not a masterpiece, but it is certainly an improvement.

IN THIS CHAPTER

The font-related properties

Text color

Text line settings such as line height, indents, and alignment

Underlines and overlines

Capitalization

Letter and word spacing

Descendant (contextual), ID, and class selectors

Specificity 101

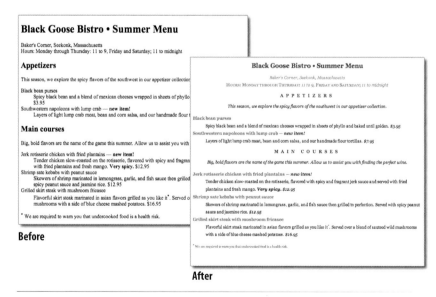

Before

After

Figure 12-1. Before and after views of the Black Goose Bistro menu that we'll be working on in this chapter.

AT A GLANCE

The font-related properties:
- `font-family`
- `font-size`
- `font-weight`
- `font-style`
- `font-variant`
- `font`

A Word About Property Listings

Each new property listing in this book is accompanied by information on how it behaves and how to use it. Here is a quick explanation of each part of property listings.

Values

These are the accepted values for the property according to the CSS2.1 specification. Predefined values appear in code font (for example, `small`, `italic`, or `small-caps`) and must be typed in exactly as shown.

Default

This is the value that will be used for the property by default, that is, if no other value is specified. Note that the browser uses a style sheet with values that may vary from the defaults defined in CSS.

Applies to

Some properties apply only to certain types of elements, such as block or table elements.

Inherits

This indicates whether the property will be passed down to the selected element's descendants. See Chapter 11, Cascading Style Sheets Orientation for an explanation of inheritance.

The Font Properties

When I design a text document (especially for print, but also for the Web), one of the first things I do is specify the font. In CSS, fonts are specified using a little bundle of font-related properties for typeface, size, weight, and font style. There is also a shortcut property that lets you specify all of the font attributes in one fell swoop.

The nature of the Web makes specifying type tricky, if not downright frustrating, particularly if you have experience designing for print (or even formatting text in a word processing program). Because you have no way of knowing which fonts are loaded on users' machines, you can't be sure that everyone will see text in the font you've chosen. And because the default font size varies by browser and user preferences, you can't be sure how large or small the type will appear, as well. We'll address the best practices for dealing with these font challenges as we go along.

Specifying the font name

Choosing a typeface, or font family as it is called in CSS, is a good place to start. Let's begin with the easy part: using the property `font-family` and its values.

`font-family`

Values: one or more font or generic font family names, separated by commas | `inherit`
Default: depends on the browser
Applies to: all elements
Inherits: yes

Use the `font-family` property to specify a font or list of fonts by name as shown in these examples.

```
body { font-family: Arial; }
tt { font-family: Courier, monospace; }
p { font-family: "Trebuchet MS", Verdana, sans-serif; }
```

All font names, with the exception of generic font families, must be capitalized. For example, use "Arial" instead of "arial". Notice that font names that contain a character space (such as Trebuchet MS in the third example) must appear within quotation marks. Use commas to separate multiple font names as shown in the second and third examples. You might be asking, "Why specify more than one font?" That's a good question, and it brings us to one of the challenges of specifying fonts for web pages.

Font limitations

Browsers are limited to displaying fonts that are already installed on the user's machine. So, although you may want the text to appear in Futura, if Futura is not installed on the user's computer, the browser's default font will be used instead.

Fortunately, CSS allows you to provide a list of back-up fonts should your first choice not be available. In the third example above, if the browser does not find Trebuchet MS, it will use Verdana, and if Verdana is not available, it will substitute some other sans-serif font.

Generic font families

That last option, "some other sans-serif font," bears more discussion. "Sans-serif" is just one of five generic font families that you can specify with the `font-family` property. When you specify a generic font family, the browser chooses an available font from that stylistic category. Figure 12-2 shows examples from each family. Generic font family names do not need to be capitalized.

All of the font properties are related to the shapes of characters.

serif

Examples: Times, Times New Roman, Georgia

Serif typefaces have decorative serifs, or slab-like appendages, on the ends of certain letter strokes.

sans-serif

Examples: Arial, Arial Black, Verdana, Trebuchet MS, Helvetica, Geneva

Sans-serif typefaces have straight letter strokes that do not end in serifs. They are generally considered easier to read on computer monitors.

monospace

Examples: Courier, Courier New, and Andale Mono

In monospace (also called constant width) typefaces, all characters take up the same amount of space on a line. For example, a capital W will be no wider than a lowercase i. Compare this to proportional typefaces (such as the one you're reading now) that allot different widths to different characters.

cursive

Examples: Apple Chancery, Zapf-Chancery, and Comic Sans

Cursive fonts emulate a script or handwritten appearance. These are rarely specified for professional web pages.

fantasy

Examples: Impact, Western, or other decorative font

Fantasy fonts are purely decorative and would be appropriate for headlines and other display type. Fantasy fonts are rarely used for web text due to cross-platform availability and legibility.

Figure 12-2. Examples of the five generic font families.

Font specifying strategies

The best practice for specifying fonts for web pages is to start with your first choice, provide some similar alternatives, then end with a generic font family that at least gets users in the right stylistic ballpark. Here's another example of this strategy in action. With this style rule, I specify that I'd prefer that users see all the text in Verdana, but I'd settle for Arial, or Helvetica, or, if all else fails, I'll let the browser choose an available sans-serif font for me.

    body { font-family: Verdana, Arial, Helvetica, sans-serif; }

Because a font will only show up if it's on a user's hard drive, it makes sense to specify fonts that are the most commonly available. Although there are countless fonts out there, the fact is that because licensed copies of fonts cost big bucks, most users stick with the fonts that are installed by their operating system or other applications. Font copyright also prevents designers from just making cool fonts available for download.

For these reasons, web designers tend to specify fonts from the Microsoft Core Web Fonts collection. These come installed with Windows, Internet Explorer, and Microsoft Office, so it is likely that they will find their way onto all Windows and even most Apple and Linux computers. Not only are they widely available, they were designed to be legible on low-resolution computer screens. Table 12-1 lists the fonts in the collection.

Table 12-1. Core Web Fonts from Microsoft

Serif	Georgia, Times New Roman
Sans Serif	Arial, Arial Black, Trebuchet MS, Verdana
Monospace	Courier New, Andale Mono
Miscellaneous	Comic Sans, Impact, Webdings

So, as you see, specifying fonts for the Web is more like merely suggesting them. You don't have absolute control over which font your users will see. It's one of those web design quirks you learn to live with.

Now seems like a good time to get started formatting the Black Goose Bistro menu. We'll add new style rules one at a time as we learn each new property.

NOTE

There are techniques for using graphics and even small Flash movies for headlines in order to achieve more stylized typography than can be handled with CSS alone. These image replacement techniques are not appropriate for large amounts of text, however. Read more about image replacement in Chapter 17, CSS Techniques.

exercise 12-1 | **Formatting a menu**

In this exercise, we'll add font properties to the Black Goose Bistro menu document, *menu-summer.html*, that you marked up back in Chapter 5. A fresh and validated copy, complete with DOCTYPE declaration, is available at *www.learningwebdesign. com/materials*. Open the document in a text editor. You can also open it in a browser to see its "before" state. It should look similar to the page shown in Figure 12-1. Hang onto this document, because this exercise will continue as we pick up additional font properties.

1. We're going to use an embedded style sheet for this exercise. Start by adding a **style** element with its required **type** attribute to the **head** of the document (remember, the only place a **style** element can go is in the **head**), like this:

```
<head>
  <title>Black Goose Bistro</title>
  <style type="text/css">

  </style>
</head>
```

NOTE

If your browser is configured to use Verdana or a sans-serif font as its default font, you won't see much of a change after adding this rule. Hang in there, more changes are to come.

CSS Units of Measurement

CSS2 provides a variety of units of measurement. They fall into two broad categories: absolute and relative.

Absolute units

Absolute units have predefined meanings or real-world equivalents.

pt points (1/72 inch in CSS2.1)

pc picas (1 pica = 12 points)

mm millimeters

cm centimeters

in inches

Absolute units should be avoided for web page style sheets because they are not relevant on computer screens. However, if you are creating a style sheet to be used when the document is printed, they may be just the ticket.

Relative units

Relative units are based on the size of something else, such as the default text size, or the size of the parent element.

em a unit of measurement equal to the current font size.

ex approximately the height of a lowercase "x" in the font.

px pixel, considered relative because it varies with display resolution, particularly between low resolution screens and high resolution print output.

% percentage values, although not a unit of measurement, are another way to specify relative size.

It is recommended that you stick with ems, percentage values, or a combination of the two when specifying text size.

2. I would like all the text on the page to appear in Verdana or some other sans-serif font. Instead of writing a rule for every element in the document, we will write one rule for the **body** element that will be inherited by all the elements it contains. Add this rule to the embedded style sheet.

```
<style type="text/css">
  body {font-family: Verdana, sans-serif;}
</style>
```

Save the document and reload the page in the browser. It should look like Figure 12-3. We'll work on the font size in the next installment.

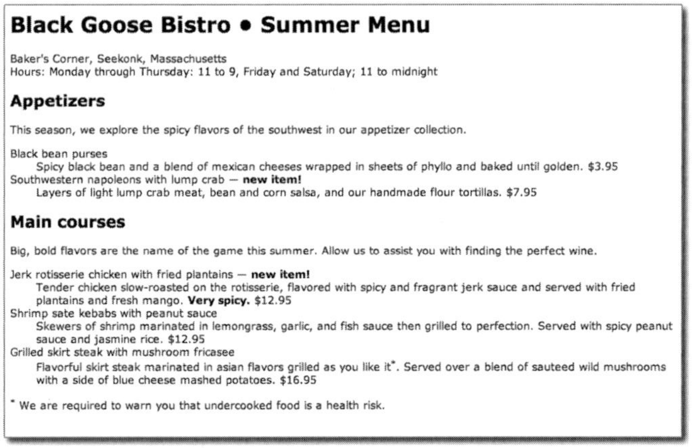

Black Goose Bistro • Summer Menu

Baker's Corner, Seekonk, Massachusetts
Hours: Monday through Thursday: 11 to 9, Friday and Saturday; 11 to midnight

Appetizers

This season, we explore the spicy flavors of the southwest in our appetizer collection.

Black bean purses
    Spicy black bean and a blend of mexican cheeses wrapped in sheets of phyllo and baked until golden. $3.95
Southwestern napoleons with lump crab — **new item!**
    Layers of light lump crab meat, bean and corn salsa, and our handmade flour tortillas. $7.95

Main courses

Big, bold flavors are the name of the game this summer. Allow us to assist you with finding the perfect wine.

Jerk rotisserie chicken with fried plantains — **new item!**
    Tender chicken slow-roasted on the rotisserie, flavored with spicy and fragrant jerk sauce and served with fried
    plantains and fresh mango. **Very spicy.** $12.95
Shrimp sate kebabs with peanut sauce
    Skewers of shrimp marinated in lemongrass, garlic, and fish sauce then grilled to perfection. Served with spicy peanut
    sauce and jasmine rice. $12.95
Grilled skirt steak with mushroom fricasee
    Flavorful skirt steak marinated in asian flavors grilled as you like it*. Served over a blend of sauteed wild mushrooms
    with a side of blue cheese mashed potatoes. $16.95

* We are required to warn you that undercooked food is a health risk.

Figure 12-3. The menu in the Verdana or sans-serif font.

Specifying font size

Use the aptly-named font-size property to specify the size of the text.

font-size

Values: length unit | percentage | xx-small | x-small | small | medium | large | x-large | xx-large | smaller | larger | inherit

Default: medium

Applies to: all elements

Inherits: yes

You can specify text size in several ways:

- At a specific size using one of the CSS length units (see the sidebar, CSS Units of Measurement, for a complete list), as shown here:

      h1 { font-size: 1.5em; }

When specifying a number of units, be sure the unit abbreviation immediately follows the number, with no extra character space in between:

INCORRECT h1 { font-size: 1.5 em; } /*space before the em*/

- As a percentage value, sized up or down from the element's default or inherited font size:

      h1 { font-size: 150%; }

- Using one of the absolute keywords (xx-small, x-small, small, medium, large, x-large, xx-large). On most current browsers, medium corresponds to the default font size:

      h1 { font-size: x-large; }

- Using a relative keyword (larger or smaller) to nudge the text larger or smaller than the surrounding text:

      strong { font-size: larger; }

I'm going to cut to the chase and tell you that, despite all these options, the only acceptable values for font-size in contemporary web design are em measurements, percentage values, and keywords. These are preferred because they allow users to resize text using the text-zoom feature on their browser. This means you can size the text as you prefer it (generally smaller than the most common default 16 pixel text), but still rest assured that users can make it larger if they have special needs or preferences.

While it may be tempting to specify text in actual pixel measurements, Internet Explorer (all versions) does not allow text-zoom on type sized in pixels. That means users are stuck with your 10 or 11 pixel type, even if they are unable to read it. That's a big no-no in terms of accessibility. In addition, all of the absolute units such as pt, pc, in, mm, and cm are out because they are irrelevant on computer monitors (although they may be useful for print style sheets).

Working with keywords

Many web designers like to specify type size using one of the predefined absolute keywords: xx-small, x-small, small, medium, large, x-large, xx-large. The keywords do not correspond to particular measurements, but rather are scaled consistently in relation to one another. The default size is medium in current browsers. Figure 12-4 shows how each of the absolute keywords renders in a browser when the default text is set at 16 pixels. I've included samples in Verdana and Times to show that, even with the same base size, there is a big difference in legibility at sizes small and below.

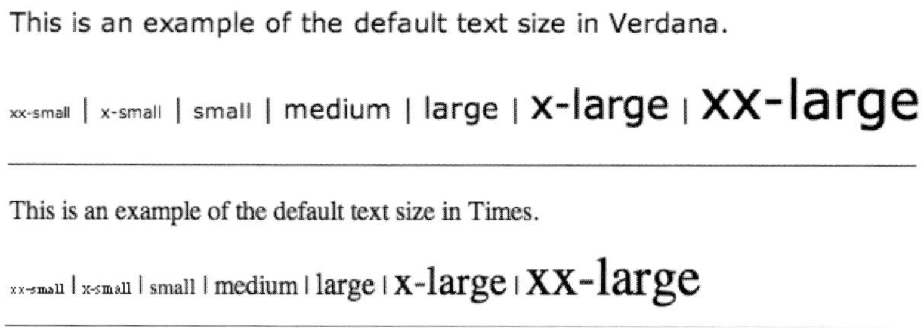

This is an example of the default text size in Verdana.

xx-small | x-small | small | medium | large | x-large | xx-large

This is an example of the default text size in Times.

xx-small | x-small | small | medium | large | x-large | xx-large

Figure 12-4. Text sized with absolute keywords.

The benefit of keywords is that current browsers in Standards Mode will never let text sized in keywords render smaller than 9 pixels, so they protect against illegible type (although I would still opt for Verdana for better readability).

On the downside, the size keywords are imprecise and unpredictable. For example, while most browsers scale each level up by 120%, some browsers use a scaling factor of 150%. Another notable problem is that Internet Explorer 5 and 5.5 for Windows use `small` as the default (not `medium`), meaning your text will display a lot smaller for users with those browsers. Fortunately, with the introduction of IE 7, these old versions are slowly going away.

The relative keywords, `larger` and `smaller`, are used to shift the size of text relative to the size of the parent element text. The exact amount of the size change is determined by each browser, and is out of your control. Despite that limitation, it is an easy way to nudge type a bit larger or smaller if the exact proportions are not critical.

Figure 12-5 shows the result of this simple bit of markup (note that the inline styles were used just to keep the example compact).

```
<p>There are two relative keywords:
 <span style="font-size: larger">larger</span> and
 <span style="font-size: smaller">smaller</span>. They are used to
shift the size of text relative to the parent element.</p>
```

There are two relative keywords: larger and smaller. They are used to shift the size of text relative to the parent element.

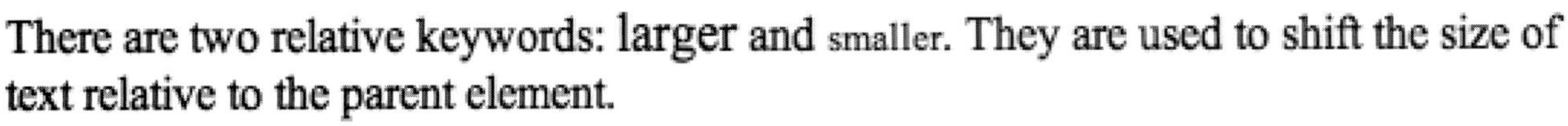

Figure 12-5. Relative size keywords make text slightly larger or smaller than the surrounding text.

Working with percentages and ems

By far the most popular way to specify font sizes for the Web is using em measurements or percentage values, or a combination of the two. Both ems and percentages are relative measurements, which means they are based on another font size, namely, the `font-size` of the parent element.

NOTE

Don't confuse the em unit of measurement with the em *(X)HTML element used to indicate emphasized text. They are totally different things.*

In this example, the `font-size` of the h1's parent element (`body`) is 16 pixels, so the resulting size of the h1 would be 150% of that, or 24 pixels.

```
body { font-size: 16px; }
h1 { font-size: 150%; }  /* 150% of 16 = 24 */
```

If no `font-size` properties have been specified, relative measurements are based on the browser's base font size, which is 16 pixels in most browsers. Of course, users can resize their base font as small or as large as they like, so there is no guaranteed starting size, only a reasonable guess.

An em is a relative unit of measurement that, in traditional typography, is based on the width of the capital letter M (thus, the name "em"). In the CSS specification, an em is calculated as the distance between baselines when the font is set without any extra space between the lines (also known as leading). For text with a font size of 16 pixels, an em measures 16 pixels; for 12 pixel text, an em equals 12 pixels, and so on, as shown in Figure 12-6.

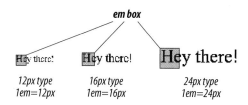

Figure 12-6. An em is based on the size of the text.

Once the dimensions of an em for a text element is calculated by the browser, it can be used for all sorts of measurements, such as indents, margins, the width of the element on the page, and so on.

For text sizing, an em value works like a scaling factor, similar to a percentage. As in the previous example, if the base font size is 16 pixels, giving `h1` elements a `font-size` of 1.5 ems makes them 24 pixels high.

```
body { font-size: 16px; }
h1 { font-size: 1.5em; }   /* 1.5 x 16 = 24 */
```

For the most part, ems and percentages can be used interchangeably when specifying type size. It's mostly a matter of preference.

There are a few snags to working with ems. One is that due to rounding errors, there is a lot of inconsistency among browsers and platforms when text size is set in fractions of an em. There are also documented problems in Internet Explorer when `font-size` is specified at sizes smaller than 1em. It is safest to use ems to scale text larger.

For both ems and percentages, there is the lingering issue of not knowing the base font size. We are left with best guesses, and the assumption that users probably have their default font size set to a size that is comfortable to read, and we probably shouldn't muck around with it too much. There is much more to the font size story. The Font Sizing Techniques sidebar lists some good resources for further research.

NOTE

Although I've set the size of the `body` *text in pixels in the previous two examples for explanation purposes, you wouldn't want to do that in the real world because the text could not be zoomed in Internet Explorer.*

In the meantime, we can add some `font-size` properties to the sample menu in the continuation of Exercise 12-1.

Font Sizing Techniques

Sizing type for web pages is problematic and the subject of much debate even among seasoned web designers.

One popular method for sizing text is to make the text slightly smaller globally (using the `body` element) with a percentage value, then size all the elements *up* as appropriate using em measurements. The following articles provide slightly different takes on that method.

- *How to Size Text Using Ems*, by Richard Rutter (*www.clagnut.com/blog/348*) is a detailed how-to that makes em increments easy to use. The comments to this blog entry are also informative and give good insight into the varying opinions on how web text should be sized.

- Owen Briggs' article on *Text Sizing* is the result of exhaustive cross-browser testing. Hundreds of screenshots are available if you want the proof. This article is a little dated, but still brings up relevant issues. Read it at *www.thenoodleincident.com/tutorials/box_lesson/font/index.html*.

If keywords are vexing you, read Todd Fahrner's classic article, *CSS Design: Size Matters* on *A List Apart* (*www.alistapart.com/articles/sizematters/*). It is a little dated (for example, support in Netscape 4 figures prominently), but it provides some useful background information and workarounds.

exercise 12-1 | **Formatting a menu (continued)**

Let's refine the size of some of the text elements to give the online menu a more sophisticated appearance. Open *menu_summer.html* in a text editor and follow the steps below. You can save the document at any point and take a peek in the browser to see the results of your work. You should also feel free to try out other size values along the way.

1. I would prefer that the body text for the document appear smaller than the common 16 pixel default. I am going to set the size of the **body** to `small`, which renders at approximately 12 pixels on most current browsers. If it ends up too small for some users, they can always zoom the text up, since it was specified with a keyword. Insert the new declaration to the body rule we've already created.

   ```
   body { font-family: Verdana, sans-serif; font-size: small; }
   ```

2. Now let's get that giant **h1** under control. I'm going to make it one and a half times larger than the **body** text size with an em measurement. I could also use font-size: 150% to accomplish the same thing.

   ```
   h1 { font-size: 1.5em; }
   ```

Figure 12-7 shows the result of our font sizing efforts.

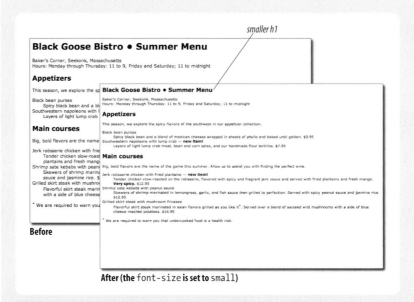

Figure 12-7. The online menu after a few minor font-size changes.

I want to point out that at this point, I don't really know exactly how many pixels tall the **h1**s will be for every user. They're likely to be 18 pixels, but they may be smaller or much larger. The important part is that I've set my desired proportion of **h1** elements to the surrounding text. If the user resizes or zooms the text, that proportion stays the same.

Font weight (boldness)

After font families and size, the remaining font properties are straightforward. For example, if you want a text element to appear in bold, use the `font-weight` property to adjust the boldness of type.

font-weight

Values: normal|bold|bolder|lighter|100|200|300|400|500|600|700|800|900|inherit

Default: normal

Applies to: all elements

Inherits: yes

As you can see, the `font-weight` property has many predefined values, including descriptive terms (`normal`, `bold`, `bolder`, and `lighter`) and nine numeric values (`100` to `900`) for targeting various weights of a font if they are available. Because most fonts common on the Web have only two weights, normal (or roman) and bold, the only font weight value you will use in most cases is `bold`. You may also use `normal` to make text that would otherwise appear in bold (such as strong text or headlines) appear at a normal weight.

The numeric chart is an interesting idea, but because there aren't many fonts with that range of weights and because browser support is spotty, they are not often used. In general, numeric settings of 600 and higher result in bold text, although even that can vary by browser, as shown in Figure 12-8.

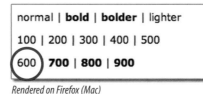

Rendered on Safari   Rendered on Firefox (Mac)

Figure 12-8. *The effect of* font-weight *values.*

About inherit

You will see that CSS properties include `inherit` in their list of keyword values. The `inherit` value allows you to explicitly force an element to inherit a style property value from its parent. This may come in handy to override other styles applied to that element and to guarantee that the element always matches its parent.

---

exercise 12-1 | **Formatting a menu (continued)**

Back to the menu. I've decided that I'd like all of the menu item names to be in bold text. What I'm *not* going to do is wrap each one in **<b>** tags... that would be so 1996! I'm also not going mark them up as **strong** elements... that is not semantically accurate. Instead, the right thing to do is simply apply a style to the semantically correct **dt** (definition term) elements to make them all bold at once. Add this rule to your style sheet, save the file, and try it out in the browser (Figure 12-9).

    dt { font-weight: bold; }

Figure 12-9. Applying the font-weight *property to* dt *elements in the menu.*

Font style (italics)

The font-style property affects the posture of the text, that is, whether the letter shapes are vertical (normal) or slanted (italic and oblique).

font-style

Values: normal|italic|oblique|inherit

Default: normal

Applies to: all elements

Inherits: yes

Italic and oblique are both slanted versions of the font. The difference is that the italic version is usually a separate typeface design with curved letter forms, while oblique text takes the normal font design and just slants it. The truth is that in most browsers, they may look exactly the same (see Figure 12-10). You'll probably only use the font-style property to make text italic or to make text that is italicized by default (such as emphasized text) display as normal.

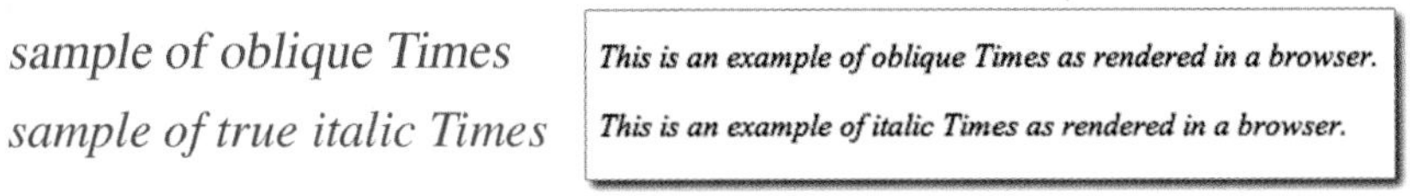

Figure 12-10. Italic and oblique text.

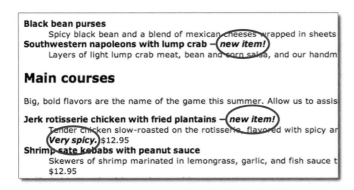

Figure 12-11. *Applying the* font-style *property to the* strong *elements.*

exercise 12-1 |
Formatting a menu (continued)

Now that all the menu item names are bold, some of the text I've marked as **strong** isn't standing out very well, so I think I'll make them italic for further emphasis. To do this, simply apply the **font-style** property to the **strong** element.

    strong { font-style: italic;
    }

Once again, save and reload. It should look like the detail shown in Figure 12-11.

Font Variant (Small Caps)

Some typefaces come in a "small caps" variant. This is a separate font design that uses small uppercase-style letters in place of lowercase letter designs. The one-trick-pony font-variant property is intended to allow designers to specify such a small-caps font for text elements.

font-variant

Values:	normal|small-caps|inherit
Default:	normal
Applies to:	all elements
Inherits:	yes

In most cases, a true small caps font is not available, so browsers simulate small caps by scaling down uppercase letters in the current font, as you'll see when we add some small caps text to the menu next. To typography sticklers, this is less than ideal and results in inconsistent stroke weights, but you may find it an acceptable option for adding variety to small amounts of text.

h1 in small caps

BLACK GOOSE BISTRO • SUMMER MENU

Baker's Corner, Seekonk, Massachusetts
Hours: Monday through Thursday: 11 to 9, Friday and Saturday; 11 to midnight

Figure 12-12. *Using* font-variant *for small caps.*

exercise 12-1 |
Formatting a menu (continued)

Just for kicks, let's set the first level heading (**h1**) in small caps so we can try out this **font-variant** property. Remember that you can add this property to the existing **h1** rule. The result is shown in Figure 12-12. If you find it kind of clunky, don't worry, we'll be undoing it later.

    h1 {
        font-size: 1.5em;
        font-variant: small-caps;
    }

The shortcut font property

Specifying multiple font properties for each text element could get repetitive and lengthy, so the creators of CSS provided the shorthand `font` property that compiles all the font-related properties into one rule.

font

Values: *font-style font-weight font-variant font-size/line-height font-family (see also values in System Fonts sidebar)* | *inherit*

Default: *depends on default value for each property listed*

Applies to: *all elements*

Inherits: *yes*

The value of the `font` property is a list of values for all the font properties we just looked at, separated by character spaces. In this property, the order of the values is important:

```
{ font: style weight variant size/line-height font-family }
```

At minimum, the `font` property *must* include a `font-size` value and a `font-family` value, in that order. Omitting one or putting them in the wrong order causes the entire rule to be invalid. This is an example of a minimal font property value:

```
p { font: 1em sans-serif; }
```

Once you've met the size and family requirements, the other values are optional and may appear in any order *prior* to the `font-size`. When style, weight, or variant are omitted, they will revert back to `normal`. There is one value in there, `line-height`, that we have not seen before. As it sounds, it adjusts the height of the text line from baseline to baseline. It appears just after `font-size`, separated by a slash, as shown in these examples.

```
h3 { font: oblique bold small-caps 1.5em/1.8em Verdana, Arial,
sans-serif; }
```

```
h2 { font: bold 1.75em/2 sans-serif; }
```

Let's use the shorthand `font` property to make some changes to the h2 headings.

System Fonts

The `font` property also allows designers to specify fonts from the operating system of the user's computer or other viewing device. This may be useful when designing a web application that blends in with the surrounding desktop environment. The system font values for the `font` property are:

`caption`
used for captioned controls (buttons, menus, etc.)

`icon`
used to label icons

`menu`
used in drop-down menus and menu lists

`message-box`
used in dialog boxes

`small-caption`
used for labeling small controls

`status-bar`
used in window status bars

exercise 12-1 | **Formatting a menu (continued)**

One last tweak to the menu, then we'll take a brief break. I want the **h2** headings to be in a bold, Georgia (serif) typeface to stand out from the surrounding text. I also want it to be 1.2 times larger than the **body** font. Instead of writing out three declarations, we'll combine them in one shorthand font property. Add this rule to the style sheet, save your work, and take another look in the browser (Figure 12-13). Notice that the **font-size** and **font-family** are next to one another and are the last things in the list of values.

```
h2 { font: bold 1.2em Georgia, serif; }
```

You might find it redundant that I included the **bold** font-weight value in this rule. After all, the **h2** elements were already bold, right? The thing about shorthand properties is that if you omit a value, it is reset to the default value for that property; it doesn't just leave it the way it was before. In this case, the default value for **font-weight** is **normal**. Because a style sheet rule we've written overrides the browser's default bold rendering of headings, the **h2**s would appear in normal weight text if we don't explicitly make them **bold** in the **font** property. Shorthand properties can be tricky that way... pay attention that you don't leave something out and override a default or inherited value you were counting on.

h2 before

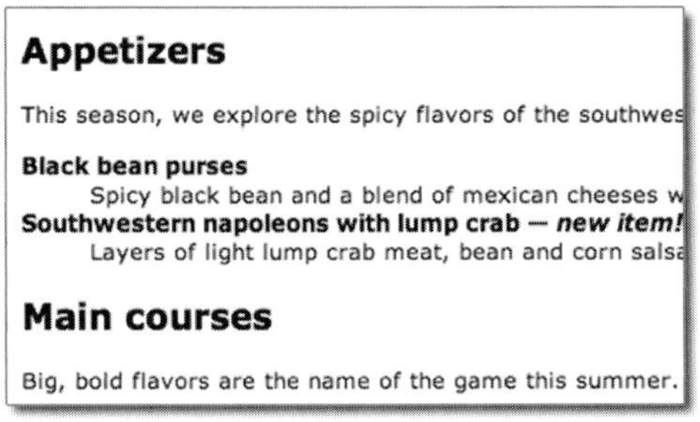

Appetizers

This season, we explore the spicy flavors of the southwes

Black bean purses
    Spicy black bean and a blend of mexican cheeses w
Southwestern napoleons with lump crab — *new item!*
    Layers of light lump crab meat, bean and corn salsa

Main courses

Big, bold flavors are the name of the game this summer.

h2 after {font: bold 1.2em Georgia, serif;}

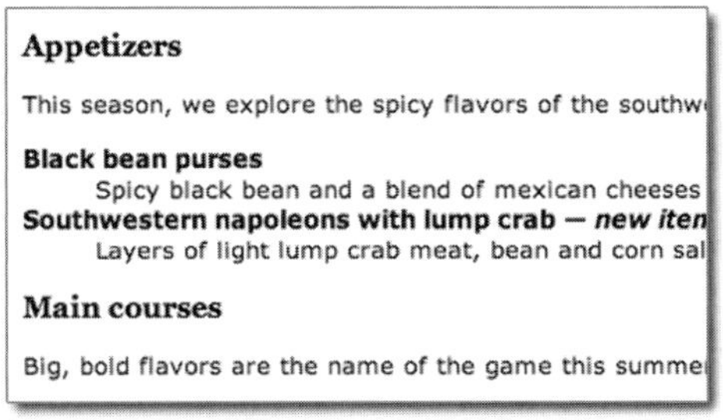

Appetizers

This season, we explore the spicy flavors of the southw

Black bean purses
    Spicy black bean and a blend of mexican cheeses
Southwestern napoleons with lump crab — *new iten*
    Layers of light lump crab meat, bean and corn sal

Main courses

Big, bold flavors are the name of the game this summe

Figure 12-13. Changing multiple properties for h2 *elements with the shorthand* font *property*

Changing Text Color

You got a glimpse of how to change text color in Chapter 11, and to be honest, there's not a lot more to say about it here. You change the color of text with the color property.

color

Values:	*color value (name or numeric)* | inherit
Default:	*depends on the browser and user's preferences*
Applies to:	*all elements*
Inherits:	*yes*

Using the color property is very straightforward. The value of the color property can be one of 17 predefined color names or a numeric value describing a specific RGB color. Here are a few examples, all of which make the h1 elements in a document gray:

```
h1 { color: gray; }

h1 { color: #666666; }

h1 { color: #666; }
```

Don't worry about the numeric values for now—I just wanted you to see what they look like. RGB color is discussed in detail in Chapter 13, Colors and Backgrounds, so in this chapter, we'll just stick with the fairly limited list of color names (see sidebar) for demonstration purposes.

Color is inherited, so you could change the color of all the text in a document by applying the color property to the body element, as shown here:

```
body { color: fuchsia; }
```

OK, so you probably wouldn't want all your text to be fuchsia, but you get the idea.

AT A GLANCE

Color Names

The 17 standard color names defined in CSS2.1:

black	silver	gray
white	maroon	red
purple	fuchsia	green
lime	olive	yellow
navy	blue	teal
aqua	orange (*2.1 only*)	

For the sake of accuracy, I want to point out that the color property is not strictly a text-related property. In fact, according to the CSS specification, it is used to change the foreground (as opposed to the background) color of an element. The foreground of an element consists of both the text it contains as well as its border.

When you apply a color to an element (including image elements), that color will be used for the border as well, unless there is a specific border-color property that overrides it. We'll talk more about borders and border color in Chapter 14, Thinking Inside the Box.

Before we add color to the online menu, I want to take a little side trip and introduce you to a few more types of selectors that will give us much more flexibility in targeting elements in the document for styling.

A Few More Selector Types

So far, we've been using element names as selectors. In the last chapter, you saw how selectors can be grouped together in a comma-separated list so you can apply properties to several elements at once. Here are examples of the selectors you already know.

element selector	`p { color: navy; }`
grouped selectors	`p, ul, p, td, th { color: navy; }`

The disadvantage of selecting elements this way, of course, is that the property (in this case, navy blue text) will apply to every paragraph and other listed elements in the document. Sometimes, you want to apply a rule to a particular paragraph or paragraphs. In this section, we'll look at three selector types that allow us to do just that: descendant selectors, ID selectors, and class selectors.

Descendant selectors

A character space between element names means that the second element must be contained within the first.

A descendant selector targets elements that are contained within (therefore descendants of) another element. It is an example of a contextual selector, because it selects the element based on its context or relation to another element. The sidebar, Other Contextual Selectors, lists some more.

Descendant selectors are indicated in a list separated by a character space. This example targets emphasized text (em) elements, but *only* when they appear in list items (li). Emphasized text in paragraphs and other elements would be unaffected (Figure 12-14).

    li em { color: olive; }

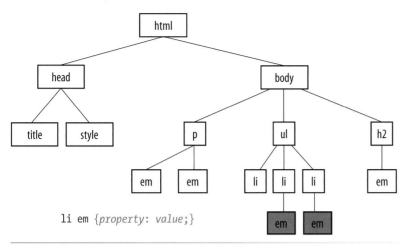

$$li\ em\ \{property:\ value;\}$$

Figure 12-14. Only em elements within li elements are selected. The other em elements are unaffected.

Here's another example that shows how contextual selectors can be grouped in a comma-separated list, just as we saw earlier. This rule targets em elements, but only when they appear in h1, h2, and h3 headings.

```
h1 em, h2 em, h3 em { color: red; }
```

It is also possible to nest descendant selectors several layers deep. This example targets em elements that appear in anchors (a) in ordered lists (ol).

```
ol a em { font-variant: small-caps; }
```

ID selectors

Way back in Chapter 5, Marking Up Text, we learned about the id attribute that gives an element a unique identifying name (its id reference). The id attribute can be used with any (X)HTML element, and it is commonly used to give meaning to the generic div and span elements. (We also saw it used in Chapter 6, Adding Links to create document fragments and in Chapter 9, Forms to associate a text label with its respective form control.)

ID selectors allow you to target elements by their id values. The symbol that identifies ID selectors is the octothorpe (#), also called a hash symbol.

Here is an example of a list item with an id reference.

```
<li id="catalog1234">Happy Face T-shirt</li>
```

Now you can write a style rule just for that list item using an ID selector, like so (notice the # preceding the id reference):

```
li#catalog1234 { color: red; }
```

Because id values must be unique in the document, it is acceptable to omit the element name. This rule is equivalent to the last one:

```
#catalog1234 { color: red; }
```

Other Contextual Selectors

Descendant selectors are one of three types of contextual selectors. The other two, child selectors and adjacent sibling selectors, are defined in CSS2.1 but unfortunately, are not supported in Internet Explorer 6 and earlier. They are supported in IE7.

A child selector is similar to a descendant selector, but it targets only the direct children of a given element (there may be no other hierarchical levels in between). They are indicated with the greater than symbol (>). This rule affects emphasized text, but only when it is directly contained in a p element. The em elements in other elements, such as list items (li) or anchors (a) would not be affected.

```
p > em {font-weight: bold; }
```

An adjacent sibling selector is used to target an element that comes directly after another element with the same parent. It is indicated with a plus (+) sign. This rule gives special treatment just to paragraphs that follow an h1. Other paragraphs are unaffected.

```
h1 + p {font-style: italic;}
```

The # symbol identifies an ID selector.

REMINDER

ID values must start with a letter (A-Z or a-z). In addition to letters, the name may contain digits (0-9), hyphens (-), underscores (_), colons (:), and periods (.).

You can also use an ID selector as part of a contextual selector. In this example, a style is applied only to li elements that appear within any element identified as "sidebar." In this way, you can treat list items in the sidebar differently than all the other list items on the page without any additional markup.

```
#sidebar li { margin-left: 10px; }
```

You should be beginning to see the power of selectors and how they can be used strategically along with well-planned, semantic markup.

Class selectors

The period (.) symbol indicates a class selector.

One last selector type, then we can get back to text style properties. The other element identifier you learned about in Chapter 5 is the $class$ identifier, used to classify elements into a conceptual group. Unlike the id attribute, multiple elements may share a $class$ name. Not only that, an element may belong to more than one class.

You can target elements belonging to the same class with, you guessed it, a class selector. Class names are indicated with a period (.) in the selector. For example, to select all paragraphs with $class="special"$, use this selector (the period indicates the following word is a class selector):

```
p.special { color: orange; }
```

To apply a property to *all* elements of the same class, omit the element name in the selector (be sure to leave the period; it's the character that indicates a class). This would target all paragraphs and any other element that has been marked up with $class="special"$.

```
.special { color: orange; }
```

Specificity 101

In Chapter 11, I introduced you to the term specificity, which refers to the fact that more specific selectors have more weight when it comes to handling style rule conflicts. Now that you know a few more selectors, it is a good time to revisit this very important concept.

The actual system CSS uses for calculating selector specificity is quite complicated, but this list of selector types from most to least specific should serve you well in most scenarios.

- **ID selectors** are more specific than (and will override)
- **Class selectors**, which are more specific than (and will override)
- **Contextual selectors**, which are more specific than (and will override)
- **Individual element selectors**

So, for example, if a style sheet has two conflicting rules for the $strong$ element,

```
strong { color: red;}
h1 strong { color: blue; }
```

CSS TIP

Try using a contextual (descendant) selector before adding unnecessary $class$ attributes to your markup. It will keep your markup simple and your style sheet streamlined. To read more, see Tantek Çelik's blog post, Context before Class, at *tantek.com/log/2002/12.html#atoc_cbeforec*. It is a few years old, but still relevant.

The Universal Selector

CSS2 introduced a universal element selector (*) that matches any element (like a wildcard in programming languages). The style rule

```
* {color: gray; }
```

makes every element in a document gray. It is also useful as a contextual selector, as shown in this example that selects all elements in an intro section:

```
#intro * { color: gray; }
```

The universal selector causes problems with form controls in some browsers. If your page contains form inputs, the safest bet is to avoid the universal selector.

the contextual selector (`h1 strong`) is more specific and therefore has more weight than the element selector.

You can use specificity strategically to keep your style sheets simple and your markup minimal. For example, it is possible to set a style for an element (`p`, in this example), then override when necessary by using more specific selectors.

```
p { line-height: 1.2em; }
blockquote p { line-height: 1em; }
p.intro { line-height: 2em; }
```

In these examples, `p` elements that appear within a `blockquote` have a smaller line height than ordinary paragraphs. However, all paragraphs with a `class` of "intro" will have a 2em line height, even if it appears within a blockquote, because class selectors are more specific than contextual selectors.

Understanding the concepts of inheritance and specificity are critical to mastering CSS. There is a lot more to be said about specificity, including a tutorial by Andy Clarke that uses a Star Wars analogy to bring the point home. References are provided in the More About Specificity sidebar.

Now, back to the menu. Fortunately, our Black Goose Bistro has been marked up thoroughly and semantically, so we have a lot of options for selecting specific elements. Give these new selectors a try in Exercise 12-2.

More About Specificity

The specificity overview in this chapter is enough to get you started, but when you get more experienced and your style sheets become more complicated, you may find that you need a more thorough understanding of the inner workings.

For the very technical explanation of exactly how specificity is calculated, see the CSS Recommendation at *www.w3.org/TR/CSS21cascade. html#specificity*.

Eric Meyer provides a thorough, yet more digestible, description of this system in his book, *Cascading Style Sheets, The Definitive Guide, 2nd Edition* (O'Reilly Media).

I also recommend the online article, *CSS: Specificity Wars*, by Andy Clarke which explains specificity in terms of "Sith power" using characters from Star Wars (*www. stuffandnonsense.co.uk/archives/ css_specificity_wars.html*). He also provides a list of links to further specificity resources.

exercise 12-2 | **Using selectors**

This time, we'll add a few more style rules using descendant, ID, and class selectors combined with the font and color properties we've learned about so far.

1. I'd like to add some color to the "new item!" elements next to certain menu item names. They are marked up as **strong**, so we can apply the color property to the **strong** element. Add this rule to the embedded style sheet, save the file, and reload it in the browser.

   ```
   strong { color: maroon; }
   ```

   That worked, but now the **strong** element "Very spicy" in the description is maroon, too, and that's not what I want. The solution is to use a contextual selector that targets only the **strong** elements that appear in **dt** elements. Try this and take a look.

   ```
   dt strong { color: maroon; }
   ```

2. Look at the document source and you will see that the content has been divided into three unique **div**s: **header**, **appetizers**, and **entrees**. We can use these to our advantage when it comes to styling. For now, let's do something simple and make all the text in the **header** teal. Because color inherits, we only need to apply the property to the **div** and it will be passed down to the **h1** and **p**.

   ```
   #header { color: teal; }
   ```

3. Now let's get a little fancier and make the paragraph inside the header italic in a way that doesn't affect the other paragraphs on the page. Again, a contextual selector is the answer. This rule selects only paragraphs contained within the **header** section of the document.

   ```
   #header p { font-style: italic; }
   ```

4. I want to give special treatment to all of the prices on the menu. Fortunately, they have all been marked up with **span** elements, like this:

```
<span class="price">$3.95</span>
```

So now all we have to do is write a rule using a class selector to change the font to Georgia or some serif font and make them italic.

```
.price {
   font-style: italic;
   font-family: Georgia, serif;
}
```

5. Similarly, I can change the appearance of the text in the header that has been marked up as belonging to the "label" class to make them stand out.

```
.label {
   font-weight: bold;
   font-variant: small-caps;
   font-style: normal;
}
```

6. Finally, there is a footnote at the bottom of the page that I want to make small and red. It has been given the class "warning," so I can use that as a selector to target just that paragraph for styling.

```
p.footnote, {
   font-size: x-small;
   color: red;
}
```

Figure 12-15 shows the results of all these changes.

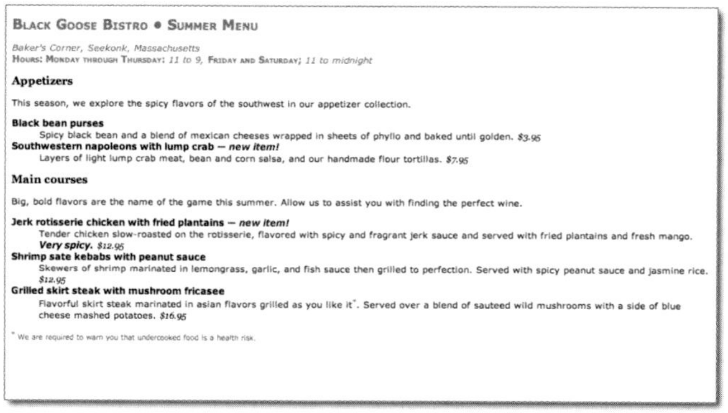

BLACK GOOSE BISTRO • SUMMER MENU

Baker's Corner, Seekonk, Massachusetts
HOURS: MONDAY through THURSDAY: 11 to 9, FRIDAY AND SATURDAY: 11 to midnight

Appetizers

This season, we explore the spicy flavors of the southwest in our appetizer collection.

Black bean purses
Spicy black bean and a blend of mexican cheeses wrapped in sheets of phyllo and baked until golden. *$3.95*
Southwestern napoleons with lump crab — *new item!*
Layers of light lump crab meat, bean and corn salsa, and our handmade flour tortillas. *$7.95*

Main courses

Big, bold flavors are the name of the game this summer. Allow us to assist you with finding the perfect wine.

Jerk rotisserie chicken with fried plantains — *new item!*
Tender chicken slow-roasted on the rotisserie, flavored with spicy and fragrant jerk sauce and served with fried plantains and fresh mango. ***Very spicy.*** *$12.95*
Shrimp sate kebabs with peanut sauce
Skewers of shrimp marinated in lemongrass, garlic, and fish sauce then grilled to perfection. Served with spicy peanut sauce and jasmine rice. *$12.95*
Grilled skirt steak with mushroom fricasee
Flavorful skirt steak marinated in asian flavors grilled as you like it*. Served over a blend of sauteed wild mushrooms with a side of blue cheese mashed potatoes. *$16.95*

* We are required to warn you that undercooked food is a health risk.

Figure 12-15. The current state of the Black Goose Bistro online menu.

Text Line Adjustments

The next batch of text properties has to do with the treatment of whole lines of text rather than the shapes of characters. They allow web authors to format web text with indents, extra leading (space between lines), and different horizontal alignments, similar to print.

Line height

The `line-height` property defines the minimum distance from baseline to baseline in text. A baseline is the imaginary line upon which the bottoms of characters sit. Line height in CSS is similar to leading in traditional typesetting. Although the line height is calculated from baseline to baseline, most browsers split the extra space above and below the text, thus centering it in the overall line height (Figure 12-16).

The `line-height` property is said to specify a "minimum" distance because if you put a tall image on a line, the height of that line will expand to accommodate it.

`line-height`

Values:	number | length measurement | percentage | normal | inherit
Default:	normal
Applies to:	all elements
Inherits:	yes

These examples show three different ways of making the line height twice the height of the font size.

```
p { line-height: 2; }

p { line-height: 2em; }

p { line-height: 200%; }
```

When a number is specified alone, as shown in the first example, it acts as a scaling factor that is multiplied by the current font size to calculate the line-height value. Line heights can also be specified in one of the CSS length units, but once again, the relative em unit is your best bet. Ems and percentage values are based on the current font size. In the three examples, if the text size is 16 pixels, the calculated line height would be 32 pixels (see Figure 12-16).

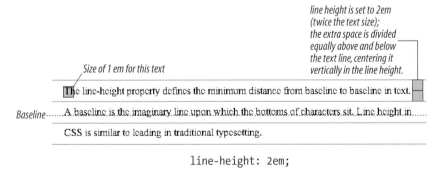

Figure 12-16. *In CSS, line height is measured from baseline to baseline, but browsers center the text vertically in the line height.*

WARNING

There is a bug in Internet Explorer 6 and earlier that causes line height to get screwy when the element contains an inline image (or other replaced element). For details, see positioniseverything.net/explorer/lineheightbug.html.

Indents

The `text-indent` property indents the first line of text by a specified amount (see note).

NOTE

The `text-indent` *property indents just the first line of a block. If you want space along the whole side of the text block, use one of the* `margin` *or* `padding` *properties to add it.*

Designers may be accustomed to specifying indents and margins in tandem, but to be consistent with how CSS handles them, margins will be discussed as part of the box model in Chapter 16.

`text-indent`

Values:	*length measurement | percentage* | inherit
Default:	0
Applies to:	*block-level elements, table cells, and inline blocks*
Inherits:	*yes*

You can specify a length measurement or a percentage value for `text-indent`. Percentage values are calculated based on the width of the *parent* element. Here are a few examples. The results are shown in Figure 12-17.

```
p#1 { text-indent: 2em; }

p#2 { text-indent: 25%; }

p#3 { text-indent: -35px; }
```

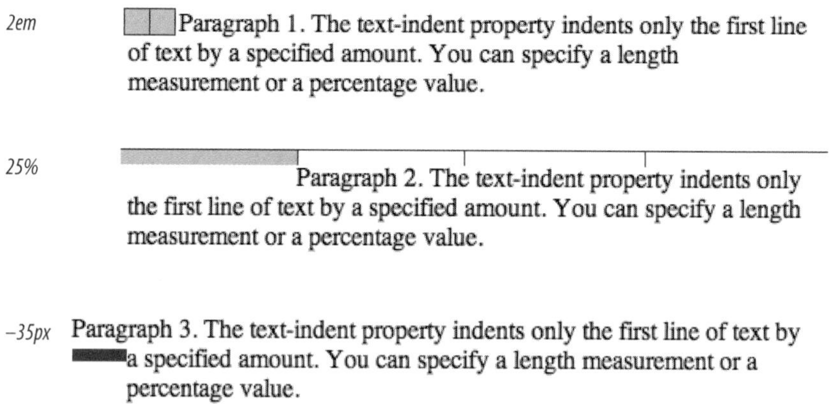

2em Paragraph 1. The text-indent property indents only the first line of text by a specified amount. You can specify a length measurement or a percentage value.

25% Paragraph 2. The text-indent property indents only the first line of text by a specified amount. You can specify a length measurement or a percentage value.

–35px Paragraph 3. The text-indent property indents only the first line of text by a specified amount. You can specify a length measurement or a percentage value.

Figure 12-17. Examples of the `text-indent` *property.*

DESIGN TIP

If you use a hanging indent, be sure that there is also a left margin applied to the element. Otherwise, the hanging text may disappear off the left edge of the browser window.

Notice in the third example, a negative value was specified and that's just fine. It will cause the first line of text to hang out to the left of the left text edge (also called a hanging indent).

The `text-indent` property inherits, but it is worth noting that the calculated values will be passed on to descendant elements. So if a `div` is set to 800 pixels wide with a 10% indent, a `text-indent` of 80 pixels will be passed down (not the 10% value).

Horizontal Alignment

You can align text for web pages just as you would in a word processing or desktop publishing program with the `text-align` property.

text-align

Values: left | right | center | justify | inherit

Default: left *for languages that read left to right;* right *for languages that read right to left;*

Applies to: *block-level elements, table cells, and inline blocks*

Inherits: *yes*

This is a fairly straightforward property to use. The results of the various text-align values are shown in Figure 12-18.

text-align: left   aligns text on the left margin

text-align: right   aligns text on the right margin

text-align: center   centers the text in the text block

text-align: justify   aligns text on both right and left margins

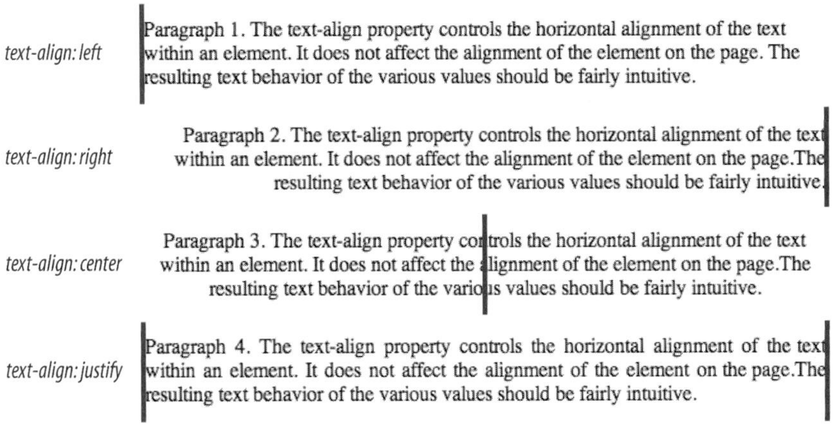

text-align: left

Paragraph 1. The text-align property controls the horizontal alignment of the text within an element. It does not affect the alignment of the element on the page. The resulting text behavior of the various values should be fairly intuitive.

text-align: right

Paragraph 2. The text-align property controls the horizontal alignment of the text within an element. It does not affect the alignment of the element on the page. The resulting text behavior of the various values should be fairly intuitive.

text-align: center

Paragraph 3. The text-align property controls the horizontal alignment of the text within an element. It does not affect the alignment of the element on the page. The resulting text behavior of the various values should be fairly intuitive.

text-align: justify

Paragraph 4. The text-align property controls the horizontal alignment of the text within an element. It does not affect the alignment of the element on the page. The resulting text behavior of the various values should be fairly intuitive.

Figure 12-18. Examples of text-align *values.*

Good news—only four more text properties to go! Then we'll be ready to try a few of them out in the Black Goose Bistro menu.

Underlines and Other "Decorations"

If you want to put a line under, over, or through text, or if you'd like to turn the underline off under links, then the text-decoration is the property for you.

text-decoration

Values: none | underline | overline | line-through | blink | inherit

Default: none

Applies to: *all elements*

Inherits: *no, but since lines are drawn across child elements they may look like they are "decorated" too*

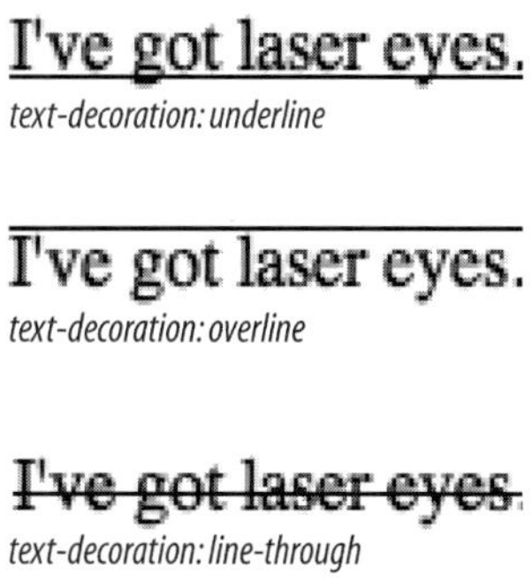

I've got laser eyes.

text-decoration: underline

I've got laser eyes.

text-decoration: overline

~~I've got laser eyes.~~

text-decoration: line-through

Figure 12-19. *Examples of* text-decoration *values.*

If you turn off underlines under links, do so with care because the underline is a strong visual cue that something is clickable.

The values for `text-decoration` are intuitive and are shown in Figure 12-19

`text-decoration: underline`	underlines the element
`text-decoration: overline`	draws a line over the text
`text-decoration: line-through`	draws a line through the text
`text-decoration: blink`	makes text flash on and off

The most popular use of the `text-decoration` property is turning off the underlines that appear automatically under linked text, as shown here:

```
a { text-decoration: none; }
```

There are a few cautionary words to be said regarding `text-decoration`.

- First, be sure there are other cues such as color, weight, or a bottom border to compensate.

- On the flip-side, because underlines are such a strong visual cue to "click here," underlining text that is *not* a link may be misleading and frustrating. Consider whether italics may be an acceptable alternative.

- Finally, there is no reason to make your text blink. Internet Explorer won't support it anyway.

Changing Capitalization

I remember when desktop publishing programs introduced a nifty feature that let me change the capitalization of text on the fly. This made it easy to see how my headlines might look in all capital letters without needing to retype them. CSS includes this feature as well with the `text-transform` property.

`text-transform`

Values: none|capitalize|lowercase|uppercase|inherit

Default: none

Applies to: all elements

Inherits: yes

When you apply the `text-transform` property to a text element, it changes its capitalization when it renders without changing the way it is typed in the source. The values are as follows (Figure 12-20):

`text-transform: none`	as it is typed in the source
`text-transform: capitalize`	capitalizes the first letter of each word
`text-transform: lowercase`	makes all letters lowercase
`text-transform: uppercase`	makes all letters uppercase

And I know what you're thinking.

text-transform: none (as was typed in)

And I Know What You'Re Thinking.

text-transform: capitalize

and i know what you're thinking.

text-transform: lowercase

AND I KNOW WHAT YOU'RE THINKING.

text-transform: uppercase

Figure 12-20. The text-transform *property changes the capitalization of characters when they are displayed, regardless of how they are typed in the source.*

Spaced Out

The final two text properties in this chapter are used to insert space between letters (letter-spacing) or words (word-spacing) when the text is displayed.

letter-spacing

Values:	*length measurement* | normal | inherit
Default:	normal
Applies to:	*all elements*
Inherits:	*yes*

word-spacing

Values:	*length measurement* | normal | inherit
Default:	normal
Applies to:	*all elements*
Inherits:	*yes*

The best way to get to know these properties is by example. When you provide a length measurement, that much space will be added between the letters of the text (letter-spacing) or words in a line (word-spacing). Figure 12-21 shows the results of these rule examples applied to the simple paragraph shown here.

The style sheet

```
p { letter-spacing: 8px; }
p { word-spacing: 1.5em; }
```

The markup

```
<p>Black Goose Bistro Summer Menu</p>
```

It is worth noting that when you specify em measurements, the calculated size is passed down to child elements, even if they have a smaller font size than the parent.

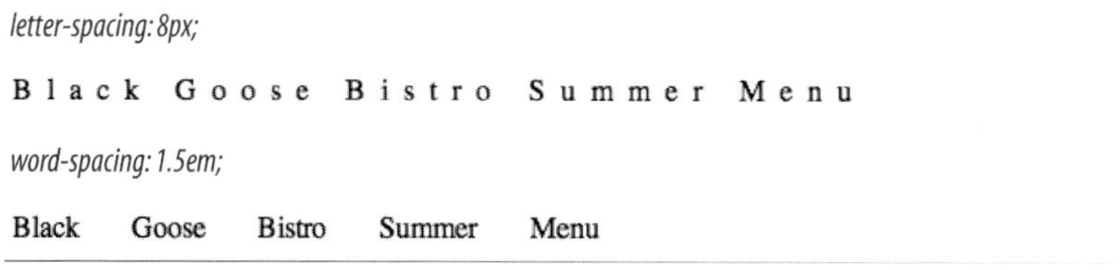

letter-spacing: 8px;

B l a c k G o o s e B i s t r o S u m m e r M e n u

word-spacing: 1.5em;

Black   Goose   Bistro   Summer   Menu

Figure 12-21. `letter-spacing` *(top) and* `word-spacing` *(bottom).*

In Exercise 12-3, we'll make one last trip back to the Black Goose Bistro menu to add some of these new properties and make a few tweaks.

The Other Text Properties

In the interest of saving space and keeping this an introductory-level book, these properties were not given the full treatment. But being the type of author who doesn't hold anything back, I'm including them here. Learn more about them at the W3C site (*www.w3.org/TR/CSS21/*).

vertical-align

Values: baseline | sub | super | top | text-top | middle | text-bottom | bottom | *percentage* | *length* | inherit

Specifies the vertical alignment of an inline element's baseline relative to the baseline of the surrounding text. It is also used to set the vertical alignment of content in a table cell (`td`).

white-space

Values: normal | pre | nowrap | pre-wrap | pre-line | inherit

Specifies how white space in the element source is handled in layout. For example, the `pre` value preserves the character spaces and returns found in the source, similar to the `pre` (X)HTML element.

visibility

Values: visible | hidden | collapse | inherit

Used to hide the element. When set to `hidden`, the element is invisible, but the space it occupies is maintained, leaving a hole in the content. The element is still there; you just can't see it.

direction

Values: ltr | rtl | inherit

Specifies the direction the text reads, left to right (`ltr`) or right to left (`rtl`).

unicode-bidi

Values: normal | embed | bidi-override | inherit

Related to bi-directional features of Unicode. The Recommendation states that it allows the author to generate levels of embedding within the Unicode embedding algorithm. If you have no idea what this means, don't worry. Neither do I. But I guess it's there should you need it for seriously multi-lingual sites.

exercise 12-3 | Finishing up the menu

Let's add a few finishing touches to the online menu, *menu_summer.html*. It might be useful to save the file and look at it in the browser after each step to see the effect of your edits and to make sure you're on track. The finished style sheet is provided in Appendix A.

1. First, I have a few global changes to the **body** element in mind. I've had a change of heart about the **font-family**. I think that a serif font such as Georgia would be more sophisticated and appropriate for a bistro menu. Let's also use the **line-height** property to open up the text lines and make them easier to read. Make these updates to the **body** style rule, as shown:

```
body {
    font-family: Georgia, serif;
    font-size: small;
    line-height: 175%;

}
```

2. I also want to redesign the header section of the document. First, remove the teal color setting by deleting that whole rule. Get rid of the **font-variant** property for the **h1** element as well. Once that is done, make the **h1** purple and the paragraph in the header gray. You can just add color declarations to the existing rules.

```
#header { color: teal; }  /* delete */

h1 {
    font-size: 1.5em;
    font-variant: small-caps;  /* delete */
    color: purple; }

#header p {
    font-style: italic;
    color: gray; }
```

3. Next, to imitate a fancy print menu, I'm going to center a few key elements on the page using the **text-align** property. Write a rule with a grouped selector to center the whole header **div**, the **h2** elements, and the paragraphs contained within the "appetizer" and "entrees" **div**s, like this:

```
#header, h2, #appetizers p, #entrees p {
    text-align: center; }
```

4. I want to make the "Appetizer" and "Main Courses" **h2** headings kind of special. Instead of large, bold type, I'm actually going to reduce the **font-size**, and use all uppercase letters, extra letter spacing, and color to call attention to the headings. Here's the new rule for **h2** elements that includes all of these changes.

```
h2 {
    font: bold 1em Georgia, serif;      /* reduced from 1.2 em */
    text-transform: uppercase;
    letter-spacing: 8px;
    color: purple; }
```

5. We're really close now; just a few more tweaks. Add a rule using contextual selectors that makes the paragraphs in the Appetizers and Main Courses sections italic.

```
#appetizers p, #entrees p {
    font-style: italic; }
```

6. Finally, we'll add a softer color to the menu item names (in **dt** elements). Note that the **strong** elements in those **dt** elements stay maroon because the color applied to the **strong** elements overrides the color inherited by their parents.

```
dt {
    font-weight: bold;
    color: olive;}
```

And we're done! Figure 12-22 shows how the menu looks now...an improvement over the unstyled version, and we used text properties to do it. Notice that we didn't touch a single character of the document markup in the process. That's the beauty of keeping style separate from structure.

DESIGN TIP

Adding letter spacing to small type is one of my favorite heading design tricks. It is a good alternative to large type for drawing attention to the element.

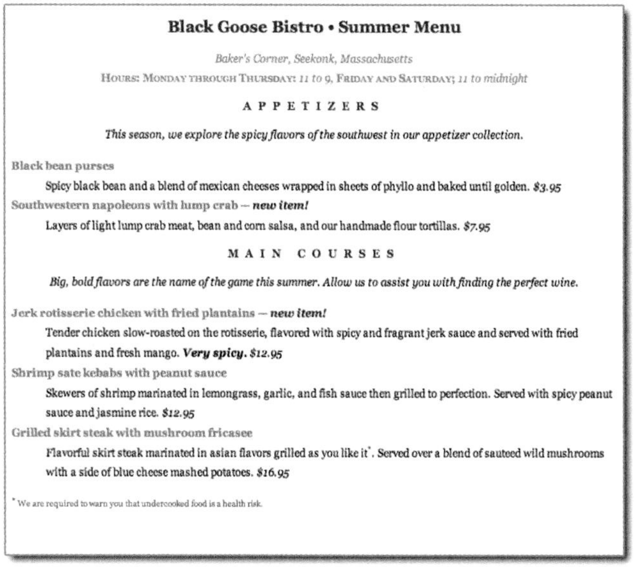

Figure 12-22. The formatted Black Goose Bistro menu.

Black Goose Bistro • Summer Menu

Baker's Corner, Seekonk, Massachusetts

HOURS: MONDAY THROUGH THURSDAY: *11 to 9*, FRIDAY AND SATURDAY; *11 to midnight*

A P P E T I Z E R S

This season, we explore the spicy flavors of the southwest in our appetizer collection.

Black bean purses

Spicy black bean and a blend of mexican cheeses wrapped in sheets of phyllo and baked until golden. *$3.95*

Southwestern napoleons with lump crab — *new item!*

Layers of light lump crab meat, bean and corn salsa, and our handmade flour tortillas. *$7.95*

M A I N   C O U R S E S

Big, bold flavors are the name of the game this summer. Allow us to assist you with finding the perfect wine.

Jerk rotisserie chicken with fried plantains — *new item!*

Tender chicken slow-roasted on the rotisserie, flavored with spicy and fragrant jerk sauce and served with fried plantains and fresh mango. *Very spicy. $12.95*

Shrimp sate kebabs with peanut sauce

Skewers of shrimp marinated in lemongrass, garlic, and fish sauce then grilled to perfection. Served with spicy peanut sauce and jasmine rice. *$12.95*

Grilled skirt steak with mushroom fricasee

Flavorful skirt steak marinated in asian flavors grilled as you like it*. Served over a blend of sauteed wild mushrooms with a side of blue cheese mashed potatoes. *$16.95*

* We are required to warn you that undercooked food is a health risk.

Test Yourself

Here are a few questions to see how well you picked up the fundamentals of selectors and text formatting.

1. Here is a chance to get a little practice writing selectors. Using the diagram shown in Figure 12-23, write style rules that makes each of the elements described below red (`color: red;`). Write the selector as efficiently as possible. I've done the first one for you.

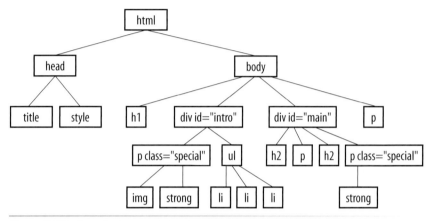

Figure 12-23. Sample document structure.

    a. All text elements in the document   ***body {color: red;}***

    b. `h2` elements

    c. `h1` elements and all paragraphs

    d. Elements belonging to the class "special"

    e. All elements in the "intro" section

    f. `strong` elements in the "main" section

    g. Extra credit: Just the paragraph that appears after an `h2` (hint: this selector will not work in Internet Explorer 6)

2. Match the style property with the text samples in Figure 12-24.

    a. _____ {font-size: 1.5em;}

    b. _____ {text-transform: capitalize;}

    c. _____ {text-align: right;}

    d. _____ {font-family: Verdana; font-size: 1.5em;}

    e. _____ {letter-spacing: 3px;}

    f. _____ {font: bold italic 1.2em Verdana;}

    g. _____ {text-transform: uppercase;}

    h. _____ {text-indent: 2em;}

    i. _____ {font-variant: small-caps;}

Default font and size

Look for the good in others and they'll see the good in you.

1 Look For The Good In Others And They'll See The Good In You.

2 Look for the good in others and they'll see the good in you.

3 Look for the good in others and they'll see the good in you.

4 Look for the good in others and they'll see the good in you.

5 Look for the good in others and they'll see the good in you.

6 LOOK FOR THE GOOD IN OTHERS AND THEY'LL SEE THE GOOD IN YOU.

7 Look for the good in others and they'll see the good in you

8 LOOK FOR THE GOOD IN OTHERS AND THEY'LL SEE THE GOOD IN YOU.

9 *Look for the good in others and they'll see the good in you.*

Figure 12-24. Text samples.

CSS Review: Font and Text Properties

In this chapter, we covered the properties used to format text elements. Here is a summary in alphabetical order.

Property	Description
font	A shorthand property that combines font properties
font-family	Specifies a typeface or generic font family
font-size	The size of the font
font-style	Specifies italic or oblique fonts
font-variant	Specifies a small-caps font
font-weight	Specifies the boldness of the font
letter-spacing	Inserts space between letters
line-height	The distance between baselines of neighboring text lines
text-align	The horizontal alignment of text
text-decoration	Underlines, overlines, and lines through
text-direction	Whether the text reads left-to-right or right-to-left
text-indent	Amount of indentation of the first line in a block
text-transform	Changes the capitalization of text when it displays
unicode-bidi	Works with Unicode bidirectional algorithms
vertical-align	Adjusts vertical position of inline elements relative to the baseline
visibility	Whether the element is rendered or is invisible
white-space	How white space in the source is displayed
word-spacing	Inserts space between words

COLORS AND BACKGROUNDS
(Plus Even More Selectors and External Style Sheets)

Did you happen to see the Web back in 1993? It was a fairly dreary affair back then, where every background was gray and all the text was black. Then came the Netscape Navigator browser and, with it, a handful of attributes that allowed rudimentary (but welcome) control over font colors and backgrounds. For years, we made do.

But thankfully, now we have style sheet properties that blow those old attributes out of the water. So if you happen to view the source of a web page and see attributes such as `bgcolor`, `background`, `link`, and `vlink` floating around, ignore them. They are relics of the past. Believe me, you're much better off without them.

We're going to cover a lot of ground in this chapter. Of course, I'll introduce you to all of the properties for specifying colors and backgrounds. This chapter also rounds out your collection of selector types and shows you how to create an external style sheet as well as a style sheet just for print. Oh, and there will be cabbages...lots and lots of cabbages (you'll see).

Our first order of business is to talk about the options for specifying color in CSS, including a primer on the nature of color on computer monitors.

Specifying Color Values

There are two main ways to specify colors in style sheets: with a predefined color name as we have been doing so far:

```
color: red;        color: olive;        color: blue;
```

or, more commonly, with a numeric value that describes a particular RGB color (the color model on computer monitors). You've probably seen color values that look like these:

```
color: #FF0000;        color: #808000;        color: #00F;
```

We'll get to all the ins and outs of RGB color in a moment, but first, a short and sweet section on the standard color names.

Color names

The most intuitive way to specify a color is to call it by name. Unfortunately, you can't make up just any color name and expect it to work. It has to be one of the color keywords predefined in the CSS Recommendation. CSS1 and CSS2 adopted the 16 standard color names originally introduced in HTML 4.01. CSS2.1 tossed in orange for a total of 17. Color names are easy to use—just drop one into place as the value for any color-related property:

```
color: silver;

background-color: gray;

border-bottom-color: teal;
```

Figure 13-1 shows printed approximations of the 17 color keywords in CSS2.1 (they will look different on computer screens, of course). I threw in their numeric values for good measure.

Extended Color Names

CSS Level 3 has a new color module that gives you a whopping 140 color names to choose from. The module uses a set of color keywords originally introduced by the X Window System. These colors have historically been supported by browsers as (X)HTML attribute values, but this is the first time they've been standardized for CSS. Some day, we'll be able to specify names like blanchedalmond, burlywood, and papayawhip. Won't that be special?

Unfortunately, they're not well supported for use in style sheets at this time, but if you're curious, you can see the full list online at www.*learningwebdesign.com/ colornames.html* or in the CSS3 proposal at *www.w3.org/TR/css3-color/#svg-color*.

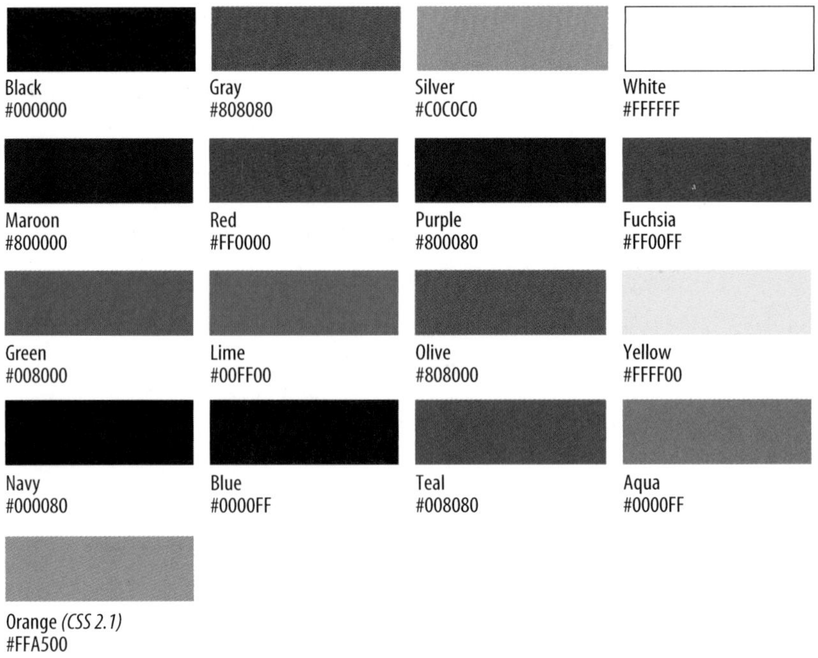

Black #000000

Gray #808080

Silver #C0C0C0

White #FFFFFF

Maroon #800000

Red #FF0000

Purple #800080

Fuchsia #FF00FF

Green #008000

Lime #00FF00

Olive #808000

Yellow #FFFF00

Navy #000080

Blue #0000FF

Teal #008080

Aqua #0000FF

Orange *(CSS 2.1)* #FFA500

Figure 13-1. The 17 standard color names in CSS2.1.

RGB color values

Names are easy, but as you can see, they are limited. By far, the most common way to specify a color is by its RGB value. It also gives you millions of colors to choose from.

For those who are not familiar with how computers deal with color, I'll start with the basics before jumping into the CSS syntax.

The RGB color model

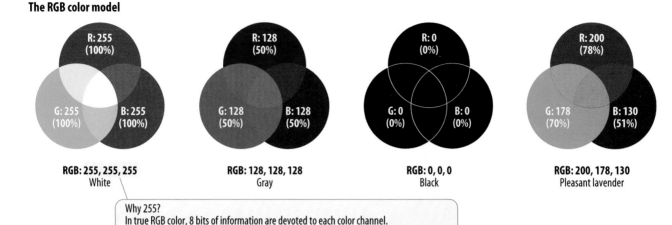

| RGB: 255, 255, 255 | RGB: 128, 128, 128 | RGB: 0, 0, 0 | RGB: 200, 178, 130 |
| White | Gray | Black | Pleasant lavender |

Why 255?
In true RGB color, 8 bits of information are devoted to each color channel.
8 bits can describe 256 shades ($2^8=256$), so colors are measured on a scale from 0 to 255.

Figure 13-2. Colors on computer monitors are made by mixing different amounts of red, green, and blue light (thus, RGB). The color in the middle of each diagram shows what happens when the three color channels are combined. The more light in each channel, the closer the combination is to white.

A word about RGB color

Computers create the colors you see on a monitor by combining three colors of light: red, green, and blue. This is known as the RGB color model. You can provide recipes (of sorts) for colors by telling the computer how much of each color to mix in. The amount of light in each color "channel" is typically described on a scale from 0 (none) to 255 (full-blast), although it can also be provided as a percent. The closer the three values get to 255 (100%), the closer the resulting color gets to white (Figure 13-2).

Any color you see on your monitor can be described by a series of three numbers: a red value, a green value, and a blue value. This is one of the ways that image editors such as Adobe Photoshop keep track of the colors for every pixel in an image. With the RGB color system, a pleasant lavender can be described as 200, 178, 230.

Picking a color

The easiest way to pick a color and find its RGB color values is to use an image editing tool such as Adobe Photoshop, Photoshop Elements, or Corel Paint Shop Pro Photo. Most image tools provide a Color Picker similar to Photoshop's shown in Figure 13-3. When you select a color from the spectrum in the Color Picker, the red (R), green (G), and blue (B) values are listed, as pointed out in the figure. And look next to the # symbol—those are the same values, converted so they are ready to go in a style sheet. I'll explain the 6-digit hex values in a moment.

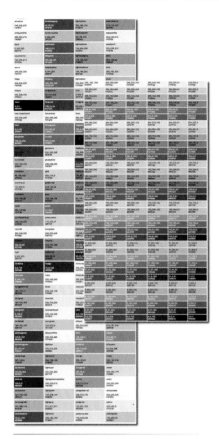

Figure 13-4. If you don't have an image editing program, you could pick a color from the charts provided at www. learningwebdesign.com.

RGB is one of four color models provided in the Color Picker (the others are HSB, Lab, and CMYK).

The RGB values listed here

The same RGB values, ready to be inserted in a style sheet

Figure 13-3. The Color Picker in Adobe Photoshop provides the RGB values for a selected pixel color.

Another cool tool for finding RGB values is Colorzilla, a free extension to the Firefox browser that gives you the values for any pixel color in the browser window (among many other features). Download it at *www.iosart.com/fire-fox/colorzilla/*.

If you don't have these programs, you could pick a color from a chart of colors, such as the ones provided on the web site for this book (Figure 13-4). Between the Color Names chart (*www.learningwebdesign.com/colornames.html*) and the Web Palette Colors chart (*www.learningwebdesign.com/webpalette.html*), there are more than 300 color samples. If you see something you like, copy down the RGB values listed.

Writing RGB values in style sheets

CSS allows RGB color values to be specified in a number of formats. Going back to that pleasant lavender, we could add it to a style sheet by listing each value on a scale from 0 to 255.

```
color: rgb(200, 178, 230);
```

You can also list them as percentage values, although that is less common.

```
color: rgb(78%, 70%, 90%);
```

Or, you can provide the web-ready version that we saw in the Color Picker. These six digits represent the same three RGB values, except they have been converted into hexadecimal (or hex, for short) values. I'll explain the hexadecimal system in the next section. Note that hex RGB values are preceded by the # symbol and do not require the rgb() notation shown above.

```
color: #C8B2E6;
```

There is one last shorthand way to specify hex color values. If your value happens to be made up of three pairs of double-digits, such as:

```
color: #FFCC00; or color: #993366;
```

you can condense each pair down to one digit. These examples are equivalent to the ones listed above:

```
color: #FC0;  or  color: #936;
```

About hexadecimal values

It's time to clarify what's going on with that six-digit string of characters. What you're looking at is actually a series of three, two-digit numbers, one each for red, green, and blue. But instead of decimal (base-10, the system we're used to), these values are written in hexadecimal, or base-16. Figure 13-5 shows the structure of the hex RGB value.

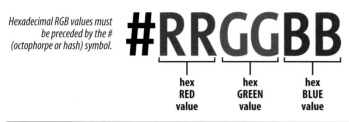

Hexadecimal RGB values must be preceded by the # (octophorpe or hash) symbol.

Figure 13-5. Hexadecimal RGB values are made up of three two-digit numbers, one for red, one for green, and one for blue.

The hexadecimal numbering system uses 16 digits: 0–9 and A–F (for representing the quantities 10–15). Figure 13-6 shows how this works. The hex system is used widely in computing because it reduces the space it takes to store certain information. For example, the RGB values are reduced from three to two digits once they're converted to hexadecimal.

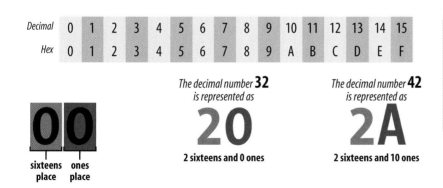

Figure 13-6. The hexadecimal numbering system is base-16.

Now that most graphics and web development software provides easy access to hexadecimal color values (as we saw in Figure 13-3), there isn't much need to translate RGB values to hex yourself, as we needed to do back in the old days. But should you find the need, the sidebar Hexadecimal Calculators should help you out.

Hexadecimal Calculators

In Windows, the standard calculator has a hexadecimal converter in the Scientific view. Mac users can download the free "Mac Dec Bin Calculator" for OSX (search for it at *versiontracker.com*).

Just enter the decimal number for each color value and click the HEX conversion button. Make a note of the resulting two-digit hex value.

Of course, you could calculate a hex value yourself by dividing your number by 16 to get the first digit, and then using the remainder for the second digit. For example, 200 converts to C8 because 200=(16 × 12) + 8. That's {12,8} in base-16, or C8 in hexadecimal. Whew! I think I'll be sticking with my Color Picker.

TIP

Handy Hex Values

White = #FFFFFF or #FFF
(the equivalent of 255,255,255)

Black = #000000 or #000
(the equivalent of 0,0,0)

The Web Palette

You will certainly come across the Web Palette or Web Safe Colors while reading about web design or using such web production tools as Dreamweaver or Photoshop. Web-safe values are easy to spot. They are made up exclusively of the hex values 00, 33, 66, 99, CC, and FF.

The web palette is a set of 216 colors that browsers use to render color on low-end monitors that are capable of displaying only 256 colors at a time. The 216 colors consist of the cross-section of colors used by both Windows and Macintosh operating systems.

Back when most users had low-end monitors, web designers stuck with web-safe colors because they rendered smoothly and predictably. However, because fewer than 1% of users have 256-color monitors as of this writing, browsers rarely need to remap colors in web pages to the web palette. That means there is no longer the need to restrict your color choices—improved technology has made the web palette obsolete.

WARNING

You can change the foreground color of an entire page by applying the color property to the body *element. Be aware, however, that on some older browsers, table elements do not properly inherit properties from the body, so text within tables would go back to the default color. To be on the safe side, make a color declaration for the* body *and relevant table elements, like this:*

```
body, table, td, th {
  color: #999;
}
```

Summing up color values

It took us a few pages to get here, but the process for picking and specifying colors in style sheets is actually easy.

- Pick one of the 17 color names,

  or

- Use a color chart or an image editor like Photoshop to select a color, and copy down the RGB values (preferably the six-digit hex values). Put those values in the style rule using one of the four RGB value formats, and you're done.

Oh, and don't worry about web-safe colors or the web palette; that's another relic from the past (see the Web Palette sidebar).

Foreground Color

Now that we know how to write color values, let's get to the color-related properties. You can specify the foreground and background colors for any (X)HTML element. There are also border-color properties that take color values, but we'll get to those in Chapter 14, Thinking Inside the Box.

The foreground of an element consists of its text and border (if one is specified). You specify a foreground color with the color property, as we saw in the last chapter when we rolled it out to make the text pretty. Here are the details for the color property one more time.

color

Values:	*color value (name or numeric)* | inherit
Default:	*depends on the browser and user's preferences*
Applies to:	*all elements*
Inherits:	*yes*

In the following example, the foreground of a blockquote element is set to a nice green with the values R:80, G:140, and B:25 (we'll use the hex code #508C19). You can see that by applying the color property to the blockquote element, the color is inherited by the p and em elements it contains (Figure 13-7). The thick dashed border around the whole blockquote is green as well; however, if we were to apply a border-color property to this same element, that color would override the green foreground setting.

The style rule

```
blockquote {
  border: 4px dashed;
  color: #508C19;
}
```

The markup

```
<blockquote>
  <p>I'd recommend Honey Gold cereal to anyone who likes cereal. It's
```

```
the <em>only</em> way to start the day!</p>
  <cite>&mdash; Jennifer Robbins, happy consumer</cite>
</blockquote>
```

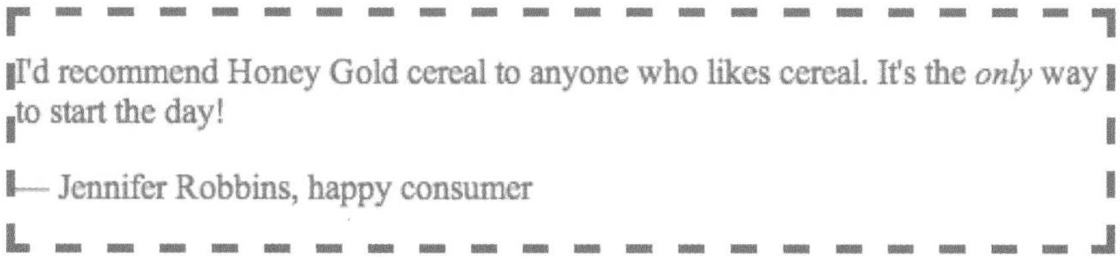
I'd recommend Honey Gold cereal to anyone who likes cereal. It's the only way to start the day!
— Jennifer Robbins, happy consumer

Figure 13-7. Applying a color to the foreground of an element.

Background Color

Before style sheets, you could apply a background color only to the entire page. Now, with the `background-color` property, you can apply background colors to any element.

background-color

Values: *color value (name or numeric)* | `transparent` | `inherit`

Default: `transparent`

Applies to: *all elements*

Inherits: *no*

A background color fills the canvas behind the element that includes the content area, and any padding (extra space) added around the content, extending behind the border out to its outer edge. Let's see what happens when we use the `background-color` property to make the background of the same sample `blockquote` light blue (Figure 13-8).

```
blockquote {
  border: 4px dashed;
  color: #508C19;
  background-color: #B4DBE6;
}
```

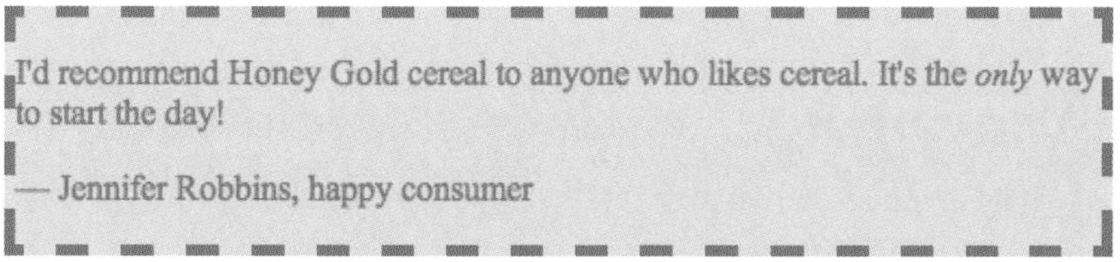
I'd recommend Honey Gold cereal to anyone who likes cereal. It's the only way to start the day!
— Jennifer Robbins, happy consumer

Figure 13-8. Adding a light blue background color to the sample blockquote.

As expected, the background color fills the area behind the text, all the way to the border. Look closely at the gaps in the border, and you'll see that the background color actually goes all the way to its outer edge. But that's where

DESIGN TIP

Using Color

Here are a few quick tips related to working with color:

- Limit the number of colors you use on a page. Nothing creates visual chaos faster than too many colors. I tend to choose one dominant color and one highlight color. I may also use a couple of shades of each, but I resist adding too many different hues.
- When specifying a foreground and background color, make sure that there is adequate contrast. People tend to prefer reading dark text on very light backgrounds online. My sample in Figure 13-8, although making its point, actually fails the contrast test.
- It is a good idea to specify the foreground color and the background color (particularly for whole pages) in tandem. This will avoid possible color clashes and contrast problems if the user has one or the other set with a user style sheet.

the background stops; if we apply a margin to this element, the background will not extend into the margin. When we talk about the CSS box model, we'll revisit all these components of an element. For now, just know that if your border has gaps, the background will show through.

To color the background of the whole page, apply the background-color *property to the* body *element.*

It's worth noting that background colors do not inherit, but because the default background setting for all elements is transparent, the parent's background color shows through its descendant elements. For example, you can change the background color of a whole page by applying the background-color property to the body element. The color will show through all the elements on the page.

In addition to setting the color of the whole page, you can change the background color of any element, both block-level (like the blockquote shown in the previous example) as well as inline. In this example, I've used the color and background-color properties to highlight a word marked up as a "glossary" term. You can see in Figure 13-9 that the background color fills the little box created by the dfn element.

The style rule

```
.glossary {
    color: #7C3306;          /* dark brown */
    background-color: #F2F288;  /* light yellow */
}
```

The markup

```
<p>A <dfn class="glossary">baseline</dfn> is the imaginary line upon
which characters sit.</p>
```

A baseline is the imaginary line upon which characters sit.

Figure 13-9. Applying the background-color *property to an inline element.*

In a moment, we'll be applying colors and backgrounds to that king of inline elements, the hypertext link. While it is possible simply to apply styles to the a element, we're going to look at a new batch of selectors that let us apply different styles to links depending on whether they've been visited and whether the user is hovering over the link or clicking on it.

Introducing.... Pseudoclass Selectors

Have you ever noticed that a link is often one color when you click on it and another color when you go back to that page? That's because, behind the scenes, your browser is keeping track of which links have been clicked (or "visited," to use the lingo). The browser keeps track of other link states too, such as whether the user's cursor is over the link, or whether it's in the process of being clicked.

AT A GLANCE

Here is a quick summary of the selector types we've covered already:

Element type selector
```
p {property: value;}
```

Grouped selectors
```
p, h1, h2 {property: value;}
```

Descendant (contextual) selector
```
ol li {property: value;}
```

ID selector
```
#sidebar {property: value;}
div#sidebar {property:
value;}
```

Class selector
```
p.warning {property: value;}
.warning {property: value;}
```

Universal selector
```
* {property: value;}
```

In CSS, you can apply styles to links in each of these states using a special kind of selector called a pseudoclass selector. It's an odd name, but you can think of it as though links in a certain state belong to the same class. However, the class name isn't in the markup—it's something the browser keeps track of. So it's *kinda* like a class, a *pseudo*class.

In this section, we'll be looking at the anchor-related pseudoclasses because they are the most useful and best supported, but there are a few others as listed in the sidebar, CSS2.1 Pseudoclasses.

Anchor pseudoclasses

There are four main pseudoclasses that can be used as selectors:

`a:link`	Applies a style to unclicked (unvisited) links
`a:visited`	Applies a style to links that have already been clicked
`a:hover`	Applies a style when the mouse pointer is over the link
`a:active`	Applies a style while the mouse button is pressed

Pseudoclass selectors are indicated by the colon (`:`) character.

The `:link`, `:visited`, and `:active` pseudoselectors replace the old presentational `link`, `vlink`, and `alink` attributes, respectively, that were once used to change link colors. But with CSS, you can change more than just color. Once you've selected the link state, you can apply any of the properties we've covered so far (and more).

Let's look at an example of each. In these examples, I've written some style rules for links (`a:link`) and visited links (`a:visited`). I've used the `text-decoration` property to turn off the underline under both link states. I've also changed the color of links (blue by default) to maroon, and visited links will now be gray instead of the default purple.

```
a:link {
  color: maroon;
  text-decoration: none;
}
a:visited {
  color: gray;
  text-decoration: none;
}
```

The `:hover` selector is an interesting one (see note). It allows you to do cool rollover effects on links that were once possible only with JavaScript. If you add this rule to the ones above, the links will get an underline and a background color when the mouse is hovered over them, giving the user feedback that the text is a link.

```
a:hover {
  color: maroon;
  text-decoration: underline;
  background-color: #C4CEF8;
}
```

NOTE

According to CSS2, :hover may be used with elements other than anchors, but this use is not supported in Internet Explorer 6 and earlier or Netscape Navigator 4. Internet Explorer 7 does support :hover on all elements, but unfortunately, it will be a while before all the old versions of IE go away.

Finally, this rule using the `:active` selector makes links bright red (consistent with maroon, but more intense) while the link is being clicked. This style will be displayed only for an instant, but it can give a subtle indication that something has happened. Figure 13-10 shows the results.

```
a:active {
    color: red;
    text-decoration: underline;
    background-color: #C4CEF8;
}
```

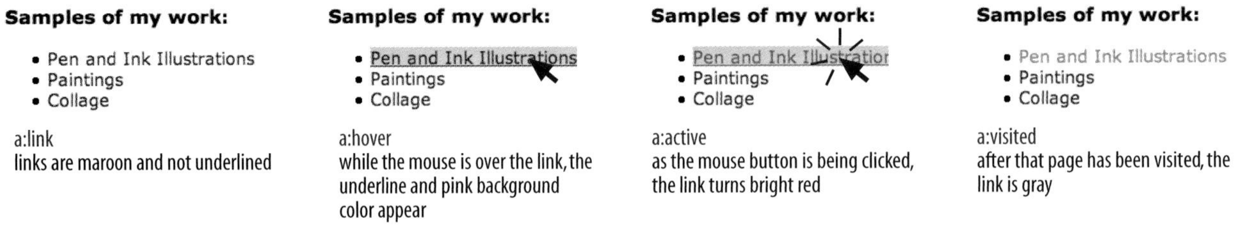

Samples of my work:

- Pen and Ink Illustrations
- Paintings
- Collage

a:link
links are maroon and not underlined

Samples of my work:

- Pen and Ink Illustrations
- Paintings
- Collage

a:hover
while the mouse is over the link, the underline and pink background color appear

Samples of my work:

- Pen and Ink Illustration
- Paintings
- Collage

a:active
as the mouse button is being clicked, the link turns bright red

Samples of my work:

- Pen and Ink Illustrations
- Paintings
- Collage

a:visited
after that page has been visited, the link is gray

Figure 13-10. Changing the colors and backgrounds of links with pseudoclass selectors.

NOTE

The :active pseudoclass selector is not used much any more. This is due in part to the fact that links remain "active" in older versions of Internet Explorer for Windows. A link clicked to activate a JavaScript function (such as a pop-up window) will also remain active until you click elsewhere on the page.

Love, HA!

If you want to use all four anchor pseudoclasses in a single style sheet, they need to appear in a particular order in order to function properly. The initials LVHA (or according to a popular mnemonic, *love, Ha!*) remind us that the required order is `:link`, `:visited`, `:hover`, `:active`. This has to do with rule order and specificity. Putting `:link` or `:visited` last would override the `:hover` and `:active` states, preventing those styles from appearing.

Pseudoelement Selectors

Pseudoclasses aren't the only kind of pseudo selectors. There are also four pseudoelements that act as though they are inserting fictional elements into the document structure for styling. Pseudoelements are also indicated with a colon (:) symbol.

First letter and line

Two of the pseudoelements are based on context and are used to select the first letter or the first line of text of an element.

`:first-line`

This selector applies a style rule to the first line of the specified element. The only properties you can apply, however, are:

color	font	background
word-spacing	letter-spacing	text-decoration
vertical-align	text-transform	line-height

`:first-letter`

This applies a style rule to the first letter of the specified element. The properties you can apply are limited to:

`color`	`font`	`text-decoration`
`line-height` *(CSS2.1)*	`vertical-align`	`text-transform`
`background`	`margin`	`padding`
`border`	`float`	
`letter-spacing` *(CSS2.1)*	`word-spacing` *(CSS2.1)*	

NOTE

There are a few properties in this list that you haven't seen yet. We'll cover the box-related properties (margin, padding, border) in Chapter 14, Thinking Inside the Box. The `float` property is introduced in Chapter 15, Floating and Positioning.

Figure 13-11 shows examples of `:first-line` and `:first-letter` pseudoelement selectors.

```
p:first-line {letter-spacing: 8px;}
```

S n o w   W h i t e   w a s   b a n i s h e d   f o r   b e i n g
most beautiful, fell in with seven dwarves, ate a poison apple, and fell asleep in a glass coffin until the handsome prince kissed her, married her, and they lived happily ever after.

```
p:first-letter {font-size: 300%; color: orange;}
```

Snow White was banished for being most beautiful, fell in with seven dwarves, ate a poison apple, and fell asleep in a glass coffin until the handsome prince kissed her, married her, and they lived happily ever after.

***Figure 13-11.** Examples of `:first-line` and `:first-letter` pseudoelement selectors.*

You've collected nearly all of the selector types. There are a few more, but because they are advanced and not well supported, they have been moved into informative sidebars (see Generated Content with :before and :after and Attribute Selectors).

NOTE

Appendix B provides a useful overview of all the selector types.

But now, I think it's time to try out foreground and background colors as well as some of these new selector types in Exercise 13-1.

exercise 13-1 | Adding color to a document

In this exercise, we'll start with a simple black-and-white article and warm it up with an earthy palette of foreground and background colors (Figure 13-13). You should have enough experience writing style rules by this point, that I'm not going hold your hand as much as I have in previous exercises. This time, you write the rules. You can check your work against the finished style sheet provided in Appendix A.

Open the file ***cabbage.html*** (available at *www.learningwebdesign.com/materials*) in a text editor. You will find that there is already an embedded style sheet that provides basic text formatting (there's even a preview of the **`margin`** and **`padding`** properties that we'll be getting to in the next chapter). With the text all set, all you'll need to do is work on the colors. Feel free to save the document at any step along the way and view your progress in a browser.

Generated Content with :before and :after

CSS2 introduced the `:before` and `:after` pseudoelements that are used to insert content before or after a specified element without actually adding the characters to the source document (this is called **generated content** in CSS). Generated content can be used to insert language-appropriate quotation marks around a quote, insert automatic counters, or even display URLs next to links when a document is printed. Unfortunately, the `:before` and `:after` pseudoelements are *not* supported in Internet Explorer for Windows (including IE7), but they are supported by all other modern browsers.

Here's a simple example that inserts the words "Once upon a time:" before a paragraph and "The End." at the end of the paragraph (Figure 13-12).

The style sheet:
```
p:before {
    content: "Once upon a time: ";
    font-weight: bold;
    color: purple;
}
p:after {
    content: " The End.";
    font-weight: bold;
    color: purple;
}
```

The markup:
```
<p>Snow White was banished for being the most
beautiful, ... and they lived happily ever after.
</p>
```

Generated content isn't something you're likely to take on in your first web site projects, but if you are interested in learning more, see these resources (and keep in mind that IE users won't see the generated content even if they are using version 7).

- The very dry CSS2 Recommendation: *www.w3.org/TR/REC-CSS2/generate.html*
- A generated content tutorial at WestCiv: *www.westciv.com/style_master/academy/css_tutorial/advanced/generated_content.html*
- For instructions on how to show the URLs for links in a print style sheet, see the *A List Apart* article, "CSS Design: Going to Print" by Eric Meyer (*www.alistapart.com/articles/goingtoprint/*)

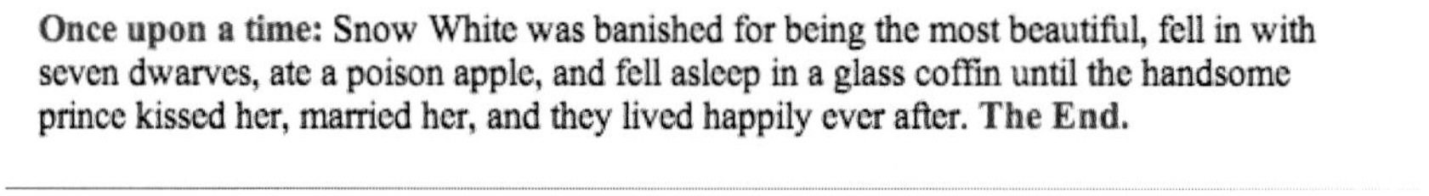

Once upon a time: Snow White was banished for being the most beautiful, fell in with seven dwarves, ate a poison apple, and fell asleep in a glass coffin until the handsome prince kissed her, married her, and they lived happily ever after. **The End.**

Figure 13-12. Generated content added with the `:before` *and* `:after` *pseudoselectors, shown in the Firefox browser (Macintosh)*

Attribute Selectors

CSS2 introduced a system for targeting specific attribute names or values. Unfortunately, they are not supported in Internet Explorer 6 and earlier, which still make up a significant share of web traffic as of this writing. There are four types of attribute selectors.

Simple attribute selector

Targets elements with a particular attribute regardless of its value

    element[attribute]

Ex. `img[title] {border: 3px solid;}`
Selects any image with a title attribute.

Exact attribute value

Selects elements with specific value for the attribute

    element[attribute="exact value"]

Ex. `img[title="first grade"] {border: 3px solid;}`
Selects images with exactly the title value "first grade".

Partial attribute value

Allows you to specify one part of an attribute value

    element[attribute~="value"]

Ex. `img[title~="grade"] border: 3px solid;}`
Looks for the word "grade" in the title, so images with the title values "first grade" and "second grade" would be selected.

Hyphen-separated attribute value

Targets hyphen-separated values

    element[attribute|="value"]

Ex.. `*[hreflang|="es"]`
Selects any element that specifies a variation on the Spanish language.

1. Make the **h1** heading orange (R: 204, G:51, B:0, or **#CC3300**). Note that because this value has all double digits, you can (and should) use the condensed version (**#C30**) and save a few bytes in the style sheet.

2. Make the **h2** headings brown (R:102, G:51, B:0, or **#663300**).

3. Make the background of the entire page a light green (R: 187, G:224, B:159, or **#BBE09F**). Note that although there is one double digit in this hex value, you cannot condense it; all three values must be double-digits to use the abbreviated version.

4. Make the background of the "titlepage" **div** an even lighter green (R:212, G:248, B:185, or **#D4F8B9**).

5. Make links dark green (**#003300**).

6. Make visited links a dull green (**#336633**).

7. When the mouse is placed over links, remove the underline, keep the text green (**#003300**), and add a medium green background color (**#87B862**).

8. As the link is clicked, make the link turn the same orange as the **h1**.

When you are done, your page should look like the one in Figure 13-13. We'll be adding background images to this page later, so if you'd like to continue experimenting with different colors on different elements, make a copy of this document and give it a new name.

WARNING

Don't forget the # character before hex values. The rule won't work without it.

NOTE

If you are interested in raising cabbages, the full text of this treatise is available online from Project Gutenburg at www.gutenberg.org/etext/19006.

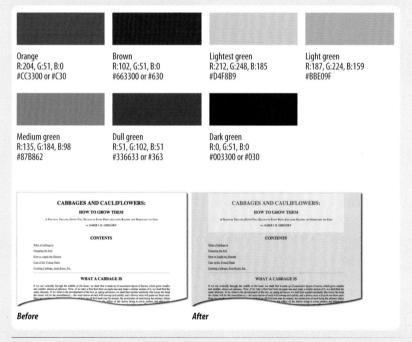

Orange
R:204, G:51, B:0
#CC3300 or #C30

Brown
R:102, G:51, B:0
#663300 or #630

Lightest green
R:212, G:248, B:185
#D4F8B9

Light green
R:187, G:224, B:159
#BBE09F

Medium green
R:135, G:184, B:98
#87B862

Dull green
R:51, G:102, B:51
#336633 or #363

Dark green
R:0, G:51, B:0
#003300 or #030

Before   After

Figure 13-13.   An earthy palette of colors for the Cabbages and Cauliflowers article (shown before and after).

Background Images

CSS really beats (X)HTML hands-down when it comes to background images (but then, (X)HTML really shouldn't have been dealing in background images in the first place). With CSS, you're not stuck with a repeating tile pattern, and you can position a background image wherever you like. You can also apply a background image to any element in the document, not just the whole page.

In this section, we'll look at the collection of properties used to place and push around background images, starting with the basic `background-image` property.

Adding a background image

The `background-image` property is used to add a background image to an element. Its primary job is to provide the location of the image file.

`background-image`

Values: *URL (location of image)* | none | inherit

Default: none

Applies to: *all elements*

Inherits: *no*

The value of `background-image` is a sort of url-holder that contains the URL of the image. The URL is relative to the (X)HTML document that the image is going into, not the style sheet document (see related Tip).

These examples and Figure 13-14 show background images applied behind a whole page (`body`) and a single `blockquote` element with padding and a border applied.

```
body {
    background-image: url(star.gif); }

blockquote {
    background-image: url(dot.gif);
    padding: 2em;
    border: 4px dashed;}
```

Here you can see the default behavior of `background-image`. The image starts in the top, left-hand corner and tiles horizontally and vertically until the entire element is filled (although you'll learn how to change that in a moment). Like background colors, tiling background images fill the area behind the content area, the extra padding space around the content, and extend to the outer edge of the border (if there is one).

If you provide both a `background-color` and a `background-image` to an element, the image will be placed on top of the color. In fact, it is recommended that you *do* provide a backup color that is similar in hue, in the event the image fails to download.

NOTE

The proper term for that "url-holder" is a functional notation. *It is the same syntax used to list decimal and percentage RGB values.*

TIP

Providing site root relative URLs for images ensures that the background image can be found regardless of location of the (X)HTML document it's going into. The root directory is indicated by a slash at the beginning of the URL. For example:

`background-image:`
`url(/images/background.jpg)`

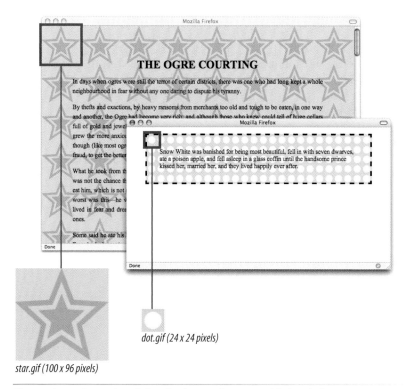

dot.gif (24 x 24 pixels)

star.gif (100 x 96 pixels)

Figure 13-14. *Examples of tiling background images added with the* `background-image` *property.*

DESIGN TIP

Background Images

When working with background images, keep these guidelines and tips in mind:

- Use a simple image that won't interfere with the legibility of the text over it.

- Always provide a `background-color` value that matches the primary color of the background image. If the background image fails to display, at least the overall design of the page will be similar. This is particularly important if the text color would be illegible against the browser's default white background.

- As usual for the Web, keep the file size of background images as small as possible.

exercise 13-2 |
Working with background images

In this exercise, we're going to add and manipulate tiling background images in the Cabbages article from the last exercise. We'll revisit this document several times to give you a chance to try out each background image property. The images provided for this exercise should be in the same directory as the *cabbage.html* document.

Add a declaration to the **body** style rule that makes the image *cabbage_A.jpg* tile in the background of the page.

```
background-image: url(cabbage_A.
jpg)
```

Easy, isn't it? When you save and view the page in the browser, it should look like Figure 13-15. For extra credit, take the image out of the page background and put it in the **div** at the top of the page.

Figure 13-15. *The article with a simple tiling background image.*

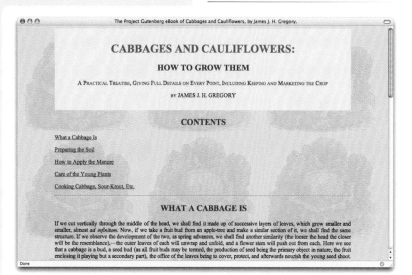

Background Tiling

As we saw in the last figure, images tile up and down, left and right when left to their own devices. You can change this behavior with the background-repeat property.

background-repeat

Values: repeat | repeat-x | repeat-y | no-repeat | inherit

Default: repeat

Applies to: all elements

Inherits: no

If you want a background image to appear just once, use the no-repeat keyword value, like this.

```
body {
   background-image: url(star.gif);
   background-repeat: no-repeat;
}
```

You can also restrict the image to tiling only horizontally (repeat-x) or vertically (repeat-y) as shown in these examples.

```
body {
   background-image: url(star.gif);
   background-repeat: repeat-x;
}
body {
   background-image: url(star.gif);
   background-repeat: repeat-y;
}
```

Figure 13-16 shows examples of each of the keyword values. Notice that in all the examples, the tiling begins in the top-left corner of the element (or browser window when an image is applied to the body element). But the background image doesn't necessarily need to start there.

exercise 13-2 | (continued)

Now let's try some slightly more sophisticated tiling on the sample article page. This time, we'll remove that busy tile in the background of the whole page and add a more subtle pattern just within the "titlepage" **div**.

1. Remove the **background-image** declaration in the **body** or **div** style rules.

2. In the **div#titlepage** rule, add the image *cabbage_B.gif* and set it to repeat horizontally only.

   ```
   div#titlepage {
      padding: 1em;
      background-color: #D4F8B9;
      background-image: url(cabbage_B.gif);
      background-repeat: repeat-x;
   }
   ```

3. Save the file and look at it in the browser. It should look like Figure 13-17. Try changing it to repeat vertically, then make it not repeat at all.

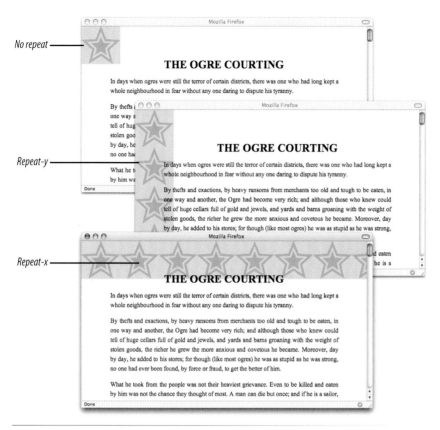

No repeat

Repeat-y

Repeat-x

Figure 13-16. *Turning off automatic tiling with* no-repeat *(top), vertical-axis tiling with* repeat-y *(middle), and horizontal-axis tiling with* repeat-x *(bottom).*

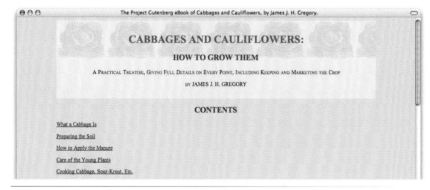

Figure 13-17. *Adding a horizontal tiling image to the* div*.*

Background Position

The background-position property specifies the position of the origin image in the background. You can think of the origin image as the first image that is placed in the background from which tiling images extend. Here is the property and its various values.

`background-position`

Values:	*length measurement* | *percentage* | left | center | right | top | bottom | inherit
Default:	0% 0% *(same as* left top*)*
Applies to:	*all elements*
Inherits:	*no*

In general, you provide both horizontal and vertical values that describe where to place the origin image, but there are a variety of ways to do it. Examples of each method are shown in Figure 13-18.

Keyword positioning

The keyword values (left, right, top, bottom, and center) position the origin image relative to the edges of the element's padding. For example, left positions the image all the way to the left edge of the background area.

Keywords are typically used in pairs, as in these examples:

```
{ background-position: left bottom; }
{ background-position: right center; }
```

If you provide only one keyword, the missing keyword is assumed to be center. Thus, `background-position: right` has the same effect as the second example above.

Length measurements

You can also specify the position by its distance from the top-left corner of the element using pixel measurements. When providing length values, the horizontal measurement always goes first.

```
{ background-position: 200px 50px; }
```

Percentages

Percentage values are provided in horizontal/vertical pairs, with 0% 0% corresponding to the top-left corner and 100% 100% corresponding to the bottom-right corner. It is important to note that the percentage value applies to both the canvas area and the image itself. For example, the 100% value places the bottom-right corner of the image in the bottom-right corner of the canvas. As with keywords, if you only provide one percentage, the other is assumed to be 50% (centered).

```
{ background-position: 15% 100%; }
```

Figure 13-18 shows the results of each of the `background-position` examples listed above with the `background-repeat` set to `no-repeat` for clarity. It is possible to position the origin image and let it tile from there, in both directions or just horizontally or vertically. When the image tiles, the position of the initial image won't be obvious, but you can use `background-position` to make a tile pattern start at a point other than the left edge of the image.

CSS TIP

To ensure best performance in modern browsers, always supply the horizontal measurement first for all value types.

`background-position: right center;`

`background-position: top left;`

`background-position: 50px 50px;`

`background-position: 15% 100%;`

Figure 13-18. Positioning a non-repeating background image

exercise 13-2 | (continued)

You guessed it... we're going to have fun with the position of the background image in the cabbage article (are you hungry for sauerkraut yet?). For this exercise, I've prepared several variations on the cabbage illustration that will look nice when tucked along various edges of the page (see Figure 13-19). All of these GIF images are transparent, so when you use them as background images, the background color will show through. I'll give you a few things to try, but feel free to experiment with different placements and types of position values on your own.

1. Put a non-repeating image in the top, left corner of the page. Use the image named *cabbage_C_topleft.gif*. I'll give you the rule for this first one. Then try putting *cabbage_C_topright.gif* in the top, right corner.

```
body {
    margin-left: 10%;
    margin-right: 10%;
    background-color: #BBE09F;
    background-image: url(cabbage_C_topleft.gif);
    background-repeat: no-repeat;
    background-position: left top;
}
```

2. Change the above rule to place the image *cabbage_C_rightside.gif* on the right edge of the page and 100 pixels down from the top (this is the screenshot shown in Figure 13-19).

The CSS Recommendation allows combined value types (for example, `background-position: right 100px`). Just make sure you always put the horizontal value first. Older browsers may have a problem with mixed values, so be sure to test this on your target browsers. You can try the same thing on the left side of the page using *cabbage_C_leftside.gif*. Experiment with different vertical values.

3. Change that same rule to place the image *cabbage_C.gif* in the center of the **body** element. Note that it will be centered vertically in the height of the whole **body** element, not in the browser window, so you'll have to scroll down to see it.

4. Now let's get fancy. Change the position of *cabbage_C.gif* to **center 85px** to center it near the top of the page. Now, add the same image to the shaded **div** at the top of the page, setting its position to **center 75px**.

```
div#titlepage {
    padding: 1em;
    background-color: #D4F8B9;
    background-image: url(cabbage_C.gif);
    background-repeat: no-repeat;
    background-position: center 75px; }
```

The images may not match up exactly, but with this image, it's difficult to tell. Try scrolling the page, and pay attention to what happens to the background images. We'll play with this concept more in the next installment of Exercise 13-2.

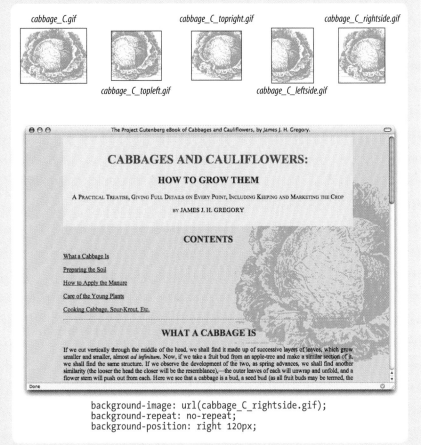

cabbage_C.gif cabbage_C_topright.gif cabbage_C_rightside.gif

cabbage_C_topleft.gif cabbage_C_leftside.gif

```
background-image: url(cabbage_C_rightside.gif);
background-repeat: no-repeat;
background-position: right 120px;
```

Figure 13-19. The collection of background images designed to be positioned in various places in the document, as well as an example of the image cabbage_C_rightside.gif positioned on the right edge of the document.

NOTE

Notice in Figure 13-18 that when an origin image is placed in the corner of an element, it is placed inside the border. Only repeated images extend under the border to its outer edge.

Background attachment

In the previous exercise, I asked you to scroll the page and watch what happens to the background image. As expected, it scrolls along with the document and off the top of the browser window, which is its default behavior. However, you can use the background-attachment property to free the background from the content and allow it to stay fixed in one position while the rest of the content scrolls.

background-attachment

Values:	scroll | fixed | inherit
Default:	scroll
Applies to:	all elements
Inherits:	no

With the background-attachment property, you have the choice of whether the background image scrolls or is fixed. When an image is fixed, it stays in the same position relative to the viewing area of the browser (as opposed to being relative to the element it fills). You'll see what I mean in a minute.

In the following example, a large, non-tiling image is placed in the background of the whole document (the body element). By default, when the document scrolls, the image scrolls too, moving up and off the page, as shown in Figure 13-20. However, if you set the value of background-attachment to fixed, it stays where it is initially placed, and the text scrolls up over it.

```
body {
    background-image: url(images/bigstar.gif);
    background-repeat: no-repeat;
    background-position: center 300px;
    background-attachment: fixed; }
```

You can fix the position of a background image for any element, not just body, but unfortunately, it won't work for users with Internet Explorer 6 and earlier for Windows. Fixed background images in non-body elements are supported in the latest IE7 release, thankfully.

A large non-repeating background image in the body of the document.

background-attachment: scroll;

By default, the background image is attached to the body element and scrolls off the page when the page content scrolls.

background-attachment: fixed;

When background-attachment is set to "fixed," the image stays in its position relative to the browser viewing area and does not scroll with the content

Figure 13-20. Preventing the background image from scrolling with the background-attachment *property.*

exercise 13-2 | (continued)

When we last left the cabbage article, we had applied the same background image to the **body** and **div** elements. We'll leave it just like that, but we'll use the **background-attachment** property to fix the image in the background of the page.

```
body {margin-left: 10%;
   margin-right: 10%;
   background-color: #BBE09F;
   background-image: url(cabbage_C.gif);
   background-repeat: no-repeat;
   background-position: center 85px;
   background-attachment: fixed;
}
```

Save the document, open it in the browser, and now try scrolling. The background image stays put in the viewing area of the browser.

Now for the *pièce de résistance*—make the background image in the **div** fixed as well. You can use the *cabbage_C.gif* image or change it to *cabbage_D.gif*, which is a little lighter.

```
div#titlepage {
   padding: 1em;
   background-color: #D4F8B9;
   background-image: url(cabbage_D.gif);
   background-repeat: no-repeat;
   background-position: center 75px;
   background-attachment: fixed;
}
```

Save the file and reload it in the browser window. Now look at what happens when you scroll the page. Windows users, you're going to need a browser other than Internet Explorer 6 (or earlier) to see the effect. (I recommend downloading the Firefox browser at *www.firefox.com*.)

READ MORE

Eric Meyer provides a more in-depth discussion of fixed background images at *www.meyerweb.com/eric/css/edge/complexspiral/glassy.html*.

Watch Out for Overrides

The background property is efficient, but use it carefully. Because it is a shorthand property, when you omit a value, that property will be reset with its default. Be careful that you do not accidentally override style rules earlier in the style sheet with a later shorthand rule that reverts your settings to the defaults.

In this example, the background image dots.gif will *not* be applied to h3 elements because by omitting the value for background-image, it essentially set that value to none.

```
h1, h2, h3 { background: red
url(dots.gif) repeat-x;}
```

```
h3 {background: green;}
```

To override particular properties, use the specific background property you intend to change. For example, if the intent in the above example was to change just the background color of h3 elements, the background-color property would be a better choice.

When using this or any shorthand property, pay attention to related rules earlier in the style sheet, or be sure that every property is specified.

exercise 13-2 | (continued)

This one is easy. Replace all of the background-related declarations in the **body** of the cabbage article with a single **background** property declaration.

```
body {
margin-left: 10%;
margin-right: 10%;
background: #BBE09F
url(cabbage_C.gif) no-repeat
center 85px fixed;
}
```

Do the same for the **div** element, and you're done.

The Shorthand background Property

You can use the handy background property to specify all of your background styles in one declaration.

background

Values: background-color background-image background-repeat background-attachment background-position | inherit

Default: see indiviual properties

Applies to: all elements

Inherits: no

As for the shorthand font property, the value of the background property is a list of values that would be provided for the individual background properties listed above. For example, this one background rule:

```
body { background: black url(arlo.jpg) no-repeat right top fixed; }
```

replaces this rule with five separate declarations:

```
body {
   background-color: black;
   background-image: url(arlo.jpg);
   background-repeat: no-repeat;
   background-position: right top;
   background-attachment: fixed;
}
```

All of the property values for background are optional and may appear in any order. The only restriction is that when providing the coordinates for the background-position property, the horizontal value must appear first, immediately followed by the vertical value. Be aware that if a value is omitted, it will be reset to its default (see Watch Out for Overrides).

Finally, External Style Sheets

Back in Chapter 11, Cascading Style Sheets Orientation, I told you that there are three ways to connect style sheets to (X)HTML markup: inline with the style attribute, embedded with the style element, and as an external *.css* document linked to or imported into the document. In this section, we finally get to that third option.

External style sheets are by far the most powerful way to use CSS, because you can make style changes across an entire site simply by editing a single style sheet document. That is the advantage to having all the style information in one place, and not mixed in with the document source.

First, a little bit about the style sheet document itself. An external style sheet is a plain-text document with at least one style sheet rule. It may *not* include any (X)HTML tags (there's no reason to, anyway). It may contain comments, but they must use the CSS comment syntax that you've seen already:

```
/* This is the end of the section */
```

The style sheet should be named with the *.css* suffix (there are some exceptions to this rule, but you're unlikely to encounter them as a beginner). Figure 13-21 shows how a short style sheet document looks in my text editor.

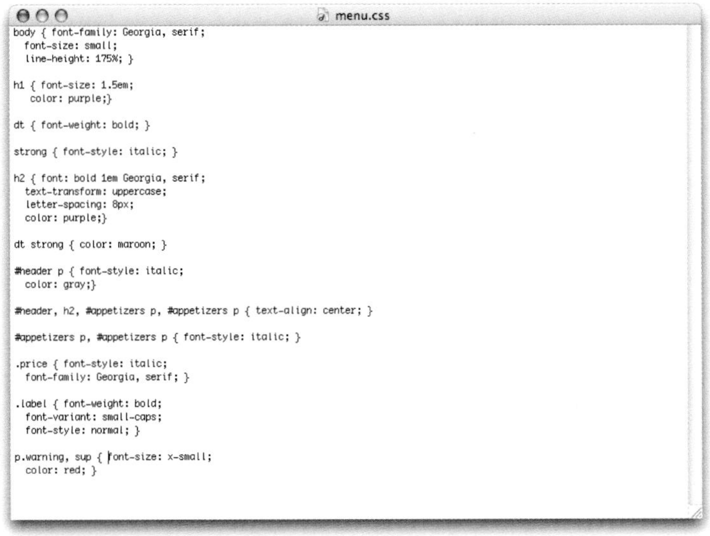

```
body { font-family: Georgia, serif;
    font-size: small;
    line-height: 175%; }

h1 { font-size: 1.5em;
    color: purple;}

dt { font-weight: bold; }

strong { font-style: italic; }

h2 { font: bold 1em Georgia, serif;
    text-transform: uppercase;
    letter-spacing: 8px;
    color: purple;}

dt strong { color: maroon; }

#header p { font-style: italic;
    color: gray;}

#header, h2, #appetizers p, #appetizers p { text-align: center; }

#appetizers p, #appetizers p { font-style: italic; }

.price { font-style: italic;
    font-family: Georgia, serif; }

.label { font-weight: bold;
    font-variant: small-caps;
    font-style: normal; }

p.warning, sup { font-size: x-small;
    color: red; }
```

Figure 13-21. External style sheets contain only CSS rules and comments in a plain text document.

There are two ways to refer to an external style sheet from within the (X) HTML document: the `link` element and an `@import` rule. Let's look at both of these attachment methods.

Using the link Element

The best-supported method is to create a link to the *.css* document using the `link` element in the `head` of the document, as shown here:

```
<head>
<link rel="stylesheet" href="/path/stylesheet.css" type="text/css" />
<title>Titles are required.</title>
</head>
```

You need to include three attributes in the `link` element:

`rel="stylesheet"`

Defines the linked document's relation to the current document. The value of the `rel` attribute is always `stylesheet` when linking to a style sheet.

`href="url"`

Provides the location of the *.css* file.

PRODUCTION TIP

Design with Embedded Styles; Finish with an External Style Sheet

It is common web development practice to use an embedded style sheet while you are designing the page because it keeps everything in one place, and your changes will show instantly when you reload the page in the browser. But once the design is all set, the style rules are then cut and pasted into an external *.css* document so they can be linked or imported to multiple documents on the site.

NOTE

The `link` element is empty, so you need to terminate it with a trailing slash in XHTML documents, as shown in this example. Omit the trailing slash in HTML documents.

exercise 13-3 |
Making an external style sheet

As noted in an earlier tip, it is common practice to create an embedded style sheet while designing a site, then to move the rules to an external style sheet once the design is finished.

We'll do just that for the cabbages style sheet.

1. Open the latest version of **cabbages.html**. Select and cut all of the rules within the **style** element, but leave the **<style>...</style>** tags, because we'll be using them in a moment.

2. Create a new text document and paste all of the style rules. Make sure that no element tags got in there by accident.

3. Save this document as **cabbage. css** in the same directory as the **cabbage.html** document.

4. Now, back in **cabbage.html**, we'll add an **@import** rule to attach the external style sheet like this:

   ```
   <style type="text/css">
     @import url(cabbage.css);
   </style>
   ```

Save the file and reload it in the browser. It should look exactly the same as it did when the style sheet was embedded. If not, go back and make sure that everything matches the examples.

5. Delete the whole style element and this time, we'll add the style sheet with a **link** element in the **head** of the document.

   ```
   <link rel="stylesheet"
   type="text/css"
   href="cabbage.css" />
   ```

Again, test your work by saving the document and viewing it in the browser. If you want more practice, try doing the same for the style sheet for the Black Goose Bistro online menu from Chapter 12, Formatting Text.

```
type="text/css"
```
This identifies the data (MIME) type of the style sheet as "text/css" (currently the only option).

You can include multiple link elements to different style sheets and they'll all apply. If there are conflicts, whichever one is listed last will override previous settings due to the rule order and the cascade.

Importing with @import

The other method for attaching external style sheets to a document is to import it with an @import rule in the style element, as shown in this example:

```
<head>
<style type="text/css">
    @import url("http://path/stylesheet.css");
    p { font-face: Verdana;}
</style>
<title>Titles are required.</title>
</head>
```

In this example, an absolute URL is shown, but it could also be a relative URL (relative to the current (X)HTML document). The example above shows that an @import rule can appear in a style element with other rules, but it *must come before any selectors*. Again, you can import multiple style sheets and they all will apply, but style rules from the last file listed take precedence over earlier ones.

You can also use the @import function within a .*css* document to reference other .*css* documents. This lets you pull style information in from other style sheets.

NOTE

You can also supply the URL without the url( ) *notation:*

```
@import "/path/style.css";
```
Again, absolute pathnames, beginning at the root, will ensure that the .css document will always be found.

You can try both the link and @import methods in Exercise 13-3.

Modular Style Sheets

Because you can compile information from multiple external style sheets, modular style sheets have become popular for style management. With this method, one external style sheet attached to an (X)HTML document accesses style rules from multiple .*css* files. You can use this method strategically to reuse collections of styles that you like to use frequently in a mix-and-match style with other collections.

For example, frequently used styles related to navigation could be stored in a navigation style sheet. Basic typography settings could be stored in another, form styles in another, and so on. These style modules are added to the main style sheet with individual `@import` rules. Again, the `@import` rules need to go before rules that use selectors.

Content of clientsite.css:

```
/* basic typography */
@import url("type.css");

/* form inputs */
@import url("forms.css");

/* navigation */
@import url("list-nav.css");

/* site-specific styles */
body { background: orange; }
```

... more style rules...

Style Sheets for Print (and Other Media)

Colors and fancy backgrounds are nice for web pages, but they are often a nuisance when the page is printed. There has been a common convention on the Web to provide a "printer friendly" version for pages that are information-rich and likely to be printed. The print version was usually a separate (X)HTML document that was text-only, or at the very least, stripped of all the bells and whistles, and reduced to a single column of content.

Now that CSS is widely supported, you can make a version of the document that is customized for print without having to make a separate (X)HTML document. It's all handled with a separate style sheet that gets used only when the document is sent to a printer.

In fact, CSS2 introduced the ability to target "print" and eight other different media types (see the CSS for Other Media sidebar). This is done using the `media` attribute in the `link` element or a `media` keyword in an `@import` rule in the style sheet.

In this very simplified example, I've created a separate style sheet for the *cabbage.html* document that gets used when the document is printed. This is the contents of *cabbage_print.css*:

```
body {
    margin-left: 10%;
    margin-right: 10%; }

div#titlepage {
    padding: 1em;
    border: thin double black; }
```

CSS for Other Media

CSS2 introduced the ability to target style sheets to nine different media. Currently, only `screen`, `print`, and `all` are widely supported; however, `handheld` is getting more attention. The complete list is as follows:

`all`
  Used for all media.

`aural`
  Used for screen readers and other audio versions of the document.

`braille`
  Used with braille tactile devices.

`embossed`
  Used with braille printers.

`handheld`
  Used for web-enabled cell phones or PDAs.

`print`
  Used for printing or print previews.

`projection`
  Used for slideshow-type presentations.

`screen`
  Used for display on a computer monitor.

`speech`
  Introduced in CSS2.1 to eventually replace `aural`.

`tty`
  Used for teletype printers or similar devices.

`tv`
  Used for presentation on a television.

For more information about media-specific style sheets, see the W3C pages at *www.w3.org/TR/CSS21/media.html*.

```
a {
  text-decoration: none;}

div#titlepage p {
  text-align: center;
  font-variant: small-caps; }

p {
  text-align: justify; }

h1,h2,h3,h4,h5,h6 {
    text-transform: uppercase;
    text-align: center; }
```

This print style sheet differs from the previous version in these ways:

- All color and background properties have been removed.
- A border has been added to the "titlepage" div to make it stand out.
- Links are not underlined.

Once the media-specific style sheets are created, I attach them to the source document and specify which style sheet is used for which media. Here are two ways to do it:

Linking to media-dependent style sheets

Use the media attribute in the link element to specify the target medium. Here, I added a new link element to *cabbage.html* that targets print (the previous one is now targeting screen):

```
<head>
<link rel="stylesheet" type="text/css"
href="cabbage.css" media="screen" />

<link rel="stylesheet" type="text/css"
 href="cabbage_print.css" media="print" />
</head>
```

Using an @import rule

Another way to attach target external style sheets is with @import rules in the style element (or in another external style sheet):

```
<style type="text/css">
@import url(cabbage.css) screen;
@import url(cabbage_print.css) print;
</style>
```

You should already be pretty familiar with how this document looks in the browser. Figure 13-22 shows how it looks when it is printed.

This is a very simplified example of what can be done with print style sheets. For more information on this rich topic, see the Style Sheets for Print box.

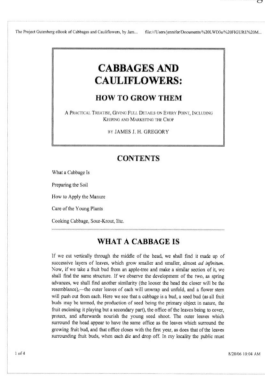

Figure 13-22. What cabbage.html looks like when printed. The print-specific style sheet removes the colors and puts a rule around the "titlepage" div.

Test Yourself

This time we'll test your background prowess entirely with matching and multiple-choice questions.

1. Which of these areas gets filled with a background color?

    a. the area behind the content

    b. any padding added around the content

    c. under the border

    d. the margin around the border

    e. all of the above

    f. a and b

    g. a, b, and c

2. Which of these is *not* a way to specify the color white in CSS?

    a. #FFFFFF   b. #FFF   c. rgb(255, 255, 255)

    d. rgb(FF, FF, FF)   e. white   f. rgb(100%, 100%, 100%)

3. Match the pseudoclass with the elements it targets.

    a. `a:link`   1. links that have already been clicked

    b. `a:visited`   2. elements that are highlighted and ready for input

    c. `a:hover`   3. the first child element of a parent element

    d. `a:active`   4. a link with the mouse pointer over it

    e. `:focus`   5. links that have not yet been visited

    f. `:first-child`   6. links that are in the process of being clicked

4. Match the following rules with their respective samples shown in Figure 13-23 (right). All of the samples in the figure use the same source document consisting of one paragraph element to which some padding and a border have been applied.

    a. `body {background-image: url(graphic.gif);}`

    b. `p {background-image: url(graphic.gif); background-repeat: no-repeat; background-position: 50% 0%;}`

    c. `body {background-image: url(graphic.gif); background-repeat: repeat-x;}`

    d. `p {background: url(graphic.gif) no-repeat right center;}`

    e. `body {background-image: url(graphic.gif); background-repeat: repeat-y;}`

    f. `body { background: url(graphic.gif) no-repeat right center;}`

5. Which rule will not work in Internet Explorer 6 and earlier (Windows) due to lack of support?

    a. `p.highlight:hover {background-color: yellow}`

    b. `li:first-child {background-color: #CCCCCC;}`

    c. `div#contents {background: url(daisy.gif) no-repeat fixed;}`

    d. `blockquote: before {content: "%8220;"; font-size: x-large; color: purple;}`

    e. all of the above

Review: Color and Background Properties

Here is a summary of the properties covered in this chapter, in alphabetical order.

Property	Description
background	A shorthand property that combines background properties
background-attachment	Specifies whether the background image scrolls or is fixed
background-color	Specifies the background color for an element
background-image	Provides the location of an image to use as a background
background-position	Specifies the location of the origin background image
background-repeat	Whether and how a background image repeats (tiles)
color	Specifies the foreground (text and border) color

THINKING INSIDE THE BOX
(Padding, Borders, and Margins)

In Chapter 11, Cascading Style Sheets Orientation, I introduced the box model as one of the fundamental concepts of CSS. According to the box model, every element in a document generates a box to which properties such as width, height, padding, borders, and margins can be applied. You probably already have a feel for how element boxes work, from adding backgrounds to elements. This chapter covers all the box-related properties. Once we've covered the basics, we will be ready to move boxes around in Chapter 15, Floating and Positioning.

We'll begin with an overview of the components of an element box, then take on the box properties from the inside out: content dimensions, padding, borders, and margins.

IN THIS CHAPTER

The components of an element box

Setting box dimensions

Adding padding around content

Adding borders

Adding margins

Assigning display roles

The Element Box

As we've seen, every element in a document, both block-level and inline, generates a rectangular element box. The components of an element box are diagrammed in Figure 14-1. Pay attention to the new terminology—it will be helpful in keeping things straight later in the chapter.

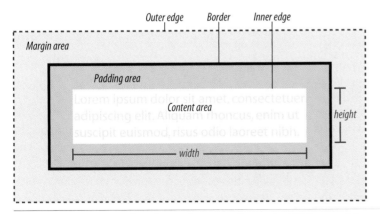

Figure 14-1. The parts of an element box according to the CSS box model.

261

content area

At the core of the element box is the content itself. In Figure 14-1, the content area is indicated by text in a white box.

inner edges

The edges of the content area are referred to as the inner edges of the element box. This is the box that gets sized when you apply `width` and `height` properties. Although the inner edges are made distinct by a color change in Figure 14-1, in real pages, the edge of the content area would be invisible.

padding

The padding is the area held between the content area and an optional border. In the diagram, the padding area is indicated by a yellow-orange color. Padding is optional.

border

The border is a line (or stylized line) that surrounds the element and its padding. Borders are also optional.

margin

The margin is an optional amount of space added on the *outside* of the border. In the diagram, the margin is indicated with light-blue shading, but in reality, margins are always transparent, allowing the background of the parent element to show through.

outer edge

The outside edges of the margin area make up the outer edges of the element box. This is the total area the element takes up on the page, and it includes the width of the content area plus the total amount of padding, border, and margins applied to the element. The outer edge in the diagram is indicated with a dotted line, but in real web pages, the edge of the margin is invisible.

All elements have these box components; however, as you will see, some properties behave differently based on whether the element is block or inline. In fact, we'll see some of those differences right off the bat with box dimensions.

The total width of an element includes the width of the content plus the total amount of padding, borders, and margins applied to the element.

Setting the Content Dimensions

Use the `width` and `height` properties to specify the width and height (naturally) of the content area of the element. You can specify the width and height only of block-level elements and non-text inline elements such as images. The `width` and `height` properties do not apply to inline text (a.k.a. non-replaced) elements and will be ignored by the browser. In other words, you cannot specify the width and height of an anchor (a) or `strong` element (see note).

width

Values: *length measurement | percentage* | auto | inherit

Default: auto

Applies to: *Block-level elements and replaced inline elements (such as images)*

Inherits: *no*

height

Values: *length measurement | percentage* | auto | inherit

Default: auto

Applies to: *Block-level elements and replaced inline elements (such as images)*

Inherits: *no*

By default, the width and height of a block element is calculated automatically by the browser (thus the default auto value). It will be as wide as the browser window or other containing block element, and as high as necessary to fit the content. However, you can use the width and height properties to make the content area of an element a specific width or height. Em, pixel, and percentage values are the most common ways to size elements.

The width and height properties are straightforward to use, as shown in these examples and Figure 14-2. I've added a background color to the elements as well, to make the boundaries of the content area more clear.

```
p#A {width: 400px; height: 100px; background: #C2F670;}

p#B {width: 150px; height: 300px; background: #C2F670;}
```

width: 400px; height: 100px;

Applying the masks to the glasses is the most labor-intensive part of the process. Not only do you have to measure, place, and burnish on each mask, but you also need to completely cover the remainder of the glass in heavy paper. Any exposed areas (even inside) will get scratched by the flying sand, so it has to be a good seal.

Applying the masks to the glasses is the most labor-intensive part of the process. Not only do you have to measure, place, and burnish on each mask, but you also need to completely cover the remainder of the glass in heavy paper. Any exposed areas (even inside) will get scratched by the flying sand, so it has to be a good seal.

width: 150px; height: 300px;

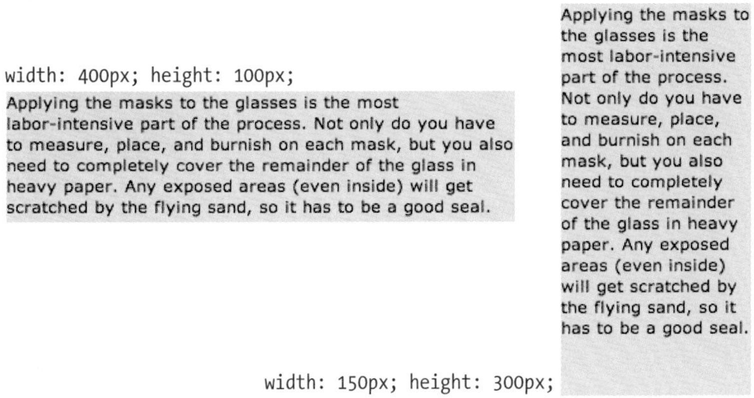

Figure 14-2. Specifying the width and height of paragraph elements.

The main thing to keep in mind when specifying the width and height is that it applies to the *content area only*. Any padding, border, and margins you apply to the element will be added to the width value. So, for example, if you set the width of an element to 200 pixels, and add 10 pixels of padding, a 1-pixel border, and 20 pixels of margin, the total width of the element box will be 262 pixels, calculated as follows:

$$20px + 1px + 10px + 200px \; width + 10px + 1px + 20px = 262px$$

NOTE

Actually, there is a way to apply width *and* height *properties to anchors by forcing them to behave as block elements with the* display *property, covered at the end of this chapter.*

Maximum and Minimum Dimensions

CSS2 introduced properties for setting minimum and maximum heights and widths for block elements. They may be useful if you want to put limits on the size of an element.

max-height, max-width, min-height, min-width

Values: *percentage | length* | none | inherit

These properties work with block level and replaced elements (like images) only. The value applies to the content area, so if you apply padding, borders, or margins, it will make the overall element box larger, even if a max-width or max-height property have been specified.

Unfortunately, these properties are not supported by Internet Explorer 6 and earlier. There is a workaround for max-width that uses a non-standard IE extension, which you can read about in this article by Svend Tofte at *www.svendtofte.com/code/max_width_in_ie/*. The css-discuss archive offers links to several min-width workarounds here: *css-discuss.incutio.com/?page=MinWidth.*

NOTE

Standards and Quirks Mode are covered in detail in Chapter 10, Understanding the Standards.

This is the way it is documented in the CSS2 Recommendation, and the way it works in all standards-compliant browsers (Firefox, Netscape 6+, Safari, Opera, and Internet Explorer 6 and 7 in Standards Mode). However, it is important to know that there is a well-known inconsistency in the way IE 5, 5.5 and 6 (in Quirks Mode) interprets width and height values. See the IE/Windows Box Model sidebar for details and a workaround.

The IE/Windows Box Model

One of the most notorious browser inconsistencies is that Internet Explorer for Windows (all versions except 6 and 7 running in Standards Mode) has its own implementation of the box model.

In these versions, the `width` property is applied to the outer edges of the *borders*, not to the content area as established in the CSS Recommendations. This causes major discrepancies between how the element is sized in standards-compliant browsers and how it will appear in IE/Windows.

Take the `div` from an earlier example that has its width set to 200 pixels, with a 20 pixel margin, a 1 pixel border, and 10 pixels of padding. On standards-compliant browsers, the visible element box would measure 222 pixels (200 + 2 + 20), and the entire element box including the margin would be 262 pixels.

But IE 5 and 5.5 (Windows only) applies the 200px width value to the outer edges of the borders (see Figure 14-3). The padding and border are subtracted, leaving a content area that's 178 pixels wide. The outer edges of the element box would measure 240 pixels, not 262. You can see how this would present a problem in page layouts with precisely sized columns or page widths.

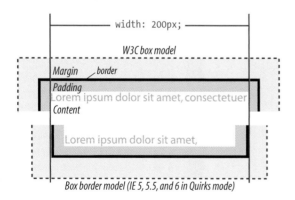

Figure 14-3. Box model interpretation in WinIE 5 and 5.5.

To deal with these discrepancies, the first thing to do is make sure you use a proper DOCTYPE declaration to ensure IE 6 and 7 (the vast majority of IE traffic as of this writing) will switch into Standards Mode and display the element widths as you'd expect.

If for some reason you must support IE 5 and 5.5, you can use a conditional comment to direct an IE 5/5.5-specific style sheet containing adjusted `width` values to just those browsers. Other browsers will interpret the contents as a regular comment and ignore it, but IE versions are programmed to pay attention to what's inside.

In this example, the IE5/5.5 style sheet contains a rule that sets the width of the `div` to 222 pixels. When IE 5/5.5 subtracts the border and padding widths, the content area will end up 200 pixels wide, as desired.

```
div { width: 222px; }
```

Name the style sheet clearly, such as *ie5.css*, or similar. In the real world, chances are this style sheet will have more than one rule, but we'll keep this example simple.

Next, link that style sheet to the document, but contain the `link` element in a conditional comment that calls on the special style sheet only "if the IE version is less than 6."

```
<!--[if lt IE 6]>
<link rel="stylesheet" type="text/css"
media="screen" href="/css/ie5.css" />
<![endif]-->
```

Obviously, there's more to it than I've covered here, so I encourage you to read more at these resources:

- The Microsoft tutorial on conditional comments (*msdn. microsoft.com/workshop/author/dhtml/overview/ ccomment_ovw.asp*)

- Conditional Comments article at Quirksmode.com (*www. quirksmode.org/css/condcom.html*)

Specifying height

In general practice, it is less common to specify the height of elements. It is more in keeping with the nature of the medium to allow the height to be calculated automatically, based on the size of the text and other contents. This allows it to change based on the font size, user settings, or other factors. If you do specify a height for an element containing text, be sure to also consider what happens should the content not fit. Fortunately, CSS gives you some options, as we'll see in the next section.

Handling overflow

When an element is set to a size that is too small for its contents, it is possible to specify what to do with the content that doesn't fit, using the overflow property.

overflow

Values: visible | hidden | scroll | auto | inherit

Default: visible

Applies to: Block-level elements and replaced inline elements (such as images)

Inherits: no

Figure 14-4 demonstrates the predefined values for overflow. In the figure, the various values are applied to an element that is 150 pixels square. The background color makes the edges of the content area apparent.

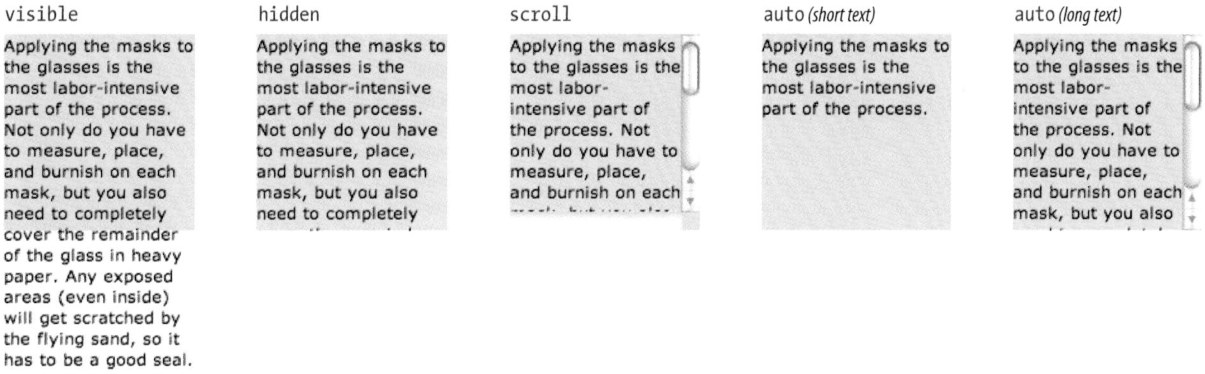

The Future of the Box Model

CSS3 includes a new box-sizing property that lets authors choose whether width and height dimensions are applied to the content area (as is the current model) or to the outer edges of the border (as implemented by IE 5/5.5). For a good overview of this new feature, read Peter-Paul Koch's article "Box Model Tweaking" at *www. quirksmode.org/css/box.html*.

visible

Applying the masks to the glasses is the most labor-intensive part of the process. Not only do you have to measure, place, and burnish on each mask, but you also need to completely cover the remainder of the glass in heavy paper. Any exposed areas (even inside) will get scratched by the flying sand, so it has to be a good seal.

hidden

Applying the masks to the glasses is the most labor-intensive part of the process. Not only do you have to measure, place, and burnish on each mask, but you also need to completely

scroll

Applying the masks to the glasses is the most labor-intensive part of the process. Not only do you have to measure, place, and burnish on each

auto *(short text)*

Applying the masks to the glasses is the most labor-intensive part of the process.

auto *(long text)*

Applying the masks to the glasses is the most labor-intensive part of the process. Not only do you have to measure, place, and burnish on each mask, but you also

Figure 14-4. Options for handling content overflow.

visible

> The default value is visible, which allows the content to hang out over the element box so that it all can be seen.

hidden

> When overflow is set to hidden, the content that does not fit gets clipped off and does not appear beyond the edges of the element's content area.

scroll

When scroll is specified, scrollbars are added to the element box to let users scroll through the content. Be aware that when you set the value to scroll, the scrollbars will always be there, even if the content fits in the specified height just fine.

auto

The auto value allows the browser to decide how to handle overflow. In most cases, scrollbars are added only when the content doesn't fit and they are needed.

Padding

Padding is the space between the content area and the border (or the place the border would be if one isn't specified). I find it helpful to add a little padding to elements when using a background color or a border. It gives the content a little breathing room, and prevents the border or edge of the background from bumping right up against the text.

You can add padding to the individual sides of any element (block-level or inline). There is also a shorthand padding property that lets you add padding on all sides at once.

padding-top, padding-right, padding-bottom, padding-left

Values:	*length measurement* | *percentage* | inherit
Default:	0
Applies to:	*all elements except table-row, table-row group, tabel-header-group, table-footer-group, table-column, and table-column-group*
Inherits:	*no*

padding

Values:	*length measurement* | *percentage* | inherit
Default:	0
Applies to:	*all elements*
Inherits:	*no*

With the padding-top, padding-right, padding-bottom, and padding-left properties, you can specify an amount of padding for each side of an element as shown in this example and Figure 14-5 (note that I've also added a background color to make the edges of the padding area apparent).

```
blockquote {
    padding-top: 1em;
    padding-right: 3em;
    padding-bottom: 1em;
    padding-left: 3em;
    background-color: #D098D4;
}
```

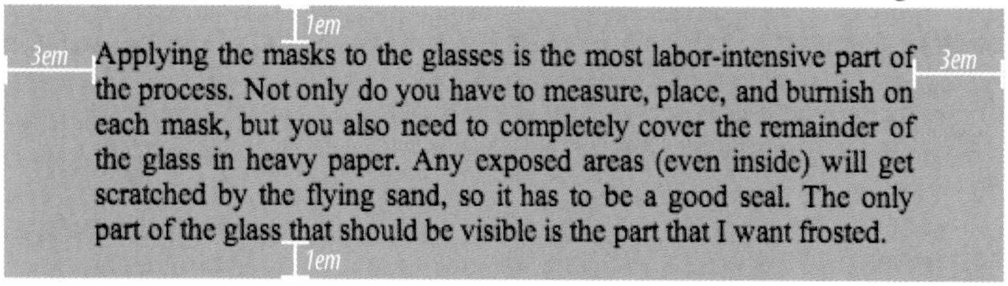

1em
3em Applying the masks to the glasses is the most labor-intensive part of *3em*
the process. Not only do you have to measure, place, and burnish on
each mask, but you also need to completely cover the remainder of
the glass in heavy paper. Any exposed areas (even inside) will get
scratched by the flying sand, so it has to be a good seal. The only
part of the glass that should be visible is the part that I want frosted.
1em

Figure 14-5. Adding padding around an element.

You can specify padding in any of the CSS length units (see the At a Glance sidebar for a refresher) or as a percentage of the *width* of the parent element. Yes, the width is used as the basis even for top and bottom padding, and if the width of the parent element should change, so will the padding values on all sides of the child element.

The shorthand padding property

As an alternative to setting padding one side at a time, you can use the shorthand `padding` property to add padding all around the element. The syntax is kind of interesting; you can specify four, three, two, or one value for a single `padding` property. Let's see how that works, starting with four values.

When you supply four `padding` values, they are applied to each side in clockwise order, starting at the top. Some people use the mnemonic device "TRouBLe" for the order *top right bottom left*.

    { padding: *top right bottom left*; }

Using the `padding` property, we could reproduce the padding specified with the four individual properties in the previous example like this:

```
blockquote {
    padding: 1em 3em 1em 3em;
    background-color: #D098D4;
}
```

If the left and right padding are the same, you can shorten it by supplying only three values. The value for "right" (the second value in the string) will be mirrored and used for "left" as well. It is as though the browser assumes "left" value is missing, so it just uses the "right" value on both sides. The syntax for three values is as follows:

    { padding: *top right/left bottom*; }

This rule would be equivalent to the previous example because the padding on the left and right edges of the element should be set to 3em.

```
blockquote {
    padding: 1em 3em 1em;
    background-color: #D098D4;
}
```

Continuing with this pattern, if you provide only two values, the first one is used for the top and the bottom edges, and the second one is used for the left and right edges:

    { padding: *top/bottom right/left*; }

Again, the same effect achieved by the previous two examples could be accomplished with this rule.

```
blockquote {
    padding: 1em 3em;
    background-color: #D098D4;
}
```

padding: 10px 10px 10px 50%;

> Applying the masks to the glasses is the most labor-intensive part of the process. Not only do you have to measure, place, and burnish on each mask, but you also need to completely cover the remainder of the glass in heavy paper. Any exposed areas (even inside) will get scratched by the flying sand, so it has to be a good seal.

padding: 100px 10px 10px 100px;

> Applying the masks to the glasses is the most labor-intensive part of the process. Not only do you have to measure, place, and burnish on each mask, but you also need to completely cover the remainder of the glass in heavy paper. Any exposed areas (even inside) will get scratched by the flying sand, so it has to be a good seal.

padding: 100px 5px;

> Applying the masks to the glasses is the most labor-intensive part of the process. Not only do you have to measure, place, and burnish on each mask, but you also need to completely cover the remainder of the glass in heavy paper. Any exposed areas (even inside) will get scratched by the flying sand, so it has to be a good seal.

padding: 10px 33%;

> Applying the masks to the glasses is the most labor-intensive part of the process. Not only do you have to measure, place, and burnish on each mask, but you also need to completely cover the remainder of the glass in heavy paper. Any exposed areas (even inside) will get scratched by the flying sand, so it has to be a good seal.

Figure 14-6. Extreme padding.

Note that all of the previous examples have the same visual effect as shown in Figure 14-5.

Finally, if you provide just one value, it will be applied to all four sides of the element. This declaration applies 15 pixels of padding on all sides of a `div` element.

```css
div#announcement {
  padding: 15px;
  border: 1px solid;
}
```

Padding doesn't need to be so conservative or symmetrical. You can use padding to dramatic effect for pushing content around inside its own border or colored background. The examples in Figure 14-6 are a little more "out there" and may give you a different perspective on how padding can be used.

exercise 14-1 | **Adding a little padding**

In this exercise, we'll use basic box properties to improve the appearance of a fictional shopping site, JenWARE.com. I've given you a big headstart by marking up the source document and creating a style sheet that handles text formatting and backgrounds. The document, *jenware.html*, is available in the *materials* directory (*www.learningwebdesign.com/materials*).

Figure 14-7 shows before and after shots of the JenWARE home page. It's going to take a few steps to get this page into presentable shape, and padding is just the beginning.

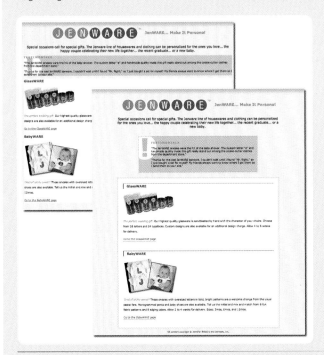

Figure 14-7. Before and after shots of the JenWARE home page.

1. Start by opening *jenware.com* in a browser and a text editor to see what you've got to work with. The document has been divided into three **div** elements ("intro," "testimonials," and "products"). Background colors have been added to the **body**, testimonials, and products sections. There is also a horizontally repeating background image along the top of the **body** that creates the gradient (color fade) at the top of the page, and an exclamation point image in the top-left corner of the testimonials section. The remaining rules are for formatting text.

2. The first thing we'll do is add padding to the "products" **div**. Two ems of padding all around ought to be fine. Find the **#products** selector and add the **padding** declaration.

   ```
   #products {
       padding: 2em;
       background-color: #FFF;
       line-height: 2em;
   }
   ```

3. Next, we'll get a little fancier with the "testimonials" section. I want to clear some space in the left side of the **div** so that my nifty exclamation point background image is visible. There are several approaches to applying different padding amounts to each side, but I'm going to do it in a way that gives you practice at deliberately overriding earlier declarations.

   Use the **padding** shorthand property to add 1 em of padding on all sides of the testimonials **div**. Then write a second declaration that adds 60 pixels of padding to the left side only. Because the **padding-left** declaration comes second, it will override the 1em setting applied with the **padding** property.

   ```
   #testimonials {
       padding: 1em;
       padding-left: 60px;
       background: #FFBC53 url(images/ex-circle-corner.gif) no-repeat left
   top;
       line-height: 1.2em;
   }
   ```

4. Save your work and look at it in the browser. The testimonials and product descriptions should look a little more comfortable in their boxes. Figure 14-8 highlights the padding additions.

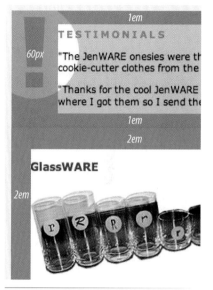

Figure 14-8. The pink area indicates padding added to the testimonials section. Blue indicates the products section padding.

Borders

A border is simply a line drawn around the content area and its (optional) padding. Thankfully, it doesn't have to be as boring as that last sentence makes it sound. You can choose from eight border styles and make them any width and color you like. You can apply the border all around the element or just a particular side or sides. You can even apply different border styles to sides of the same element. We'll start our border exploration with the various border styles.

Border style

The style is the most important of the border properties because, according to the CSS specification, if there is no border style specified, the border does not exist. In other words, you must always declare the style of the border, or the other border properties will be ignored.

Border styles can be applied one side at a time or by using the shorthand border-style property.

border-top-style, border-right-style,
border-bottom-style, border-left-style

Values: none|dotted|dashed|solid|double|groove|ridge|inset|outset|inherit

Default: none

Applies to: all elements

Inherits: no

border-style

Values: none|dotted|dashed|solid|double|groove|ridge|inset|outset|inherit

Default: none

Applies to: all elements

Inherits: no

The value of the border-style properties is one of ten keywords describing the available border styles, as shown in Figure 14-9.

WARNING

There is a bug in Internet Explorer 6 for Windows that causes borders specified as dotted *to render as* dashed.

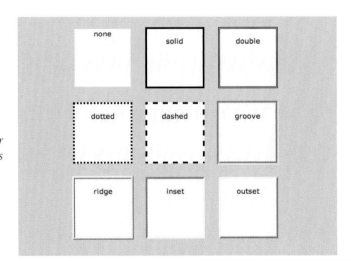

Figure 14-9. The available border styles (shown at the default medium width) .

You can use the side-specific border style properties (border-top-style, border-right-style, border-bottom-style, and border-left-style) to apply a style to one side of the element. If you do not specify a width, the default medium width will be used. If there is no color specified, the border uses the foreground color of the element (same as the text).

In the following example, I've applied a different style to each side of an element to show the single-side border properties in action (Figure 14-10).

```
div#silly {
  border-top-style: solid;
  border-right-style: dashed;
  border-bottom-style: double;
  border-left-style: dotted;
  width: 300px;
  height: 100px;}
```

The `border-style` shorthand property works on the clockwise (TRouBLe) system described for `padding` earlier. You can supply four values for all four sides or fewer values when the left/right and top/bottom borders are the same. The silly border effect in the previous example could also be specified using the `border-style` property as shown here, and the result would be the same as shown in Figure 14-10.

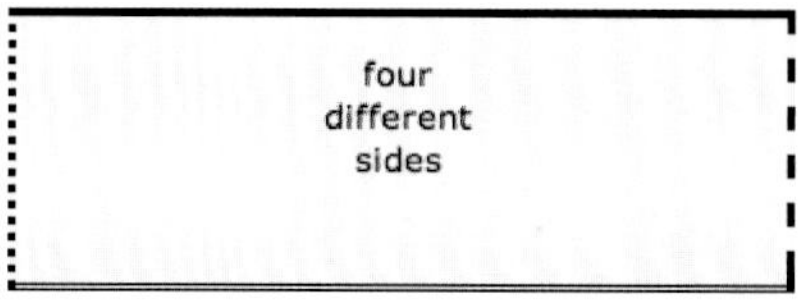

Figure 14-10. Border styles applied to individual sides of an element.

```
border-style: solid dashed double dotted;
```

Border width (thickness)

Use one of the border width properties to specify the thickness of the border. Once again, you can target each side of the element with a single-side property, or specify several sides at once in clockwise order with the shorthand `border-width` property.

`border-top-width, border-right-width,`
`border-bottom-width, border-left-width`

Values:	*length units* | thin | medium | thick | inherit
Default:	medium
Applies to:	*all elements*
Inherits:	*no*

`border-width`

Values:	*length units* | thin | medium | thick | inherit
Default:	medium
Applies to:	*all elements*
Inherits:	*no*

The most common way to specify the width of borders is using a pixel measurement; however, you can also specify one of the keywords (`thin`, `medium`, or `thick`) and leave the rendering up to the browser.

I've included a mix of values in this example (Figure 14-11). Notice that I've also included the `border-style` property because if I didn't, no border would render at all.

```
div#help {
  border-top-width: thin;
  border-right-width: medium;
  border-bottom-width: thick;
  border-left-width: 12px;
  border-style: solid;
  width: 300px;
  height: 100px; }
```

or

```
div#help {
    border-width: thin  medium thick 12px;
    border-style: solid;
    width: 300px;
    height: 100px; }
```

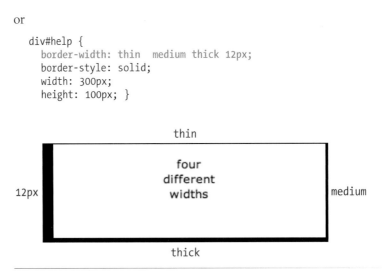

Figure 14-11. Specifying the width of borders.

Border color

Border colors are specified in the same way: using the side-specific properties or the `border-color` shorthand property. When you specify a border color, it overrides the foreground color as set by the `color` property for the element.

`border-top-color, border-right-color, border-bottom-color, border-left-color`

Values:	*color name or RGB value* | transparent | inherit
Default:	*the value of the* `color` *property for the element*
Applies to:	*all elements*
Inherits:	*no*

`border-color`

Values:	*color name or RGB value* | transparent | inherit
Default:	*the value of the* `color` *property for the element*
Applies to:	*all elements*
Inherits:	*no*

You know all about specifying color values, and you should be getting used to the shorthand properties as well, so I'll keep this example short and sweet (Figure 14-12). Here, I've provided two values for the shorthand `border-color` property to make the top and bottom of a `div` maroon and the left and right sides aqua.

```
div#special {
    border-color: maroon aqua;
    border-style: solid;
    border-width: 6px;
    width: 300px;
    height: 100px;
}
```

NOTE

CSS2 added the `transparent` *keyword value for border colors that allows the background of the parent to show through the border, yet holds the width of the border as specified. This may be useful when creating rollover (`:hover`) effects with CSS because the space where the border will appear is maintained when the mouse is not over the element.*

Unfortunately, the `transparent` *value is not supported by Internet Explorer for Windows (versions 6 and earlier). Support in IE7 is not yet documented as of this writing, so you'll have to test it out yourself.*

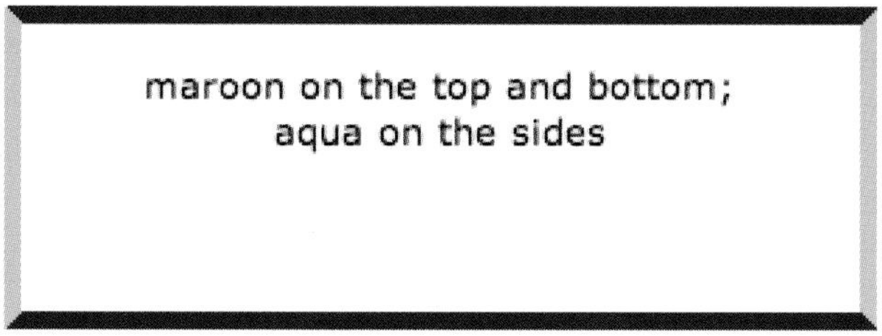

Figure 14-12. Specifying the color of borders.

Combining style, width, and color

The authors of CSS didn't skimp when it came to border shortcuts. They also created properties for providing style, width, and color values in one declaration. Again, you can specify the appearance of specific sides, or use the border property to change all four sides at once.

border-top, border-right, border-bottom, border-left

Values: border-style border-width border-color | inherit

Default: defaults for each property

Applies to: all elements

Inherits: no

border

Values: border-style border-width border-color | inherit

Default: defaults for each property

Applies to: all elements

Inherits: no

The values for border and the side-specific border properties may include style, width, and color values in any order. You do not need to declare all three, but keep in mind that if the border style value is omitted, no border will render.

The border shorthand property works a bit differently than the other shorthand properties that we covered in that it takes one set of values and always applies them to all four sides of the element. In other words, it does not use the clockwise, "TRBL" system that we've seen with other shorthand properties.

Here is a smattering of valid border shortcut examples to get an idea for how they work.

    h1 { border-left: red .5em solid; }   *left border only*

    h2 { border-bottom: 1px solid; }   *bottom border only*

    p.example { border: 2px dotted #663; } *all four sides*

Now it is time to try your hand at borders. Exercise 14-2 will not only give you some practice, but it should also give you some ideas on the ways borders can be used to add graphic interest to CSS-based page designs.

NOTE

Internet Explorer 6 users will see dashed borders instead of dotted borders under links due to buggy support for the dotted *keyword.*

exercise 14-2 | **Border tricks**

In this exercise, we'll have some fun with borders on the JenWARE home page. In addition to putting subtle borders around content sections on the page, we'll use borders to beef up the product headlines and as an alternative to underlines under links.

1. Open *jenware.html* in a text editor if it isn't already. We'll start simple by using the shorthand **border** property to add an orange (#F26521) dashed rule around the testimonials section. Add the new declaration to the rule for the "testimonials" **div**.

```
#testimonials {
   border: 1px dashed #F26521;
   padding: 1em;
   padding-left: 60px;
   background: #FFBC53 url(images/ex-circle-corner.gif) no-repeat left
top;
   line-height: 1.2em;
   }
```

2. Next, add a double rule around the "products" area that is an even lighter orange (#FFBC53) so as not to call too much attention to itself.

```
#products {
   border: double #FFBC53;
   padding: 2em;
   background-color: #FFF;
   line-height: 2em;
   }
```

3. Just for fun (and practice), we'll add decorative borders on two sides of the headlines in the products section. I want the borders to be the same color as the text, so we don't need to specify the **border-color**. Find the existing rule for **h2** elements in the "products" **div**, and add a declaration that adds a 1-pixel solid rule on the top of the headline. Add another declaration that adds a thicker, 3-pixel solid rule on the left side. Finally, to prevent the text from bumping into that left border, we can add a little bit of padding (1em) to the left of the headline content.

```
#products h2 {
   border-top: 1px solid;
   border-left: 3px solid;
   padding-left: 1em;
   font-size: 1.2em;
   color: #921A66;
   }
```

4. The last thing we'll do is replace the standard text underline under links with a decorative bottom border.

   You will find that there are already rules in the style sheet for changing the colors of the four link states. Start by turning the underline off for all of the link states by setting the **text-decoration** to **none** in each of the rules.

   ```
   text-decoration: none;
   ```

   Next, add a 1-pixel dotted border to the bottom edge of each state by adding this declaration to each link rule:

   ```
   border-bottom: 1px dotted;
   ```

Notice that because we want the border to have the same color as the links, we do not need to specify a color. However, if you try this on your own pages, you can easily change the color and style of the bottom border.

As is often the case when you add a border to an element, it is a good idea to also add a little padding to keep things from bumping together. Add some padding to the bottom edges only, like so:

```
padding-bottom: .25em;
```

I'm noticing that there are a lot of redundant declarations here, and although it isn't necessary, let's take the time to condense our style sheet by grouping the selectors for these underline effects, then use separate rules to change only the colors (and background for the :hover state) . The final links section of the style sheet should look like this:

```
a:link, a:visited, a:hover, a:active {
    text-decoration: none;
    border-bottom: 1px dotted;
    padding-bottom: .25em;
}

a:link, a:active {
    color: #CC0000;
}

a:visited {
    color: #921A66;
}

a:hover {
    background-color: #FCF191;
    color: #921A66;
}
```

See Figure 14-13 for what the page looks like.

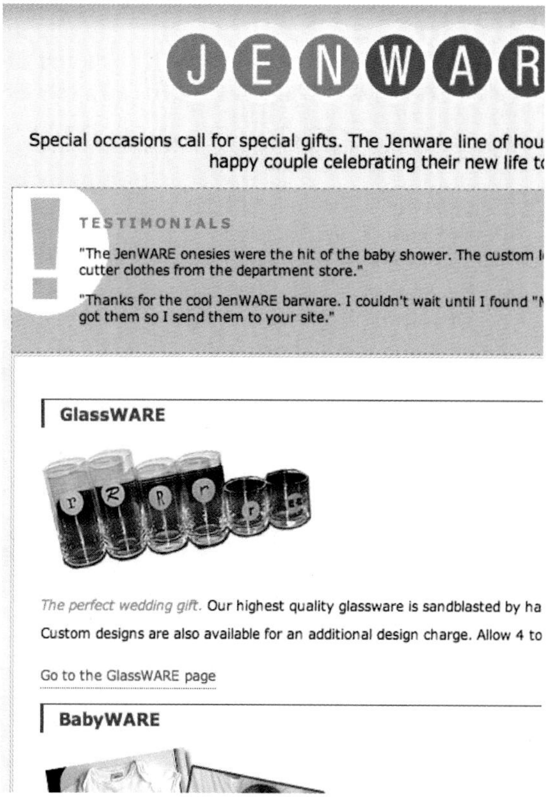

Margins

The last remaining component of the element box is its margin, which is an optional amount of space that you can add on the outside of the border. Margins keep elements from bumping into one another or the edge of the browser window. You can even use margins to make space for another column of content (we'll see how that works in Chapter 16, Page Layout with CSS). In this way, margins are an important tool in CSS-based page layout.

The side-specific and shorthand `margin` properties work much like the padding properties we've looked at already, however, margins have some special behaviors to be aware of.

`margin-top, margin-right, margin-bottom, margin-left`

Values: *length measurement* | *percentage* | auto | inherit

Default: auto

Applies to: *all elements*

Inherits: *no*

Figure 14-13. The results of our border additions.

`margin`

Values: *length measurement* | *percentage* | auto | inherit

Default: auto

Applies to: all elements except elements with table display types other than table-caption, table, and inline-table

Inherits: no

Adding a margin to the body *element adds space between the page content and the edges of the browser window.*

The margin properties are very straightforward to use. You can specify an amount of margin to appear on each side of the element, or use the `margin` property to specify all sides at once.

The shorthand `margin` property works the same as the `padding` shorthand. When you supply four values, they are applied in clockwise order (top, right, bottom, left) to the sides of the element. If you supply three values, the middle value applies to both the left and right sides. When two values are provided, the first is used for the top and bottom, and the second applies to the left and right edges. Finally, one value will be applied to all four sides of the element.

As for most web measurements, em units are your best bet for providing margin amounts that scale along with the text. Pixel values are commonly used as well. You can also provide a percentage value, but it should be noted that, as for padding, the percentage value is calculated based on the *width* of the parent element. If the parent's width changes, so will the margins on all four sides of the child element. The `auto` keyword allows the browser to fill in the amount of margin necessary to fit or fill the available space.

Figure 14-14 shows the results of the following margin examples. Note that I've added a light dotted rule to indicate the outside edge of the margin for clarity purposes only, but they would not appear on a real web page.

Ⓐ
```
p#A {
    margin: 4em;
    border: 1px solid red;
    background: #FCF2BE;
}
```

Ⓑ
```
p#B {
    margin-top: 2em;
    margin-right: 250px;
    margin-bottom: 1em;
    margin-left: 4em;
    border: 1px solid red;
    background: #FCF2BE;
}
```

Ⓒ
```
body {
    margin: 0 10%;
    border: 1px solid red;
    background-color: #BBE09F;
}
```

Ⓐ

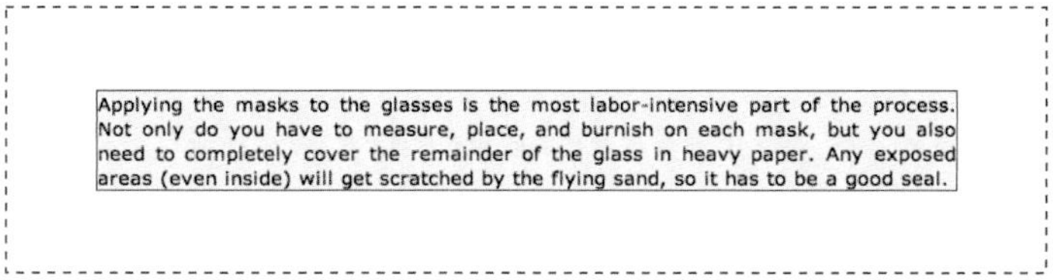

Applying the masks to the glasses is the most labor-intensive part of the process. Not only do you have to measure, place, and burnish on each mask, but you also need to completely cover the remainder of the glass in heavy paper. Any exposed areas (even inside) will get scratched by the flying sand, so it has to be a good seal.

`margin: 4em;`

Ⓑ

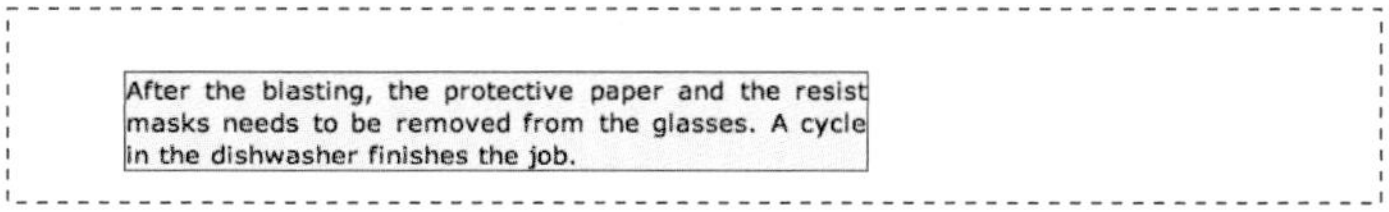

After the blasting, the protective paper and the resist masks needs to be removed from the glasses. A cycle in the dishwasher finishes the job.

```
margin-top: 2em;
margin-right: 250px;
margin-bottom: 1em;
margin-left: 4em;
```

Ⓒ

The Project Gutenberg eBook of Cabbages and Cauliflowers, by James J. H. Gregory.

CABBAGES AND CAULIFLOWERS:

HOW TO GROW THEM

A PRACTICAL TREATISE, GIVING FULL DETAILS ON EVERY POINT, INCLUDING KEEPING AND MARKETING THE CROP

BY JAMES J. H. GREGORY

CONTENTS

What a Cabbage Is

Preparing the Soil

How to Apply the Manure

Care of the Young Plants

Cooking Cabbage, Sour-Krout, Etc.

Done

`body: {margin: 0 10%}`

Adding margins to the body puts space between the element and the edges of the viewing area of the browser window. The red border shows the boundary of the body element (there is no padding applied).

Figure 14-14. Applying margins to the body and to individual elements.

Margin behavior

While it is easy to write rules that apply margin amounts around (X)HTML elements, it is important to be familiar with margin behavior.

Collapsing margins

The most significant margin behavior to be aware of is that the top and bottom margins of neighboring elements collapse. This means that instead of accumulating, adjacent margins overlap, and only the largest value will be used.

Using the two paragraphs from the previous figure as an example, if the top element has a bottom margin of 4 ems, and the following element has a top margin of 2 ems, the resulting margin space between elements does not add up to 6 ems. Rather, the margins collapse and the resulting margin between the paragraphs will be 4 ems, the largest specified value. This is demonstrated in Figure 14-15.

Figure source
Applying the masks to the glasses is the most labor-intensive part of the process. Not only do you have to measure, place, and burnish on each mask, but you also need to completely cover the remainder of the glass in heavy paper. Any exposed areas (even inside) will get scratched by the flying sand, so it has to be a good seal.
4em
After the blasting, the protective paper and the resist masks needs to be removed from the glasses. A cycle in the dishwasher finishes the job.
Adjacent vertical margins collapse

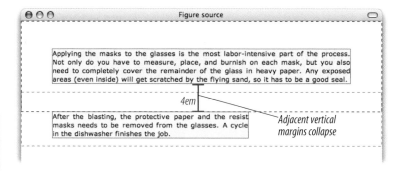

Figure 14-15. Vertical margins of neighboring elements collapse so that only the larger value is used.

> **FURTHER READING**
>
> ## Collapsing Margins
>
> When spacing between and around elements behave unpredictably, collapsing margins are often to blame. Here are a few articles that dig deep into collapsing margin behavior. They may help you understand what is happening behind the scenes in your layouts.
>
> - "No Margin for Error" by Andy Budd (*www.andybudd.com/archives/2003/11/no_margin_for_error/*)
> - "Uncollapsing Margins" by Eric Meyer (*www.complexspiral.com/publications/uncollapsing-margins/*)
> - "CSS: Auto-height and Margin-collapsing," by Minz Meyer (*www.researchkitchen.de/blog/archives/css-autoheight-and-margincollapsing.php*)

The only time top and bottom margins don't collapse is for floated or absolutely positioned elements (we'll get to floating and positioning in Chapter 15). Margins on the left and right sides never collapse, so they're nice and predictable.

Margins on inline elements

You can apply top and bottom margins to inline text elements (or "non-replaced inline elements", to use the proper CSS terminology), but it won't add vertical space above and below the element, and the height of the line will not change. However, when you apply left and right margins to inline text elements, margin space *will* be held clear before and after the text in the flow of the element, even if that element breaks over several lines.

Just to keep things interesting, margins on replaced elements, such as images, do render on all sides, and therefore do affect the height of the line. See Figure 14-16 for examples of each.

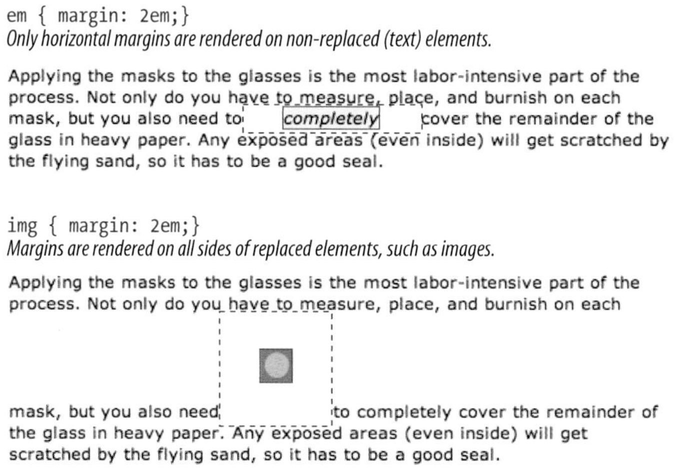

em { margin: 2em;}
Only horizontal margins are rendered on non-replaced (text) elements.
Applying the masks to the glasses is the most labor-intensive part of the process. Not only do you have to measure, place, and burnish on each mask, but you also need to completely cover the remainder of the glass in heavy paper. Any exposed areas (even inside) will get scratched by the flying sand, so it has to be a good seal.
img { margin: 2em;}
Margins are rendered on all sides of replaced elements, such as images.
Applying the masks to the glasses is the most labor-intensive part of the process. Not only do you have to measure, place, and burnish on each mask, but you also need to completely cover the remainder of the glass in heavy paper. Any exposed areas (even inside) will get scratched by the flying sand, so it has to be a good seal.

Figure 14-16. Margins applied to inline text and image elements.

Negative margins

It is worth noting that it is possible to specify negative values for margins. When you apply a negative margin, the content, padding, and border are moved in the opposite direction that would have resulted from a positive margin value.

This will be more clear with an example. Figure 14-17 shows two neighboring paragraphs with different colored borders applied to show their boundaries. In the left view, I've added a 4-em bottom margin to the top paragraph and it has the effect of pushing the following paragraph *down* by that amount. If I specify a negative value (-4em), the following element moves *up* by that amount, and overlaps the element with the negative margin.

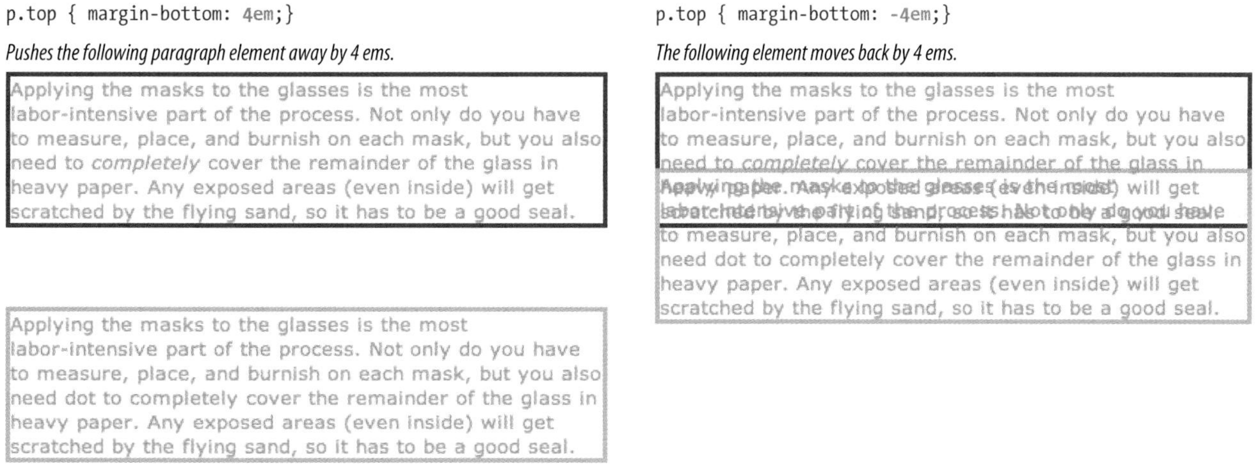

```
p.top { margin-bottom: 4em;}
```

Pushes the following paragraph element away by 4 ems.

> Applying the masks to the glasses is the most labor-intensive part of the process. Not only do you have to measure, place, and burnish on each mask, but you also need to *completely* cover the remainder of the glass in heavy paper. Any exposed areas (even inside) will get scratched by the flying sand, so it has to be a good seal.

> Applying the masks to the glasses is the most labor-intensive part of the process. Not only do you have to measure, place, and burnish on each mask, but you also need dot to completely cover the remainder of the glass in heavy paper. Any exposed areas (even inside) will get scratched by the flying sand, so it has to be a good seal.

```
p.top { margin-bottom: -4em;}
```

The following element moves back by 4 ems.

> Applying the masks to the glasses is the most labor-intensive part of the process. Not only do you have to measure, place, and burnish on each mask, but you also need to *completely* cover the remainder of the glass in heavy paper. Any exposed areas (even inside) will get scratched by the flying sand, so it has to be a good seal.
>
> Applying the masks to the glasses is the most labor-intensive part of the process. Not only do you have to measure, place, and burnish on each mask, but you also need dot to completely cover the remainder of the glass in heavy paper. Any exposed areas (even inside) will get scratched by the flying sand, so it has to be a good seal.

Figure 14-17. Using negative margins.

This may seem like a strange thing to do, and in fact, you probably wouldn't make blocks of text overlap as shown. The point here is that you can use margins with both positive and negative values to move elements around on the page. This is the basis of many CSS layout techniques.

Now let's use margins to add some space between parts of the JenWARE home page in Exercise 14-3. You'll also see how margins are used to properly center an element in the width of the browser window.

exercise 14-3 | **Adding margin space around elements**

Open *jenware.html* in your text editor if it isn't open already, and we'll get some margins in there. We'll be using a variety of properties and values along the way. Feel free to save the page and look at it in the browser after each step.

1. First, we'll add some space between the browser window and the sides of the content. Making the margins 12% of the browser window should give it plenty of space, and it will scale proportionally for different browser widths. To add space around the whole page, you use the **body** element, of course.

   ```
   body {
       margin-left: 12%;
       margin-right: 12%;
       font: 76% Verdana, sans-serif;
       background: #FCF191 url(images/top-background.gif) repeat-x;
   }
   ```

2. Now let's add some space above and below the "intro" section of the page. This time, we'll use the shorthand **margin** property to add 3-em margins to the top and bottom edges only.

   ```
   #intro {
       margin: 3em 0;
       text-align: center;
   }
   ```

3. So far, we've been using measurement values exclusively for the **margin** property. Another option is to use the **auto** keyword and let the browser apply as much margin as is necessary to fill the available space. If you set the margin to **auto** on the left and right sides of an element, it has the effect of keeping the element centered in the width of the browser window or other containing element. In fact, that is the proper method for centering elements horizontally.

   We'll use this technique to center the testimonials box on the page. First, set the **width** of the element to 500 pixels. Then, apply a 2-em margin to the top and bottom, and **auto** margin left and right. You can use the **margin** property as shown here. Note that you have to declare a width so the browser knows how to calculate the **auto** distances.

   ```
   #testimonials {
       width: 500px;
       margin: 2em auto;
       border: 1px dashed #F26521;
       padding: 1em;
       padding-left: 60px;
       background: #FFBC53 url(images/ex-circle-corner.gif) no-repeat left
   top;
       line-height: 1.2em;
   }
   ```

   This isn't the most beautiful design, but it's only temporary. In the next chapter, we'll be putting this testimonials box into its own column in a two-column layout.

4. Finally, I'd like 3 ems of space above the product category **h2** elements (particularly since there may be more in the future). By this point, I bet you could write this one without my help, but for thoroughness' sake, here is the new declaration added to **h2**s in the "products" section.

NOTE

When the value is 0, you don't need to provide a specific unit.

To center an element in the browser window, apply a width *to the element and set its left and right margins to* auto.

```
#products h2 {
    margin-top: 3em;
    border-left: 3px solid;
    border-top: 1px solid;
    padding-left: 1em;
    font-size: 1.2em;
    color: #921A66;
}
```

5. Save and look at it in the browser. There's more space above the product category headings now, but I don't like all that extra space above the first one. Fortunately, that heading has been marked up as belonging to the class "first", so we can write another rule that applies zero margin above just that heading.

This somewhat complicated selector targets **h2** elements with the class "first" but only when they appear in the **div** with the **id** "products".

```
#products h2.first {
    margin-top: 0;
}
```

Save the document again and it should look something like the one in Figure 14-18 (the width of your page may be different depending on your browser and monitor size). The final style sheet for this page is available in Appendix A.

Figure 14-18. The JenWARE home page after adding padding, borders, and margins.

A good understanding of padding, borders, and margins is the first step to mastering CSS layouts. In the next chapter, we'll learn about the properties used to float and position elements on the page. We'll even turn the JenWARE page into a two-column layout. But before we move on, there is one more property to get out of the way.

Assigning Display Roles

As long as we're talking about boxes and the CSS layout model, this is a good time to introduce the display property. You should already be familiar with the display behavior of block and inline elements in (X)HTML. However, not all XML languages assign default display behaviors (or display roles, to use the proper term from the CSS specification) to the elements they contain. For this reason, the display property was created to allow authors to specify how elements should behave in layouts.

display

Values: inline|block|list-item|run-in|inline-block|table|inline-table| table-row-group|table-header-group|table-footer-group|table-row |table-column-group|table-column|table-cell|table-caption|none| inherit

Default: inline

Applies to: all elements

Inherits: yes

The `display` property defines the type of element box an element generates in the layout. In addition to the familiar `inline` and `block` display roles, you can also make elements display as list items or the various parts of a table (list and table display roles are addressed in Chapter 17, CSS Techniques).

In general, the W3C discourages the random reassigning of display roles for (X)HTML elements. However, in certain scenarios, it is benign and has even become commonplace. For example, it is common practice to make `li` elements (which usually display as block elements) display as inline elements to turn a list into a horizontal navigation bar. You may also make an otherwise inline `a` (anchor) element display as a block in order to give it a specific width and height. These techniques are demonstrated in Chapter 17.

WARNING

Bear in mind that changing the presentation of an (X)HTML element with the CSS `display` property does not change the definition of that element as block-level or inline in (X)HTML. Putting a block-level element within an inline element will always be invalid (X)HTML, regardless of its display role.

Another useful value for the display property is `none`, which removes the content from the normal flow entirely. Unlike `visibility: hidden`, which just makes the element invisible, but holds the space it would have occupied blank, `display: none` removes the content, and the space it would have occupied is closed up.

One popular use of `display: none` is to prevent certain content from appearing when the source document is displayed in specific media. For example, you could have a paragraph that appears when the document is printed, but is not part of the page when it is displayed on a computer screen.

The Box Model in Review

At this point you should have a good feel for element boxes and how to manipulate the space within and around them. These are the raw tools you'll need to do real CSS-based layouts. In the next chapter, we'll start moving the boxes around on the page, but first, why not get some practice at writing rules for padding, borders, and margins in the following test.

Test Yourself

In this test, your task is to write the declarations that create the effects shown in each example. All the paragraphs shown here share a rule that sets the dimensions and the background color for each paragraph. You need only to provide the box-related property declarations. Answers, as always, appear in Appendix A.

Lorem ipsum dolor sit amet, consectetuer adipiscing elit. Praesent porttitor venenatis mi. Nunc semper, orci a adipiscing tempus, magna nulla varius nisl, imperdiet fermentum nisi erat vel arcu.

All of the samples in this exercise start out styled as shown here and share the properties listed below.

```
p { background-color: #C2F670;
    width: 200px;
    height: 200px;}
```

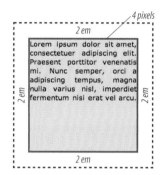

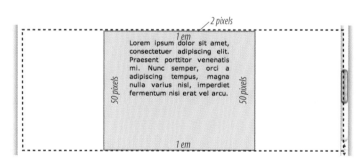

Some useful hints: outer margin edges are indicated by dotted blue lines. All necessary measurements are provided in dark red. Borders use one of the 17 standard color names.

Review: Basic Box Properties

The following is a summary of the properties covered in this chapter related to the basic box model.

Property	Description
`border`	A shorthand property that combines border properties
`border-top,` `border-right,` `border-bottom,` `border-left`	Combine border properties for each side of the element
`border-color`	Shorthand property for specifying the color of borders
`border-top-color,` `border-right-color,` `border-bottom-color,` `border-left-color`	Specify the border color for each side of the element
`border-style`	Shorthand property for specifying the style of borders
`border-top-style,` `border-right-style,` `border-bottom-style,` `border-left-style`	Specify the border style for each side of the element
`border-width`	Shorthand property for specifying the width of borders
`border-top-width,` `border-right-width,` `border-bottom-width,` `border-left-width`	Specify the border width for each side of the element
`display`	Defines the type of element box an element generates
`height`	Specifies the height of the element's content area
`margin`	Shorthand property for specifying margin space around an element
`margin-top,` `margin-right,` `margin-bottom,` `margin-left`	Specify the margin amount for each side of the element
`max-height`	Specifies the maximum height of an element
`max-width`	Specifies the maximum width of an element
`min-height`	Specifies the minimum height of an element
`min-width`	Specifies the minimum width of an element
`overflow`	How to handle content that doesn't fit in the content area
`padding`	Shorthand property for specifying space between the content area and the border
`padding-top,` `padding-right,` `padding-bottom,` `padding-left`	Specify the padding amount for each side of the element
`width`	Specifies the width of an element's content area

FLOATING AND POSITIONING

At this point, you've learned dozens of CSS properties that allow you to change the appearance of text elements and the boxes they generate. But so far, we've merely been decorating elements as they appear in the flow of the document.

In this chapter, we'll look at floating and positioning, the CSS methods for breaking out of the flow and arranging elements on the page. Floating an element moves it to the left or right, and allows the following text to wrap around it. Positioning is a way to specify the location of an element anywhere on the page with pixel precision.

We'll start by examining the properties responsible for floating and positioning, so you'll get a good feel for how the CSS layout tools work. In Chapter 16, Page Layout with CSS, we'll broaden the scope and see how these properties are used to create common multicolumn page layouts.

Before we start moving elements around, let's be sure we are well acquainted with how they behave in the normal flow.

IN THIS CHAPTER

Floating elements to the left and right

Clearing floated elements

Relative positioning

Absolute positioning and containing blocks

Fixed positioning

Normal Flow

We've covered the normal flow in previous chapters, but it's worth a refresher. In the CSS layout model, text elements are laid out from top to bottom in the order in which they appear in the source, and from left to right (in left-to-right reading languages*). Block elements stack up on top of one another and fill the available width of the browser window or other containing element. Inline elements and text characters line up next to one another to fill the block elements.

When the window or containing element is resized, the block elements expand or contract to the new width, and the inline content reflows to fit (Figure 15-1).

---

* For right-to-left reading languages such as Arabic and Hebrew, the normal flow is top to bottom and right to left.

Dealing with Browser Bugs

This is a good time to address the unfortunate topic of browser bugs. This book presents the way CSS is *supposed* to work, but in reality, browsers have bugs and uneven support for the CSS2.1 standard that make getting a layout to behave consistently a major headache.

Although no browser is perfect, all eyes turn to Internet Explorer for Windows because it makes up the lion's share of web traffic (over 80% as of this writing). It also has a host of notorious bugs related to page layout such as the IE5/5.5 Box Model Problem, the "Guillotine Bug," the "Peekaboo Bug," and the "Double Float-Margin Bug," just to name a few.

Unfortunately, the techniques for dealing with browser bugs are beyond the scope of this book (in fact, they could fill a small book in themselves). In addition, bug workaround best practices change frequently, so information in a book is likely to get stale.

However, I do encourage you to become famiilar with the ways your pages (especially those with floats and positioned elements) are likely to misbehave in popular browsers. In many cases, you can adapt your design to avoid the bug. There are also techniques for giving specific browsers the CSS rules they need (or make sure they don't get the ones they don't understand).

The following resources are good starting places to get up to speed on the browser issues developers care about most, and what fixes are available.

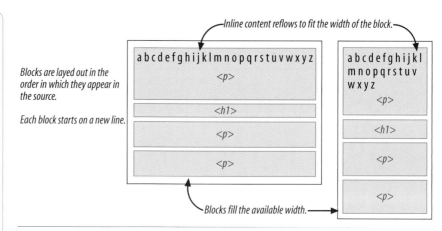

Figure 15-1. *One more example of the normal flow behavior.*

Objects in the normal flow affect the layout of the objects around them. This is the behavior you've come to expect in web pages—elements don't overlap or bunch up, they make room for one another.

We've seen all of this before, but in this chapter we'll be paying attention to whether elements are in the flow or removed from the flow. Floating and positioning changes the relationship of elements to the normal flow in different ways. Let's first look at the special behavior of floated elements (or "floats" for short).

Floating

Simply stated, the `float` property moves an element as far as possible to the left or right, allowing the following content to wrap around it. It is not a positioning scheme *per se*, but a unique feature built into CSS with some interesting behaviors. Floats are one of the primary tools of modern CSS-based web design, used to create multicolumn layouts, navigation toolbars from lists, and table-like alignment without tables. It's exciting stuff. Let's start with the `float` property itself.

float

Values:	`left`|`right`|`none`|`inherit`
Default:	`none`
Applies to:	*all elements*
Inherits:	*no*

The best way to explain floating is to demonstrate it. In this example, the `float` property is applied to an `img` element to float it to the right. Figure 15-2 shows how the the paragraph and the contained image is rendered by default (top) and how it looks when the `float` property is applied (bottom).

The markup

```
<p><img src="crown.gif" alt="" />They went down, down,...</p>
```

The style sheet

```
img {
  float: right;
}

p {
  padding: 15px;
  background-color: #FFF799;
  border: 2px solid #6C4788;
}
```

Inline image in the normal flow

space next to the image is held clear

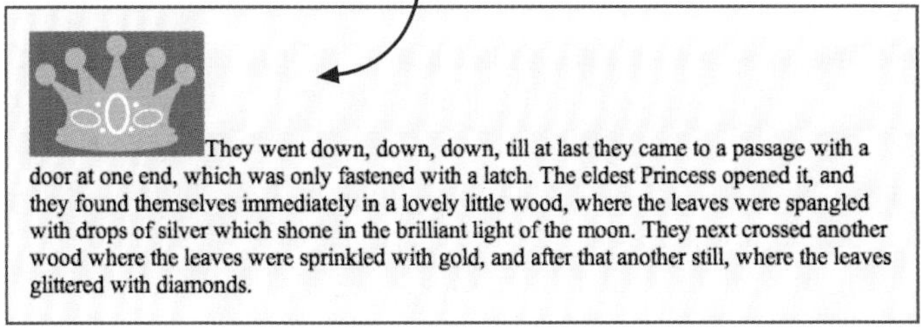

They went down, down, down, till at last they came to a passage with a door at one end, which was only fastened with a latch. The eldest Princess opened it, and they found themselves immediately in a lovely little wood, where the leaves were spangled with drops of silver which shone in the brilliant light of the moon. They next crossed another wood where the leaves were sprinkled with gold, and after that another still, where the leaves glittered with diamonds.

Inline image floated to the right.

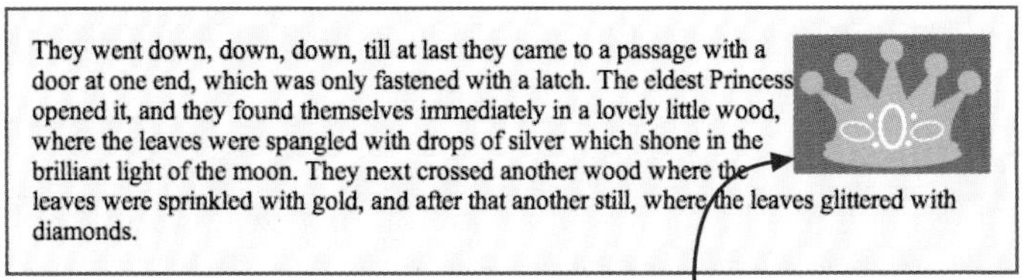

They went down, down, down, till at last they came to a passage with a door at one end, which was only fastened with a latch. The eldest Princess opened it, and they found themselves immediately in a lovely little wood, where the leaves were spangled with drops of silver which shone in the brilliant light of the moon. They next crossed another wood where the leaves were sprinkled with gold, and after that another still, where the leaves glittered with diamonds.

image moves over and text wraps around it

Figure 15-2. The layout of an image in the normal flow (top), and with the `float` *property applied (bottom).*

That's a nice effect... we've gotten rid of a lot of wasted space on the page, but now the text is bumping right up against the image. How do you think you would add some space between the image element and the surrounding text? If you guessed "add a margin," you're absolutely right. I'll add 10 pixels of space on all sides of the image using the `margin` property (Figure 15-3). You can begin to see how all the box properties work together in page layout.

```
img {
  float: right;
  margin: 10px;
}
```

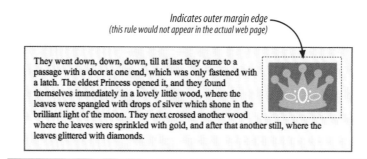

Indicates outer margin edge — (this rule would not appear in the actual web page)

They went down, down, down, till at last they came to a passage with a door at one end, which was only fastened with a latch. The eldest Princess opened it, and they found themselves immediately in a lovely little wood, where the leaves were spangled with drops of silver which shone in the brilliant light of the moon. They next crossed another wood where the leaves were sprinkled with gold, and after that another still, where the leaves glittered with diamonds.

Figure 15-3. Adding a 10-pixel margin around the floated image.

Some key behaviors of floated elements are apparent in the previous two figures:

A floated element is like an island in a stream.

First and foremost, you can see that the image is both removed from its position in the normal flow, yet continues to influence the surrounding content. The subsequent paragraph text reflows to make room for the floated img element. One popular analogy compares floats to islands in a stream—they are not in the flow, but the stream has to flow around them. This behavior is unique to floated elements.

Floats stay in the content area of the containing element.

It is also important to note that the floated image is placed within the content area (the inner edges) of the paragraph that contains it. It does not extend into the padding area of the paragraph.

Margins are maintained.

In addition, the margin is held on all sides of the floated image, as indicated in Figure 15-3 by the blue, dashed line. In other words, the entire element box, from outer edge to outer edge, is floated.

More floating examples

Those are the basics...let's look at more examples and explore some additional floating behaviors. Before style sheets, the only thing you could float was an image by using the deprecated align attribute. With CSS, it is possible to float any (X)HTML element, both inline and block-level, as we'll see in the following examples.

Floating an inline text element

In the previous example, we floated an inline image element. This time, let's look at what happens when you float an inline text (non-replaced) element (Figure 15-4).

The markup

```
<p><span class="disclaimer">Disclaimer: The existence of silver, gold,
and diamond trees is not confirmed.</span>They went down, down, down,
till at last they came to a passage... </p>
```

The style sheet

```
span.disclaimer {
  float: right;
  margin: 10px;
  width: 200px;
  color: #FFF;
  background-color: #9D080D;
  padding: 4px;
}

p {
  padding: 15px;
  background-color: #FFF799;
  border: 2px solid #6C4788;
}
```

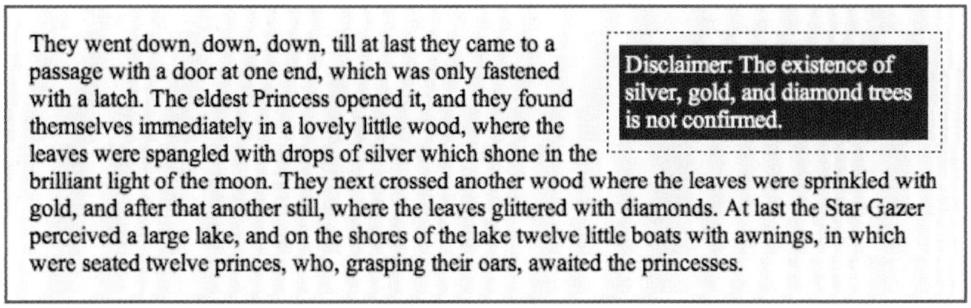

They went down, down, down, till at last they came to a passage with a door at one end, which was only fastened with a latch. The eldest Princess opened it, and they found themselves immediately in a lovely little wood, where the leaves were spangled with drops of silver which shone in the brilliant light of the moon. They next crossed another wood where the leaves were sprinkled with gold, and after that another still, where the leaves glittered with diamonds. At last the Star Gazer perceived a large lake, and on the shores of the lake twelve little boats with awnings, in which were seated twelve princes, who, grasping their oars, awaited the princesses.

Disclaimer: The existence of silver, gold, and diamond trees is not confirmed.

Figure 15-4. Floating an inline text (non-replaced) element.

From the looks of things, it is behaving just the same as the floated image, which is what we'd expect. But there are some subtle things at work here that bear pointing out.

Always provide a width for floated text elements.

First, you'll notice that the style rule that floats the `span` includes the `width` property. In fact, it is necessary to specify a width for floated text elements because without one, the content area of the box expands to its widest possible width (or, on some browsers, it may collapse to its narrowest possible width). Images have an inherent width, so we didn't need to specify a width in the previous example (although we certainly could have).

Floated inline elements behave as block elements.

Notice that the margin is held on all four sides of the floated `span` text, even though top and bottom margins are usually not rendered on inline elements (see Figure 14-16 in the previous chapter). That is because all floated elements behave like block elements. Once you float an inline element, it follows the display rules for block-level elements, and margins are rendered on all four sides. Margins on floated elements do *not* collapse, however.

And speaking of block-level elements...

It is necessary to specify the width for floated text elements.

Floating block elements

Let's look at what happens when you float a block within the normal flow. In this example, a whole paragraph element is floated to the left (Figure 15-5).

The markup:

```
<p>ONCE upon a time....</p>
<p id="float">As he had a white skin, blue eyes,...</p>
<p>The fact was he thought them very ugly...</p>
```

The style sheet:

```
p#float {
    float: left;
    width: 200px;
    margin-top: 0px;
    background: #A5D3DE;
}

p {
    border: 1px solid red;
}
```

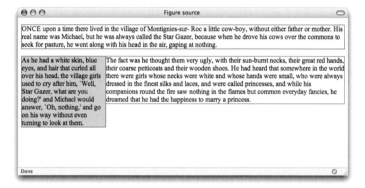

Figure 15-5. Floating a block-level element.

I've added a red rule around all p elements to show their boundaries. In addition, I set the top margin on the float to 0 (zero) to override the browser's default margin settings on paragraphs. This allows the floated paragraph to align with the top of the following paragraph. There are a few other things I want to point out in this example.

Just as we saw with the image, the paragraph moves off to the side (left this time) and the following content wraps around it, even though blocks normally stack on top of one another. There are two things I want to point out in this example.

You must provide a width for floated block elements.

If you do not provide a width value, the width of the floated block will be set to auto, which fills the available width of the browser window or other containing element. There's not much sense in having a full-width floated box since the idea is to wrap text next to the float, not start below it.

Elements do not float higher than their reference in the source.

A floated block will float to the left or right relative to where it occurs in the source allowing the following elements in the flow to wrap around it. It will stay below any block elements that precede it in the flow (in effect, it is "blocked" by them). That means you can't float an element up to the top corner of a page, even if its nearest ancestor is the body element. If you want a floated element to start at the top of the page, it must appear first in the document source.

Floating multiple elements

It's perfectly fine to float multiple elements on a page or even within a single element. When you float multiple elements, there is a complex system of behind-the-scenes rendering rules that ensure floated elements do not overlap. You can consult the CSS2.1 specification for the details, but the upshot of it is that floated elements will be placed as far left or right (as specified) and as high up as space allows.

Figure 15-6 shows what happens when a series of sequential paragraphs are floated to the same side. The first three floats start stacking up from the left edge, but when there isn't enough room for the fourth, it moves down and to the left until it bumps into something; in this case, the edge of the browser window. However, if one of the floats, such as "P2," had been very long, it would have bumped up against the edge of the long float instead.

The source

```
<p>P1</p>
<p class="float">P2</p>
<p class="float">P3</p>
<p class="float">P4</p>
<p class="float">P5</p>
<p>P6</p>
<p>P7</p>
<p>P8</p>
<p>P9</p>
<p>P10</p>
```

The style sheet:

```
p.float {
   float: left;
   width: 200px;
   margin: 0px;
   background: #CCC;}

p {border: 1px solid red;}
```

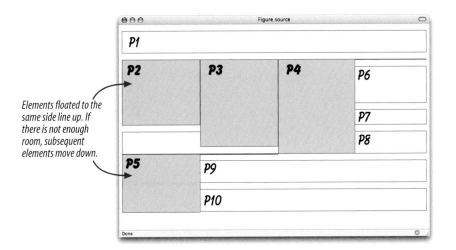

Elements floated to the same side line up. If there is not enough room, subsequent elements move down.

Figure 15-6. Multiple floated elements line up and do not overlap.

This lining-up effect is used strategically in CSS-based web design to create multicolumn layouts and horizontal navigation bars out of floated list items. We'll look at these techniques in Chapter 16, Page Layout with CSS and Chapter 17, CSS Techniques, respectively.

Clearing floated elements

The last thing you need to know about floated elements is how to turn the text wrapping *off* and get back to layout as usual. This is done by clearing the element that you want to start below the float. Applying the clear property to an element prevents it from appearing next to a floated element, and forces it to start against the next available "clear" space below the float.

clear

Values:	left|right|both|none|inherit
Default:	none
Applies to:	block-level elements ony
Inherits:	no

NOTE

The clear property replaces the depre-cated clear attribute once used in the br element to clear aligned images.

Keep in mind that you apply the clear property to the element you want to start below the floated element, not the floated element itself. The left value starts the element below any elements that have been floated to the left. Similarly, the right value makes the element clear all floats on the right edge of the containing block. If there are multiple floated elements, and you want to be sure an element starts below all of them, use the both value to clear floats on both sides.

In this example, the clear property has been used to make h2 elements start below left-floated elements. Figure 15-7 shows how the h2 heading starts at the next available clear edge below the float.

```
img {
    float: left;
    margin-right: 10px;
}

h2 {
    clear: left;
    margin-top: 2em;
}
```

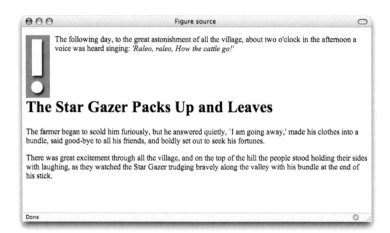

Figure 15-7. Clearing a left-floated element

Notice in Figure 15-7 that although there is a 2-em top margin applied to the h2 element, it is not rendered between the heading and the floated image. That's the result of collapsing vertical margins. If you want to make sure space is held between a float and the following text, apply a bottom margin to the floated element itself.

It's time to give floating a try in Exercise 15-1.

exercise 15-1 | **Floating elements**

In this exercise, we'll make further improvements to the JenWARE home page that we worked on in Chapter 14. If you did not follow along with the exercises in the previous chapter, there is a fresh copy in its most recent state, called *jenware_2.html*, in the Chapter 15 materials (*www.learningwebdesign.com/materials*).

1. Open the JenWARE home page document in a text editor and browser (it should look like Figure 14-18 in the previous chapter).

   We'll start by removing wasted vertical space next to the product images by floating the images to the left. We'll use a contextual selector to make sure that we only float the images in the "products" section of the page. While we're at it, let's add a little margin on the bottom and right sides using the **margin** shorthand property.

   ```
   #products img {
      float: left;
      margin: 0 6px 6px 0;
   }
   ```

   Save the document and take a look at it in the browser. You should see the product descriptions wrapping to the right of the images.

2. Next, I'd like the "Go to the (product) page" links to always appear below the images so they are clearly visible on the left side of the products section. This change is going to require a little extra markup, because we need a way to target just the paragraphs that contain "go to" links. Scroll down to the markup section of the document and add the class name "goto" to each of the paragraphs that contain links. Here is the first one:

   ```
   <p class="goto"><a href="#">Go to the GlassWARE
   page </a></p>
   ```

   Now we can use a class selector to make those paragraphs clear the floated images.

   ```
   #products p.goto {
      clear: left;
   }
   ```

3. Time to take on that "testimonials" **div** box. Instead of taking up valuable space "above the fold," let's move it off to the side and let the products section move up into the spotlight. Start by removing the **margin** property and changing the **width** from 500 to 150 pixels. Finally, float the **div** to the right with the **float** property. Figure 15-8 shows the results.

   ```
   #testimonials {
      float: right;
      width: 500px 150px;
      margin: 2em auto;
      border: 1px dashed #F26521;
      padding: 1em;
      padding-left: 60px;
      background: #FFBC53
      url(images/ex-circle-corner.  gif) no-repeat
      left top;
      line-height: 1.2em;
   }
   ```

Figure 15-8. *The results of floating the testimonials* div.

There are some interesting behaviors to observe here. First, let's keep in mind that although it looks a little like the "testimonials" **div** is being floated in the products box, it is actually floated within the content area of the **body** element (the nearest block-level ancestor). This is the same floated block element behavior we saw in Figure 15-6.

Look at how the "products" **div** behaves: its content wraps around the float, but its element box (indicated by the border and white background color) is not reshaped around the float. In fact, the background of the "products" **div** appears to be behind or under the floated box. This is the normal behavior for floats and wrapped content: the content reflows, but the element box is not changed.

The other behavior of note here is that the "testimonials" **div** was floated relative to its position in the source... it can't float up higher than the block-level paragraph element that preceded it. The testimonials box moved off to the right edge of the **body** content area, and the following **div** moved up in its space.

4. There is one last change to make to this page that's going to make a big difference in its appearance. Let's add some space between the products and testimonial areas so they don't appear to overlap. We'll do this by adding a margin on the right of the "products" **div** that is wide enough to accommodate the "testimonials" box.

How wide does the margin need to be? We'll need to calculate the width of the "testimonials" element box.

150 pixel width + **2** pixels of border + **60** pixels left padding + approximately **12** pixels (1 em) right padding = approx. **224** pixels

Setting the right margin on the "products" **div** to 250 pixels should do the trick.

```
#products {
    margin-right: 250px;
    border: double #FFBC53;
    padding: 2em;
    background-color: #FFF;
    line-height: 2em;
}
```

The results are shown in Figure 15-9. Hey, look at that!... your first two-column layout, created with a float and a wide margin. This is the basic concept behind many CSS-based layout templates as you'll see in Chapter 16.

Figure 15-9. A new two-column layout for the JenWARE home page, created with a float and a wide margin on the following content.

That covers the fundamentals of floating. Let's move on to the other approach to moving elements around on the page—positioning.

Positioning Basics

CSS provides several methods for positioning elements on the page. They can be positioned relative to where they would normally appear in the flow, or removed from the flow altogether and placed at a particular spot on the page. You can also position an element relative to the browser window (technically known as the viewport in the CSS Recommendations) and it will stay put while the rest of the page scrolls.

Unfortunately, not all positioning methods are well supported, and inconsistent and buggy browser implementation can make it challenging to achieve the results you're after. The best thing to do is get acquainted with the way positioning *should* work according to the specification, as we'll do in the following sections, starting with the basic `position` property.

Types of positioning

`position`

Values:	`static`|`relative`|`absolute`|`fixed`|`inherit`
Default:	`static`
Applies to:	all elements
Inherits:	no

The `position` property indicates that an element is to be postioned, and specifies which positioning method should be used. I'll introduce each keyword value briefly here, then we'll take a more detailed look at each method in the remainder of this chapter.

`static`

This is the normal positioning scheme in which elements are positioned as they occur in the normal document flow.

`relative`

Relative positioning moves the box relative to its original position in the flow. The distinctive behavior of relative positioning is that the space the element would have occupied in the normal flow is preserved.

`absolute`

Absolutely positioned elements are removed from the document flow entirely and positioned relative to a containing element (we'll talk more about this later). Unlike relatively positioned elements, the space they would have occupied is closed up. In fact, they have no influence at all on the layout of surrounding elements.

NOTE

Positioning is another CSS feature that can trigger unexpected browser behavior. Consult the sites listed in the Dealing with Browser Bugs sidebar for known browser bugs and workarounds.

fixed

> The distinguishing characteristic of fixed positioning is that the element stays in one position in the window even when the document scrolls. Fixed elements are removed from the document flow and positioned relative to the browser window (or other viewport). rather than another element in the document.

Specifying position

Once you've established the positioning method, the actual position is specified with four offset properties.

top, right, bottom, left

Values: length measurement | percentage | auto | inherit

Default: auto

Applies to: Positioned elements (where position value is relative, absolute, or fixed)

Inherits: no

NOTE

Negative values are acceptable and move the element in the opposite directions. For example, a negative value for top *would have the effect of moving the element up.*

The values provided for each of the offset properties defines the distance the element should be moved *away* from that respective edge. For example, the value of top defines the distance the top outer edge of the positioned element should be offset from the top edge of the browser or other containing element. A positive value for top results in the element box moving *down* by that amount. Similarly, a positive value for left would move the positioned element to the right (toward the center of the containing block) by that amount.

Further explanations and examples of the offset properties will be provided in the discussions of each postioning method. We'll start our exploration of positioning with the fairly straightforward relative method.

Relative Positioning

As mentioned previously, relative positioning moves an element relative to its original spot in the flow. The space it would have occupied is preserved and continues to influence the layout of surrounding content. This is easier to understand with a simple example.

Here I've positioned an inline em element (a background color makes its boundaries apparent). First, I used the position property to set the method to relative, then I used the top offset property to move the element 30 pixels down from its initial position, and the left property to move it 60 pixels to the right. Remember, offset property values move the element away from the specified edge, so if you want something to move to the right, as I did here, you use the left offset property. The results are shown in Figure 15-10.

```
em {
  position: relative;
  top: 30px;
  left: 60px;
  background-color: fuchsia;
}
```

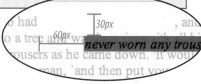

Figure 15-10. When an element is positioned with the relative method, the space it would have occupied is preserved.

I want to point out a few things that are happening here.

The original space in the document flow is preserved.

You can see that there is a blank space where the emphasized text would have been if the element had not been positioned. The surrounding content is laid out as though the element were still there, therefore we say that the element still "influences" the surrounding content.

Overlap happens.

Because this is a positioned element, it can potentially overlap other elements, as shown in Figure 15-10.

The empty space left behind by relatively positioned objects can be a little awkward, so this method is not used as often as floating and absolute positioning. However, relative postioning is commonly used to create a positioning context for an absolutely positioned element, as I'll explain in the next section.

Absolute Positioning

Absolute positioning works a bit differently and is actually a more flexible method for achieving page layouts than relative positioning. Now that you've seen how relative positioning works, let's take the same example as shown in Figure 15-10, only this time we'll change the value of the position property to absolute.

```
em {
  position: absolute;
  top: 30px;
  left: 60px;
  background-color: fuchsia;
}
```

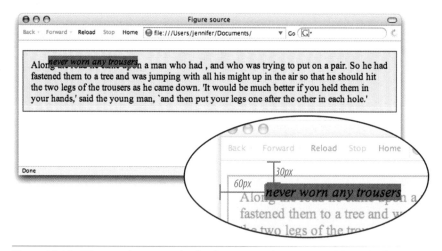

Figure 15-11. When an element is absolutely positioned, it is removed from the flow and the space is closed up.

As you can see in Figure 15-11, the space once occupied by the em element is now closed up, as is the case for all absolutely positioned elements. In its new position, the element box overlaps the surrounding content. In the end, absolutely positioned elements have no influence whatsoever on the layout of surrounding elements.

The most significant difference here, however, is the location of the positioned element. This time, the offset values position the em element 30 pixels down and 60 pixels to the right of the top-left corner of the browser window.

But, wait. Before you start thinking that absolutely positioned elements are always placed relative to the browser window, I'm afraid that there's more to it than that.

What actually happens in absolute positioning is that the element is positioned relative to its nearest containing block. It just so happens that the nearest containing block in Figure 15-11 is the root (html) element (also known as the initial containing block), so the offset values position the em element relative to the whole browser window area.

Getting a handle on the containing block concept is the first step to taking on absolute positioning

Containing blocks

The CSS2.1 Recommendation states, "The position and size of an element's box(es) are sometimes calculated relative to a certain rectangle, called the containing block of the element." It is critical to have an awareness of the containing block of the element you want to position.

CSS2.1 lays out a number of intricate rules for determining the containing block of an element, but it basically boils down to this:

- If the positioned element is *not* contained within another positioned element, then it will be placed relative to the initial containing block (created by the `html` element).

- But if the element has an ancestor (i.e. is contained within an element) that has its position set to `relative`, `absolute`, or `fixed`, the element will be positioned relative to the edges of *that* element instead.

Figure 15-11 is an example of the first case: the p element that contains the absolutely positioned `em` element is *not* positioned itself, and there are no other positioned elements higher in the hierarchy, therefore the `em` element is positioned relative to the initial containing block, which is equivalent to the browser window area.

Let's deliberately turn the p element into a containing block and see what happens. All we have to do is apply the `position` property to it; we don't have to actually move it. The most common way to make an element into a containing block is to set the `position` to `relative`, but don't move it with offset values. (By the way, this is what I was talking about earlier when I said that relative positioning is most often used to create a context for an absolutely positioned element.)

We'll keep the style rule for the `em` element the same, but we'll add a `position` property to the p element, thus making it the containing block for the positioned `em` element. Figure 15-12 shows the results.

```
p {
    position: relative;
    padding: 15px;
    background-color: #DBFDBA;
    border: 2px solid #6C4788;
}
```

NOTE

Some browsers base the initial containing block on the body *element. The net result is the same in that it fills the browser window.*

Or, to put it another way...

The containing block for an absolutely positioned element is the nearest *positioned* ancestor element (that is, any element with a value for `position` other than `static`).

If there is no containing block present (in other words, if the positioned element is *not* contained within another positioned element), then the initial containing block (created by the `html` element) will be used instead.

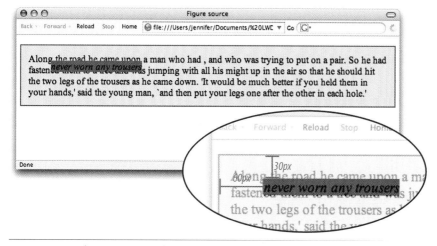

Figure 15-12. The positioned p *element acts as a containing block for the* em *element.*

You can see that the em element is now positioned 30 pixels down and 60 pixels from the top-left corner of the paragraph box, not the browser window. Notice also that it is positioned relative to the *padding edge* of the paragraph (just inside the border), not the content area edge. This is the normal behavior when block elements are used as containing blocks (see note).

I'm going to poke around at this some more to reveal additional aspects of absolutely positioned objects. This time, I've added width and margin properties to the positioned em element (Figure 15-13).

NOTE

When inline elements are used as containing blocks (and they can be), the positioned element is placed relative to the content area edge, not the padding edge.

```
em {
    width: 200px;
    margin: 25px;
    position: absolute;
    top: 30px;
    left: 60px;
    background-color: fuchsia;
}
```

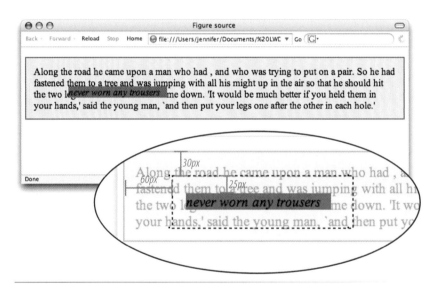

Figure 15-13. Adding a width and margins to the positioned element.

Here we can see that:

- The offset values apply to the outer edges of the element box (from margin edge to margin edge), and

- Absolutely positioned elements always behave as block-level elements. For example, the margins on all sides are maintained even though this is an inline element. It also permits a width to be set for the element.

It is important to keep in mind that once you've positioned an element, it becomes the new containing block for all the elements it contains. Consider this example in which a `div` named "content" is positioned in the top-left corner of the page. When a positioned list item within that `div` is given offset values that place it in the top-right corner, it appears in the top-right corner of the contents `div`, not the entire page (Figure 15-14). That is because once the `div` is positioned, it acts as the containing block for the `li` element.

The markup:

```
<div id="preface">
    <h1>Old-Fashioned Fairy Tales</h1>
    <p>As the title...</p>
    <p>Except for the use...</p>
    <p>They have appeared...</p>
    <p>First,...</p>
</div>

<div id="content">
<h2>Contents</h2>
<ul>
    <li>The Nix in Mischief</li>
    <li id="special">The Ogre Courting</li>
    <li>Murdoch's Wrath</li>
    <li>The Little Darner</li>
    <li>The Magic Jar</li>
</ul>
</div>
```

The style sheet:

```
body {
    background-color: #F9FEB0;
}

div#content {
    width: 200px;
    position: absolute;
    top: 0;    /* positioned in the top-left corner */
    left: 0;
    background-color: #AFD479;
    padding: 10px;
}

li#special {
    position: absolute;
    top: 0;      /* positioned in the top-right corner */
    right: 0;
    background-color: fuchsia;
}

div#preface {
    margin-left: 225px;   /* makes room for the contents box */
}
```

The li element is positioned in the top-right corner of the "contents" div.

The positioned "contents" div becomes the containing block for the positioned li element and creates a new positioning context.

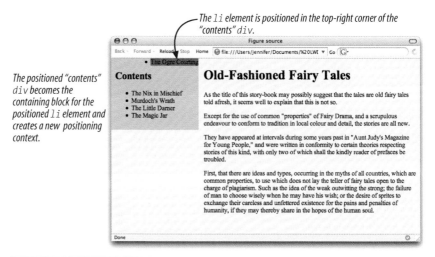

Figure 15-14. *Positioned elements become the containing block for the elements they contain. In this example, the list item is positioned relative to the containing div element, not the whole page.*

Specifying Position

Now that you have a better feel for the containing block concept, let's take some time to get better acquainted with the offset properties. So far, we've only seen an element moved a few pixels down and to the right, but that's not all you can do, of course.

Pixel measurements

As mentioned previously, positive offset values push the positioned element box *away* from the specified edge and toward the center of the containing block. If there is no value provided for an edge, it is set to `auto`, and the browser adds enough space to make the layout work. In this example, I've used pixel length for all four offset properties to place the positioned element at a particular spot in its containing element (Figure 15-15).

```
div#a {
    position: relative;    /* creates the containing block */
    height: 120px;
    width: 300px;
    border: 1px solid;
    background-color: #CCC;
}

div#b {
    position: absolute;
    top: 20px;
    right: 30px;
    bottom: 40px;
    left: 50px;
    border: 1px solid;
    background-color: teal;
}
```

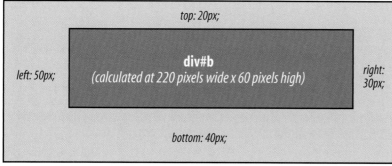

Figure 15-15. Setting offset values for all four sides of a positioned element.

Notice that by setting offsets on all four sides, I have indirectly set the dimensions of the positioned `div#b` (it fills the 220 × 60 pixel space that is left over within the containing block after the offset values are applied). If I had also specified a width and other box properties for `div#b`, there is the potential for conflicts if the total of the values for the positioned box and its offsets do not match the available space within the containing block.

The CSS specification provides a daunting set of rules for handling conflicts, but the upshot is that you should just be careful not to over-specify box properties and offsets. In general, a width (plus optional padding, border, and margin) and one or two offset properties are all that are necessary to achieve the layout you're looking for. Let the browser take care of the remaining calculations.

Percentage values

You can also specify positions with percentage values. In the first example in Figure 15-16, the image is positioned half-way down the left edge of the containing block. In the second example on the right, the `img` element is positioned so that it always appears in the bottom right corner of the containing block.

```
img#A {
  position: absolute;
  top: 50%;
  left: 0%;   /* the % symbol could be omitted for a 0 value */
}

img#B {
  position: absolute;
  bottom: 0%;  /* the % symbol could be omitted for a 0 value */
  right: 0%;   /* the % symbol could be omitted for a 0 value */
}
```

WARNING

Be careful when positioning elements at the bottom of the initial containing block (the `html` *element). Although you may expect it to be positioned at the bottom of the whole page, browsers actually place the element in the bottom corner of the browser window. Results may be unpredictable. If you want something positioned in a bottom corner of your page, put it in a containing block element at the end of the document source, and go from there.*

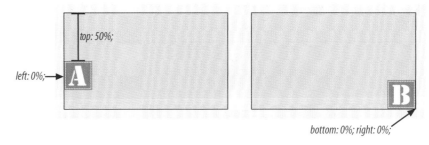

top: 50%;

left: 0%;→

bottom: 0%; right: 0%;

Figure 15-16. Using percentage values to position an element in the bottom corner of the containing block.

In Exercise 15-2, we'll have some more fun with the JenWARE home page, this time using absolute positioning.

exercise 15-2 | **Absolute positioning**

In this exercise, we'll use absolute positioning to add an award graphic to the site and to create a two-column layout. Open the latest version of *jenware.html* (or *jenware_2.html* if you were using that version in the previous exercise) in a text editor to get started.

1. Let's pretend that JenWARE.com won the "Awesome Site of the Week" award, and now we have the option of displaying a little award banner on the home page. Because it is new content, we'll need to add it to the markup. Because it is non-essential information, we'll add the image in a new **div** at the very end of the document, after the copyright paragraph.

   ```
   <div id="award"><img src="images/awesomesite.gif"
   alt="awesome site of the week" /></div>
   ```

Just because it is at the end of the document source doesn't mean it needs to display at the bottom of the page. We can use absolute positioning to place the "award" **div** in the top, left corner of the browser window for all to see by adding a new rule to the style sheet that positions the **div**, like so:

```
#award {
    position: absolute;
    top: 35px;
    left: 25px;
}
```

Save the document and take a look (Figure 15-17). Resize the browser window very narrow and you will see that the positioned award image overlaps the header content. Notice also that when you scroll the document, the image scrolls with the rest of the page. Try playing around with other offset properties and values to get a feel for positioning in the browser window (or the "initial containing block" to use the correct term).

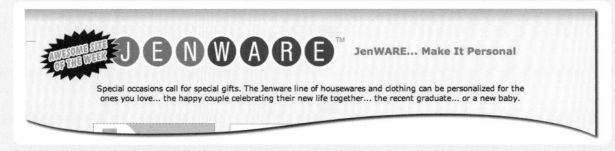

Figure 15-17. An absolutely positioned award graphic.

2. The floated testimonials box is working just fine, but for fun, let's see if we can do the same thing with absolute positioning. In this case, positioning within the initial containing block is not quite feasible because we want it to always appear under the intro `div` (regardless of its size) and to stay within the margins of the page, which are also flexible. What we need is a new positioning context under the intro, so let's create a new containing block for the positioned testimonials box.

   This is going to require some changes to the markup. Wrap the testimonials and products divs in a new `div` with an `id` of content. The structure of the document should look like this:

   ```
   <div id="content">
     <div id="testimonials">... </div>
     <div id="products"> ... </div>
   </div>
   ```

3. Now we can turn the "content" `div` into a containing block simply by positioning it with the "unmoved-relative-position" trick:

   ```
   #content {
     position: relative;
   }
   ```

4. We know that according to the normal flow, the "content" `div` will always appear below the preceding block-level "intro" `div` element, regardless of its size. What we want to do is position the "testimonials" `div` in the top, right corner of the "content" `div` containing block, so we add these properties to the `#testimonials` rule (delete the `float` property from the previous exercise first).

   ```
   #testimonials {
     position: absolute;
     top: 0;
     right: 0;
     float: right;
     width: 150px;
     border: 1px dashed #F26521;
     padding: 1em;
     padding-left: 60px;
     background: #FFBC53 url(images/ex-circle-corner.
   gif) no-repeat left top;
     line-height: 1.2em;
   }
   ```

Save the document and look at it in the browser (Figure 15-18). It should look just the same as the float exercise, but you have the satisfaction of knowing you have experience of creating a column with absolute positioning.

Figure 15-18. *Two column format created by absolutely positioning the testimonials box.*

Extra credit: Try switching the position of the columns by positioning the testimonials box on the left. (Hint: you'll need to change the `margin` setting on the "products" `div`, too).

Reality Check

Before you get too excited about the ease of creating multi-column layouts with absolute positioning, let me point out that this exercise represents a best-case scenario in which the positioned side-column is pretty much guaranteed to be shorter than the main content. There is also no significant footer to worry about. If the sidebar were to grow longer with more testimonials, it would overlap any full-width footer that might be on the page, which is not ideal. Consider this a heads-up that there's more to the story, as we'll see in Chapter 16.

Stacking order

Before we close the book on absolute positioning, there is one last related concept that I need to introduce. As we've seen, absolutely positioned elements overlap other elements, so it follows that multiple positioned elements have the potential to stack up on one another.

By default, elements stack up in the order in which they appear in the document, but you can change the stacking order with the `z-index` property. Picture the z-axis as a line that runs perpendicular to the page, as though from the tip of your nose, through this page, and out the other side.

`z-index`

Values: (number) | auto | inherit

Default: auto

Applies to: positioned elements

Inherits: no

The value of the `z-index` property is a number (positive or negative). The higher the number, the higher the element will appear in the stack. Lower numbers and negative values move the element lower in the stack. Let's look at an example to make this clear (Figure 15-19).

Here are three paragraph elements, each containing a letter image (A, B, and C, respectively) that have been positioned in a way that they overlap on the page. By default, paragraph "C" would appear on top because it appears last in the source. However, by assigning higher `z-index` values to paragraphs "A" and "B," we can force them to stack in our preferred order.

Note that the values of `z-index` do not need to be sequential, and they do not relate to anything in particular. All that matters is that higher number values position the element higher in the stack.

The markup:

```
<p id="A"><img src="A.gif" alt="A" /></p>
<p id="B"><img src="B.gif" alt="B" /></p>
<p id="C"><img src="C.gif" alt="C" /></p>
```

The style sheet:

```
#A {
    z-index: 10;
    position: absolute;
    top: 200px;
    left: 200px;
}

#B {
    z-index: 5;
    position: absolute;
    top: 225px;
    left: 175px;
}
```

```
#C {
  z-index: 1;
  position: absolute;
  top: 250px;
  left: 225px;
}
```

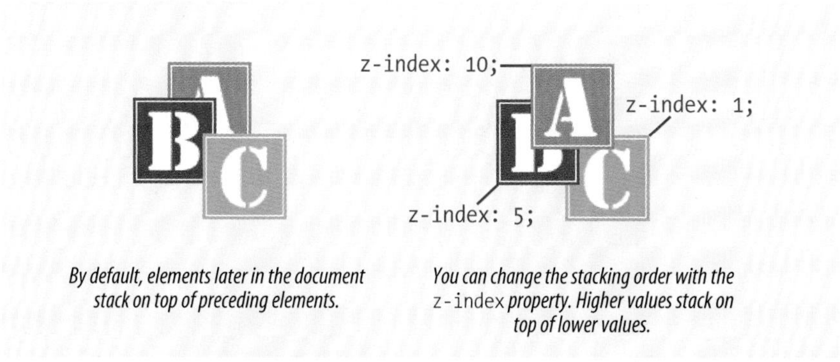

z-index: 10;

z-index: 1;

z-index: 5;

By default, elements later in the document stack on top of preceding elements.

You can change the stacking order with the z-index property. Higher values stack on top of lower values.

Figure 15-19. Changing the stacking order with the z-index *property.*

To be honest, the z-index property is not often required for most page layouts, but you should know it's there if you need it. If you want to guarantee that a positioned element always ends up on top, just assign it a very high z-index value, such as:

```
img#essential {
  z-index: 100;
  position: absolute;
  top: 0px;
  left: 0px;
}
```

Fixed Positioning

We've covered relative and absolute positioning, now it's time to take on the remaining method: fixed positioning.

For the most part, fixed positioning works just like absolute positioning. The significant difference is that the offset values for fixed elements are always relative to the browser window (or other viewport), which means the positioned element stays put even when the rest of the page scrolls. By contrast, you may remember that when you scrolled the JenWARE page in Exercise 15-2, the award graphic scrolled along with the document—even though it was positioned relative to the initial containing block (equivalent to the browser window). Not so with fixed positioning where the position is, well, *fixed*.

Let's switch the award graphic on the JenWARE page to fixed positioning to see the difference.

WARNING

Unfortunately, fixed positioning is not supported in IE for Windows, versions 6 and earlier. It is, however, supported in IE7 in Standards mode, so it will be a more reliable positioning method as older IEWin versions fade away.

exercise 15-3 | **Fixed positioning**

This should be simple. Open *jenware.html* (or *jenware_2.html*) and edit the style rule for the award **div** to make it **fixed** rather than **absolute**.

```
#award {
  position: fixed;
  top: 35px;
  left: 25px;
}
```

Save the document and open it in a browser (Windows users, you'll need to download Firefox or another non-Internet Explorer 6 browser to play along). At first look, it should appear the same as in Exercsise 15-2. However, when you scroll the page, you will see that the award now stays put where we positioned it in the browser window (Figure 15-20).

Figure 15-20. The award graphic stays in the same place in the top-left corner of the browser window when the document scrolls.

Now you've been introduced to all the tools of the trade for CSS-based layout: floating and three types of positioning (relative, absolute, and fixed). You should have a good feel for how they work for when we start putting them to use in the various design approaches and templates in Chapter 16.

Test Yourself

Before we move on, take a moment to see how well you absorbed the principles in this chapter.

1. Which of the following is *not* true of floated elements?

   a. All floated elements behave as block elements.

   b. Floats are positioned against the padding edge (just inside the border) of the containing element.

   c. Inline elements flow around a float, but the element box is unchanged.

   d. You must provide a width property for floated block elements.

2. Which of these style rules is incorrect? Why?

   a. `img { float: left; margin: 20px;}`

   b. `img { float: right; width: 120px; height: 80px; }`

   c. `img { float: right; right: 30px; }`

   d. `img { float: left; margin-bottom: 2em; }`

3. How do you make sure a "footer" `div` starts below a floated sidebar?

4. Write the name of the positioning method or methods (static, relative, absolute, or fixed) that best matches each of the following descriptions.

   a. Positions the element relative to a containing block.

   b. Removes the element from the normal flow.

   c. Positions the element relative to the viewport.

   d. The positioned element may overlap other content.

   e. Positions the element in the normal flow.

f. The space the element would have occupied in the normal flow is preserved.

g. The space the element would have occupied in the normal flow is closed up.

h. You can change the stacking order with z-index.

i. Positions the element relative to its original position in the normal flow.

5. Calculate the width of the "sidebar" div element box based on this style rule.

```
div#sidebar { width: 200px;
   margin: 25px;
   padding-left: 30px;
   padding-right: 10px;
   border: 1px solid #FFF;
}
```

Extra credit: What width would you have to provide for Internet Explorer 5 and 5.5 (Windows) to compensate for its box model problem?

Review: Basic Layout Properties

Here is a summary of the properties covered in this chapter, in alphabetical order.

Property	Description
float	Moves the element to the right or left and allows the following text to flow around it.
clear	Prevents an element from being laid out next to a float.
position	Specifies the positioning method to be applied to the element
top, bottom, right, left	Specifies the offset amount from each respective edge.
z-index	Specifies the order of appearance within a stack of overlapping positioned elements.

PAGE LAYOUT WITH CSS

Now that you understand the principles of moving elements around on the page using CSS floats and positioning, we can put these tools to use in some standard page layouts. This chapter looks at the various approaches to CSS-based web design and provides some simple templates that will get you on your way to building basic two- and three-column web pages.

Before we get started, it must be said that there are seemingly endless variations on creating multicolumn layouts with CSS. This chapter is intended to be a "starter kit." The templates presented here are simplified and may not work for every situation (although I've tried to point out the relevant shortcomings of each). You may know of better approaches. In fact, because there is so much to be said about CSS page layout, I've provided pointers to additional samples and tutorials on the Web. New techniques turn up regularly.

Page Layout Strategies

Way back in Chapter 3, The Nature of Web Design, we established the fact that there is no way of knowing exactly how wide, skinny, tall, or short a user's browser window will be. Users may set their browsers to fill the monitor at one of the standard resolutions or have them set to some other comfortable dimension. The precise size of any given web page is an unknown. In addition, there is no way of knowing how large your text will be. You may prefer small tidy text, but a portion of your users will make their text larger, possibly much larger, to make it comfortable to read. Changing text size is likely to have an impact on the layout of your page.

Over time, three general page layout approaches have emerged to deal with these inescapable facts. Liquid pages resize along with the browser window. Fixed pages put the content in a page area that stays a specific pixel width regardless of the browser's dimensions. Finally, elastic pages have areas that get larger or smaller when the text is resized. Let's look at how each strategy works as well as the reasons for and against using each of them. I'll also briefly introduce zoom layouts that address the needs of users with low vision.

IN THIS CHAPTER

Fixed, liquid, and elastic page layouts

Two- and three-column layout templates using floats

Two- and three-column layout templates using absolute positioning

Centering a fixed-width page

Optimal Line Length

Line length is a measure of the number of words or characters in a line of text. The rule of thumb is that the optimal line length is 10 to 12 words or between 60 and 75 characters.

When line lengths grow too long, the text becomes more difficult to read. Not only is it hard to focus long enough to get to the end of a long line, it is also requires extra effort to find the beginning of the next line again.

Line length is at the heart of the debate over which layout technique is superior. In liquid layouts, line lengths might get too long when the browser is sized very wide. In fixed width designs, line lengths may become awkwardly short if the text is sized large within narrow and rigid column widths. The elastic layout introduced later in this chapter, however, offers predictable line lengths even when the text is sized larger. This makes it a popular option for balancing design and accessibility priorities.

Create a liquid layout by specifying widths in percentages or not at all.

Liquid page design

Liquid page layouts (also called fluid layouts) follow the default behavior of the normal flow. In other words, the page area and/or columns within the page are allowed to get wider or narrower to fill the available space in the browser window. There is no attempt to control the width of the content or line breaks—the text is permitted to reflow as required. Figure 16-1 shows *W3.org*, which is a good example of a liquid layout.

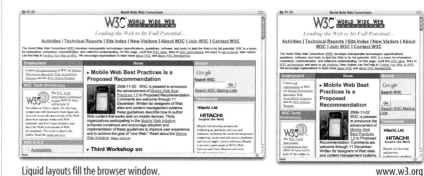

Liquid layouts fill the browser window.
Content reflows when the browser window and columns resize.

www.w3.org

Figure 16-1. Example of a liquid layout.

Proponents of liquid web pages feel strongly that this is the best formatting method because it is consistent with the nature of the medium. Of course, it has both advantages and disadvantages.

Advantages	Disadvantages
You don't have to design for a specific monitor resolution.	On large monitors, line lengths can get very long and uncomfortable to read. See the sidebar for more information.
You avoid potentially awkward empty space because the text fills the window.	They are less predictable. Elements may be too spread out or too cramped at extreme browser dimensions.
Liquid pages keep with the spirit and nature of the medium.	

How to create liquid layouts

Create a liquid layout by specifying widths in percentage values. You can also not specify a width at all, in which case the width will be set to the default `auto` setting, and the element will fill the available width of the window or other containing element. Here are a few examples.

In this two-column layout (Figure 16-2), the width of each `div` has been specified as a percentage of the available page width. The main column will always be 70% of the width of the window, and the right column fills 25% (the remaining 5% is used for the margin between the columns), regardless of the window size.

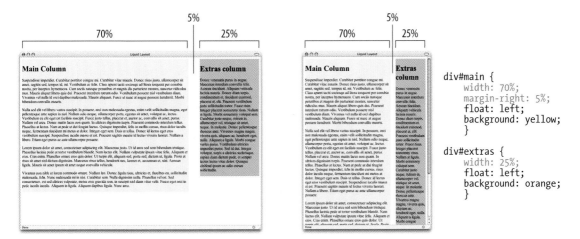

```
div#main {
    width: 70%;
    margin-right: 5%;
    float: left;
    background: yellow;
    }

div#extras {
    width: 25%;
    float: left;
    background: orange;
    }
```

Figure 16-2. Liquid layout using percentage values.

In the example in Figure 16-3, the secondary column on the left is set to a specific pixel width, and the main content area is set to auto and fills the remaining space in the window (I could have also left it unspecified for the same result). Although this layout uses a fixed width for one column, it is still considered liquid because the width of the page is based on the width of the browser window.

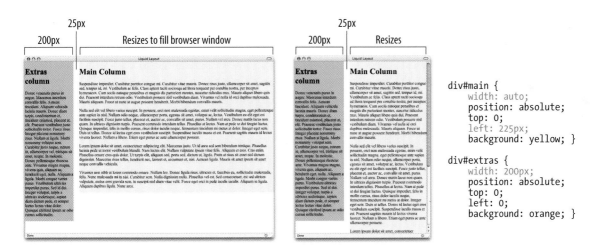

```
div#main {
    width: auto;
    position: absolute;
    top: 0;
    left: 225px;
    background: yellow; }

div#extras {
    width: 200px;
    position: absolute;
    top: 0;
    left: 0;
    background: orange; }
```

Figure 16-3. Liquid layout combining fixed-width and auto sized columns.

Dealing with line lengths

Although long line lengths are possible in liquid layouts, it's certainly a manageable situation and not a reason to reject this layout approach.

In the vast majority of cases, users have their browsers sized reasonably, that is, somewhere between 800 and 1250 pixels. If your page is two or more columns, you're in luck, because it will be difficult for the line lengths to get too out of hand at these "reasonable" browser widths. Sure, line lengths will change when the browser is resized, and they may not be in the ideal range of 60 to 75 characters per line, but text is unlikely to be unreadable.

If your page consists of only one column, I suggest using left and right margins (in the 10 to 20% range, depending on preference) to reduce the resulting line length and also add valuable white space around the text.

Finally, you can use the `max-width` property to limit the width of the content containers. Unfortunately, it is not supported by Internet Explorer (Windows) 6 and earlier, but those versions will eventually fall out of significant use.

Fixed Layouts

Fixed-width layouts, as the name implies, stay put at a specified pixel width as determined by the designer. This approach is based on traditional guiding principles of graphic design, such as a constant grid, the relationship of page elements, and comfortable line lengths. When you set your page to a specific width, you need to decide a couple of things.

First, you need to pick a page width, usually based on common monitor resolutions. Most fixed-width web pages as of this writing are designed to fit in an 800×600 pixel browser window, although more and more sites are venturing into a (roughly) 1000 pixel page width.

You also need to decide where the fixed-width layout should be positioned in the browser window. By default, it stays on the left edge of the browser, with the extra space to the right of it. Some designers opt to center the page, splitting the extra space over left and right margins, which may make the page look as though it better fills the browser window. Figure 16-4 shows two fixed width layouts. Both use fixed-width pages, but position the content differently in the browser window.

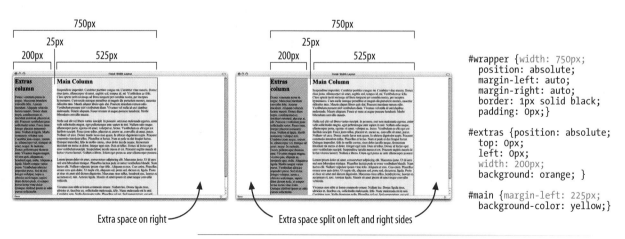

Figure 16-4. Examples of fixed layouts (left-aligned and centered).

One of the main concerns with using fixed-width layouts is that if the user's browser window is not as wide as the page, the content on the right edge of the page will not be visible. Although it is possible to scroll horizontally, it may not always be clear that there is more content there in the first place.

Take a look at O'Reilly Media's web site (*www.oreilly.com*) in Figure 16-5. The page was designed to fill a browser window maximized to a 1024 × 768 monitor. Given the nature of the content and the audience it is intended for, it is a completely appropriate design decision. However, the figure on the right shows what a user with an 800 × 600 monitor would see. The entire right column is hidden. Fortunately, O'Reilly uses the right column for interesting, yet non-critical information, so even if it is overlooked, there is no serious harm done.

Fixed-width layouts are created by specifying width values in pixel units.

Figure 16-5. Users may miss out on content on the right edge of a fixed layout if the browser is not as wide as the page area.

Let's review the pros and cons of using the fixed-width strategy.

Advantages	Disadvantages
The layout is predictable.	Content on the right edge will be hidden if the browser window is smaller than the page.
It offers better control over line length.	
Trends come and go; however, it is worth noting that many of the most well-known web designers use fixed-width designs as of this writing.	Text elements still reflow if the user resizes the font size, so it doesn't guarantee the layout will stay exactly the same.
	Line lengths may grow awkwardly short at very large text sizes.

How to create fixed-width layouts

Fixed-width layouts are created by specifying width values in pixel units. Typically, the content of the entire page is put into a `div` (often named "content," "container," "wrapper," or "page") that can then be set to a specific pixel width. This `div` may also be centered in the browser window. Widths of column elements, and even margins and padding, are also specified in pixels. We will see examples of this technique later in this chapter.

Elastic Layouts

A third layout approach is growing in popularity because it marries resizable text with predictable line lengths. Elastic (also called jello) layouts expand or contract with the size of the text. If the user makes the text larger, the box that contains it expands proportionally. Likewise, if the user likes her text size very small, the containing box shrinks to fit. The result is that line lengths (in terms of words or characters per line) stay the same regardless of the text size. This is an advantage over liquid layouts where line lengths can get too long, and fixed layouts where very large text may result in awkwardly few characters per line.

Figure 16-6 shows the Elastic Lawn design by Patrick Griffiths at CSS Zen Garden (*www.csszengarden.com/?cssfile=/063/063.css*), an often-referenced example of an elastic layout at work. Notice that when the text size gets bigger in each sample, so does the content area of the page. However, instead of rewrapping in the larger layout space, the line breaks are the same.

NOTE

AOL.com also uses an elastic layout (as of this writing), demonstrating that this approach is a viable option for large sites with lots of detailed information on the home page.

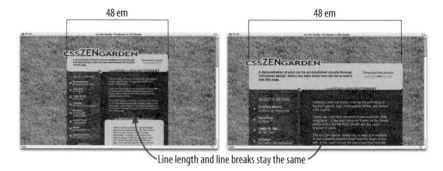

Figure 16-6. The Elastic Lawn design by Patrick Griffiths at CSS Zen Garden is a classic example of elastic page layout.

As any layout approach, elastic layouts come with their own pros and cons:

Advantages	Disadvantages
Provide a consistent layout experience while allowing flexibility in text size. Tighter control over line lengths than liquid and fixed layouts.	Images don't lend themselves to automatic rescaling along with the text and the rest of the layout (but there are methods to achieve this). The width of the layout might exceed the width of the browser window at largest text sizes. This can be prevented with proper planning and/or the `max-width` property (unsupported in IE6 and earlier).

How to create elastic layouts

The key to elastic layouts is the em, a unit of measurement that is based on size of the text. For example, for an element with 12-pixel text, an em is 12 pixels. In Chapter 12, Formatting Text, we learned that it is always preferable to specify font size in ems because it allows the text to be resized with the zoom feature in all modern browsers (remember that IE6 and earlier do not zoom text sized in pixels). In elastic layouts, the dimensions of containing elements are specified in ems as well. That is how the widths can respond to the text size.

Elastic layouts are created by specifying widths in em units.

For example, if the text size is set to 76% (equal to about 12 pixels on most browsers), and the page is set to 40 em, the resulting page width would be 480 pixels (40 em x 12px/em). If the user resizes the text up to 24 pixels, the page grows to 960 pixels. Note that this is getting close to the available canvas space in browsers on 1024-pixel wide monitors. If the page were set much more than 40 ems wide, there would be the risk of the right edge extending beyond the browser window at extremely large text sizes.

Zoom Layouts for Low-Vision Users

Users who are totally blind may use screen readers to access web content. However, there are many visually impaired users who have enough vision to view sites on computer monitors as long as the type is large and the contrast is good.

A new layout technique, called zoom layouts (Figure 16-7), has emerged to address the special requirements of these low-vision users. The hallmarks of zoom layouts include:`

- A single column layout
- Extremely large type (set in ems for scalability)
- High-contrast text and background (both light-on-dark and dark-on-light versions are often supplied)
- Simplified navigation that appears at the beginning of the document
- Some visual elements such as color and simple graphics to create an experience consistent with that of the site's normal presentation.

Zoom layouts are usually provided as an alternative to the site's normal design. They're made accessible to those who need it via a link at the top of the page.

The champion of the zoom layout is accessibility expert, Joe Clark. For more information, these links to Mr. Clark's publications are a good place to start.

The Zoom Layout Page
joeclark.org/access/webaccess/zoom/

Zoom Layout presentation at @media 2005
joeclark.org/appearances/atmedia/atmedia-NOTES-2.html

"Big, Stark, and Chunky," article at *A List Apart*
alistapart.com/articles/lowvision

Figure 16-7. A zoom layout designed by Doug Bowman at stopdesign.com.

The Liquid vs. Fixed Debate

The "liquid or fixed" question has sparked impassioned debate among professionals in the web design community. There has been an undeniable trend toward fixed-width layouts (presumably to control line lengths), but there are still staunch proponents of liquid designs as best for a medium where the canvas size is unknown. Many designers from both sides are switching to elastic layouts as a solid compromise solution.

To get caught up with both sides of the debate, start with these articles and blog entries (they all have links to additional points of view):

- "On Fixed vs. Liquid Design," by Doug Bowman (experimenting with fixed width design at *www.stopdesign.com/log/2003/12/15/fixedorliquid.html*)

- "More on fixed widths," by Richard Rutter (pro–liquid design article at *clagnut.com/blog/269/*)

- "Fixed Fashion," by Jeremy Keith (pro–liquid designpost at *www.adactio.com/journal/980*)

Which one should I use?

As you can see, each layout approach has its own advantages and drawbacks. Developers tend to have their favorites, and if you read through comments left on CSS-design-related web sites, you'll find that there are some passionate opinions for and against each approach (see the sidebar, The Liquid vs. Fixed Debate).

I'm of the opinion that there is no "right" way to lay out all web pages. I find that the best solution is usually a function of the nature of content and design of the site I am working on. You will probably find the same thing to be true. But now you know the various options and can take them into consideration when it is time to lay out the page.

Page Layout Templates

Here it is... the section you've been waiting for: how to create two- and three-column layouts using CSS and absolutely no tables. The code examples in this section should give you a good head start toward formatting your pages, but they are not universal solutions. Your content may dictate more complicated solutions. You may also prefer one of the more robust templates listed in the More Layout Templates and Tutorials sidebar.

This section provides templates and techniques for the following:

- Multicolumn layouts using floats (two- and three-column)

- Multicolumn layouts using positioning (two- and three-column, with and without footer)

- A centered fixed width page

Using the templates

The sample pages in this section aren't pretty. In fact, I've stripped them down to their bare minimum to help make the structure and strategy as clear as possible. Here are a few notes regarding the templates and how to use them.

Simplified markup

The DOCTYPE declaration, and other document structure markup (`html`, `head`, `title`, and `body` elements) have been omitted from the templates to save space. Be sure that your documents have the proper structural markup.

Headers and footers

I've included a header and footer element on many of these examples, but either one or both could easily be omitted for a minimal two- or three-column layout.

Dominant main column

One thing to be aware of is that all of these examples are based on the best-case scenario where the main content column is longer than the side column(s), which of course is not always the case in the real world. If your side columns are longer, you may need to make adjustments or use a different structure altogether.

Color-coding

I've included two views of each layout. The one on the left is plain and simple and shows off the potential of the layout. In the right view, I've added a garish background color to help you match the markup and style sheet code with what is happening in the browser. The background colors are also helpful for visualizing the boundaries and placement of element boxes.

Make it yours

The example style sheets contain the minimum number of rules to create a flexible and usable page structure. There is obviously a lot more that could be done with text, backgrounds, margins, padding, and borders to make these pages more appealing. Once you've laid a framework with these templates, you should feel free to change the measurements and add your own styles. Values that can be replaced are indicated in italics in the style sheet examples.

Multicolumn Layouts Using Floats

The most popular way to create a column is to float an element to one side and let the remaining content wrap around it. A wide margin is used to keep the area around the floated column clear.

One of the advantages of floats is that it is easier to start page elements such as a footer below the columned area of the page. The drawback of float-based layouts is that they are dependent on the order in which the elements appear in the source. Getting the layout effect you are after may result in the document source not being in the optimal order for users of non-visual browsers.

The templates in this section reveal the general strategy for approaching two- and three-column layouts using floats and should serve as a good head start toward implementing your own layouts.

Two-column with footer
Method: FLOAT
Layout: LIQUID

The markup and styles in this example produce a liquid two-column layout with a header area, a main column of content, a sidebar, and footer for copyright information as shown in Figure 16-8.

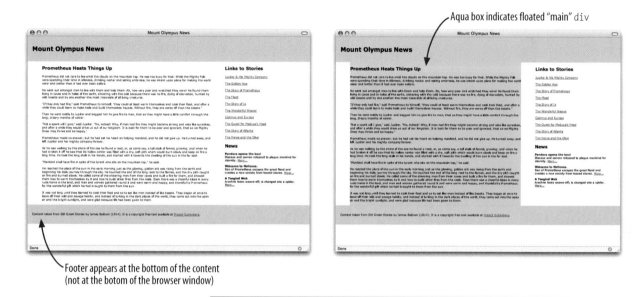

Aqua box indicates floated "main" div

Footer appears at the bottom of the content (not at the botom of the browser window)

Figure 16-8. Two-column layout with footer.

The Markup

```
<div id="header">
Masthead and headline
</div>

A <div id="main">
Main article...
</div>

<div id="extras">
List of links and news
</div>

<div id="footer">
Copyright information
</div>
```

Markup Notes:

The source document has been divided into four divs, one each for the header, content, extras, and footer.

Ⓐ The main content appears before the extras in the source document so that it is accessed first by users with non-graphical browsers. That means that we can't float the "extras" `div` because it will not float above the preceding block element to the top of the page. Instead, the main content `div` is floated and the following text (the "extras" `div`) wraps around it.

The Style Sheet

```
#header {
    background: #CCC;
    padding: 15px; }
```

Ⓑ
```
#main {
    background-color: aqua;
    float: left;   /* floats the whole main article to the left */
    width: 60%;
    margin-right: 5%;   /* adds space between columns */
    margin-left: 5%; }
```

Ⓒ
```
#footer {
    clear: left; /* starts the footer below the floated content */
    padding: 15px;
    background: #CCC; }
```

Ⓓ
```
#extras {
    margin-right: 5%} /* space on the right of the side column */
```

Ⓔ
```
body {
    font-family: Verdana, sans-serif;
    margin: 0; /* clears default browser margins */
    padding: 0; }
```

```
li {
    list-style: none;
    margin: 10px 0; }
```

Style Sheet Notes:

Ⓑ The main content `div` is floated to the left and set to 60% of the page width. A margin is applied to the left and right sides of the floated "main" `div` to add space between columns.

Ⓒ The "footer" `div` is cleared (with the `clear` property) so that it starts below the floated main content column.

Ⓓ A margin is added on the right edge of the "extras" `div` to add space between it and the browser window.

Ⓔ The margin and padding on the `body` element have been set to zero to clear the default browser settings. This allows the shaded header and footer areas to go right up to the edge of the browser window without any white gaps.

Three-column with footer
Method: FLOAT
Layout: FIXED

This example uses floated elements to create a fixed-width three-column layout (a main content column flanked by left and right sidebars) with optional header and footer (Figure 16-9).

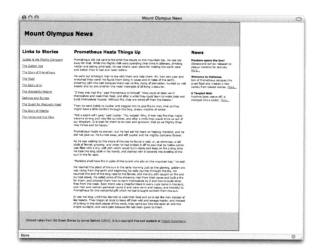 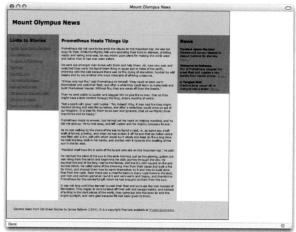

Figure 16-9. Three-column layout using floats.

The Markup

Ⓐ `<div id="container">`

    `<div id="header">`
    Masthead and headline
    `</div>`

Ⓑ   `<div id="links">`
    List of links
    `</div>`

    `<div id="main">`
    Main article...
    `</div>`

    `<div id="news">`
    News and announcements...
    `</div>`

    `<div id="footer">`
    Copyright information
    `</div>`

`</div>`

Markup Notes

Ⓐ All of the content elements in the document have been placed in a "container" `div` to which the fixed-width measurement will be applied.

Ⓑ Remember that with floating, the order that the elements appear in the source document is significant. To get the narrow sidebars on either side of the content, I needed to move the "links" `div` before the "content" `div` to keep the style sheet straightforward. There are methods that allow the content to appear in any order, but they tend to get complicated. The last three resources listed in the More Layout Templates and Tutorials sidebar address this issue.

The Style Sheet

```
    #container {
      width: 750px;
❻   border: solid 1px; }

    #header {
      background: #CCC;
      padding: 15px; }

❼ #links {
      background-color: fuchsia;
      float: left;
❽   width: 175px; }

❼ #main {
      background-color: aqua;
      float: left;
❽   width: 400px; }

❼ #news {
      background-color: green;
      float: left;
❽   width: 175px; }

❾ #footer {
      clear: both;    /* starts the footer below the floated content */
      padding: 15px;
      background: #CCC; }

    body {
      font-family: Verdana, sans-serif;
      font-size: small;
      margin: 0;
      padding: 0;}

❿ h2, ul, p {
      padding: 0px 8px; }     /* adds space around content */

    li {
      list-style: none;
      margin: 10px 0; }
```

Style Sheet Notes

❻ A border has been added to the container to reveal its edges in this demonstration, but it can easily be removed.

❼ The style sheet floats the "links" "main," and "news" `div`s to the left. The result is that they accumulate against the left edge of the containing block, thus creating three columns.

❽ Because there are no padding, border, or margin settings for each floated element, the sum of their widths is equal to the width of the outer container.

❾ The `clear: both` property has been added to the footer to make sure it starts below all of the floated elements.

❿ Space within each content `div` is added by applying padding on the elements it contains (`h2`, `ul`, `p`, etc.).

Now it's your turn to give it a try. In Exercise 16-1, you'll use the same content to create a hybrid of the previous examples: a two-column, fixed-width layout using floats.

exercise 16-1 | **Float-based Layout**

In this exercise, we'll create the fixed-width layout shown in Figure 16-10. The source document for this exercise, *olympus.html*, is available online at *www.learningwebdesign.com/materials/*. It contains the basic markup and the start of the style sheet for all the exercises in this chapter.

1. Open *olympus.html* in your text editor and save it as a new file called *2col-olympus.html* (that will keep a copy of the starter document fresh for the next exercise). We'll start by getting the markup all set. Because this is a fixed-width layout, wrap all of the content (from the first h1 to the end of the last paragraph) in a div identified as the "container" (with the id attribute) just as we did in the three-column template earlier. Be sure to include the closing </div> tag.

2. Next, add divs that identify the four content sections. Name them "header," "main," "extras," and "footer." Note that the "extras" div in this example contains both Links and News.

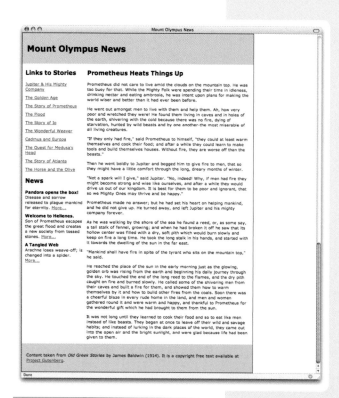

Figure 16-10. Two-column, fixed-width layout.

3. With the markup in place, you can move on to the style sheet. The style element and some basic text formatting rules have been added for you. Apply a width to the container div. This sets the width of the page area. Also, apply a border to make the boundaries of the page area clear (you can always remove it later).

   ```
   #container {
     width: 750px;
     border: 1px solid; }
   ```

4. Next, let's make the header and footer stand out. Give them some padding and a light background color. I'm using gray, but you can use any color you like.

   ```
   #header {
     padding: 15px;
     background: #CCC; }

   #footer {
     padding: 15px;
     background: #CCC; }
   ```

5. Now give the main content div a width and float it to the right to make the second column,

   ```
   #main {
     float: right;
     width: 550px; }
   ```

   and clear the footer so it appears below the floated content,

   ```
   #footer {
     clear: both;
     padding: 15px;
     background: #CCC; }
   ```

6. Save the document and take a look at it in the browser. It should look almost like the sample in Figure 16-10. The only problem is that the text is bumping up against the edges of the columns and the browser. We can fix that. Add margins on both sides of the floated main column and on the left side of the "extras" **div**.

```
#main {
  float: right;
  width: 530px;
  margin: 0 10px; } /* adds 0 pixels top/bottom and 10px left/right */

#extras {
  margin-left: 10px; }
```

7. Save the document again, and take a look. You should have a page that matches the example.

8. The layout is officially done, but let's play around with it a bit to get a better feel for what's happening. First, make the background of the "main" **div** yellow by adding **background-color: yellow;** to the **#main** rule. Save the file and look at it in the browser. You should see that the color goes behind the content area of the floated box, but does not extend into the margin area, as expected.

9. Now, make the background of the "extras" **div** red by adding **background-color: red;** to the **#extras** rule. Save the file and look at it in your browser. You will see that the red background color goes all the way across the page area, behind the floated column (as shown in Figure 16-11). This is because the sidebar text is just wrapping around the float. The normal behavior for wrapped text is that the content moves out of the way of the float, but the element box still takes up its normal width. The background of the wrapped text appears behind the float. You may remove the background colors once you've gotten the point.

NOTE

The margin will be added on the outside of the 550 pixel-wide content block. That means that the side column will be reduced by 20 pixels. If you want the left and right columns to stay 200 and 550 pixels respectively, you need to reduce the width of the main div *to 530px. We'll talk about this more in the final 3-column template example.*

EXERCISE TIPS

- If things aren't working, make sure that you didn't miss a semicolon (;) at the end of a property or a curly bracket (}) at the end of a rule.

- Try saving and viewing the document after each step to see the effects of each change that you make.

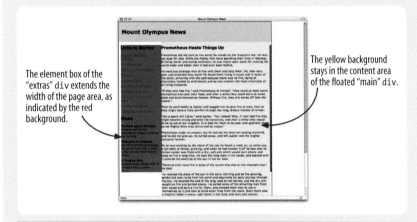

The element box of the "extras" div extends the width of the page area, as indicated by the red background.

The yellow background stays in the content area of the floated "main" div.

Figure 16-11. Adding background colors to reveal element structure.

Obviously, there is more you could do to pretty up this page with color, text formatting, images, and so on. What is important here is that you get a feel for creating the structure using floats. Later in the chapter, I'll show you a trick for adding colors to columns using a background image. We'll also learn how to center a fixed-width layout like this one in the browser window.

Layouts Using Absolute Positioning

Absolute positioning can also be used to create a multicolumn page. The advantage is that the order of the source document is not as critical as it is in the float method, because element boxes can be positioned anywhere. The disadvantage is that you run the risk of elements overlapping and content being obscured. This makes it tricky to implement full-width elements below columns (such as the footer in the previous example), because it will get overlapped if a positioned column grows too long.

When working with absolute positioning, remember that every element you position is removed from the normal flow. If content you expect to be at the bottom of the page is sitting at the very top, it's because you positioned (and thus removed) all the elements above it that were "holding it down." This is something to keep in mind while troubleshooting.

Two-column with narrow footer
Method: POSITIONED
Layout: LIQUID

The example in this section creates a right sidebar column using absolute positioning. The resulting layout is shown in Figure 16-12. Note that the footer design has been modified for the sake of simplifying the template (full-width footers are problematic, as mentioned earlier).

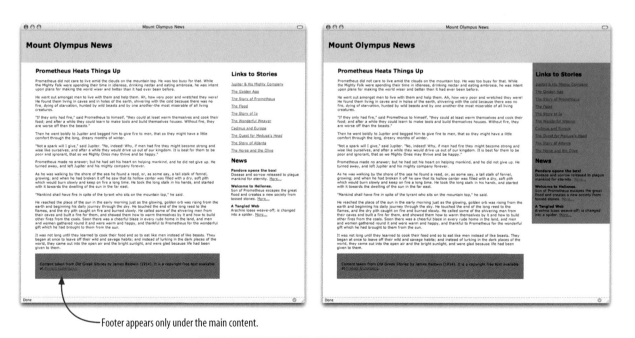

Footer appears only under the main content.

Figure 16-12. Two-column layout with absolute positioning.

The Markup

```
<div id="header">
Masthead and headline
</div>

<div id="main">
Main article...
</div>

Ⓐ <div id="extras">
List of links and news
</div>

<div id="footer">
Copyright information
</div>
```

The Style Sheet

```
Ⓑ #header {
    height: 70px;
    padding: 15px;    /* height of header = 100 (15+70+15) */
    background: #CCC;}

Ⓒ #main {
    margin-right: 30%; /* makes room for the positioned sidebar */
    margin-left: 5%; }

Ⓓ #extras {
    position: absolute;
    top: 100px;    /* places the extras div below the header */
    right: 0px;    /* places it against right edge of the window */
    width: 25%;
    background: green;
    padding: 10px;}   /* adds space within colored box */

Ⓔ #footer {
    margin-right: 30%; /* keeps the footer aligned with content */
    margin-left: 5%;
    padding: 15px;
    background: #666; }

body {
    font-family: Verdana, sans-serif;
    font-size: small;
    margin: 0;
    padding: 0;}

ul { padding: 0px; }

li {
    list-style: none;
    margin: 10px 0; }
```

Markup Notes

Ⓐ This style sheet absolutely positions the "extras" div element against the right side of the page and 100 pixels down from the top to leave room for the header element. The "main" content div is given a right margin wide enough to make a space for the newly positioned box.

Style Sheet Notes

Ⓑ In this example, we know that the header is exactly 100 pixels tall (70 height plus 30 pixels of padding).

Ⓒ The 30% right margin makes space for the column that is 25% of the page plus 5% space between the columns.

Ⓓ The "extras" div is positioned absolutely 0 pixels from the right edge of the browser and exactly 100 pixels down from the top.

Ⓔ The margins applied to the main content were also applied to the footer div. That is to prevent the footer from being overlapped by a long sidebar.

WARNING

Because this template places columns a specific pixel measurement from the top, it may not be appropriate for pages with headers that may expand taller. The solution is to create another containing div after the header just for the columns, so that the sidebar can be placed in its top-right corner. This will keep the sidebar below the header regardless of its size. The trade-off is a bit of unnecessary markup.

Three-column (narrow footer)
Method: POSITIONED
Layout: LIQUID

In this template, both sidebar columns are absolutely positioned, and margins are applied to both sides of the main content to make way for the sidebars. The resulting layout is shown in Figure 16-13.

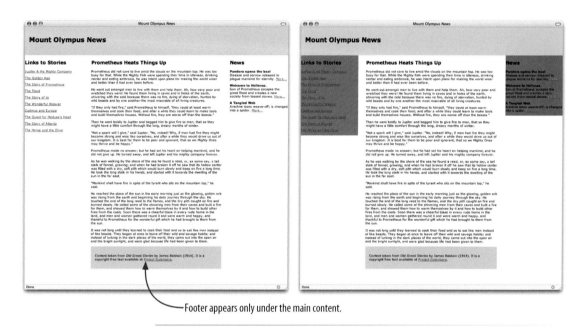

Footer appears only under the main content.

Figure 16-13. Positioning two sidebars in a three-column layout.

The Markup

```
<div id="header">
Masthead and headline
</div>
```

Ⓐ
```
<div id="main">
Main article...
</div>
```

Ⓑ
```
<div id="links">
List of links
</div>
```

Ⓑ
```
<div id="news">
News and announcements...
</div>
```

```
<div id="footer">
Copyright information
</div>
```

Markup Notes

Ⓐ Because absolute positioning is not order-dependent, the main content `div` can appear in its preferable position first in the document source.

Ⓑ Only the "links" and "news" `div` elements are positioned in this layout.

The Style Sheet

```
#header {
  height: 70px;
  padding: 15px;    /* height of header = 100 (15+70+15) */
  background: #CCC;
}

#main {
  margin-left: 25%; /* makes room for the left sidebar */
  margin-right: 25%; /* makes room for the right sidebar */
}

#links {
  position: absolute;
  top: 100px;    /* places the sidebar below the header */
  left: 0px;     /* places it against left edge of the window */
  width: 22%; /* less than main margins to add space between cols */
  background: fuchsia;
}

#news {
  position: absolute;
  top: 100px;    /* places the sidebar below the header */
  right: 0px;    /* places it against right edge of the window */
  width: 22%;
  background: green;
}

#footer {
  margin-right: 25%; /* keeps the footer aligned with content */
  margin-left: 25%;
  padding: 15px;
  background: #CCC;
}

body {
  font-family: Verdana, sans-serif;
  font-size: small;
  margin: 0;
  padding: 0;}

ul { padding: 0px; }

li {
  list-style: none;
  margin: 10px 0; }
```

Style Sheet Notes

The style sheet is essentially the same as that for the previous example, with the exception that margins have been applied to both sides of the "main" and "footer" div elements to make room for columns on both sides. The comments within the style sheet provide information on what key properties are doing.

- **C** The "links" and "news" divs are positioned against the left and right edges of the browser window (technically, it's the initial-containing block), respectively.

- **D** The width of the positioned columns is narrower than the margins on the main content div to allow space between columns.

- **E** The footer gets the same margin treatment as the main content column to make sure the side columns do not overlap it.

Three-column with rules and padding between columns
Method: POSITIONED
Layout: FIXED

In this three-column layout, all three columns are absolutely positioned in a fixed layout. In addition, borders and padding have been added between columns. For reasons of simplicity, the footer has been omitted altogether in this example because there is no way to keep it at the bottom of the page without using JavaScript or jumping through some CSS hoops that are beyond the scope of this chapter. The result is shown in Figure 16-14.

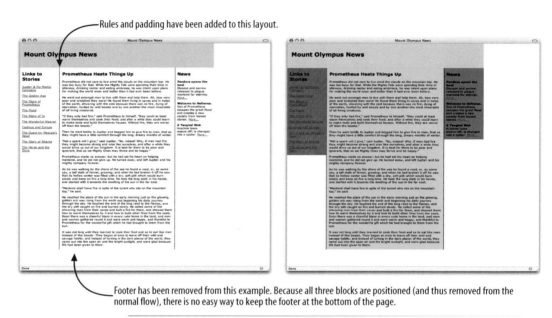

Rules and padding have been added to this layout.

Footer has been removed from this example. Because all three blocks are positioned (and thus removed from the normal flow), there is no easy way to keep the footer at the bottom of the page.

Figure 16-14. Three positioned columns in a fixed-width layout.

The Markup

Ⓐ `<div id="container">`

`<div id="header">`
Masthead and headline
`</div>`

Ⓑ `<div id="main">`
Main article...
`</div>`

Ⓑ `<div id="links">`
List of links
`</div>`

Ⓑ `<div id="news">`
News and announcements...
`</div>`

`</div>`

Markup Notes

A Because this is a fixed-width layout, all of the content has been wrapped in a "container" `div`.

B All three content-containing `div` elements are absolutely positioned. The main content `div` can appear first in the source document.

The Style Sheet

```
C  #container {
      position: relative;   /* makes "container" a containing block */
      width: 750px; }

   #header {
      height: 70px;
      padding: 15px;   /* total height = 100 (15+70+15) */
      background: #CCC; }

   #main {
D     position: absolute;
      top: 100px;
E     left: 150px;
F     width: 428px;   /* 450 minus 2px of border and 20px of padding */
      border-left: solid 1px black;
      border-right: solid 1px black;
      padding: 0px 10px; /* 10 pixels padding left and right */
      background-color: aqua; }

   #links {
D     position: absolute;
      top: 100px;
E     left: 0px;
F     width: 134px; /* 150 minus 16 px total padding */
      padding: 0 8px;    /* 8 px padding left and right */
      background: fuchsia; }

   #news {
D     position: absolute;
      top: 100px;
E     left: 600px;   /* makes room for other 2 columns */
F     width: 134px;   /* 150 minus 16 px total padding */
      padding: 0 8px;    /* 8 px padding left and right */
      background: green; }

   body {
      font-family: Verdana, sans-serif;
      font-size: small;
      margin: 0;
      padding: 0; }

   ul { padding: 0px; }

   li {
      list-style: none;
      margin: 10px 0; }
```

Style Sheet Notes

⊙ The "container" `div` has a fixed width (750 pixels) and its position is set to `relative` to establish it as a containing block for the positioned column elements.

⊙ All three content `div`s ("links," "main," and "news") are absolutely positioned below the header.

⊙ The values for `left` (that is, the distance from the left edge of the containing block area) are relative to the left edge of the entire *element* box (including margins) for each `div`, not just the content area.

⊙ Whenever you add padding, margins, or borders to a fixed-width layout structure, you need to do some math to make sure the sum of the element widths plus all their extras does not exceed the total container width. In the example, the 750 pixel overall width is divided into two 150 pixel sidebars and a 450 pixel main column. Although it may be tempting to set the width of each `div` to these values, unfortunately, that won't work. The `width` property applies only to the content area.

Figure 16-15 breaks down all the measurements that span the width of the "container" `div`. You can easily match the values in the figure to the ones used in the preceding style sheet.

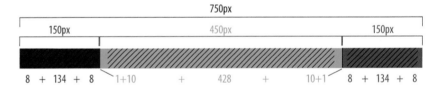

Figure 16-15. Calculating widths, margins, borders, and padding.

WARNING

If you need to support Internet Explorer 5 and 5.5 for Windows, your work isn't finished. IE5 incorrectly implements the box model and applies the `width` *property to the outer edges of the element. A workaround for providing a different set of width properties just for IE5/5.5(Win) is provided in Chapter 14, Thinking Inside the Box. With the release of IE7, many developers have chosen to stop supporting IE5, but of course, whether you choose to support it or not depends on the nature of your site and your own server statistics.*

exercise 16-2 | **Elastic layout with positioned column**

Now you should be ready to take on an absolutely positioned layout. In this exercise, we'll use the same content to create a two-column, elastic layout (Figure 16-16) using absolute positioning.

1. Open *olympus.html* and save it as a new document named *elastic-olympus.html*.

2. Delete the copyright information paragraph at the end of the document. This layout does not include a footer.

3. Next, add the necessary markup. Once again, add a **div** named "container" around everything, and divide the content into three **div**s: "header," "main," and "extras."

4. In the style sheet, set up the page by giving the "container" **div** a **width** and setting its **position** to **relative** to establish a containing block for the positioned columns. Because this is an elastic layout, the **width** should be specified in em units. We'll use a conservative 40em so that the layout can be resized larger a few intervals before running off the typical 1024-pixel wide monitor.

```
#container {
    width: 40em;
    position: relative;
}
```

5. Give the header a height (also in em units), padding, and a background color as we've been doing throughout this chapter.

```
#header {
    height: 4em;
    padding: 1em;
    background-color: #CCC;
}
```

6. Now we can position the "extras" **div**. Add this rule to your style sheet to position the sidebar box below the header and give it a width of 10em with 1 em of padding on the left side.

```
#extras {
    width: 10em;
    position: absolute;
    top: 6em;
    left: 0;
    padding-left: 1em;
}
```

7. Finally, make room for the positioned sidebar by adding a margin on the left edge of the "main" content **div**. I've added an 12em margin to make room for the 11em-wide sidebar plus 1em space between columns.

```
#main {
    margin-left: 12em;
}
```

8. Save the file and open it in a browser. It should look like the layout shown in Figure 16-16. Try using the text zoom feature on your browser to make the text larger and smaller and see the elastic layout at work.

The page width expands when text is sized larger.

Figure 16-16. Two-column, elastic layout.

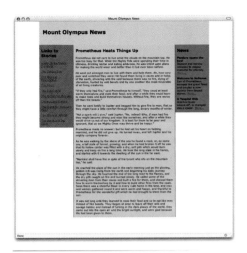

Figure 16-17. *Centering a fixed-width page element.*

Centering a Fixed-Width Page

All of the fixed-width examples we've seen so far have been aligned on the left side of the browser window with empty space to the right of it. Although you see plenty of left-aligned pages, many designers choose to center their fixed-width pages in the browser window to split up that potentially awkward left-over space.

This section looks at two methods for centering a fixed-width page: the official CSS way and an effective creative solution that works in all CSS-compliant browsers (even Netscape Navigator 4). We'll use these methods to center the fixed-width three-column page we made earlier (Figure 16-17).

Top-to-Bottom Column Backgrounds

Adding color to columns is an effective way to further emphasize the division of information and bring a little color to the page. I have added background colors to the column elements in some of the template demonstrations, but as you have seen, the color stops at the end of the element box and does not extend to the bottom of the page. This is not the effect I am after.

Unfortunately, there is no supported way of setting the height of an element to 100% of the page height, and while there are CSS layout templates and JavaScript workarounds that produce full-height column elements, they are beyond the scope of this chapter.

But don't fret. There is a reliable solution known as the "faux columns" trick that will work with any of the fixed-width templates in this chapter. In this technique, column colors are added using a tiling image in the background of the page or containing element (such as the "container" `div` in the examples).The Faux Columns method was first introduced by Dan Cederholm in his article for *A List Apart*, and in his book, *Web Standards Solutions*.

Here's how it works. The column shading in Figure 16-18 is the result of a horizontal image with bands of color that match the width of the columns. When the image is set to tile vertically in the background, the result is vertical stripes over which a multicolumn layout may be positioned. Of course, this only works when the width of the column or page is set in a specific pixel measurement.

You may recognize the layout in Figure 16-18. It is the layout we created in Exercise 16-1. If you'd like to give this a try, I've included the image file, *2col_bkgd.gif*, with the materials for this chapter. Make sure that it is in the same directory as your

document *2col-olympus.html*, then open the HTML file and add the image to the background of the container `div` like so:

```
#container {
    width: 750px;
    border: solid 1px;
    background-image: url(2col_bkgd.gif);
    background-repeat: repeat-y;
}
```

2col_bkgd.gif

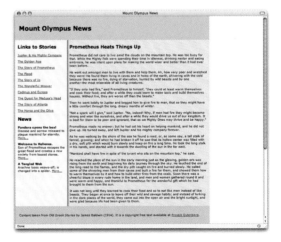

Figure 16-18. *A tiling background image is used to create colored columns.*

In CSS, the proper way to center a fixed-width element is to specify a `width` for the `div` element that holds all the page's contents, then set the left and right margins to `auto`. According to the CSS visual formatting model, this will have the net effect of centering the element in the initial containing block.

```
#container {
  position: relative;
  width: 750px;
  margin-right: auto;
  margin-left: auto;
}
```

This method works for all current standards-compliant browsers, including Internet Explorer 6 when it is in "compliance" mode (see Chapter 10, Understanding the Standards, about triggering compliance mode). It will not work in IE 6 in "quirks" mode or any earlier version.

An alternative method uses negative margins to effectively center a containing block on the page for all browsers that support basic absolute positioning (including Netscape Navigator 4). First, the "container" (the name of the `div` in the examples) is absolutely positioned so its left edge is 50% across the width of the browser window. Then, a negative left margin is applied that pulls the page back to the left by half its width, thus aligning the mid-point of the block with the mid-point of the window. And *voila*, it's centered.

```
#container {
  position: absolute;
  left: 50%;
  width: 750px;
  margin-left: -375px;     /* half the width measurement */
}
```

Exercise 16-3 lets you apply these methods to the pages you created in the previous two exercises.

CSS Layouts in Review

Using these templates as starting points, you should be able to create a wide variety of page types: liquid, fixed, or elastic; two- or three-column (or more). Whether you choose to do a float-based or positioned layout may depend on the order of your source document and whether you need elements to appear at the bottom of the page.

Again, there are many more options for creating page layouts as listed in the More Layout Templates and Tutorials sidebar earlier in the chapter. Be sure to test your layouts in several browsers, because floats and positioning can cause some browser hiccups (see the Dealing with Browser Bugs sidebar in Chapter 15).

---

exercise 16-3 | Centering layouts

In this exercise, you can center the elastic layout you created in Exercise 16-2. We'll use the proper CSS method that works in all standards compliant browsers (the DOCTYPE at the beginning of the document will ensure IE6-Win switches into Standards Mode and plays along).

1. Open the document *elastic-olympus.html* that you just created.

2. To center the whole page, simply set the left and right margins to **auto**, and there... you're done. Save the file and open it in a browser to see the centered page.

   ```
   #container {
     width: 40em;
     position: relative;
     margin-left: auto;
     margin-right: auto;
   }
   ```

If you have time and interest, you can try centering the layout in Exercise 16-1 (*2col-olympus.html*) using the second method listed above.

NOTE

The negative-margin method is taken from The Zen of CSS Design by Dave Shea and Molly Holzschlag (Peachpit Press). It was originally used by Jon Hicks in his Zen Garden submission. It is also useful for centering an element vertically in the browser window by applying a top offset and setting a negative top margin.

Test Yourself

If you successfully created multiple-column layouts in the exercises, then you've gotten the main point of this chapter. Here are a few questions to make sure you got the finer details.

1. Match each layout type with the factor that determines the final size of the page area.

   Fixed-width layouts   a. The browser window

   Liquid layouts   b. Font size

   Elastic layouts   c. The designer

2. Match each layout type with the unit of measurement used to create it.

   Fixed-width layouts   a. Ems

   Liquid layouts   b. Pixels

   Elastic layouts   c. Percentages and/or auto

3. Match each layout type with its potential advantage.

   Fixed-width layouts   a. Predictable line lengths

   Liquid layouts   b. No awkward "leftover" space

   Elastic layouts   c. Predictable layout grid

4. Match each layout type with its potential disadvantage.

   Fixed-width layouts   a. Uncomfortably long line lengths

   Liquid layouts   b. Images don't resize with the page

   Elastic layouts   c. Awkwardly short lines at large text sizes

5. Based on the techniques in this chapter, which CSS layout method would you choose for each situation (floats or positioning)?

   My page has a full-width footer: _____

   I don't want to change the order of my source code: _____

   I don't want to have to worry about overlapping elements: _____

CSS TECHNIQUES

By now you have a solid foundation in writing style sheets. You can style text, element boxes, and even create page layouts using floats and positioning. But there are a few more properties and common CSS techniques that I want you to know about before we move on to creating web graphics in Part IV.

This chapter is a grab bag of sorts. It starts with the CSS properties specifically related to table and list formatting. It then moves on to common CSS-based design practices such as using lists as the basis for horizontal navigation bars, using images in place of text in a way that is accessible to screen readers, and using the `:hover` pseudoselector to create rollovers (an effect that used to require JavaScript).

NOTE

This chapter merely scratches the surface of CSS techniques, so I encourage you to further your education starting with the CSS resources listed at the end of Chapter 11, Cascading Style Sheets Orientation.

Style Properties for Tables

We've already covered the vast majority of style properties you'll need to style content in tables. For example, the appearance and alignment of the content within the cells can be specified using properties we covered in Chapter 12, Formatting Text and Chapter 13, Colors and Backgrounds. In addition, you can treat the table and cells themselves with padding, margins, and borders as covered in Chapter 14, Thinking Inside the Box.

There are a few CSS properties, however, that were created specifically for tables. Some of them are fairly esoteric and are briefly introduced in the sidebar, Advanced Table Properties. This section focuses on properties that directly affect table display; specifically, the treatment of borders.

IN THIS CHAPTER

Style properties for tables

Changing list bullets and numbers

Turning lists into navigation bars

Replacing text with images

CSS rollovers

Advanced Table Properties

There are a few more properties related to the CSS table model that you are not likely to need if you are just starting out (or perhaps ever).

Table layout

The `table-layout` property allows authors to specify one of two methods of calculating the width of a table. The `fixed` value bases the table width on `width` values provided for the table, columns, or cells. The `auto` value bases the width of the table on the minimum width of the contents of the table. Auto layout may display nominally more slowly because the browser must calculate the default width of every cell before arriving at the width of the table.

Table display values

Chapter 14 introduced the `display` property used to specify what kind of box an element generates in the layout. CSS is designed to work with all XML languages, not just (X)HTML. It is likely that other languages will have the need for tabular layouts, but will not have elements like `table`, `tr`, or `td` in their vocabularies.

To this end, there are a variety of table-related `display` values that allow authors of XML languages to assign table layout behavior to any element. The table-related `display` values are: `table`, `inline-table`, `table-row-group`, `table-header-group`, `table-footer-group`, `table-row`, `table-column-group`, `table-column`, `table-cell`, and `table-caption`. You could assign these display roles to other (X) HTML elements, but it is generally discouraged. Browser support for table display values is incomplete as of this writing.

Separated and collapsed borders

CSS provides two methods for displaying borders between table cells: separated or collapsed. When borders are separated, a border is drawn on all four sides of each cell and you can specify the space between the borders. In the collapsing border model, the borders of adjacent borders "collapse" so that only one of the borders is visible and the space is removed (Figure 17-1).

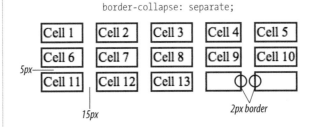

Figure 17-1. Separated borders (top) and collapsed borders (bottom).

The `border-collapse` property allows authors to choose which of these border rendering methods to use.

border-collapse

Values: separate | collapse | inherit

Default: separate

Applies to: table and inline-table elements

Inherits: yes

Separated border model

Tables render with separated borders by default, as shown in the top table in Figure 17-1. You can specify the amount of space you'd like to appear between cells using the `border-spacing` property. Unfortunately, Internet Explorer 6 (and earlier) for Windows does not support the `border-spacing` property, so the effect will be lost for those users. It is supported in IE7.

border-spacing

Values: length length | inherit

Default: 0

Applies to: table and inline-table elements

Inherits: yes

The values for border-spacing are two length measurements. The horizontal value comes first and applies between columns. The second measurement is applied between rows. If you provide one value, it will be used both horizontally and vertically. The default setting is 0, causing the borders to double up on the inside grid of the table.

These are the style rules used to create the custom border spacing shown in the top table in Figure 17-1.

```
table {
  border-collapse: separate;
  border-spacing: 15px 5px;
  border: none;  /* no border around the table itself */
}
td {
  border: 2px solid purple;  /* borders around the cells */
}
```

NOTE

Although the border-spacing default is zero, browsers add two pixels of space for the cellspacing attribute by default. If you want to see the doubling-up effect, you need to set the cellspacing attribute to 0 in the table element.

Collapsed border model

When the collapsed border model is chosen, only one border appears between table cells. This is the style sheet that created the bottom table in Figure 17-1.

```
table {
  border-collapse: collapse;
  border: none;  /* no border around the table itself */
}
td {
  border: 2px solid purple;  /* borders around the cells */
}
```

Notice that although each table cell has a 2-pixel border, the borders between cells measure a total of two pixels, not four. Borders between cells are centered on the grid between cells, so if cells are given a 4-pixel border, two pixels will fall in one cell and two pixels in another. For odd numbers of pixels, the browser decides where the extra pixel falls.

In instances where neighboring cells have different border styles, a complicated pecking order is called in to determine which border will display. If the border-style is set to hidden for either of the cells, then no border will display. Next, border width is considered: wider borders take precedence over narrower ones. Finally, if all else is equal, it comes down to a matter of style. The creators of CSS rated the border styles from most to least precedence as follows: double, solid, dashed, dotted, ridge, outset, groove, and (the lowest) inset.

Empty cells

For tables with separated borders, you can decide whether you want empty cells to display their backgrounds and borders using the empty-cells property.

`empty-cells`

Values: show|hide|inherit

Default: show

Applies to: table cell elements

Inherits: yes

For a cell to be "empty," it may not contain any text, images, or nonbreaking spaces. It may contain carriage returns and space characters.

Figure 17-2 shows the previous separated table border example with its empty cells (what would be Cell 14 and Cell 15) set to `hide`.

```
table {
  border-collapse: separate;
  border-spacing: 15px 3px;
  empty-cells: hide;
  border: none;
}
td {
  border: 1px solid purple;
}
```

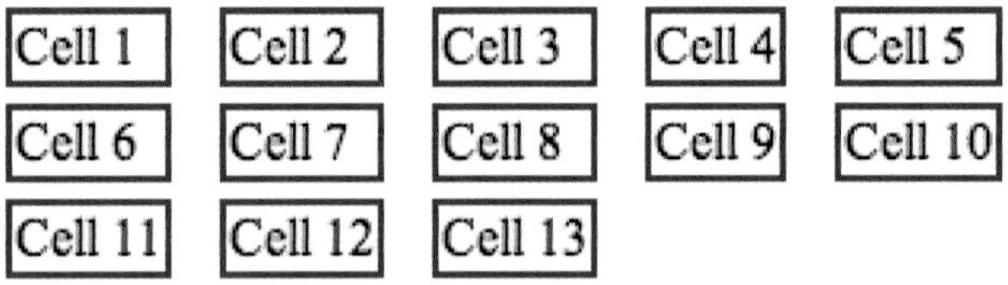

Cell 1	Cell 2	Cell 3	Cell 4	Cell 5
Cell 6	Cell 7	Cell 8	Cell 9	Cell 10
Cell 11	Cell 12	Cell 13		

Figure 17-2. Hiding empty cells with the `empty-cells` *property.*

Before we move on, take a moment to get acquainted with table formatting, using these properties and many of the others we've covered so far, in Exercise 17-1.

Changing List Bullets and Numbers

As you know, browsers automatically insert bullets before unordered list items and numbers before items in ordered lists. For the most part, the rendering of these markers is determined by the browser. However, CSS provides a few properties that allow authors to choose the type and position of the marker, or replace the bullet with a custom graphic.

Choosing a Marker

Use the `list-style-type` property to select the type of marker that appears before each list item. This property replaces the deprecated `type` attribute in (X)HTML.

list-style-type

Values: none|disc|circle|square|decimal|decimal-leading-zero|
lower-alpha|upper-alpha|lower-latin|upper-latin|lower-roman|
upper-roman|lower-greek |inherit

Default: disc

Applies to: ul, ol, *and* li *(or elements whose display value is list-item)*

Inherits: yes

---

exercise 17-1 | Styling a table

This exercise gives you a chance to apply all of your style sheet knowledge to match the table samples in Figure 17-3. The starter document, *imagetable.html*, is available with the materials for this chapter at *www.learningwebdesign.com/materials/*. I recommend you save the document after each step to see the effects of each change. The final style sheet is in Appendix A.

Format	Suffix	Color depth	Transparency	Good for
GIF	.gif	8-bit (256 colors)	Yes	Images with flat colors and hard edges
JPEG	.jpg or .jpeg	24-bit (millions of colors)	No	Images with color gradations and soft edges, such as photographs
PNG	.png	8-bit, 24-bit, or 32-bit	Yes	All images

The sample table after Step 5

Format	Suffix	Color depth	Transparency	Good for
GIF	.gif	8-bit (256 colors)	Yes	Images with flat colors and hard edges
JPEG	.jpg or .jpeg	24-bit (millions of colors)	No	Images with color gradations and soft edges, such as photographs
PNG	.png	8-bit, 24-bit, or 32-bit	Yes	All images

The final table after Step 7

Figure 17-3. *Write the style rules to match these examples.*

1. Open the file *imagetable.html* in a text editor. The document contains the marked up table and a style rule for the table that sets its width and the font properties for its content. Note that the **cellpadding** and **cellspacing** attributes have been set to zero to remove default space added by the browser. Before you start adding styles, open the document in a browser to see your starting point. It's kind of a jumbled mess, but we'll fix that one step at a time.

2. Start by writing a rule that formats the table cells (**td** elements) in the following ways:
   - Apply 6 pixels of padding to the top and bottom of each cell, but only 3 pixels on the left, and 12 pixels on the right. Use the shorthand **padding** property.
   - Make sure the cell contents stay at the top of each cell (**vertical-align: top;**).

   - Add a 1-pixel solid olive border around each cell with the **border** shorthand property.

3. Next, let's whip those table headers into shape. Write a rule that formats **th** elements as follows:
   - Make the background "olive" (**background-color**) and the text white (**color**).
   - Left-align the text in each cell (**text-align** property).
   - Apply 3 pixels of padding on the top, left, and bottom and 12 pixels on the right edge (**padding**).
   - Make sure the text falls at the bottom of each cell (**vertical-align**).

4. Now we'll add alternating background colors to the rows. Look in the markup and you'll see that each **tr** element has been assigned a class of "odd" or "even." Using class identifiers, write style rules to:
   - Give "odd" rows a background color of **#F3F3A6** (yellow-green).
   - Give "even" rows a background color of **#D4D4A2** (pale olive green).

5. Save the document and look at it in a browser. The table is looking pretty good, but let's play around with the border spacing to see what else we can do with it. First, in the rule for the **table** element, set the **border-collapse** property to **separate** and add 4 pixels of space between cells with the **border-spacing** property. If you use Internet Explorer 6 or earlier, you won't see the effect of this change, but those using IE7, Firefox, or another standards-compliant browser should see a table that looks like the one in the top of Figure 17-3.

6. Change the **border-collapse** property to **collapse** and remove the **border-spacing** property entirely. Take another look at the table in the browser. The border between cells should be 1 pixel wide.

7. Finally, let's get rid of borders on the sides of cells altogether to give the table the streamlined look of the table at the bottom of Figure 17-3. Do this by changing the **border** property for **td** elements to **border-bottom**. Save the file and see if it matches the sample in the browser.

List Item Display Role

You may have noticed that the list style properties apply to "elements whose display value is list-item." The CSS2.1 specification allows any element to perform like a list item by setting its `display` property to `list-item`. This property can be applied to any (X)HTML element or elements in another XML language. For example, you could automatically bullet or number a series of paragraphs by setting the display property of paragraph (p) elements to `list-item` as shown in this example:

```
p.bulleted {
   display: list-item;
   list-style-type: upper-
alpha;
   }
```

NOTE

CSS2.1 also includes armenian *and* georgian *as values for list-style-type, but they are poorly supported. CSS2 included* hebrew *and various Japanese number sets, but these were dropped in CSS2.1.*

Use the `none` value to turn the marker off for a list item. This is useful when using a semantically marked up list as the basis for navigation (as we'll do later in this chapter) or form field entries.

The `disc`, `circle`, and `square` values generate bullet shapes just as browsers have been doing since the beginning (Figure 17-4). Bullet size changes with the font size. Unfortunately, there is no way to change the appearance (size, color etc.) of generated bullets, so you're basically stuck with the browser's default rendering.

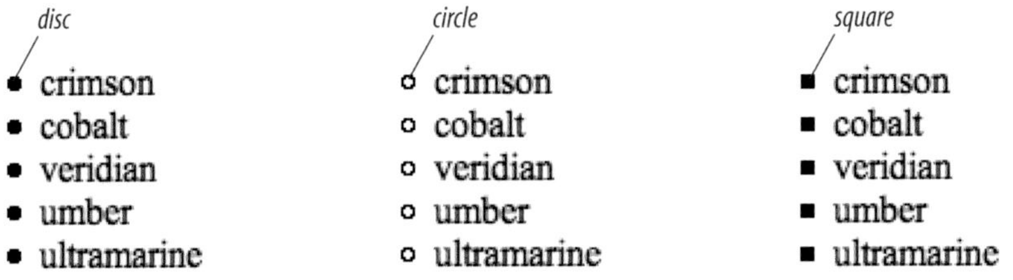

disc
- crimson
- cobalt
- veridian
- umber
- ultramarine

circle
○ crimson
○ cobalt
○ veridian
○ umber
○ ultramarine

square
■ crimson
■ cobalt
■ veridian
■ umber
■ ultramarine

Figure 17-4. *The* `list-style-type` *values* `disc`, `circle`, *and* `square`

The remaining keywords (Table 17-1) specify various numbering and lettering styles for use with ordered lists. The browser controls the presentation of generated numbers and letters, but they usually match the font properties of the associated list item.

Table 17-1. *Lettering and numbering system keywords in CSS2.1*

Keyword	System
decimal	1, 2, 3, 4, 5...
decimal-leading-zero	01, 02, 03, 04, 05...
lower-alpha	a, b, c, d, e...
upper-alpha	A, B, C, D, E...
lower-latin	a, b, c, d, e... (same as lower-alpha)
upper-latin	A, B, C, D, E... (same as upper-alpha)
lower-roman	i, ii, iii, iv, v...
upper-roman	I, II, III, IV, V...
lower-greek	α, β, γ, δ, ε...

Marker position

By default, the marker hangs outside the content area for the list item, displaying as a hanging indent. The `list-style-position` allows you to pull the bullet inside the content area so it runs into the list content.

list-style-position

Values: inside|outside|inherit

Default: outside

Applies to: ul, ol, *and* li *(or elements whose display value is list-item)*

Inherits: *yes*

An example should make this more clear. I've applied a background color to the list items in Figure 17-5 to reveal the boundaries of their content area boxes. You can see that when the position is set to outside (left), the markers fall outside the content area, and when it is set to inside, the content area box extends to include the marker.

```
li {background-color: #F99;}

ul#outside {list-style-position: outside;}

ul#inside {list-style-position: inside;}
```

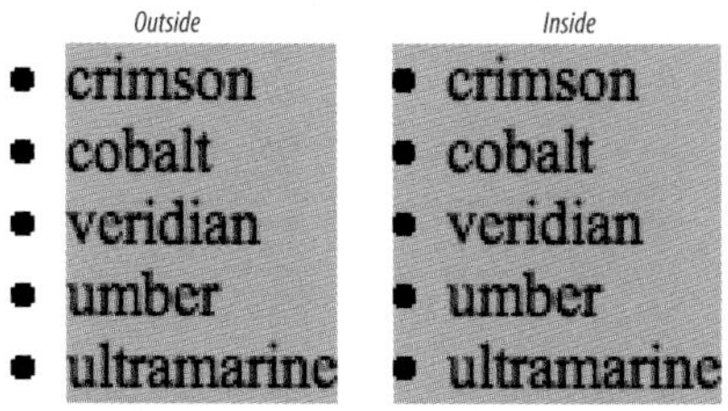

Unfortunately, there is no way to set the distance between the marker and the list item content in CSS2.1, but this functionality may be added in CSS3.

Figure 17-5. The list-style-position *property.*

WARNING

Internet Explorer for Windows (6 and earlier) always includes the bullet in the content area box. This can cause some inconsistent results when positioning list blocks or adding borders, padding, and margins to list items.

Make your own bullets

One nifty feature that CSS provides for lists is the ability to use your own image as a bullet using the list-style-image property.

list-style-image

Values: *URL*|none|inherit

Default: none

Applies to: ul, ol, *and* li *(or elements whose display value is list-item)*

Inherits: *yes*

The value of the list-style-image property is the URL of the image you want to use as a marker. The list-style-type is set to circle as a backup in case the image does not display, or the property isn't supported by the browser or other user agent. The result is shown in Figure 17-6.

```
ul {
    list-style-image: url(/images/happy.gif);
    list-style-type: circle;
    list-style-position: outside;
}
```

It is important to note that the URL is always interpreted as relative to the style sheet, whether it is embedded in the document or an external file elsewhere on the server. Site root relative URLs, as shown in the example, are the preferred method because the pathname always starts at the root directory of the server and is not dependent on the location of the style sheet.

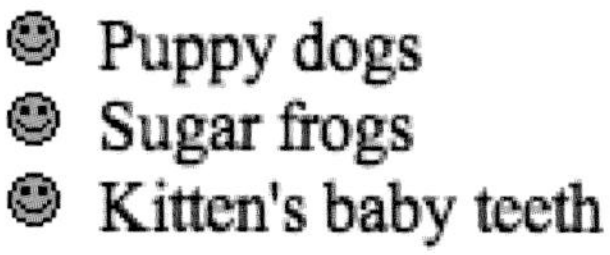

Figure 17-6. Using an image as a marker.

The list-style shorthand property

The three list properties (for type, position, and image) can be combined in a shorthand list-style property.

list-style

Values: `list-style-type list-style-position list-style-image`|inherit

Default: *see individual properties*

Applies to: `ul`, `ol`, *and* `li` *(or elements whose display value is list-item)*

Inherits: *yes*

The values for each property may be provided in any order and may be omitted. Keep in mind that omitted properties are reset to their default values in shorthand properties. Be careful not to override list style properties listed earlier in the style sheet. Each of these examples duplicates the rules from the previous example.

```
ul { list-style: url(/images/happy.gif) circle outside; }

ul { list-style: circle outside url(/images/happy.gif); }

ul { list-style: url(/images/happy.gif) circle; }
```

Using Lists for Navigation

Back in Chapter 5, Marking Up Text, I showed an example of a semantically marked up unordered list that displays as a navigation toolbar using only style sheet rules. Twelve chapters later, here I am to tell you how that's done. There are two methods for changing a list into a horizontal bar. The first makes the list items display as inline elements instead of their default block-level behavior. The second uses floats to line up the list items and the links.

All of the examples in this section use this markup for an unordered list that contains five list items. Figure 17-7 shows how it looks using default browser styles. I've omitted real URL values in the a elements to simplify the markup.

- Serif
- Sans-serif
- Script
- Display
- Dingbats

Figure 17-7. The default rendering of the example unordered list.

```
<ul id="nav">
    <li><a href="#">Serif</a></li>
    <li><a href="#">Sans-serif</a></li>
    <li><a href="#">Script</a></li>
    <li><a href="#">Display</a></li>
    <li><a href="#">Dingbats</a></li>
</ul>
```

Inline list items

Let's begin with the inline list item method. This technique uses the display property (introduced in Chapter 14) to make the list item elements behave as inline elements instead of as block elements (their default display role). As a result, they line up next to one another instead of each starting on a new line. We'll start with the minimum style rules for removing the bullets (list-

`style-type: none;`) and making the list items appear next to each other instead of in a list (`display: inline;`). The margins and padding are set to zero to prepare for styles that will be applied to the anchor (`a`) element within each `li` element. The result of the styles thus far are shown in Figure 17-8.

```
ul#nav {
  list-style-type: none;
  margin: 0px;
  padding: 0px;
}

ul#nav li {
  display: inline;
}
```

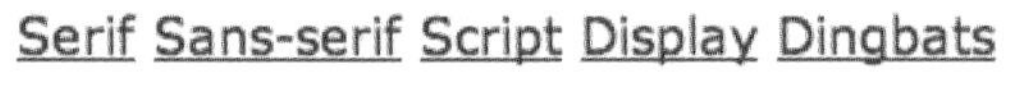

Serif Sans-serif Script Display Dingbats

Figure 17-8. Making unordered list items display inline instead of as block elements.

Now that the items are on one line, we can apply any style to the `a` (anchor) elements. In this example, the link underlines have been removed and a border, background color, and padding have been added. The resulting list is shown in Figure 17-9.

```
ul#nav li a {  /* selects only links in the "nav" list */
  padding: 5px 20px;
  margin: 0px 2px;
  border: 1px solid #FC6A08;
  background-color: #FCA908;
  text-decoration: none;
  text-align: center;
  color: black;
}
```

Serif
Sans-serif
Script
Display
Dingbats

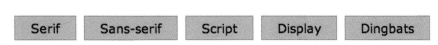

Figure 17-9. Adding styles to the inline list.

Floated list items

The other method for creating horizontal lists uses the `float` property to line up the list items next to one another. Remember that when multiple consecutive items are floated to one side, they stack up against that edge. That's the behavior we'll be taking advantage of with this example. When using `float`, it is important to set the following element in the source to `clear: both;` to ensure that no page content wraps around the list.

The following example is just one of many variations on formatting navigation with floated list items. The primary steps are:

1. Turn off the bullets (`list-style-type: none;`).

2. Float each list item (`float: left;`).

3. Make the anchor elements (`a`) display as block elements so dimensions may be set (`display: block;`).

4. Format the links with various styles.

This time, each `a` element is given a decorative background image that makes it look like a tab (Figure 17-10).

```
body {
    font-family: Verdana, Arial, Helvetica, sans-serif;
    font-size: .8em;
    background-color: #FEF6D6; }

ul#nav {
    list-style: none;
    margin: 0;
    padding: 0; }

ul#nav li {
    float: left;
    margin: 0 2px;
    padding: 0; }

ul#nav li a {
    display: block; /* to set width & height of the a element  */
    width: 100px;
    height: 28px;
    line-height: 28px;
    background: #E3A7CA url(tab.gif) no-repeat;
    text-transform: uppercase;
    text-decoration:  none;
    text-align: center; }
```

> ## BROWSER BUG
>
> There is a bug in Internet Explorer 5 for the Mac that causes this floated list item example not to work correctly as shown here.
>
> If you need (or want) to support IE5(Mac), you need to float the anchor elements as well as the list items by adding this declaration to the beginning of the `#nav li a` rule:
>
>   float: left;
>
> Then you need to add a "hack" at the end of the style sheet that overrides the earlier `float` value and sets the `float` for anchor elements back to `none` in all browsers except IE5(Mac). Be sure to copy it exactly, noting the difference between slashes and backslashes.
>
>   /* Commented backslash hack
>   hides rule from IE5-Mac */
>
>   #nav li a { float: none; }
>
>   /* End IE5-Mac hack */

SERIF   SANS-SERIF   SCRIPT   DISPLAY   DINGBATS

Figure 17-10. Tabbed navigation created with floated list items.

In this example, the list items are still block elements, but because they are all floated to the left, they line up next to one another.

Notice that the `display` property for the anchor (`a`) elements has been set to `block` (anchors are usually inline elements). This was done to allow us to apply `width` and `height` properties to the `a` elements. The remaining properties set the size of each "tab," apply the tab background image, turn off underlines, and style and center the text.

More list and tabbed navigation tutorials

The examples in this section are only the most elementary introduction to how CSS can be used to create tabbed navigation from semantically logical list markup. For more sophisticated techniques and in-depth tutorials, these are just a few of the numerous resources online.

Sliding Doors of CSS (Parts I and II), by Douglas Bowman *(www.alistapart. com/articles/slidingdoors* and *www.alistapart.com/articles/slidingdoors2)*

> A problem with the floated list example above is that if a user makes the text larger in the browser, it will bust out of the tab graphic. In this article, Doug Bowman introduces his ingenious technique for graphical tabs that resize larger with the text.

Accessible Image-Tab Rollovers, by Dan Cederholm *(www.simplebits.com/ notebook/2003/09/30/accessible_imagetab_rollovers.html)*

> This tutorial combines list-based tabbed navigation with image replacement techniques (we'll get to image replacement in the next section).

Free CSS Navigation Designs, by Christopher Ware *(www.exploding-boy. com/2005/12/15/free-css-navigation-designs/)*

> A collection of 11 navigational menus available for your downloading and customizing pleasure.

CSS Design: Taming Lists by Mark Newhouse *(www.alistapart.com/stories/ taminglists)*

> This article demonstrates a number of CSS tricks for controlling the presentation of lists, including various inline list item applications.

Image Replacement Techniques

Web designers frustrated with typography limitations on the Web have been using inline images for prettier text since the `img` element first came on the scene. The problem with swapping out real text, like an `h1` element, for an `img` is that the text is removed from the source document entirely. Providing alternative text improves accessibility, but it does not repair the damage to the semantic structure of the document. Not only that, in terms of site maintenance, it's preferable to control matters of presentation from the style sheet and leave the source free of purely decorative elements.

The year 2003 saw the dawn of CSS image replacement (IR) techniques that replace text with a background image specified in a style sheet. The text element itself is still present in the source document, so it is accessible to screen readers and search engine indexers, but it is prevented from displaying in graphical browsers via some CSS sleight-of hand. There are many techniques for hiding the text such as negative margins, covering it up with a graphic, negative letter-spacing, and so on. We'll be looking at a popular technique that hides the text with a large negative text indent.

NOTE

For an explanation and comparison of image replacement techniques, see David Shea's (of CSS Zen Garden fame) list and articles at www.mezzoblue.com/tests/revised-image-replacement/.

It should be noted that as of this writing, there is no ideal solution for CSS image replacement, just different approaches and trade-offs. Most techniques rely on users being able to read the content in images when the text is hidden, which means users who have CSS turned *on* but images turned *off* (or who are simply waiting for images to load over a slow connection) are not well served. This problem remains to be solved.

The IR technique with the most widespread use was created by Mike Rundle for use on his Phark site (it is commonly called the Phark or Rundle/Phark method). It hides the element text by setting an extremely large negative `text-indent` that pushes the text off the screen to the left where it can't be seen (Figure 17-11). In this example, the text is set off by -5000 pixels (some authors prefer -999em because it saves a character and results in a larger distance).

The Future of Image Replacement

In CSS Level 3, image replacement may be accomplished using the expanded capabilities of automatically generated content. To replace an `h1` element with an image in CSS3, the rule would look like this;

```
h1 {
    content: url(headline.gif);
}
```

Unfortunately, current browsers do not support this use of generated content well enough for it to be a viable option as of this writing. Hopefully, one day that will change and the image replacement trickery in this chapter will be a quaint blip in web design's past.

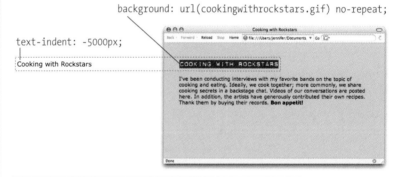

Figure 17-11. The Rundle/Phark image replacement method works by using a large negative text-indent to hide the text in a graphical browser. The background image containing a more attractive version of the text appears in place.

The style sheet

```
body {
    font-family: Verdana, Arial, Helvetica, sans-serif;
    margin: 50px;
    background-color: #BEC9F1; }

#cwr {
    text-indent: -5000px; /* moves the text out of view */
    background: url(cookingwithrockstars.gif) no-repeat;
    width: 350px; /* sets the dimension of the graphic */
    height: 35px; }
```

The markup

```
<h1 id="cwr">Cooking with Rockstars</h1>
<p>I've been conducting interviews with my favorite bands on the topic
of cooking and eating. Ideally, we cook together; more commonly, we
share cooking secrets in a backstage chat. Videos of our conversations
are posted here. In addition, the artists have generously contributed
their own recipes. Thank them by buying their records. <strong>Bon
appetit!</strong></p>
```

Because the headline text is an ordinary `h1` element, it will be read by a screen reader. The other advantages to this method are that no extra markup (such as a `span` element) is required, and it doesn't require any browser hacks. The major disadvantage is that users with CSS turned on but images turned off will see *nothing*. Likewise, users with graphical browsers will see no headline at all if the image file simply fails to load.

CSS Rollovers

Chapter 13, Colors and Backgrounds briefly introduced the `:hover` pseudo-class selector used to create rollover effects when the mouse is positioned over a link (see note). In this section, we'll take an expanded look at how it can be used.

NOTE

The `:hover` pseudoclass may be applied to any element according to the CSS2.1 Recommendation, but because Internet Explorer 6 and earlier for Windows only support it on the anchor (a) element, its practical use has been limited to links. IE7 does support `:hover` correctly, so authors will have more options as older versions of IE go away. For a JavaScript-based workaround for IE6 and earlier, see the "Suckerfish :hover" article at www.htmldog.com/articles/suckerfish/hover/.

First, for a refresher, here is an example of a simple text link that has been set to display in dark red text with no underline. When someone places the mouse over the link, the `a:hover` rule brightens up the text color and adds a decorative bottom border (a more subtle effect than a real text underline). The result is shown in Figure 17-12.

```
a:link {
  text-decoration: none;
  color: #930;
}

a:hover {
  text-decoration: none;
  color: #F30;
  padding-bottom: 2px;
  border-bottom: dotted 2px #930;
}
```

sIFR Text

Another interesting image replacement technique is sIFR, which stands for Scalable Inman Flash Replacement. sIFR replaces text with small Flash movies instead of GIF, JPEG, or PNG images. The advantage is that text in Flash movies is vector-based, so it is smooth, anti-aliased, and able to resize with the page.

Using a combination of CSS, JavaScript, and Flash technology, sIFR allows authors to "insert rich typography into web pages without sacrificing accessibility, search engine friendliness, or markup semantics." sIFR (in Version 2.0 as of this writing) was created by Mike Davidson, who built upon the original concept developed by Shaun Inman (the "I" of sIFR).

sIFR is not perfect, but it is a promising technique that could lead to more powerful typography solutions. To find out more about sIFR, including how to implement it on your site, visit *www.mikeindustries.com/sifr*.

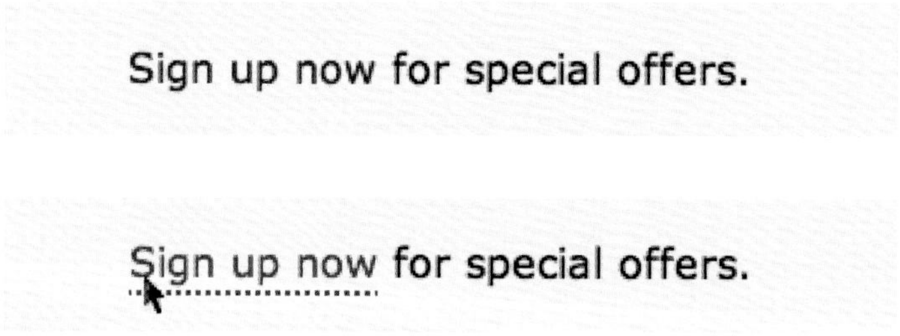

Sign up now for special offers.

Sign up now for special offers.

Figure 17-12. A simple text link as it appears when the page loads and when the mouse rolls over it.

Swapping background images

Image rollovers work on the same principle as described for text, except that the `background-image` value is changed for the hover state. Again, because Internet Explorer 6 and earlier only support `:hover` on the a element, a link is used in this example.

In this example, a background image (*button.gif*) is applied to links in a navigational toolbar. The a element is set to display as a block so that `width` and `height` values (matching the image dimensions) can be applied to it. The `a:hover` rule specifies a different background image (*button_over.gif*) to display when the mouse is over the link (Figure 17-13). It also changes the text color for better contrast with the highlighted button color.

```
#navbar li {
   list-style-type: none;
   float: left; }

#navbar a {
   color: #FFF;
   display: block;    /* allows width and height to be specified */
   width: 150px;
   height: 30px;
   background: #606 url(button.gif) no-repeat;
/* the next properties center the text horizontally and vertically*/
   text-align: center;
   text-decoration: none;
   line-height: 30px;
   vertical-align: middle; }

#navbar a:hover {
   color: #000;
   background: #f0f url(button_over.gif) no-repeat; }
```

button.gif

products

button_over.gif

products

Figure 17-13. Simple image rollover.

WARNING

Changing the anchor (a) element to display as a block means that you can't apply this method to inline links because each link will start on a new line. This method is most useful for links that will be floated to form a horizontal toolbar, as we saw previously in this chapter.

To clear vertical space for background images in inline a elements, try adjusting the line-height *for the containing element.*

In some instances, such as graphical navigation bars, it is desirable for each link to have its own background and rollover images. In this case, it is necessary to give each li (or other containing element) a unique id value.

```
<li id="info"><a href="#">more info</a></li>
<li id="contact"><a href="#">contact us</a></li>

a {display: block; width: 150px; height: 30px; }

#info a {background: #666 url(info.gif) no-repeat; }
#info a:hover {background: #666 url(info_over.gif) no-repeat; }

#contact a {background: #eee url(contact.gif) no-repeat; }
#contact a:hover {background: #eee url(contact_over.gif) no-repeat; }
```

Shifting the background image

Another popular method for handling image rollovers is to put all the rollover states in one image, then change only the background-position for each link state. This avoids the need to load or preload multiple images for each rollover and can speed up display.

Figure 17-14 shows the image, *bothbuttons.gif*, that contains both the default background image and the hover state. The style rule shifts the position of the initial background image from bottom to top, revealing the appropriate portion of the image. Pretty fancy, huh?

```
a {
    display: block;
    width: 150px;
    height: 30px;
    background: #606 url(bothbuttons.gif) bottom left no-repeat;
    color: #FFF;
    text-align: center;
    text-decoration: none;
    line-height: 30px;
    vertical-align: middle; }

a:hover {
    background: #f0f url(bothbuttons.gif) top left no-repeat;
    color: #000; }
```

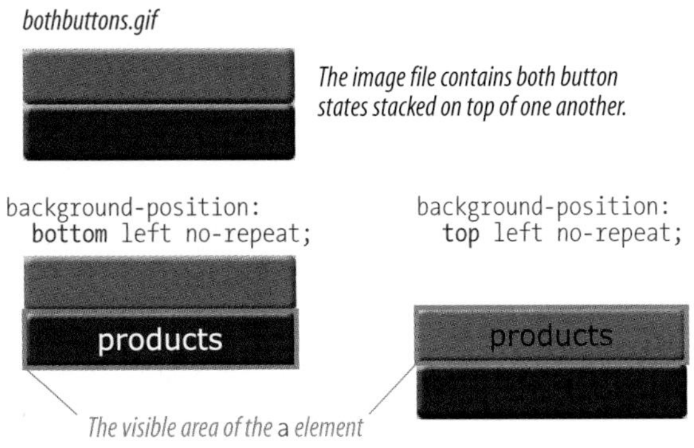

NOTE

This technique was introduced by Petr Staniček [aka "Pixy"] in his article "Fast Rollovers without Preload" (wellstyled. com/css-nopreload-rollovers.html).

WARNING

Applying rollovers to background images can cause a flickering effect in Internet Explorer 6 on Windows. One solution is to apply the background image to both the link (a) and its containing element; however, increased font size could result in both images showing. For an in-depth look at this problem and possible solutions, see the article, Minimize Flickering CSS Background Images in IE6 by Ryan Carver at www.fivesevensix.com/studies/ ie6flicker/.

bothbuttons.gif

The image file contains both button states stacked on top of one another.

background-position:
  bottom left no-repeat;

background-position:
  top left no-repeat;

products

products

The visible area of the a element

Figure 17-14. Containing all rollover states in one image.

exercise 17-2 | **Putting it together**

You've seen horizontal lists... you've seen CSS rollovers. Now put them together in this exercise. As a bonus, I've thrown in a chance to do an image replacement, too. The starter document, *designerrific.html*, and its respective *images* directory are provided with the materials for this chapter, and the resulting style sheets are in Appendix A.

In this exercise, we'll create a typical page header that consists of an **h1** and a list. Figure 17-15 shows the unstyled document and two designs we'll create entirely with style sheet rules. It will take us a few steps to get there, but I promise at least one *A-ha!* moment along the way.

1. Open *designerrific.html* in a text editor. The first thing we'll do is write some rules for the **body** element to set the font for the whole page to Verdana (or some sans-serif font) and set the margin to zero. This will allow us to place elements right against the browser window.

   ```
   body {
       font-family: Verdana, sans-serif;
       margin: 0;   }
   ```

2. Next, use the Phark image replacement technique to replace the **h1** text with an image that contains the company's logotype (*designerrific-trans.gif*, located in the *images* directory). Set the dimensions of the element to 360 pixels wide by 70 pixels high to reveal the whole image.

   ```
   h1#ds {
       text-indent: -5000px;
       background: url(images/designerrific_trans.gif)
                         no-repeat;
       width: 360px;
       height: 70px; }
   ```

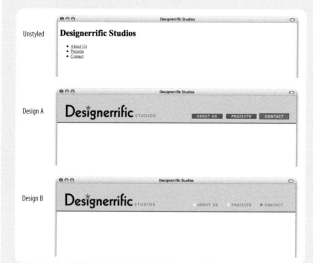

Unstyled

Design A

Design B

Save the document and take a look in the browser. You should see the logo shown in Figure 17-15 in place of the **h1** text. If not, go back and make sure that you aren't missing any semicolons or brackets in your style rule and that the pathname to the image file is correct.

3. Now we'll turn the unordered list into navigation using the inline method outlined earlier. Set the stage by removing the bullets from the **ul** and changing the **display** of the list items to **inline**.

   ```
   ul#nav {
       list-style-type: none;   }

   ul#nav li {
       display: inline; }
   ```

   In Design A, each anchor is styled as a dark teal (#0A6D73) rectangular box with white type and a white 1-pixel border. The linked text should be resized to 76% its default size and underlines removed for a clean look. In addition, text is centered and transformed to uppercase with 2 pixels of letter spacing added for interest. Finally, padding is added around the content (2 pixels top and bottom, and 20 pixels left and right) and a 2-pixel margin is added to keep the links from bumping into one another. Take a try at writing these style rules yourself, then check your work against this code:

   ```
   ul#nav li a {
       background-color: #0A6D73;
       border: 1px solid #FFF;
       color: white;
       font-size: 76%;
       text-decoration: none;
       text-align: center;
       text-transform: uppercase;
       letter-spacing: 2px;
       padding: 2px 20px;
       margin: 0px 2px;
   }
   ```

   Save the document and open it in a browser. You should see the links lined up in rectangles as shown in Design A (they'll be under the logotype because we haven't moved them yet).

DESIGN TIP

Design B is a good example of how small background images can be tucked off into a corner of an element. That little star changing color offers good feedback that the link is clickable, but it is more subtle and streamlined than the big 3-D button shown in the earlier example.

Figure 17-15. The Designerrific Studios header before and after styling.

4. Let's add a rollover effect to those links too. When the mouse passes over the "button", it will turn bright pink (#F8409C) to match the star in the logo, and the border will turn dark maroon (#660000, or #600 shorthand) to match the logo text.

```
ul#nav li a:hover {
   background-color: #F8409C;
   border: 1px solid #600;
}
```

When you save the document and refresh it in the browser, you should see the highlighted pink color when you mouse over the links. Exciting!

5. Now that we have the pieces built, we can assemble them in the header layout as shown in Figure 17-15. There are several approaches to doing this, but we'll use absolute positioning to place the **h1** and the **ul** right where we want them.

First, let's set up the shaded masthead area by styling the **div** (**id="header"**) that holds the headline and navigation list. Give it a light teal background color (#9CD8CD) and a double bottom border that matches the logo (#600). Set its height to 100 pixels. In addition, set its **position** to **relative** to establish it as a containing block for the elements it contains.

```
#header {
   position: relative;
   background: #9cd8cd;
   border-bottom: 3px double #600;
   height: 100px;}
```

Save the document and look at it again in the browser. You will see a shaded masthead area waiting for the elements to be positioned in it. You'll also see that it doesn't go all the way to the top of the browser window as we had wanted. That extra space is actually coming from the default margin that the browser is applying to the **h1** element. Therefore, we will set the margin on the **h1** (and the **ul** for good measure) to zero to eliminate that problem.

Add this declaration to the rules for **h1#ds** and **ul#nav**. Now when you save and refresh, the extra space is removed and the shaded header should go all the way to the top of the window.

```
margin: 0;
```

6. Finally, we'll absolutely position the **h1** and the **ul**. I've done the finagling for you and arrived at the following positions:

```
h1#ds {
   text-indent: -5000px;
   background: url(images/designerrific_trans.gif)
no-repeat;
   width: 360px;
   height: 70px;
   margin: 0;
   position: absolute;
   top: 25px;
   left: 25px;
}
```

```
ul#nav {
   list-style-type: none;
   margin: 0;
   position: absolute;
   top: 65px;
   right: 25px;
}
```

This time when you save and refresh, you'll find that your page looks just like Design A in Figure 17-1. That wasn't too bad, was it?

Design B is essentially the same as Design A, except it uses as subtle image swap (the white star turns pink) in the rollover. Save a copy of your document as *designerrific-B.html* and we'll make those changes.

CSS TIP

It is common to set the margin on elements to zero to override the browser's default spacing. This makes positioning and floating elements more predictable.

---

7. Remove the background and border from the links and change the text color to dark teal (#1A7E7B). Remove the background and border from the **a:hover** rule as well. (The resulting rules are shown after Step 8.)

8. Add the non-repeating *star-white.gif* background image to the left edge of each anchor, centered in the height of the element. To the **a:hover** rule, add the *star-pink.gif* in the same position. The resulting rules are as follows:

```
ul#nav li a {
   color: #1A7E7B;
   font-size: 76%;
   text-decoration: none;
   text-align: center;
   text-transform: uppercase;
   letter-spacing: 2px;
   padding: 2px 20px;
   margin: 0px 2px;
   background: url(images/star-white.gif) left
center no-repeat;
}
```

```
ul#nav li a:hover {
   background: url(images/star-pink.gif) left
center no-repeat;
}
```

Save the document, and *voila*! You've created the style sheet for Design B.

Wrapping Up Style Sheets

We've come to the end of our style sheet exploration. By now, you should be comfortable formatting text and even doing basic page layout using CSS. The trick to mastering style sheets, of course, is lots of practice and testing. If you get stuck, you will find that there are many resources online (I've listed many throughout Part III) to help you find the answers you need.

In Part IV, we'll set the source document and style sheets aside and turn our attention to the world of web graphics production. But first, a little final exam to test your CSS techniques chops.

Test Yourself

See how well you picked up the CSS techniques in this chapter with these questions. As always, the answers are available in Appendix A.

1. Match the style rules with their respective tables in Figure 17-16.

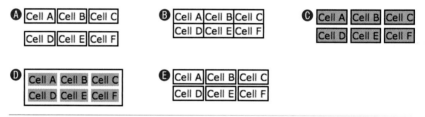

Figure 17-16. Match these tables with the code examples in Question 1.

```
table { border-collapse: collapse;}        _____
td { border: 2px black solid; }

table { border-collapse: separate; }       _____
td { border: 2px black solid; }

table {                                     _____
   border-collapse: separate;
   border-spacing: 2px 12px; }
td { border: 2px black solid; }

table {                                     _____
   border-collapse: separate;
   border-spacing: 5px;
   border: 2px black solid; }
td { background-color: #99f; }

table {                                     _____
   border-collapse: separate;
   border-spacing: 5px; }
td {
   background-color: #99f;
   border: 2px black solid; }
```

2. Match the style rules with the resulting lists in Figure 17-17.

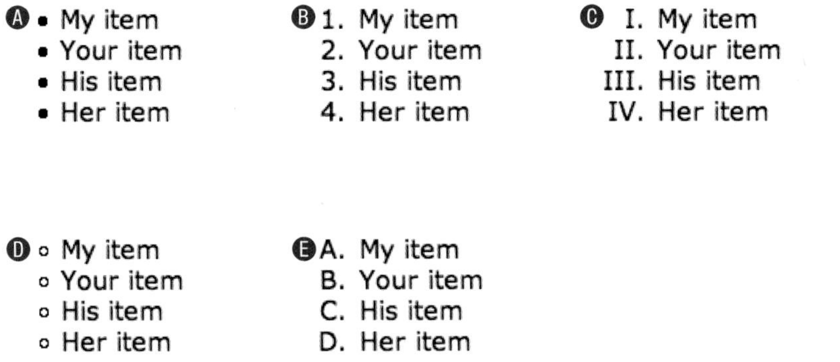

Ⓐ • My item   **Ⓑ** 1. My item   **Ⓒ** I. My item
   • Your item   2. Your item   II. Your item
   • His item   3. His item   III. His item
   • Her item   4. Her item   IV. Her item

Ⓓ ○ My item   **Ⓔ** A. My item
   ○ Your item   B. Your item
   ○ His item   C. His item
   ○ Her item   D. Her item

Figure 17-17. Match these lists with the code examples in Question 2.

```
list-style-type: upper-alpha        _____

list-style-type: circle             _____

list-style-type: decimal            _____

list-style-type: disc               _____

list-style-type: upper-roman        _____
```

3. What does the `display` property do?

4. Name two ways to get unordered list items to line up like a horizontal navigation bar.

5. Which of these is responsible for creating CSS rollover effects?

    A.   the `rollover` property

    B.   the `:hover` property

    C.   the `:hover` selector

    D.   the `onmouseover` attribute

Review: Table and List Properties

The following is a summary of the properties covered in this chapter.

Property	Description
border-collapse	Whether borders between cells are separate or collapsed
border-spacing	The space between cells set to render as separate
empty-cells	Whether borders and backgrounds should render for empty cells
list-style-type	The type of marker (bullet or numbering system)
list-style-position	Whether the marker is inside or outside the element box
list-style-image	Specifies an image to be used as a marker
list-style	A shorthand property for defining list-style-type, list-style-position, and list-style-image

CREATING WEB GRAPHICS

PART **IV**

WEB GRAPHICS BASICS

Unless you plan on publishing text-only sites, chances are you'll need to know how to create web graphics. For many of you, that might mean getting your hands on an image-editing program for the first time and acquiring some basic graphics production skills. If you are a seasoned designer accustomed to print, you may need to adapt your style and process to make graphics that are appropriate for web delivery.

This chapter covers the fundamentals of web graphics production, beginning with some options for finding and creating images. From there, it introduces the file formats available for web graphics and helps you decide which to use. You'll also learn the basics of image resolution, resizing, and transparency.

As always, there are step-by-step exercises along the way. I want to point out, however, that I write with the assumption that you have some familiarity with an image-editing program. I use Adobe Photoshop (the industry standard) in the examples and exercises, but you can follow along with most steps using other tools listed in this chapter. If you are starting at square one, I recommend spending time with the manual or third-party books about your graphics software.

Image Sources

You have to *have* an image to save an image, so before we jump into the nitty-gritty of file formats, let's look at some ways to get images in the first place. There are many options: from scanning, shooting, or illustrating them yourself, to using available stock photos and clip art, or just hiring someone to create images for you.

Creating your own images

In most cases, the most cost-effective way to generate images for your site is to make your own from scratch. The added bonus is that you know you have full rights to use the images (we'll address copyright again in a moment). Designers may generate imagery with scanners, digital cameras, or using an illustration or photo editing program.

IN THIS CHAPTER

Where to get images

An overview of GIF, JPEG, and PNG formats

Image size and resolution

Resizing images in Photoshop

Binary and alpha transparency

Preventing "halos"

359

Scanning Tips

If you are scanning images for use on the Web, these tips will help you create images with better quality.

- Because it is easier to maintain image quality when resizing smaller than resizing larger, it is usually a good idea to scan the image a bit larger than you actually need. This gives you more flexibility for resizing later. Don't go overboard, however, because if you have to reduce its size too much, you'll get a blurry result. Issues of image size are discussed in more detail in the Image Size and Resolution section later in this chapter.

- Scan black and white images in grayscale (8-bit) mode, not in black-and-white (1-bit or bitmap) mode. This enables you to make adjustments in the midtone areas once you have sized the image to its final dimensions and resolution. If you really want only black and white pixels, convert the image as the last step.

- If you are scanning an image that has been printed, you will need to eliminate the dot pattern that results from the printing process. The best way to do this is to apply a slight blur to the image (in Photoshop, use the Gaussian Blur filter), resize the image slightly smaller, then apply a sharpening filter. This will eliminate those pesky dots. Make sure you have the rights to use the printed image, too, of course.

Scanning

Scanning is a great way to collect source material. You can scan almost anything, from flat art to 3-D objects. Beware, however, the temptation to scan and use found images. Keep in mind that most images you find are probably copyright-protected and may not be used without permission, even if you modify them considerably. See the Scanning Tips sidebar for some how-to information.

Digital cameras

You can capture the world around you and pipe it right into an image-editing program with a digital camera. Because the Web is a low-resolution environment, there is no need to invest in high-end equipment. Depending on the type of imagery, you may get the quality you need with a standard consumer digital camera.

Electronic illustration

If you have illustration skills, you can make your own graphics in a drawing or photo-editing application. The sidebar, Tools of the Trade, introduces some of the most popular graphics programs available today. Every designer has her own favorite tools and techniques. I sometimes create my logos, illustrations, and type effects in Adobe Illustrator, then bring the image into Photoshop to create the web-ready version. However, for most image types, Photoshop has all I need, so it is where I spend the majority of my design time.

Stock photography and illustrations

If you aren't confident in your design skills, or you just want a head-start with some fresh imagery, there are plenty of collections of ready-made photos, illustrations, buttons, animations, and textures available for sale or for free. Stock photos and illustrations generally fall into two broad categories: rights-managed and royalty-free.

Rights-managed means that the copyright holder (or a company representing them) controls who may reproduce the image. In order to use a rights-managed image, you must obtain a license to reproduce it for a particular use and for a particular period of time. One of the advantages to licensing images is that you can arrange to have exclusive rights to an image within a particular medium (such as the Web) or a particular business sector (such as the health care industry or banking). On the downside, rights-managed images get quite pricey. Depending on the breadth and length of the license, the price tag may be many thousands of dollars for a single image. If you don't want exclusive rights and you want to use the image only on the Web, the cost is more likely to be a few hundred dollars, depending on the source.

If that still sounds too steep, consider using royalty-free artwork for which you don't need to pay a licensing fee. Royalty-free artwork is available for a one-time fee that gives you unlimited use of the image, but you have no control over who else is using the image. Royalty-free images are available from the top-notch professional stock houses such as Getty Images for as little as 30 bucks an image, and from other sites for less (even free).

Following is a list of a few of my favorite resources for finding high-quality stock photography and illustrations, but it is by no means exhaustive. A web search will turn up plenty more sites with images for sale.

IStockPhoto *(www.istockphoto.com)*

> If you're on a tight budget (and even if you're not), there's no better place to find images than IStockPhoto. The photo collections are generated by ordinary people who contribute to the site and all the images are royalty-free. Prices start at just a buck a pop! It's my personal favorite image resource.

Getty Images *(www.gettyimages.com)*

> Getty is the largest stock image house, having acquired most of its competitors over recent years. It offers both rights-managed and royalty-free photographs and illustrations at a variety of price ranges.

Jupiter Images *(www.jupiterimages.com)* and PictureQuest *(www.picturequest.com)*

> Jupiter Images and its PictureQuest division offer high quality rights-managed and royalty-free photo collections.

JuicyStock.com *(www.juicystock.com)*

> This is a great resource for affordable, royalty-free photographs of people and places from around the globe.

Veer *(www.veer.com)*

> I like Veer because it tends to be a little more hip and edgy than its competitors. It offers both rights-managed and royalty-free photographs, illustrations, fonts, and stock video.

Clip art

Clip art refers to collections of royalty-free illustrations, animations, buttons, and other doo-dads that you can copy and paste into a wide range of uses. Nowadays, there are huge clip-art collections available specifically for web use. A trip to your local software retail store or a browse through the pages of a software catalog will no doubt turn up royalty-free image collections, some boasting 100,000 pieces of art. Clip art collections may also come bundled with your graphics software.

There are a number of resources online, and the good news is that some of these sites give graphics away for free, although you may have to suffer through a barrage of pop-up ads. Others charge a membership fee, anywhere from $10 to $200 a year. The drawback is that a lot of them are poor quality or kind of hokey (but then, "hokey" is in the eye of the beholder). The following are just a few sites to get you started.

Clipart.com (*www.clipart.com*)

This service charges a membership fee, but is well-organized and tends to provide higher quality artwork than the free sites.

Original Free Clip Art (*www.free-clip-art.net*)

As the name says, they've got free clip art. This site has been around a while, unlike many others that come and go.

#1 Free Clip Art (*www.1clipart.com*)

Another no-frills free clip art site.

Hire a designer

Finding and creating images takes time and particular talents. If you have more money than either of those things, consider hiring a graphic designer to generate the imagery for your site for you. If you start with a good set of original photos or illustrations, you can still use the skills you learn in this book to produce web versions of the images as you need them.

Meet the Formats

Once you've got your hands on some images, you need to get them into a format that will work on a web page. There are dozens of graphics file formats out in the world. For example, if you use Windows, you may be familiar with BMP graphics, or if you are a print designer, you may commonly use images in TIFF and EPS format. On the Web, you have only three choices: GIF (pronounced "jif"), JPEG ("jay-peg"), and PNG ("ping"). If this sounds like alphabet soup to you, don't worry. By the end of this section, you'll know a GIF from a JPEG and when to use each one. Here is a quick rundown:

GIF images are most appropriate for images with flat colors and hard edges or when transparency or animation is required.

JPEGs work best for photographs or images with smooth color blends.

PNG files can contain any image type and are often a good substitute for the GIF format. They can also contain images with transparent or partially transparent areas.

These formats have emerged as the standards because they are platform-independent (meaning they work on Windows, Macs, and Unix operating systems) and they condense well to be easily ported over a network. The remainder of this section tackles terminology and digs deeper into the features and functions of each format. Understanding the technical details will help you make the highest-quality web graphics at the smallest sizes.

Name Files Properly

Be sure to use the proper file extensions for your image files. GIF files must be named with the *.gif* suffix. JPEG files must have *.jpg* (or the less common *.jpeg*) as a suffix. PNG files must end in *.png*. Browsers look at the suffix to determine how to handle various media types, so it is best to stick with the standardized suffixes for image file formats.

The ubiquitous GIF

The GIF (Graphic Interchange Format) file is the habitual favorite for web pages. Although not designed specifically for the Web, it was the first format was quickly adopted for its versatility, small file sizes, and cross-platform compatibility. GIF also offers transparency and the ability to contain simple animations.

Because the GIF compression scheme excels at compressing flat colors, it is the best file format to use for logos, line art, graphics containing text, icons, etc. (Figure 18-1). You can save photographs or textured images as GIFs, too, but they won't be saved as efficiently, resulting in larger file sizes. These are best saved as JPEGs, which I'll get to next. However, GIF does work well for images with a combination of small amounts of photographic imagery and large flat areas of color.

To make really great GIFs, it's important to be familiar with how they work under the hood and what they can do.

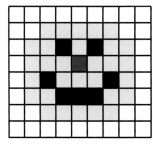

Figure 18-1. The GIF format is great for graphical images comprised mainly of flat colors and hard edges.

8-bit, indexed color

In technical terms, GIF files are indexed color images that contain 8-bit color information (they can also be saved at lower bit depths). Let's decipher that statement a term at a time. 8-bit means GIFs can contain up to 256 colors—the maximum number that 8 bits of information can define (2^8=256). Lower bit depths result in fewer colors and also reduce file size.

Indexed color means that the set of colors in the image, its palette, is stored in a color table (also called a color map). Each pixel in the image contains a numeric reference (or "index") to a position in the color table. This should be made clear with a simple demonstration. Figure 18-2 shows how a 2-bit (4-color) indexed color image references its color table for display. For 8-bit images, there are 256 slots in the color table.

Color table

The pixels in an indexed color image contain numerical references to the color table for the image.

The color table matches numbers to RGB color values. This is the map for a 2-bit image with only 4 colors.

The image displays with the colors in place.

Figure 18-2. A 2-bit image and its color table.

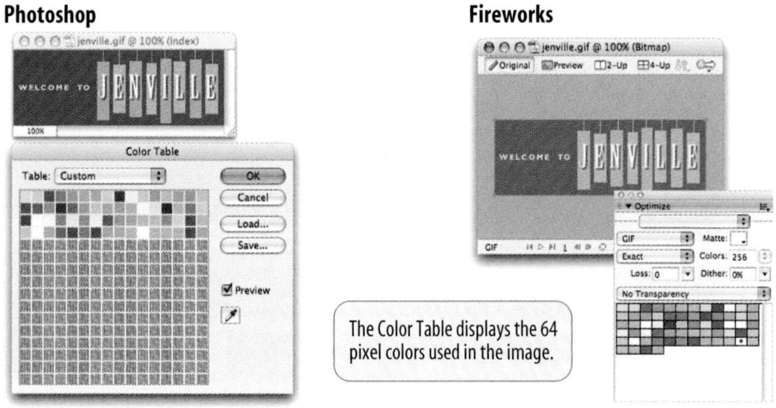

Photoshop

Fireworks

The Color Table displays the 64 pixel colors used in the image.

Figure 18-3. A view of the Color Table in Photoshop and Fireworks.

When you open an existing GIF in Photoshop, you can view (and even edit) its color table by selecting Image → Mode → Color Table (Figure 18-3). You also get a preview of the color table for an image when you use Photoshop's Save for Web & Devices to export an image in GIF format, as we'll be doing later in this chapter. In Fireworks (and the discontinued ImageReady, not shown), the color table is displayed in the Optimize panel.

Most source images (scans, illustrations, photos, etc.) start out in RGB format, so they need to be converted to indexed color in order to be saved as a GIF. When an image goes from RGB to indexed mode, the colors in the image are reduced to a palette of 256 colors or fewer. In Photoshop, Fireworks, and (now retired) ImageReady, the conversion takes place when you save or export the GIF, although you can see a preview of the final image and its color table. Other image editing programs may require you to convert the image to indexed color manually first, then export the GIF as a second step.

In either case, you will be asked to select a palette for the indexed color image. The sidebar, Common Color Palettes, outlines the various palette options available in the most popular image tools. It is recommended that you use Selective or Perceptual in Photoshop, Adaptive in Fireworks, and Optimized Median Cut in Paint Shop Pro Photo for the best results for most image types.

GIF compression

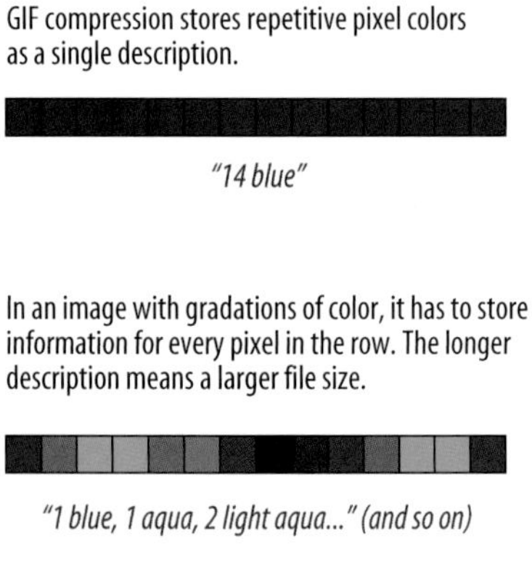

GIF compression stores repetitive pixel colors as a single description.

"14 blue"

In an image with gradations of color, it has to store information for every pixel in the row. The longer description means a larger file size.

"1 blue, 1 aqua, 2 light aqua…" (and so on)

Figure 18-4. A simplified demonstration of LZW compression used by GIF images.

GIF compression is "lossless," which means that no image information is sacrificed in order to compress the indexed image (although some image information may be lost when the RGB image is converted to a limited color palette). Second, it uses a compression scheme (called "LZW" for Lempel-Ziv-Welch) that takes advantage of repetition in data. When it encounters a string of pixels of identical color, it can compress that into one data description. This is why images with large areas of flat color condense better than images with textures.

To use an extremely simplified example, when the compression scheme encounters a row of 14 identical blue pixels, it makes up a shorthand notation that means "14 blue pixels." The next time it encounters 14 blue pixels, it uses only the code shorthand (Figure 18-4). By contrast, when it encounters a row that has a gentle gradation from blue to aqua and green, it needs to store a description for every pixel along the way, requiring more data. What actually happens in technical terms is more complicated, of course, but this example is a good mental model to keep in mind when designing GIF images for maximum compression.

Transparency

You can make parts of GIF images transparent so that the background image or color shows through. Although all bitmapped graphics are rectangular by nature, with transparency, you can create the illusion that your image has a more interesting shape (Figure 18-5). GIF transparency is discussed in detail later in this chapter.

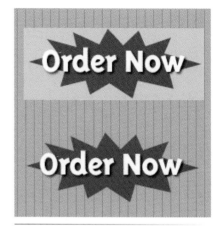

Figure 18-5. Transparency allows the striped background to show through the image on the bottom.

Common Color Palettes

All 8-bit indexed color images use palettes to define the colors in the image, and there are several standard palettes to choose from. Some are methods for producing a custom palette based on the colors in the image. Others apply a preexisting palette to the image.

Exact. Creates a custom palette out of the actual colors in the image if the image already contains fewer than 256 colors.

Adaptive. Creates a custom palette using the most frequently used pixel colors in the image. It allows for color-depth reduction while preserving the original character of the image.

Perceptual (Photoshop/ImageReady only). Creates a custom color table by giving priority to colors for which the human eye has greater sensitivity. Unlike Adaptive, it is based on algorithms, not just a pixel count. It generally results in images with better color integrity than Adaptive palette images.

Selective (Photoshop/ImageReady only). This is similar to Perceptual, but it gives preference to areas of broad color and the preservation of web-safe colors.

Web, Restrictive, or Web216. Creates a palette of colors exclusively from the web-safe palette (see Chapter 13, Colors and Backgrounds for more information on the web palette). It is no longer necessary to use colors from the web palette, so this is not recommended.

Web Adaptive (Fireworks only). This adaptive palette converts colors to the nearest web palette color. Because the web palette is obsolete and limited, this is no longer recommended.

Uniform. Creates a palette that contains an evenly stepped sampling of colors from the RGB spectrum.

Custom. This allows you to load a palette that was previously saved and apply it to the current image. Otherwise, it preserves the current colors in the palette.

System (Windows or Macintosh). Uses the colors in the specified system's default palette.

Optimized Median Cut (Paint Shop Pro Photo only). This reduces the image to a few colors using something similar to an Adaptive palette.

Optimized Octree (Paint Shop Pro Photo only). Use this palette if the original image has just a few colors and you want to keep those exact colors.

Figure 18-6. Interlaced GIFs display in a series of passes, each clearer than the pass before.

FURTHER READING

Animated GIFs

With so much to say about Cascading Style Sheets, I ran out of room in this edition for a chapter on animated GIFs. The good news is that you can download a PDF of the *Animated GIFs* chapter from the second edition of *Learning Web Design* at *www.learningwebdesign.com*. The chapter includes detailed explanations of the animation settings and step-by-step instructions for how to create animations.

Interlacing

Interlacing is an effect you can apply to a GIF that makes the image display in a series of passes. Each pass is clearer than the pass before until the image is fully rendered in the browser window (Figure 18-6). Without interlacing, some browsers may wait until the entire image is downloaded before displaying the image. Others may display the image a few rows at a time, from top to bottom, until the entire picture is complete.

Over a fast connection, these effects (interlacing or image delays) may not even be perceptible. However, over slow modem connections, interlacing large images may be a way to provide a hint of the image to come while the entire image downloads.

Whether you interlace or not is your design decision. I never do, but if you have an especially large image and an audience with a significant percentage of dial-up connections, interlacing may be worthwhile.

Animation

Another feature built into the GIF file format is the ability to display simple animations (Figure 18-7). Many of the spinning, blinking, fading, or otherwise moving ad banners you see are animated GIFs (although Flash movies have become increasingly popular for web advertising).

Figure 18-7. All the frames of this simple animation are contained within one GIF file.

Animated GIFs contain a number of animation frames, which are separate images that, when viewed together quickly, give the illusion of motion or change over time. All of the frame images are stored within a single GIF file, along with settings that describe how they should be played back in the browser window. Settings include whether and how many times the sequence repeats, how long each frame stays visible (frame delay), the manner in which one frame replaces another (disposal method), whether the image is transparent, and whether it is interlaced.

Adobe Photoshop CS3, Fireworks, and the discontinued ImageReady have interfaces for creating animated GIFs. Another highly recommended tool is GIFmation by BoxTop Software, available at *www.boxtopsoft.com*.

The photogenic JPEG

The second most popular graphics format on the Web is JPEG, which stands for Joint Photographic Experts Group, the standards body that created it.

Unlike GIFs, JPEGs use a compression scheme that loves gradient and blended colors, but doesn't work especially well on flat colors or hard edges. JPEG's full-color capacity and compression scheme make it the ideal choice for photographic images (Figure 18-8).

24-bit Truecolor images

JPEGs don't use color palettes like GIFs. Instead, they are 24-bit images, capable of displaying colors from the millions of colors in the RGB color space (also referred to as the Truecolor space, see note). This is one aspect that makes them ideal for photographs—they have all the colors you'll ever need. With JPEGs, you don't have to worry about limiting yourself to 256 colors the way you do with GIFs. JPEGs are much more straightforward.

Figure 18-8. The JPEG format is ideal for photographs (color or grayscale) or any image with subtle color gradations.

Lossy compression

The JPEG compression scheme is lossy, which means that some of the image information is thrown out in the compression process. Fortunately, this loss is not discernible for most images at most compression levels. When an image is compressed with high levels of JPEG compression, you begin to see color blotches and squares (usually referred to as artifacts) that result from the way the compression scheme samples the image (Figure 18-9).

NOTE

RGB color is explained in Chapter 14, Colors and Backgrounds.

Original

Maximum compression

Figure 18-9. JPEG compression discards image detail to achieve smaller file sizes. At high compression rates, image quality suffers, as shown in the image on the right.

You can control how aggressively you want the image to be compressed. This involves a trade-off between file size and image quality. The more you compress the image (for a smaller file size), the more the image quality suffers. Conversely, when you maximize quality, you also end up with larger files. The best compression level is based on the particular image and your objectives for the site. Compression strategies are discussed in more detail in Chapter 19, Lean and Mean Web Graphics.

Progressive JPEGs

Progressive JPEGs display in a series of passes (like interlaced GIFs), starting with a low-resolution version that gets clearer with each pass as shown in Figure 18-10. In some graphics programs, you can specify the number of passes it takes to fill in the final image (3, 4, or 5).

Photo courtesy of Liam Lynch

Figure 18-10. Progressive JPEGs render in a series of passes.

The advantage to using progressive JPEGs is that viewers can get an idea of the image before it downloads completely. Also, making a JPEG progressive usually reduces its file size slightly. The disadvantage is that they take more processing power and can slow down final display.

Decompression

JPEGs need to be decompressed before they can be displayed; therefore, it takes a browser longer to decode and assemble a JPEG than a GIF of the same file size. It's usually not a perceptible difference, however, so this is not a reason to avoid the JPEG format. It's just something to know.

The amazing PNG

The last graphic format to join the web graphics roster is the versatile PNG (Portable Network Graphic). Despite getting off to a slow start, PNGs are now supported by all browsers in current use. In addition, image-editing tools are now capable of generating PNGs that are as small and full-featured as they ought to be. Thanks to better support across the board, PNGs are finally enjoying the mainstream popularity they deserve.

WARNING

Cumulative Image Quality Loss

Be aware that once image quality is lost in JPEG compression, you can never get it back again. For this reason, you should avoid resaving a JPEG as a JPEG. You lose image quality every time.

It is better to hang onto the original image and make JPEG copies as needed. That way, if you need to make a change to the JPEG version, you can go back to the original and do a fresh save or export. Fortunately, Photoshop's Save for Web & Devices feature does exactly that. Fireworks and ImageReady also preserve the originals and let you save or export copies.

PNGs offer an impressive lineup of features:

- The ability to contain 8-bit indexed, 24-bit RGB, 16-bit grayscale, and even 48-bit color images

- A lossless compression scheme

- Simple on/off transparency (like GIF) or multiple levels of transparency

- Progressive display (similar to GIF interlacing)

- Gamma adjustment information

- Embedded text for attaching information about the author, copyright, and so on

This section takes a closer look at each of these features and helps you decide when the PNG format is the best choice for your image.

Multiple image formats

The PNG format was designed to replace GIF for online purposes and TIFF for image storage and printing. A PNG can be used to save many image types: 8-bit indexed color, 24- and 48-bit RGB color, and 16-bit grayscale.

8-bit indexed color images

Like GIFs, PNGs can store 8-bit indexed images with a maximum of 256 colors. They may be saved at 1-, 2-, and 4-bit depths as well. Indexed color PNGs are generally referred to as PNG-8.

RGB/Truecolor (24- and 48-bit)

In PNGs, each channel (red, green, and blue) can be defined by 8- or 16-bit information, resulting in 24- or 48-bit RGB images, respectively. In graphics programs, 24-bit RGB PNGs are identified as PNG-24. It should be noted that 48-bit images are useless for the Web, and even 24-bit images should be used with care. JPEG offers smaller file sizes with acceptable image quality for RGB images.

Grayscale

PNGs can also support 16-bit grayscale images—that's as many as 65,536 shades of gray (2^{16}), enabling black-and-white photographs and illustrations to be stored with enormous subtlety of detail, although they are not appropriate for the Web.

Transparency

Like GIFs, PNGs can contain transparent areas that let the background image or color show through. The killer feature that PNG has over GIF, however, is the ability to contain multiple levels of transparency, commonly referred to as alpha-channel (or just alpha) transparency.

PNGs in Motion

One of the only features missing in PNG is the ability to store multiple images for animation. The first effort to add motion to PNGs was the MNG format (Multiple-image Network Graphic). It gained some browser support, but its popularity suffered from the fact that MNGs were not backward compatible with PNGs. If a browser didn't support MNG, it would display a broken graphic.

More recently, there has been a proposed extension to PNG called APNG (Animated Portable Network Graphic) that addresses the issue of backward compatibility. If a browser does not support an APNG, it displays the first frame as a static image PNG instead.

Both of these formats are in development and are not well supported as of this writing.

Figure 18-11 shows the same PNG against two different background images. The orange circle is entirely opaque, but the drop shadow contains multiple levels of transparency, ranging from nearly opaque to entirely transparent. The multiple transparency levels stored in the PNG allows the drop shadow to blend seamlessly with any background. The ins and outs of PNG transparency will be addressed in the upcoming Working with Transparency section.

WARNING

Multiple levels of transparency are not supported by Internet Explorer 6 and earlier for Windows. For details, see the Internet Explorer and Alpha Transparency sidebar in the Working with Transparency section.

Figure 18-11. Alpha-channel transparency allows multiple levels of transparency, as shown in the drop shadow around the orange circle PNG.

PNG Color Shifting

Due to incorrect gamma handling, PNGs will look darker in Internet Explorer (all versions). The upshot of it is that it is difficult to get a match between a PNG and a background color, even if the RGB values are the same. Making the edges transparent is the solution in many situations.

There is a great article written by Aaron Gustafson (*www.easy-reader. net/archives/2006/02/18/png-color-oddities-in-ie/*) that identifies the problem and serves as a great jumping-off point for further research.

Progressive display (interlacing)

PNGs can also be coded for interlaced display. When this option is selected, the image displays in a series of seven passes. Unlike interlaced GIFs, which fill in horizontal rows, PNGs fill in both horizontally and vertically. Interlacing adds to the file size and is usually not necessary, so to keep files as small as possible, turn interlacing display off.

Gamma correction

Gamma refers to the brightness setting of a monitor (see note). Because gamma settings vary by platform, the graphics you create may not look the way you intend for the end user. PNGs can be tagged with information regarding the gamma setting of the environment in which they were created. This can then be interpreted by the software displaying the PNG to make appropriate gamma compensations. When this is implemented on both the creator and end user's side, the PNG retains its intended brightness and color intensity. Unfortunately, as of this writing, this feature is poorly supported.

NOTE

Gamma is discussed in Chapter 3, The Nature of Web Design.

Embedded text

PNGs also have the ability to store strings of text. This is useful for permanently attaching text to an image, such as copyright information or a description of what is in the image. The only tools that accommodate text annotations to PNG graphics are Corel Paint Shop Pro Photo and the GIMP (a free image editor). Ideally, the meta-information in the PNG would be accessible via right-clicking on the graphic in a browser, but this feature is not yet implemented in current browsers.

When to use PNGs

PNGs pack a lot of powerful options, but competition among web graphic formats nearly always comes down to file size.

For images that would typically be saved as GIFs, 8-bit PNG is a good option. You may find that a PNG version of an image has a smaller file size than a GIF of the same image, but that depends on how efficiently your image program handles PNG compression. If the PNG is smaller, use it with confidence.

Although PNG does support 24-bit color images, its lossless compression scheme nearly always results in a dramatically larger file than JPEG compression applied to the same image. For web purposes, JPEG is still the best choice for photographic and continuous tone images.

The exception to the "smallest file wins" rule is if you want to take advantage of multiple levels of transparency. In that case, PNG is your only option and may be worth a slightly heftier file size.

The following section takes a broader look at finding the best graphic format for the job.

Choosing the best format

Part of the trick to making quality web graphics that maintain quality and download quickly is choosing the right format. Table 18-1 provides a good starting point.

Table 18-1. Choosing the best file format

If your image...	use...	because...
Is graphical, with flat colors	GIF or 8-bit PNG	They excel at compressing flat color.
Is a photograph or contains graduated color	JPEG	JPEG compression works best on images with blended color. Because it is lossy, it generally results in smaller file sizes than 24-bit PNG.
Is a combination of flat and photographic imagery	GIF or 8-bit PNG	Indexed color formats are best at preserving and compressing flat color areas. The dithering that appears in the photographic areas as a result of reducing to a palette is usually not problematic.
Requires transparency	GIF or PNG	Both GIF and PNG allow on/off transparency in images.
Requires multiple levels of transparency	PNG	PNG is the only format that supports alpha-channel transparency.
Requires animation	GIF	GIF is the only format that can contain animation frames.

Work in RGB Mode

Regardless of the final format of your file, you should always do your image-editing work in RGB mode (grayscale is fine for non-color images). To check the color mode of the image in Photoshop, select Image → Mode and make sure there is a checkmark next to RGB Color.

JPEG and PNG-24 files compress the RGB color image directly. If you are saving the file as a GIF or PNG-8, the RGB image must be converted to indexed color mode, either manually or as part of the Save for Web or Export process.

If you need to edit an existing GIF or PNG-8, you should convert the image to RGB before doing any edits. This enables the editing tool to use colors from the full RGB spectrum when adjusting the image. If you resize the original indexed color image, you'll get lousy results because the new image is limited to the colors from the existing color table.

If you have experience creating graphics for print, you may be accustomed to working in CMYK mode (printed colors are made up of Cyan, Magenta, Yellow, and blacK ink). CMYK mode is irrelevant and inappropriate for web graphics.

Saving an image in your chosen format

Virtually every up-to-date graphics program allows you to save images in GIF, JPEG, and PNG format, but some give you more options than others. If you use Photoshop, Fireworks or Corel Paint Shop Pro Photo, be sure to take advantage of special web graphics features instead of doing a simple "Save As...".

Start with an RGB image that is at an appropriate size for a web page (image size is discussed in the next section). Edit the image as necessary (resizing, cropping, color correction, etc.), and when you are finished, follow these instructions for saving it as GIF, JPEG, or PNG.

NOTE

This feature was called simply "Save for Web" in Photoshop versions 6 through CS2.

Photoshop (versions 6 and higher, see note)

Open Photoshop's Save for Web & Devices dialog box (File → Save for Web & Devices) (Figure 18-12) and select the file type from the pop-up menu. When you choose a format, the panel displays settings appropriate to that format. The Save for Web window also shows you a preview of the resulting image and its file size. You can even do side-by-side comparisons of different settings; for example, a GIF and PNG-8 version of the same image. Once you have selected the file type and made your settings, click Save and give the file a name.

Photoshop CS3
Select the file type in the **Save for Web & Devices** dialog box. You can change the settings and compare resulting images before you Save.

We'll see the Save for Web & Devices dialog box again later in this chapter when we resize images and work with transparency. It also pops up in Chapter 19 when we discuss the various settings related to optimization.

Figure 18-12. Selecting a file type in Photoshop's handy Save for Web & Devices dialog box.

Fireworks (all versions)

With the image open and the Preview tab selected, the file type can be selected from the Optimize panel (Figure 18-13). When you are finished with your settings, select Export from the File menu and give the graphic file a name.

Fireworks 8
Select a file type in the **Optimize** panel prior to Exporting the graphic.

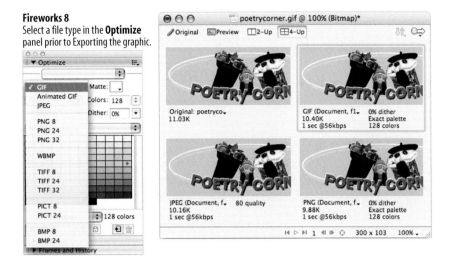

Figure 18-13. Select a file type in the Fireworks Optimize panel.

Paint Shop Pro Photo

The GIF Optimizer, JPEG Optimizer, and PNG Optimizer are accessed from the Export option in the File menu. Each opens a multipanel dialog box with all the settings for the respective file type and a preview of a portion of the compressed image. The Colors panel of the GIF optimizer is shown in Figure 18-14. When you have made all your settings, click OK. Note that you need to choose your file type *before* accessing the settings, and there is no way to compare image type previews as is possible in Photoshop and Fireworks.

Image Size and Resolution

One thing that GIF, JPEG, and PNG images have in common is that they are all bitmapped (also called raster) images. When you zoom in on a bitmapped image, you can see that it is like a mosaic made up of many pixels (tiny, single-colored squares). These are different from vector graphics that are made up of smooth lines and filled areas, all based on mathematical formulas. Figure 18-15 illustrates the difference between bitmapped and vector graphics.

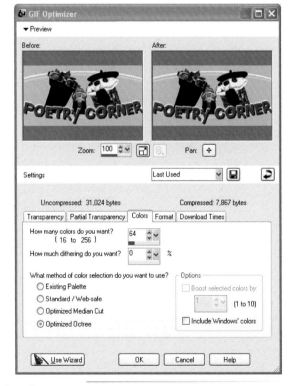

Figure 18-14. Web optimization options in Corel Paint Shop Pro Photo.

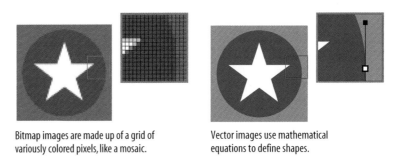

Bitmap images are made up of a grid of variously colored pixels, like a mosaic.

Vector images use mathematical equations to define shapes.

Figure 18-15. Bitmapped and vector graphics.

Goodbye inches, hello pixels!

If you've used bitmapped images for print or the Web, you may be familiar with the term resolution, the number of pixels per inch. In the print world, image resolutions of 300 and 600 pixels per inch (ppi) are common.

On the Web, however, images need to be created at much lower resolutions. 72 ppi has become the standard, but in reality, the whole notion of "inches" and therefore "pixels per inch" becomes irrelevant in the web environment. In the end, the only meaningful measurement of a web image is its actual pixel dimensions. This statement deserves a bit more explanation.

When an image is displayed on a web page, the pixels map one-to-one with the display resolution of the monitor (see note). Because the monitor resolution varies by platform and user, the image will appear larger or smaller depending on the configuration, as the following example demonstrates.

NOTE

Some modern browsers have a feature that scales large images to fit inside the browser window. If this feature is turned on, the one-to-one pixel matching no longer applies.

I have created a graphic that is 72 pixels square (Figure 18-16). Although I may have created that image at 72 pixels per inch, it's likely that it will never measure precisely one inch when it is displayed on a monitor (particularly the higher-resolution monitors that are prevalent today). On the high-resolution monitor, the pixels are smaller and the "one-inch" square graphic ends up less than three-quarter-inch square.

Dots Per Inch

Because web graphics exist solely on the screen, it is correct to measure their resolutions in pixels per inch (ppi).

When it comes to print, however, devices and printed pages are measured in dots per inch (dpi), which describes the number of printed dots in each inch of the image. The dpi may or may not be the same as the ppi for an image.

In your travels, you may hear the terms dpi and ppi used interchangeably (albeit incorrectly so). It is important to understand the difference.

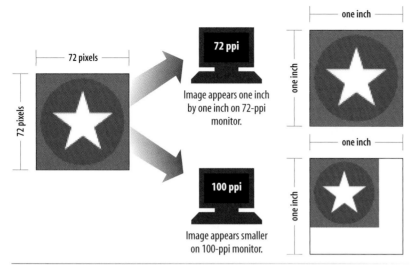

Figure 18-16. The size of an image is dependent on the monitor resolution.

For this reason, it is useless to think in terms of "inches" on the Web. It's all relative. And without inches, the whole notion of "pixels per inch" is thrown out the window as well. The only thing we know for sure is that the graphic is 72 pixels across, and it will be twice as wide as a graphic that is 36 pixels across.

After this example, it should be clear why images fresh from a digital camera are not appropriate for web pages. I commonly shoot images at 1600×1200 pixels with a resolution of 180 ppi. With browser windows commonly as small as 800 pixels wide, all those extra pixels are unnecessary and would cause half the image to hang outside a typical browser window. Users would have to scroll vertically and horizontally to see it. Even though some modern browsers scale the image down to fit the browser window, that doesn't solve the problem of forcing an unnecessarily large download on users when a much smaller file will do.

Resizing images

The images you get from a digital camera, scanner, or stock photo company are generallly too large for web use, so you need to resize them smaller. In fact, I'd say that resizing images smaller makes up a large portion of the time I spend doing graphics production, so it's a good basic skill to have.

In Exercise 18-1, I'll show you an easy way to resize an image using Photoshop's "Save For Web & Devices" feature. With this method, the exported web graphic is resized, but the original remains unaltered. Adobe Photoshop Elements has a similar feature, so you can follow along if you have either of these programs. For other programs, or if you want more control over the final image quality, see the Using Image Size sidebar following the exercise.

Working in Low Resolution

Despite the fact that resolution is irrelevant, creating web graphics at 72 ppi puts you at a good starting point for images with appropriate pixel dimensions. The drawback to working at a low resolution is that the image quality is lower because there is not as much image information in a given space. This tends to make the image look more grainy or pixelated and, unfortunately, that is just the nature of the Web. On the upside, image edits that are noticeable in high-resolution graphics (such as retouching or cloning) are virtually seamless at low resolution. In addition, low resolution means smaller file sizes, which is always a concern for media shared over a network.

NOTE

If you don't have Photoshop, you can download a free trial version at www. adobe.com/downloads.

exercise 18-1 | **Resizing an image smaller in Photoshop**

In this exercise, we'll take a high-resolution photo and size it to fit on a web page. The source image, *ninja.tif*, is available with the materials for this chapter at *www.learningwebdesign.com/materials/*.

1. Open the file *ninja.tif* in Photoshop. A quick way to find the pixel dimensions of the image is to open the Image Size dialog box (Image → Image Size) shown in Figure 18-17 **A**. This image is 1600 x 1600 pixels, which is too big for a web page. Close the Image Size box for now (we were only using it to peek at our starting point). The Info window (not shown) also shows pixel dimensions when the whole image is selected.

2. Now we'll resize the image and save it as a JPEG in one fell swoop. Select Save for Web & Devices from the File menu. Because this image is a photograph, select JPEG **B** from the Formats pop-up menu. The default High/60 compression setting is fine for this example.

3. With the format chosen, it's time to get to the resizing. Click on the Image Size tab in the bottom half of the settings column **C**. Enter the dimensions that you'd like the final JPEG to be when it is saved. I'm going to set the width to 400 pixels. When "constrain proportions" is checked, the height changes automatically when you enter the new width.

4. Next, select the Quality **D**. I usually go for Bicubic or Bicubic Sharper for the best results then click Apply **E**. You will see the resized image in the Optimized Image view (select the tab at the top if it isn't already).

5. Click Save **F**, give the file a name, and select a directory in which to save it. You can close the original image without saving, or save it to preserve the Save for Web settings.

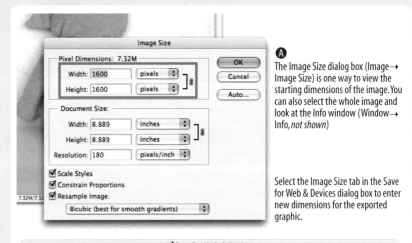

A The Image Size dialog box (Image→ Image Size) is one way to view the starting dimensions of the image. You can also select the whole image and look at the Info window (Window→ Info, *not shown*)

Select the Image Size tab in the Save for Web & Devices dialog box to enter new dimensions for the exported graphic.

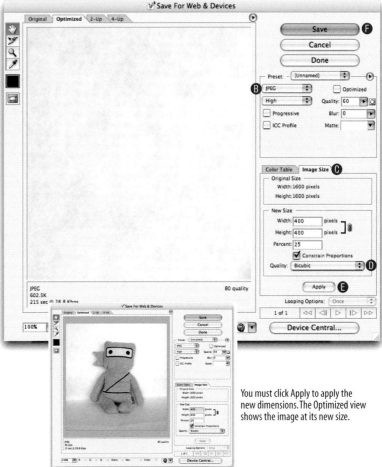

You must click Apply to apply the new dimensions. The Optimized view shows the image at its new size.

Figure 18-17. Using the Save for Web & Devices dialog box to resize an image.

Working with Transparency

Both GIF and PNG formats allow parts of an image to be transparent, allowing the background color or image to show through. In this section, we'll take a closer look at transparent graphics, including tips on how to make them.

The first thing to know is that there are two types of transparency. In binary transparency, pixels are either entirely transparent or entirely opaque, like an on/off switch. Both GIF and PNG files support binary transparency.

In alpha (or alpha-channel) transparency, a pixel may be totally transparent, totally opaque, or up to 254 levels of opaqueness in between (a total of 256 opacity levels). Only PNGs support alpha transparency. The advantage of PNGs with alpha transparency is that they blend seamlessly with any background color or pattern, as shown back in Figure 18-11.

In this section, you'll become familiar with how each type of transparency works, and learn how to make transparent images using Photoshop.

How binary transparency works

Remember that the pixel colors for GIFs and PNG-8s are stored in an indexed color table. Transparency is simply treated as a separate color, occupying a position in the color table. Figure 18-18 shows the color table in Photoshop for a simple transparent GIF. The slot in the color table that is set to transparent is indicated by a checker pattern. Pixels that correspond to that position will be completely transparent when the image displays in the browser. Note that only one slot is transparent—all the other pixel colors are opaque.

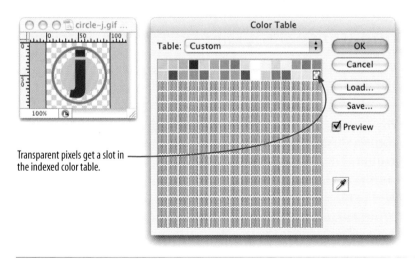

Transparent pixels get a slot in the indexed color table.

Figure 18-18. Transparency is treated as a color in the indexed color table.

Using Image Size

The disadvantage to the method shown in Exercise 18-1 is that you lose control over the quality of the image. If you are an image quality control freak (like me), you may prefer resizing the image using the Image Size dialog box (Figure 18-17 Ⓐ). In Fireworks, Modify → Canvas... → Image Size... gives you a similar set of options.

Although you can set the pixel dimensions right at the top, it is better to take care of a few other settings first.

Be sure that Resample Image and Constrain Proportions are checked at the bottom, select Bicubic (or Bicubic Sharper) as the Quality setting, then set the Resolution to 72 pixels/inch. Then enter the desired final pixel dimensions at the top of the box and click OK. Double-clicking on the magnifying glass tool (not shown) displays the resized image at 100%.

Now you can apply sharpening filters and other effects and use Save For Web to output the image in a web format.

I find that resizing a very large image in a couple of steps helps preserve quality. First, I resize it to an in-between dimension and sharpen it with a sharpening filter. Then I resize it to its final dimensions and sharpen again. You can't do that with the Save For Web method.

Remember that the Image Size settings resize the *original* image. Don't save it, or you'll lose your high-quality version! Be sure to "Save As" in order to keep a copy of your original.

Internet Explorer and Alpha Transparency

Alpha transparency is really cool, but unfortunately, it comes with one major headache—it is not supported in Internet Explorer 6 and earlier for Windows. Users with those browsers (and there are a *lot* of them) will see the PNG as entirely opaque.

There is a workaround using Microsoft's proprietary AlphaImageLoader filter. The details of the process are beyond the scope of this chapter, but these resources are good places to start if you want to ensure cross-browser support for your transparent PNGs.

Start with the AlphaImageLoader filter documentation on the MSDN (Microsoft Developers Network) site at *http://msdn.microsoft.com/en-us/library/ms532969.aspx*.

These articles introduce variations and alternative techniques:

- "Cross-browser Variable Opacity with PNG: A Real Solution," by Michael Lovitt at *www.alistapart.com/articles/pngopacity*.

- "PNG Behavior," *webfx.eae.net/dhtml/pngbehavior/pngbehavior.html*.

NOTE

The principles and settings outlined in Exercise 18-2 are nearly identical in Fireworks, so the same general instructions apply, although the interface is slightly different.

How alpha transparency works

RGB images, such as JPEGs and PNG-24s, store color in separate channels, one for red, one for green, and one for blue. PNG-24 files add another channel, called the alpha channel, to store transparency information. In that channel, each pixel may display one of 256 values, which correspond to 256 levels of transparency when the image is displayed. The black areas of the alpha channel mask are transparent, the white areas are opaque, and the grays are on a scale in between. I think of it as a blanket laid over the image that tells each pixel below it how transparent it is (Figure 18-19).

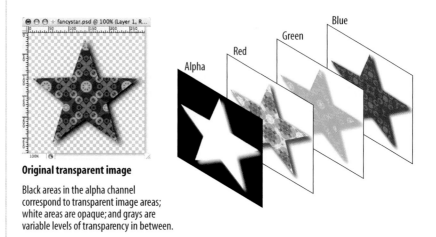

Original transparent image

Black areas in the alpha channel correspond to transparent image areas; white areas are opaque; and grays are variable levels of transparency in between.

Figure 18-19. Transparency information is stored as a separate (alpha) channel in 24-bit PNGs.

Making transparent GIFs and PNGs

The easiest way to make parts of an image transparent is to design them that way from the start and preserve the transparent areas when you create the GIF or PNG version of the image. Once again, Photoshop's Save for Web & Devices feature or Firework's Optimize panel are perfect tools for the job.

It is possible to add transparent areas to a flattened opaque image, but it may be difficult to get a seamless blend with a background. We'll look at the process for making portions of an existing image transparent later in this section.

But first, follow along with the steps in Exercise 18-2 that demonstrates how to preserve transparent areas and guarantee a good match with the background using Photoshop's Save for Web & Devices dialog box. There are some new concepts tucked in there, so even if you don't do the exercise, I recommend giving it a read, particularly steps 5, 6, and 7.

exercise 18-2 | **Creating transparent images**

In this exercise, we're going to start from scratch, so you'll get the experience of creating a layered image with transparent areas. I'm going to keep it simple, but you can apply these techniques to fancier designs, of course.

1. Launch Photoshop and create a new file (File → New...). There are a few settings in the New dialog box (Figure 18-20) that will set you off in the right direction for creating transparent web graphics.

   - First, make your new graphic 500 pixels wide and 100 pixels high to match the example in this exercise **A**.

   - Set the resolution to 72 pixels/inch because web graphics are low-resolution **B**.

   - Make sure the color mode is RGB Color, 8-bit **C**.

   - Finally, and most importantly for this exercise, select Transparent from the Background Contents options **D**. This option creates a layered Photoshop file with a transparent background. It is much easier to preserve transparent areas in an image than to add it later. The transparent areas (in this case, the whole area, since we haven't added any image content yet) is indicated by a gray checkerboard pattern **E**.

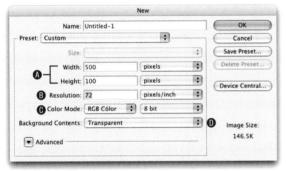

Figure 18-20. Creating a new image with a transparent background.

2. Now we'll add some text and give it a drop shadow (Figure 18-21, following page).

   - Use the type tool **F** and type your name. Open the Character window **G** (Window → Character) to change the look of the font. With the text selected, choose a bold typeface (something chunky) and set the size large enough to fill the space, as shown in the example. Click the swatch next to Color, and use the Color Picker to choose a color for the text that is not too light and not too dark. I'm using a medium pink.

   - Next, add a soft drop shadow to the text. Open the Layers window **H** (Window → Layers) if it isn't open already. You will see the layer containing your text in the list. Add a drop shadow by clicking the Layer Style button (it looks like an FX) at the bottom of the Layers window and select "Drop Shadow..." **I**. In the Layer Style dialog box **J**, you can play around with the settings, but I recommend setting the Distance and Size to at least 5 to get the most out of the rest of the exercise. When you are done, click OK.

3. Save the image as a Photoshop file to preserve the layers for easier editing later, if necessary. I'm naming mine *jennifer.psd* (use the *.psd* suffix). With a nice source image saved, we are ready to start making the web versions.

4. With the new file still open, select Save for Web & Devices from the File menu. Click on the 4-Up tab at the top to compare the original image to several other versions (Figure 18-22, following page). Note, your previews may display in a grid instead of a stack.

5. Let's see how the image looks as a GIF with and without transparency. Click on the second preview to select it, then set the file type to GIF and set the number of colors to 32. Now, toggle the checkmark next to Transparency off and on (Figure 18-23 on page 381).

   - When Transparency is off (not checked, as shown on the left), the Matte color is used to fill in the transparent areas of the original image. Set the Matte color to white to match my example.

   - When Transparency is on (checked, as shown on the right), a checker pattern appears in the transparent areas of the image, indicating where the background color or pattern of the web page will show through. If you look carefully at the drop shadow area, you will see that the shades of gray are blended with the white Matte color. Try changing the Matte color and watch what happens in the drop shadow area.

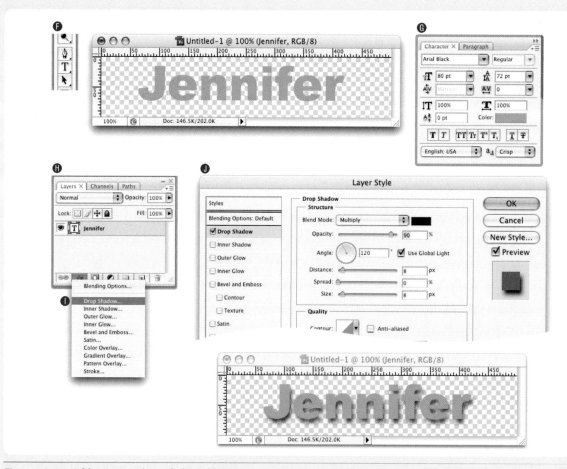

Figure 18-21. Adding text with a soft drop shadow.

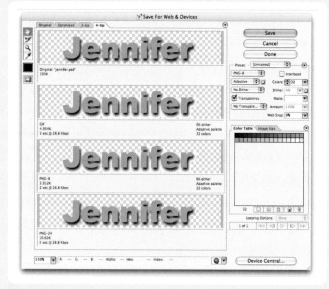

Figure 18-22. The "4-up" tab in the Save for Web & Devices dialog box allows you to compare four different versions of the same image.

6. Leave the GIF preview alone for a moment and select the next preview. Set the file type to PNG-8 and try toggling the Transparency checkbox. As expected, it behaves exactly the same as the GIF because both formats use binary transparency. The previews should look like those shown in Figure 18-23.

7. Now select the fourth preview, make it a PNG-24, and toggle the Transparency checkbox (Figure 18-24). When it is unchecked (left), the Matte color fills in the transparent areas of the original image. But when Transparency is checked (right), the checkerboard pattern shows through the drop shadow blend. So, too, will the background of a web page. When Transparency is selected, the Matte tool is no longer available, because there is no need to specify the background color of the page...the PNG with alpha transparency will blend with anything.

Take a moment to note the file size of the transparent PNG-24. Mine is nearly 10.6 KB, while my transparent GIF version is 5 KB, and the transparent PNG-8 came in at just 3.3 KB. The significantly larger file size is the price you pay for the versatility of the alpha transparency.

8. Save the PNG-24 with Transparency turned on and name the file with the *.png* suffix (mine is *jennifer.png*). Open the Save for Web & Devices dialog box again and save a GIF version of the image with Transparency turned on (make sure that Matte is set to white). Name the file with the *.gif* suffix. We'll be using these graphics again in the next section.

The translucent grays in the drop shadow get blended with the color specified by the Matte setting

Figure 18-23. Previews of transparency turned off (left) and on (right) in a GIF.

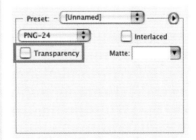

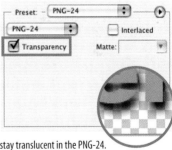

The translucent grays in the drop shadow will stay translucent in the PNG-24.

Figure 18-24. Previews of Transparency turned off (left) and on (right) in a PNG-24.

DESIGN TIP

The trick to getting a transparent GIF to blend seamlessly with a background is to use the RGB values from the web page's background color (or the dominant color from a background image) for the Matte color. If your page background is a multi-colored pattern or is otherwise difficult to match, opt for a Matte color that is slightly darker than the predominant background color.

NOTE

Fireworks gives you a choice of Index or Alpha Transparency for PNG-8 graphics. See the PNG-8 "Alpha" Transparency sidebar for details.

PNG-8 "Alpha" Transparency

Technically, variable levels of transparency are *not* limited to 24-bit PNGs. PNG-8 files can do it too. Instead of using an alpha channel, they store different transparency levels in multiple slots in the index color table. The resulting file size is potentially smaller than the same image saved as a PNG-24 with an alpha channel.

As of this writing, only Fireworks allows you to create PNG-8s with multiple levels of transparency, and browser support is poor. Most browsers display them as though they have simple binary transparency. For now, this is another cool PNG feature that remains virtually untapped due to lagging software support.

Avoiding "halos"

Now that I've got some transparent graphics, I'm going to try them out on a minimal web page with a white background. If you want to work along, open a text editor and create an HTML document like the one shown here (I've omitted the DOCTYPE and character set information to save space):

```
<html>
<head>
  <title>Transparency test</title>
  <style type="text/css">
    body {
      background-color: white;
    }
  </style>
</head>
<body>
  <p><img src="jennifer.png" alt="" /></p>
  <p><img src="jennifer.gif" alt="" /></p>
</body>
</html>
```

TERMINOLOGY

Anti-aliasing

Anti-aliasing is a slight blur applied to rounded edges of bitmapped graphics to make smoother transitions between colors. Aliased edges, by contrast, have stair-stepped edges. Anti-aliasing text and graphics can give your graphics a more professional appearance.

When I open the file in a browser, the graphics look more or less the same against the white background (Figure 18-25, left). But, if I change the background color of the web page to teal (`background-color: teal;`), the difference between the alpha and binary transparency becomes very clear (right).

Figure 18-25. The difference between binary and alpha transparency becomes very clear when the background color of the page changes.

When the background color changes, the GIF no longer matches the background, resulting in an ugly fringe commonly called a halo. Halos are the result of anti-aliased edges that have been blended with a color other than the background color of a page. They are a potential hazard of binary transparency, whether GIF or PNG-8.

Prevention is the name of the game when it comes to dealing with binary transparency and halos. As you've just seen, the Matte color feature in Photoshop and Fireworks makes it easy to blend the edges of the graphic to a target background color. If the background color changes, you can re-export the GIF or PNG-8 with the new Matte color. See the Matte Alternative sidebar for options if your tool doesn't have a Matte setting.

Another option is to save your image as a PNG-24 with variable transparency. That way, you don't have to worry about the background color or pattern, and it will be no problem if it changes in the future. The trade-off, of course, is the larger file size to download. In addition, alpha transparency does not work in Internet Explorer 6 and earlier without the aid of some proprietary and/or JavaScript workarounds (see the Internet Explorer and Alpha Transparency sidebar earlier in this chapter). This will become less of an issue of course as those versions go away.

Adding transparency to flattened images

It is possible to add transparent areas to images that have already been flattened and saved as a GIF or PNG. The GIF containing a yellow circle on a purple background in Figures 18-26 and 18-27 blends in fine against a solid purple background, but would be an obvious square if the background were changed to a pattern. The solution is to make the purple areas transparent to let the background show through. Fortunately, most graphics tools make it easy to do so by selecting a pixel color in the image, usually an eyedropper tool, that you'd like to be transparent.

In Photoshop, the transparency eyedropper is found on the Color Table dialog box (Image → Mode → Color Table). Click on the eyedropper, then on a pixel color in the image, and it magically turns transparent (Figure 18-26). To save the new transparent graphic, use the Save For Web & Devices feature as demonstrated earlier.

> **Matte Alternative**
>
> If you are using a graphics tool that doesn't have the Matte feature, create a new layer at the bottom of the layer "stack" and fill it with the background color of your page. When the image is flattened as a result of changing it to Indexed Color, the anti-aliased edges blend with the proper background color. Just select that background color to be transparent during export to GIF or PNG format and your image should be halo-free.

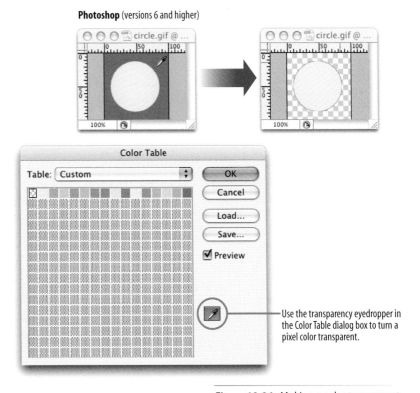

Figure 18-26. Making a color transparent in Photoshop.

In Fireworks, the transparency eyedropper is located at the bottom of the Optimize panel (Figure 18-27). The Add to Transparency tool allows you to select more than one pixel color to make transparent. The Subtract from Transparency dropper turns transparent areas opaque again. When you are finished, export the transparent graphic (File → Export).

Fireworks

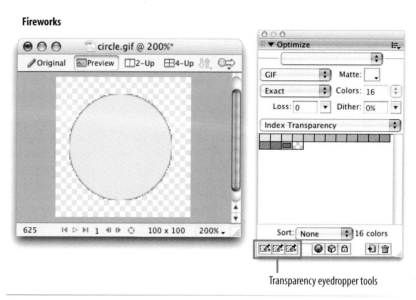

Transparency eyedropper tools

Figure 18-27. Making colors transparent in Fireworks.

If you look closely, you can see that there is a fringe of pixels still anti-aliased to purple, which means that this graphic will work well only against purple backgrounds. On other background colors, there will be a pesky halo. Unfortunately, the only way to fix a halo in an image that has already been flattened is to get in there and erase the anti-aliased edges, pixel by pixel. Even if you get rid of the fringe, you may be left with unattractive stair-stepped edges. You could also select the image area (the yellow circle in this example) with a marquee tool that has the "feathering" set to 1 or 2 pixels. Copy the image area and paste it to a new transparent layered image file, then use Save for Web & Devices to output a new graphic with the Matte set to match the background color.

If you are concerned with the professional appearance of your site, I'd say it's better to recreate the graphic from scratch, taking care to prevent halos, than to waste time trying to fix them. This is another reason to always save your layered files.

Web Graphics 101 Summary

If I've done my job, you should now have a good foundation in web graphics, including where to find an image, what file format to save it in, and how to resize it so it is appropriate for the Web. You also know the difference between binary and alpha transparency, and how to make graphics that blend well with the background of a web page.

In Chapter 19, we'll take graphics production to the next level and explore all the ways to make images as small as possible for faster downloads. But first, a little quiz.

Test Yourself

Answer the following questions to see if you got the big picture on web graphics. The answers appear in Appendix A.

1. What is the primary advantage to using rights-managed images?

2. What does ppi stand for?

3. Which graphic is more appropriate for placement on a web page: a 7-inch wide graphic at 72 ppi or a 4-inch wide graphic at 300 ppi?

4. What is "indexed color?" What file formats use it?

5. How many colors are in the color table for an 8-bit graphic? For a 5-bit graphic?

6. Name two things you can do with a GIF that you can't do with a JPEG.

7. JPEG's lossy compression is cumulative. What does that mean? Why is it important to know?

8. Name three types of image the PNG format can store.

9. What is the difference between binary and alpha transparency?

10. Pick the best graphic file format for each of the images in Figure 18-28. You should be able to make the decision just by looking at the images as they're printed here and explain your choice.

ABOUT THIS SITE

Ⓐ

Ⓑ

Ⓒ

Ⓓ

Ⓔ

Figure 18-28. Choose the best file format for each image.

LEAN AND MEAN WEB GRAPHICS

Because a web page is published over a network, it needs to zip through the lines as little packets of data in order to reach the end user. It is fairly intuitive, then, that larger amounts of data will require a longer time to arrive. And guess which part of a standard web page packs the most bytes—that's right, the graphics.

Thus is born the conflicted relationship with graphics on the Web. On the one hand, images make a web page more interesting than text alone, and the ability to display graphics is one of the factors contributing to the Web's success. On the other hand, graphics also try the patience of surfers with slow Internet connections. The user can hang in there and wait, turn graphics off in their browsers, or simply surf somewhere else.

This chapter covers the strategies and tools available for making web graphic files as small as possible (a process known as optimizing) while maintaining acceptable image quality. Maybe you're thinking, "Why bother? Everyone has broadband these days, right?!" After you read the next section, I think you'll be eager to learn the general and format-specific optimizing techniques that follow. If you're going to make web graphics, why not do it like the pros?

Why Optimize?

Despite the popularity of high-bandwidth connections, dial-up modem connections still make up a significant percentage of web traffic (20 to 30% as of this writing). In addition to dial-up connections, designers need to consider the performance of their web page designs on mobile devices where connection and processing speeds tend to lag behind the desktop experience.

What it boils down to is this: it is well worth your while to wring every unnecessary byte out of your graphics files to keep download times as short as possible.

In fact, many corporate clients set a kilobyte limit (or K-limit) that the sum of all the files on the page may not exceed. I know of one corporate site that set its limit to a scant 15 kilobytes (KB, or commonly just K) per page—that

IN THIS CHAPTER

Why you should optimize your graphics

General optimization strategies

Optimizing GIFs

Optimizing JPEGs

Optimizing PNGs

Optimizing to a target file size

NOTE

Optimization is not just for graphics. Professional (X)HTML, CSS, and JavaScript authors take measures to keep superfluous code and extra characters out of the text documents that make up web sites as well.

includes the (X)HTML document and all the graphics combined. Similarly, many sites put stingy K-limits on the ad banners they'll accept. Even if keeping graphic files small is not a priority for you, it may be for your clients. You've got to be prepared.

How Long Does It Take?

It's impossible to say exactly how long a graphic will take to download over the Web. It depends on many factors, including the speed of the user's connection, the speed of the user's computer, the amount of activity on the web server, and the general amount of traffic on the Internet itself.

The general rule of thumb is to figure that a graphic could take 1 second per kilobyte (KB) under worst-case conditions (say, over a 28.8 Kbps modem connection). That would mean a 30 KB graphic would take 30 seconds to download, which is a long time for a user to be staring at a computer screen.

Use the 1 sec/KB guideline only to get a ballpark estimate for the lowest common denominator. Actual times are likely to be a lot better, and may be a lot worse.

General Optimization Strategies

Regardless of the image or file type, there are a few basic strategies to keep in mind for limiting file size. In the broadest of terms, they are:

Limit dimensions

Although fairly obvious, the easiest way to keep file size down is to limit the dimensions of the image itself. There aren't any magic numbers; just don't make images any larger than they need to be. By simply eliminating extra space in the graphic in Figure 19-1, I was able to reduce the file size by 3K (23%).

600 x 200 pixels (**13 KB**)

500 x 136 pixels (**10 KB**)

Figure 19-1. You can reduce the size of your files simply by cropping out extra space.

Reuse and recycle

If you use the same image repeatedly in a site, it is best to create only one image file and point to it repeatedly wherever it is needed. This allows the browser to take advantage of the cached image and avoid additional downloads. Caching is explained in the Taking Advantage of Caching sidebar in Chapter 7, Adding Images.

Design for compression

One of the best strategies for making files as small as possible is to design for efficient compression. For example, because you know that GIF compression likes flat colors, don't design GIF images with gradient color blends when a flat color will suffice. Similarly, because JPEG likes soft transitions and no hard edges, you can try strategically blurring images that will be saved in JPEG format. These strategies are discussed in more detail later in this chapter.

Use web graphics tools

If you know you will be doing a lot of web production work, it is worth investing in image editing software such as Adobe Photoshop or Adobe (Macromedia) Fireworks.

Figure 19-2 shows the Save for Web & Devices dialog box in Photoshop CS3 and the Optimize and Preview panels in Fireworks 8. We used the Save for Web function in Chapter 18, Web Graphics Basics to resize an image and to make transparency settings. In this chapter, we'll explore the settings that pertain to keeping file sizes as small as possible.

Save for Web & Devices dialog box in Photoshop CS3

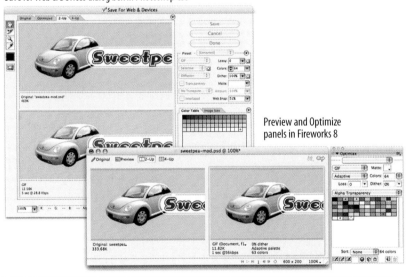

Preview and Optimize panels in Fireworks 8

Figure 19-2. Web graphics optimizing tools in Photoshop CS3 and Fireworks 8

Both tools allow you to preview the final image and its respective file size as you make your optimization settings, so you can tweak settings and see the results instantly. The set of options varies by file type, so I'll explain them one format at a time, starting with that old favorite, GIF.

NOTE

Adobe ImageReady, the web graphics tool bundled with Photoshop versions 6 through CS2, has been discontinued in favor of Fireworks, which Adobe acquired from Macromedia. For this reason, this book sticks with Photoshop and Fireworks. If you have a copy of ImageReady, you will find that the optimization options are a close match to Photoshop's Save for Web & Devices.

JPEG Optimization Tools

If you are really concerned with making the smallest JPEGs possible while maximizing image quality, I recommend checking out specialized compression utilities. These tools have been programmed specifically to work with JPEGs, so they've got fancy algorithms that can compress files much smaller than Photoshop alone.

ProJPEG by BoxTop Software
www.boxtopsoft.com

JPEG Cruncher by Spinwave
www.spinwave.com

Optimizing GIFs

Photoshop CS3

Fireworks 8

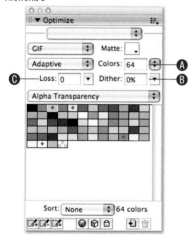

Figure 19-3. GIF optimization options in Photoshop and Fireworks.

When optimizing GIF images, it is useful to keep in mind that GIF compression works by condensing strings of repetitive pixel colors. Many optimization strategies work by creating more areas of solid color for the compression scheme to sink its teeth into.

The general methods for keeping GIF file sizes in check are:

- Reducing the number of colors (the bit-depth) of the image
- Reducing dithering in the image
- Applying a "lossy" filter
- Designing with flat colors

This section looks at each of these options using Photoshop's Save for Web & Devices and Fireworks' Optimize panels as springboards (Figure 19-3). When a feature is specific to these tools, I will note it; otherwise, the approaches shown here should be achievable with most image editing software.

Reducing the number of colors

The most effective way to reduce the size of a GIF file, and therefore the first stop in your optimization journey, is to reduce the number of colors in the image.

Although GIFs can contain up to 256 colors, there's no rule that says they have to. In fact, by reducing the number of colors (bit-depth), you can significantly reduce the file size of an image. One reason for this is that files with lower bit depths contain less data. Another byproduct of the color reduction is that more areas of flat color are created by combining similar, abutting pixel colors. More flat color areas mean more efficient compression.

Nearly all graphics programs that allow you to save or export to GIF format will also allow you to specify the number of colors or bit depth. In Photoshop and Fireworks, the color count and the color table are revealed in the settings panel. Click on the Colors pop-up menu Ⓐ to select from a standard list of numbers of colors. Some tools give you a list of bit-depths instead. See the Bit Depth sidebar for how bit-depths match up to numbers of colors. When you select smaller numbers, the resulting file size shrinks as well.

If you reduce the number of colors too far, of course, the image begins to fall apart or may cease to communicate effectively. For example, in Figure 19-4, once I reduced the number of colors to eight, I lost the rainbow, which was the whole point of the image. This "meltdown" point is different from image to image.

| 256 colors: 21 KB | 64 colors: 13 KB | 8 colors: 6 KB |

Figure 19-4. Reducing the number of colors in an image reduces the file size.

You'll be surprised to find how many images look perfectly fine with only 32 pixel colors (5-bit). That is usually my starting point for color reduction, and I go higher only if necessary. Some image types fare better than others with reduced color palettes, but as a general rule, the fewer the colors, the smaller the file.

NOTE

The real size savings kick in when there are large areas of flat color. Keep in mind that even if your image has 8-pixel colors, if it has a lot of blends, gradients, and detail, you won't see the kind of file size savings you might expect with such a severe color reduction.

Reducing dithering

When the colors in an image are reduced to a specific palette, the colors that are *not* in that palette get approximated by dithering. Dithering is a speckle pattern that results when palette colors are mixed to simulate an unavailable color.

In photographic images, dithering is not a problem and can even be beneficial; however, dithering in flat color areas is usually distracting and undesirable. In terms of optimization, dithering is undesirable because the speckles disrupt otherwise smooth areas of color. Those stray speckles stand in the way of GIF compression and result in larger files.

One way to shave extra bytes off a GIF is to limit the amount of dithering. Again, nearly all GIF creation tools allow you to turn dithering on and off. Photoshop and Fireworks go one step further by allowing you to set the specific amount of dithering on a sliding scale (Figure 19-3, **B**). You can even preview the results of the dither setting, so you can decide at which point the degradation in image quality is not worth the file size savings (Figure 19-5). In images with smooth color gradients, turning dithering off results in unacceptable banding and blotches.

Bit Depth

Bit depth is a way to refer to the maximum number of colors a graphic can contain. This chart shows the number of colors each bit depth can represent:

1-bit	2 colors
2-bit	4 colors
3-bit	8 colors
4-bit	16 colors
5-bit	32 colors
6-bit	64 colors
7-bit	128 colors
8-bit	256 colors

NOTE

If you've been paying attention, you may be thinking that the photo of the barn in this section should be saved as a JPEG, not a GIF. You're absolutely right. Normally, I wouldn't make this photo a GIF, but I'm using it in the examples for this section because it reveals the effects of optimization more dramatically than an image with flat colors. Thank you for bearing with me.

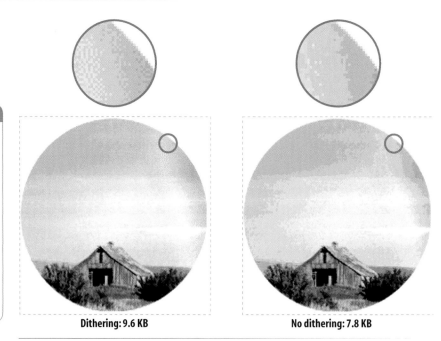

Finding the "Sweet Spot"

You will see that finding the best optimization for a given image requires adjusting all of these attributes (bit-depth, dithering, lossiness) in turn until the best image quality at the smallest file size is achieved. It takes time and practice, but eventually, you will find the "sweet spot" for each image.

Dithering: 9.6 KB　　　　**No dithering: 7.8 KB**

Figure 19-5. Turning off or reducing the amount of dithering reduces the file size. Both images have 32 pixel colors and use an adaptive palette.

Lossy set to 0%: 13.2 KB

Using the lossy filter

As we discussed in Chapter 18, GIF compression is lossless, which means every pixel in the indexed color image is preserved during compression. You can force some pixels to be thrown out prior to compression, however, using the Lossy setting in Photoshop or Loss in Fireworks (Figure 19-3, ❸).

Again, throwing out stray pixels is all in the name of maximizing repetition in strings of pixel colors, allowing GIF compression to do its stuff. Depending on the image, you can apply a loss value of 5% to 30% without seriously degrading the image. Figure 19-6 shows the results of applying Photoshop's Lossy setting to the barn image.

This technique works best for continuous tone art (but then, images that are all continuous tone should probably be saved as JPEGs anyway). You might try playing with lossiness on an image with a combination of flat and photographic content.

Lossy set to 25%: 7.5 KB

Figure 19-6. File size without and with the Lossy setting applied in Photoshop.

Designing for GIF compression

Now that you've seen how high bit-depths and dithering bloat GIF file sizes, you have a good context for my next tip. Before you even get to the point of making optimization settings, you can be proactive about optimizing your graphics by designing them to compress well in the first place.

Keep it flat

I've found that as a web designer, I've changed my illustration style to match the medium. In graphics where I might have used a gradient blend, I now opt for a flat color. In most cases, it works just as well, and it doesn't introduce unflattering banding and dithering or drive up the file size (Figure 19-7). You may also choose to replace areas of photos with subtle blends, such as a blue sky, with flat colors if you need to save them as GIFs (otherwise, the JPEG format may be better).

This GIF has gradient blends and 256 colors. Its file size is **19 KB.**

Even when I reduce the number of colors to 8, the file size is **7.6 KB.**

When I create the same image with flat colors, the size is only **3.2 KB.**

Figure 19-7. You can keep file sizes small by designing in a way that takes advantage of the GIF compression scheme.

Horizontal stripes

Here's an esoteric little tip. When you are designing your web graphics, keep in mind that GIF compression works best on horizontal bands of color. If you want to make something striped, it's better to make the stripes horizontal rather than vertical (Figure 19-8). Silly, but true.

Summing up GIF optimization

The GIF format offers many opportunities for optimization. Designing with flat colors in the first place is a good strategy for creating small GIFs. The next tactic is to save the GIF with the fewest number of colors possible to keep the image intact. Adjusting the amount of dithering and applying a loss filter are additional ways to squeeze out even more bytes.

Exercise 19-1 on the following page gives you a chance to try out some of these techniques.

280 bytes

585 bytes

Figure 19-8. GIFs designed with horizontal bands of color will compress more efficiently than those with vertical bands.

asian.psd; target: **4 to 5 KB**

info.psd; target: **<300 bytes**

bunny.psd; target: **5 to 6 KB**

Figure 19-9. Create GIFs that are optimized to the target file sizes.

Optimizing JPEGs

JPEG optimization is slightly more straightforward than GIF. The general strategies for reducing the file size of JPEGs are:

- Be aggressive with compression

- Use Weighted (Selective) Optimization if available

- Choose Optimized if available

- Soften the image (Blur/Smoothing)

This section explains each approach, again using Photoshop's and Fireworks' optimization tools, shown in Figure 19-10. Notice that there is no color table for JPEGs because they do not use palettes.

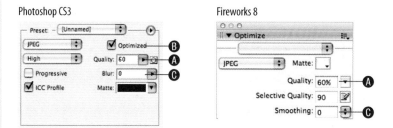

Figure 19-10.   JPEG optimization options in Photoshop's Save for Web & Devices dialog box (left) and Fireworks' Optimize panel (right).

Before we get to specific settings, let's take a look at what JPEG compression is good at. This will provide some perspective for later techniques in this section.

Getting to know JPEG compression

The JPEG compression scheme loves images with subtle gradations, few details, and no hard edges. One way you can keep JPEGs small is to start with the kind of image it likes.

Avoid detail

JPEGs compress areas of smooth blended colors much more efficiently than areas with high contrast and sharp detail. In fact, the blurrier your image, the smaller the resulting JPEG. Figure 19-11 shows two similar graphics with blended colors. You can see that the image with contrast and detail is more than four times larger at the same compression/quality setting.

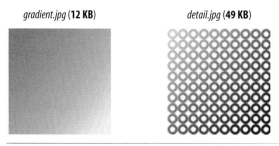

*gradient.jpg (**12 KB**)*   *detail.jpg (**49 KB**)*

Figure 19-11. JPEG compression works better on smooth blended colors than hard edges and detail.

Avoid flat colors

It's useful to know that totally flat colors don't fare well in JPEG format because the colors tend to shift and get mottled as a result of the compression, particularly at higher rates of compression (Figure 19-12). In general, flat graphical images should be saved as GIFs because the image quality will be better and the file size smaller.

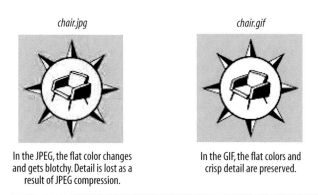

chair.jpg   *chair.gif*

In the JPEG, the flat color changes and gets blotchy. Detail is lost as a result of JPEG compression.

In the GIF, the flat colors and crisp detail are preserved.

Figure 19-12. The same flat graphical image saved as both a JPEG and a GIF.

Be aggressive with compression

The primary tool for optimizing JPEGs is the Quality setting (Figure 19-10, **Ⓐ**). The Quality setting allows you to set the rate of compression; lower quality means higher compression and smaller files. Figure 19-13 shows the results of different quality (compression) rates as applied in Photoshop and Fireworks.

Notice that the image holds up reasonably well, even at very low quality settings. Notice also that the same settings in each program produce different results. This is because the quality rating scale is not objective—it varies from program to program. For example, 1% in Photoshop is similar to 30% in Fireworks and other programs. Furthermore, different images can withstand different amounts of compression. It is best to go by the way the image looks rather than a specific number setting.

Unpredictable Color in JPEGs

In GIF images, you have total control over the colors that appear in the image, making it easy to match RGB colors in adjoining GIFs or in an inline GIF and a background image or color.

Unfortunately, flat colors shift around and get somewhat blotchy with JPEG compression, so there is no way to control the colors precisely. Even pure white can get distorted in a JPEG.

This means there is no guaranteed way to create a perfect, seamless match between a JPEG and another color, whether in a GIF, PNG, another JPEG, or even an RGB background color. If you need a seamless match between the foreground and background image, consider switching formats to GIF or PNG to take advantage of transparency to let the background show through.

Photoshop CS3

Fireworks 8

100% (38.8 KB)   80% (20.7 KB)   100% (51.5 KB)   80% (12.3 KB)

60% (12.8 KB)   40% (8 KB)   60% (7.7 KB)   40% (5 KB)

20% (5.9 KB)   1% (3.4 KB)   20% (1.8 KB)   1% (1.2 KB)

Figure 19-13. A comparison of various compression levels in Photoshop and Fireworks.

Weighted optimization (selective JPEGs)

Not all image areas are created equal. You may wish to preserve detail in one area, such as a person's face, but compress the heck out of the rest of the image. To this end, Photoshop (versions 6 and higher) gives us Weighted Optimization. In Fireworks, it's called Selective Quality. Both methods apply different amounts of JPEG compression within a single image—one setting for a selected area and another setting for the rest of the image.

In both programs, the process starts by using a selection tool to select the area of the image you'd like to preserve. From there, the programs work a little differently.

Using weighted optimization (Photoshop)

In Photoshop, once you've selected the higher-quality areas of the image, save the selection to a new channel (Select → Save Selection) (Figure 19-14, **Ⓐ**) and give the channel a name **Ⓑ**. The white areas of the mask correspond to the highest image quality, while dark areas describe the lowest (gray areas are on a linear scale in between) **Ⓒ**.

In the JPEG options in the Save for Web & Devices dialog box, there is a Mask button next to the Quality setting **Ⓓ**. Clicking the Mask button gives you the Modify Quality Setting dialog box **Ⓔ** where you can set the quality levels for the black (low quality) areas and white (high quality) areas of the masked image. Selecting the Preview option allows you to see the results of your settings. When you are done, click OK, then Save.

NOTE

*Photoshop offers weighted optimization GIFs as well (Fireworks does not). Look for the Mask button like the one pictured in Figure 19-14 **Ⓓ** next to the Palette, Lossy, and Dither options to access the respective settings. Refer to the Photoshop documentation for more detailed instructions.*

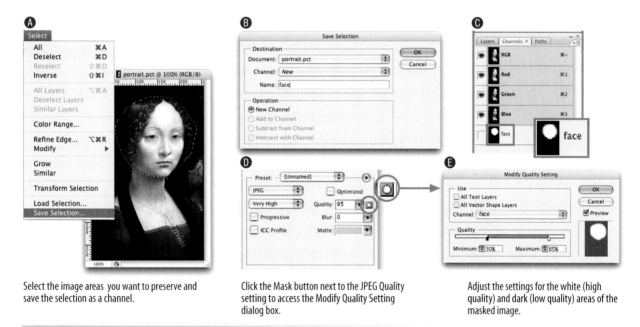

Select the image areas you want to preserve and save the selection as a channel.

Click the Mask button next to the JPEG Quality setting to access the Modify Quality Setting dialog box.

Adjust the settings for the white (high quality) and dark (low quality) areas of the masked image.

Figure 19-14. Using Weighted Optimization in Photoshop CS3.

Using selective quality (Fireworks)

Fireworks has a set of options for creating what it calls "selective JPEGs" (Figure 19-15). Select the areas of the image you want to preserve **Ⓐ**, then select Modify → Selective JPEG → Save Selection as JPEG Mask **Ⓑ**. In the Optimize panel, you can set the Selective Quality for your selection or click the adjacent icon **Ⓒ** to access the Selective JPEG dialog box with a full set of options, such as preserving type and button quality and selecting a color for the masked area. The regular Quality setting will be used for all other areas of the image.

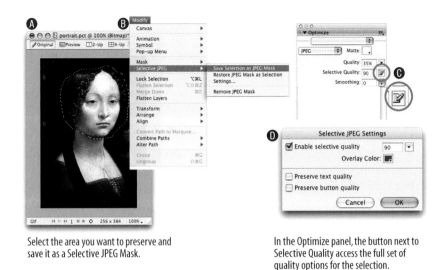

Select the area you want to preserve and save it as a Selective JPEG Mask.

In the Optimize panel, the button next to Selective Quality access the full set of quality options for the selection.

Figure 19-15. *Using Selective Quality in Fireworks 8.*

Quality: 20; Blur: 0 (9.3 KB)

This JPEG was saved at low quality (20% in Photoshop) with no Blur applied.

Choose optimized JPEGs

Optimized JPEGs have slightly smaller file sizes and better color fidelity (although I've never been able to see the difference) than standard JPEGs. For this reason, you should select the Optimized option if your image software offers it (Figure 19-10, **B**). Look for the Optimized option in Photoshop and third-party JPEG compression utilities. Fireworks does not offer the option as of this writing.

Blurring or smoothing the image

Because soft images compress smaller than sharp ones, Photoshop and Fireworks make it easy to blur the image slightly as part of the optimization process. In Photoshop, the tool is called Blur (Figure 19-10, **C**); in Fireworks, it's Smoothing (Figure 19-10, **C**). Blurring makes the JPEG compression work better, resulting in a smaller file (Figure 19-16). If you don't have these tools, you can soften the whole image yourself by applying a slight blur to the image with the Gaussian Blur filter (or similar) manually prior to export.

Quality: 20; Blur: .5 (7.2 KB)

With a Blur setting of only .5, the resulting file size is 22% smaller. In Fireworks, use Smoothing for similar results.

Figure 19-16. *Blurring the image slightly before exporting as a JPEG results in smaller file sizes.*

The downside of Blur and Smoothing filters is that they are applied evenly to the entire image. If you want to preserve detail in certain areas of the image, you can apply a blur filter just to the areas you don't mind being blurry. When you're done, export the JPEG as usual. The blurred areas will take full advantage of the JPEG compression, and your crisp areas will stay crisp. Try combining this selective blurring technique with Weighted Optimization or Selective JPEGs for even more file savings.

Summing up JPEG optimization

Your primary tool for optimizing JPEGs is the Quality (compression) setting. If your tools offer them, making the JPEG Optimized or applying Blur or Smoothing will make them smaller. Again, if JPEG images are central to your site and both size and quality are priorities, you may find that specialized JPEG utilities (listed in the JPEG Optimization Tools sidebar) are worth the investment. They generally produce smaller file sizes with better image quality than Photoshop and Fireworks.

Now it's your turn to play around with JPEGs in Exercise 19-2.

exercise 19-2 | Optimizing JPEGs

Once again, see if you can use the techniques in this section to save the JPEGs in Figure 19-17 in the target file size range. There are no right answers, so follow your preferences. What is important is that you get a feel for how file size and image quality react to various settings.

falcon.tif
target: 35–40 KB

Imagine that this image is going on a site that sells poster where it would be important to preserve the type and painting detail throughout the image. The result is you can't compress it as far as other images.

boats.psd
target: 24–30 KB

Watch for JPEG artifacts around the lines and masts of the boats. Try to keep those lines clean.

penny.tif
target: 12–18 KB

This image is a good candidate for some manual blurring of the background prior to compression.

Figure 19-17. Match the file sizes.

Photoshop CS3

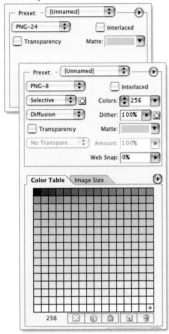

Fireworks 8

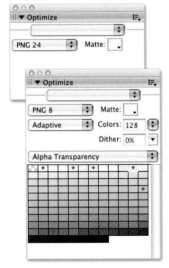

Figure 19-18. PNG-24 and PNG-8 settings in Photoshop and Fireworks.

Optimizing PNGs

As discussed in the previous chapter, there are two types of PNG files: 24-bit PNGs (PNG-24) that contain colors from the millions of colors in the RGB color space, and 8-bit indexed PNGs (PNG-8) with a palette limited to 256 colors. This section looks at what you can (and can't) do to affect the file size both kinds of PNG files.

PNG-24

PNG's lossless compression makes PNG-24 a wonderful format for preserving quality in images, but unfortunately, it makes it a poor option for web graphics. A PNG-24 will always be significantly larger than a JPEG of the same image because no pixels are sacrificed in the compression process. Therefore, your first "lean and mean" strategy is to avoid PNG-24 for photographic images and choose JPEG instead.

The big exception to this rule is if you want to use multiple levels of transparency (alpha transparency). In that case, given today's tools and browsers, PNG-24 is your only option.

There aren't any tricks for reducing the file size of a PNG-24, as evidenced by the lack of options on the PNG-24 export panels (Figure 19-18). You'll have to accept the file size that your image editing tool cranks out.

PNG-8

Indexed color PNGs work similarly to GIFs, and in fact, usually result in smaller file sizes for the same images, making them a good byte-saving option. The general strategies for optimizing GIFs also apply to PNG-8s:

- Reduce the number of colors
- Reduce dithering
- Design with flat colors

You can see that the list of export options for PNG-8s is more or less the same as for GIF (Figure 19-18). The notable exception is that there is no "lossy" filter for PNGs as there is for GIFs. Otherwise, all of the techniques listed in the Optimizing GIFs section apply to PNGs as well.

It is worth noting that making a PNG interlaced significantly increases its file size, by as much as 20 or 30 percent. It is best to avoid this option unless you deem it absolutely necessary to have the image appear in a series of passes.

NOTE

I have not included an exercise specifically for PNGs because there are no new settings or strategies to explore. However, you should feel free to try making PNG-8s and PNG-24s out of the images in the previous two exercises, and see how they compare to their GIF and JPEG counterparts.

Optimize to File Size

One last optimizing technique is good to know about if you use Photoshop or Fireworks.

In some instances, you may need to optimize a graphic to hit a specific file size, for example, when designing an ad banner with a strict K-limit. Both Photoshop and Fireworks offer an Optimize to File Size function. You just set the desired file size and let the program figure out the best settings to use to get there, saving you lots of time finagling with settings.

This feature is pretty straightforward to use. In Photoshop, choose "Optimize to File Size" from the Options pop-up menu in the Save for Web & Devices dialog box . In Fireworks, choose "Optimize to Size" from the Options pop-up menu in the Optimize panel (Figure 19-19). All you need to do is type in your desired target size and click OK. The tool does the rest.

Photoshop also asks if you'd like to start with your own optimization settings or let Photoshop select GIF or JPEG automatically. Curiously, PNG is not an option for automatic selection, so start with your own settings if you want to save as PNG.

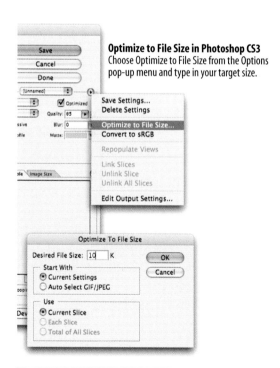

Optimize to File Size in Photoshop CS3
Choose Optimize to File Size from the Options pop-up menu and type in your target size.

Optimize to Size in Fireworks 8
Choose Optimize to Size from the Options pop-up menu and type in your target size.

Figure 19-19. Optimizing to a specific file size (in Photoshop and Fireworks).

Optimization in Review

If this collection of optimization techniques feels daunting, don't worry. After a while, they'll become part of your standard production process. You'll find it's easy to keep your eye on the file size and make a few setting tweaks to bring that number down. Now that you have the added advantage of understanding what the various settings are doing behind the scenes, you can make informed and efficient optimization decisions.

Combine your new graphics production skills with your knowledge of (X) HTML and style sheets, and you've got what it takes to put together a complete web site. But we're not quite through. In Part V, we'll take a birds-eye view at the web site production process as well as how to get your site on the Web.

Test Yourself

Now that you're acquainted with the world of graphics optimization, it's time to take a little test. I know you'll ace it.

1. Why do professional web designers optimize their graphics?

2. How does dithering affect the file size of a GIF?

3. How does the number of pixel colors affect the file size of a GIF?

4. What is the most effective setting for optimizing a JPEG?

5. How does the Blur or Smoothing setting affect JPEG size?

6. What is the best way to optimize a PNG-8? A PNG-24?

FROM START TO FINISH

PART V

THE SITE DEVELOPMENT PROCESS

By now you are familiar with (X)HTML and CSS, but markup and visual design are only pieces of the whole web design process. In this chapter and the following, we'll broaden the scope to consider the big picture of how sites get built and published to the Web.

Web sites come in all shapes and sizes—from a single page résumé to megasites conducting business for worldwide corporations and everything in between. Regardless of the scale, the process for developing a site involves the same basic steps:

1. Conceptualize and research.

2. Create and organize content.

3. Develop the "look and feel."

4. Produce a working prototype.

5. Test it.

6. Launch the site.

7. Maintain.

Of course, depending on the nature and scale of the site, these steps will vary in sequence, proportion, and number of people required, but in essence, they are the aspects of a typical journey in the creation of a site. This chapter examines each step of the web design process.

1. Conceptualize and Research

Every web site begins with an idea. It's the result of some*one* wanting to get some*thing* online, be it for personal or commercial ends. This early phase is exciting. You start with the core idea ("photo album for my family," "shopping site for skateboarding gear," "online banking," etc.) then brainstorm on how it's going to manifest itself as a web site. This is a time for lists and sketches, whiteboards and notebooks. What's going to make it exciting? What's going to be on the first page?

IN THIS CHAPTER

The standard steps in the web design process:

Conceptualization and research

Content organization and creation

Art direction

Prototype building

Testing

Site launch

Maintenance

Some Questions Before You Begin

This is just a small sampling of the questions you should ask yourself or your clients during the research phase of design.

Strategy

- Why are you creating this web site? What do you expect to accomplish?
- What are you offering your audience?
- What do you want users to do on your web site? After they've left?
- What brings your visitors back?

General Site Description

- What kind of site is it? (Purely promotional? Info-gathering? A publication? A point of sale?)
- What features will it have?
- What are your most important messages?
- Who are your competitors? What are they doing right? What could be improved upon?

Target Audience

- Who is your primary audience?
- How Internet-savvy are they? How technically savvy?
- Can you make assumptions about an average user's connection speed? Platform? Monitor size? Browser use?
- How often do you expect them to visit your site? How long will they stay during an average visit?

Content

- Who is responsible for generating original content?
- How will content be submitted (process and format)?
- How often will the information be updated (daily, weekly, monthly)?

Resources

- What resources have you dedicated to the site (budget, staff, time)?
- Does the site require a full content management system?
- Can maintenance be handled by the client's staff?
- Do you have a server for your site?
- Have you registered a domain name for your site?

Graphic Look and Feel

- Are you envisioning a certain look and feel for the site?
- Do you have existing standards, such as logos and colors, that must be incorporated?
- Is the site part of a larger site or group of sites with design standards that need to be matched?
- What are some other web sites you like? What do you like about them? What sites do you not like?

Many web development and design firms spend more time on researching and identifying clients' needs than on any other stage of production.

Don't bother launching an HTML editor until you have your ideas and strategy together. This involves asking your client (or yourself) a number of questions regarding resources, goals, and, most importantly, audience. The Some Questions Before You Begin sidebar provides just a sampling of the sorts of questions you might ask before you start a project.

Many large web development and design firms spend more time on researching and identifying clients' needs than on any other stage of production. For large sites, this step may include case studies, interviews, and extensive market research. There are even firms dedicated to developing web strategies for emerging and established companies.

You may not need to put that sort of effort (or money) into a web site's preparation, but it is still wise to be clear about your expectations and resources early on in the process, particularly when attempting to work within a budget.

2. Create and Organize Content

The most important part of a web site is its content. Despite the buzz about technologies and tools, content is still king on the Internet. There's got to be something of value, whether it's something to read, something to do, or something to buy that attracts visitors and keeps them coming back. Even if you are working as a freelancer, it is wise to be sensitive to the need for good content.

The most important part of a web site is its content.

Content creation

When creating a site for a client, you need to immediately establish who will be responsible for generating the content that goes on the site. Some clients arrive full of ideas but empty-handed, assuming that you will create the site and all of the content in it. Ideally, the client is responsible for generating its own content and will allocate the appropriate resources to do so. Solid copy writing is an important, yet often overlooked component of a successful site.

Solid copy writing is an important, yet often overlooked component of a successful site.

Information design

Once you've got content—or at least a very clear idea of what content you will have—the next step is to organize the content so it will be easily and intuitively accessible to your audience. For large sites, the information design may be handled by a specialist in information architecture. It might also be decided by a team made up of designers and the client. Even personal sites require attention to the division and organization of information.

Again, this is a time for lists and sketchbooks. Get everything that you want in the site out there on the table. Organize it by importance, timeliness, category, and so on. Decide what goes on the home page and what gets divided into sections. Think about how your users would expect to find information on your site and design with their needs and assumptions in mind.

The result of the information design phase may be a diagram (often called a site map) that reveals the overall "shape" of the site. Pages in diagrams are usually represented by rectangles; arrows indicate links between pages or sections of the site. The site map gives designers a sense of the scale of the site and how sections are related, and aids in the navigation design.

Figure 20-1 is a diagram of a small self-promotional site. It is tiny compared to the diagrams for sprawling corporate or e-commerce sites, but it demonstrates how pages and the connections between pages are represented. I once saw a site diagram for a high-profile commercial site that, despite using postage stamp–sized boxes to represent pages, filled the length and height of the hallway.

DESIGN TIP

Viva la Pen and Paper!

There's still no beating pen and paper when it comes to firing up and documenting the creative process. Before you delve into the (X)HTML and GIFs, there's no better way to hash out your ideas quickly than in your handy notepad, on a napkin or whiteboard, or whatever surface is available. It's about creativity.

Make lists. Draw diagrams. Figure out that home page. Do it fast and loose, or include every minute detail and copy it faithfully online. It all comes down to your personal style.

The effectiveness of a site's organization can make or break it. Don't underestimate the importance of this step.

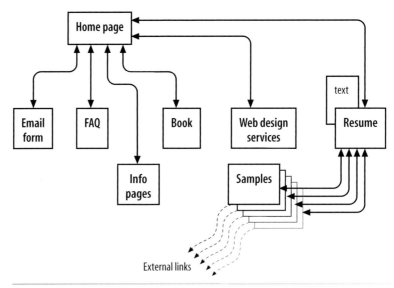

Figure 20-1. A simple site diagram.

3. Develop the "Look and Feel"

The look and feel of a site refers to its graphic design and overall visual appearance, including its color scheme, typography, and image style (for example, photographic versus illustrative). You may also hear the visual design of a site referred to as the theme or skin. As in the print world, this phase of design is often referred to as art direction.

Sketch it

This is another chance to get out pads of paper and markers. Or perhaps you prefer to work out ideas right in Photoshop. Either way, it's your chance to be creative and try things. The result is one or more sketches (sometimes called a look and feel study) that show off your proposed visual style for the site.

A sketch is usually just a flat graphic file in the approximate dimensions of the browser window. When it is necessary to show interactivity (such as a "rollover" button effect), some designers use a layer in Photoshop that can be switched on and off to simulate the effect.

In some cases, it may be necessary to create a prototype home page in HTML to show off interactive and animated features, particularly if you have a client with no imagination (but a big budget to cover development costs). Keep in mind that the art direction phase is for exploring how the site will look, so flat graphic sketches are usually adequate.

The art direction process

In most professional web development jobs, the client receives two or three sketches showing its home page in various visual styles. In some cases, a second- or third-level design might be included if it is important to show how the design plays out through several levels. Figure 20-2 shows a set of look-and-feel studies I created for a women's site several years ago.

Ideally, the graphic designer is given a list of what must appear on the page, including required images, navigational elements, and a manuscript for the text. There may also be a wireframe diagram of the functionality as worked out by an interface designer. That is the best case scenario; don't be surprised if you are asked to make stuff up on occasion.

After reviewing the sketches, the client picks one sketch, often with a list of changes, requiring another round of design until the final design is agreed upon. In my experience, clients usually see elements they like in each style and ask for some sort of hybrid. Some clients request more and more sketches. See the sidebar, Get It in Writing, for tips on keeping the process under control.

4. Produce a Working Prototype

Once the design is approved and the content is ready to go, the site enters the production phase. For small sites, the production may be done by one person (see the sidebar, Solo Production Process). It is more common in commercial web design to have a team of people working on specialized tasks.

The art department uses its graphics tools to create all the graphics needed for the site. The production department marks up the content with (X)HTML and formats the text with style sheets. They may create final pages or simply templates that get filled out with content on the fly. Programmers write the scripts and server-side applications necessary to make the site function as intended. There may also be multimedia elements such as videos or Flash movies. In short, all of the parts of the site must be built.

At some point, all the pieces are brought together into a working site. This is not necessarily a distinct step; it is more likely to be an ongoing process. As in software design, the first prototype is often called the "alpha" release. It might be made available only to people within the web team for review and revisions before it is released to the client. After changes, the second release is called the "beta." The client should certainly be involved by this phase, if not sooner. At this point, there is still plenty to do before the site is ready to go live

Figure 20-2. *As part of the art direction phase, I created three sketches for this women's site, demonstrating how the same material might look in three different visual styles.*

on the Web. There are also sites out there, often web applications and services, that make their beta versions open to the public or a limited subscriber base in order to gather valuable feedback.

Solo Production Process

It is perfectly possible to create an entire web site by yourself; in fact, that is one of the cool things about the Web. If you are flying solo, as I do, your production process might go something like this:

1. Sketch out the structure of the home page and second-level pages. You might do this as a simple sketch on paper or you might develop the page structure and its look in Photoshop.

2. Create the (X)HTML documents and images. If you are using a style sheet, you should start it as well. Same goes for scripts.

3. Put the pieces together and look at the page in the browser. If you are using a WYSIWYG web authoring tool, you should still open it in a browser since the layout view is not always accurate. There are some styles and behaviors that can be tested only in the browser.

4. Make changes as necessary to the (X)HTML documents, images, styles, and scripts.

5. Save your changes and reload in the browser (or several browsers).

6. Repeat steps 4 and 5 until the pages are finished.

7. Upload it to the server and test it again.

5. Test It

All web sites need to be tested before they are ready for the public. Professional web developers build time and resources into the production schedule for rigorous testing, but even personal pages need to be taken for a spin around the block before the official launch. Whether formally or informally, sites should be tested for basic functionality, performance in different browsing environments, and how easy they are to use.

The site may be tested locally (on your own hard drive) prior to uploading to its final home on the web server. It is also useful to set up a hidden testing site on the server so that the kinks can be worked out in its natural environment before making it live.

Basic quality check

At minimum, all sites should be tested to make sure they work. In the web design biz, checking a site for basic functionality is one part of what is often called the QA (short for quality assurance) phase of production.

The following questions address some of the minimal requirements before publishing a site to the Web.

Is all the content there? Make sure that none of your content is missing, whether as the result of a markup glitch or miscommunication.

Are there typos or grammar errors? The importance of proofreading a site is often overlooked, but errors in copy can seriously damage the perceived credibility of your site. Make sure all copy is read carefully, preferably by more than one person.

Do all the links work? It's very easy to leave links un-linked during the production process. It is also possible that some files may have been moved around but the links were not updated. Before you go live, have someone click every link on every page to make sure there are no dead ends.

Are all the images showing? Confirm that all the graphic files are in the proper directory and that the correct pathname is used in the `img` elements to avoid missing image icons.

Are all the scripts and applications functioning properly? Run the pages through a few typical user scenarios (filling out forms, buying a product, or whatever interaction make sense for your site) to be sure that everything is working as it should.

Browsing environment testing

As discussed in Chapter 3, The Nature of Web Design, your site will be viewed on a wide range of browsing environments that will impact the way it looks and functions. Another part of quality assurance is to test your pages under as many conditions as possible.

Professional developers typically maintain computers running different operating systems and numerous browser versions for testing purposes. If you are a solo or hobbyist web designer, you will benefit from just looking at your site on a friend's computer that has a different operating system and browser than you used when you created your site.

A robust site will fare well when tested according to the following criteria.

How does the page look in different browsers? On another platform? Browsers are notoriously uneven in their support of Cascading Style Sheets, so if you use CSS for page layout, it is critical that you view your pages in as many graphical browsers as possible. I often use a service called Browsercam (*browsercam.com*) that allows me to view my page in many browser versions without needing to run them on my own machines.

How does the site work in different browsers? On another platform? Similarly, there are browser differences in script support, so run your functionality tests under more than browser/platform configuration. (Unfortunately, Browsercam won't test functionality.)

What happens to the pages when the browser window is resized very large? Very small? What happens if the text is zoomed very large or very small? Can your site withstand a certain amount window and text resizing? Does content fall off the screen? Does the page fall apart?

Is the site usable on a text-only browser? What will users see if they access your page with a mobile phone or PDA? If you've written your (X)HTML documents well, they should be accessible on all manner of browsing devices. Still, it's worthwhile to look at your site under minimal conditions to see if you can make any tweaks to improve the experience.

Is the site usable with the graphics turned off? Some users with slower connections may surf the Web with graphics turned off in the browser to speed up the content display. Some browsers display the alternative text for each image element, but others don't. Have you accommodated those users?

What happens if the user is not able to view the multimedia elements? It would be nice if every user was guaranteed to have the plug-ins required to view media such as Flash movies or Windows Media, but unfortunately, that is not the case. Do you provide help getting the plug-ins they need? Are there alternative versions of your content for those unable to view the media?

What is it like to look at your site on a dial-up modem connection? There is still a significant portion of users accessing the Web over slow connections. Is there anything you can do to make your pages load more quickly?

User testing

Another type of testing that is important to perform is user testing. This process involves sitting people down with your site and seeing how easily they can find information and complete tasks. Ideally, user testing is conducted as early in the development process as possible so the site design can be adjusted before the serious production begins. It is not uncommon to do additional usability testing at regular intervals throughout the production process and even after the site has launched, so that the site can be tweaked to better serve the needs of its visitors.

There are companies that you can hire to run controlled tests for you, but the price is usually steep, making it an option only for commercial web sites with serious budgets. However, it is possible to run informal user testing on your family members, friends, coworkers, and anyone you can get to sit in front of the computer and answer a few questions.

There are two general kinds of user testing: general observed behavior and task-oriented testing. In the first, you sit the testing subject down with the site and let them explore it on their own. They provide feedback as they go along, noting what they like, don't like, what's clear, what's confusing.

In task-oriented testing, users are given a series of tasks of varying difficulty to perform on the site, such as "Find out if there are any upcoming workshops on glassblowing," or, "Find out who is offering the best price on camcorders." An observer takes notes on how efficiently the task is completed, as well as the links the user followed in the course of completing the task.

Some questions you might want to answer through user testing are:

- Can users tell at a glance what the site is about?

- Are there any obstacles in the way of accomplishing goals? Can they quickly find critical information or make a purchase?

- Do the test subjects seem to enjoy using the site?

- Is there a particular task or site feature that seems to be tripping up multiple users?

FURTHER READING

User testing is a rich and complex topic well beyond the scope of this chapter. For more insight, I recommend the book *Observing the User Experience* by Mike Kuniavsky (Morgan Kaufmann Publishers, 2003).

6. Launch the Site

Once you have all the kinks worked out of the site, it's time to upload it to the final server and make it available to the world.

It's a good idea to do one final round of testing to make sure everything was transferred successfully and the pages function properly under the configuration of the final server. This may seem like extra work, but if the reputation of your business (or your client's business) is riding on the success of the web site, attention to detail is essential.

With the working site online, it's time to take yourself or your team out for a a good dinner or a round of drinks (well, that's what I would do).

7. Maintain the Site

A web site is never truly "done;" in fact, the ability to make updates and keep content current is one of the advantages of the web medium. It is important to have a strategy for what will happen with the site after its initial launch.

Although maintenance is an ongoing process that happens after the site is initially created, decisions regarding maintenance should be made early in the development process. For instance, you should be clear up front about who will be responsible for site upkeep. If you are a freelancer, this should be included in the contract you sign when you begin the job. You should also decide what parts of the site will be updated, and how frequently. The refresh rate will affect the way you organize information and design the site.

You should also consider the lifespan of the site. If it is a site promoting a specific event, what happens to the site when the event is over? Even sites that are designed to be around a while will usually require a redesign after a few years to keep up with changes in content and current publishing practices.

The Development Process in Review

Hopefully, this chapter gives you a feel for all of the work that goes into a typical site. Regardless of the role you play in the process, it is important to be familiar with the other steps along the way. As I mentioned earlier, the steps may not occur in exactly the same order listed here. You should also be prepared for any given step to entail a great deal of work, particularly for larger commercial sites.

Test Yourself

How familiar are you with these basic terms in the web design process? Answers can be found in Appendix A.

1. What is a site diagram for? At what point in the process would you make one?

2. What is a "look and feel" study?

3. Name three things that should be done or decided before the first HTML document is created.

4. What is a beta release? Who is likely to look at it?

5. Name four things for which *every* web site should be tested.

GETTING YOUR PAGES ON THE WEB

Because your browser can display documents right from your hard drive (in other words, you can view them locally), you do not need an Internet connection to create web pages. However, eventually, you'll want to get them out there for the world to see. That is the point, right?

Putting a page on the Web is easy... just transfer your files to your web server and *ta da*—you're on the Web! But what if you don't have a web server? This chapter will tell you where to look for one (you might even have server space and not know it). You might also want your own domain name. For example, I have littlechair.com and several others.

This chapter tells you what you need to know about registering a domain name and getting a server for your web site. We'll also look at the steps involved in the typical web publishing process, including how to use FTP programs to transfer files.

IN THIS CHAPTER

Registering your own domain name

Finding a server to host your web site

The general web publishing process, step-by-step

Using FTP to upload files

www."YOU".com!

Your home page address is your identity on the Web. If you are posting a just-for-fun page and want to save money, having your own personal corner at some larger domain (such as *www.earthlink.com/members/~littlechair* or *littlechair.blogspot.com*) might be fine. More likely, you'll want your own domain name that better represents your business or content. For a small yearly fee, anyone can register a domain name.

What's in a name?

A domain name is a human-readable name associated with a numeric IP address (the "IP" stands for Internet Protocol) on the Internet. While computers know that my site is on a server at Internet point 66.226.64.6, you and I can just call it "littlechair.com." The IP address is important, though, because you'll need one (well, two, usually) to register your domain name.

How Much Does a Domain Cost?

While it may seem overwhelming to choose from all the competing domain name sellers, the up side is that it has resulted in lower prices. The base price for registering a domain is about $35 per year; however, there are usually deep discounts for registering for more than one year. The longest any domain can be secured is 10 years.

There are domain registries that offer rock-bottom rates, but you may pay the price of being bludgeoned with advertising for their other services, such as web hosting.

There are also optional additional fees to be aware of. For instance, registrars now offer a service in which they keep your contact information private for about $10 a year (as of this writing). Without that service, the information you provide (including your address) is accessible to the public.

TIP

Because there are so many sources for domain names, it is easy to end up with domains registered with several different companies. While there is no rule against this, people who maintain multiple domains find it more convenient to have all their names registered at the same place. This makes it easier to handle billing and keep up with expirations and renewals.

Registering a domain

Registering a domain name is easy and fairly inexpensive. There are two ways to go about it: have your hosting company do it for you or get one directly from a registrar.

It has become common for companies that provide web hosting to register domain names as part of the process of setting up an account. They offer this service for your one-stop-shopping convenience. But be sure to ask specifically—some still require you to register your domain on your own.

You can also register one yourself directly from a domain name registrar. Domain name registries are regulated and overseen by ICANN (Internet Corporation for Assigned Names and Numbers). ICANN also makes sure that domain names are assigned to a single owner. There used to be just one domain name registrar, Network Solutions, but now there are hundreds of ICANN accredited registrars and countless more resellers.

You'll have to do your own research to find a registrar you like. To see the complete list of accredited registrars, go to *www.internic.net/regist.html*. Some of the most popular are Network Solutions (*www.networksolutions.com*), the original domain registrar; Register.com (*www.register.com*), which has also been around a long time; and GoDaddy (*www.godaddy.com*), known for its rock-bottom prices.

All registrars in the U.S. can register domain names ending in *.com*, *.net*, or *.org*, while some offer newer and international extensions (see the sidebar, Dot What?).

A domain registration company will ask you for the following:

- An administrative contact for the account (name and address)

- A billing contact for the account (name and address)

- A technical contact for the account (generally the name and address of your hosting service)

- Two IP addresses

If you don't have IP addresses, most domain registry services will offer to "park" the site for you for an additional fee. Parking a site means that you have reserved the domain name, but you can't actually *do* anything with it until you get a real server for the site. Basically, you're paying for the privilege of borrowing some IP addresses. Be sure to shop wisely. In addition to the $35 per year registration fee, do not spend more than $35 to $50 per year to park a site. As mentioned earlier, some domain registration companies also offer basic hosting services.

Is it available?

You might have already heard that the simple domain names in the coveted *.com* top-level domain are heavily picked over. Before you get too attached to a specific name, you should do a search to see if it is still available. All of the domain name registration sites feature a domain name search right on the front page. This is the first step for setting up a new domain.

If "your-domain-name" at ".com" is not available, try one of the other top level domain suffixes, such as *.org*, *.info*, or *.us*. You may also try variations on the name itself. For example, if I found that *jenrobbins.com* wasn't available, I might be willing to settle for *jenrobbinsonline.com* or *jenniferrobbins.com*. Some registrar sites will provide a list of available alternatives for you.

If you have your heart set on a domain name and a budget to back it up, you might offer to purchase the domain from its owner. To find out who owns a domain name, you can do a WhoIs search on that domain. The WhoIs database lists the name and contact information for every domain (unless the owner paid extra to keep the contact information private). You can find a WhoIs search function on most registrars' sites.

Finding Server Space

For your pages to be on the Web, they must reside on a web server. Although it is possible to run web server software on your desktop computer (in fact, every new Mac comes with web server software installed; the same is true for almost all GNU/Linux distributions and to some extent Windows), it's more likely that you'll want to rent some space on a server that is dedicated to the task. Looking for space on a web server is also called finding a host for your site.

Fortunately, there are many hosting options, ranging in price from free to many thousands of dollars a year. The one you choose should match your publishing goals. Will your site be business or personal? Will it get a few hits a month or thousands? Do you need services such as e-commerce or streaming media? How much can you (or your client) afford to pay for hosting services?

If you are working as a freelancer, your clients will probably assume the responsibility of setting up server space for their sites. Smaller clients may ask for your assistance in finding space, so it is good to be familiar with the available options.

In this section, I'll introduce you to some of the options available for getting your web pages online. This should give you a general idea of what type of service you need. However, you should still count on doing a fair amount of research to find the one that's right for you.

NOTE

With hosting services offering to register domain names, and domain registrars offering hosting services, the line has really blurred between these two services. But be aware that getting your domain name and finding a server for your web site are indeed separate tasks. It is fine to get hosting from one company and your domain from someone else.

Dot What?

The majority of web sites that you hear about end with *.com*, but there are other suffixes available for different purposes. These suffixes, used for indicating the type of site, are called top-level domains (or TLDs). The most common top-level domains in the United States are the original six generic TLDs established in the 1980s:

.com	commercial/business
.org	nonprofit organization
.edu	educational institutions
.net	network organizations
.mil	military
.gov	government agencies

Since then, additional TLDs have been added, including .aero, .biz, .cat, .coop, .info, .int, .jobs, .mobi, .museum, .name, .pro, .travel, plus scores of two-letter country code TLDs.

To view the current complete list of TDS, see *www.icann.org/registries/top-level-domains.htm*.

In your own backyard

You may not need to shop around for hosting at all. If one of these scenarios describes you, you may have server space there for the taking.

Student account. If you are a student, you may be given some space to publish personal pages as part of your school account. Ask the department that gives you your email account how to take advantage of web space.

Online services and ISPs. If you have an account with an online service such as America Online (*www.aol.com*) or CompuServe (*www.compuserve.com*), you probably already have some web server space just waiting to be filled. Apple Computer offers web space for Mac owners with .Mac accounts. The online services usually provide tools, templates, and other assistance for making web pages and getting them online. Likewise, ISPs (Internet Service Providers) such as Earthlink provide as much as 10 MB of web server space for their members.

Company servers. If you are working as an in-house web designer, it is likely that there will be a server connected to your company's network. If this is the case, you can just copy your files to the specified server machine. Web design firms usually have servers for testing purposes.

Professional hosting services

If you are working on a serious business site, or if you are just serious about your personal web presence, you will need to rent server space from a professional hosting service. What you're paying for is some space on one of their servers, an amount of bandwidth per month over their Internet connection, and technical support. They may also provide such additional services as mailing lists, shopping carts, and so on. The hosting service is responsible for making sure your site is online and available around the clock, 24/7.

Hosting companies usually offer a range of server packages, from just a few megabytes (MB) of space and one email address to full-powered e-commerce solutions with lots of bells and whistles. Of course, the more server space and more features, the higher your monthly bill will be, so shop wisely.

ISPs vs. Hosting Services

There are two types of Internet services, and they are easily confused.

An ISP (Internet Service Provider) is the company you go to if you want access to the Internet from your home or office. You can think of an ISP as a provider of a pipeline from your computer to the worldwide network of the Internet via dial-up, DSL, cable modem, or ISDN connections. AOL, CompuServe, and Earthlink are examples of nationwide ISPs, but there are also smaller, local ISPs in nearly every urban area.

In this chapter, we're talking about hosting services. Their business is based on renting out space on their computers. They take care of the server software, keeping the lines working, and so on. They also provide email accounts and may also include special features such mailing lists or e-commerce solutions for your site. There are thousands of hosting services out there.

The slightly confusing part is that many ISPs also give you some space on a server to host your personal pages. If you put your pages here, you will be stuck with the ISP name in your URL. In other words, they generally don't host other domain names; you need a hosting service for that.

Professional hosting services, however, do not tend to offer Internet access. They expect you to take care of that yourself. In most cases, you'll need both an ISP and a hosting company.

Advantages:

Scalable packages offer solutions for every size of web site. With some research, you can find a host that matches your requirements and budget.

You get your own domain name (for example, *littlechair.com*).

Disadvantages:

Finding the right one requires research (see the Shopping for Hosting Services sidebar).

Robust server solutions can get expensive, and you need to watch for hidden charges.

Shopping for Hosting Services

When you set out to find a host for your web site, you should begin by assessing your needs. The following are some of the first questions you should ask yourself or your client:

Is it a business or personal site? Some hosting services charge higher rates for business sites than for personal sites. Make sure you are signing up for the appropriate hosting package for your site, and don't try to sneak a commercial site onto a personal account.

Do you need a domain name? Check to see whether the hosting company will register a domain name for you as part of the package price. This saves you a step and the extra charge for domain registration somewhere else.

How much space do you need? Most small sites will be fine with 10 MB or 15 MB of server space. You may want to invest in more if your site has hundreds of pages, a large number of graphics, or a significant number of audio and video files that take up more space.

Do you need a dedicated server? Most hosting plans are for shared servers, which, as it sounds, means that your site will share space on a computer with many other sites. For most sites, this is fine, although it is important to be aware that excessive traffic to another site on the server may impact your site's performance. Some larger commercial sites where performance is critical opt for a dedicated server so they can take advantage of the full processing power of that machine. Dedicated server plans tend to be significantly more expensive than shared plans, but it may be money well spent for processing-intensive sites.

How much traffic will you get? Be sure to pay attention to the amount of data transfer you're allowed per month. This is a function of the size of your files and the amount of traffic you'll get (i.e., the number of downloads to browsers). Most hosting services offer 5–10 gigabytes (GB) of throughput a month, which is perfectly fine for low- or moderate-traffic sites, but after that, they start charging per megabyte. If you are serving media files such as audio or video, this can really add up. I once ran a popular site with a number of movies that turned out to have over 30 GB of data transferred a month. Fortunately, I had a service with unlimited data transfer (there are a few out there), but with another hosting company I could have racked up an extra $500 per month in fees.

How many email accounts do you need? Consider how many people will want email at that domain when you're shopping for the right server package. If you need many email accounts, you may need to go with a more robust and higher-priced package.

Do you need extra functionality? Many hosting services offer special web site features—some come as part of their standard service and others cost extra money. They range from libraries of spiffy scripts (for email forms or guestbooks) all the way up to complete, secure e-commerce solutions. When shopping for space, consider whether you need extra features, such as shopping carts, secure servers (for credit card transactions), a streaming media server (for streaming audio and video), mailing lists, and so on.

Do you feel comfortable with their level of technical support? Take a look at the hosting company's policies and record on technical support. Do they provide a phone number (preferable), live online chat with technicians, or just an email address for customer service? It is important to know that your hosting company will be there to answer your questions promptly.

Will they do regular backups? Ask whether the hosting company does regular backups of your data in case there is a problem with the server.

Do you want to be a reseller? If you run a web design business and anticipate finding server space for multiple clients, you may want to become a hosting reseller. Many hosting companies have programs in which they provide multiple server plans at discount prices. You can pass the savings along to your clients or mark up the price to compensate yourself for the administrative overhead.

Once you've identified your needs, it's time to do some hunting. First, ask your friends and colleagues if they have hosting services that they can recommend. There's nothing like firsthand experience from someone you trust. After that, the Web is the best place to do research. The following sites provide reviews and comparisons of various hosting services; they can be good starting points for your server shopping spree:

CNET Web Hosting Reviews
www.cnet.com (look for Web Hosting under Reviews)

HostIndex
www.hostindex.com

TopHosts.com
www.tophosts.com

Free hosting options

If you just want to publish a personal site and don't want to sink any money into it, there are many services out there that offer free space on the Web.

Free hosting services. Believe it or not, some companies give server space away for free! The downsides are that you can not have your own domain name, and they may put their advertising on your pages. A good place to start looking for free web hosting is *www.freewebspace.net* or do a web search for "free web hosting."

Blogging services. If you just want to publish a blog (short for web log, an online journal), you can take advantage of one of the free blogging services. They allow you to publish the type of information typically found on a blog page: entries, comments, blogroll (list of similar blogs), etc. Some of the most popular are *Blogger.com*, *LiveJournal.com*, and *Typepad.com* (which charges a small monthly fee), but if you do a web search for "free blog hosting," you'll find many more to explore.

Online community sites. Online community sites such as Yahoo! GeoCities (*geocities.yahoo.com*) or Tripod (*www.tripod.lycos.com*) organize their members' sites into categories, so people with similar interests can find each other. In exchange for free space, they put ads on the members' content.

Social network sites. Another arena for publishing your blogs, photos, music, and so on is to join one of the popular social network sites. These sites link their members together by friend (and friend-of-a-friend) connections. Some popular social network sites as of this writing are *MySpace.com*, *Friendster.com*, and *Facebook.com*; however, this is a rapidly expanding use of the Web, so they may not be the latest and greatest networks by the time you are reading this book. These services may place limitations on the type of content you can publish and offer varying levels of customization, so it's not the same as publishing your own site on their servers.

The Publishing Process

So, you've got your domain and your hosting all lined up... what now? This is a good time to review the typical steps involved in creating and publishing a site to the Web. Not every site follows these exact steps, but this will give you a general idea of the process.

❶ **Create a directory (folder) for the site on your computer.** This will be your local root directory. "Local" means it resides on your hard drive, and "root" is the technical term used to refer to a top-level directory for site. This is where you save all of the documents that make up the site and will be transferred to the actual web server. Additional files related to the site, such as layered Photoshop files, raw content documents, and other miscellaneous development documents should be kept in a separate directory. In Figure 21-1, I named my local root directory *jenskitchen*.

Advantages:

It's free!

Good for personal and hobbyist web pages. Also a good option for teens with limited budgets.

Depending on the service you choose, you could potentially find people with similar interests.

Disadvantages:

You may be stuck with annoying ad banners or pop-up windows.

You may be limited in the type of content you can publish.

You may have limited control over page layout and navigation.

You generally don't get your own domain name.

Not appropriate for business sites.

NOTE

On the Web, it is more appropriate to use the terms "directory" and "subdirectory" rather than "folder" and "subfolder." This is due to the fact that servers have come to be discussed using UNIX terminology, whereas folders are a convention of operating systems with graphical interfaces, such as Windows or MacOS.

❷ **Create the web page(s).** This is the step that takes all the hard work, as you know from reading the rest of this book. It's important to note that all the HTML and image files for this simple site have been saved in the local root directory, *jenskitchen*.

❸ **Check the page locally.** Before making the page live, it is a good idea to check the page in a browser while it's still on your own machine. Just launch your favorite browser and open the (X)HTML file for the page from your hard drive, as shown in Figure 21-1. If it needs some adjustments, go back and edit the (X)HTML and/or CSS files and save them. You must save the files in order to see changes in the browser (be sure to save it in the same directory so it overwrites the old version). Now click Refresh or Reload in the browser to see how it looks.

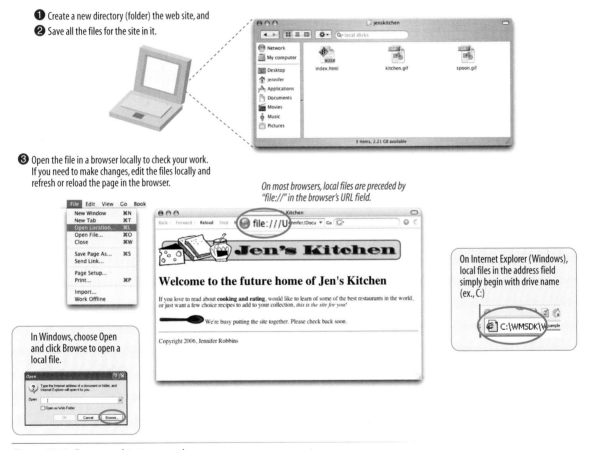

Figure 21-1. Create and test your web page on your own computer.

❹ **Upload the files.** When everything looks fine in the browser, you're ready to upload the page to the remote server that is hosting your site (Figure 21-2). Use a file transfer (FTP) program to upload your files (we'll go over the ins and outs of FTP in the next section). Just be sure to put all the files in your site's root directory on the server. The hosting company or server administrator will tell you the name of your site's root directory when you set up the account.

NOTE

If you have organized your local files into subdirectories, the same subdirectory structure will need to be set up on the remote root directory as well (see the sidebar Organizing and Uploading a Whole Site).

❺ **Check it out live on the Web.** Once all the files have been transferred to the server, you (and anyone else) can see it by typing your URL in the browser. Tell your friends!

❹ When the page is ready, you can upload it to the proper directory on the server using FTP.

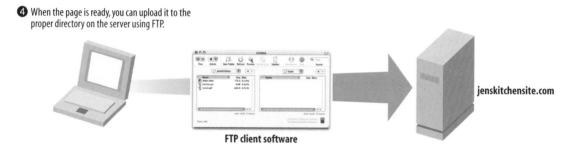

FTP client software

jenskitchensite.com

❺ Once the files are on the web server, you can open the web page using its URL.

Figure 21-2. Uploading and viewing a page from the remote server.

Testing on the Server

In the example in this chapter, the web page was tested locally and became "live" as soon as it was moved to the server. As another option, web developers may create a special test site (also called a *development* or *staging* site) on the server. The advantage is that the site can be tested on the actual server and tweaked before it is made live to the public. Staging sites are also useful when the site is being created and tested by a group

of developers, because the whole team has access to it.

The staging site might be in a separate directory or in a subdomain (for example, *dev.jenskitchensite.com*). When the site is ready to go, all the files can be moved to the root directory on the server.

Transferring Files with FTP

Most likely, your server will be in a remote location, accessible via the Internet. Files are transferred between computers on the Internet via a protocol called FTP (File Transfer Protocol). You may also hear "FTP" used casually as a verb, as in "I'll FTP those files by this afternoon."

NOTE

If you are in an office or at a school that has a web server as part of its network, you may be able to move the files directly over the network without using FTP.

You'll need some information handy to transfer files with FTP:

The name of your web server (host). For example, *www.jenware.com*.

Your login name or user ID. You'll get a login name from the server administrator when you set up your server account, often via an email. If you're a freelancer, you'll need access to your client's login.

Your password. This will also be provided by the server administrator or client.

The directory where your web pages reside. Your server administrator may also tell you which directory to use for your web pages, in other words, the name of the root directory for your site. Often, it's www or html. It is also possible that your server is set up to send you to the correct directory automatically when you log in, in which case, you won't need to enter a directory name. Again, get directions from the administrator.

The type of data transfer. In most cases, you will use FTP for uploading, but some hosting services require SFTP (see sidebar). This information will be provided to you with the login and FTP instructions for your account.

FTP software

Because FTP is an Internet protocol, you need to use special FTP software (called an FTP client) designed specifically for the job of transfering files.

The better WYSIWYG web-authoring tools such as Dreamweaver from Adobe, Microsoft Expression Web, and the open source Nvu (pronounced N-view) have FTP clients built in. This is a great feature, because you can build your pages and upload them all in one program.

If you haven't yet invested in one of these tools, there are a number of stand-alone FTP client utilities with simple interfaces that make file transfer as easy as moving files around on your own computer. For the Mac, Transmit, Fetch and Interarchy allow "drag and drop" transfers. On Windows, WS_FTP, CuteFTP, and Filezilla are quite popular. You can download these programs at CNET's *www.download.com*.

Two-way Street

Although this section focuses on uploading files to a server, FTP can be used to download files from the server to your local computer as well. FTP clients use the terms "download" or "get," or may provide down-arrow icons for downloading.

TERMINOLOGY

SFTP

SFTP, or SSH File Transfer Protocol, is a network protocol that offers more secure file transfer than ordinary FTP. It uses the SSH, Secure Shell, protocol that establishes a secure line between a local and remote computer. SFTP also allows basic server management such as deleting remote files and creating and naming remote directories.

ONLINE RESOURCE

FTP Clients

For a comprehensive list of FTP clients sorted by platform and protocol support, see the "Comparison of FTP Clients" page at Wikipedia (*en.wikipedia.org/wiki/Comparison_of_FTP_clients*).

Organizing and Uploading a Whole Site

We uploaded only one document in this example, but chances are your site will consist of more than one page. If your site contains more than a dozen or so documents and graphics files, you should organize your files into directories and subdirectories. This requires some work and careful planning, but it makes site management much easier in the long run.

One common convention is to keep all of the graphic files in a directory called *images* or *graphics*. In most cases, the overall directory structure is based on the structure of the site itself. For instance, if you have a "News" category on your site, there would be a corresponding news directory for those files.

The good news is that you can upload an entire site in one go. When you select a directory to be FTP'd, it will upload *everything* within that directory—leaving the subdirectory structure intact. Follow the FTP instructions in this section, but select the directory name instead of a single filename for upload.

The FTP program checks the format of each file and selects text or raw data/binary as appropriate during the upload.

It is a good idea to set up your site directory structure as you want it on your local hard drive first, then upload everything to the final server once it is ready.

Using FTP, step by step

FTP clients have slightly different interfaces and use different terminology, but they essentially work the same. Again, these steps should give you the general picture.

Step 1: Make sure you are online. You may have a network or cable connection that is always online, but you may need to dial in over a modem. You can launch your FTP program before or after getting online.

Step 2: Open a connection to the server and enter your information. This is usually the point at which you are asked to enter the server name, login, password, and the optional settings mentioned earlier. Some FTP programs allow you to save the settings and give the connection a name to make it easy to connect later. Your tool may call this process setting up a new "site" or "connection." The window at the top of Figure 21-3 shows the server settings in Transmit, but your tool may use a multiscreen "wizard" process for collecting and saving site settings.

Step 3: Navigate to your local and remote root servers. Many FTP clients feature two windows: one gives you a view of the files on your local hard drive, the other is a view of the files on the remote server (Figure 21-3). The windows typically also provide methods for navigating through the directories. Some clients, such as Fetch, show a view only of the remote server. Whatever tool you use, make sure that the root directory on your server (or the appropriate directory within the root) is selected.

Step 4: Select the file on your local hard drive and upload it. FTP programs vary on how the upload option is presented once your file is selected, but it's usually fairly intuitive. Some ask you to select Upload, Send, or Put from a menu or push-button; others use an up arrow or right arrow to indicate the transfer direction from your computer to the remote server. You may also be able to drag and drop the file from the local window to the server window to start the upload.

NOTE

Some FTP clients, such as Fetch, may also ask you to indicate the format or type of file being transferred. HTML documents should be sent as Text or ASCII. For images and other media, choose Binary or Raw Data. Many FTP clients choose the format for you automatically.

Step 5: Watch it upload. Once you click the Upload button or arrow, your file starts whizzing over the lines and onto the server. Your FTP client will probably provide some sort of feedback that shows the progress of the upload. When the file shows up in the file list in the remote server window, and the file size matches that shown on your local computer, you know that it has arrived.

When you open a new connection, you will be asked for your server settings (shown here in the Transmit FTP client for the Mac).

When you are connected, you can see the contents of your local hard drive and the remote server. Use the navigation tools to make sure the proper directories are selected.

To upload in Transmit, select File > Upload or drag the file from the local window to the remote window. Other tools may provide arrow buttons for moving files between computers.

WS_FTP (left) and Dreamweaver site manager (right) also provide side-by-side windows.

Figure 21-3. Three popular FTP client interfaces.

Step 6: Check it in a browser. Now the document is officially on the Web. Just to be sure, check it with a browser. Open a browser and enter your URL, and there it is! If you need to make changes, do so on the local document, save it, then upload it again.

Test Yourself

Before we move on, let's see if the important parts of this chapter have been uploaded to your brain. Answers appear in Appendix A.

1. There are basic services that you need if you want to get yourself and your own site online. Match the following services with the companies that provide them. Note that some services may have more than one answer.

   A. Hosting company   B. ISP   C. Domain registrar

   Get connected to the Internet _____

   Find out if yourname.com is available _____

   Get yourname.com for 3 years _____

   Get space on a web server _____

2. Name two ways in which servers are identified on the Internet.

3. What does it mean to look at a page locally?

4. What three pieces of information are required to FTP files to a server? What else may you need to know?

5. What format should you select to upload a graphic file? An audio file? An HTML file?

6. How do you upload a whole directory of files at once?

7. We know the saying "no free lunches." Name at least three potential sacrifices you might need to make in exchange for free hosting.

ANSWERS

Chapter 1: Where Do I Start?

1. B, D, A, C

2. The W3C guides the development of Web-related technologies.

3. C, D, A, E, B

4. Frontend design is concerned with aspects of a site that appear in or are related to the browser. Backend development involves the programming required on the server for site functionality.

5. A web authoring tool provides a visual interface for creating entire web pages, including the necessary (X)HTML, CSS, and scripts. HTML editors provide only shortcuts to writing (X)HTML documents manually.

Chapter 2: How the Web Works

1. c, 2. i, 3. g, 4. h, 5. f, 6. b, 7. a, 8. d, 9. e

Chapter 3: The Nature of Web Design

1. You need to be aware that your page may look and work differently from browser to browser. Sticking to the standards will ensure a similar (although not identical) experience on modern standards-compliant browsers. For the rest, be sure that your content is available and accessible.

2. The platform on which your page is viewed can affect how certain page and form elements are rendered, the size of the text, availability of fonts and plug-ins, and the brightness of colors. Some technologies developed for Windows may not be as well supported on Mac or Unix platforms.

3. Users' browser settings will override the settings you make in your style sheets by default. It is easy for users to change the fonts, background colors, and size of the text. Users can also choose to turn off functionality such as Java, JavaScript, and image display.

4. Because browser windows can be resized, you never know how large your web page's screen area will be.

5. As many as 30% of Internet users are still using dial-up connections, so you should always take time to optimize your images, audio/video, even your (X)HTML documents for the quickest download possible.

6. Be sure that your content is accessible to all users, regardles of the devices they may be using to read, navigate, and input information. The best way to ensure accessibility is to stick with the standards, make sure your source document is logical, and follow the guidelines set out by the WAI.

Chapter 4: Creating a Simple Page (HTML Overview)

1. A tag is part of the markup used to delimit an element. An element consists of the content and its markup.

2. The minimal markup of an (X)HTML document is as follows:

```
<html>
<head>
  <title>Title</title>
</head>
<body>
</body>
</html>
```

3. a. *Sunflower.html*—Yes

   b. *index.doc*—No, it must end in *.html* or *.htm*

   c. *cooking home page.html*—No, there may be no character spaces

   d. *Song_Lyrics.html*—Yes

   e. *games/rubix.html*—No, there may be no slashes in the name

   f. *%whatever.html*—No, there may be no percent symbols

4. All of the following markup examples are incorrect. Describe what is wrong with each one, then write it correctly.

   a. It is missing the src attribute before the file name and the alt attribute to be valid: `<img src="birthday.jpg" alt="description of photo>`

   b. The slash in the end tag is missing: `<i>Congratulations!</i>`

   c. There should be no attribute in the end-tag: `<a href="file.html">linked text</a>`

   d. The slash should be a forward-slash: `<p>This is a new paragraph</p>`

5. Make it a comment: `<!-- product list begins here -->`

Exercises 4-1 through 4-5

```
<html>

<head>
<title>Black Goose Bistro</title>

<style type="text/css">
body { background-color: #C2A7F2;
       font-family: sans-serif;}
h1 { color: #2A1959;
     border-bottom: 2px solid #2A1959;}
h2 { color: #474B94;
     font-size: 1.2em;}
h2, p { margin-left: 120px;}
</style>
```

```
</head>

<body>
<h1><img src="blackgoose.gif" alt="black goose logo">Black Goose Bistro</h1>

<h2>The Restaurant</h2>
<p>The Black Goose Bistro offers casual lunch and dinner fare in a hip atmosphere. The menu changes regularly to
highlight the freshest ingredients.</p>

<h2>Catering</h2>
<p>You have fun... <em>we'll handle the cooking.</em> Black Goose Catering can handle events from snacks for bridge
club to elegant corporate fundraisers.</p>

<h2>Location and Hours</h2>
<p>Seekonk, Massachusetts;
Monday through Thursday 11am to 9pm, Friday and Saturday, 11am to midnight</p>
</body>

</html>
```

Chapter 5: Marking Up Text

1. ```
   <p>People who know me know that I love to cook.</p>
   <hr />
   <p>I've created this site to share some of my favorite
       recipes.</p>
   ```

2. Deprecated means that an element or attribute is being phased out and is discouraged from use.

3. A `blockquote` is a block-level element used for long quotations or quoted material that may consist of other block elements. The `q` (quote) element is for short quotations that go in the flow of text and do not cause line breaks.

4. `pre`

5. The `ul` element is an unordered list for lists that don't need to appear in a particular order. They display with bullets by default. The `ol` element is an ordered list in which sequence matters. The browser automatically inserts numbers for ordered lists.

6. Use a style sheet to remove bullets from an unordered list.

7. `<acronym title="World Wide Web Consortium">W3C</acronym>`

8. A `dl` is the element used to identify an entire definition list. The `dt` element is used to identify just one term within that list.

9. The `id` attribute is used to identify a unique element in a document, and the name in its value may appear only once in a document. `class` is used to classify multiple elements into conceptual groups.

10. `&mdash;`   em dash —

    `&amp;`   ampersand &

    ` `   non-breaking space

    `&copy;`   copyright ©

    `&bull;`   bullet •

    `&trade;`   trademark symbol ™
   ```

Exercise 5-1

```
<html>
<head><title>Tapenade Recipe</title></head>
<body>

<h1>Tapenade (Olive Spread)</h1>

<p>This is a really simple dish to prepare and it's always a big hit at parties. My father recommends:</p>

<blockquote><p>"Make this the night before so that the flavors have time to blend. Just bring it up to room
temperature before you serve it. In the winter, try serving it warm."</p></blockquote>

<h2>Ingredients</h2>

<ul>
  <li>1 8oz. jar sundried tomatoes</li>
  <li>2 large garlic cloves</li>
  <li>2/3 c. kalamata olives</li>
  <li>1 t. capers</li>
</ul>

<h2>Instructions</h2>

<ol>
  <li>Combine tomatoes and garlic in a food processor. Blend until as smooth as possible.</li>

  <li>Add capers and olives. Pulse the motor a few times until they are incorporated, but still retain some
texture.</li>

  <li>Serve on thin toast rounds with goat cheese and fresh basil garnish (optional).</li>
</ol>

</body>
</html>
```

Exercise 5-2

The seven changes were:

1. The h1 is missing an end tag.

2. The closing p tag is missing a slash.

3. The strong element would be better than the b element.

4. Add the abbr element for Mass.

5. The book title would be better as a cite element than in italic text

6. The prize code example would be better as a kbd or samp element.

7. The text marked as italic in the last line should be emphasized (em).

```
<h1>You Won!</h1>
<p><strong>Congratulations!</strong> You have just won dinner for two at the highly acclaimed Blue Ginger
restaurant in Wellesley, <abbr title="Massachusetts">Mass.</abbr> In addition to dinner, you will receive
an autographed copy of Ming Tsai's book, <cite>Blue Ginger</cite>. To redeem your prize, go to our site and
enter your prize code (Example: <kbd>RPZ108-BG</kbd>). We're sure you're going to <em>love</em> it!</p>
```

Exercise 5-3

```html
<html>
<head>
<title>Black Goose Bistro Summer Menu</title>
</head>
<body>

<div id="header">
<h1>Black Goose Bistro &bull; Summer Menu</h1>

<p>Baker&rsquo;s Corner Seekonk, Massachusetts<br />Hours: M-T: 11 to 9, F-S; 11 to midnight</p>
</div>

<div id="appetizers">
<h2>Appetizers</h2>

<dl>
<dt class="newitem">Southwestern Napoleons</dt>
<dd>Spicy black bean and a blend of mexican cheeses wrapped in sheets of phyllo and baked until golden. <span
class="price">$3.95</span></dd>

<dt>Southwestern napoleons with lump crab &mdash; <strong>new item!</strong></dt>
<dd>Layers of light lump crab meat, bean and corn salsa, and our handmade flour tortillas. <span
class="price">$7.95</span></dd>
</dl>

</div>

<div id="main">

<h2>Main courses</h2>

<dl>
<dt>Shrimp sate kebabs with peanut sauce</dt>
<dd>Skewers of shrimp marinated in lemongrass, garlic, and fish sauce then grilled to perfection. Served with
spicy peanut sauce and jasmine rice. <span class="price">$12.95</span></dd>

<dt>Grilled skirt steak with mushroom fricasee</dt>
<dd>Flavorful skirt steak marinated in asian flavors grilled as you like it<sup>*</sup>. Served over a blend
of sauteed wild mushrooms with a side of blue cheese mashed potatoes. <span class="price">$16.95</span></dd>

<dt class="newitem">Jerk rotisserie chicken with fried plantains &mdash; <strong>new item!</strong></dt>
<dd>Tender chicken slow-roasted on the rotisserie, flavored with spicy and fragrant jerk sauce and served with
fried plantains and fresh mango. <span class="price">$12.95</span></dd>
</dl>

</div>

<div id="warnings">
<p class="footnote"><sup>*</sup> We are required to warn you that undercooked food is a health risk.</p>
</div>

</body>
</html>
```

Chapter 6: Adding Links

1. `<a href="tutorial.html">...</a>`

2. `<a href="examples/instructions.html">...</a>`

3. `<a href="examples/french/family.html">...</a>`

4. `<a href="/examples/german/numbers.html">...</a>`

5. `<a href="../index.html">...</a>`

6. `<a href="http://www.learningwebdesign.com">...</a>`

7. `<a href="../instructions.html">...</a>`

8. `<a href="../../index.html">...</a>`

9. `<img src="images/arrow.gif" alt="" />`

10. `<img src="../images/arrow.gif" alt="" />`

11. `<img src="../../images/bullet.gif" alt="" />`

Exercise 6-1

```
<li><a href="http://www.epicurious.com">Epicurious</a></li>
```

Exercise 6-2

```
<p><a href="index.html">Back to the home page</a></p>
```

Exercise 6-3

```
<li><a href="recipes/tapenade.html">Tapenade (Olive Spread)</a></li>
```

Exercise 6-4

```
<li><a href="recipes/pasta/linguine.html">Linguine with Clam Sauce</a></li>
```

Exercise 6-5

```
<p><a href="../index.html">[Back to the home page]</a></p>
```

Exercise 6-6

```
<p><a href="../../index.html">[Back to the home page]</a></p>
```

Exercise 6-7

1. `<p><a href="tapenade.html">Go to the Tapenade recipe</a></p>`

2. `<p><a href="../salmon.html">Go to the Salmon recipe</a></p>`

3. `<p><a href="pasta/linguine.html">Go to the Linguine recipe</a></p>`

4. `<p><a href="../../about.html">Go to the About page</a></p>`

5. `<p><a href="http://www.allrecipes.com">Go to the All Recipes web site</a></p>`

Chapter 7: Adding Images

1. The `src` and `alt` attributes are required for the document to be valid. If the `src` attribute is omitted, the browser won't know which image to use. You may leave the value of the `alt` attribute empty if alternative text would be meaningless or clumsy when read in context.

2. `<img src="furry.jpg" alt="" />`

3. 1) It improves accessibility by providing a description of the image if it is not available or not viewable, and 2) because HTML documents are not valid if the `alt` attribute is omitted.

4. It allows the browser to render the rest of the content while the image is being retrieved from the server, which can speed up the display of the page.

5. The three likely causes for a missing image are: 1) the URL is incorrect, so the browser is looking in the wrong place or for the wrong file name (names are case-sensitive); 2) the image file is not in an acceptable format; and 3) the image file is not named with the proper suffix (.gif, .jpg, .jpeg, or .png, as appropriate).

6. It indicates that the image is used as an imagemap and provides the name of the applicable map.

Exercise 7-1

In *index.html*:

```
<h2>Pozzarello</h2>
<p><a href="window.html"><img src="thumbnails/window_100.jpg" alt="view from the bedroom window" width="75"
height="100"/></a></p>
<p>The house we stayed in was called Pozzarello and it was built around the year 1200 as the home of the
gardner who tended the grounds of the adjacent castle. The thick walls kept us nice and cool inside, despite
the blistering mid-day heat. This is the view from our bedroom window.</p>

<h2>On the Road</h2>
<p><a href="countryside.html"><img/ src="thumbnails/countryside_100.jpg" alt="photo of countryside"
width="100" height="75"/></a></p>
<p>This is the scene on the way to Montalcino (all roads lead to Montalcino!). It looks a lot like the
scene on the way to Sienna, and the scene on the way to the grocery store. We were surrounded by beautiful
countryside for most of our travels.</p>

<h2>Sienna</h2>
<p><a href="sienna.html"><img/ src="thumbnails/sienna_100.jpg" alt="photo of Sienna" width="75"
height="100"></a><a href="duomo.html"> <img/ src="thumbnails/duomo_100.jpg" alt="the Duomo cathedral
in Sienna" width="75" height="100"/></a></p>
<p>The closest city to our villa was Sienna, about 30 minutes away. We spent many days exploring the steep
and crooked streets, sampling the local cuisine at outdoor restaurants, and stopping in the dark and echoey
Duomo to escape the sun.</p>
```

In *countryside.html*:

```
<h1>The Tuscan Countryside</h1>
<p><img/ src="photos/countryside.jpg" alt="photo of the countryside on the way to Montalcino"
width="500" height="375"/></p>
```

In *sienna.html*:

```
<h1>The Streets of Sienna</h1>
<p><img/ src="photos/sienna.jpg" alt="view of the narrow winding streets of Sienna" width="375"
height="500"/></p>
```

In *duomo.html*:

```
<h1>A View of the Duomo</h1>
<p><img src="photos/duomo.jpg" alt="view of the Duomo cathedral in Sienna" width="375"
height="500"></p>
```

Chapter 8: Basic Table Markup

1. The table itself (table), rows (tr), header cells (th), data cells (td), and an optional caption (caption).

2. Professional designers no longer use tables for layout because they are not semantically correct, they can get overly complicated and be a barrier to accessibility, and style sheets are now supported well enough that they offer a superior alternative.

3. Captions are for short titles and they display in the browser. Summaries are for longer descriptions and they do not display but may be read aloud by a screen reader.

4. If you want to add additional information about the structure of a table, to specify widths to speed up display, or to add certain style properties to a column of cells.

5. 1) The caption should be the first element inside the table element; 2) There can't be text directly in the table element. It must go in a th or td; 3) The th elements must go inside the tr element; 4) There is no colspan element. This should be a td with a colspan attribute; 5) The second tr element is missing a closing tag.

Exercise 8-1

```
<table>
    <tr>
        <th>Album</th>
        <th>Year</th>
    </tr>
    <tr>
        <td>Rubber Soul</td>
        <td>1965</td>
    </tr>
    <tr>
        <td>Revolver</td>
        <td>1966</td>
    </tr>
    <tr>
        <td>Sgt. Pepper's</td>
        <td>1967</td>
    </tr>
    <tr>
        <td>The White Album</td>
        <td>1968</td>
    </tr>
    <tr>
        <td>Abbey Road</td>
        <td>1969</td>
    </tr>
</table>
```

Exercise 8-2

```html
<table>
    <tr>
        <td colspan="3">The Sunday Night Movie</td>
    </tr>
    <tr>
        <td>Perry Mason</td>
        <td>Candid Camera</td>
        <td>What's My Line?</td>
    </tr>
    <tr>
        <td>Bonanza</td>
        <td colspan="2">The Wackiest Ship in the Army</td>
    </tr>
</table>
```

Exercise 8-3

```html
<table>
    <tr>
        <td>apples</td>
        <td rowspan="3">oranges</td>
        <td>pears</td>
    </tr>

    <tr>
        <td>bananas</td>
        <td rowspan="2">pineapple<td>
    </tr>
    <tr>
        <td>lychees</td>
    </tr>
</table>
```

Exercise 8-4

```html
<html>
<head>
    <title>Table Challenge</title>
    <style type="text/css">
        td, th { border: 1px solid #CCC }
        table {border: 1px solid black }
    </style>
</head>

<body>
<table border="0" cellspacing="4">
    <caption>Your Content Here</caption>
  <tr>
    <th rowspan="2"> </th>
    <th colspan="2">A common header for two subheads</th>
    <th rowspan="2">Header 3</th>
  </tr>
  <tr>
    <th>Header 1</th>
    <th>Header 2</th>
  </tr>
  <tr>
```

```
      <th scope="row">Thing A</th>
      <td>data A1</td>
      <td>data A2</td>
      <td>data A3</td>
    </tr>
    <tr>
      <th scope="row">Thing B </th>
      <td>data B1</td>
      <td>data B2</td>
      <td>data B3</td>
    </tr>
    <tr>
      <th scope="row">Thing C</th>
      <td>data C1</td>
      <td>data C2</td>
      <td>data C3</td>
    </tr>
  </table>
  </body>
  </html>
```

Chapter 9: Forms

1. A form for accessing your bank account online: POST (because of security issues)

    A form for sending t-shirt artwork to the printer: POST (because it uses the file selection input type)

    A form for searching archived articles: GET (because you may want to bookmark search results)

    A form for collecting essay entries: POST (because it is likely to have a length text entry)

2. Which form control element is best suited for the following tasks?

    Choose your astrological sign from 12 signs: Pull-down menu (`<select>`)

    Indicate whether you have a history of heart disease (yes or no):   Radio buttons (`<input type="radio">`)

    Write up a book review: `<textarea>`

    Select your favorite ice cream flavors from a list of eight flavors.   Eight checkboxes

    Select your favorite ice cream flavors from a list of 25 flavors.   Scrolling menu (`<select multiple="multiple">`)

3. Each of these markup examples contains an error. Can you spot what it is?

```
<input name="country" value="Your country here" />
```
    The type attribute is missing.

```
<checkbox name="color" value="teal" />
```
    Checkbox is not an element name; it is a value of the type attribute in the input element.

```
<select name="popsicle">
    <option value="orange" />
    <option value="grape: />
    <option value="cherry" />
</select>
```
    The option element is not empty. It should contain the value for each option (for example,
    `<option>Orange</option>`).

```
<input type="password" />
```

The required name attribute is missing.

```
<textarea name="essay" height="6" width="100">Your story.</textarea>
```

The width and height of a text area are specified with the cols and rows attributes, respectively.

Exercises 9-1 through 9-3: Final source document

```
<!DOCTYPE html PUBLIC "-//W3C//DTD XHTML 1.0 Strict//EN"
    "http://www.w3.org/TR/xhtml1/DTD/xhtml1-strict.dtd">
<html xmlns="http://www.w3.org/1999/xhtml" lang="en" xml:lang="en">
<head>
<meta http-equiv="content-type" content="text/html;charset=utf-8" />
    <title>Contest Entry Form</title>
<style type="text/css">
  ol, ul { list-style-type: none;}
</style>
</head>
<body>

<h1>"Pimp My Shoes" Contest Entry Form</h1>

<p>Want to trade in your old sneakers for a custom pair of Forcefields? Make a case for why your shoes have
got to go and you may be one of ten lucky winners.</p>

<form action="http://www.learningwebdesign.com/contest.php" method="post">

<fieldset>
<legend>Contest Entry Information</legend>
<ol>
<li><label for="form-name">Name:</label> <input type="text" name="name" id="form-name" /></li>
<li><label for="form-city">City:</label> <input type="text" name="city" id="form-city" /></li>
<li><label for="form-state">State:</label> <input type="text" name="state" id="form-state" /></li>
<li><label for="form-story">My shoes are SO old...</label><br />
<textarea name="story" rows="5" cols="60" id="story">(Make us feel sorry for your shoes.)</textarea></li>
</ol>
</fieldset>

<h2>Design your custom Forcefields:</h2>

<fieldset>
<legend>Custom shoe design</legend>
<fieldset>
<legend>Color <em>(choose one)</em></legend>
<ul>
  <li><label><input type="radio" name="color" value="red" /> Red</label></li>
  <li><label><input type="radio" name="color" value="blue" /> Blue</label></li>
  <li><label><input type="radio" name="color" value="black" /> Black</label></li>
  <li><label><input type="radio" name="color" value="silver" /> Silver</label></li>
</ul>
</fieldset>

<fieldset>
<legend>Features <em>(Choose as many as you want)</em></legend>
<ul>
```

```
   <li><label><input type="checkbox" name="features" value="laces" /> Sparkley laces</label></li>
   <li><label><input type="checkbox" name="features" value="logo" checked="checked"/> Metallic logo</label></
li>
   <li><label><input type="checkbox" name="features" value="heels" /> Light-up heels</label></li>
   <li><label><input type="checkbox" name="features" value="mp3" /> MP3-enabled</label></li>
</ul>
</fieldset>

<fieldset>
<legend>Size</legend>
<label for="size">(sizes reflect standard men's sizes):</label>
   <select name="size" id="size">
       <option>5</option>
       <option>6</option>
       <option>7</option>
       <option>8</option>
       <option>9</option>
       <option>10</option>
       <option>11</option>
       <option>12</option>
       <option>13</option>
   </select>
</fieldset>

</fieldset>
<p><input type="submit" value="Pimp my shoes!" />  <input type="reset" /></p>
</form>
</body>
</html>
```

Chapter 10: Understanding the Standards

1. Netscape Navigator and Microsoft Internet Explorer were the major players in the Browser Wars.

2. HTML 4.01 Transitional includes the deprecated presentational elements and attributes that have been removed from the Strict version.

3. HTML 4.01 Strict and XHTML 1.0 Strict the same in that they have the same elements and attributes listed in three DTD versions. They are different in that XHTML is an XML language that has more stringent syntax requirements.

4. The major syntax requirements in XHTML are:

   • Element and attribute names must be lowercase.

   • All elements must be closed (terminated), including empty elements.

   • Attribute values must be in quotation marks.

   • All attributes must have explicit attribute values.

   • Elements must be nested properly.

   • Always use character entities for special characters.

   • Use id instead of name as an identifier.

   • Scripts must be contained in a CDATA section.

5. Look at these valid markup examples and determine whether each is HTML or XHTML:

   `<IMG SRC="panda.jpg" ALT="panda eating leaves">`   HTML

   `<img src="orchid.jpg" alt="orchid" width=100 height=150 >`   HTML

   `<img src="flipflop.gif" alt="closeup of foot in sandal" />`   XHTML

6. The html element must include the `xmlns`, `lang`, and `xml:lang` attributes in XHTML documents.

7. Include a correct DOCTYPE declaration at the beginning of a document to trigger a browser to use Standards Mode.

8. XHTML offers the benefits of XML, including the ability to be combined with other XML languages, be parsed and used by any XML parsing software, and transform information from XML applications to a web page. It is also consistent with future web technologies, requires better coding practices, and is better for accessibility and use on handheld devices.

9. ISO 8859-1 is the character encoding of the 256 characters commonly used in Western languages.

Exercise 10-1

The following changes must be made to the markup:

1. Convert all elements and attributes to lowercase.

2. Add XHTML attributes to the `html` element.

3. Convert the & in the title to its character entity, `&amp;`

4. In the `img` element, put the `width` and `height` values in quotation marks

5. Terminate the `img` element by adding a space and trailing slash before the closing bracket.

6. Close the `li` elements in the unordered list and the final `p` element.

```
<html xmlns="http://www.w3.org/1999/xhtml" lang="en" xml:lang="en">

<head>
<title>Popcorn &amp; Butter</title>
</head>

<body>
<h1>Hot Buttered Popcorn</h1>

<p><img src="popcorn.jpg" alt="bowl of popcorn" width="250" height="125" /></p>

<h2>Ingredients</h2>
<ul>
   <li>popcorn</li>
   <li>butter</li>
   <li>salt</li>
</ul>

<h2>Instructions</h2>

<p>Pop the popcorn. Meanwhile, melt the butter. Transfer the popped popcorn into a bowl, drizzle with melted
butter, and sprinkle salt to taste.</p>

</body>
</html>
```

Chapter 11: CSS Orientation

1. selector: `blockquote`, property: `line-height`, value: `1.5`, declaration: `line-height: 1.5`

2. The paragraph text will be gray because when there are conflicting rules of identical weight, the last one listed in the style sheet will be used.

3. a. Use one rule with multiple declarations applied to the p element.

   ```
   p {font-family: sans-serif;
       font-size: 1em;
       line-height: 1.2em;}
   ```

   b. The semicolons are missing.

   ```
   blockquote {
       font-size: 1em;
       line-height: 150%;
       color: gray;
   }
   ```

   c. There should not be curly braces around every declaration, only around the entire declaration block.

   ```
   body {background-color: black;
      color: #666;
      margin-left: 12em;
      margin-right: 12em;}
   ```

   d. This could be handled with a single rule with a grouped element type selector.

   ```
   p, blockquote, li {color: white;}
   ```

   e. This inline style is missing the property name.

   ```
   <strong style="color: red">Act now!</strong>
   ```

4.   `div#intro { color: red; }`

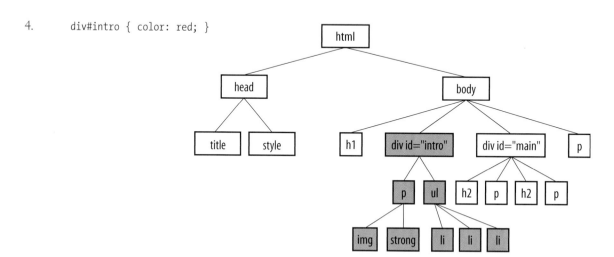

Chapter 12: Formatting Text

1. a. All text elements in the document: `body {color: red;}`

   b. h2 elements: `h2 {color: red;}`

   c. h1 elements and all paragraphs: `h1, p {color: red;}`

   d. Elements belonging to the class "special": `.special {color: red;}`

   e. All elements in the "intro" section: `#intro {color: red;}`

   f. Strong elements in the "main" section: `#main strong {color: red;}`

   g. Extra credit: Just the paragraph that appears after the "main" section (hint: this selector will not work in Internet Explorer 6): `h2 + p {color: red;}`

2. a. ❹ `{font-size: 1.5em;}`

   b. ❶ `{text-transform: capitalize;}`

   c. ❼ `{text-align: right;}`

   d. ❸ `{font-family: Verdana; font-size: 1.5em;}`

   e. ❷ `{letter-spacing: 3px;}`

   f. ❾ `{font: bold italic 1.2em Verdana;}`

   g. ❽ `{text-transform: uppercase;}`

   h. ❺ `{text-indent: 2em;}`

   i. ❻ `{font-variant: small-caps;}`

Exercises 12-1 through 12-3:

```
<style type="text/css">

body { font-family: Georgia, serif;
  font-size: small;
  line-height: 175%; }

h1 { font-size: 1.5em;
   color: purple;}

dt { font-weight: bold; color: olive; }

strong { font-style: italic; }

h2 { font: bold 1em Georgia, serif;
  text-transform: uppercase;
  letter-spacing: 8px;
  color: purple;}

dt strong { color: maroon; }

#header p {
  font-style: italic;
  color: gray;}
```

```
#header, h2, #appetizers p, #appetizers p #entrees p { text-align: center; }

#appetizers p, #appetizers p #entrees p { font-style: italic; }

.price {
  font-style: italic;
  font-family: Georgia, serif; }

.label {
  font-weight: bold;
  font-variant: small-caps;
  font-style: normal; }

p.warning, sup {
  font-size: x-small;
  color: red;}

</style>
```

Chapter 13: Colors and Backgrounds

1. g.   a, b, and c

2. d.   rgb(FF, FF, FF)

3. a.–5, b.–1, c.–4, d.–6, e.–2, f.–3

4. a. –1, b.–3, c.–2, d.–6, e.–5, f.–4

5. e.   all of the above

Exercise 13-1

```
<style type="text/css">

    body {margin-left: 10%; margin-right: 10%; background-color: #BBE09F;}

    div#titlepage { padding: 1em; background-color: #D4F8B9;}

    div#titlepage p {text-align: center; font-variant: small-caps;}

    p {text-align: justify;}

    h1,h2,h3,h4,h5,h6 {text-transform: uppercase; text-align: center;}

    h1 { color:#C30;}
    h2 { color:#630;}

    a:link {color:#030;}
    a:visited {color:#363;}
    a:hover {color:#030; background-color:#87B862; text-decoration:none;}
    a:active {color:#C30;}

</style>
```

Exercise 13-2, page 247

```
body { margin-left: 10%; margin-right: 10%; background-color: #BBE09F; background-image: url(cabbage_A.jpg);}
```

Extra credit:

```
div#titlepage { padding: 1em; background-color: #D4F8B9; background-image: url(cabbage_A.jpg); }
```

Exercise 13-2, continued on page 248

Step 2:

```
div#titlepage { padding: 1em; background-color: #D4F8B9; url(cabbage_B.gif); background-repeat: repeat-x; }
```

Step 3 (vertical repeat):

```
div#titlepage { padding: 1em; background-color: #D4F8B9; url(cabbage_B.gif); background-repeat: repeat-y; }
```

Step 3 (no repeat):

```
div#titlepage { padding: 1em; background-color: #D4F8B9; url(cabbage_B.gif); background-repeat: no-repeat; }
```

Exercise 13-2, continued on page 251

Step 1:

```
body { margin-left: 10%; margin-right: 10%; background-color: #BBE09F; background-image: url(cabbage_C_
topright.gif); background-repeat: no-repeat; background-position: right top; }
```

Step 2:

```
body { margin-left: 10%; margin-right: 10%; background-color: #BBE09F; background-image: url(cabbage_C_
rightside.gif); background-repeat: no-repeat; background-position: right 100px; }
```

```
body { margin-left: 10%; margin-right: 10%; background-color: #BBE09F; background-image: url(cabbage_C_
leftside.gif); background-repeat: no-repeat; background-position: left 100px; }
```

Step 3:

```
body { margin-left: 10%; margin-right: 10%; background-color: #BBE09F; background-image: url(cabbage_C.gif);
background-repeat: no-repeat; background-position: center center; }
```

Step 4:

```
body { margin-left: 10%; margin-right: 10%; background-color: #BBE09F; background-image: url(cabbage_C.gif);
background-repeat: no-repeat; background-position: center 85px; }
```

```
div#titlepage { padding: 1em; background-color: #D4F8B9; background-image: url(cabbage_C.gif); background-
repeat: no-repeat; background-position: center 75px; }
```

Exercise 13-2 (pages 253 and 254)

(All code is provided in the exercise itself.)

Exercise 13-3

(All code is provided in the exercise itself.)

Chapter 14: Thinking Inside the Box

1. `border: double black medium;`

2. `overflow: scroll;`

3. `padding: 2em;`

4. `padding: 2em; border: 4px solid red;`

5. `margin: 2em; border: 4px solid red;`

6. `padding: 1em 1em 1em 6em; border: 4px dashed; margin: 1em 6em;`

   or

   `padding: 1em; padding-left: 6em; border: 4px dashed; margin: 1em 6em;`

7. `padding: 1em 50px; border: 2px solid teal; margin: 0 auto;`

Exercise 14-3

```
<style type="text/css">

body {
  margin-left: 12%;
  margin-right: 12%;
  font: 76% Verdana, sans-serif;
  background: #FCF191 url(images/top-background.gif) repeat-x; }

/* styles for the intro section */
#intro {
  margin: 3em 0;
  text-align: center; }

#intro h1 {
  font-size: 1.5em;
  color: #F26521; }

#intro img {
  vertical-align: middle; }

#intro p {
  font-size: 1.2em; }

/* styles for the testimonials box */

#testimonials {
  width: 500px;
  margin: 2em auto;
  border: 1px dashed #F26521;
  padding: 1em;
  padding-left: 60px;
  background: #FFBC53 url(images/ex-circle-corner.gif) no-repeat left top;
  line-height: 1.2em; }

#testimonials h2 {
  font-size: 1em;
  text-transform: uppercase;
  color: #F26521;
```

```
      letter-spacing: 3px; }

  /* styles for the products section */
  #products {
      border: double #FFBC53;
      padding: 2em;
      background-color: #FFF;
      line-height: 2em;}

  #products h2 {
      margin-top: 3em;
      border-left: 3px solid;
      border-top: 1px solid;
      padding-left: 1em;
      font-size: 1.2em;
      color: #921A66;}

  #products h2.first { margin-top: 0; }

  /* link styles */

  a:link, a:visited, a:hover, a:active {
      text-decoration: none;
      border-bottom: 1px dotted;
      padding-bottom: .25em;}

  a:link, a:active {
      color: #CC0000;}

  a:visited {
      color: #921A66; }

  a:hover {
      background-color: #FCF191;
      color: #921A66; }

  /* miscellaneous styles */

  em { color: #F26521; }

  p#copyright {
      color:#663333;
      font-size: 10px;
      text-align: center; }

  </style>
```

Chapter 15: Floating and Positioning

1. B., floats are positioned against the content area of the containing element (not the padding edge)

2. C., floats do not use offset properties, so there is no reason to include right.

3. Clear the footer div to make it start below a floated sidebar: div#footer { clear: both; }

4. A. absolute, B. absolute, fixed, C. fixed, D. relative, absolute, fixed, E. static, F. relative, G. absolute, fixed, H. relative, absolute, fixed, I. relative

5. The sidebar div would be 292 pixels from outer edge to outer edge. (*Extra credit:* For IE-Win 5 and 5.5, you would set the width to 242px.)

Chapter 16: Page Layout with CSS

1. Fixed, c.; Liquid, a.; Elastic, b.

2. Fixed, b.; Liquid, c.; Elastic, a.

3. Fixed, c.; Liquid, b.; Elastic, a.

4. Fixed, c.; Liquid, a.; Elastic, b.

5. Full-width footer: floats; Not change source order: positioning; No worries about overlapping: floats.

Chapter 17: CSS Techniques

1. B, E, A, D, C

2. E, D, B, A, C

3. The `display` property is used to specify how the element box should be handled in the layout; for example, as a block element starting on a new line or as an inline element staying in the text flow.

4. List items can be turned into inline elements using the `display` property, or floated to one edge so they stack up next to one another.

5. C, the `:hover` selector.

Exercise 17-1, Design A

```
<style type="text/css">

table {
   font-family: verdana, sans-serif;
   font-size: 76%;
   border-collapse: separate;
   border-spacing: 4px;
   width: 550px;}

th { text-align: left;
   color: white;
   background: olive;
   vertical-align: bottom;
   padding: 3px 12px 3px 3px; }

td { padding: 6px 12px 6px 3px;
   vertical-align: top;
   border: 1px olive solid; }

tr.odd { background-color: #F3F3A6;}
tr.even { background-color: #D4D4A2;}
</style>
```

Exercise 17-1, Design B

```
<style type="text/css">

table {
   font-family: verdana, sans-serif;
   font-size: 76%;
   width: 550px;
```

```css
  border-collapse: collapse; }

td { padding: 6px 12px 6px 3px;
  vertical-align: top;
  border-bottom: 1px olive solid; }

th { text-align: left;
  color: white;
  background: olive;
  vertical-align: bottom;
  padding: 3px 12px 3px 3px;}

tr.odd { background-color: #F3F3A6;}

tr.even { background-color: #D4D4A2;}
</style>
```

Exercise 17-2, Design A

```css
<style type="text/css">

body {font-family: Verdana, sans-serif;
  margin: 0;}

h1#ds {
  text-indent: -5000px;
  background: url(images/designerrific_trans.gif) no-repeat;
  width: 360px;
  height: 70px;
  margin: 0;
  position: absolute;
  top: 25px;
  left: 25px;}

ul#nav {
  list-style-type: none;
  margin: 0;
  position: absolute;
  top: 65px;
  right: 25px;}

ul#nav li { display: inline;}

ul#nav li a {
  background-color: #0A6D73;
  border: 1px solid #FFF;
  color: white;
  font-size: 76%;
  text-decoration: none;
  text-align: center;
  text-transform: uppercase;
  letter-spacing: 2px;
  padding: 2px 20px;
  margin: 0px 2px;}

ul#nav li a:hover {
  background-color: #F8409C;
  border: 1px solid #600; }

#header {
```

```
    position: relative;
    background: #9cd8cd;
    border-bottom: 3px double #600;
    height: 100px;}

</style>
```

Exercise 17-2, Design B

```
<style type="text/css">

body {font-family: Verdana, sans-serif;
    margin: 0;}

h1#ds {
    text-indent: -5000px;
    background: url(images/designerrific_trans.gif) no-repeat;
    width: 360px;
    height: 70px;
    margin: 0;
    position: absolute;
    top: 25px;
    left: 25px; }

ul#nav {
    list-style-type: none;
    margin: 0;
    position: absolute;
    top: 65px;
    right: 25px; }

ul#nav li {
    display: inline; }

ul#nav li a {
    color: #1A7E7B;
    font-size: 76%;
    text-decoration: none;
    text-align: center;
    text-transform: uppercase;
    letter-spacing: 2px;
    padding: 2px 20px;
    margin: 0px 2px;
    background: url(images/star-white.gif) left center no-repeat; }

ul#nav li a:hover {
    background: url(images/star-pink.gif) left center no-repeat; }

#header {
    position: relative;
    background: #9cd8cd;
    border-bottom: 3px double #600;
    height: 100px; }

</style>
```

Chapter 18: Web Graphics Basics

1. You can license to have exclusive rights to an image, so that your competitor doesn't use the same photo on their site.

2. ppi stands for "pixels per inch" and is a measure of resolution.

3. The 7-inch, 72ppi image is only 504 pixels across and would fit fine on a web page. The 4-inch, 300 ppi image is 1200 pixels across, which is too wide for most pages.

4. Indexed color is a mode for storing color information in an image that stores each pixel color in a color table. GIF and 8-bit PNG formats are indexed color images.

5. There are 256 colors in an 8-bit graphic, and 32 colors in a 5-bit graphic.

6. GIF can contain animation and transparency. JPEG cannot.

7. Lossy compression is cumulative, which means you lose image data every time you save an image as a JPEG. If you open a JPEG and save it as a JPEG again, even more image information is thrown out than the first time you saved it. Be sure to keep your full-quality original and save JPEG copies as needed.

8. PNGs can store 8-bit indexed color, RGB color (both 24- and 48-bit) and 16-bit grayscale images.

9. In binary transparency, a pixel is either entirely transparent or entirely opaque. Alpha transparency allows up to 256 levels of transparency.

10. **Ⓐ** GIF or PNG-8 because it is text, flat colors, and hard edges. **Ⓑ** JPEG because it is a photograph. **Ⓒ** GIF or PNG-8 because although it has some photographic areas, most of the image is flat colors with hard edges. **Ⓓ** GIF or PNG-8 because it is a flat graphical image. **Ⓔ** JPEG because it is a photograph.

Chapter 19: Lean and Mean Web Graphics

1. Smaller graphic files means shorter download and display times. Every second counts toward creating a favorable user experience of your site.

2. Dithering introduces a speckle pattern that interrupts strings of identical pixels, therefore the GIF compression scheme can't compress areas with dithering as efficiently as flat colors.

3. The fewer pixel colors in the image, the smaller the resulting GIF, both because the image can be stored at a lower bit depth and because there are more areas of similar color for the GIF to compress.

4. The Quality (compression) setting is the most effective tool for controlling the size of a JPEG.

5. JPEG compression works effectively on smooth or blurred areas, so introducing a slight blur allows the JPEG compression to work more efficiently, resulting in smaller files.

6. Just as you would do for an indexed GIF, optimize a PNG-8 by designing with flat colors, reducing the number of colors, and avoiding dithering. There are no strategies for optimizing a PNG-24 because they are designed to store images with lossless compression.

Chapter 20: The Web Development Process

1. A site diagram is useful for planning and visualizing how information is organized on the site. It should be done very early in the design process, as soon as the content and functionality of the site have been determined. The site diagram becomes a valuable reference for the whole production team.

2. A look and feel study is a sketch or series of sketches that propose graphic styles for the site. It focuses on how the site looks rather than how it works.

3. There are many things that should be determined before production begins, including answers to questions like those in the Some Questions Before You Begin sidebar, but some other general tasks include: determining the site idea and strategy, getting information about your target audience, generate content, organize site content, create a site diagram that reflects the organization, create wireframe diagrams to show page layout and functionality, and develop the graphic look and feel.

4. The beta release incorporates changes from the initial alpha prototype and is close to a working version of the site. At the very least, the client is invited to review it, but some sites choose to make beta releases available to a broader audience.

5. At minimum, sites should be checked to make sure that all the content is there and accessible, that there are no typos or errors, that all the links work, that images are visible, and that scripts and applications are functioning properly. Beyond that, it is also important to test the site's look and performance on a wide variety of browsing environments and conditions.

Chapter 21: Getting Your Pages on the Web

1. Get connected to the Internet   B

   Find out if yourname.com is available   C

   Get yourname.com for three years   C (and sometimes A)

   Get space on a web server   A (and sometimes B or C)

2. By numeric IP address and by domain name.

3. To open a file that is stored on your own hard drive. Pages that are on an external computer or server are said to be remote.

4. You must know the name of the server, your login, and password. You may also need to know the name of the root directory and the type of FTP transfer.

5. Upload graphics and audio files as "binary" or "raw data," depending on what your FTP client calls it. HTML files should be uploaded as "text" or "ASCII."

6. Select the directory name in the FTP client.

7. In order to publish content on the Web for free, you may need to accept their advertising on your pages, you may be limited as to what type of content you can publish, you may have limited control over the page layout and navigation, and you usually do not get your own domain name.

CSS2.1 SELECTORS

Selector	Type of Selector	Description
*	Universal selector	Matches any element `* {font-family: serif;}`
A	Element type selector	Matches the name of an element. `div {font-style: italic;}`
A, B	Grouped selectors	Matches elements A and B `h1, h2, h3 {color: blue;}`
A B	Descendant selector	Matches element B only if it is a descendant of element A. `blockquote em {color: red;}`
A>B	Child selector	Matches any element B that is a child of element A. `div.main>p {line-height: 1.5;}`
A+B	Adjacent sibling selector	Matches any element B that immediately follows any element A. `p+ul {margin-top: 0;}`
.classname A.classname	Class selector	Matches the value of the class attribute in all elements or in a specified element. `p.credits {font-size: 80%;}`
#idname A#idname	ID selector	Matches the value of the id attribute in an element. `#intro {font-weight: bold;}`
A[att]	Simple attribute selector	Matches any element A that has the given attribute defined, whatever its value. `table[border] {background: white;}`
A[att="val"]	Exact attribute value selector	Matches any element A that has the specified attribute set to the specified value. `table[border="3"] {background: yellow;}`
A[att~="val"]	Partial attribute value selector	Matches any element A that has the specified value as one of the values in a list given to the specified attribute. `table[class~="example"] {background: yellow;}`
A[att|="val"]	Hyphenated prefix attribute selector	Matches any element A that has the specified attribute with a value that is equal to or begins with the provided value. It is most often used to select languages, as shown here. `a[lang|="en"] {background-image: url(en_icon.png);}`
a:link	Pseudoclass selector	Specifies a style for links that have not yet been visited. `a:link {color: maroon;}`

451

Selector	Type of Selector	Description
`a:visited`	Pseudoclass selector	Specifies a style for links that have already been visited. `a:visited {color: gray;}`
`:active`	Pseudoclass selctor	Specifies a style for any element that has been activated by the user, such as a link as it is being clicked. `a:active {color: red;}`
`:focus`	Pseudoclass selector	Specifies any element that currently has the input focus, such as a selected form input. `input[type="text"]:focus {background: yellow;}`
`:hover`	Pseudoclass selector	Specifies a style for elements (typically links) that appears when the mouse is placed over them. `a:hover {text-decoration: underline;}`
`:lang(xx)`	Pseudoclass selector	Selects an element that matches the two-character language code. `a:lang(de) {color: green;}`
`:first-child`	Pseudoclass selector	Selects an element that is the first child of its parent element in the flow of the document source. `p:first-child {line-height: 2em;}`
`:first-letter`	Pseudoelement selector	Selects the first letter of the specified element. `p:first-letter {font-size: 4em;}`
`:first-line`	Pseudoelement selector	Selects the first line of the specified element. `blockquote: first-line {letter-spacing: 4px;}`
`:before`	Pseudoelement selector	Inserts generated text at the beginning of the specified element and applies a style to it. `p.intro:before {content: "start here"; color: gray;}`
`:after`	Pseudoelement selector	Inserts generated content at the end of the specified element and applies a style to it. `p.intro:after {content: "fini"; color: gray;}`

INDEX

About the Author

Jennifer Niederst Robbins was one of the first designers for the Web. As the designer of O'Reilly's Global Network Navigator (GNN), the first commercial web site, she has been designing for the Web since 1993. She is the author of the bestselling *Web Design in a Nutshell* (O'Reilly), and has taught web design at the Massachusetts College of Art in Boston and Johnson and Wales University in Providence. She has spoken at major design and Internet events including SXSW Interactive, Seybold Seminars, the GRAFILL conference (Geilo, Norway), and one of the first W3C International Expos.

Colophon

Our look is the result of reader comments, our own experimentation, and feedback from distribution channels. Distinctive covers complement our distinctive approach to technical topics, breathing personality and life into potentially dry subjects. The photo cover of a leaf is from Photos.com. The text font is Linotype Birka; the heading font is Adobe Myriad Pro.